FIGURE E.2

The New Layout dialog box

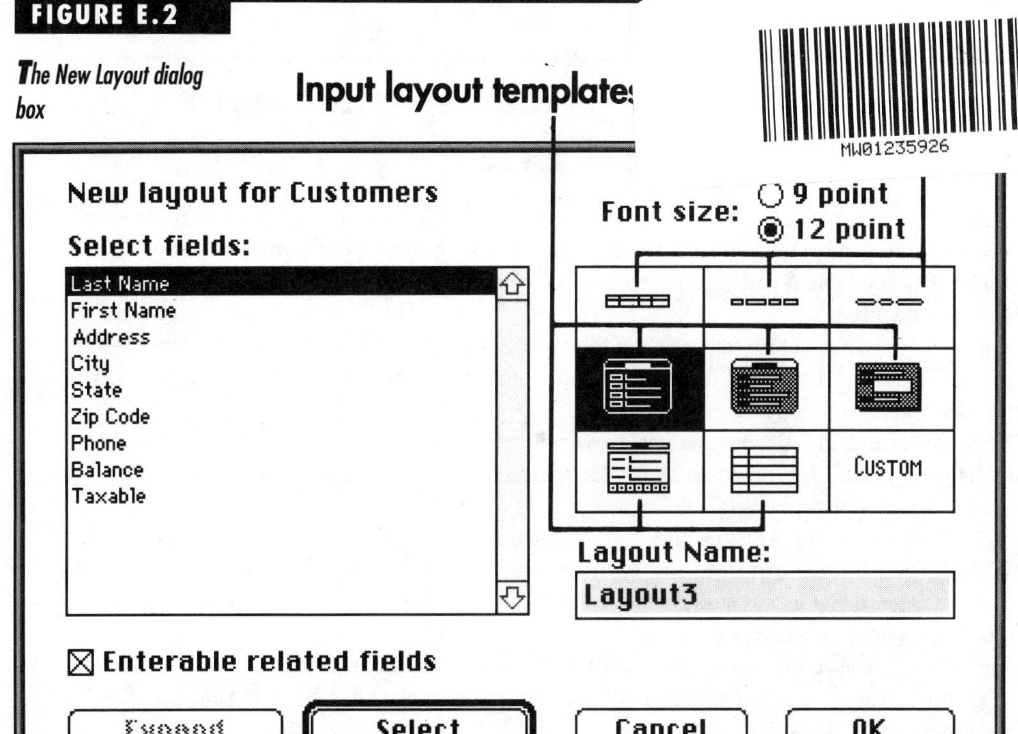

FIGURE E.3

The output control lines

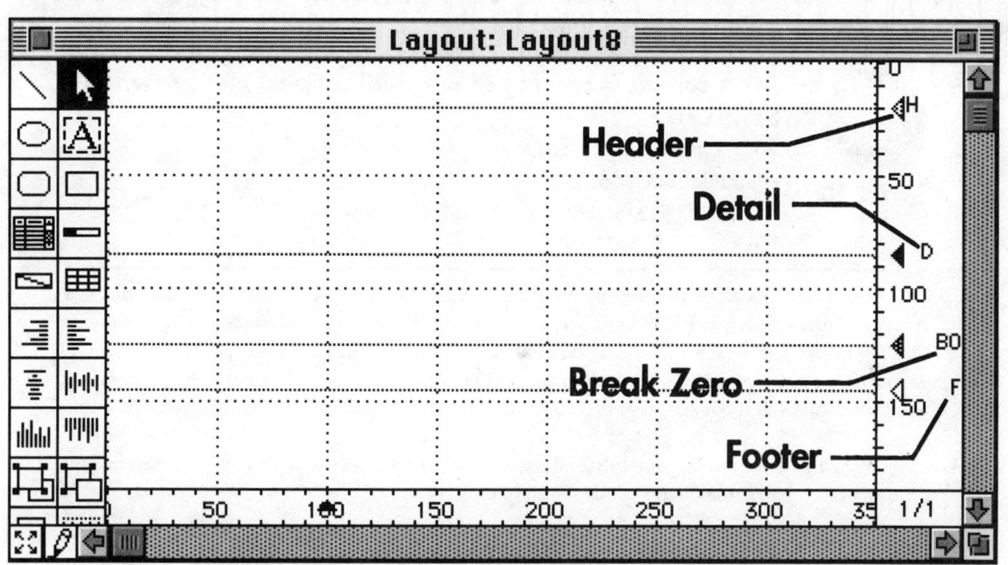

For every kind of computer user, there is a SYBEX book.

All computer users learn in their own way. Some need straightforward and methodical explanations. Others are just too busy for this approach. But no matter what camp you fall into, SYBEX has a book that can help you get the most out of your computer and computer software while learning at your own pace.

Beginners generally want to start at the beginning. The **ABC's** series, with its step-by-step lessons in plain language, helps you build basic skills quickly. Or you might try our **Quick & Easy** series, the friendly, full-color guide.

The **Mastering** and **Understanding** series will tell you everything you need to know about a subject. They're perfect for intermediate and advanced computer users, yet they don't make the mistake of leaving beginners behind.

If you're a busy person and are already comfortable with computers, you can choose from two SYBEX series—**Up & Running** and **Running Start**. The **Up & Running** series gets you started in just 20 lessons. Or you can get two books in one, a step-by-step tutorial and an alphabetical reference, with our **Running Start** series.

Everyone who uses computer software can also use a computer software reference. SYBEX offers the gamut—from portable **Instant References** to comprehensive **Encyclopedias, Desktop References**, and **Bibles**.

SYBEX even offers special titles on subjects that don't neatly fit a category—like **Tips & Tricks**, the **Shareware Treasure Chests**, and a wide range of books for Macintosh computers and software.

SYBEX books are written by authors who are expert in their subjects. In fact, many make their living as professionals, consultants or teachers in the field of computer software. And their manuscripts are thoroughly reviewed by our technical and editorial staff for accuracy and ease-of-use.

So when you want answers about computers or any popular software package, just help yourself to SYBEX.

For a complete catalog of our publications, please write:

SYBEX Inc.
2021 Challenger Drive
Alameda, CA 94501
Tel: (510) 523-8233/(800) 227-2346 Telex: 336311
Fax: (510) 523-2373

SYBEX is committed to using natural resources wisely to preserve and improve our environment. As a leader in the computer book publishing industry, we are aware that over 40% of America's solid waste is paper. This is why we have been printing the text of books like this one on recycled paper since 1982.

This year our use of recycled paper will result in the saving of more than 15,300 trees. We will lower air pollution effluents by 54,000 pounds, save 6,300,000 gallons of water, and reduce landfill by 2,700 cubic yards.

In choosing a SYBEX book you are not only making a choice for the best in skills and information, you are also choosing to enhance the quality of life for all of us.

Inside 4th Dimension 3.1

INSIDE 4th DIMENSION® 3.1

Second Edition

Geoff Perlman

San Francisco • Paris • Düsseldorf • Soest

ACQUISITIONS EDITOR: Dianne King
DEVELOPMENTAL EDITOR: Kenyon Brown
EDITORS: David Krassner, Michelle Nance
TECHNICAL EDITOR: Chris Boccucci
BOOK DESIGNER: Lisa Jaffe
CHAPTER ART: Claudia Smelser
PRODUCTION ART: Charlotte Carter
SCREEN GRAPHICS: Aldo Bermudez and John Corrigan
TYPESETTERS: Deborah Maizels, Stephanie Hollier
PROOFREADER/PRODUCTION COORDINATOR: Catherine Mahoney
COVER DESIGNER: Ingalls + Associates
COVER ILLUSTRATION: Hank Osuna

Library of Congress Card Number: 93-86588
ISBN: 0-7821-1455-5

Manufactured in the United States of America

10 9 8 7 6 5 4 3 2 1

To Sandra

ACKNOWLEDGMENTS

The book you are holding in your hands is a product of the efforts of many people beyond myself. Those individuals deserve credit for helping produce this book from start to finish, and they are David Krassner, my editor at SYBEX, whose constant feedback and support made writing this book much easier; Kenyon Brown, my developmental editor and Dianne King, my acquisitions editor at SYBEX, who rolled the dice on an unpublished writer; and all of the people at SYBEX involved in the production of this book, including Chris Boccucci, technical editor; Lisa Jaffe, book designer; Claudia Smelser, chapter art; Charlotte Carter, production art; Aldo Bermudez and John Corrigan, screen graphics; Deborah Maizels and Stephanie Hollier, typesetters; Catherine Mahoney, proofreader and production coordinator; Nancy Guenther, indexer; and Hank Osuna of Ingalls + Associates, who designed the cover.

Also, thanks to Laurent Ribardière, the author of 4th Dimension; and Marylène Delbourg-Delphis, the president of ACI, without whom this book would certainly not have been written; as well as Ron Dell'Aquila and Dave Terry, both former ACI employees, who have over the last few years been excellent sources of knowledge and ideas; Gary Brocks and Basil Bourque, both ACI trainers, whose feedback, suggestions, and friendship have been both helpful and appreciated; and to those of you who attended my 4D training classes over the past two-and-a-half years. The questions you asked and experience you gave me are very much a part of this book.

Finally, much credit and appreciation to Sandra Scheld, whose seemingly endless supply of encouragement (keeping my nose to the grindstone), ideas, and support were instrumental in the completion of this book. I could not have done it without you.

Geoff Perlman

TABLE OF CONTENTS

FOREWORD

When Geoff told me that he was writing a book on 4D, I was glad. If anyone can make 4th Dimension even more accessible to an even wider audience, Geoff can. However, I knew that for a 4D expert there is a difference between the thought of writing a book and seeing that thought through to completion.

4th Dimension is the best selling relational database on the Macintosh, and it is used by hundreds of thousands of people around the world. But you will notice that there are few books about it. It's not that no one wants to write about 4D. On the contrary, what tends to happen is that people start books but then get so involved in 4th Dimension that they become 4D developers, spending all their hours creating solutions for their customers. They have no time left to be authors.

So, I had a few doubts about how Geoff's project would go. Geoff literally lives with 4D. He does training for ACI all over the United States. He builds training materials and practical examples for users, both novice and expert. He does this year round. I was secretly worried that his project might go the way of so many others. My doubts were unfounded. He has met the challenge. That he would spend his nights with 4th Dimension, as well as his days, truly shows the depth of his 4D evangelical zeal.

Geoff genuinely wants to share this passion for 4th Dimension. But his enthusiasm has not prevented him from communicating with clarity. His book takes you by the hand and gently introduces you to the 4D world. Geoff does not assume that everybody knows what a database is. He does not assume that everybody understands computer jargon. He writes for people in the real world and shows you how business problems can be translated into 4D concepts. You will not be intimidated by this book. You are taking control of your Macintosh to streamline your life.

I have the impression that when he was working on this book, Geoff was thinking of how he solved the problems of his brother's business. He started programming in BASIC. A tough start indeed. Then he discovered 4th Dimension. He remembers how stunned he was that the program provided him with so much capability with so little effort. How surprised he was that a data management system could be so open to novice users, welcoming them to a world where they are rarely invited. What Geoff tells you in this book is that you should not be afraid of 4D. That when starting out with 4th Dimension, you should remember the small note you may have seen before you went for your driving test: *Millions of people have passed it. Why not you?*

Marylène Delbourg-Delphis
President, ACI

INTRODUCTION

4th Dimension (or *4D* for short) version 3.1 is the third major revision of the 4th Dimension database management system. With each new version of 4th Dimension, performance has increased and features have been added to make it easier for you to create powerful database applications quickly. You probably purchased 4th Dimension to create a database for a specific task. At first, you will ask yourself, "What can I do with 4th Dimension?" The more you learn about 4th Dimension, though, the more you will begin to ask yourself, "What can't I do with 4th Dimension?" The purpose of this book is to give you the knowledge you need to get the most out of 4th Dimension. 4th Dimension is like a tool kit. The better you understand what tools are available to you and how they work, the more productive you will be.

If you have already looked through the documentation that comes with 4th Dimension, you have probably figured out that it is a large and powerful application. Its power comes from the large number of tools that the application provides. I know that understanding 4th Dimension can be frustrating and confusing at times, especially if you are new to it. The purpose of this book is to help you understand 4th Dimension and its tools and help you get started building your own database applications.

WHO SHOULD USE THIS BOOK?

This book is for users who are interested in increasing their understanding of 4th Dimension. If you are new to 4th Dimension, this book will guide you from understanding basic database management to creating a very customized database application. By the time you finish with this book, you will feel very comfortable with your understanding of 4th Dimension.

If you are an experienced 4th Dimension user, this book will help solidify your understanding. You will find tips and techniques that will help you get even more out of 4th Dimension. This book also covers the changes and new features in version 3.1 and gives you ideas on how you might use these new features to make your existing applications even more powerful.

THE STRUCTURE OF THIS BOOK

This book is written as a tutorial and as a reference. You will get the most out of it if you read the chapters in the order that they appear in the book. How much of the book you read really depends on how much you need to get out of 4th Dimension. For some of you, this book will cover more than you will ever need. For others, it will provide you with the knowledge you need to begin your journey into the 4th Dimension. The book is organized as follows:

Chapter 1: Understanding Database Management covers basic database concepts, including simple steps to learning 4th Dimension, and gives you some idea about what 4th Dimension can do.

Chapter 2: Entering 4th Dimension introduces you to the files that 4D creates and the three areas of 4th Dimension.

In *Chapter 3: Creating a Database File* you will learn how to create files, add fields, choose their data types, and assign field attributes.

In *Chapter 4: Adding and Changing Records* you begin adding records and learning how to makes changes to them later.

Chapter 5: Searching for Records teaches you all about locating records you have already entered. This chapter covers all of the different ways you can search for records.

In *Chapter 6: Sorting Records* you will learn how to rearrange (sort) your records so that they are in some kind of order.

Chapter 7: Changing Groups of Records teaches you how to remove records from your database files and how to make changes to many records all at once.

A database is not much good without the ability to print out reports. In *Chapter 8: Creating and Printing Reports* you will learn about 4D's powerful and easy to use report editor.

At some point, you may need to print mailing labels from records in your database. *Chapter 9: Creating and Printing Labels* covers 4D's label editor.

If you are keeping track of numbers in your database, you may want to create graphs. *Chapter 10: Creating Graphs* introduces the graph editor.

You may need to exchange information with other programs on your computer. *Chapter 11: Importing and Exporting Records* teaches you how to use 4D's import editor (for bringing data into your database) and export editor (for sharing your data with other programs).

4D gives you the ability to customize the screens you create to interact with your data. In *Chapter 12: Creating and Customizing Layouts* you will learn about 4D's layout editor.

Your database files can share information. *Chapter 13: Managing Related Files* teaches you how to create file relations so your files can share and store information more efficiently.

Computers are terrific at performing calculations quickly and accurately. *Chapter 14: Adding Automatic Calculations Using Scripts* teaches you how to add automatic calculations to your databases.

If you have used a Macintosh, you are familiar with pull-down menus. *Chapter 15: Adding Custom Menus* shows you how to add your own pull-down menus to your database.

4th Dimension has a long list of commands that do a variety of tasks. *Chapter 16: Adding Power with 4D Commands* teaches you how to figure out which commands to use to get different jobs done.

4th Dimension has its own programming language. If you have never done any programming before, *Chapter 17: Programming Techniques* will get you started.

If you plan to store sensitive information in your database, you will want to be able to protect it. *Chapter 18: Adding Passwords* introduces you to 4th Dimension's password system.

Chapter 19: Increasing Performance with the 4D Compiler covers another supporting program called the 4D Compiler. If you use 4D's programming language, you can use the 4D Compiler to "turbo-charge" your programming.

There are several other support programs you can buy to use with 4th Dimension. *Chapter 20: Adding Functionality with the 4D Modules* describes these programs and gives you ideas on where you might use them.

Chapter 21: Allowing Multiple Users with the 4D Server. The 4D Server allows you to have more than one user accessing the database at the same time. This chapter explains how 4D Server works and how it is different from 4D.

Part of using a database is maintaining it. *Chapter 22: Database Maintenance* explains making backup copies of your data and gives you steps to take if some data becomes corrupted.

Appendix A: 4D Development Utilities lists some of the development utilities available for 4th Dimension.

Appendix B: Changes in 4D Version 3.x explains all the changes that have been made between version 2.0 and 3.1. The experienced user may wish to review this chapter to quickly find out what's new in version *3.x.*

Appendix C: 4D Commands and Functions briefly summarizes all the commands and functions in 4th Dimension.

Appendix D: ASCII Chart contains the full ASCII character set, to assist you in writing scripts.

Appendix E: 4th Dimension Keyboard Shortcuts and Icons lists shortcuts for accessing important 4th Dimension features and covers the 4D icons and their functions.

SPECIAL FEATURES

This book has several features to make understanding and learning easier.

The Mac Tracks at the beginning of each chapter summarize specific skills and techniques covered within that chapter. Experienced 4th Dimension users can use this to find specific information in the chapter. Beginners will want to refer back to this after they have read the chapter as a reminder on how to perform specific tasks.

Also at the beginning of each chapter, you will find a Featuring list, which enumerates the topics covered in the chapter.

Four special visual icons are used in this book to identify notes:

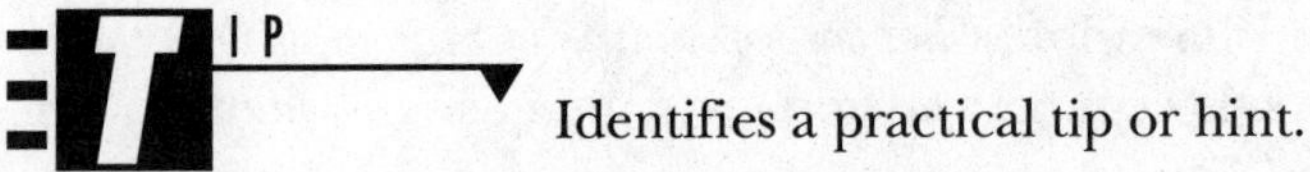

Identifies a practical tip or hint.

Identifies a special note that augments information in the text or presents reminders about previous techniques.

Identifies a warning about a potential problem.

Identifies a new feature or change specific to version 3.x of 4th Dimension.

Finally, we have used a shorthand convention in alluding to menu commands; it follows this format: *menu* ➤ *command*. So, for example, if we want you to choose the New command from the File menu, we would ask you to choose File ➤ New.

A SAMPLE DISK

This book shows many examples of databases, forms, reports, menus, and programming. If you would like to use these examples without having to create them yourself, you can purchase a disk with the examples completed for you.

The sample disk also contains chapter databases. For every chapter in the book there is one database named with the chapter it goes with. Each chapter database is finished up to the chapter that it belongs to. For example, the *Chapter 5* database has been completed through the end of Chapter Four. These databases allow you to start working in the tutorial from any chapter. They also give you examples to look at to make sure that the database you are creating is coming out right. This disk can be ordered by sending US$30.00 to: S2 Software, 19672 Stevens Creek Blvd., Suite 275, Cupertino, CA 95014. California residents, please add 8.25% sales tax.

If you have questions about 4th Dimension or about the sample disk, contact the distributor in your country from the list below.

FRANCE

ACI
5, Rue Beaujon
75008 Paris, France
Tel: 1/42-27-37-25
Fax: 1/42-27-38-54
AppleLink: ACI.SALESF

GERMANY

ACI GmbH
Hanns-Braun-str.52
D-8056 Neufahrn Bei Freising
Tel: 49/81-65-30-01
Fax: 49/81-65-62-475
AppleLink: GER.XSE0005

ENGLAND

ACI UK
St Ann's House
Parsonage Green
Wilmslow SK9 1HT
Tel: 44/625-536-178
Fax: 44/625-536-497
AppleLink: UK0074

U.S.A.

ACI
10351 Bubb Road
Cupertino, CA 95014
Tel: 1/408 252-4444
Fax: 1/408 252-0831
AppleLink: D4444

SWEDEN

ACI AB
Botkyrkavägen 4
S-143 30 Vårby
Sweden
Tel: 46 (8) 740 4075
Fax: 46 (8) 740 1975

If your country is not listed, call ACI in Paris, France for the location of the nearest distributor.

If you have any comments about this book, you can reach me through electronic mail. The list below indicates the mail addresses to use for different mail systems.

MAIL SYSTEM	ADDRESS
AppleLink	76307.65@COMPUSERVE.COM@INTERNET#
America On-Line	76307.65@COMPUSERVE.COM
Internet	76307.65@COMPUSERVE.COM
CompuServe	76307,65
MCI Mail	To: Geoff Perlman (EMS)
	EMS: internet
	Mbx: 76307.65@COMPUSERVE.COM

UNDERSTANDING DATABASE MANAGEMENT

1

TRACKS 

A database is 4

An organized collection of information.

A database management system is 4

A set of tools to help you access and manipulate data in a database more easily.

4th Dimension stores your information 6

In files on your computer disk.

A database has three major functions: 6

Entering data, *manipulating* data, and *reporting* on data.

TRACKS **MAC** TRACKS

4th Dimension files contain information in 7

Records or *rows.*

Records are separated into 7

Fields or *columns.*

To get the most out of your computer 8

You must give it instructions in a way that it can understand them. 4th Dimension makes this very intuitive!

To effectively manage your 4th Dimension files 9

You must learn how to do the following basic tasks: Adding information; changing information; searching for information; sorting information; and printing information.

Databases

Database management systems

The major functions of a database

Records and fields

What you'll need to learn to be an efficient 4D user

4TH DIMENSION IS a powerful application that you can use to build almost any kind of database for quickly and accurately managing large amounts of data. You might use 4th Dimension to track: customers, invoices, inventory, accounting information, test results, schedules, events, and just about anything else you can imagine. 4th Dimension is a *database management system.* It sounds a lot more complicated than it really is.

A database is an organized collection of information. You use many databases every day. For example, when you look through your check register to find the last check you wrote, you are accessing a database. When you call information to find a telephone number, you are accessing a database. You may have file cabinets at your office in which you organize related information. Customer records may be in one file and invoices in another. Reference books, phone books, even your own memory are all examples of databases.

A database management system is a set of tools to help you access your data more efficiently. You can think of a database as a card file. Each card has a person's name, address, and phone number on it. Figure 1.1 shows an example of a Rolodex-style card. You add new cards, remove cards, and put them into alphabetical order. When you need to add a new card, you take blank card, fill it out and insert it into your card file in the correct alphabetical position. When you no longer need a card, you remove it from your card file and throw it away. You keep your

FIGURE 1.1

An example of a Rolodex-style card

Mrs. Sally N. Jones
123 University Avenue
Irvine, CA 92715
714-555-4657

cards in alphabetical order to make finding cards faster. Figure 1.2 shows a card file sorted alphabetically by last name. Occasionally you update cards in your card file because someone has moved or changed phone numbers.

If you were going to have an open house for your business, you might look through your card file to search for people you want to invite and then write down their names, addresses, and phone numbers so you can contact them. When you add, update, remove, and refer to the cards in your card file, you are *managing* the information in it.

Cards can also be used to keep track of other kinds of data. You might have cards with recipes on them. How you organize the cards would depend on how you are going to use them. You might sort them alphabetically by name or by category. A collection of cards can be used

FIGURE 1.2

A card file sorted by last name

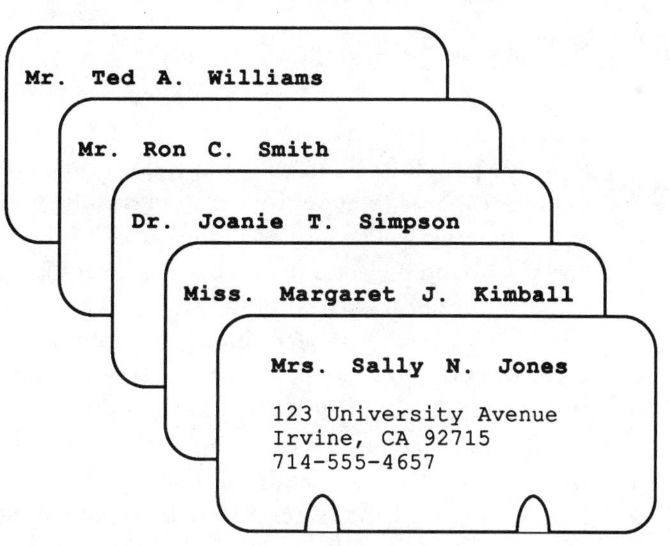

to keep track of just about any kind of information. You might easily have several files of cards each storing information belonging to a particular category. For example, you might have a file of cards with information on customers and another with information on vendors. If your business sells parts, you might have yet another file with information about inventory items. All of these files collectively represent your company database.

Obviously 4th Dimension does not use cards to keep track of information. Instead of cards, 4D keeps information in electronic records on disk. A record is the computer equivalent of a Rolodex-style card. In 4th Dimension you can add, update, remove, and access the records. These records are organized into files. The files are put together to form a database.

A database has three major functions:

- **Entering data:** For example, when you write names and addresses on cards and insert the cards into your card file, you are *entering* data.
- **Manipulating data:** When you put your cards into alphabetical order or search through them to look for party guests, you are *manipulating* or managing your data.
- **Reporting on data:** When you write down the party guests from your cards, you are *reporting* on the data in your database.

When you add cards to a Rolodex-style holder, you use tools. Your eyes locate a blank card and your hand then picks up the card. You use a pen or pencil to fill in information on the card. Finally, your eyes scan the card for whatever information is going to be used to determine where the card will be located in the card file (the last name for example) and your hand picks up the card and puts it into the right place. You use these and other tools to remove cards, update cards, and so on.

Analogously, with a computer, a database management system is a set of tools designed to help you manage information in a database file. It gives you the ability to enter information once and then to manipulate it just about any way you can think of (and perhaps in some ways you haven't). As you go through this book, you will learn about all the different tools 4th Dimension provides for managing your information.

A database management system is to a computer what your eyes and fingers are to a set of Rolodex-style cards.

A database management system such as 4th Dimension allows you to quickly perform tasks like adding, changing, searching, sorting, and reporting on the information in your database.

UNDERSTANDING DATABASE FILES

4th Dimension doesn't store your information on Rolodex-style cards. Information in a 4th Dimension database is stored on your computer disk.

A 4th Dimension database is made up of files. Each file contains *records* (or *rows*) of information. Records are separated into *fields* (or *columns*) of information. Figure 1.3 shows a database file that contains names, addresses, and phone numbers.

The first record in the file is Tony Banks. There are five records in all. The information in Figure 1.3 is broken down into seven fields or columns:

Last Name

First Name

Address

City

State

Zip Code

Phone Number

The information needs to be separated into fields because a computer can't tell the difference between an address and a phone number just by looking at it the way you and I can.

FIGURE 1.3

Records in a database file

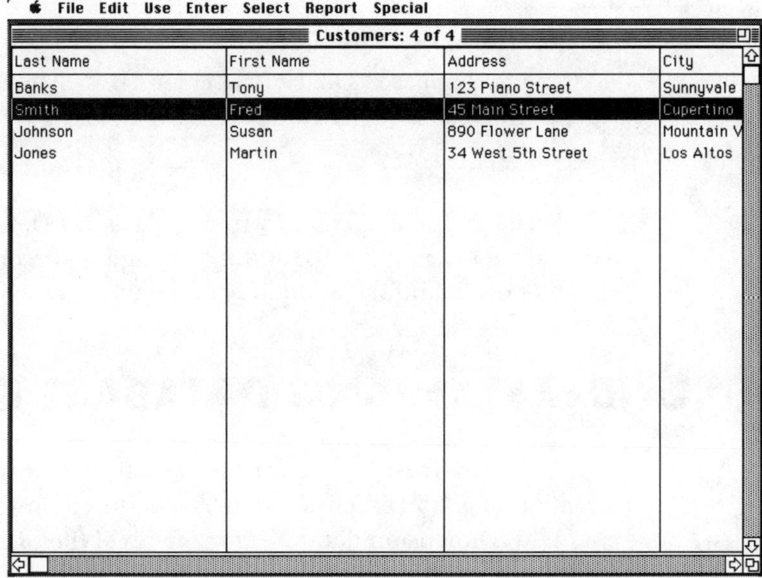

File Edit Use Enter Select Report Special
Customers: 4 of 4
Last Name
First Name
Address
City
Banks
Tony
123 Piano Street
Sunnyvale
Smith
Fred
45 Main Street
Cupertino
Johnson
Susan
890 Flower Lane
Mountain V
Jones
Martin
34 West 5th Street
Los Altos

For a large part of the population, computers are mysterious and intelligent machines that can do practically anything. In the movies, we have seen computers like C3PO from Star Wars that can think. These kind of computers are just what they appear to be, fantasy. One day we will probably have computers like C3PO, but today's computers, generally speaking, can't figure things out by themselves. They need to have information separated into meaningful fields in order to allow us to give the computer instructions on what to do with that data. Things that are mysterious to us are usually things that we just don't know enough about. By reading this book, you will understand more about computers and more about 4th Dimension, and perhaps both will seem less mysterious.

DATABASES IN BUSINESS

Businesses manage enormous amounts of information. A typical business has information on customers, orders, invoices, inventory, vendors, purchase orders, employees, and so on. This information might be entered onto forms that are put into folders and stored in file cabinets. This information can also be stored in files in a 4th Dimension database.

Business information is more than a bunch of forms. It starts out on a form and ends up in many different places. Forms are used to gather information together to allow it to be used in many different ways. Invoices, applications, and orders are all examples of forms used to gather information. The boxes you fill out on a form are like the fields in a database.

The data gathered together with forms is then used to create reports. Forms that have data relevant to a particular report are gathered together and sorted into some kind of order. Certain pieces of information from these forms are then re-entered on a report. The benefit of using a database is that the information is only entered once and then saved onto a computer disk. Later, you can retrieve the information and use it to create numerous different kinds of reports, without having to re-enter anything.

LEARNING 4TH DIMENSION

If you are new to computers, you are probably wondering what computers can do. Well, computers can do a lot of amazing things (and do them terribly fast) if we humans give them enough information. One of the things you will learn in this book is how we give computers the instructions they need in order to perform the tasks we want them to do.

If you have been using computers for a while, you're probably comfortable with your knowledge of what computers can do, although you might feel unsure of exactly how they do it. This book attempts to take away some of the mystery of how we tell computers what to do. By learning how to get 4th Dimension to do what you want, you will better understand how computers really work.

There are a few basic tasks that you need to learn to effectively manage your 4th Dimension files. These are:

- Adding information
- Changing information
- Searching for information

- Sorting information
- Printing information

Once you understand these basic tasks, you can then be very productive. With this knowledge, you can enter your data, manage it, and get the reports you need to get the job done. These basic tasks all work in the same way for all the database files you will create. After learning these tasks, you will be able to quickly create databases for all of your information and manage it faster than ever before.

In the beginning, you may think that you will never be able to use a computer to do the tasks that you have been doing without one. Believe it or not, it's easier than you think. Using 4th Dimension is as simple as using the Macintosh. You simply select menus and type simple instructions to tell 4th Dimension what to do. Before long, you will be surprised at how much you have learned and how much you can do. Learning 4th Dimension will take much of the mystery out of computers and make you feel empowered.

WHAT YOU CAN DO WITH 4TH DIMENSION

Computers are not very smart, though. They can do only what we humans tell them to do. There are things that any five year old would understand perfectly that would leave a computer scratching its memory. What computers are good at is doing things very, very fast. This is the main reason for using a computer in the first place. With 4th Dimension, you can add to, change, report on, and analyze your data in a fraction of the time it would take you to do it by hand. For example, suppose you had 100,000 items in inventory. If you needed to create a report showing only those items that were priced over five dollars and then sort them in alphabetical order by vendor, it would take you days to do by hand. With 4th Dimension, you could get the same job done in just a few minutes! It's the incredible speed at which a computer operates that makes it an almost magical and certainly wonderful invention.

ENTERING 4TH DIMENSION

2

TRACKS MAC

TRACKS **MAC** TRACKS

Structure and data files

4D's three environments: Design, User, and Runtime

Quick tours of the three environments and their menus

Installing 4D

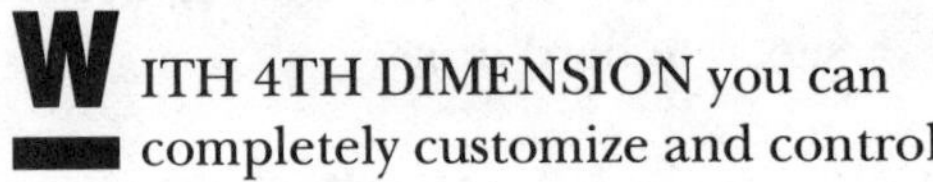
WITH 4TH DIMENSION you can completely customize and control your database files.

UNDERSTANDING 4D DESKTOP FILES

As you design and use your database, 4th Dimension will create *desktop files.* A desktop file is different from a *database file,* which is stored inside your database. You probably use a word processor. The files you create and save with it are desktop files, so called because they can be manipulated from the Macintosh desktop. Figure 2.1 shows a few sample desktop files.

The desktop files created by 4th Dimension store information for different purposes. Let's say you often search your database for information that matches a set of complex criteria. With 4D you don't have to remember this criteria; you can enter it once and save the criteria in a desktop file that can be used again later. Each type of desktop file

FIGURE 2.1

Three desktop files

4th Dimension creates has a different icon. A complete description of these files along with their icons can be found in *Appendix E.*

A 4th Dimension database requires a minimum of two desktop files, which are created automatically when you create a new database. These two files are the *structure* file and the *data* file.

THE STRUCTURE FILE

The *structure* file stores everything that describes your database. When you create a new database, the first thing 4th Dimension needs is a name for the structure file. The structure file, like all other desktop files created by 4D, has its own icon. Figure 2.2 shows an example of a structure file as you might see it inside a folder from the Macintosh desktop. A 4th Dimension database is made up of many different parts. Files, layouts, menus, and procedures are some of the components of a database. In this book you will learn how to use 4th Dimension to create these parts. These parts are stored in the structure file.

Let's say you created a database to keep track of employees in your department and another department wanted to use your database to keep track of their employees. All you would have to do is give them a copy of the structure file of your database. The actual employee information (names, addresses, and salaries) you have entered into the database is stored in another file called the *data* file.

THE DATA FILE

The *data* file stores the information you enter into your database. For example, when you enter names, addresses, phone numbers, and salaries, this data is stored in the data file. This book will teach you how

FIGURE 2.2

A sample structure file

to use 4th Dimension to set up automatic calculations based on your data. For example, you may want 4th Dimension to automatically calculate how long an employee has been with your company. If you have entered the employee's start date into a field, you can have 4th Dimension calculate how long the employee has worked at your company and then store this information in another field. All of the data that goes into your database, whether typed in or calculated by 4th Dimension, is stored in the data file. The data file is a desktop file just like the structure file. 4th Dimension gives the data file the same name as the structure file and adds the word *.data* to the end of the name (similar to an file extension in DOS). Figure 2.3 shows an example of the data file (as viewed from the Macintosh desktop) that would be created along with the example structure file from Figure 2.2.

You can take advantage of the distinction that 4th Dimension makes between structure files and data files when exchanging information with others. For example, if you wanted to give someone a copy of your database layout, but not the actual data stored in it, you could just give them a copy of the structure file.

As I mentioned before, if another department wanted to use the database you have created to track employees, you wouldn't want to give them a copy of your database with its private employee information in it. You could make a copy of the database and, after deleting all of the information, give the other department the copy. But this might be time-consuming if the database had a lot of information in it. Instead, you simply give them a copy of the structure file from your database. When

FIGURE 2.3

A sample data file

the other department uses the database for the first time, 4th Dimension will automatically create a data file for their data.

4th Dimension keeps the structure of your database separate from its information to make re-using easy. This also makes updating your database easy.

Let's say you have created a database that will be used by someone else in your organization. After creating the database, the user begins entering information. After a large amount of data has been entered, the user realizes that he forgot to include a few fields (columns) of information that need to be in the database. You could update his copy of the database and then update your copy, but this would be inefficient. Instead, because the structure of your database is separate from the data, you can update your copy of the database and simply give the user a new copy of the structure file to replace his old one. After replacing the old structure file with the new updated one, the user will be able to take advantage of the changes you have made.

THREE ENVIRONMENTS OF 4TH DIMENSION

4th Dimension has three areas or *environments* that are used to perform different tasks. An *environment* is simply a group of functions that go together. 4D's three environments are called *Design, User,* and *Runtime.* Each environment has its own set of pull-down menus that perform special functions. The Design environment provides menus that allow you to make changes to the design of your database. The menus in the User environment give you the ability to add records, print reports, etc. When you access the Runtime environment, 4th Dimension replaces its menus with the menus that you have created. In this book, you will be using each of these environments to create and use a database. Let's take a closer look at each of these environments.

THE DESIGN ENVIRONMENT

The *Design* environment is where you create the database. You can think of it as the "hard-hat" area. Before you can enter information into a database, you need to tell 4th Dimension:

- How you want to organize the information (files and fields)
- How you want to access the information (layouts)
- What kind of calculations or special functions you want (scripts and procedures)
- What pull-down menus you want

In the Design environment you will create files, add fields to files, create layouts to allow the user to enter and view data in the files, write calculations, create pull-down menus and all the parts of the database that define its utility. As you read and work through the exercises in this book, you will be spending quite a bit of time in the Design environment.

A Quick Tour of the Design Environment Menus

Let's take a quick tour of the Design environment's menus. This will help you become familiar with the basic organization of the Design environment. I will discuss the menus in more detail later in the book.

The File Menu

The *File* menu allows you to:

- Create new databases
- Open existing databases
- Close all the design environment windows
- Save changes to the database structure
- Set up general preferences
- Specify the page setup
- Print the database structure
- Quit 4th Dimension and return to the Finder

Figure 2.4 shows the File menu in the Design environment.

FIGURE 2.4

The File menu in the Design environment

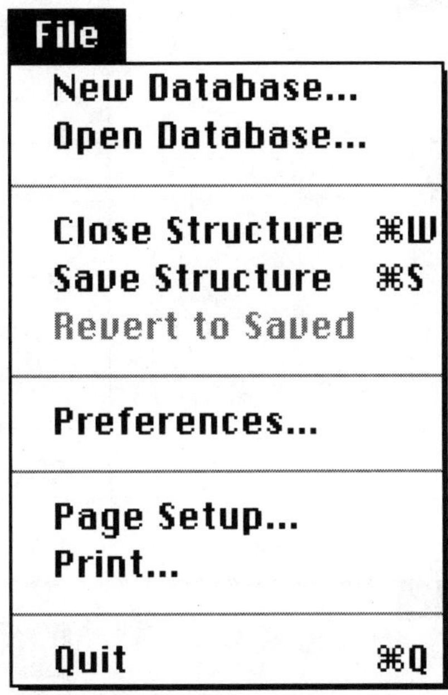

The Edit Menu The *Edit* menu, shown in Figure 2.5, allows you to cut, copy, and paste selected text to the Clipboard.

The Use Menu The *Use* menu, shown in Figure 2.6, allows you to move between the Design environment and the User environment.

The Design Menu The *Design* menu allows you to create and modify all of the pieces of your database other than the data itself such as:

- Database files
- Layouts
- Procedures
- Menus
- Passwords
- Lists
- Processes

FIGURE 2.5

The Edit menu in the Design environment

Edit
Undo ⌘Z
Cut ⌘X
Copy ⌘C
Paste ⌘V
Clear
Select All ⌘A
Show Clipboard

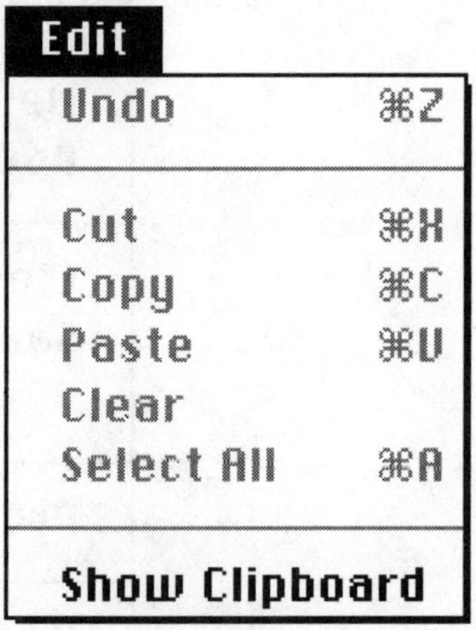

FIGURE 2.6

The Use menu in the Design environment

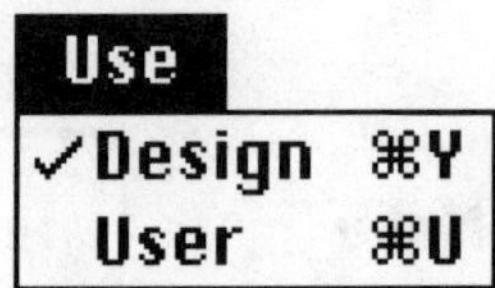

Figure 2.7 shows the Design menu.

The Structure Menu The *Structure* menu, shown in Figure 2.8, allows you to create, rename, and control access to files, as well as to create and modify the fields that make up the files.

Don't be too concerned about trying to understand what each of these menus does. Each menu item will be discussed in detail later in the book.

The Data Menu The Data menu, shown in Figure 2.9, allows you to divide your data file into several segments which can be placed on separate hard disks.

FIGURE 2.7

The Design menu in the Design environment

Design
✓Structure
Layout... ⌘L
Procedure... ⌘P
Menu... ⌘M
Passwords
Lists
Process

FIGURE 2.8

The Structure menu in the Design environment

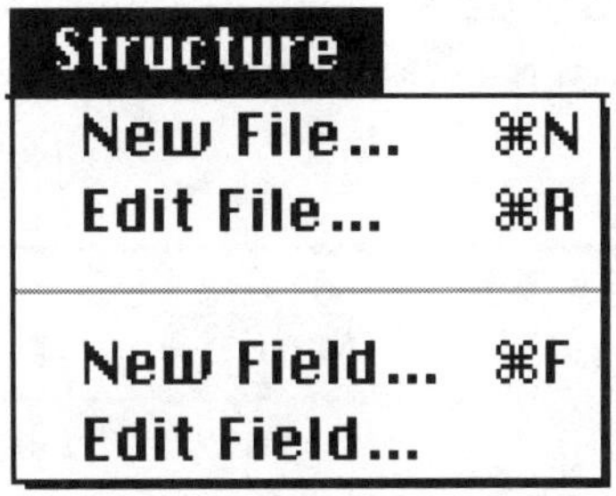

Structure
New File... ⌘N
Edit File... ⌘R
New Field... ⌘F
Edit Field...

FIGURE 2.9

The Data menu

Data
Segments...

THE USER ENVIRONMENT

The *User* environment is the area where you use the database that you have created in the Design environment. In the User environment, you can add records, delete records, change records, search and sort records, print reports, print labels, print graphs, and perform many other functions on your database. The User environment gives you all the functions you need to use your database.

You might end up using only the Design and User environments of 4th Dimension. After creating a database in the Design environment, you can enter data into the database and use that data to print reports and do all of the things that you would expect (and some things you might not expect) a database to do. These two environments give you everything you need to create a database and manage the data that is entered.

A Quick Tour of the User Environment Menus

Let's take a quick tour of the User environment's menus. This will help you become familiar with the basic organization of the User environment. I will discuss the menus in more detail later in the book.

The File Menu The *File* menu, shown in Figure 2.10, allows you to create new databases and open existing databases, move data in and out

FIGURE 2.10

The File menu in the User environment

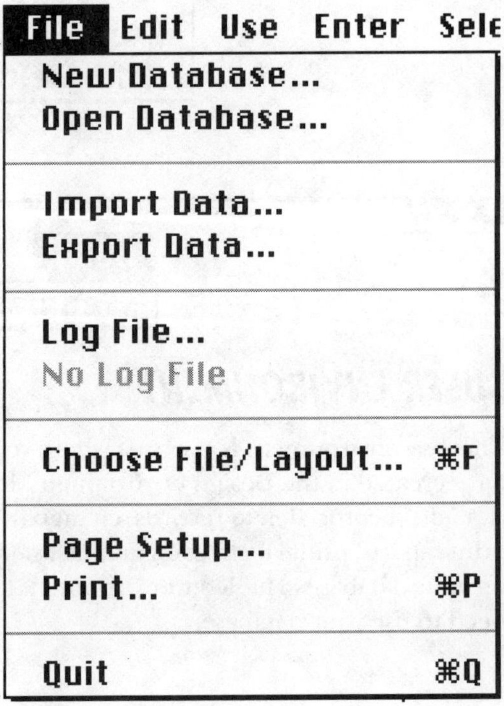

of your database, create a log file to track changes to your data, and print information from your database.

The Use Menu The *Use* menu in the User environment is almost the same as the Use menu in the Design environment with one important difference. In the User environment, the Use menu allows you to move between the Design, User, and Runtime environments (see Figure 2.11).

FIGURE 2.11

The Use menu in the User environment

The Enter Menu The *Enter* menu, illustrated in Figure 2.12, allows you to add new records and modify existing records in several different ways.

FIGURE 2.12

The Enter menu in the User environment

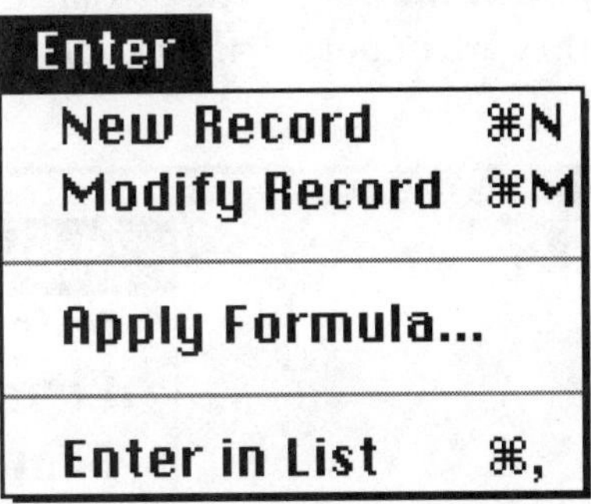

The Select Menu The *Select* menu allows you to select records from a file in your database (see Figure 2.13). You can list all the records, search for specific records, and sort records. You will use this menu when

FIGURE 2.13

The Select menu in the User environment

Select	Report	Special
Show All	⌘G	
Show Subset	⌘H	
Search Editor...	⌘S	
Search by Layout...	⌘L	
Search and Modify...		
Search by Formula...		
Sort Selection...	⌘T	

you want to gather records together for a specific purpose, such as printing a report.

The Report Menu The *Report* menu allows you to create custom reports, labels, and graphs from the data in your database (see Figure 2.14).

The Special Menu The *Special* menu allows you to change characters as they are imported and exported (see Figure 2.15). It also allows

FIGURE 2.14

The Report menu in the User environment

Report	
Quick...	⌘R
Labels...	⌘J
Graph...	⌘K

FIGURE 2.15

The Special menu in the User environment

Special	
Edit Output ASCII Map...	
Edit Input ASCII Map...	
Execute Procedure...	⌘E

you to run procedures you have created using 4th Dimension's procedural language (which we will discuss in detail in *Chapter 13*).

Again, don't be too concerned about trying to understand what each of these menus does. Each menu item will be discussed in detail later in the book.

THE RUNTIME ENVIRONMENT

The *Runtime* environment gives you absolute control over what the user can do with your database. The User environment gives you a complete set of pull-down menus to perform typical database functions. However, you may create your own menus and define (using 4th Dimension's programming language) what the menus can do. When you use the Runtime environment, 4th Dimension replaces the User environment's menus with the custom menus that you have created. With your custom menus in place, you have almost complete control over what the user can do and how they do it. Later in this book, you will be creating custom menus and then writing procedures to make the menus work.

BEFORE YOU BEGIN

Now that you understand a bit about databases and 4th Dimension's environments, it's time to create a database. By now you should have installed 4th Dimension on your Macintosh hard disk. If you haven't, you will need to take the time to do this before going further. 4th Dimension comes with complete installation instructions.

This tutorial is full of example screens to help you learn. The example screens were created on a Macintosh IIci running version 7.0 of the Macintosh operating system. Consequently, some of the sample screens that involve operating-system dialog boxes for opening files, printing, and such will look slightly different from yours if you are not running system 7.0. 4th Dimension does not require system 7.0 to run. However, it does require that you are running system 6.0.4 or greater. There are a few features in 4th Dimension that you can only use if you are running system 7.0. These features are not going to stop you from creating and getting a lot of productivity out of your database, and I will point them out as they are discussed.

CREATING A DATABASE FILE

3

TRACKS MAC

To open an existing database called Learn 4D 34

1. To open the Learn 4D*f* folder, double-click on the folder icon. Another list box will appear, displaying the Learn 4D database icon.
2. Double-click on the icon to open the Learn 4D database. 4D opens Learn 4D to the last place you were working when you quit the database. Now you can continue from where you left off in the book.

To formulate a legal field name, you must keep in mind that 38

- The name cannot be more than 15 characters long.
- The first character must be a letter, but numbers can be used after that.
- The only characters allowed in field names are the letters *A* through *Z*, the numbers 0 through 9, spaces and underscores (_).
- Field names can contain both uppercase and lowercase letters.

To rename a file 45

1. Click anywhere on File1 to select it.
2. Choose Structure ➤ Rename File (⌘-R).

3. Type **Customers** as the new name for File1.
4. Click **OK** or press the Return key.

To add a field 46

1. Click anywhere on the Customers file to select it.
2. Choose Structure ➤ New Field (⌘-F).
3. Type **Last Name** as the name for Field1.
4. Click the Mandatory and Indexed attributes to select them.
5. Click the OK & Next button or press the Return key.

To zoom out on a structure window 49

1. Click the **Show Page** button. The database structure will appear reduced.
2. Click on the reduced image of the Customers file and drag to the lower-right corner.
3. Click **OK**.

To change data types 50

Double-click on the field name you want to change in the structure window. This will bring up the Field dialog box. Then simply select one of the other data types. This works best when you are working with empty fields.

Creating a simple database

Saving your work

Opening an existing database

Adding fields

Changing data types

IN THIS CHAPTER, you will begin creating your first database. You will need to launch (run) 4th Dimension on your computer. There may be conditions that prevent 4D from running. 4th Dimension requires 1500 kilobytes (1500K) of random-access memory (RAM) to run. If you don't have this much memory available when you attempt to run 4D, the system software will display the message: *There is not enough memory to run 4D.* If you see this message (or something like it) you may want to quit other applications to make more memory available. If you are not running any other applications and you are still getting a message like this, you may need to install more memory into your machine. Don't worry if this turns out to be the case. Memory is very inexpensive and getting cheaper every day.

4th Dimension will take advantage of all of the memory you allow it to use. If you have plenty of memory available, you might want to give 4D an extra megabyte of memory for better performance.

CREATING A NEW DATABASE

As mentioned in the last chapter, a 4D database is made up of two desktop files (the *structure* file and the *data* file) that hold all of your files, fields, screens, calculations, menus, and data. Creating your first database requires a few simple steps. First, you will need to run 4D, then create a new database and give it a name.

When you launch 4D, a large *4D* will appear on the screen. After a few seconds, the *4D* will vanish and the Open Database dialog box will appear as shown in Figure 3.1. This dialog box gives you the option of opening an existing database or creating a new one. Don't worry if the files listed in Figure 3.1 are different from the ones on your screen.

Call your first database *Learn 4D.* Create it by following these steps:

1. Double-click on the 4th Dimension icon to launch 4D.
2. Click the **New** button.
3. Type **Learn 4D** as the name for your new database.
4. Press the return key or click the **Save** button to save the structure file.
5. Press the return key or click the **Save** button to save the data file.

FIGURE 3.1

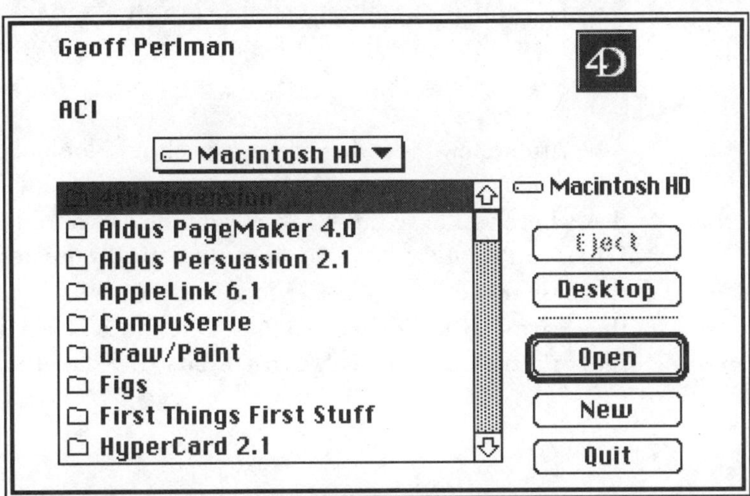

You can either open an existing database or create a new one in the Open Database dialog box.

Try to keep your file names fairly short; this will make them easier to read in the Finder!

The name you enter for a database must follow these rules which also apply to any desktop files you create on your Macintosh:

- The name can be a maximum of 31 characters. You should try to keep the name short, though (around 15 characters). It will be easier to read when you are viewing your 4th Dimension files from the desktop.
- The name can contain numbers (0 to 9) and any other characters, including spaces, but it may not contain colons (:).
- You can use uppercase and lowercase letters.

Don't try to remember these rules. 4D will not allow you to enter a name that doesn't conform to them.

Make sure these two files are always in the same folder. If they're not, 4D will ask you to locate the missing file.

After a few seconds, your screen should look like Figure 3.2. 4th Dimension has created your database. At the location on your hard disk where you have put 4D, you will now find a folder called *Learn 4Df*. When you create a database, 4D automatically creates a folder with the database name and adds an *f* to the end (the *f* stands for folder). Inside the Learn 4D*f* folder are two files. One file is **Learn 4D** (the structure file) and the other file is **Learn 4D.data** (the data file).

FIGURE 3.2

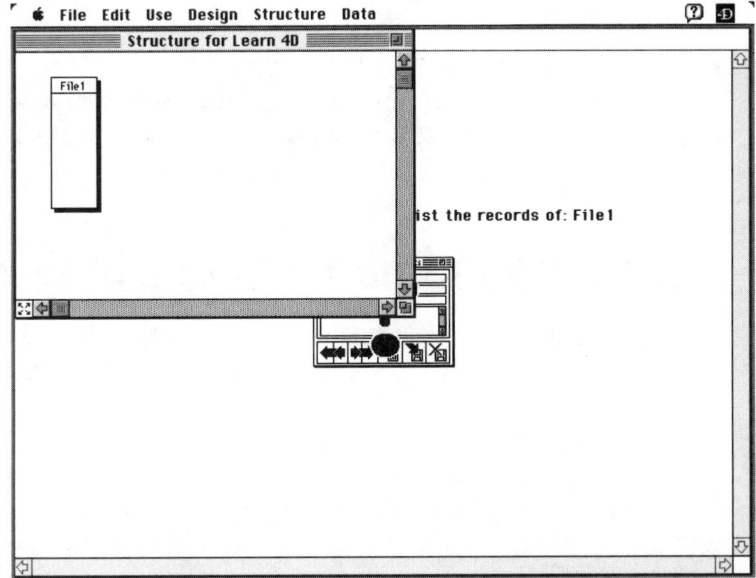

The Structure window

As mentioned in the last chapter, 4D has three environments. When you create a new database, 4D begins in the Design environment and displays the *structure window.* Behind the structure window is the *User window.* You will use the User window to access the data in your database, using the files you have created in the structure window.

TAKING BREAKS

Anytime you want to take a break from the exercises in this book, you can quit 4D by choosing File ➤ Quit. Some applications ask you if you want to save the file you are working on before you quit. 4D will not ask you this as it saves all of your work automatically.

Always quit 4th Dimension before shutting off your computer. If you don't, you might lose some of your work.

RETURNING TO THE LEARN 4D DATABASE

To get back to your database, launch 4D. When the Open Database dialog box appears, follow these steps to open the Learn 4D database:

1. To open the Learn 4D*f* folder, double-click on the folder icon. Another list box will appear, displaying the Learn 4D database icon.
2. Double-click on the icon to open the Learn 4D database. 4D opens Learn 4D to the last place you were working when you quit the database. Now you can continue from where you left off in the book.

DESIGNING A DATABASE FILE

As you learned in previous chapters, a database contains files. Files are divided up into *fields* and contain *records*. Before you can enter any information into a file, you must add at least one field. There are few basic rules to consider when designing a database file. We'll discuss these rules as you create a file in the following sections.

DEFINING FIELDS

When designing a file, the most important point is to put each unique piece of information into a separate field. Don't worry about putting information into fields based on how you will want to print the information. You can easily reorganize the information when you want to print.

By separating unique pieces of information into fields, you will have much greater flexibility in managing your data.

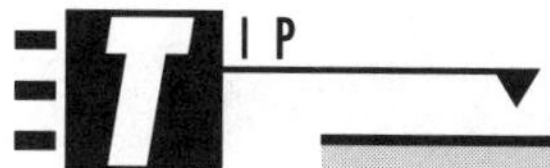

The Tab key will jump you from field to field in dialog boxes.

Let's say you are creating a database to keep track of names and addresses. It may seem logical to create a single field called Name and enter the names like this:

Name

Sally Jones

Ted Williams

Joanie Simpson

Ron Smith

Margaret Kimball

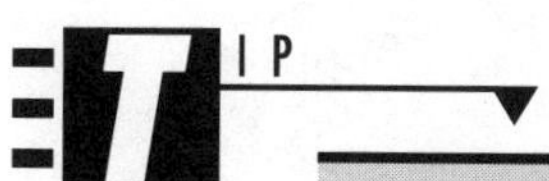

The information you enter into a field is considered to be *one piece of information.*

There are a couple of problems with using only one field, though. First, there is no way to have 4th Dimension sort the information by last name, because the information in the name field begins with the first name. For the same reason, there is no way to quickly search for a last name. This type of organization is a common beginner's mistake. Be aware that the information you enter into a field is considered to be *one piece of information.* If you want to be able to search and sort the first name and last name, they will need to be in two separate fields like this:

First Name	**Last Name**
Sally	Jones
Ted	Williams
Joanie	Simpson
Ron	Smith
Margaret	Kimball

Now that the first name and last name are in separate fields, you can search and sort them separately. If you want to add titles, such as *Mr.*, *Dr.*, and *Ms.*, or middle initials, you should create separate fields for these as well:

Title	**First Name**	**Middle Initial**	**Last Name**
Ms.	Sally	N.	Jones
Mr.	Ted	A.	Williams
Dr.	Joanie	T.	Simpson
Mr.	Ron	C.	Smith
Ms.	Margaret	J.	Kimball

Each file can have up to 511 fields. So don't worry about running out.

By separating the names into four different fields, you have a great deal of flexibility. If you are printing form letters, you can put all four fields together to create a name like *Ms. Margaret J. Kimball* or use just one field for a greeting, as in *Dear Margaret:*.

Another common mistake people make with name and address files is to group the city, state, and zip code into one field like this:

CityStateZip

Irvine, CA 92715

Sunnyvale, CA 94086

Anchorage, AK 99510

Newport News, VA 23606

Framingham, MA 01701

Again, grouping the data into one field causes problems. You couldn't sort the information by state. You couldn't find all the records for people in a particular zip code because the zip code is not isolated.

To make sure you have the most flexibility for searching and sorting, separate the city, state and zip code into three separate fields. (Don't worry about typing a comma at the end of a city name. You can add it back when you print the city field.)

City	**State**	**Zip**
Irvine	CA	92715
Sunnyvale	CA	94086
Anchorage	AK	99510
Newport News	VA	23606
Framingham	MA	01701

WHAT GOES IN A DATABASE FILE?

You can put any information you want into a database. All the information you use in your business can be stored in a database. 4D allows you to create up to 255 files in a single database. Therefore it is not necessary (and definitely not recommended) to put all of your data into one file in your database. Look at the way you store your information now. You don't mix customers records and invoice records together. You have a file for customer information and another for invoices. Information is broken down into separate files to make it easier to manage. The same principle holds true in a computer database.

The number of files you need and best way to organize them may not always be obvious. Later in the book we will talk more about how to separate your information into separate files and how to get your files to share information with each other.

ASSIGNING FIELD NAMES

4th Dimension does not require that fields have unique names. It's a good idea, though, to get into the habit of assigning unique names to each field to keep things from getting confusing—can you imagine having two children with the same name? The name you assign to a field must conform to the following rules:

- The name can not be more than 15 characters long.
- The first character must be a letter, but numbers can be used after that.
- The only characters allowed in field names are the letters *A* through *Z*, the numbers 0 through 9, spaces and underscores (_).
- Field names can contain both uppercase and lowercase letters.

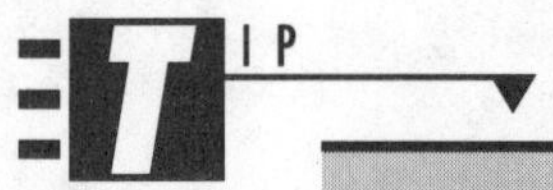

Some database products don't allow spaces in field names. If you have used one of these products, you are probably in the habit of using underscores instead of spaces. Remember, 4D allows spaces in field names, which make the names easier to read.

Again, don't worry about remembering these rules, 4th Dimension will not allow you to enter names that don't adhere to these rules.

CHOOSING FIELD TYPES

You must choose a *field type* for each field in each of your database files. 4th Dimension has ten different field types:

Alphanumeric can contain letters, numbers, and practically anything else you can type from the keyboard. Numbers that are entered cannot be used in calculations. The maximum number of characters that can be entered is eighty. Examples: *John Smith, Hoopy Frude, 123 Main Street.*

Text has the same limitations as an alphanumeric field, except that a text field can contain up to 32,000 characters.

Real can contain any number with any number of decimal places. Real numbers can be used in mathematical calculations. Examples: *5, –45, 7843, 600, 450.586.*

Integer can contain only whole numbers (no decimal values are allowed) that are within the range –32,767 and +32,767. Examples: *45, –5768, 30,000.*

Long Integer can contain whole numbers only (no decimal values are allowed) that are within the range –2,147,483,648 and +2,147,483,647. Examples: *5, –600, 55,987.*

Date can store dates in MM/DD/YY format. While the dates are entered and stored in this format, they can be displayed in six different formats. Dates must be within the range 01/01/100 to 12/31/32767. Examples: *1/1/95, 12/31/95, 1/1/2000.*

Time can store time in HH:MM:SS format. While the times are entered and stored in this format, they can be displayed in five different formats. Time values must be within the range 00:00:00 to 596523:00:00. Examples: *1:10:00, 12:01:05, 325:45:52.*

Boolean stores true or false. By default, a Boolean field is false. A Boolean field is used when you need to store one of two values. Examples: *True or False, Male or Female, Paid or Unpaid.*

Picture can store bitmaps (like MacPaint creates) and PICT images (like MacDraw creates).

Subfile isn't really a field type. A Subfile is a connecting point for another file that has it own subfields. The records entered into a Subfile are part of the record that the Subfile belongs to. Subfiles will be discussed in more detail later.

In most cases the appropriate field type will be obvious, but sometimes it can be a bit tricky. For example, if you are choosing a field type for a phone number or zip code field, you might be tempted to select one of the three numeric formats (real, integer, or long integer). This seems to make sense because phone numbers and zip codes are numbers. Actually, phone numbers and zip codes are *not* true numbers.

To 4th Dimension, a true number is a quantity, an age, or a temperature in degrees. These numbers can contain the digits 0 through 9, they may have decimal values and they may have a leading minus (–) sign. Other characters, such as letters and punctuation marks, are not allowed. Phone numbers might contain parentheses or even letters, as in *(415) 777-FILM.* Nine-digit zip codes contain a hyphen, as in *94086-4179.*

You would not want to choose a numeric field type for a phone number or zip code because this would limit what you could enter into the field. It could even cause problems with the data you entered. For example, some zip codes begin with a zero. If you chose a numeric field type and entered a zip code like 03456, 4D would drop the leading zero as it is unnecessary when entering a number. Before assigning a numeric (real, integer, or long integer) field type to a field, ask yourself if you are going to want to perform calculations on this field. If not, then use an alphanumeric field type instead of a numeric field type. Alphanumeric fields allow you to enter both numbers and letters. You are not going to want totals on phone numbers or zip codes. Basically, you should use numeric field types only for fields you want to perform mathematical equations on.

If you choose a field type and later decide you have chosen the wrong one, don't worry. You can change a field's data type. Picture and Subfile are the only data types that can't be changed once they are selected.

You may be wondering how you are going to be able to sort your records by zip code if the zip code field is not a number. Don't worry, 4th Dimension knows that 12345 comes before 12346 in sort order, even if the field is alphanumeric.

CHOOSING FIELD ATTRIBUTES

Attributes control how a field is going to respond during data entry. 4th Dimension provides many different attributes that can be assigned to a field. While you must select a data type for a field, you do not have to choose any attributes. A field may have several attributes or none at all. There are seven attributes that can be assigned to a field:

Mandatory fields require the user to enter a value in order to save the record. Select this attribute when you want to be absolutely sure that a value is entered into a particular field. 4th Dimension will display a message to let the user know that the field is mandatory should they try to save a record without entering a value.

Display Only can't be changed by the user. When a field is display only, the user can view the contents of the field, but cannot alter them. This attribute is commonly used for fields that hold the result of a calculation. Later in this book, you will learn how to create automatic calculations. Some of your calculations will store their results in fields. Because the computer is calculating the value stored in the field, you would not want to accidentally type over the value.

In most cases, you won't assign a field as Mandatory and Display Only. With both selected, the user must fill in a value but can't because the field is Display Only! Catch-22.

Can't Modify allows you to enter a value into the field only once for each record. Once you enter a value into the field and save the record, you can no longer change it from the keyboard. I say "from the keyboard" because you can change Can't Modify fields with 4th Dimension's programming language which will learn about in a later chapter, see *Chapter 13.*

Indexed can greatly decrease the time it takes to search or sort the field. When you select this attribute, 4D creates an index for the field similar to an index at the back of a reference book. This allows 4D to quickly locate records by using the index instead of looking at each record individually. Text, Picture, and Subfiles cannot be indexed. Indices will be discussed in more detail later in this chapter.

Unique prevents the user from entering a value into a field that already exists in that field in another record. Because the user cannot enter duplicate values, the values in the field are unique. A field must be indexed in order to be unique. The reason for this is simple. When a value is entered into a unique field, 4D must search the file to see if another record already has that value. Because this search is occurring while you are entering data, it needs to be very fast. If the field were not indexed, this search would take too long.

Choices allows you to attach a list of values to the field. The list will be displayed when the user is entering data into this field. Instead of typing a value into the field, the user selects from a list of choices. Choices lists are created with the List editor, which is discussed in a *Chapter 12.*

Invisible allows you to have control over when a field is displayed. 4th Dimension has several built-in editors for searching records, sorting records, creating reports and so on. Normally, the user will have access to all the fields in a file when using one of these editors. Invisible fields will not be displayed in any of the built-in editors. In the Structure window, invisible fields appear in italics.

Invisible fields can be used for data entry and reporting. They don't appear in any of 4D's built-in editors.

WHAT IS AN INDEX?

An index is an table of data arranged to make searching and sorting significantly faster. You have probably used the index at the back of a reference book. Subjects are arranged in alphabetical order to make finding them in the index fast. Next to each subject is one or more page numbers where you will find information about that subject. You can locate the page or pages in a book that contain information on subject you are interested in by using the index. Without the index, you would have to look at every page to find all the pages that contain information on the subject. This could take quite a while especially if the book had hundreds of pages.

When you index a field, 4D creates an index table for that field. As you enter data into the indexed field, 4D updates the index table. When you search using an indexed field, 4D uses the index to locate records rather than looking through each record, one at a time. This makes searching and sorting records much faster. You will not see the index tables that 4D creates, because it stores them inside your data file and uses them transparently. Should you remove the index attribute from a field, 4D will stop updating the index table and searching and sorting on that field will be slower.

At this point you are probably asking yourself, "Why not index every field?" There are two reasons:

- Indices can greatly increase the size of the data file and consequently, increase the amount of disk space required for your database.
- Each time a record is saved, 4D must also update the index tables for any indexed fields that have changed. The more indexed fields, the longer it will take to save a record.

The answer is to index only the fields that you will be searching and sorting most often. If you don't know which fields will need to be indexed right now, don't worry. You can index a field at any time, even after you have entered data. Should you decide to index a field after you have already entered records into your database, 4D will create the index table based on the existing data.

Even when you search using a field that is not indexed, the search is still very fast. Imagine how long it would take you to search through a stack of 100,000 invoices looking for the invoices for a particular customer. It would probably take several days and you would look like a train wreck by the time you finished. 4D can complete the same search, even on a field that is not indexed, in a few minutes. If the field is indexed, 4D can complete the search in a few seconds!

CREATING A FILE

Now that you have created the Learn 4D database, you are ready to create your first file. Because a 4D database needs at least one file, 4D goes ahead and creates the first file for you. In Figure 3.2, there is a box titled "File1" with a scroll bar. This box graphically represents the first (and at this point, the only) file and will eventually display the names of the fields (as well as other useful information) that belong to this file.

RENAMING A FILE

4D assigns default names to files as you add them to your database. These default names begin with the word *File* and end with the number of the file. The first file is named "File1", the second "File2", and so on. These names are not very meaningful; fortunately, you can give them more explicit names. The first file in your database is going to hold information about customers. Let's rename File1 now. Remember, if you make a mistake as you type the file name, use the arrow keys or the Backspace key to make corrections.

1. Click anywhere on File1 to select it.
2. Choose Rename File (⌘-R) from the Structure menu.
3. Type **Customers** as the new name for File1.
4. Click **OK** or press the Return key.

Figure 3.3 shows the File Attributes dialog box. This dialog is used to rename files, to control access to records in files, and to control access to the file structure itself. Record access and structure access are controlled by the password system, which is discussed in a later chapter.

FIGURE 3.3

The File Attributes dialog box

File Attributes
Filename: Customers
☐ Invisible file ☒ Completely delete
Record Access
Load: All Groups
Save: All Groups
Add: All Groups
Delete: All Groups
File Definition Access
Owner: All Groups
Cancel
OK

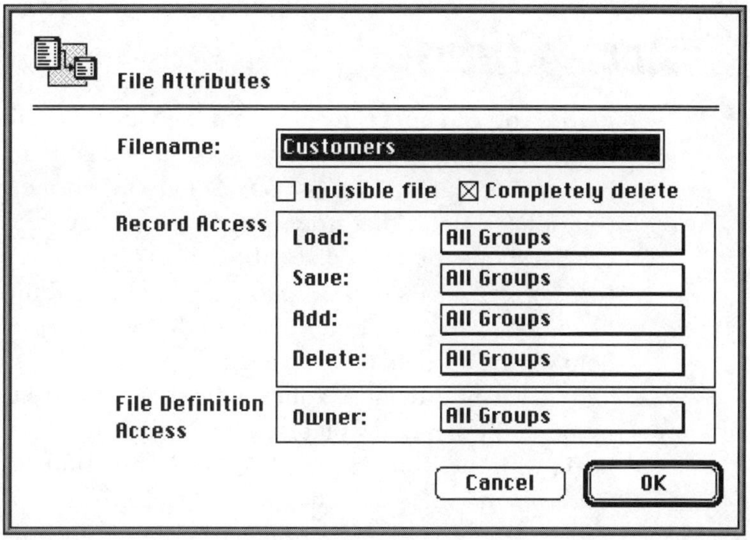

The Invisible check box allows you to make the file invisible. This means that the user will not be able to access the file or any of its fields when using any of 4th Dimension's built-in editors. (These file names appear in italics in the Structure window.)

The Completely Delete check box allows you to control how 4D updates your data file after records are deleted using the programming language. For more information on this option, see the 3.1 addendum file that came with your copy of 4D.

Notice that File1 is now the Customers file. You can name files anything you want, but follow these rules mentioned earlier for fields

- The name can not be more than 15 characters long.
- The first character must be a letter, but numbers can be used after that.
- The only characters allowed in file names are the letters *A* through *Z*, the numbers 0 through 9, spaces and underscores (_).
- File names can contain both uppercase and lowercase letters.

Again, don't worry about remembering these rules, 4th Dimension will not allow you to enter names that aren't kosher. File names can be changed at any time so don't worry if you cannot think of the most meaningful name right away.

ADDING FIELDS

Before you can enter any data into the Customers file, you will need to add fields. At first, the Customers file will contain fields named Last Name, First Name, Address, City, State, Zip, Phone, and Taxable. Later, you will add fields that store other kinds of data for each person. Figure 3.4 shows the Field dialog box. This dialog box is used to rename fields, assign a field type and to assign field attributes. With the Field dialog box you can also add balloon help for the field. Adding balloon help will be covered in *Chapter 12*.

4D assigns default names to fields as you add them to your database in much the same way that it assigns names to files. Default field names begin with the word *Field* and end with the number of the field. The first field is named "Field1", the second "Field2", and so on.

FIGURE 3.4

The Field dialog box

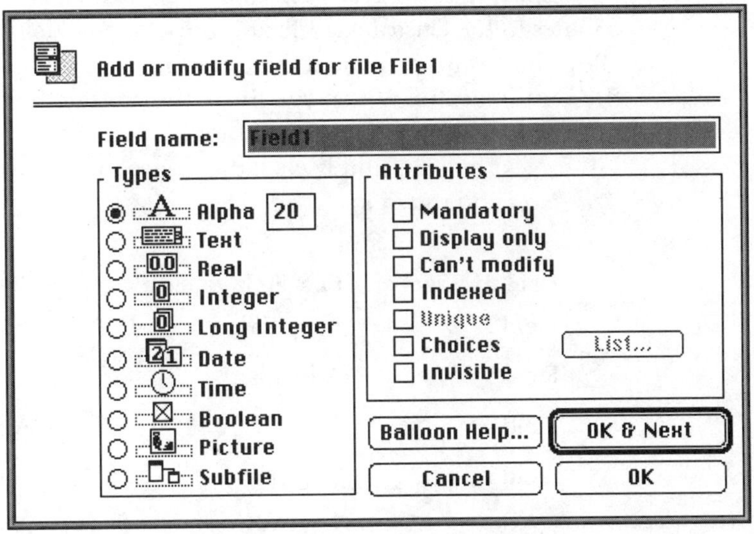

Let's add the first field:

1. Click anywhere on the Customers file to select it.
2. Choose New Field (⌘-F) from the Structure menu.
3. Type **Last Name** as the name for Field1.
4. Click the Mandatory and Indexed attributes to select them.
5. Click the **OK & Next** button or press the Return key.

You have just added your first field to the Customers file. The Last Name field will store the person's last name. Names are alphanumeric. It was not necessary for you to choose Alpha because 4D defaults to Alpha. The default length for an Alpha field is twenty characters. This should be fine for most last names. If you find that you need to enter a first name that is longer than twenty characters, don't worry. 4D allows you to change the length of an Alpha field at any time.

You selected Mandatory to ensure that the Last Name is always entered. Indexed was selected because you will search the Customers file most often by Last Name.

Clicking the **OK & Next** button adds the Last Name field and its attributes to the Customers file and presents the Field dialog box again to allow you to enter the next field. It's time to add the rest of the fields for the Customers file. When you finish the Taxable field, click the **OK** button instead of the OK & Next button. If you should accidentally click the OK & Next button, simply click the **Cancel** button to cancel the new field.

Now add the fields listed below:

Field Number	New Field Name	Field Type
Field2	First Name	Alpha 20
Field3	Address	Alpha 20
Field4	City	Alpha 20
Field5	State	Alpha 2
Field6	Zip Code	Alpha 9
Field7	Phone	Alpha 10
Field8	Balance	Real
Field9	Taxable	Boolean

4D displays the fields for the Customers file and places a letter next to each field indicating the fields data type. The following letters are used to represent different data types:

Letter	Data Type
A	Alphanumeric
T	Text
R	Real
I	Integer
L	Long integer
D	Date
H	Time

Letter	**Data Type**
B	Boolean
P	Picture
*	Subfile

The Last Name field appears in bold as a visual indication that the field is indexed.

4th Dimension allows you to have up to 255 files in a database. It would seem that the more files you add to your database, the more cluttered your structure window will get. The structure window will hold all the files you add to your database. Depending on how large you make the structure window, you may only be able to view one section of your database structure at a time. Fortunately, you can scroll the structure window allowing you to view all of your files. You can also zoom in and out of the structure window. *Zoom*, in this case, means to reduce or enlarge an image. You can reduce the structure to an image small enough to allow you to see all of your files at once. The **Show Page** button allows you to do this. The Show Page button is located in the lower-left corner of the structure window. It looks like four arrows pointed in all different directions. Let's try it:

1. Click the **Show Page** button. The database structure will appear reduced.
2. Click on the reduced image of the Customers file and drag to the lower-right corner.
3. Click **OK**.

You are now viewing the lower-right portion of the structure window. the window appears blank because there are no files here. When you clicked the Show Page button, 4D displayed a reduced image of the database structure. When you dragged the image with the mouse, you probably noticed that you were moving a rectangle from the upper-left corner of the window to the lower-right corner. This rectangle is the viewing area. Anything inside this rectangle will be enlarged when you click the **OK** button. As you add more and more files to your database, you can use this technique to view different areas of your database structure.

Now, use the Show Page button or the scroll bars to move back to the Customers file:

1. Click the **Show Page** button. The database structure will appear reduced. A rectangle appears in the lower-right corner indicating the area of the database structure that is being displayed.
2. Click on the rectangle and drag it to the upper-left corner.
3. Click **OK**.

You can rearrange your files in the structure window by clicking on a file name and dragging with the mouse.

MAKING CHANGES AND CORRECTIONS

Occasionally, you will make mistakes as you create your file structure. You might choose the wrong data type or attributes for a field. You might add more fields or files than you need. You might add the fields you want, but in the wrong order. Fortunately, 4D allows you to correct these mistakes.

Changing Data Types and Attributes

Changing each field's data type is simple. Double-clicking on the field name in the structure window will display the Field dialog box. To change the data type, simply select one of the other data types.

The effect of the change can be more complicated if you are changing the type after you have entered data into the field. The reason for this is that 4D will have to convert the data that has already been entered into the field into the data type. The problem arises when you change the data type of a field to a type that cannot hold some of the data that has already been entered. For example, if you have an Integer field and you decide (after entering data into the field) to change it to a Long integer field, 4D will convert the data from Integers to Long integers. In this case you would not notice any difference in your data because Integer values can be entered into Long integer fields. However, if you changed a Real field to an Integer field, you might lose some of your data, because not all Real numbers can be entered into Integer fields. Real numbers can include decimal values and can be above 32,767 and can be below –32,767. If you entered *34.96* into a Real field and then changed the field to an Integer field, the *.96* would be lost and the 34 would remain. If you entered 50,000 into a Real field and then changed it to an Integer field, the number would be converted to zero.

Not all data types can be changed. Once you create a Picture field, it cannot be changed to any other type of field. This rule also applies to Subfiles. So be careful when selecting these data types.

Of course, you will have to worry about how 4D is going to convert your data only if you are changing the data type after entering it. Once you have had some experience with 4D, you will feel more comfortable changing fields from one data type to another when necessary. In the beginning, however, I suggest you make a backup copy of your database before you change the data type of any fields. Making backup copies of your database is absolutely critical. I will discuss this topic in more detail in *Chapter 21*.

4D can now build indices transparently; so if you choose a field with data and change its attribute to Indexed, you won't have to wait for it to finish building the index. This process will go on in the background, allowing you to do other work.

Changing attributes is simple and has very little effect on your data. Attributes mostly govern the way a field behaves during data entry. Consequently, you don't have to worry about the possible ill effects of data conversion when changing attributes. The only attribute whose change might have any noticeable effect is the Indexed attribute. As you enter records into files in your database, 4th Dimension automatically updates indices for any fields that are indexed. However, should you choose to select the Indexed attribute after entering records, 4D will need to build the index from data that is already entered. As 4D builds the index, it will display a progress dialog box on the screen to let you know which field is being indexed and how far along in the process it is. 4D may take anywhere from a few seconds to a few minutes to build the index, depending on how much data has been entered into the field. Fortunately, you do not have to wait for 4th Dimension to finish building the index because a new feature in version 3 allows 4D to build indices in the background. This means that 4D can build the index while you are doing other things.

There are two ways to change a field's data type or attributes. Let's try both methods:

1. Click once on the Address field to select it.
2. Choose Structure ➤ Edit Field.
3. Press the Tab key.
4. Type **30** as the maximum length for the Address field.
5. Click the **OK** button.

As mentioned earlier, clicking the **OK** button saves any changes you have made to the field and closes the Field dialog box. The **OK & Next** button will save the changes to the field and then display the next field in the file to allow you to change it.

Another way to display the Field dialog box is to double-click on a field in the structure window. After trying both methods I think you will find that double-clicking the field to display the Field dialog box is the easier of the two. Let's change the length of the Address field back to 20:

1. Double-click on the Address field.
2. Press the Tab key.
3. Type **20** as the maximum length for the Address field.
4. Click the **OK** button.

As you can see, 4D allows you to easily change the data type and attributes of a field with minimal effect on your data. In most cases, the appropriate data type and attributes for a field will be obvious. As you use and learn more about 4D, you find will find yourself choosing data types and attributes more accurately.

Deleting Files and Fields

4D does not allow files or fields to be deleted once they have been created. Should you decide that a particular field is no longer necessary (or create an extra field by accident), you will want to make sure you remove this field from any layouts that it is used on. As your database becomes larger and more complex, it can get difficult to keep track of which layouts a particular field is displayed on. A support product for 4th Dimension called 4D Insider creates a complete cross reference of your database showing you (among many other things) on which layouts each field is displayed. Having this product will make managing changes to your database structure easy and less time-consuming.

Removing a field from a layout does *not* mean deleting it from the structure.

4th Dimension has several built-in editors for searching, sorting, printing labels, and so on, that display the fields from the file you are using. You will not want unused fields to appear in these editors. You can use the Invisible attribute to prevent these fields from appearing in 4D's built-in editors. By making a field invisible and removing it from all layouts, you are virtually deleting it. While you will always know it is there, the user will never see it.

Because Boolean fields take up the least room, change the data type of unused fields to Boolean to save disk space.

Luckily, there is very little penalty for having unused files and fields in your database, because unlike other databases, records in 4D are only as long as they need to be. In most other database products, fields have a fixed length and will store more data than you actually enter into the field. You will want to make sure that unused fields are taking up the least amount of room possible. Boolean fields take up the least amount of room so change the data type of any unused fields to Boolean.

Later when you need to add more fields to a file or more files to your database, you can use these unused files and fields instead of adding new ones.

Changing the Order of Fields

Sometimes you will create all the necessary fields for a file only to later discover that they are in the wrong order in the file. Perhaps you forgot to create a field for State in a Customers file and adding it now would put it after the Phone field. Fields in a file cannot be reordered. However, this usually doesn't matter because you can control the order that the fields appear in on layouts. The only place you cannot control the order of the fields is in 4D's built-in editors.

Fortunately, where there is a will there is usually a way. Using 4D's procedural language you can exchange the data in two fields and then rename them from the Structure editor, thus effectively changing their order in the file. It's not a very complicated task and you will understand how to do this as you learn more about 4D.

TAKING A BREAK

If you want to take a break at this point, you can save your work and come back to it later. To do this, simply choose File ➤ Quit. You don't have to worry about saving your changes before you quit. 4th Dimension automatically saves your changes when you quit.

Later, when you want to return to your work, just follow the instructions in the section titled *Returning to the Learn 4D Database* at the beginning of this chapter.

ADDING AND CHANGING RECORDS

4

MAC TRACKS MAC

To save a new record once you have entered it **63**

Press the Enter key or click the Save button at the bottom of the screen.

To move from one field to the next or previous field **63**

Press Tab or Shift-Tab. Note that if the field is not a Text field, you can use Return and Shift-Return, too.

To add a carriage return in a Text field **64**

Press the Return key. Note that you can jump to the next field only by pressing the Tab key.

To close a record without saving changes **65**

Press ⌘-period (.).

To move from character to character when entering data **65**

Use the arrow keys.

To erase what you have typed one character at a time **66**

Press the Backspace key.

To open the current input layout for a file and display a record for editing **70**

Double-click on the record in the output layout.

To "undo" an erroneous edit **70**

Press ⌘-Z.

If you really botch up a record and cannot undo your mistakes **70**

Press ⌘-period.

To display all the records in the file you are viewing **72**

Choose Select ➤ Show All.

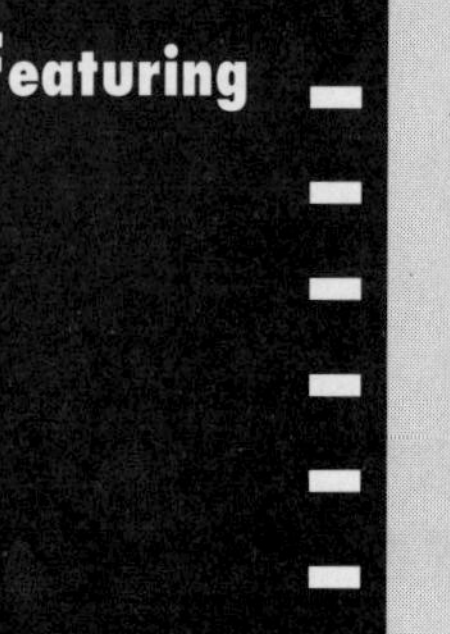

Featuring

- *Adding and saving new records*
- *Important keys for data entry*
- *Traversing fields*
- *Editing fields*
- *Input and output layers*
- *4D's (almost) unlimited capacity*

IN THIS CHAPTER you will learn how to add records to your database and then make changes to them when necessary. In the previous chapter you created your first file in the Design environment. To begin using your database, you will need to access the User environment. The User environment gives you access to the records in your database and provides you with menus for adding records, searching for records, sorting records, printing records in reports, and many other database management functions.

ACCESSING THE USER ENVIRONMENT

In case you have taken a break and don't have your database open, let's go through the steps to open the database and access the User environment. Once there, you can try adding a few records.

1. Locate the Learn 4D*f* folder and double-click the folder icon to open it.
2. Locate the Learn 4D file and double-click on it to open it.
3. Select Use ➤ User.

You have just crossed over into the User environment. When you switch to the User environment, 4D changes the menu bar to display menus that allow you to manage the data in your database. Figure 4.1 displays the User environment as you should now see it.

When you enter the User environment, 4D will display records in a list for the first file in the database. Because you have not yet entered any records into the Customers file, instead of showing the list 4D displays a message indicating that there are no records to display. This "list" is actually a layout that 4D creates for you automatically. After you have entered at least one record, 4D will replace the message you see now with a layout that displays records in a list (columnar) format. You will learn more about layouts after you have entered a few records.

FIGURE 4.1

The User environment displaying the Customers file

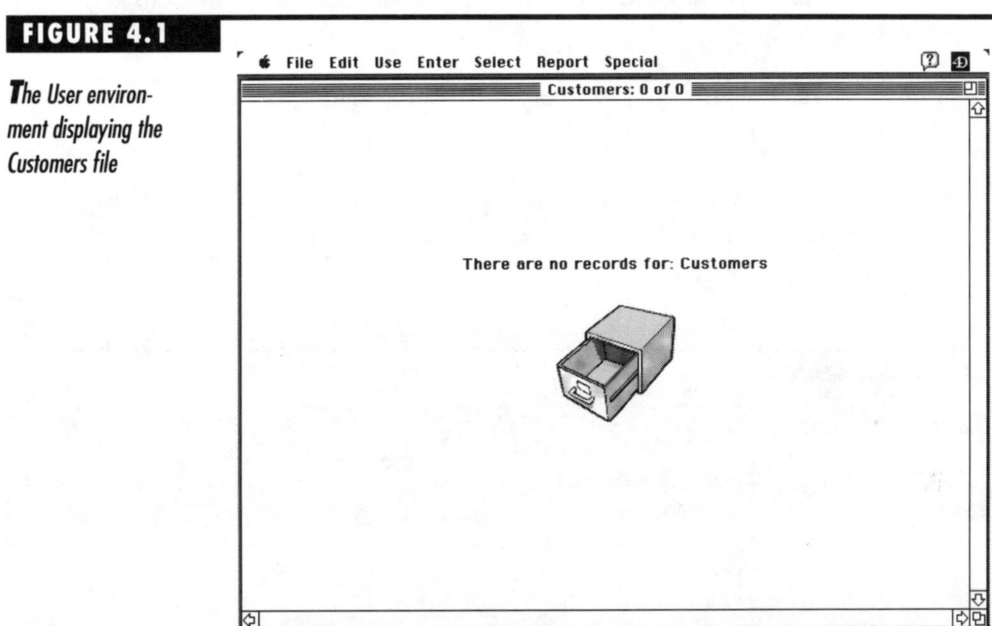

ADDING NEW RECORDS

Adding records to a file is easy. Let's add the following record to the Customers file:

1. Choose Enter ➤ New Record.

2. Type **Brown** in the Last Name field and press the Tab key to move to the next field.
3. Type **John** in the First Name field and press the Tab key.
4. Type **123 Disk Drive** in the Address field and press the Tab key.
5. Type **Sunnyvale** in the City field and press the Tab key.
6. Type **CA** in the State field and press the Tab key.
7. Type **94086** in the Zip Code field and press the Tab key.
8. Type **4085551234** in the Phone field and press the Tab key.
9. Type **9000** in the Balance field and press the Tab key.
10. Press the spacebar or use the mouse to select Yes in the Taxable field.

Your screen should now look like Figure 4.2. If it doesn't, use the keyboard and mouse to change the record so that it matches the example in Figure 4.2.

FIGURE 4.2

Entering your first record

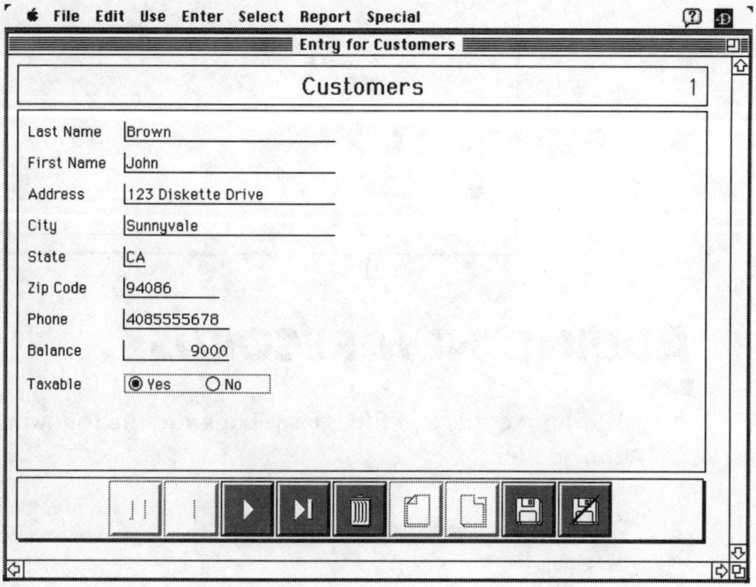

Now let's save the record:

1. Press the Enter key to save the record.
2. While holding down the ⌘ key, press the period key to cancel the next new record.

That's all there is to it. Entering information into your database is simple. You can also see that getting from no database to entering data is not a long journey. The database you have created is fairly simple but also very powerful. Now that you are entering data, you will be able to do all kinds of productive tasks with this database without much effort and in a fraction of the time it would take you to do them by hand.

Each time you save a new record, 4D creates another new record. This makes data entry go faster because you don't have to choose Enter ➤ New Record over and over when you are entering a series of records all at once. Once you have entered the last new record that you want to enter for now, you will press the Enter key to save the record. 4D will save the record and create another new one for you. You don't want to enter any more records so you can cancel this new record by pressing ⌘-period (.). After entering one or more new records, 4D displays the records as in list format. With this list format (called an *output layout*) you can look at a summary of several records all at once. I will talk about this output layout in more detail later on.

IMPORTANT KEYS FOR DATA ENTRY

You have just entered your first record into the Customers file. You used a few special keys to complete the data entry. These special keys each have a specific purpose.

The Tab Key

The Tab key is used to move the cursor from one field to another. But how does 4D know which field to move to next? In most cases, the first field for data entry will be the field in the upper-left corner of the layout. Data entry typically begins in the upper-left corner and ends in the lower-right corner. This makes sense because it's the same way we read (from upper-left to lower-right). However, with 4th Dimension you can change the tab order allowing you to design your layouts so that data entry begins in any field you wish and ends in any field you wish. I will explain tab order (which is actually called *entry order*) in *Chapter 12.*

If you want to move back to the last field you entered data into, hold down the Shift key and press Tab. Pressing Tab to move forward and Shift-Tab to move back is standard procedure in most applications.

The Return Key

The Return key works almost exactly the same way that the Tab key does. Pressing the Return key moves the cursor to the next field in the entry order. Pressing Shift-Return moves the cursor to the previous field in the entry order. So what's the difference between the Tab key and the Return key? The difference is how each deals with Text fields. A Text field allows you to enter up to 32,000 characters. A Text field is also the only field that allows you to enter carriage returns. Pressing the Tab key in a Text field will move the cursor to the next field. Pressing the Return key in a Text field however, inserts a carriage-return into the text field, moving the cursor down one line.

It would seem that there is no reason to have the Return key move the cursor from one field to the next if it is not going to do it consistently with all field types. The reason that the Return key is used is that most people find it easier to press the Return key instead of the Tab key. Later, you will be entering a few more records. When you do this, you will use the Return key instead of the Tab key. This will allow you to judge for yourself which is more comfortable for you.

The Enter Key

Pressing the Enter key saves the record to disk. When you chose Enter ➤ New Record, 4D didn't actually create a new record. In fact, at that point the record is not in the database yet. What it created could be thought of as a "potential record". The record has been created in the computer's memory but has not been saved to disk for permanent storage. Pressing the Enter key is a way of telling 4D that you have accepted this record and want it saved so you can access it later. As you were entering the record, you may have noticed a series of icons at the bottom of the screen. These icons are actually buttons that you can click to perform different tasks. The button that is second from the right and looks like a computer disk is the "Accept" or "Save" button. Clicking this button with the mouse is equivalent to pressing the Enter key. In both cases, the record will be saved to disk.

Don't confuse the Return and Enter keys. The Return key moves the cursor to the next field. The Enter key saves the record.

The ⌘-Period Key Combination

Pressing ⌘-period cancels a record. You know that the Enter key is used to save a record to disk. You also need a way to tell 4D not to save a record to disk. For example, you might begin entering a new customer into your Customers file then suddenly remember that you have already entered them before. You don't want to have a duplicate record so you want to tell 4D to cancel this new record you have created. By holding down the ⌘ key (the key with an apple on one side and a cloverleaf on the other) and pressing the period key, you are telling 4D to cancel the new record and consequently, it is not saved to disk.

If you have been using a Macintosh for any length of time you have probably already figured out that in most cases, pressing ⌘-period cancels that action being taken. By holding down a key (like the ⌘ key) and pressing another key, you are modifying the action of the second key. So while pressing the period key will type a period, pressing ⌘-period does something completely different. The ⌘ key is called a *modifier* key. A modifier key does not do anything when pressed alone. Rather, it modifies the action of another key. The other modifier keys are Option, Shift, and the Control key.

Other Keys

There are a few other keys you might use when entering data. You can use the arrow keys to move from character to character. The right arrow key moves the cursor forward one character. The left arrow key moves the cursor back one character. The Backspace key also moves the cursor back one character and erases as it goes.

VIEWING A LIST OF RECORDS

When you are in the User environment, 4th Dimension displays a list of records for the file you are currently accessing. From the list you can choose a record and modify (edit) it. After you enter one or more new records, 4D displays a list showing you the last record you entered. This helps you to keep track of where you are as you enter new records.

When you are viewing records in a list or editing just one record, you are using layouts.

WHAT ARE LAYOUTS?

When you Chose Enter ➤ New Record, 4th Dimension created a new record and displayed a layout designed as a form for you to use to enter the information for the new record. You entered the information into fields and pressed the Enter key to save the record to disk. 4th Dimension then displayed another layout designed to display records in list format. The layout used to enter the record is the files' *input* layout and the layout used to list records is the files' *output* layout.

If you are familiar with dBASE, an *input layout* is like an edit screen and an *output layout* is like a browse screen.

When you add a file to a 4D database, 4D automatically creates an input layout and an output layout for you, unless you create your own. Let's take a brief look at these two types of layouts. Later, we will be examining input and output layouts in more detail.

UNDERSTANDING INPUT LAYOUTS

To 4th Dimension, all layouts are created equal. This means that layouts don't come in different types. However, layouts are designed for different purposes. A layout that is designed to look like a form is called an *input* layout. An input layout is used to input information. You might design many different input layouts for each file in your database. Only one of these input layouts can be used at a time. You designate one layout as the current input layout for each file. By your indicating a layout as the current input layout, 4D knows which layout to use to display a record for editing. If you need to use a different layout for data entry, you can change the current input layout to any other layout that belongs to the file you are using. Figure 4.3 shows an example of an input layout.

FIGURE 4.3

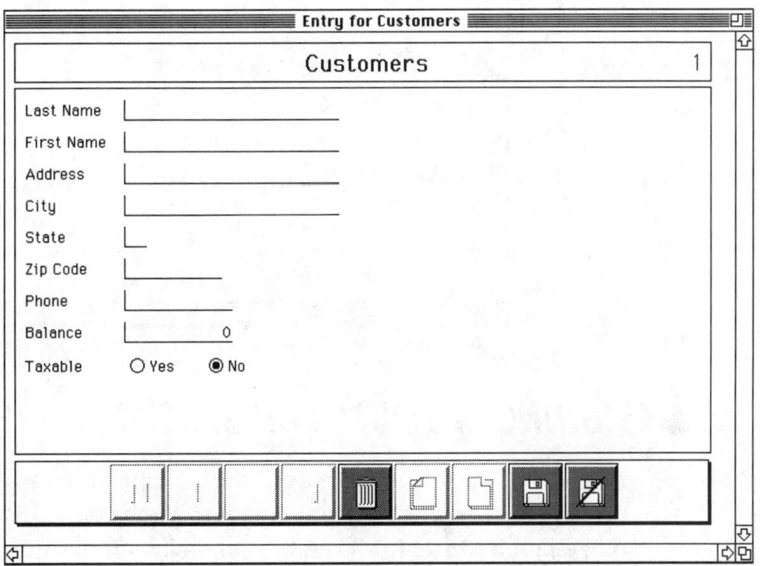

An example of an input layout

UNDERSTANDING OUTPUT LAYOUTS

Output layouts output information. Typically output layouts are designed to display information in a columnar format. An output layout will sometimes look like a form. For example, you might have one layout that displays a list of invoices on the screen and another layout designed to print invoices that you will give to your customers. Both of these layouts are output layouts. The first sends data to the screen and the second sends data to the printer. At any time, only one layout can be the current output layout for the file you are using. Figure 4.4 shows an example of an output layout.

FIGURE 4.4

An example of an output layout

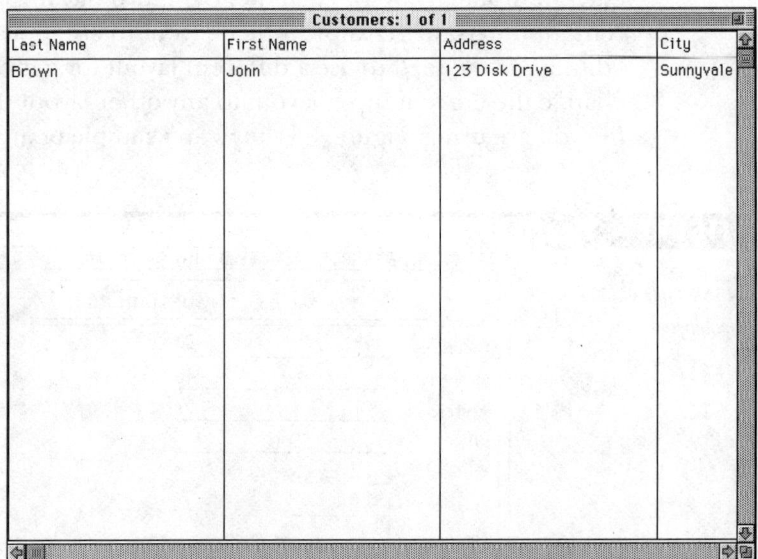

DESIGNING LAYOUTS FOR SPECIFIC PURPOSES

As you can see, layouts are designed for specific purposes. You could use an output layout as an input layout or visa-versa. This probably wouldn't make much sense, however, because a layout designed to look like a form for data entry is going to take up most of the vertical space on the screen. Consequently, you wouldn't be able to look at very many records as a list. Conversely, a layout designed for output as a list would not work well as an input layout if there were many fields, because you would not be able to look at all the fields on the screen at once as you entered the record.

4D allows you to have up to 32,000 layouts per database. That is more than you will ever need. 4D also stores them in a very compact format, so don't worry about creating extra layouts if you need them.

Output layouts are generally designed to summarize data, allowing you to choose one or more records to perform a task on. Input layouts are designed to show all the detail for one specific record and are used to edit the record.

CHANGING EXISTING RECORDS

Now that you know how to add new records to a file, you will also need to know how to make changes to existing records. To edit an existing record, you need to open the record into the input layout. As I mentioned earlier, the input layout is used to display detailed information about a record and allow you to edit that information. Right now you are viewing a list of records in the output layout. Let's make a few changes to the record that you just finished entering.

1. Double-click on John Brown's record.
2. Tap the Tab key a few times until the Address field is highlighted.
3. Type **123 Diskette Drive** as the new address.
4. Tap the Tab key a few more times until the Phone field is highlighted.
5. Type **4085555678** as the new phone number.
6. Tap the Enter key (or click the Save button) to save the record and return to the output layout.

Double-clicking is a standard method for opening files and folders on the Macintosh. Double-clicking on a record in the output layout opens the current input layout for the file and displays the record for editing. After you have changed some of the values in the fields, pressing the Enter key or clicking the Save button replaces the old version of the record with the new one.

In the next chapter, you will learn about the different ways you can locate the records you have entered in your database. Once you have located a record, you can use the same technique you just used to edit the record.

UNDOING AN EDIT

Occasionally, as you are entering information you will type over some existing information only to realize that you have changed the wrong information and can't remember what was there before. This is a common mistake with a simple solution. Provided that you haven't moved out of the field yet, you can press ⌘-Z to "undo" the edit. The new information you have entered will be replaced by the information that was in the field originally.

If you're like most people, you will occasionally do a very professional job of messing a record up completely. In this case, you can't use ⌘-Z to undo the changes because this works only with the field you are currently typing in. Instead, press ⌘-period to cancel the record. This will cancel any changes you have made to the record. After canceling the record, you can reopen it and start over.

GETTING SOME PRACTICE

It would be a good idea at this point to get some practice entering new records into your database and then making a few changes to them. Enter the records listed below. Remember to press the Enter key or click the **Save** button to save each record. Do *not* type the words *Phone, Taxable,* and *Balance.*

The Save button is also called the Accept button; we will talk more about the Accept button in *Chapter 12.*

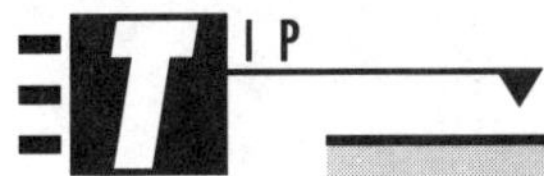

When you use key combinations (like ⌘-N), it is not necessary to enter the letter in uppercase. The computer knows that ⌘-N and ⌘-n are the same thing.

1. Choose Enter ➤ New Record (⌘-N).
2. Enter the records listed below:

   Jones, Sally
   56 Green Apple Road
   Irvine, CA 92715
   Phone: 7145559890
   Balance: 5500
   Taxable: No

   Williams, Ted
   4501 Evelyn Avenue
   Sunnyvale, CA 94086
   Phone: 4085558303
   Balance: 1500
   Taxable: Yes

   Simpson, Joanie
   921 Maple Street
   Anchorage, AK 99510
   Phone: 9045553245
   Balance: 6750
   Taxable: No

Smith, Ron
29 Old Town #4
Newport News, VA 23606
Phone: 7035553890
Balance: 8877
Taxable: Yes

Kimball, Margaret
8990 Main Street
Framingham, MA 01701
Phone: 5085557890
Balance: 1050
Taxable: No

3. Press the **Save** button after entering each record.
4. Once you have entered the last record, press the **Cancel** button (⌘-period) to cancel the new record.

After entering the last record, 4th Dimension returns you to the output layout and displays the last record you entered. If you were in the middle of entering several records and you decided to take a break, when you returned to continue entering records you would know exactly where you left off.

At this point you may want to review the records you have entered. Choose Select ➤ Show All.

The Show All menu item displays all the records in the file that you are viewing. Now that you can see all of the records you just finished entering, let's practice making a few changes.

1. Double-click Ron Smith's record to open it.
2. Change the Address field to **29 Old Town #5**.
3. Save the record.
4. Double-click on Margaret Kimball's record.
5. Change the Address field to **22 East Main Street**.
6. Save the record.

USING THE ENTER IN LIST FEATURE

There will be times when you need to make a few small changes to several records. You could double-click on each record, change it, and then save the record and go on to the next record that needs to be edited. However, there is a faster way. The Enter In List menu item allows you to make changes to records from the output layout. This method can be faster because you don't have to open each record.

Let's make a few changes to your records using the Enter In List feature.

1. Choose Enter In List from the Enter menu.
2. Click on Joanie in the First Name field.
3. Change *Joanie* to **Joan**.
4. Highlight **56 Green Apple Road** in the Address field.
5. Change the address to **14 Pear Street**.
6. Choose Enter ➤ Enter In List (⌘-,).

When you choose Enter In List, 4D puts a check mark next to the Enter In List menu item to indicate that you are in "Enter In List" mode. While in this mode, you can make changes to records in the output layout. You can use the Tab key to move from one field to another. If you have used a spreadsheet program like Microsoft Excel, this kind of editing will seem familiar. 4D stays in this mode until you choose Enter In List again.

You may be wondering why 4D requires you to choose Enter In List when you want to make changes using the output layout rather than letting you make changes anytime you want. Normally, clicking on a record highlights the entire record, indicating that the record is selected. By selecting one or more records, you can tell 4D to perform some task on only those records you have selected.

Enter In List needs to be a mode because clicking on a record is going to have a different effect when you are editing the values of that record. While editing in "Enter In List" mode, clicking on a field in the record puts the insertion point (cursor) into the field, allowing you to type instead of highlighting the entire record.

HOW MANY RECORDS CAN 4D HOLD?

So far, you have entered six records into the Customers file in your database. Each file you create in your database can hold up to 16 million records. This is probably more records than you will ever need. For example, if each record took one minute to enter, 16 million records would take over 30 years of non-stop typing! Needless to say, 4D can hold all of the records you can enter into it.

SEARCHING FOR RECORDS

5

MAC TRACKS MAC

To perform a simple search — 81

1. Choose Select ➤ Search And Modify.
2. Type the search text in the box next to the field you wish to search.
3. Click the **OK** button or press the Enter key.

To show all the records in a file — 82

Choose Select ➤ Select Show All

To use the input layout as a form for filling in search criteria — 83

1. Choose Select ➤ Search By Layout.
2. Using the Tab key or the mouse, position the cursor in the field you wish to search in.
3. Type the search text in the field.
4. Press the Enter key or click the **Save** button (the disk button) to perform the search.

To perform a simple search with the Search Editor — 85

1. Choose Select ➤ Search Editor (⌘-S).
2. Choose Edit ➤ Clear.
3. Click on a field.

4. Click on one of the comparators.
5. Type the search text in the Value field.
6. Click **OK** or press the Enter key to perform the search.

To narrow a search to the current selection — 94

Just remember to click the **Search in selection** check box in the Search Editor.

To save criteria you have entered in the Search Editor for use in future searches — 96

1. Choose Select ➤ Search Editor.
2. Click the **Save** button.
3. Type a name for the search document.
4. Click **OK** to save the file to disk.

To recall a search criteria file from disk — 96

1. Click the **Load** button.
2. Click on the name of the search criteria file.
3. Click the **OK** button to load the criteria.

Featuring

- *Searching for records*
- *The current selection in a file*
- *The current record in a file*
- *Saving and recalling search criteria*
- *Using ranges, conjunctions, comparators, and wildcards to narrow searches*

IN THIS CHAPTER you will learn how to locate records in your database. 4th Dimension provides you with several different ways to locate records in your database files. In database terminology, locating records is called *searching.*

Searching for records means finding those records in a file that have information you want. Because files are made up of fields, you need to decide which field or fields might contain the information you are looking for. You may want to locate all of the customers in your Customers file that are located in the state of California so you can send letters to them announcing a special sale.

You search for records using a *criterion.* A criterion is an expression that results in a true or false answer. For example, if you wanted to search for all the customers in California, you would tell 4th Dimension to find all of the records in the Customers file where the State field has the value *CA.* 4D would then look at each record in the file and compare the value in the State field to the value you asked for (CA). In essence, 4D is looking at each record and asking itself "Is it true that the State field has the value CA?" If the answer is yes, 4D remembers that this record matches the search criteria. If 4D finds any records that match, it groups these records together, allowing you to perform tasks on only the records that were found. After searching for records, you could perform many database management functions, including the following:

- Printing the records in a report
- Sorting the records

- Deleting the records
- Editing the records

Searching is a basic function of any database and 4D gives you many different ways to perform this function.

USING SEARCH AND MODIFY

The simplest way to perform a search is using the Search And Modify menu item in the User environment. Search And Modify displays a window listing all the indexed fields in the file you are searching. Figure 5.1 shows the Search And Modify window as it looks for the Customers file.

You enter your search criteria by typing the value you are searching for in the box next to the field you want 4D to search. When you press the **OK** button, 4D will perform the search. If any records are found, 4D will open the input layout and display the first record it has found. Once the records are there, you can edit them; click the **Next Record** button to display the next record found or click the **Save** or **Cancel** button to return to the output layout. The output layout will display all of the records that 4D found when it performed the search. In case you have taken a break and don't have your database open, let's go through the steps to open the database and access the User Environment. Once

FIGURE 5.1

The Search And Modify window

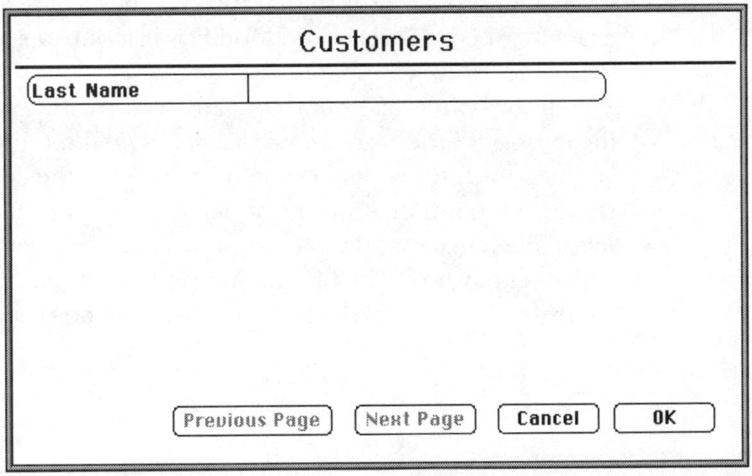

there, we can try Search and Modify. If you haven't left 4D, you can skip the first three steps.

1. Locate the Learn 4D*f* folder and double-click the folder icon to open it.
2. Locate the Learn 4D file and double-click on it to open it.
3. Select Use ➤ User.
4. Choose Select ➤ Search And Modify.
5. Type **Kimball** in the box next to Last Name.
6. Click the **OK** button or press the Enter key.

4th Dimension locates the first (and in this case, the only) record where the Last Name field is equal to *Kimball.* Once the record is found, the input layout is opened to display the record. If more than one customer had the last name *Kimball,* you could use the **Next Record** button to display the next Kimball in the database. Now close the input layout and return to the output layout.

7. Click the **Cancel** button or press ⌘-period.

Notice that the record that was found is now displayed in the output layout. You access the records in your files by moving back and forth from the output layout to the input layout. 4D presents you with a summary list of records so that you can choose a record to open and examine or edit. Search And Modify is just one of several ways you can locate records in your database files.

If the search had not found any records, 4D would have displayed the message *There are no selected records for the file: Customers.* Don't be alarmed by this message. It doesn't mean that the customers file has no records in it; rather, it means none of the records in the file are currently selected. Notice that the picture shows a file cabinet with records in it and an empty box. The file cabinet represents the Customers file and the empty box represents the fact that there are no records selected.

UNDERSTANDING THE CURRENT SELECTION

When you search for records in a file, 4th Dimension locates all of the records in the file that match the criterion you have entered. The result of the search is a selection of records from the file. This selection of records is known as the *current selection.* Note that *all* files have a current selection; it might be empty, however, if you haven't performed a search or selected Select ➤ Show All.

The purpose of the current selection is to establish a group of records that you will want 4D to perform functions on. For example, you might search for all of your customers in California and then print labels for a special mailing.

Each file in your database has a current selection at all times. Choosing Select ➤ Show All makes the current selection contain all the records. The records are then displayed in the output layout because it is currently on the screen. If you performed a search that did not find any records, the current selection for the file you were searching would be empty. Say you had a database with 10,000 customer records. If you searched the database using a criterion and found 500 records, the current selection would be those 500 records.

The concept that each file has a current selection is an important one and is central to the design for 4th Dimension. When you print a report, it is the records in the current selection that are printed. When you sort records, it is the records in the current selection that are sorted. The process of performing a database task on existing records, therefore, usually consists of two steps. First, you create a current selection (perhaps by searching a file in your database) and secondly, you perform some function on the records in the current selection. Let's perform a search to demonstrate the current selection.

1. Choose Select ➤ Search By Layout (⌘-L).
2. Type **CA** into the State field.
3. Press the Enter key or click the **Save** button.

The three records found represent the current selection. Now change the current selection to all the records in the file by choosing Select ➤ Show All.

If you take a list with you when you go grocery shopping, you probably check off the items on the list as you find them. You can think of the current selection as the checkmarks on your list. The checkmarks indicate the items. The current selection is a list of the records found.

All the records in the file are displayed. You have just changed the current selection from the customers in California to all the records in the Customers file.

UNDERSTANDING THE CURRENT RECORD

The *current record* is the record you are working with. Just as each file has a current selection, each file also has a current record. For example, when you double-click on a record in the output layout to modify it in the input layout, that record becomes the current record.

The concept that each file has a current record is equally as important as the concept of the current selection. Don't worry if these concepts don't seem clear enough right now. You are just beginning with 4th Dimension and these concepts will become clearer as you learn more.

USING SEARCH BY LAYOUT

Search By Layout lets you use the input layout as a form for filling in a search criterion. This might be easier to use since it is typically the same layout used for data entry. When you choose Select ➤ Search By Layout, 4D displays the current input layout to allow you to enter values into the fields you want to search in. Let's try using Search By Layout to find all of the customers that live in California.

1. Choose Select ➤ Search By Layout.
2. Using the Tab key or the mouse, position in the cursor in the State field.
3. Type **CA** in the State field.
4. Press the Enter key or click the **Save** button (the disk button) to perform the search.

Once the layout is accepted, 4D performs the search using the values entered into the fields. The records found by the search are then displayed in the output layout.

In some cases you may want to perform a search with a more specific criterion. Let's say you wanted to find only those customers who were in Sunnyvale, California. You could enter *Sunnyvale* into the city field to perform the search. This may not be accurate however, because there could be a city called Sunnyvale in a state other than California. To make sure that you find only customers who live Sunnyvale, California, you will need to give 4D multiple criteria.

1. Choose Select ➤ Search By Layout.
2. Type **Sunnyvale** into the City field.
3. Press the Tab key once to move to the State field.
4. Type **CA** into the State field.
5. Press the Enter key or click the **Save** button.

By entering both the city and state you were looking for, you gave 4D a more specific criterion. In this case, 4D searched for records where the City field was equal to Sunnyvale *and* the State field was equal to CA. When records have to match one criterion *and* another, it is called an *AND search.*

Search By Layout allows you to fill in as many fields as you require to specify what you are searching for. If you had also clicked Yes for the Taxable field, 4D would have added this to the search criteria and only found customers who lived in Sunnyvale, California and were taxable.

You can perform other types of searches with Search By Layout. For example, let's say you wanted to search for all customers whose Balance is greater than or equal to 6000. You can perform this type of search by typing >= in the field you want to search before entering the value want to search for. The >= is called a *comparator,* because 4D is going to use this test as it compares the value in the field to the value you are searching for. Let's try it.

1. Select Search By layout from the Select menu.
2. Position the cursor in the Balance field.
3. Type **>=6000** in the Balance field.
4. Press the Enter key or click the **Save** button.

As you can see, the records found are only those that have a balance greater than or equal to 6000.

Here is a list of other comparators that can be used in a search:

Comparator	**Meaning**	**Example**
<	Less than	<5
>	Greater than	>500
<=	Less than or equal to	<=12/01/94
>=	Greater than or equal to	>=

If you perform these types of searches on Alpha fields or Text fields, the search is alphabetical. For example, entering **>=Jones** in the Last Name field would locate all the Customers whose last name comes after *Jones* alphabetically.

By the way, you may have noticed that the cursor turned into an eye while you were entering your search criterion. This is 4th Dimension's way of reminding you that you are entering a search criteria and not a new record. The eye means that you are "looking" for records.

USING THE SEARCH EDITOR

The Search Editor is designed for more complex criteria. Search And Modify and Search By Layout are great when the criteria are simple. There will be times however, when the search criteria are more complex. The Search Editor allows you to perform searches that could not be performed with Search And Modify or Search By Layout. You can also save the criteria you create and reuse them later. Figure 5.2 shows the Search Editor.

The Search Editor has several parts to it. The top half of the Search Editor displays the criteria as you build it with the Search Editor. The left scrollable area displays the fields from the file you are accessing. The center scrollable area displays the comparators. The right area displays conjunctions. To enter a search criterion, you select a field and a comparator and then enter the value for the criterion. 4D makes it easy to know which of these areas you need to select from by blinking the rectangle that surrounds an area. Let's try a simple search.

1. Choose Select ➤ Search Editor (⌘-S).
2. Choose Edit ➤ Clear.
3. Click on the State field.

FIGURE 5.2

The Search Editor with search criteria

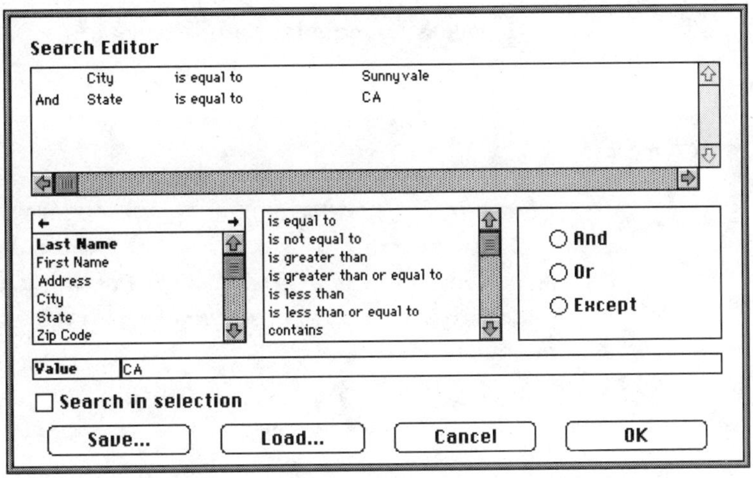

Search Editor

	City	is equal to	Sunnyvale
And	State	is equal to	CA

Last Name
First Name
Address
City
State
Zip Code

is equal to
is not equal to
is greater than
is greater than or equal to
is less than
is less than or equal to
contains

And
Or
Except

Value CA

Search in selection

Save... Load... Cancel OK

4. Click on the **is not equal to** comparators.
5. Type the **CA** in the Value field.
6. Click **OK** or press the Enter key to perform the search.

When you opened the Search Editor, you probably noticed that there was already a criterion there. The criterion is actually the one you entered when you used Search By Layout. When you use Search By Layout, 4D takes the criterion you enter and passes it along to the Search Editor. Selecting Edit ➤ Clear deletes the criterion, allowing you to enter a new one.

After the search is completed, 4D displays the records that match the criteria. Because you are viewing the output layout, 4D displays the records in the output layout. If you access the Search Editor from the input layout, 4D will use the input layout to display the first record it finds. From there you can use the **Next Record** button to move to the next record in the current selection. Let's try it.

1. Double-click on the first record to display it in the input layout.
2. Choose Select ➤ Search Editor.
3. Click on **is not equal to** in the criteria box at the top of the Search Editor to highlight it.
4. Click **is equal to** in the comparator scrollable area to replace **is not equal to** with **is equal to**.
5. Click **OK** or press the Enter key.

The Search Editor is more complicated than Search And Modify or Search By layout, but it allows you to perform more complex searches than the other two methods.

Notice that you can replace pieces of criteria in the Search Editor without clearing the criteria and retyping it again. This can save you time if the criteria are many and you are performing similar searches.

After the search is completed, 4D displays the first record in the current selection in the input layout. Figure 5.3 shows the input layout with the **Next Record** button labeled. Try moving to the next record in the current selection by clicking the Next Record button.

FIGURE 5.3

The input layout displaying the first record found

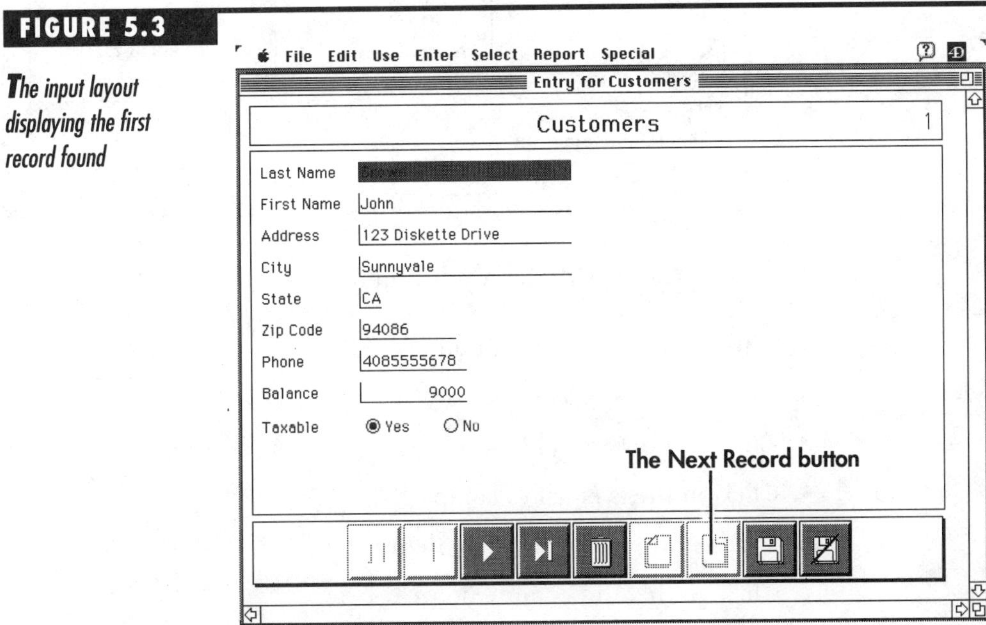

THE AND CONJUNCTION

The *And* conjunction is used to find records that match more than one criteria. When you used Search By Layout, you learned about AND searches. When you used Search By Layout to perform an AND search, you searched for Customers whose City was Sunnyvale *and* whose State was CA. The Search Editor can also do AND searches. Let's try the same search using the Search Editor. Figure 5.4 shows what the Search Editor looks like with these criteria entered.

FIGURE 5.4

The Search Editor displaying an AND search

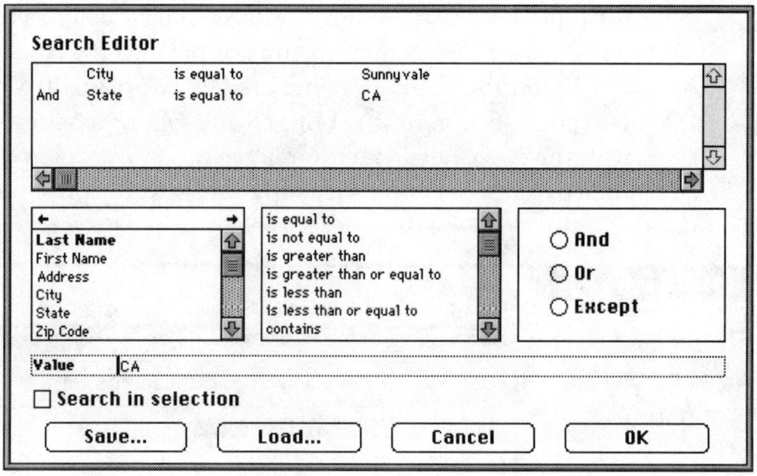

Let's try a search with the AND conjunction:

1. Choose Select ➤ Search Editor (⌘-S).
2. Choose Edit ➤ Clear.
3. Click on the City field.
4. Click on the **is equal to** comparator.
5. Type **Sunnyvale** in the value field.
6. Click on the **And** conjunction.
7. Click on the State field.
8. Click on the **is equal to** comparator.
9. Type **CA** in the value field.
10. Click **OK** or press the Enter key.

4th Dimension displays the records found in the search, including only those for whom the customer's City is Sunnyvale **and** the State is CA.

You may want to find all of the records where a field matches any one of a list of values. For example, you might want to find all of the Customers in both California and Virginia. At first, it appears that you would use the And conjunction because you are searching for Customers in California **and** Virginia. Let's try this kind of search.

1. Choose Select ➤ Search Editor (⌘-S).
2. Choose Edit ➤ Clear.
3. Click on the State field.
4. Click on the **is equal to** comparator.
5. Type **CA** in the value field.
6. Click on the **And** conjunction.
7. Click on the State field.
8. Click on the **is equal to** comparator.
9. Type **VA** in the value field.
10. Click **OK** or press the Enter key to perform the search.

No records were found that match that criteria. Why? Well, think about how the criteria reads: *State is equal to California And State is equal to Virginia.* This would never find any records because the value in the State field for a record can not be equal to both California and Virginia. To perform the type of search we really want to do, you will use the *Or* conjunction.

THE OR CONJUNCTION

The *Or* conjunction allows you to search for records that match any one of several criteria. You know now that the AND conjunction is not going to work if you are trying to find customers who live in California and Virginia. In fact, it not grammatically correct to say that we are looking for Customers who live in California and Virginia. This would be true only if for some reason we were trying to find customers who are part time residents of both states.

What we are really looking for are our customers who live in *either* California *or* Virginia. In this case, we will use the Or conjunction. With the Or conjunction, you might be looking for records where a particular field matches one of many values. You might be looking for records where different fields match different values. What is important is that if any one of the criteria is true, the record will be found. Let's try an Or search.

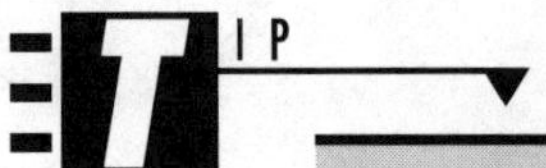

The And and Or conjunctions are often confused. If a search is not finding the records you are looking for, try switching from one to the other and trying your search again.

1. Choose Select ➤ Search Editor.
2. Click on the **And** conjunction in the top half of the Search Editor.
3. Click the **Or** radio button to replace the And conjunction with the Or conjunction.
4. Click **OK** or press the Enter key to perform the search.

THE EXCEPT CONJUNCTION

The *Except* conjunction allows you to search for records that do not match a criteria. Using the Except conjunction is no different from using the **is not equal to** comparator. For example, the criterion **State is not equal to CA** will find the same records as **Except State is equal to CA**. If they are the same, why have both? The Except conjunction exists mostly to make criteria read more clearly. It is easier to understand the criteria **State is equal to CA Except Zip Code is equal to 94086** than **State is equal to CA And Zip Code is not equal to 94086**. Figures 5.5 and 5.6 show these two criteria. Let's try a search using Except.

1. Choose Select ➤ Search Editor (⌘-S).
2. Choose Edit ➤ Clear.
3. Click on the State field.
4. Click on the **is equal to** comparator.

FIGURE 5.5

Search using the "is not equal to" comparator

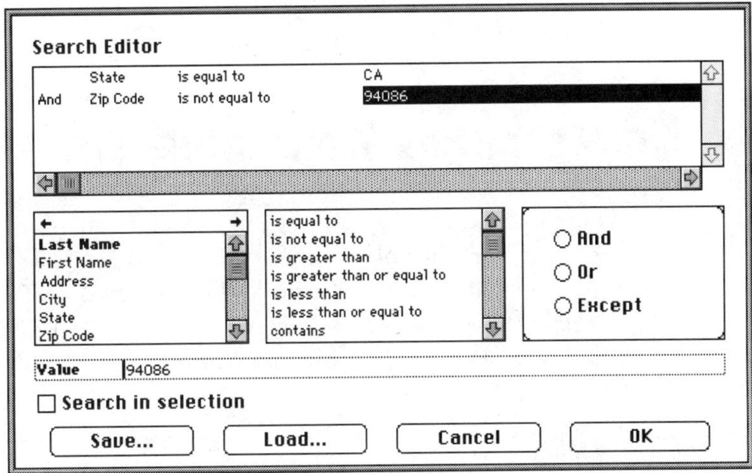

FIGURE 5.6

Search using the Except conjunction

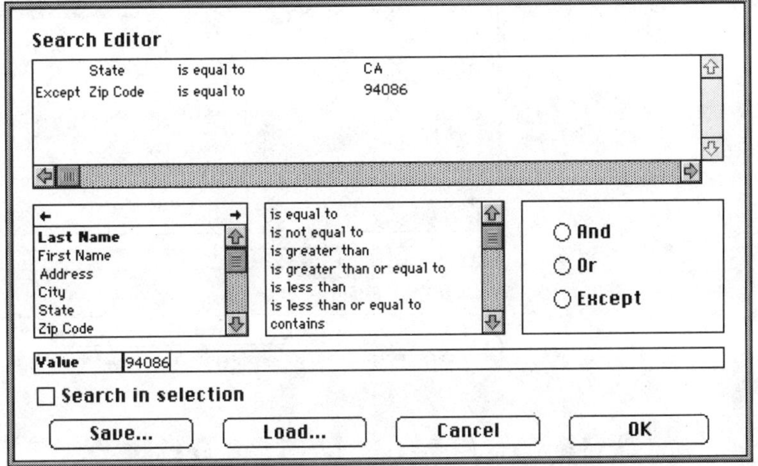

5. Type **CA** in the value field.
6. Click on the **Except** conjunction.
7. Click on the Zip Code field.
8. Click on the **is equal to** comparator.

9. Type **94086** in the value field.

10. Click **OK** or press the Enter key to perform the search.

COMBINING AND AND OR SEARCHES

There may be cases where it would make sense to use *And* and *Or* together. For example, suppose you want to see all the records for customers in California or Virginia who are Taxable. The criteria read as *Locate customers whose State field is equal to CA or VA and whose Taxable field is equal to Yes.* Figure 5.7 shows how these criteria would look.

FIGURE 5.7

***A** search for customers in California or Virginia who are taxable*

Search Editor

	State	is equal to	CA
Or	State	is equal to	VA
And	Taxable	is equal to	False

Address
City
State
Zip Code
Phone
Taxable

is equal to
is not equal to
is greater than
is greater than or equal to
is less than
is less than or equal to
contains

And
Or
Except

Value Yes No

Search in selection

Save... Load... Cancel OK

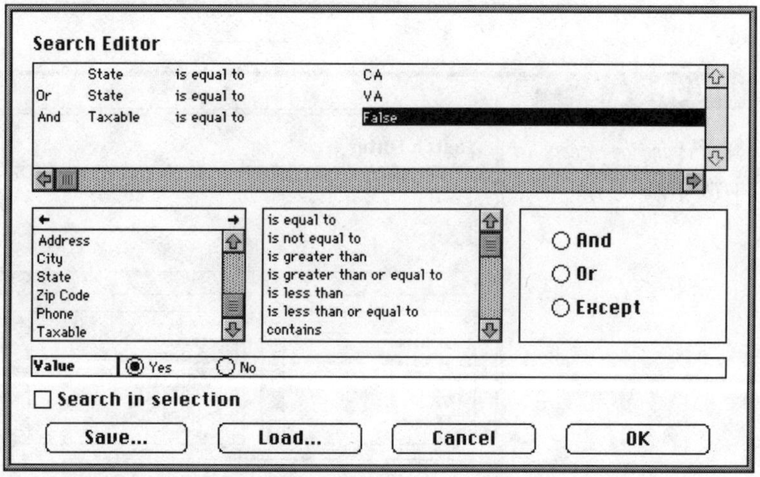

NARROWING A SEARCH

The Search Editor normally searches the entire file, but it can also be used to search only the current selection. For example, you may have just searched for all the customers in California or Virginia. Now you want to find the customers in California or Virginia that are taxable. You could perform the search again adding the taxable criteria. However, it will be faster and easier to have 4th Dimension simply search only through the records you have already found, looking for customers that are taxable.

This is called *narrowing* a search. You started with a selection of records that contained customers in California and Virginia. Now you want to narrow down the selection to only those customers out of this group that are taxable. Let's try this type of search.

1. Choose Select ➤ Search Editor (⌘-S).
2. Choose Edit ➤ Clear.
3. Click the State field.
4. Click the **is equal to** comparator.
5. Type **CA** in the value field.
6. Click the **Or** conjunction.
7. Click the State field again.
8. Click the **is equal to** comparator.
9. Type **VA** in the value field.
10. Click the **OK** button or press the Enter key to perform the search.

4D finds all the records for customers in California or Virginia. These records are now the current selection for the Customers file. The next step is to perform another search for the customers in this selection that are taxable.

1. Choose Select ➤ Search Editor (⌘-S).
2. Choose Edit ➤ Clear.
3. Click the Taxable field.
4. Click the **is equal to** comparator.
5. Click on the **Yes** radio button in the value field.
6. Click the **Search in selection** check box.
7. Click on the **OK** button or press the Enter key to perform the search.

If the fields you are searching are not indexed, the search will take longer as you enter more and more records. You may want to index the fields you are searching often.

This time, 4th Dimension searched only through the current selection looking for customers that are taxable. The current selection has been reduced to only the records found in the first search that also matched the criteria in the second search. From here you could continue to perform searches to further narrow the selection down. As long as you click the **Search in selection** check box, 4D will search through the records in the current selection only.

SEARCHING FOR RANGES

Another common type of search is a *range search.* A range search is one where you search for records in which a field contains any one of a range of values. A range search is also called a *betweens* search because you are searching for records where a field is between two values. For example, you might want to find all the customers whose last name starts with the letters *A–M.* Figure 5.8 shows what this criterion would look like in the Search Editor.

It might seem at first that you would be looking for customers whose last name is greater than *A* and less than *M.* Notice, though, that the criteria in Figure 5.8 use *greater than or equal to* and *less than or equal to.* If you were to use *greater than* instead of *greater than or equal to,* you would never find any customers whose last name begins with *A,* because the criterion would be looking only for last names beyond the letter *A. Greater than or equal to* and *less than or equal to* are used to include the value you are searching on, while *greater than* and *less than* are used to exclude the value.

A common range search is using date fields. Suppose you want to find all the invoices for last year. The criteria might be *Invoice Date greater than or equal to 1/1/93 And Invoice Date less than or equal to 12/31/93,* as seen in Figure 5.9. Another example might be searching for all the employees whose salary is between $25,000 and $50,000.

FIGURE 5.8

A range search in the Search Editor

Search Editor
Last Name is greater than or equal to A
And Last Name is less than or equal to M
Last Name
First Name
Address
City
State
Zip Code
is equal to
is not equal to
is greater than
is greater than or equal to
is less than
is less than or equal to
contains
And
Or
Except
Value M
Search in selection
Save...
Load...
Cancel
OK

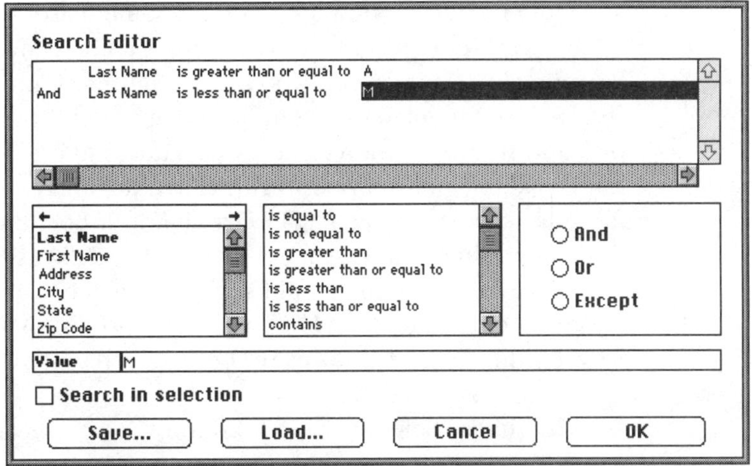

FIGURE 5.9

A range search using Date fields

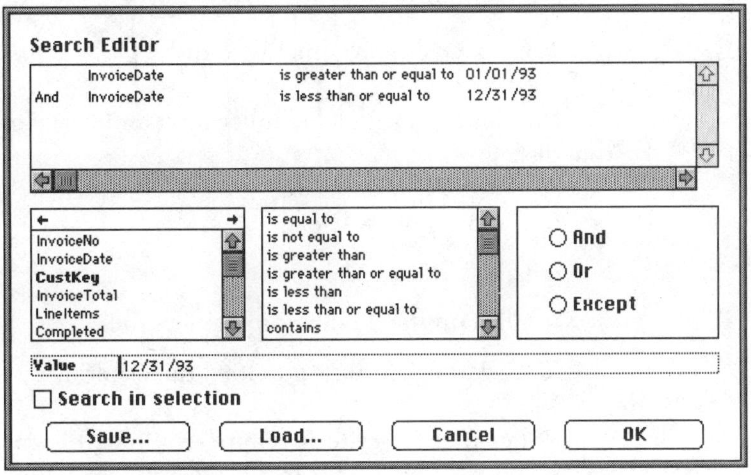

Search Editor
InvoiceDate is greater than or equal to 01/01/93
And InvoiceDate is less than or equal to 12/31/93
InvoiceNo
InvoiceDate
CustKey
InvoiceTotal
LineItems
Completed
is equal to
is not equal to
is greater than
is greater than or equal to
is less than
is less than or equal to
contains
And
Or
Except
Value 12/31/93
Search in selection
Save...
Load...
Cancel
OK

SAVING SEARCHES FOR FUTURE USE

Sometimes your search criteria get extensive and complex. Once you enter a long criteria list, you won't want to have to remember it and enter it again the next time you want to do the same search. If it is long enough or complex enough, you might not enter it correctly the second time. Fortunately, 4D allows you to save the search criteria you enter so that you can use them later without having to re-enter them. By now you have probably noticed the **Save** and **Load** buttons in the Search Editor. These buttons allow you to save the criteria as a document and load it from that file later when you need it. The search editor documents are files on the desktop just like your Learn 4D structure and data files. These Search Editor files are very small and use a minimal amount of disk space. Let's try saving criteria to disk. The last criteria used should still be in the Search Editor. If not, go back to the last exercise and re-enter them.

1. Choose Select ➤ Search Editor.
2. Click the **Save** button.
3. Type **Taxable Customers** as the name of the search document.
4. Click **OK** to save the file to disk.

Now let's clear the current criteria and try reloading the criteria from disk.

1. Choose Edit ➤ Clear.
2. Click the **Load** button.
3. Click on the **Taxable Customers** file.
4. Click the **OK** button to load the criteria.

Notice that the criteria reappear. While this particular criteria list is small, you might have a list that is several lines long. Saving criteria to disk will save you a great deal of typing. If you have never used a database before, it will be helpful to save criteria once you know they are correct. After a while, you will become comfortable with the Search Editor and will know exactly what to enter to find the records you are looking for. But for now, saving the criteria to disk will save you time and frustration trying to duplicate a search criteria that you used before.

You can, of course, save criteria anywhere on your disk. However, it's probably best to keep them in the same folder as your database to make them easy to find. If you begin to accumulate several criteria files, you might want to create a folder for them inside your database folder.

USING THE SEARCH BY FORMULA EDITOR

While the Search Editor is very powerful, it cannot perform every kind of search. When you need to search for records that match the result of a calculation, you will use the Search By Formula Editor. You can use 4D's built-in commands and functions in your calculations to perform searches that you can't perform with the Search Editor. It is shown in Figure 5.10.

FIGURE 5.10

The Search By Formula Editor

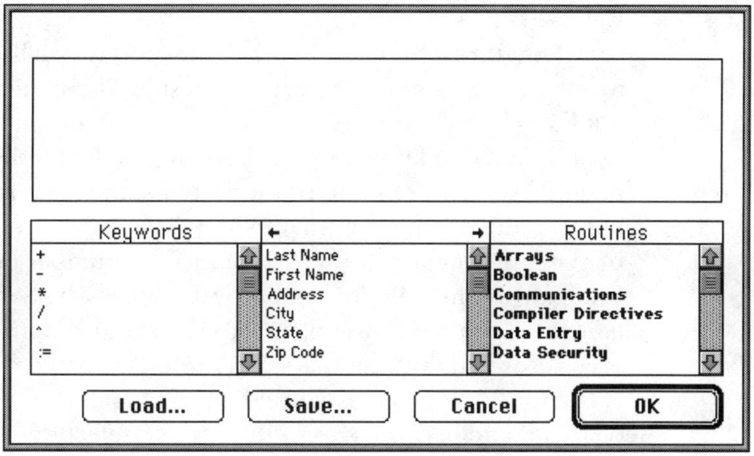

USING 4D COMMANDS AND FUNCTIONS FOR SEARCHING

What kind of searches can you perform with the Search By Formula editor? Practically any search that the Search Editor can't perform.

Say you are printing labels and you notice that some of the company names are too long to fit on the labels you have. After examining the labels you determine that names longer than 15 characters won't fit. Using the Search By Formula editor, you can search for the companies that have names longer than 15 characters. The formula would look like this:

```
Length([Customers]Company Name)>15
```

When you give a function a value to work on (like the contents of the Company Name field), we say the value is "passed" to the function.

Length is a function in 4D. A function is usually something that performs a calculation and returns the result. The Length function figures out how many characters there are in an alphanumeric or text field. The Length function knows how to calculate the length by looking in the parentheses that follow it. In the formula, the Company Name field is in between the parentheses that follow the Length function. Consequently, the Length function is going to return the number of characters in the Company Name field for the current record. The Search By Formula editor will compare this formula to each record in the file. As it moves to each record, 4D will compare this formula to the record. If the Company Name for the record has more than 15 characters, then that record will be found and become part of the current selection.

There are other functions that can be used to perform searches. Say you had a file that kept track of invoices. You would probably have an Invoice Date field. You might be interested in seeing what kind of ordering trends occur during the week. For example, you might want to know how many orders come in on Mondays. With the Search Editor, you would have to enter the date of every Monday of every year that you have invoices for. Since there are roughly 52 Mondays in every year, that could take some time! Instead, you can use another one of 4D's functions called Day number.

The Day number function will tell you what day of the week a day falls on. This function returns a 1 for dates that occur on Sundays and a 7 for dates that occur on Saturdays. So, the formula to search for all invoices that were taken on Monday would look like this:

```
Day number([Invoices]Invoice Date)=2
```

Because a calculation is involved, 4D cannot use its indexes when performing a Search By Formula. This means that the more records there are in the file, the longer the search will take.

There are many other functions built in to 4D. You can consult your Language Reference or *Appendix C* for information on other functions. With these functions and the Search By Formula editor you can perform just about any search you can think of.

WILDCARD SEARCHING

When you are searching for records, you don't always know exactly what you are looking for. When you searched for the customer whose last name was *Kimball*, you found one record. In this case, you knew the entire and exact spelling of the customer's last name. There may be times however, when you only have a piece of information to work with and not the entire thing. For example, you might remember that the person's name begins with *Kim* or ends with *ball* or that their last name has *im* somewhere in it. Fortunately, 4th Dimension has the ability to perform these types of searches.

The @ (called the *at*) symbol is a special character that allows you to tell 4th Dimension that you know only a piece of the information you are looking for. You can use the @ symbol with Search By Layout, Search And Modify, the Search Editor, and the Search By Formula Editor. Using the @ symbol, you can perform three different searches. These searches are *Begins With, Contains,* and *Ends With.*

BEGINS WITH SEARCHES

A *Begins With* is one where you are searching for records in which the value in a field begins with whatever you are searching for. You might be looking for all the customers whose company namc begins with *ACME.* In this case a Begins With search would find names like *ACME Tools, ACME Diaper Service,* and even *Acmentos Italian Restaurant.* A Begins With search is also useful when you suspect that you may have misspelled something. Suppose you entered *ACME Bakkery.* Because you misspelled *bakery,* you might have trouble finding it later. It you searched for *ACME Bakery,* 4D would report that it found no records. In case you did misspell the name, you could then use a Begins With search to look for customers whose company name begins with *ACME B.* This search would locate the record because only the first six letters have to match instead of all. Let's try a Begins With search.

1. Choose Select ➤ Search By Layout.
2. Type **S@** in the Last Name field.
3. Click the **Save** button or press the Enter key to begin the search.

Notice that the only records found were those where the Last Name begins with *S.* By entering an @ after the *S,* you are telling 4D to look for records where the Last Name begins with *S.* You can type as much of the last name as you wish followed by the @ symbol.

CONTAINS SEARCHES

A *Contains* search allows you to look for records where a field contains the value you are looking for. For example, if you were searching for the customers who have the word *computer* somewhere in their company name, you would use a Contains search. The result of this search would find names like *Apple Computer, Inc.*, *Computers Plus*, and *Super Computers, Inc.*

A common typo that wreaks havoc during searches is entering a space as the first character in a field. For example, during data entry, the user is about to enter *Smith* in the Last Name field. By accident, the user enters a space and then types the name *Smith.* On the screen everything looks normal.

Later, locating this customer will be frustrating at best because the user will be using the Search Editor to locate the customer whose last name is *Smith* not *(space)Smith.* It's even more frustrating because they will be able to scan the output layout and find the record they are looking for. Usually at this point the user thinks that the Search Editor doesn't work. The reality is that 4D did exactly what it was told to do. It searched for customers whose Last Name was equal to *Smith,* not *(space)Smith.* In a later chapter, you will learn how to have 4D remove any extra spaces at the beginning or end of an entry. Let's say however, that you already have entered many records, some of which have spaces that have been entered accidentally at the beginning of Last Name field. A Contains search makes it easy to find these records.

A Contains search works just like a Begins With search. The only difference is that you enter the @ symbol both before and after the value you are searching for. Let's try it.

1. Choose Select ➤ Search By Layout.
2. Type **@2@** in the Address field.
3. Click the **Save** button or press the Enter key to perform the search.

4D does not use the index of a field when performing a Contains search. This means that a Contains search will take longer as the number of records in the file increases, regardless of indexing.

In this case, 4th Dimension locates all of the records that have an address that contains a *2*. In some cases, the 2 was the first character in the field and in other cases it was in a different position.

ENDS WITH SEARCHES

The *Ends With* search is used to locate records where a field ends with a value. For example, you might use an Ends With search to locate all the customers whose company name ends with *Inc.*

To perform an Ends With search, the @ symbol is positioned at the beginning of the value instead of at the end. Let's try it.

1. Choose Select ➤ Search By Layout.
2. Type **@N** in the First Name field.
3. Click the **Save** button or press the Enter key to perform the search.

4D does not use the index of a field when performing an Ends With search. This means that an Ends With search will take longer as the number of records in the file increases, regardless of indexing.

Notice that 4D found only those customers whose first name ends with the letter *N*. Just like the Begins With and Contains searches, you can enter as many characters to search for as you wish. The important part is to make sure that the first character is the @ symbol.

SORTING RECORDS

MAC TRACKS MAC

To list customers in a database by Last Name 108

1. Choose Select ➤ Show All.
2. Choose Select ➤ Sort Selection (⌘-T).
3. Click on the Last Name field in the list of fields.
4. Click the **OK** button or press the Enter key to begin the sort.

To sort customers in a database by Last Name and First Name 109

1. Choose Select ➤ Show All.
2. Choose Select ➤ Sort Selection (⌘-T).
3. Click on the Last Name field.
4. Click on the First Name field.
5. Click the **OK** button or press the Enter key to perform the sort.

To sort the customer records in descending order 111

1. Choose Select ➤ Show All.
2. Choose Select ➤ Sort Selection (⌘-T).

3. Click on the Last Name field.
4. Click on the **up arrow** next to the Last Name field.
5. Click the **OK** button or press the Enter key to perform the sort.

To sort records by formula (in this case, by the length of the last name) 116

1. Choose Select ➤ Show All.
2. Choose Select ➤ Sort Selection (⌘-T).
3. Click on the **Add Formula** button.
4. Click on the word *Routines.*
5. Scroll through the list of routines until you see one called *Length.*
6. Click on the Length routine.
7. Click on the left parenthesis listed under *Keywords.*
8. Click on the Last Name field.
9. Click on the right parenthesis listed under *Keywords.*
10. Click the **OK** button to enter the formula.

Featuring

- *The Sort Editor*
- *Sorting on one field*
- *Sorting on multiple fields*
- *Sorting in ascending and descending order*
- *Expediting sorts by indexing fields*
- *Sorting by formula*

NOW THAT YOU know how to add new records and search for existing records, you need to know how to arrange the records in some kind of order. For example, you might want your customers in order by last name. Perhaps you want your invoices in order by invoice date, with the newer invoices listed first and the older invoices listed last. Arranging records in order is called *sorting*. The order is usually based on one or more fields. For example, if you wanted your customers in order by last name, you would sort the records in the Customers file by the Last Name field.

Don't confuse sorting with searching. Quite often someone will say, "I need to sort through the junk in my closet and find that old picture." What they really mean is, "I need to *search* through the junk in my closet and find that old picture." When you are looking for something, you are searching. When you are putting things in a particular order, you are sorting.

When you sort a field, the order that the records will be arranged in depends on the data type of the field. For example, if you sorted your customers by last name, the records would be arranged alphabetically by last name. Last names beginning with *A* would be at the top of the list and last names beginning with *Z* at the bottom. Figure 6.1 shows a list of last names in sorted order. When you sort records by a numeric field, such as a real number, integer, or long integer field, the order of the records will be from the lowest number to the highest. When you sort on a date field, the records will be in order from the date that is farthest in the past to the date farthest in the future.

FIGURE 6.1

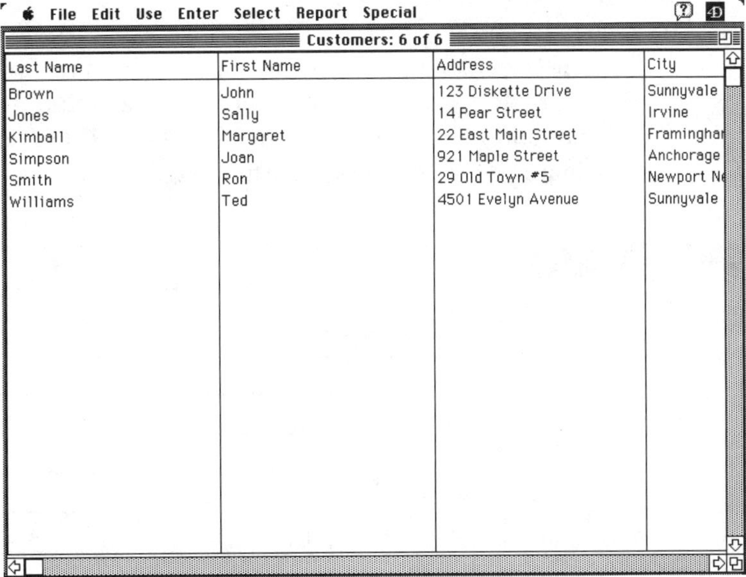

Last names sorted from A to Z

I have already talked about many different tasks you might use your database to perform. At this point, you might be wondering what kind of database tasks require sorting. Just about any time the you want to view more than one record, it's helpful to have them in some kind of order. A few examples of tasks that might require sorting include:

- Displaying a list of records on the screen
- Printing reports
- Printing address labels

When you are looking at a list of records on the screen or perhaps on a printed report, it's always helpful to have the information in order. Sorting makes it much easier to find one particular record in a list.

At this point, you will want to make sure you have the Learn 4D database up and running. If you don't have the Learn 4D database open, use the techniques described in previous chapters to open it and access the User environment.

THE SORT EDITOR

In the last chapter, you learned how to search records using 4th Dimension's built-in search editor. There is also a built-in sort editor. The Sort Editor allows you to choose which field to sort your records on, as well as including a few options for sorting. Figure 6.2 shows the Sort Editor.

FIGURE 6.2

The Sort Editor

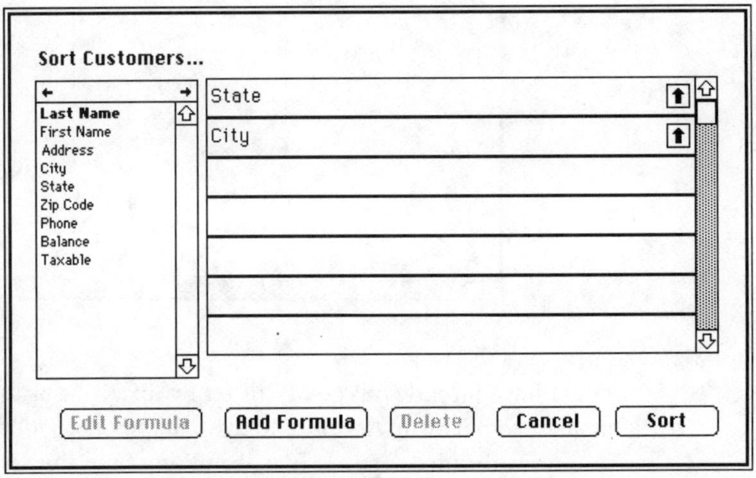

SORTING BY LAST NAME

Suppose you wanted to list all of your customers in alphabetical order (A–Z) by last name. Let's try it:

1. Choose Select ➤ Show All.
2. Choose Select ➤ Sort Selection (⌘-T).
3. Click on the Last Name field in the list of fields.
4. Click the **OK** button or press the Enter key to begin the sort.

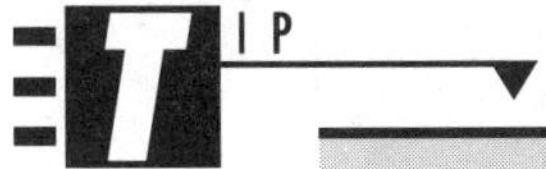

If you accidentally click on the wrong field, click on it in the scrollable area on the right and the click the Delete button.

Notice that the customers are now listed in alphabetical order by their last names. After displaying the Sort Editor you clicked the Last Name field to select it for sorting. When you pressed the Enter key, 4th Dimension sorted the records, redisplaying the output layout with the records in order by last name. That's all there is to it.

SORTING AND THE CURRENT SELECTION

In the last chapter, you learned about an important 4th Dimension concept called the *current selection.* The current selection is simply a set of records you have selected to work with from a file. I mention this again because it is important for sorting.

You might have noticed that the menu item for sorting is called Sort Selection. This means that the only records sorted will be those in the current selection. Say you use the Search Editor to find all customers in California. If you then were to sort the records, you would be sorting only the records you found (those customers in California).

You are probably beginning to understand why the current selection is such an important part of 4th Dimension. So many tasks in 4D are performed on the records in the current selection.

SORTING BY ZIP CODE

A very typical field to sort on is Zip Code. Let's say you had to send out a very large number of brochures to your customers. You can save a small fortune by using bulk mail. In order to get the bulk-mail rate from the post office, you must deliver your mail to the post office in order by zip code. If you had to do this by hand it could take hours. Luckily, your data is in a database and sorting is only a matter of a few mouse clicks. Let's try sorting the customers by the Zip Code field:

1. Choose Select ➤ Show All.
2. Choose Select ➤ Sort Selection (⌘-T).
3. Click on the Zip Code field.
4. Click the **OK** button or press the Enter key to perform the sort.

Notice that the records are now sorted numerically by the Zip Code field. Even though the Zip Code field is not a number field (real, integer, or long integer) you can still sort numerically. How is this possible? The Zip Code is not a number field but it *is* an alphanumeric field. The *numeric* in alphanumeric means that 4D knows the difference between letters and numbers. Consequently, 4D can sort the zip codes correctly, even though the field is not a number field.

PERFORMING SORTS WITHIN SORTS

There will be times when sorting on only one field will not be enough. As your database grows, you may have several people with the same last name. Take a look at Figure 6.3, which shows a list of people who all have the last name *Wong*. Notice that Betty Wong is listed after Randy Wong. Obviously, this is the wong order (sorry, the *wrong* order). In a small database, this would not cause problems, because the number of people with the name Wong would be small. However, in a very large database that has 500 Wongs (say a phone directory), it might take a while to locate any particular Wong.

When you sort a large number of records, you may want to sort the records by more than one field. If you sorted your customers by last name you could then scan down the list and look at all the customers with the last name Wong. However, if there are 500 Wongs it might take a while to find Betty Wong. You have sorted the records only by last name. So, while the records are all ordered by last name, the first names are all out of order. To make it easier to locate Betty Wong, you can sort the

FIGURE 6.3

People with the last name Wong

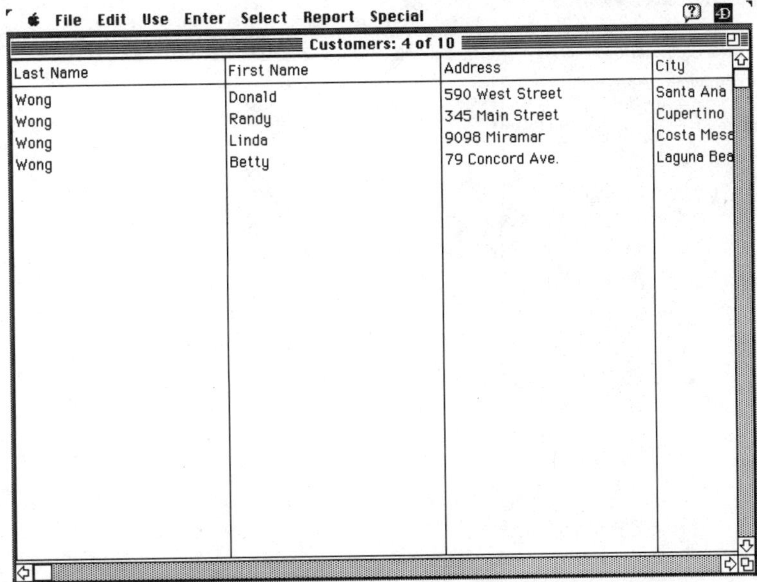

records by last name *and* first name. This way, the records will be in order first by last name then within each last name group, they will be in order by first name. Figure 6.4 shows records sorted by last name and first name.

Let's try sorting the Customers by both the Last Name and First Name fields:

1. Choose Select ➤ Show All.
2. Choose Select ➤ Sort Selection (⌘-T).
3. Click on the Last Name field.
4. Click on the First Name field.
5. Click the **OK** button or press the Enter key to perform the sort.

You really don't have enough records to notice the difference yet. If you had two customers with the same last name, you would now have them in alphabetical order by Last Name and within each group of Last Names they would be sorted by First Name.

FIGURE 6.4

Customers sorted by last name and first name

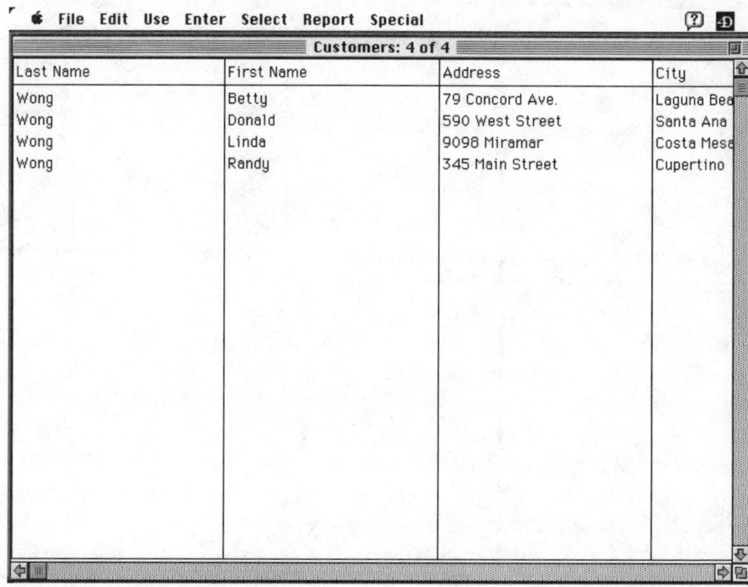

You can sort records on up to 16 fields. This means that if you had enough fields, you could sort by Last Name, First Name, Age, Hair Color, Favorite Movie, Great Grandmother's Maiden Name, and on and on. Each field you sort on is considered to be one *level*. So, if you sort on four fields, it is called a *four-level* sort.

At this point, you might want to try sorting the Customers on different fields just to see the results.

ASCENDING AND DESCENDING SORTS

You can sort your records in two different directions. When you sort from A–Z or 0–9 it's called an *ascending* sort. When sorted, the values will start low and go higher. For example, if you sorted the names *Larry, Moe,* and *Curly* in ascending order, the sorted order would be *Curly, Larry,* and *Moe.* If you sorted the numbers *45, 27,* and *99* in ascending order, the new order would be *27, 45,* and *99.*

You may have noticed the arrow buttons next to the fields being sorted in the Sort Editor. When the arrow is pointing up, the sort on that field will be in ascending order. Clicking on the arrow button changes it to point down. When the arrow is pointing down, the sort order is descending, which is the opposite of ascending. In most cases, you will sort your records in ascending order. This is 4D's default order for sorting, so you will rarely have to change it.

The other direction for sorting is *descending* order. Descending is simply the reverse of ascending. If *Larry*, *Moe*, and *Curly* where sorted in descending order, the order would be *Moe*, *Larry*, and *Curly*. You can think of descending order as reverse alphabetical order. Let's try sorting the records as we did before, but this time in descending order:

1. Choose Select ➤ Show All.
2. Choose Select ➤ Sort Selection (⌘-T).
3. Click on the Last Name field.
4. Click on the **up arrow** next to the Last Name field.
5. Click the **OK** button or press the Enter key to perform the sort.

Notice that the Names are now in reverse alphabetical order. You are probably wondering why you would ever want to sort in reverse alphabetical order. Well, say you are a teacher. You are probably used to calling on students in alphabetical order. There's that one kid in your class who was unlucky enough to be born with the last name *Adams*. This kid is the first one called on in every class he or she has ever had. Perhaps you want to give this kid a break for once. So, you might sort your students by last name but in descending order. Now Adams is at the bottom of the list and Zolwalski is at the top of the list.

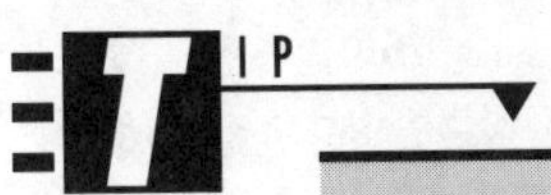

To remember the difference between *ascending* and *descending*, think about airplanes. When a plane beings its descent to land, it's at a high altitude (say 39,000 feet) and goes down to a low altitude (0 feet).

Of course, there are other more practical reasons for sorting in descending order. For example, if you wanted to see the most recently written invoices, you would sort your invoices in descending order. Newer invoices would now appear at the top of the list and older invoices at the bottom. The following list shows how the various data types treat information sorted in ascending and descending order:

Data Type	**Ascending**	**Descending**
Alphanumeric	Bob, John, Susan	Susan, John, Bob
Real	9.4, 9.7, 11.34	11.34, 9.7, 9.4
Dates	10/31/62, 01/06/64, 02/21/66	02/21/66, 01/06/64, 10/31/62

THE FASTEST POSSIBLE SORT

You might be wondering how long it will take 4D to sort your records. That is a good question and not an easy one to answer. There are many factors that come into play. For example, a Macintosh Classic cannot sort records as fast as a Macintosh Quadra 950. The Quadra is a faster machine than the Classic, so most things you might do on your computer will be faster on the Quadra.

If you sort on more than one field, 4D can't use the indexes to make the sort faster. For small databases, this won't matter but for larger ones it could take a while to sort on multiple fields. Using a process called *concatenation*, you can get the same effect as sorting one multiple fields with the speed of sorting on one indexed field. You will see an example of this in *Chapter 14*.

There is another factor that is more important than the machine itself. That factor is whether the field is indexed or not. If the field you are sorting on is not indexed, the time is takes to sort the records will increase as the number of records being sorted increases. If the field you are sorting on is indexed, the time it takes 4D to sort the records will be very short, even if you are sorting thousands of records. The reason for this is simple. The index has the data already arranged in sorted order. So, when you sort on an indexed field, there is less work for 4D to do. The fastest possible sort is when you sort on one indexed field.

SORTING BY FORMULA

There will be times when you need to sort your records by something other than the data in a field. For example, say you were printing labels from the information in your customers file. After printing the labels, you realized that some of the names were too long for the labels and were printing off the edge of the label. You might want to sort the names in such a way that would allow you to see the names in order from shortest to longest. You couldn't just sort the records by last name because that would show them in alphabetical order. What you want is to sort the customers by the length of their last names.

Sorting the customers by the length of their last name requires a calculation. We need a formula to calculate the length of the customer's last name and then sort on the result (the length) of that formula. This is called *sorting by formula*. Instead of sorting on the data in a field, you are sorting on the result of a calculation derived from a field.

Luckily, 4D has a large set of built-in commands and functions to make this job easier. This will be your first exposure to 4th Dimension's procedural language. You will use the built-in *Length* function to sort the customers by the length of their last names. You enter the formula (calculation) into the formula editor in the Sort Selection dialog box. The formula editor allows you to enter calculations to be used to determine the result that will be sorted on instead of sorting on the field itself.

Let's try it:

1. Choose Select ➤ Show All.
2. Choose Select ➤ Sort Selection (⌘-T).
3. Click on the **Add Formula** button.

If you hold down the ⌘ and Shift keys and type the first letter of a function, 4D will automatically scroll the Routines list to the first function beginning with that letter. For example, ⌘-*Shift-L* will scroll to the first function that begins with *L*.

4. Click on the word *Routines.*
5. Scroll through the list of routines until you see one called *Length.*
6. Click on the Length routine.
7. Click on the left parenthesis listed under *Keywords.*
8. Click on the Last Name field.
9. Click on the right parenthesis listed under *Keywords.*
10. Click the **OK** button to enter the formula.

You can see that the names are now sorted in order by length. If your sort didn't come out right or 4D reported an error, make sure that your formula matches the one shown in Figure 6.5.

SAVING SORT FORMULAS FOR FUTURE USE

The formula we used to sort with was simple. However, formulas can be much more complex. If you are using a complex formula, you might

FIGURE 6.5

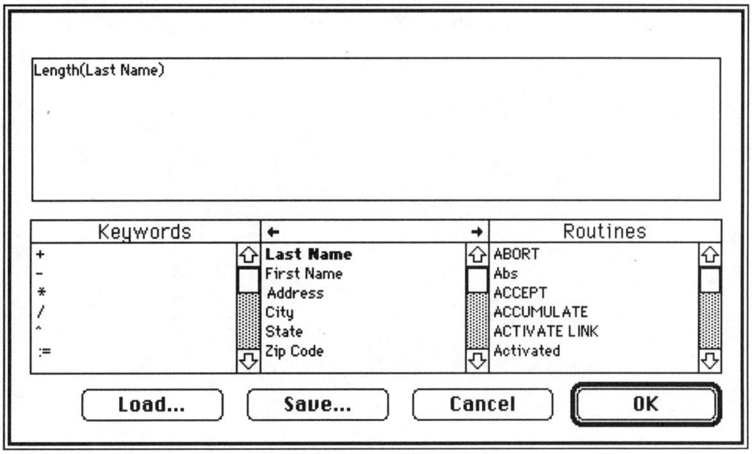

The Sort Selection dialog box displaying the sort formula

wish to type it into the formula editor in the Sort Selection dialog box every time you want to use it for sorting. 4D provides you with a way to save the formulas you create so you can use them later without having to remember them or retype them into the formula editor.

When you were entering the formula, you may have noticed two buttons, **Load** and **Save**. After entering a formula, you can click the **Save** button to save the formula to a formula file on disk. Each formula you save has its own file. These files are physical files that will appear in the folder with your database. Later, you can reuse a formula you have saved. To do so, simply go to the formula editor, click the **Load** button, and choose a formula to load into the Sort Editor. It's that simple.

You will probably find that most of the sorting you do will not require a formula. However, it's nice to have the ability to use a formula for sorting when the need arises.

HOW LONG DOES A SORT LAST?

Records are sorted in memory only. This means that the records stay in a certain order in the file but can be sorted temporarily in memory to allow you to have them in order for a report you are about to print. Once you do anything that changes the current selection, the records will be displayed in the order that they are stored in. If you use the Search, Show All or Show Subset menu items, you will change the current selection and, consequently, the records will be displayed in the order that they appear in the file.

CHANGING GROUPS OF RECORDS

MAC TRACKS MAC

To change records in your database 123

They must be in the current selection

To search for specific records 124

Use the Search Editor, Search By Layout Editor, and Search By Formula Editor.

To select contiguous records 125

1. If you are not in the User environment, choose Use ➤ User.
2. Choose Select ➤ Show All to insure that all the customers are being displayed.
3. Click on the first record to highlight it.
4. While holding down the **Shift** key, click on the last record in the group you want to select. All files in between will be highlighted.
5. Choose Select ➤ Show Subset to reduce the current selection to just the highlighted records.

To select noncontiguous records 126

1. Make sure you are viewing your file in the User environment.
2. Choose Select ➤ Show All.
3. Click on the first record to highlight it.

4. While holding down the ⌘ key, click on the other records you want to select.
5. Choose Select ➤ Show Subset to reduce the current selection to just the highlighted records.

To delete several records 129

1. Create a selection of records you want to delete.
2. **Shift**-click or ⌘-click on the other records you wish to delete.
3. Choose Select ➤ Show Subset.
4. Select Edit ➤ Clear.
5. When 4D asks, "Are you sure?," click the **Yes** button.

To change several records at once 130

Use the Apply Formula Editor.

Featuring

- *Selecting records*
- *Searching for records*
- *Deleting records*
- *Changing records*
- *Using the Apply Formula Editor*
- *Multiline formulas*

IN PREVIOUS CHAPTERS you learned how to add new records, search for records, and modify records once you located them. In this chapter, you will learn how to delete records and how to make changes to a large number of records all at once.

4D stores changes to records in an area of its memory called the *buffer*. When this buffer fills, 4D will save the information to the datafile. You can specify (in the Preferences dialog box) how often 4D saves the buffer to the datafile. By default, 4D will save every 15 minutes.

4th Dimension, unlike other applications you might have used, automatically and immediately saves the changes you make. This is beneficial, because it prevents you from losing hours of work due to a power failure or a computer error. You have probably had such catastrophes happen to you at least once. You are working for several hours on an important document when, suddenly, a system error occurs and your hours of work go down the drain. This doesn't happen with 4th Dimension because it saves your changes to your database as you make them. So, even if a system error occurs, it is unlikely you would lose any of your work. At most, you might lose the one record you are working on, but one record can be easily re-entered.

I am mentioning this because it is important to understand that the changes you make in your database are saved immediately. This means that you will want to be sure you are making the changes you really want. When you are changing just one record, this is not a worry. If you don't want to keep the changes you have made, you can simply locate the record and manually change it back. However, in this chapter you will be learning about changing and deleting large numbers of records all at once. If you change hundreds of records and then realize that you made a mistake, it might not be that easy to get the records back the way you want them.

This illustrates the importance of having a *backup* copy of your database. Just before you make any drastic changes in your database, make a copy and store it on diskettes or in another folder on your hard disk. If the changes you make don't come out the way you had expected, you will still have a copy of the database from before the changes were made.

Some changes you make are easily reversible. Say you have a database that keeps track of your employees. You have added a Bonus field to keep track of the amount of money each employee will get as his or her yearly bonus. Business was great this year so you have decided to give each employee a 10% bonus. By accident you multiplied the salary field by *10* instead of *0.10* to calculate the bonus. This type of error is easy to correct because you can simply recalculate the bonus using the correct figure.

FINDING THE RECORDS YOU WANT TO CHANGE

The first thing you need to do to make changes to your data is to locate the records you wish to change. 4th Dimension's functions for changing or deleting records work on the current selection. This means that when you want to change or delete several records at once, you will need to make these records the current selection. There are several ways to do this.

SELECTING ALL OF THE RECORDS

On some occasions, the changes you wish to make apply to all the records in a particular file in your database. Selecting all the records is simple:

1. Go to the User environment.
2. Choose the file you wish to work with.
3. Choose Select ➤ Show All.

The Show All command makes the current selection all the records in the file. Later in this chapter you will learn how to use 4D to change or delete these records.

SEARCHING FOR SPECIFIC RECORDS

You already know how to use the Search Editor, Search By Layout Editor, and Search By Formula Editor to locate records. As 4th Dimension finds records that match the search criteria you entered, it puts these records into the current selection. Once you have a current selection that contains the records you want, you can then proceed to change or delete them.

HAND-PICKING RECORDS

There may be times when you can't use the Search Editor to locate the records you want. Perhaps the information you need to choose the records you want to delete is not in the database. Perhaps the information you will use to choose the records you want is only in your head.

Say you are having an open house and want to invite only a few of your best customers. If you are keeping track of each customer's total purchases in the database, you might search for customers that have the highest purchases. But that might not give you exactly what you want. Perhaps you have a new customer who hasn't purchased much yet, but who you know will be purchasing quite a bit in the future. Using the Search editor would not locate this customer. Fortunately, 4D gives you the ability to "hand-pick" records.

You have seen that clicking on a record in the output layout highlights the record. You can also highlight several records at once. Let's try it:

1. If you are not in the User environment, choose Use ➤ User.
2. Choose Select ➤ Show All to insure that all the customers are being displayed.
3. Click on the first record to highlight it.
4. While holding down the **Shift** key, click on the fourth record.

Notice that all of the records between the first and fourth records are highlighted. Figure 7.1 shows what your screen should look like.

If you click on a record to highlight it then hold the **Shift** key and click on another record, 4D highlights all the records in between. This is call *contiguous selection.* Now let's reduce the current selection to just the highlighted records: Choose Select ➤ Show Subset. Notice that the

FIGURE 7.1

Contiguously selected records

File Edit Use Enter Select Report Special

Customers: 6 of 6

Last Name	First Name	Address	City
Brown	John	123 Diskette Drive	Sunnyvale
Jones	Sally	14 Pear Street	Irvine
Williams	Ted	4501 Evelyn Avenue	Sunnyvale
Simpson	Joan	921 Maple Street	Anchorage
Smith	Ron	29 Old Town #5	Newport N
Kimball	Margaret	22 East Main Street	Framingha

current selection has been reduced to just the records that were highlighted. Using the Shift-click method, you can select groups of records from the current selection then reduce the current selection to just the records you selected.

This method is great if the records you want to select are next to each other. There will be times however, when you need to highlight records that are not next to each other in the current selection. Here's how to do it:

1. Make sure you are viewing the Customers file in the User environment.
2. Choose Select ➤ Show All.
3. Click on the first record to highlight it.
4. While holding down the ⌘ key, click on the third and fifth records.
5. Choose Select ➤ Show Subset.

Figure 7.2 shows what your screen should look like at this point. Using the ⌘ key instead of the Shift key allows you to highlight records that are not next to each other in the current selection. This is called *noncontiguous selection.*

You can use these techniques separately or together to select any group of records you want. Let's try using the two techniques together. This time, you will select the first, second, third, and fifth records:

1. Choose Select ➤ Show All.
2. Click on the first record to highlight it.
3. **Shift**-click on the third record to highlight both the second and third records.
4. ⌘-click on the fifth record.
5. Choose Select ➤ Show Subset.

Using the Shift-click and ⌘-click techniques, you can select any group of records you want. Once they are selected, you can reduce the

FIGURE 7.2

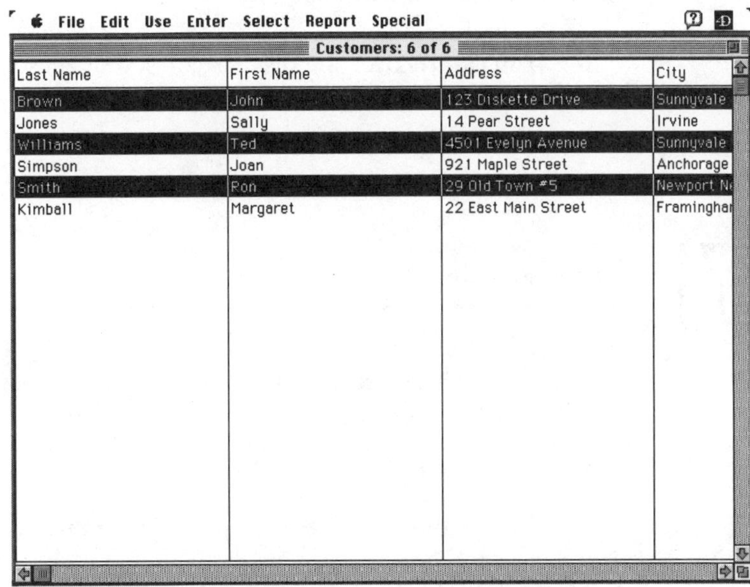

Noncontiguously selected records

current selection to just the highlighted records using the Show Subset menu item.

These techniques allow you to hand-pick the records you want to change or delete. Computers are great for quickly locating and manipulating data. However, we don't put every bit of information into our databases. So, there will be times when the Search Editor won't be able to locate the records you are looking for, because the information that matches your criteria isn't in the database. Fortunately, 4D gives you these techniques for choosing the records by hand.

DELETING RECORDS

If you keep adding more and more records to your database, there may come a time when you want to get rid of some of them. For example, you may have old records you don't need anymore. Deleting records you no longer need benefits you in two ways:

- You can recover the disk space used by these records after compacting with 4D Tools (see *Chapter 22*).
- Searching will be faster because there are fewer records to search through.

Deleting records does not reduce the size of the datafile. You need to compact the datafile to make it smaller. This will be covered in detail in *Chapter 22.*

As I mentioned before, it's a good idea to make a backup copy of your database before deleting records. If you make a mistake and delete the wrong records, you will have an intact backup copy of the database. After a while, you will feel more comfortable with your understanding 4th Dimension and you will be able to delete the right records standing on one leg. In the beginning, though, make a backup. It's better to be safe then sorry.

DELETING A SINGLE RECORD

Deleting a single record is simple. When you created your database, 4D automatically generated input and output layouts for you. On the input layout, there are several buttons, one of which looks like a trash can. That's the **Delete** button. Figure 7.3 shows an input layout with a delete button.

You can use this button to delete a record. Let's try it:

1. Make sure you are viewing the Customers file in the User environment.
2. Choose Select ➤ Show All.

FIGURE 7.3

An input layout with a delete button

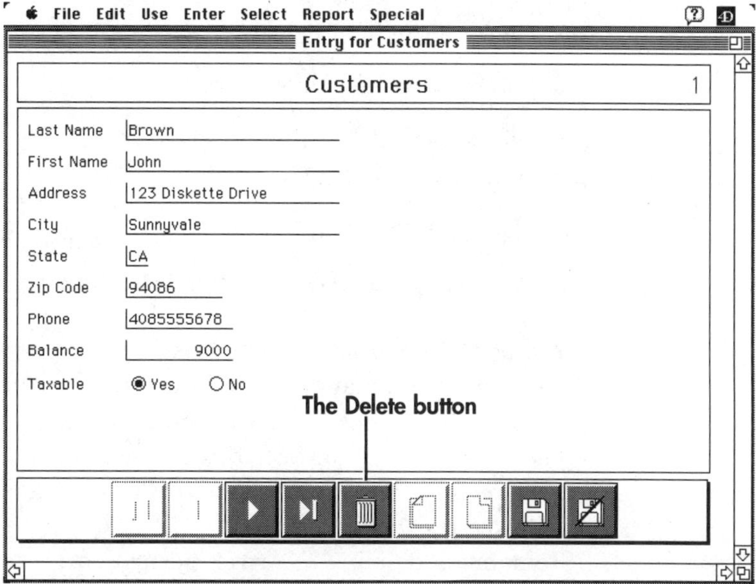

3. Double-click on the first record to display it in the input layout.
4. Click on the **Delete** button.
5. When 4D asks, "Are you sure?," click the **No** button.

Clicking the **Delete** button will delete only the record you are viewing at the time. Because deleting is an irreversible action, 4D asks you to confirm that you are sure you want to delete the record. It does this to give you the chance to change your mind. We don't want to delete the record right now so you clicked the **No** button. Had we wanted to get rid of the record, clicking **Yes** would have done so.

DELETING SEVERAL RECORDS AT ONCE

There may be times when you will want to delete several records all at once. 4th Dimension has the ability to delete all records in the current selection. The first thing you need to do is get the records you want to delete into the current selection.

1. Choose Select ➤ Show All.
2. Click on the first record.
3. **Shift**-click on the third record.
4. Choose Select ➤ Show Subset.
5. Choose Edit ➤ Select All (⌘-A).
6. Select Edit ➤ Clear.
7. When 4D asks, "Are you sure?," click the **No** button.

You used the **Shift**-click technique to select a few records. Then the Show Subset command reduced the current selection to just these records. Selecting Edit ➤ Clear deletes the records in the current selection. Just as before, 4D asks you to confirm that you are sure you want to delete the records. We don't want to really delete any records right now so you clicked the **No** button.

Remember, deleting records is permanent. You may have used other applications where you can perform an action then select Edit ➤ Undo to restore the status of the file. You can't undo after deleting records. That's why 4D asked you to confirm that you really wanted delete the records. When an application asks you to confirm some action you are about to take, it typically means that the action is irreversible; you are given a chance to change your mind. It's too bad that more things in life aren't that way.

Changing Several Records at Once

As your database grows, you may find it necessary to make a change to many records all at once. For example, when the phone company changes an area code, you may want to search your database to find all of your customers in this area code and then change their area code to a new one. If you have 500 customers in that area code, it could take some time to change every one of them by hand. Fortunately, 4th Dimension provides you with a way to make a change to several records all at the same time.

THE APPLY FORMULA EDITOR

The *Apply Formula Editor* allows you to enter a formula that 4D will execute for each record in the current selection. A formula is simply a calculation that will change a value in a particular field. You might create formulas to do simple tasks like assigning a new area code to an Area Code field. Perhaps you entered your customers' names all in capital letters and now you want them in upper- and lowercase. With a formula, you can easily make these kinds of changes quickly and apply them to as many records as you want. Instead of retyping all 500 of your customers' last names, you can create a simple formula that would handle the job in a minute or so. Figure 7.4 shows the Apply Formula Editor.

Formulas

A formula is a calculation. Formulas usually begin with a field, followed by :=. The combination of a colon and an equals sign make up the *assignment operator.* This operator is used to assign values to whatever is to the left of the assignment operator. For example, the formula

```
[Customers]Last Name:="Perlman"
```

will copy the name *Perlman* (notice it doesn't include the quotations) into the Last Name field in the Customers file. The quotations are used

FIGURE 7.4

The Apply Formula Editor

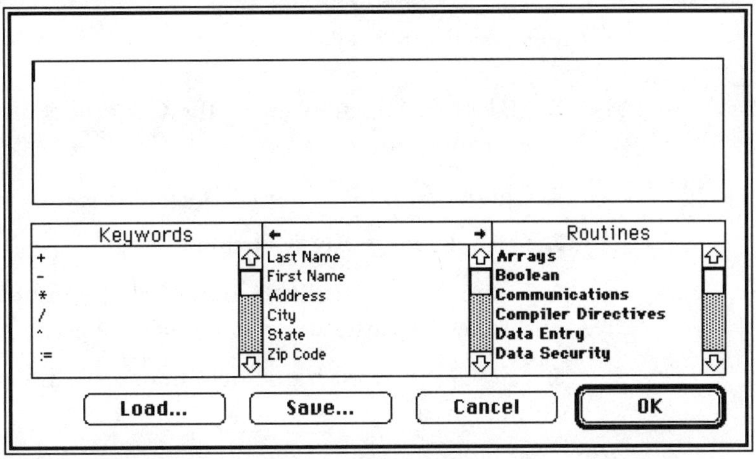

to let 4D know that *Perlman* is a constant value. Without the quotations, 4D might think that *Perlman* was something else (like a field).

4th Dimension has many functions built into it that can be used to create simple yet powerful formulas. Say you want to change all of your customers' last names to title case (first character uppercase, all other characters lowercase). To do this, you would use the *Uppercase* and *Lowercase* functions in 4D. The fastest way to perform this kind of calculation is to make the entire last name lowercase, then make the first character uppercase. The first part of the formula would look like this:

```
[Customers]Last Name:=Lowercase([Customers]Last
Name)
```

You can read this formula as "The Customers file's Last Name field (*[Customers]Last Name*) is assigned (*:=*) the lowercase value of the Customers file's Last Name field (*Lowercase([Customers]Last Name)*)." The Lowercase function needs to know what text you want in lowercase. You indicate this by adding parentheses after the Lowercase function and enclosing in the parentheses the object that contains the text (in this case the Last Name field). This formula is really three steps:

1. Make a copy of the contents of the Last Name field.
2. *Pass* the copy to the Lowercase function.
3. Assign the lowercase copy back to the Last Name field, replacing the original.

Let's try this formula:

1. Make sure you are viewing the Customers file in the User environment.
2. Choose Select ➤ Show All.
3. Select Enter ➤ Apply Formula.
4. In the middle scrollable area, click the right arrow to display the Customers file name.
5. Click on the Last Name field to enter it into the formula area.

6. Click on := in the Keywords scrollable area to enter it into the formula.
7. Click on the word *Routines* to display the list of 4D routines.
8. Scroll down through the list of routines (they are in alphabetical order) until you see the Lowercase function.
9. Click on the **Lowercase** function to add it to the formula.
10. Type an opening parenthesis "(" (don't type the quotations).
11. Click on the Last Name field to add it to the formula.
12. Type a closing parenthesis ")".
13. Click the **OK** button to apply the formula you have entered to the current selection.

You can see that the last names are in all lowercase letters. At this point, we are only half done. The next step is to make the first character uppercase for every last name. This requires another formula. The formula looks like this:

```
[Customers]Last Name≤1≥:=Uppercase([Customers]Last
Name≤1≥)
```

This formula looks very similar to the last formula we used with two important differences. First, we are using the Uppercase function instead of the Lowercase function. Secondly, we have added ≤*1*≥ to the formula in two places. The ≤ and ≥ characters are used for *character referencing* (to type these characters, hold down the option key while typing the < or > characters). Using these characters allows you to refer to a specific character in a field rather than the entire field. This formula can be read as "the first character of the Last Name field is assigned the uppercase value of the first character of the Last Name field." In other words, the first character will be replaced by an uppercase version of itself. If for some reason you wanted to replace the second character, you would simply put a *2* between the ≤ and the ≥ characters. Let's apply the second formula to the current selection:

1. Make sure you are viewing the Customers file in the User environment.

2. Choose Select ➤ Show All.
3. Select Enter ➤ Apply Formula.
4. In the middle scrollable area, click the right arrow to display the Customers file name.
5. Click on the Last Name field to enter it into the formula area.
6. Type ≤ character (Option-<).
7. Type 1.
8. Type ≥ character (Option->).
9. Click on := in the Keywords scrollable area to enter it into the formula.
10. Scroll down through the list of routines (the are in alphabetical order) until you see the Uppercase function.
11. Click on the **Uppercase** function to add it to the formula.
12. Type an opening parenthesis "(" (don't type the quotations).
13. Click on the Last Name field to add it to the formula.
14. Type ≤ character (Option-<).
15. Type 1.
16. Type ≥ character (Option->).
17. Type a closing parenthesis ")".
18. Click the **OK** button to apply the formula you have entered to the current selection.

Now the last names are in title case with the first character in uppercase and all the rest in lowercase. The Formula editor will accept only one formula at a time. Because of this, we had to enter the first formula and apply it to the selection and then enter the second formula (instead of entering both at the same time). This means that 4D has to go through the records twice instead of just once. However, there is a way to have the Formula editor execute several formulas at once.

Writing Compound Formulas in the Procedure Editor

4th Dimension has its own built-in programming language. The Uppercase and Lowercase functions are part of that language. When you want to give instructions to 4D using it's programming language, you write a *procedure.* A procedure is a set of instructions (formulas) that 4D can execute. To write a procedure you use the Procedure editor. Figure 7.5 shows the Procedure editor. We will be taking a more detailed look at 4D's programming language in *Chapter 13.*

You can also use the Procedure editor to write multiple-line formulas that can then be used by the Apply Formula menu item in the User environment. The Procedure editor is similar to the Apply Formula dialog box in that they both have the keywords, field names, and routines at the bottom of the window. Let's try creating a procedure that has both of the formulas we used earlier:

1. Choose Use ➤ Design to switch back to the Design environment.

2. Select Design ➤ Procedure.

FIGURE 7.5

The Procedure Editor

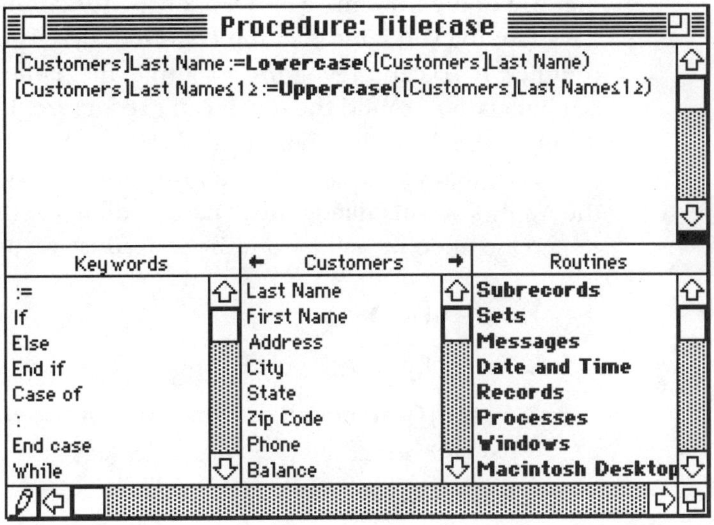

```
Procedure: Titlecase
[Customers]Last Name:=Lowercase([Customers]Last Name)
[Customers]Last Name≤1≥:=Uppercase([Customers]Last Name≤1≥)

Keywords    ← Customers →    Routines
:=          Last Name        Subrecords
If          First Name       Sets
Else        Address          Messages
End if      City             Date and Time
Case of     State            Records
:           Zip Code         Processes
End case    Phone            Windows
While       Balance          Macintosh Desktop
```

3. Click the **New** button to create a new procedure.
4. Type **Titlecase** as the name for the new procedure.
5. Click **OK.**

You have created a procedure and now have the Procedure editor on your screen. The bottom portion of the window displays the keywords, field names, and routines. The top portion is for your formulas. At this point we need to enter the two formulas. Use the keywords, field list, and routines just as you did before to enter the two formulas below:

1. Enter **[Customers]Last Name:=Lowercase([Customers]Last Name)**.
2. Press the Return key.
3. Enter **[Customers]Last Name≤1≥:=Uppercase([Customers]Last Name≤1≥)**.
4. Press the Return key.
5. Click the close box to close and save the procedure.

When you finished typing a line and pressed return, 4D changed the style of the Lowercase and Uppercase functions to bold. This is 4D's way of letting you know that it recognized these two words as built-in routines. If 4D can't recognize a routine, file name, or field name, it will put bullets (•) around the text it can't recognize. I will go into more detail on the Procedure editor in *Chapter 13*.

Now that you have written a procedure, let's go back and use it in the Apply Formula dialog box. First we will make the all the last names uppercase, then we will try out the procedure we just wrote.

1. Select Use ➤ User.
2. Select Enter ➤ Apply Formula.
3. Enter **[Customers]Last Name:=Uppercase([Customers]Last Name)**.
4. Click **OK.**

Now that the last names are in uppercase, you can test out the procedure using the Apply Formula dialog box and see it work.

1. Select Enter ➤ Apply Formula.
2. Click on **Routines** to show the list of routines.
3. Scroll down to the bottom of the list and click on the **Titlecase** procedure.
4. Click **OK**.

As you can see, the records have been changed. This time, 4D only had to make one pass through the records instead of two. By creating a procedure, you have decreased the amount of time 4D takes to apply the formulas to the records in the selection. You have also saved yourself some typing. The formulas are saved in a procedure in case you want to use them again.

In writing this procedure, you have taken your first step in programming. In *Chapter 14*, we will explore programming in more detail. If you have never done any programming before, I hope that this first experience has been a pleasant one. We tend to fear the unknown. By learning about programming, it becomes known and the fear vanishes.

CREATING AND PRINTING REPORTS

8

MAC TRACKS MAC

To open a saved quick report from disk 148

1. Choose File ➤ Open (⌘-O).
2. Select the quick report file you wish to open.
3. Click the **Open** button.

To select a single cell 156

Simply click in it.

To highlight an entire row or column 156

Click on the letter of the left-most column of the row or the title of the column.

To add a field to the sort area 158

Click and drag «**Add Sort**» from the sort area to the field on the report that you want to add and release the mouse button.

Featuring

- *Using the Quick Report Editor*
- *Arranging fields on a report*
- *Previewing and printing your work*
- *Hiding rows or columns*
- *Forcing page breaks in reports*
- *Formatting cells, rows, and columns*
- *Adding headers and footers*

THERE ARE TWO reasons for using a database. The first is to have fast access to large amounts of data. The second is to analyze large amounts of data and make decisions based on that analysis. Typically, large amounts of data are presented in a *report.* Reporting is one of the most important functions of a database system. Without the ability to generate reports, the database would not be very useful.

4th Dimension gives you two methods for printing reports. The first method is using 4D's built-in *Quick Report Editor.* This editor will quickly generate useful reports and save them for later use. In this chapter, we will be examining the Quick Report Editor in great detail.

The second method for printing reports is using *layouts.* You have already used input and output layouts to access records. 4D can also use these layouts for printing forms and reports. In *Chapter 12,* you will learn more about creating layouts for printing.

If you have quit 4D, reopen the Learn 4D database you have been creating.

USING THE QUICK REPORT EDITOR

The Quick Report Editor can be used to create *columnar* reports. A columnar report is a one that displays fields of data in columns. Figure 8.1 shows a

FIGURE 8.1

A report created with the Quick Report Editor

Last Name	First Name	State	Balance
Brown	John	CA	$9,000
Jones	Sally	CA	$5,500
Kimball	Margaret	MA	$1,050
Simpson	Joan	AK	$6,750
Smith	Ron	VA	$8,877
Williams	Ted	CA	$1,500
		Grand Total:	$32,677

typical report that was created using the Quick Report Editor.

Let's open the Quick Report Editor and begin creating a report. Follow these steps:

1. If you do not have the Learn 4D database open, open it now and choose Use ➤ User (⌘-U).
2. Choose Select ➤ Show All (⌘-G).
3. Choose Report ➤ Quick (⌘-R).

Invisible fields will not appear in the fields area. The invisible attribute prevents the field from appearing in any of 4D's built-in editors that are part of the User environment.

You should now see the Quick Report Editor. The window you see is made up of three areas: the fields area, the report area, and the sort area. Figure 8.2 shows the Quick Report Editor and points out these three areas. In the upper-left corner is the fields area. This area lists the fields from the current file. Since your database has only one file, that file is the current file by default. Later, you will add more files to your database. At that point, you could use the right and left arrow buttons above the fields to select other files in your database.

FIGURE 8.2

The Quick Report Editor

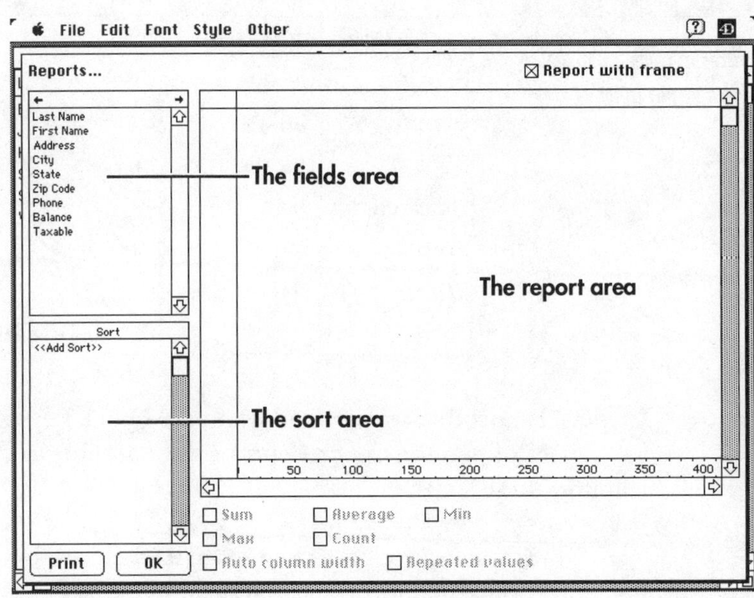

When you use the Quick Report Editor, it replaces the User environment menus with its own menus to help you create your report. When you close the Quick Report Editor, the User environment menus will reappear.

The second area is the report area. This is where you create the layout of the report. You create your report in this area by dragging fields from the fields area into the report area.

Just below the fields area is the sort area. The fields that the report will sort on before printing are listed here. As you build your first report, you use this area to select fields for sorting the records in the report.

SELECTING FIELDS

The first step in creating a report is to create columns that will be printed on the report. You do this by dragging fields from the Fields area to the report area.

Holding down the mouse button while moving the mouse is called *dragging*. Typically you use this technique to move an object from one place to another.

Let's now create a simple report, which we will print listing customers by state:

1. Click on the Last Name field and hold down the mouse button.
2. With the mouse button held down, move the mouse until the pointer is over the report area and release the mouse button.

You have just placed the Last Name field on the report. By doing this you have created a column on the report where the Last Name field will be printed. Four rows appeared when you created your first column. I will explain these rows in a moment; but first, let's finish adding fields to the report. Remember, to add a field to the report, drag it to the right of the last field you added.

1. Drag the First Name field from the Fields area and release the mouse when the pointer is to the right of the Last Name field on the report.
2. Drag the Address field to the report area.
3. Drag the City field to the report area.
4. Drag the State field to the report area.
5. Drag the Zip Code field to the report area.
6. Drag the Phone field to the report area.

7. Drag the Balance field to the report area.

Figure 8.3 shows how your report should now look.

Now that you have added fields to your report, you can print your report to see how it looks so far. 4th Dimension's Quick Report Editor has a print preview function that allows you to see your report on the screen. With this feature you can quickly get an idea of how the report is going to look without waiting for the printer and wasting paper. Let's try printing your report to the screen:

1. Click the **Print** button.
2. When the Print dialog box appears, select the Print Preview checkbox in the lower-left corner.
3. Click the **Print** button.

FIGURE 8.3

Fields arranged on a report

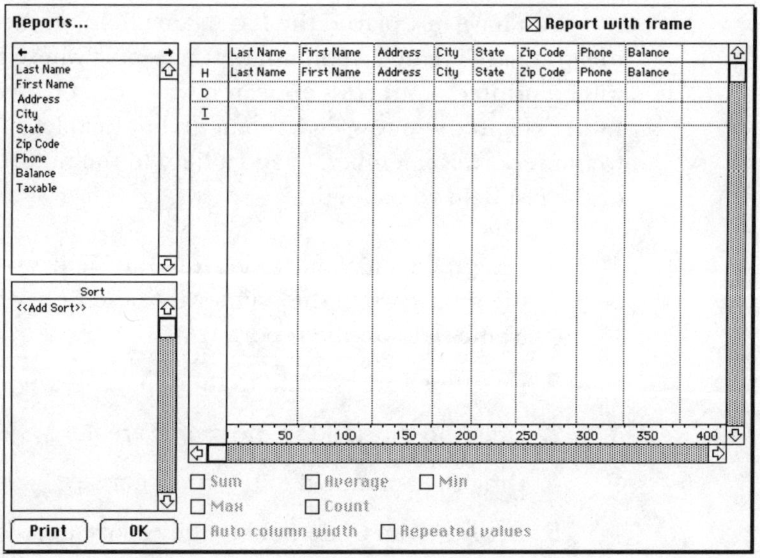

If the Print dialog box doesn't appear when you click the Print button, it means that there is no printer selected. To select a printer, select Chooser from the Apple menu. Click on the icon that represents the type of printer you have. Once you have done this, close the Chooser and print your report.

4D opens a window showing you the progress of the printing of the report. At the bottom of this window are four buttons:

Zoom	Magnifies a portion of the report, allowing you to view the report at actual size.
Next Page	Prints the next page of the report to the screen.
Stop Printing	Ends the print preview and returns to the Quick Report Editor.
Print	Prints the report to the printer.

As you can see, 4D has reduced the image of the page to make the 8½ × 11" page fit on whatever size monitor you have. In order to see the report as it will actually look when printed, you will need to use the Zoom button.

Click the **Zoom** button now.

In the print preview window there is a small, transparent rectangle on top of your report. You can move this rectangle around to zoom in on different portions of the report.

Now you can see the report as it will print. 4D automatically makes all of the columns wide enough to hold the widest piece of data being printed. 4D names the columns for you and puts a frame around each column to make the report easier to read.

1. Click anywhere to return to the print preview screen.
2. Click the **Stop Printing** button.

SAVING QUICK REPORTS FOR FUTURE USE

Quick reports can be saved and retrieved later for printing or modifying. Quick reports are not saved as part of the structure file. Each quick report is saved as an individual desktop file. At this point, it would be a good idea to save your report in case you want to take a break and come back to it later.

1. Choose File ➤ Save (⌘-S).
2. Type **Balance By State Report**.
3. Click the **Save** button to save the quick report to disk.

As you make changes to your quick report, you will probably want to save it again. To save it, simply choose File ➤ Save (⌘-S). You won't have to retype the filename because 4D already knows the name of the report file you saved. Indeed, any changes you make will overwrite the original file. So if you want to save several different versions of the same report, you must give them different names (such as *Balance by Region Report, Balance by Zip Code Report,* and so on).

Let's make sure that the report file was saved to disk. First, we will create a new, blank report to erase what is in the Quick Report Editor now. Next, we will reopen the Balance By State Report that we saved to disk.

1. Choose File ➤ New (⌘-N).
2. Choose File ➤ Open (⌘- O).
3. Select the report.

Notice that 4D brought your quick report back just as you saved it. Now you can continue to work on it and save your changes occasionally as you go.

REPORT SECTIONS

Quick Reports are made up of rows and columns. The columns are usually fields from your database files. The rows are sections of the report that are printed in a certain order.

COLUMN TITLES

The first row displays the *column titles.* In your report, this row displays the names of the fields for each column. The items in this row may not always be field names. Later you will learn how to create calculated columns that display data from calculations instead of data from fields. The column titles section is the only section that does not print. The purpose of this row is to identify the columns.

THE HEADER SECTION

The *header row* is the row with the *H* in the left-most column. This row prints at the top of each page. By default, the columns have the field names in the header row. The text in this row can be changed if needed. You might want to change a column name because it's too long or perhaps you want to enter something more meaningful than what you have. Figure 8.4 points out this row in the Quick Report Editor.

As with many other Mac programs, double-clicking a word in 4D highlights it. Also, double-clicking an individual field puts the program into edit mode for that field.

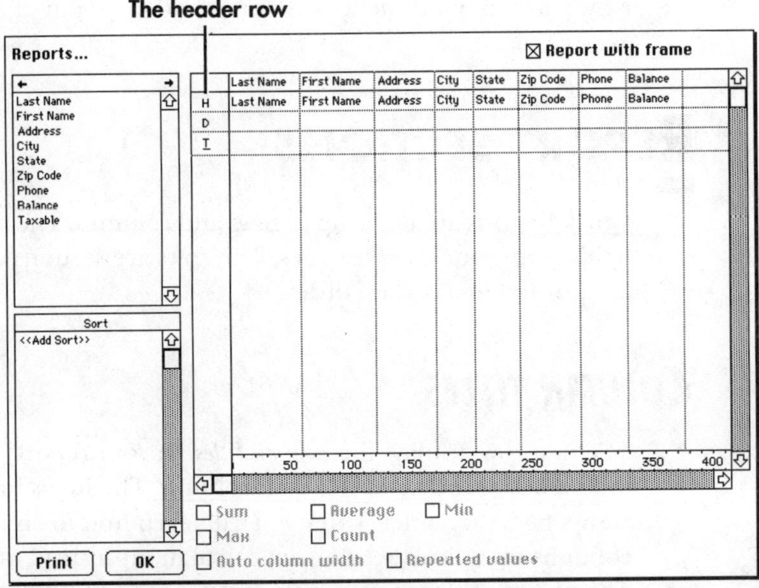

FIGURE 8.4

The header section of the Quick Report Editor

Let's try renaming some of the columns in the header row:

1. Double-click on the Last Name column in the header row.
2. Double-click on the word *Name* and press the **Delete** key to delete it.
3. Double-click on the First Name column in the header row.
4. Double-click on the word *Name* and press the **Delete** key.
5. Double-click on the Address column in the header row.
6. Click the mouse in front of the word *Address* and type **Street**.
7. Double-click on the Phone field in the header row and change it to **Telephone**.

I mentioned earlier that the Quick Report Editor will make the columns wide enough to hold the widest piece of data. If a column heading is the widest piece of information, the Quick Report Editor will adjust the size of the column to make the column title fit. If you have a column title that is longer than the data in the column, make the column title two rows instead of one:

1. Double-click on *Street Address* in the header row of the Address column.
2. Click the mouse just before the word *Address* to position the cursor in front of the *A* in *Address.*
3. Press the **Return** key.

The header is now using two lines instead of just one and the column became narrower. You can use this technique anytime you would like to add more text to the header of a column without making the column wider.

THE DETAIL SECTION

The detail section is the row with a *D* in the left-most column. The data from your database fields appear in this row. The Quick Report Editor prints this row once for each record in the current selection. At the moment, you won't be doing much with this section. Later in this chapter, you will see how you can use this section to format the data from the fields as well as change the fonts and styles used for printing. Figure 8.5 points out this row in the Quick Report Editor.

THE TOTALS SECTION

The totals section is the row with the *T* in the left-most column. The Quick Report Editor has a number of built-in functions that display their results in the Totals section. This is all you need to know about the totals section for now. Later, we will take a closer look at it and learn about the functions that use the totals section. Figure 8.6 points out this row in the Quick Report Editor. This might be a good time to save your quick report.

FIGURE 8.5

The detail section of the Quick Report Editor

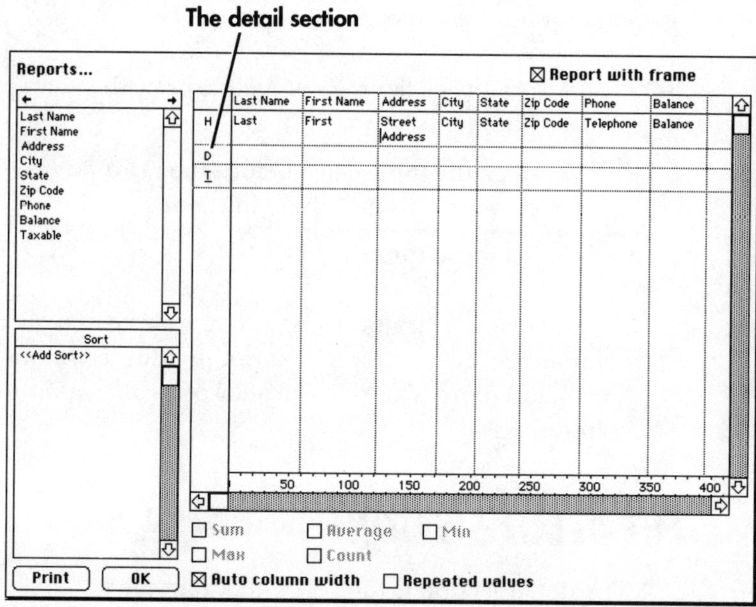

FIGURE 8.6

The totals section of the Quick Report Editor

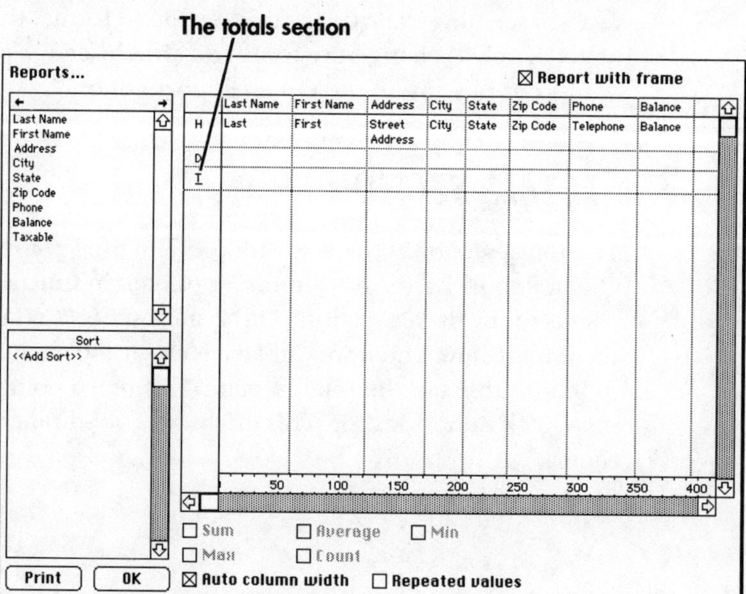

FORMATTING FIELDS

When you format a field, you are changing the way the data in the field will appear. You may want a telephone number to appear on the screen as *714-555-5768* and print on reports as *(714) 555-5768*. When you enter data into fields in your database, 4D does not store (nor do you enter) any formatting characters like *$* for dollars or */* for dates; only the data itself is stored. The benefit to this is that you can display the same data many different ways using different display formats.

4D has a number of built-in formats for different data types. There are five alphanumeric formats, eighteen numeric (real, integer, or long integer) formats, six date formats, four picture formats, and six time formats. In addition, you can create your own formats for most of the data types. There are three important characters for formatting. These characters are the pound sign (#), the zero (0), the caret (^) and the decimal (.).

THE POUND SIGN (#)

In a format, the pound sign is a placeholder for a character of data from the field. For example, you probably noticed that all the numbers in the Telephone column print together without any formatting. If we made **(###) ###-####** the format for the Telephone column, the data would be easier to read and to recognize as telephone numbers.

Because this field is alphanumeric, 4D begins on the left and fills one character from the field into each place that a pound sign holds. The pound sign holds a place for the characters in the field and is therefore called a *placeholder*.

Let's try adding this format to the Phone column:

1. Double-click in the detail row of the Phone column.
2. Enter **(###) ###-####** as the format for the detail row.
3. Print the report to the screen.
4. Use the **Zoom** button to view the Phone column.
5. Click the **Stop Printing** button when you are finished.

THE ZERO CHARACTER (0)

The zero character is also used as a placeholder in a format. When you use a zero in a format, you are telling 4D that you want a zero to appear in cases where there is no character. For example, if you were storing invoices totals and had the value *500.07* in a field, it would print just as it was entered. However, if the value were *500.70*, it would not print as entered. Why? Because 4D doesn't store *500.70*. 4D stores only what it needs to keep track of the value. Consequently, *500.70* would be stored as *500.7* and would print this way if you did not format the column on your report. By adding zeros to a format you can eliminate this problem. In the format **##0.00**, 4D treats the zeros just like the pound sign with one exception: If there is no character in the position where a zero is in the format, the zero is printed instead. If you have used just about any spreadsheet program, you are already familiar with this type of formatting. 4D handles the formatting of numbers in the same way that spreadsheets do.

THE CARET CHARACTER (^)

The caret character is used to print a blank space when there is not value for a particular position in a format. This is useful when you want to align certain character in your format. For example, if were printing a report on today's invoices and you wanted all of the dollar signs in the Invoice Total column to be aligned, you would use the format **$^^^,^^0.00**. With this format, the value *500.7* would print as **$ 500.70.**

THE DECIMAL CHARACTER (.)

The decimal character is used mostly when formatting columns that are displaying data that contains a decimal value. For example, if you had a database that was tracking invoices, you might have a report that printed a summary of the invoices that were written each day. Say an invoice had a total of $500.70. 4D wouldn't know this value represented dollars and cents so it would store the value as *500.7*. To format this field to display the data as dollars and cents on a Quick Report you would use the format **$###,##0.00**. 4D uses the decimal in the format to help apply the format to the data in the correct way.

Let's try adding a format to the Balance field on the report:

1. Double-click in the detail row of the Balance column.
2. Enter **$###,##0.00** as the format for the Detail row.
3. Print the report to the screen.
4. Use the **Zoom** button to view the Balance column.
5. Click the **Stop Printing** button when you are finished.

FORMATTING DATE COLUMNS

4D has six built-in date formats. The way you choose a date format for a column on a report is different from the way you select numeric formats. Each of the date formats has a number. To format a column using a particular date format, you simply double-click in the detail row of the column and enter the number that represents the date format you want. The table below lists the six formats:

Number	Format
1	1/06/1999
2	Wed, Jan 6, 1999
3	Wednesday, January 6, 1999
4	1/6/1999
5	January 6, 1999
6	Jan 6, 1999

CHOOSING FONTS, STYLES, AND SIZES

The place where each row and column come together is called a *cell*. Each column heading, detail, and total area is a cell. Each cell in a quick report can have it's own font, style, and size. You can set the font, style, and size for entire columns and rows all at once.

To highlight a single cell, simply click in it. To highlight an entire row, click on the letter in the left-most column of the row. To highlight an entire column, click on the column title. Once you have highlighted a portion of your report, you can use the Font and Style menus to change the way the highlighted area will print. Let's try setting the font and style for a few portions of the quick report. First, let's make the Last Name appear in boldface:

1. Click on the detail row of the Last Name column to select it.
2. Choose Style ➤ Bold.

4D places a checkmark next to Bold in the Style menu to let you know that it will print this area in bold. Practically every Macintosh application lets you set the font and style of the data being printed so this shouldn't be anything new. Now, let's make the entire detail section appear in the Helvetica font:

1. Click on the *D* in the left-most column to select entire detail section.
2. Choose Font ➤ Helvetica.

If you are printing to a laser printer, you should be sure to select fonts that will print best on it. While Geneva will print on a laser printer, the printer actually substitutes Helvetica for you. The problem is that the spacing between letters is set for Geneva which is wider than Helvetica. Consequently, the letters are too far apart. If you select the Helvetica font, the laser printer will have the correct letter spacing and your reports will look nicer.

As before, 4D places a checkmark next to Helvetica in the Font menu to indicate that the highlighted area has been set to print in this font. You may also have noticed that the format for the Phone column now appears in Helvetica instead of Geneva, which is the default font for the Quick Report Editor.

Now let's make the Last Name and First Name columns appear in italics:

1. Click on the Last Name column title to select the entire column.
2. Choose Style ➤ Italic.
3. Repeat steps one and two for the First Name column.

Now that you have made several changes to your report, let's print it to the screen again to see the effect of these changes. Figure 8.7 shows how your quick report should now look when you print it to the screen using print preview. This might be a good time to save your quick report.

1. Click the **Print** button.
2. If it is not already selected, click the **Print Preview** button.
3. Click the **Print** button to begin printing the report to the screen.
4. Click the **Zoom** button to examine the changes you have made.
5. When you are finished, click the **Stop Printing** button.

FIGURE 8.7

The changed quick report

Last	First	Street Address	City	State	Zip Code	Telephone	Balance
Brown	John	123 Diskette Drive	Sunnyvale	CA	94086	(408)-555-5678	$9,000.00
Jones	Sally	14 Pear Street	Irvine	CA	92715	(714)-555-9890	$5,500.00
Kimball	Margaret	22 East Main Street	Framingham	MA	01701	(508)-555-7890	$1,050.00
Simpson	Joan	921 Maple Street	Anchorage	AK	99510	(904)-555-3245	$6,750.00
Smith	Ron	29 Old Town #5	Newport News	VA	23606	(703)-555-3890	$8,877.00
Williams	Ted	4501 Evelyn Avenue	Sunnyvale	CA	94086	(408)-555-8303	$1,500.00

FRAMING THE REPORT

By default, 4D prints a frame around the columns and rows to make the report easier to read. If you deselect the Report with frame checkbox, 4D will print the report without the frames around each column and row.

SORTING RECORDS FOR THE REPORT

In most cases, you will probably want the records on a report printed in some kind of sorted order. The Quick Report Editor allows you to store the sort order with the report so you don't have to remember to sort the records before you print the report. In the lower-left portion on the Quick Report Editor is the sort area. This area lists the fields to be sorted on before the report is printed. To sort on a field, you click on «**Add Sort**» and drag to the field you want to sort on. 4D then adds the highlighted field to the sort order. Figure 8.8 shows how the Quick Report Editor would look if you were sorting your report by State and Last Name.

FIGURE 8.8

A report sorted by State and Last Name

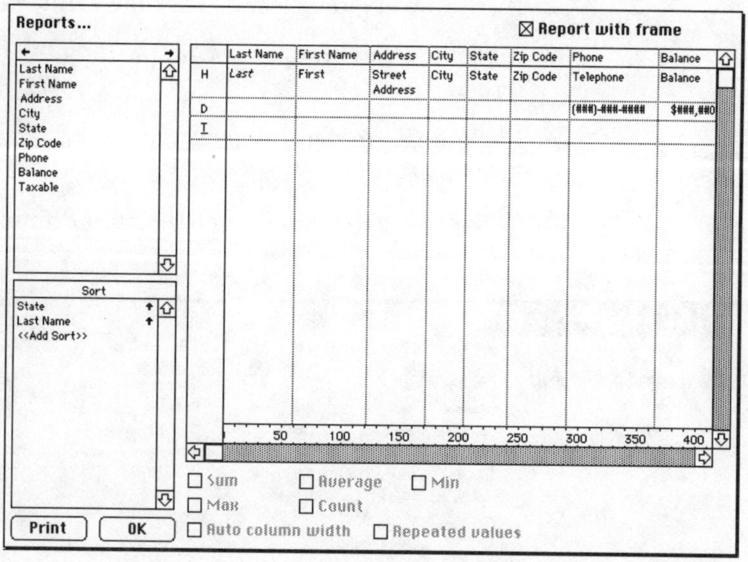

If you sort on more than one field, 4D cannot perform an indexed sort. This means that the more records you are sorting, the longer the sort will take. To make sorting as fast as possible, make sure you sort on only one field and make sure that the field is an indexed field.

Let's add the State and Last Name fields to the sort area. Follow these steps:

1. Click and drag «**Add Sort**» from the Sort area to the State field on the report then release the mouse button.
2. Click and drag «**Add Sort**» from the sort area to the Last Name field on the report and release the mouse button.

When you dragged «**Add Sort**» to a field, the field was added to the sort order. 4D also added a tiny arrow indicating that the fields would be sorted in ascending order. If you want a field sorted in descending order, simply click on the arrow next to the field.

Sometimes, when setting up the sort, you might select the fields in the wrong order; or perhaps you will select a field you didn't really want to sort on. Say for instance, you decided not to sort on the Last Name field. To remove the last Name field from the sort order, select Other ➤ Delete Last Sort.

THE REPEATED VALUES OPTION

If you print your report, you will notice that the name of the state *CA* is printed only once—for Ted Williams—it is not printed for Sally Jones or John Brown. Since you sorted by State and all of these customers are in the same state, 4D prints the state once and doesn't print it again until it changes to another state. This makes the report easier to read because it is easier to spot the point at which a sorted column changes to a new value (and it saves a little ink too).

If you don't want 4D to suppress these values, click on the State column and check the Repeated Values checkbox. This will cause 4D to print the field for every record, even if it is the same value as for the last record that printed.

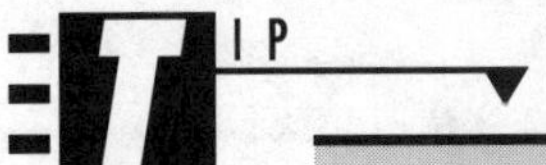

You may want to use this option if the people reading the report are misinterpreting the missing data as data that was never entered into the database.

1. Click on the State column to select it.
2. Click the Repeated Values checkbox.
3. Print the report to the screen.
4. Click the State column to select it.
5. Click the Repeated Values checkbox again to deselect it.

ADDING CALCULATED COLUMNS

Back in *Chapter 2* I explained why you would want to separate your data into individual fields rather than lumping it together in one field. The example I used was city, state, and zip code. Rather than putting this data all in one field, we have separated it into three fields to give us the ability to deal with each piece of information separately.

Having it all in one field has its advantages when printing a report, though. For example, to save room on your report and to make it easier to read, you might want the Address and City fields in one column on the report. Fortunately, this is one of the rare circumstances where you can have your cake and eat it too.

The Quick Report Editor gives you the ability to create *calculated columns.* Calculated columns are columns that don't display information directly from fields. They display information that is the result of some calculation. These columns could be used to combine several fields into one column, or to add information that doesn't exist in any field but that can be derived from a calculation. As 4D prints the report, it performs the calculations for any calculated columns. Let's change the report so that the Address and City fields all appear in one column. First, we will need to add a column that will hold the result of our calculation:

1. Click on the Address column title to highlight the entire column.
2. Choose Edit ➤ Insert Column (⌘-I).

Now that we have added a blank column, we can delete the columns we will no longer need.

1. Click on the Address column title to select it.
2. Choose Edit ➤ Delete Column.
3. Because the City column is next, it should already be highlighted, so choose Edit ➤ Delete Column.

Figure 8.9 shows how your quick report should now look.

FIGURE 8.9

The report with a new column

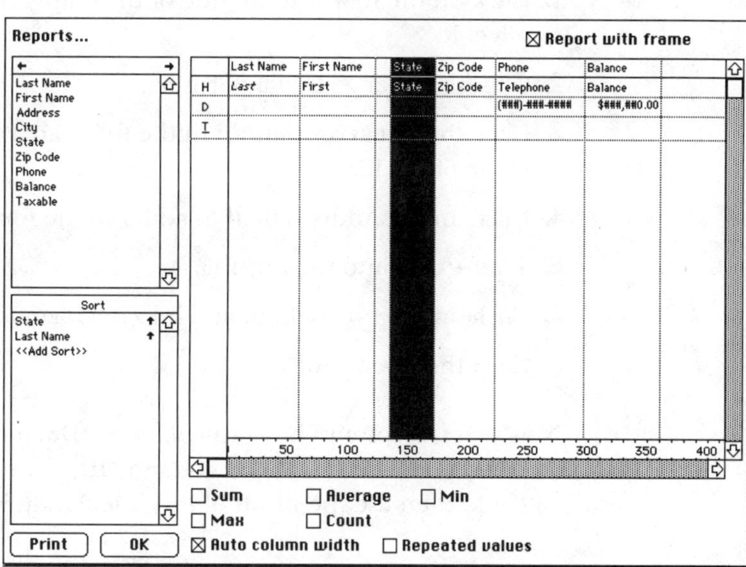

Our next step is to add a calculation to our new column that will combine the Address and City fields. Combining information together is called *concatenation.* To make the report look nice we will concatenate the Address and City fields. We will need to create a formula to do this. To make the address readable, we will add a comma and a space between the Address and the City fields. The formula will look like this:

```
[Customers]Address+", "+[Customers]City
```

When you use the plus sign (+) in a formula, 4D knows what to do based on the type of data you are using it with. If you use the plus sign with two numeric values, 4D adds them together. If you use the plus sign between two alphanumeric values, 4D combines them. In our case, we also want to add a few other characters in between the fields. Notice that we are adding ", " to the Address field before we add the City field. The quotes give us a way to tell 4D that we want to add the characters in between the quotes. The quotes themselves will not be added. So, between the Address and City fields we have added a comma and a space, and between the City and State fields we have added just a space. The Quick Report Editor uses the same Formula editor you have used in other chapters for entering formulas. Let's add this formula to our report:

1. Click on the new column title of the empty column to select it.
2. Choose Other ➤ Edit a Formula.
3. Click the **left arrow** button in the fields area to display the name of the file.
4. Click on the Address field to add it to the formula.
5. Type **+", "+** into the formula.
6. Click on the City field to add it to the formula.
7. Click the **OK** button.

Now that the column has a calculation, 4D names the column *C1.* If you created a second calculated column, 4D would name it *C2,* and so on. You could then use the result of this calculation in the formulas of the new columns. At this point the only thing left to do is to give the column an appropriate header and set its font.

1. Double-click the header row of the new column.
2. Type **Address and City**.
3. Click on the detail row of the new column.
4. Select Font ➤ Helvetica.

USING COLUMN MATH FUNCTIONS

The Quick Report Editor has five built-in math functions that can be performed on any entire numeric column. These functions place the result of the calculation in the totals area of the report. These functions are:

Function	Description
Sum	Totals all entries for the selected column.
Average	Calculates the average of all entries in the selected column.
Minimum	Calculates the lowest value in the selected column.
Maximum	Calculates the highest value in the selected column.
Count	Calculates the number of entries in the selected column that have a value greater than zero.

Using these functions is simple. Click on a column title to select the entire column, then click on the function you want for that column. The Quick Report Editor places an icon that represents the function you selected in the totals area. Let's try adding the Sum and Average functions to the Balance column:

1. Click on the Balance column title to select the entire column.

2. Click the Sum checkbox.
3. Click the Average checkbox.
4. Print the report to the screen and use the **Zoom** button to view the totals area.

You can see from the print preview that 4D has summed and averaged the Balance column. Since there is nothing that prints on the report to tell the reader what these two numbers are, it might be helpful to add a label that explains them.

1. Double-click in the cell to the left of the cell where Sum and Average are.
2. Type **Grand Total:** and press the **Return** key.
3. Type **Avg Balance:**.
4. Print the report to the screen to see how it looks now.

Figure 8.10 shows what your quick report should look like now. This is a good time to save your report.

FIGURE 8.10

The quick report with totals

Last	First	Address and City	State	Zip Code	Telephone	Balance
Simpson	Joan	921 Maple Street, Anchorage	AK	99510	(904)-555-3245	$6,750.00
Brown	John	123 Diskette Drive, Sunnyvale	CA	94086	(408)-555-5678	$9,000.00
Jones	Sally	14 Pear Street, Irvine		92715	(714)-555-9890	$5,500.00
Williams	Ted	4501 Evelyn Avenue, Sunnyvale		94086	(408)-555-8303	$1,500.00
Kimball	Margaret	22 East Main Street, Framingham	MA	01701	(508)-555-7890	$1,050.00
Smith	Ron	29 Old Town #5, Newport News	VA	23606	(703)-555-3890	$8,877.00
					Grand Total:	$32,677.00
					Avg Balance:	$5,446.16

ADDING SUBTOTALS TO REPORTS

Quite often when you create a report you will want a breakdown of totals by category. For example, in this report, you might want total balances as well as the average balance for each state. Totals by category are called *subtotals.* To create subtotals you must do two things:

- Sort on the field you want subtotals for
- Add a Break section to the report

Since you are already sorting the report on the State field, you have accomplished the first step. The second step is to add a *break section* to the report. A break section is a row that prints each time a sorted field changes value. The report is sorted by state, so each time the state changes, the break section will print. Break sections contain totals just like the totals section. The math functions in a break section calculate their totals for each sorted value. Because the report is sorted by state, you will have the result of the sum and average functions for each state. Let's try adding a break section:

1. Click on the *T* in the totals section to select the entire row.
2. Choose Edit ➤ Insert Break (⌘-B).

Notice that 4D inserts a new row. *B1* stands for *Break Level 1.* This means that each time the value changes for the first field the report is sorted on, the B1 areas will print. You can sort on up to sixteen fields in 4D and consequently, you can have up to sixteen break areas in a report.

4D copied the text you entered (*Grand Total:* and *Avg Balance:*) from the totals area to the B1 area. Grand Total is not really accurate for the B1 area, since this will really be only the subtotal for each state. Also, it might be helpful to know which state the totals area for. Let's make some changes to the text for the B1 area to make things more clear:

1. Double-click in the cell that says *Grand Total:* and *Avg Balance:* in the B1 row.
2. Double-click on the word *Grand* and drag across to highlight the word *Total.*
3. Type **Subtotal**.
4. Click at the right end of *Avg Balance:* and press the **Return** key.

5. Type **State: #.**
6. Print the report to the screen to see how it looks.

4D printed a break area each time the state changed and calculated the sum and average for each state. Also notice that the contents of the State field were printed in the space where you entered the pound sign (#). When you enter a pound sign in a break area, 4D replaces the pound sign with whatever caused the break to occur. Because you are sorting on the State field, the State field caused the break area to print.

PAGE BREAKS

All of the sections of the report you have been creating print together. There may be times, though, when you want 4D to print individual sections on individual pages. Say you had offices in each state and you wanted to send out this report so that all the offices would know which customers in their state are carrying balances and what the total and averages are for their state. You probably wouldn't want to send this entire report to each office and the have everyone looking at everyone else's information. You could use the Search Editor to search for the Customers in each individual state then print a report, but that could take a while if you have a lot of customers; besides, it's really not necessary.

The Quick Report Editor has the ability to print each sorted section of your report on a separate page. This means that each time the break area is printed, 4D will start the next section at the top of a new page. This is called a *page break.* You may have noticed that the *T* in the totals row is underlined. The underline indicates where the page break is in the report. By default, a report page breaks after the totals section is printed, which is at the end of the report. What we want is to have the report page break each time the B1 section is printed. Let's change the page break:

1. Click on *B1* in the break 1 section to highlight the entire row.
2. Choose Other ➤ Page Break.
3. Print the report to see how it looks. You will need to use the **Next Page** button to view each page of the report.

HIDING COLUMNS AND ROWS

If you have printed the entire report, you may have noticed that the Grand Totals printed on the last page of the report. This might not be convenient if you only want each of your offices to see the information for their state. Fortunately, the Quick Report Editor gives you the option to hide columns and rows. Using this feature, we can hide the totals row so that it doesn't appear on the report. Let's try it:

1. Click on the *T* in the totals area to select the entire row.
2. Choose Edit ➤ Hide line.
3. Print the report and notice that the totals section is no longer printed on the last page.

Figure 8.11 shows what your quick report should now look like. When you selected Edit ➤ Hide Line, 4D grayed the totals section as a visual indication that this section would not be printed. To hide an entire column, simply click on the column title to select the entire column, then select Edit ➤ Hide Column.

FIGURE 8.11

The quick report with the totals row hidden

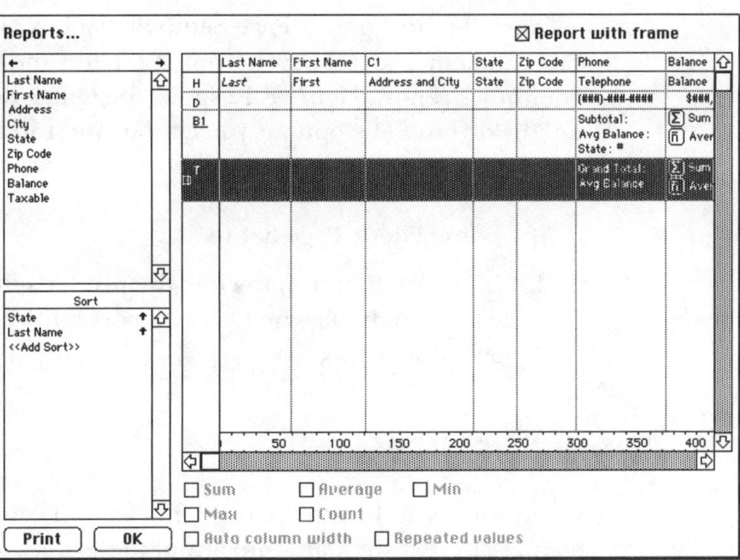

There are lots of other reasons why you might hide a line (row). You might want to sort on a field, but not print it on the report. You might want to print one report will all of the columns and then another with only selected ones. Being able to hide columns and rows gives you a lot of flexibility when creating reports.

SETTING UP THE PAGE

Quick reports have print options just like anything else you print from your Macintosh. You can select these options by choosing File ➤ Page Setup. If you have printed anything from your Macintosh before, the Page Setup options are familiar. These options change depending on the type of printer you have selected from the Chooser. If you want more information on these options, see the Apple system software manuals that came with your Macintosh.

When you select File ➤ Page Setup, 4D displays the chosen printer's Page Setup dialog box. When you click the **OK** button, 4D displays the special Page Setup dialog box for the Quick Report Editor.

THE PAGE SETUP DIALOG BOX

The Quick Report Editor's Page Setup dialog box allows you to choose options and enter text that will print at the top and bottom of each page of your quick report. Figure 8.12 shows the Quick Report Editor's Page Setup dialog box. The options you choose are stored with the report when you save it to disk and only affect the report you are working on.

1. Choose File ➤ Page Setup.
2. Click the **OK** button to close the printer's Page Setup dialog and display the Quick Report Editor Page Setup dialog box.

ADDING HEADERS

The three areas at the top are for the header of your quick report. You can enter any text you want into any of these areas and they will print in

FIGURE 8.12

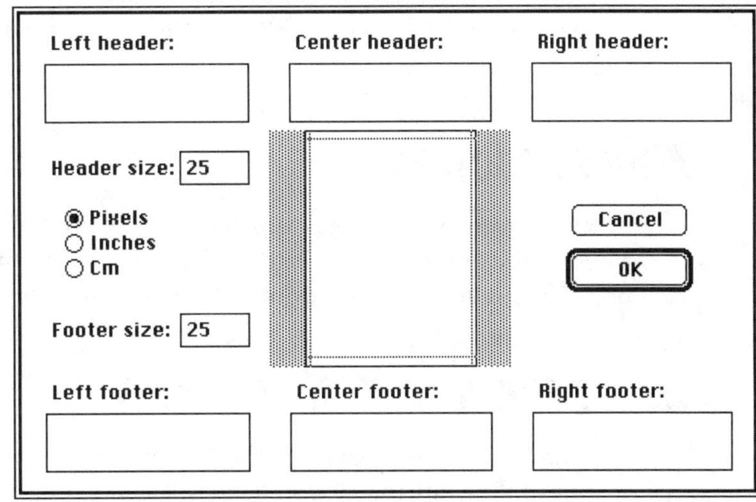

The Quick Report Editor's Page Setup dialog box

an appropriate part of each page. Any text you enter must be one line. You cannot enter carriage returns to create multi-line headers. These three areas are useful for the title of your report or perhaps the name of the person the report is for. The header size box lets you set how tall the header area will be. By default, the size is in pixels. One pixel is equal to one dot on the screen. There are 72 dots in one vertical inch of screen space. You can change the measurement from pixels to inches or centimeters. When you change it, 4D will automatically convert whatever you have entered for the header size to the selected measurement type. So, if you think about it, you have a built-in pixel-to-inches-to-centimeters converter!

The graphic in the middle of the dialog box represents the page as it will print. The purpose of this graphic is to show you how tall the header and footer areas are. If you change the header size or the footer size, this area will be updated to reflect the change. Let's try it:

1. Click **Inches**.
2. Click in the Header Size box and use the backspace key to delete the value that is there.
3. Type **.5**.

Notice that after you entered a header size of one-half inch, the small page graphic in the middle changed to show you how much of the page the header would use.

ADDING FOOTERS

At the bottom of the Page Setup dialog there are three footer areas. These three areas work just like the header areas at the top of the dialog box. The Footer Size box controls the size of the footer area.

USING FONTS, STYLES, AND SIZES

You can set the font, style, and size for the header and footer areas. To set any of these attributes, you need to click on the header or footer area on the graphic in the middle of the diàlog box to select it. Once selected, you can use the Font and Style menus to choose the font, style, and size you want of the header or footer. Let's try it:

1. Click in the center header box.
2. Type **Balances By State**.
3. Press the **Tab** key to move to the right header.
4. Type your name.
5. Click on the header area of the graphic to select it.
6. Choose Font ➤ Helvetica.
7. Choose Style ➤ Bold.
8. Choose Style ➤ 12.

You may have noticed that has you typed your header, 4D copied what you typed into the header area of the small page graphic in the middle of the dialog box. This way you can see how the size of the text relates to the size of the header area. You can use these same techniques to select font, style, and sizes for the footer area. Selecting a font will not change the way the text you typed appears in the header or footer boxes.

They will always appear in the Chicago font in this dialog box. However, rest assured that it will print on the report in the font and style you selected.

AUTOMATIC PAGE NUMBERING

Numbering the pages of a report is always useful. I have found it especially useful when, after printing a terribly long report, I dropped it, scattering the pages in all directions. 4D can number your report pages for you automatically. To put page numbers on a report, simply type **#P** in any of the header or footer areas. Let's try it:

1. Click in the Center Footer box.
2. Type **Page: #P**.

That's all there is to it. It doesn't get much simpler than that!

TIME AND DATE STAMPING REPORTS

If you print a report often, it can be very useful to have the time and date printed on the report. Time and date *stamping* a report is as easy as numbering the pages. To put the current time on the report, just enter **#H** (the *H* stands for *hours*) in any of the header or footer boxes. To put the current date on the report, type **#D**.

1. Click in the Left Footer box.
2. Type **#H**.
3. Click in the Right Footer box.
4. Type **#D**.
5. Click on the footer area in the small page graphic and select a font, style, and size from the menus.

Your computer can keep track of the current time and date because it has a five-year battery inside it. If you have your Macintosh repaired, the first thing the technician will do is remove the battery. When they are finished working on your computer, they will put the battery back. However, technicians are notorious for not resetting the time and date from the control panel under the Apple menu. If the date on your report is January 1st, 1904 (the earliest date the Macintosh knows), it means that the battery has been removed and reinstalled.

The time and date come from the clock inside your Macintosh. If either the time or date is incorrect on your report, it means that the clock is wrong in your Macintosh. Fortunately, this is easy to correct by selecting the General Controls control panel from the Apple menu. The configuration of the control panel will be different depending on which version of the operating system you are using. Again, if you need more information, look in the system software guide that came with your Macintosh.

Let's try printing the report to the screen so you can see your headers and footers:

1. Click the **OK** button to close the Page Setup dialog box.
2. Click the **Print** button to print the report to the screen.
3. Use the **Zoom** button to check the headers and footers.
4. When you are finished, click the **Stop Printing** button and then save your report.

PRINTING YOUR QUICK REPORT TO OTHER DEVICES

You already know how to print your quick reports to the screen or to your printer. There are three other ways to print your report. You can print your report using direct ASCII printing, print to a disk file, or print to a graph. You can use these print options by selecting File ➤ Print To instead of using the **Print** button or the Print menu item.

DIRECT ASCII PRINTING

Long reports can take a while to print, depending on how many records are being printed, the size of the font, the complexity of the calculations, the number of fields on the report, and the type of printer being used. If you own a serial printer (like an ImageWriter), you can use it to print your report extremely fast using direct ASCII printing. To use this print method, choose File ➤ Print To and select the Direct ASCII Printing option. With this option selected, 4D will not use any of the fonts you have chosen for your report. Instead, it will substitute a font that is built-in to the ImageWriter printer. Consequently, the printing is much, much faster.

PRINTING TO A DISK FILE

With this option selected, 4D presents a Save As file dialog box instead of the normal print dialog box when you click the **Print** button. 4D creates a text file on disk and copies all the text into the file. 4D will, by default, insert **Tab** characters between columns and insert a return character at the end of each row. 4D inserts these characters to make it easier for you to use this text file with other applications on your Macintosh. Printing to a disk file is called *exporting*; I will discuss exporting in more detail in *Chapter 11*. Let's try printing this report to a disk file:

1. Choose File ➤ Print To.
2. Click on the Disk File option.
3. Click the **OK** button.

4. Click the **Print** button.
5. Type **Balance Report File**.
6. Click the **Save** button.

Instead of being printed to your printer, the report is exported to a text file called **Balance Report File**. You can now open this file with any application that will read a text file. You might want to try opening a word processor or spreadsheet program and selecting this file to see what it looks like when it is exported. The advantage to this option is that you can use the data from the report in other documents you create with other applications.

PRINTING TO A GRAPH

When you print your report as a graph, 4D presents the built-in Graph editor and uses the data from the report to create the graph. We will take a closer look at the Graph editor in *Chapter 10.* The graph editor normally uses data from records to produce a graph. With this option, you can create graphs based on data that is the result of calculations.

HOW MANY FIELDS WILL FIT ON A QUICK REPORT?

When you print a quick report, 4D makes each column wide enough for the widest piece of information in that column. If you are printing a report with a lot of columns, they may not all fit, due to the width of the data. There are a number of things you can do to make all your columns fit on your report.

CHANGING THE PAGE ORIENTATION

The easiest way to get more columns on a page is to change the orientation of the page. By default, 4D will print the report in Portrait mode (8½×11"). However, you can also print your reports in landscape mode (11×8½"). By printing your report in landscape mode, you get more columns on the page because the page is wider. The only real disadvantage is that your report will probably take more pages to print and may not be as easy to read (depending on who the reader is). You can change your report to landscape mode by selecting File ➤ Page Setup and clicking on the icon that shows a page printing horizontally.

SETTING COLUMN WIDTHS TO A FIXED SIZE

As I mentioned, 4D calculates the width of each column automatically. This option (called Auto Column Width) can be turned off on a column-by-column basis. You can set the column width manually for any column by turning off the Auto Column Width option. If you set the column width manually and a piece of information won't fit, 4D will "wrap" the information to the next line of the column. This means that your report will require more pages to print because there will be more lines; however, you can make all the columns fit on the page.

The unit of measure for the rulers is based on the unit of measure for the headers and footers. To change the unit of measure, open the Page Setup dialog box and select points, inches, or centimeters.

You probably noticed the rulers in the Quick Report Editor. These rulers are there to help you when you are setting the column width manually. Let's try manually setting the column width for the Last Name column:

1. Click on the Last Name column title to select the entire column.
2. Click on the Auto Column Width checkbox to deselect it.
3. Move the pointer to the line between Last Name column title and the First Name column title. You will know you are

in the right place when the pointer changes to a vertical line with arrows pointing left and right.

4. Click and drag the line 1" to the right.

Using this technique, you can set the column width for all the columns on your quick report. Another advantage to setting the column width manually is speed. If you set the column width for all columns manually, 4D doesn't have to go through all of the records being printed to find the widest piece of information. Therefore, your report prints faster. If your report is several pages long, manually setting the column widths can save you several minutes.

Columns that have been set manually can easily be set back to automatically calculate the column width. Let's set the Last Name column back to automatic:

1. Click on the Last Name column title to select the entire column.
2. Click the Auto Column Width checkbox to select it.

USING CALCULATED COLUMNS TO SAVE ROOM

You have already learned one method for saving room on quick reports without even realizing it. Calculated columns can often save room because the information is displayed in a more compact form. The column you created to print the Address and City fields takes less room to print than the two columns did separately.

SO, HOW MANY FIELDS *WILL* FIT ON A QUICK REPORT?

As you can see, this is not an easy question to answer. This is one of those situations where trial and error is your best teacher. Set up your report and print it to the screen. If some of the columns don't print, try the techniques I have suggested. As you learn more about 4D, you will find that there usually several ways to solve any problem.

TAKING A BREAK

This is one of the longest chapters in the book. If you have worked straight through it, congratulations. You might want to take a break at this point. Make sure you save your quick report before you close quit 4th Dimension. if you can't remember what to do to get back into your database later, consult *Chapter 3*.

9 CREATING AND PRINTING LABELS

MAC TRACKS MAC

Generally speaking, to print labels, you 182

1. Select your page settings.
2. Choose the fields you want to print.
3. Pick the font and style.
4. Print the labels.

To specify the page setup for your labels 185

1. Choose Report ➤ Labels (⌘-J).
2. When the Page Setup dialog box appears, click **OK**.
3. Press the Tab key to move the cursor from the Label Across box to the Labels Down box.
4. Type the number of rows you want.

To change the font in a label 187

1. Choose a font from the Font popup menu.
2. Enter a type size in the Font Size box.
3. Choose any formatting you like from the Font Style popup menu.

To preview labels (print them to screen) 190

1. Click the **Print** button.
2. Click the Print Preview checkbox.
3. Click the **Print** button.

To save a label format to disk 192

1. Click the **Save** button.
2. Type a name for your file.
3. Click the **Save** button to save the file to disk.

To retrieve a label format from disk 193

Simply open the Label Editor and click the **Load** button. When the Open File dialog box appears, find the label file you want and click the **Open** button.

Featuring

- *The Label Editor*
- *Arranging labels*
- *Previewing labels*
- *Printing labels*
- *Direct ASCII printing*
- *Saving and retrieving label formats*

A COMMON TASK FOR any database is to print *labels*. If you are keeping track of customers, you might want to print labels for a mailing. If you are keeping track of inventory, you might print labels with inventory part numbers on them to mark new inventory as you receive it. Most database products give you the ability to print labels. However, none make the job as easy as 4th Dimension's Label Editor.

If you are not familiar with all the options in the Page Setup dialog box, you might want read about them in the system software guide that came with your computer. The more you know about these options, the easier it will be to print labels just the way you want them.

With the Label Editor, you simply select page settings, choose the fields you want, pick the font and style, and print. Figure 9.1 shows the Label Editor with a label already designed. You might have had a hard time printing labels with other database programs. If so, it's probably not your fault. Printing labels using any application can be a sticky business, so I will give you several helpful hints to make the job easier as we explore the Label Editor.

FIGURE 9.1

A label in the Label Editor

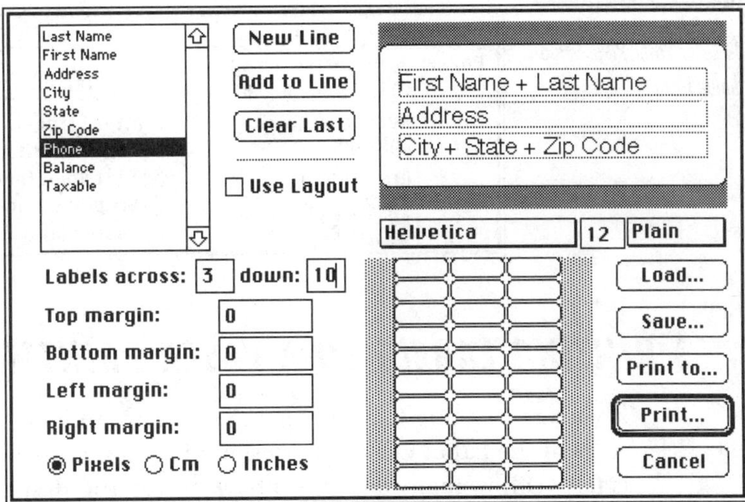

NOTE

When you click the Options button in the Page Setup dialog box, the Options dialog box appears. The little animal on the sample page is called the *Dog Cow*. It is called this because it looks both like a dog and a cow. Appropriately, the Dog Cow says, "Moof!"

SETTING UP THE PAGE

The first step in creating labels is to describe the labels you are going to print on to 4th Dimension. The size of the page is described using the standard Page Setup dialog box. Figure 9.2 shows a typical Page Setup dialog box. If you are printing on sheets of labels, select the page size that matches the size of a sheet. If you are printing on continuous labels, select a page size that is evenly divisible by the height of one label. This is to ensure that your label text will print right in the middle of the label and not slowly move down to the bottom of the label.

FIGURE 9.2

***A** LaserWriter Page Setup dialog box*

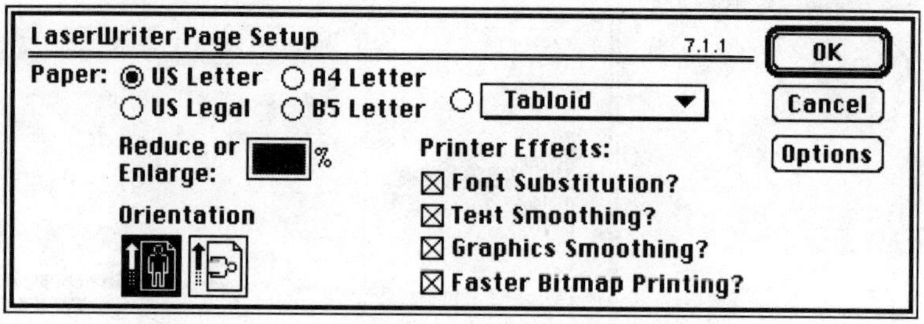

LaserWriter Page Setup 7.1.1
OK
Paper: ◉ US Letter ○ A4 Letter
○ US Legal ○ B5 Letter ○ Tabloid
Cancel
Reduce or Enlarge: %
Options
Printer Effects:
☒ Font Substitution?
Orientation
☒ Text Smoothing?
☒ Graphics Smoothing?
☒ Faster Bitmap Printing?

PRINTING LABELS TO A LASER PRINTER

If you are printing to a laser printer, you are in luck. The default page settings of the Label Editor are designed for laser labels. All you have to do is tell 4D how many labels you have across and down the page. When you purchase your labels, make sure that you buy laser labels. I mention this because often people will buy copier labels—they are usually less expensive than laser labels. However, copier labels have different margins than laser labels and are more difficult to print on. Spend a little more money on laser labels and you will save the difference in lost time and frustration.

PRINTING TO AN IMAGEWRITER OR OTHER SERIAL PRINTER

I have found that the easiest type of labels to use on an ImageWriter are called "one-up" labels. This means that there is one continuous column of tractor-feed labels. Again, make sure that the height of one label divides evenly into one of the page sizes in the ImageWriter's Page Setup dialog box.

SETTING THE PAGE SIZE AND LABEL ARRANGEMENT

The first thing we need to do is choose a page size and tell 4D how many labels we want across and down the page. As usual, if you are not in the Learn 4D database, open it and move to the User environment.

1. Choose Report ➤ Labels (⌘-J).
2. When the Page Setup dialog box appears, click **OK**.
3. Press the Tab key to move the cursor from the Label Across box to the Labels Down box.
4. Type **10**.

Notice that when you typed *10*, the area that shows a page of labels changed. Now it shows three labels across and ten labels down. This page-preview area makes it easier for you to ensure you have described your labels correctly.

CHOOSING AND ARRANGING FIELDS

In the upper-left corner of the Label Editor is a list of the fields from the file you are working with. The area to the right of the list of fields is the *label layout area.* The fields you choose to put on your labels will appear here. There are three buttons you use to place fields on a label. They are *New Line, Add To Line,* and *Clear Last.*

The **New Line** button will place the selected field on a new line on the label.

The **Add to Line** button will add the selected field to the same line as the last field added to the label. The Add to Line button also adds a space between fields automatically.

The **Clear Last** button is used to remove the last field from the label in case you make a mistake.

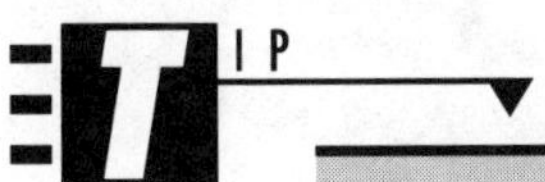

You can use the arrow keys to choose fields from the fields list instead of using the mouse.

Let's create some labels for a mailing:

1. Click on the First Name field to select it.
2. Click the **New Line** button.
3. Select the Last Name field.
4. Click the **Add to Line** to add the Last Name field to the same line that the First Name field is on.
5. Select the Address field and click the **New Line** button.
6. Select the City field and click the **New Line** button.
7. Select the State field and click the **Add to Line** button.
8. Select the Zip Code field and click the **Add to Line** button.

That's all there is to it. If you make a mistake, use the **Clear Last** button to remove the last field you placed on the label. If you make a mistake and don't realize it until after you have added more fields, you can still use the **Clear Last** button. Simply click the **Clear Last** button until you have removed all the fields up to and including the field you added by mistake. After that you can add back the fields you *do* want on the label.

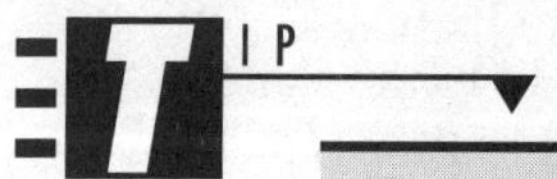

There is no way to add a comma (or any other text) *between* fields in the Label Editor. However, layouts created with the Layout Editor can contain commas and can be used with the Label Editor for printing labels. You will learn more about the Layout Editor in *Chapter 12*.

When it comes to arranging the fields on the label, trial and error seems to be the best method. Remember that the arrangement you create must accommodate the widest piece of information in each field. The Label Editor (unlike the Quick Report Editor) won't wrap information to the next line if it doesn't fit. So, it is important to arrange the fields on the label so that everything fits. One way you can get more information on a label is by selecting a smaller font size.

Choosing the Font, Size, and Style

Below the label preview area is a popup menu for choosing the font for the label. Next to it, you can enter the font size and next to that is another popup menu for the font style. Unlike in the Quick Report Editor, the font, style, and size are the same for all fields in the Label Editor. You can select the font, style, and size at any time, whether you have added fields to the label or not.

Now that you have added fields to your label, let's change the font:

1. Choose Helvetica from the Font popup menu.
2. Type **12** in the Font Size box.
3. Choose Bold from the Font Style popup menu.

Notice that you now have less room on the label. We made the font size 12 point to make the labels more readable. The default font size for a label is 9 point. By using 9 point, the fields take up less room and there is now more room for other fields. If you have many fields that need to fit on a label, this is a simple way to get more room. If you are printing labels on a laser printer, you can probably go down to 9 point or smaller and the label will still be readable. If you are printing to a dot-matrix printer like an ImageWriter, anything below 9 point may not be readable.

Setting the Margins

Setting the margins for a label format is never easy. Luckily, 4D comes with several label templates already created and set for different types of labels. If you want the job of printing labels to be as painless as possible, look over the label templates and buy labels that one of the templates was designed for.

If you have already purchased more labels than the mind can "comfortably" conceive, you will need to make some adjustments to the margins to get them just right. Increasing a margin means moving the label text towards the center of the page. However, you can also use negative margins. If you use a negative value for a margin, you are moving the label text away from the center of the page. For example, a negative right margin will pull the labels toward the right side of the page. This gives you the ability to adjust exactly where on the label the text falls.

If your labels are printing too close to the top of the page, enlarge the top margin. If they are printing too far away from the top of the page, shrink the top margin. Remember, to get the labels just where you want them on the page you may need to use a negative number for a margin. You can use negative numbers to adjust any of the margins. The label templates that come with 4D should work right out of the box; however, all printers are not created equal, so you may have to use the techniques I have described here to get your labels printing correctly on the page.

TRIED AND TRUE MARGIN SETTINGS

To make your first attempt at printing labels as successful as possible, I will give you some specific information on what labels to buy and how to set the margins. Avery Corporation's many different kinds of labels have become the standard in most offices. Avery 5160 Laser Printer labels are probably the most popular of their labels. These labels have three columns and ten rows. They are also perforated between the columns which makes it easy to separate the columns and peel off the labels. The best margins I have been able to create are (in pixels):

Top Margin	18
Bottom Margin	0
Left Margin	0
Right Margin	–30

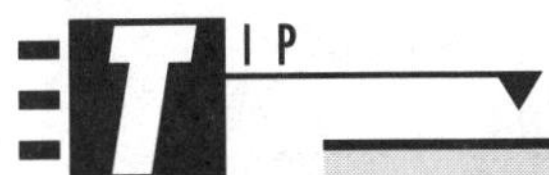

If you are not sure that the font you are using is a laser font, do the following test. When you print, deselect the Font Substitution and Text Smoothing options in the Page Setup dialog box. If the text is "jaggy" (not smooth) when you print, you are not using a laser font.

If you are printing addresses, a 10 point font is usually small enough for even some of the longer addresses. Remember to use a laser font. Laser fonts are built into the laser printer. The laser printer has special fonts it uses to print at a very high resolution. These fonts are not used on the screen, though. When you bought your laser printer, it came with a disk that had the screen fonts that matched the built-in laser fonts. Screen fonts are not built into the printer. If you use a screen font that doesn't have a matching laser font, the printer will substitute a laser font. When the printer substitutes fonts, it doesn't substitute the spacing between the letters. Consequently, the letters are more widely spaced than they would be had you used a built-in laser font. The following fonts are built-in to almost all of Apple laser printers:

Avant Garde

Bookman

Courier

Helvetica

New Century Schoolbook

New Helvetica Narrow

Palatino

Symbol

Times

Zapf Chancery

Zapf Dingbats

Apple's System 7 software has another type of font called a *True Type* font. True Type fonts print more clearly than screen fonts but not quite as nicely as laser fonts. You can identify True Type fonts by their names. In your system file, screen fonts have the font size next to the font name. True Type fonts have no size next to their name because they can appear in any size.

PRINTING THE LABELS

Printing the labels is simple. Fill your printer with labels and click the **Print** button. In most laser printers, the labels go in face up. If you are using a dot-matrix printer, feed the labels in until the print head is on the first label.

The Print Preview feature of 4D works in the Label Editor the same as in the Quick Report Editor. For the purposes of this book, we will print the labels to the screen to see how they look.

1. Click the **Print** button.
2. Click the Print Preview checkbox.
3. Click the **Print** button.

The Print Preview feature works just as it did with the Quick Report Editor. You can zoom in, zoom out, move to the next page, print the page, or stop previewing your labels.

NORMAL PRINTING

There are so many different kinds of labels and just as many different kinds of printers. Luckily, Apple sells only three basic types of printers, the LaserWriter, the ImageWriter, and the StyleWriter. This means that the number of possible label configurations is reduced. However there are still a great number of combinations. There are a few basic rules and tips when it comes to printing labels on different kinds of printers.

Printing to a Laser Printer

When printing to a laser printer, it is important to use laser labels instead of copier labels. I mentioned earlier in this chapter that the Label Editor comes set for laser labels right out of the box. There is another even more important reason to use laser labels: heat. Laser printers generate more heat than copiers do. Consequently, copier labels may not be designed to withstand the heat of a laser printer. This means that you could end up with copier labels melting inside your laser printer, a very expensive problem to fix.

Printing to an ImageWriter Printer

There is one very important point I need to make about printing to an ImageWriter printer. *Don't* print in Best mode. When you print in Best mode, the ImageWriter prints one entire line then backs up and prints the same line again. This makes the line darker and consequently, it looks nicer. There is one rather unfortunate side effect that you need to be aware of. When the printer backs up, it will sometimes reverse the direction of the labels and cause labels to peel off inside the printer and get stuck. You can't get the labels out yourself (if this happens to you, don't even try). When a label peels off inside your printer, you will need to take the printer to a technician to be repaired. This little repair job will probably cost over $100. When printing with an ImageWriter, use Draft or Faster mode.

DIRECT ASCII PRINTING

If you need to print a very large number of labels, you may want to use direct ASCII printing. This means that 4D won't use the font, font size, and font style you have selected for printing. Instead, 4D will use a font that is built into the dot-matrix printer. Because the printer doesn't have to worry about font, style, and size, it can print very fast. It doesn't look terrific but it will get the job done.

To print using direct ASCII printing, click the **Print To** button. Figure 9.3 shows the dialog box that appears and allows you to choose between a regular print mode and the direct ASCII mode. From there, you simply click **OK** to begin printing.

FIGURE 9.3

The Print Mode Selection dialog box

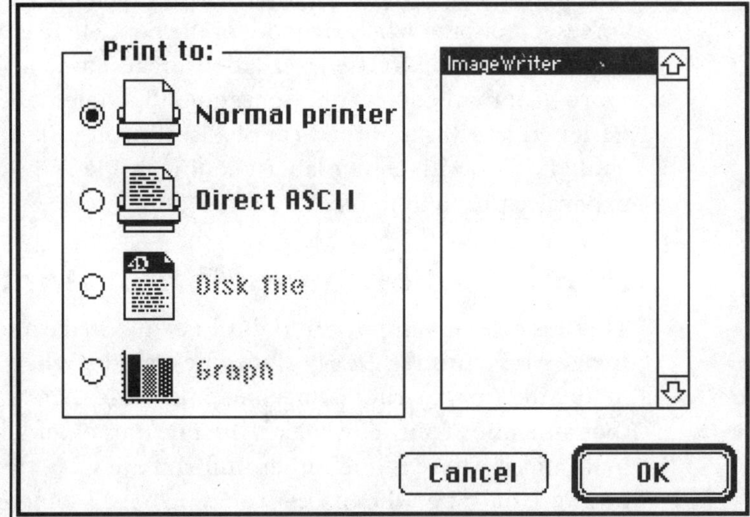

SAVING THE LABEL FORMAT

Once you have spent time making adjustments to your label format and setting the font and style just the way you want them, you will want to be able to save the label format to disk so you can use it later. Fortunately, the Label Editor provides you with this ability. Like the Quick Report Editor, the Label Editor saves the label formats as disk files. Let's save the label format you have created so you can use it later:

1. Click the **Save** button.
2. Type **3 Across Labels** as the name of the file.
3. Click the **Save** button to save the file to disk.

When the Save As dialog box appears, 4D will probably be displaying the folder where your copy of 4D is located. If you want the label format to be saved in the folder with your database, you will need to navigate to that folder before you click the Save button.

RETRIEVING AN EXISTING LABEL FORMAT

Opening a label format file is as easy as saving it. Simply open the Label Editor and click the **Load** button. When the Open File dialog box appears, find the label file you want and click the **Open** button.

CREATING LAYOUTS FOR USE AS LABEL FORMATS

You might have noticed the **Use Layout** checkbox in the Label Editor. When you click this checkbox, 4D will use the current output layout for the label setup instead of the label you have created in the label preview area. Creating a layout takes more work than using the Label Editor exclusively. However, you have much greater control over how the label looks when you use a layout. For example, by creating a layout, you could choose different fonts for each field to appear in. You could also enter text that you wanted to appear on each label (like a comma after the City field).

In *Chapter 12* you will learn all about 4th Dimension's Layout Editor. After learning about the Layout Editor, you will know how to create layouts for use with the Label Editor. For now, just keep in mind that this option is available and gives you greater control over the look of your labels.

CREATING GRAPHS

10

MAC TRACKS MAC

To choose a graph type **201**

1. Choose Quick ➤ Graph (⌘-K).
2. Click on the type of graph you wish to select.

To create a simple graph **206**

1. Click on the field you want to make the X-axis field.
2. Click on the field you want to make the Y-axis field.
3. Click the **Graph** button to create the graph.

To change the graph type on the fly **207**

Simply select a graph type from the Graph Type menu.

To create a picture graph **213**

1. Copy your picture to the Clipboard.
2. Open the Graph Editor (choose Report ➤ Graph).

3. Create a graph.
4. Choose Pictures ➤ Paste To Y1.
5. Choose Graph Type ➤ Picture.

To print a graph 214

Simply choose File ➤ Print and click **OK**.

To copy a graph into the scrapbook 215

1. Choose Edit ➤ Copy (⌘-C).
2. Choose Apple ➤ Scrapbook.
3. Choose Edit ➤ Paste (⌘-V).
4. Close the Scrapbook.

Featuring

- *Graphing in 4D*
- *The eight graph types*
- *Creating simple graphs*
- *Creating picture graphs*
- *Printing a graph*
- *Copying a graph to the scrapbook*

CREATING BUSINESS *GRAPHS* is a common database task. In most database programs, you would have to move your data out of your database and into a spreadsheet or graphing program in order to create graphs. Fortunately, 4D has a built-in Graph Editor, which allows you to create eight different types of graphs, customizing the way they are displayed and printed.

WHAT EXACTLY GETS GRAPHED?

You have seen that the current selection plays an important role in 4th Dimension databases. The Search Editor creates a current selection, the Delete Selection menu item deletes the records in the current selection, the Sort Editor sorts the records in the current selection. Also, the Quick Report Editor and the Label Editor print the records from the current selection.

The concept of a current selection in a database seems to be a necessary and obvious need for a database program. However, 4th Dimension is the only relational database program that uses this concept.

The Graph Editor also uses the current selection. The records that are graphed are those in the current selection. So, before creating a graph, you will want to select some records. You may be selecting records by hand or perhaps searching for records with the Search Editor. By now you are probably starting to see just how important the current selection concept is to 4th Dimension. Let's make sure all the records are selected so we can graph them:

1. If you aren't in the User environment, go there now.
2. Choose Select ➤ Show All (⌘-G).

CHOOSING A GRAPH TYPE

The first step in creating a graph is to decide upon one of the eight different graph types. Figure 10.1 shows the Graph Editor.

You choose a graph type by clicking on the picture that represents the type of graph you want. The table below describes the eight different graph types:

Graph Name	Description
Column	Displays one column of data per field.
Stacked Column	Stacks all the fields into one column.

FIGURE 10.1

The Graph Editor

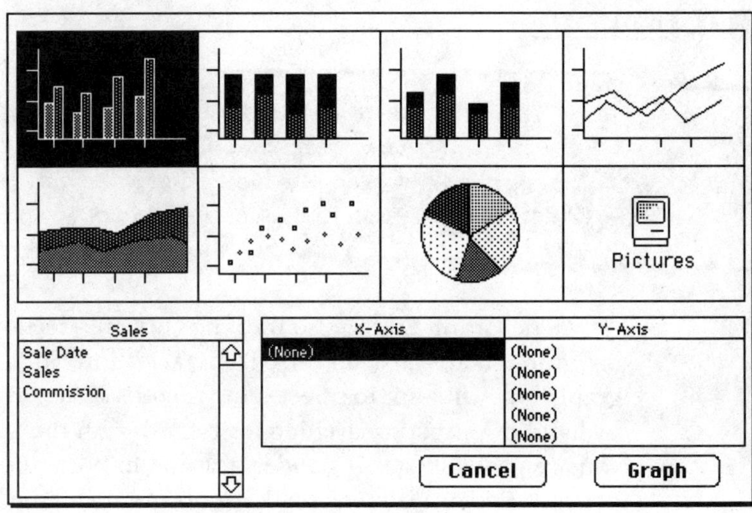

Graph Name	Description
Proportional Column	Stacks all the fields into one column, displaying each field as a portion of the entire column.
Line	Draws one line per field.
Area	Draws a shaded area for each field. An area graph is just like a line graph excepting that the portion beneath the line filled in with a pattern.
Scatter	Draws one dot per field per record. If more than one field is being graphed, the Graph Editor draws different shapes of dots for each field.
Pie	Draws a circle divided into sections that represent each bit of data as a percentage of the total.

Graph Name	Description
Picture	Picture graphs allow you to use your own graphic to create columns instead of the built-in columns. For example, if you sold computers and you were graphing computer sales, you might want to display columns that look like computers instead of the regular columns.

The table below shows sales and commissions on different dates.

Date	Sales	Commission
01/06/94	$4505	$560
01/10/94	$5679	$890
01/15/94	$7890	$745
01/22/94	$6598	$998
01/22/94	$3479	$445

This data was used to create a sample of each graph type, which appear in Figures 10.2–10.9. The Date is on the X axis and the Sales and Commissions are graphed on the Y axis.

Let's open the Graph Editor and select an area graph:

1. Choose Report ➤ Graph (⌘-K).
2. Click on the **Area** graph to select it.

FIGURE 10.2

A column graph

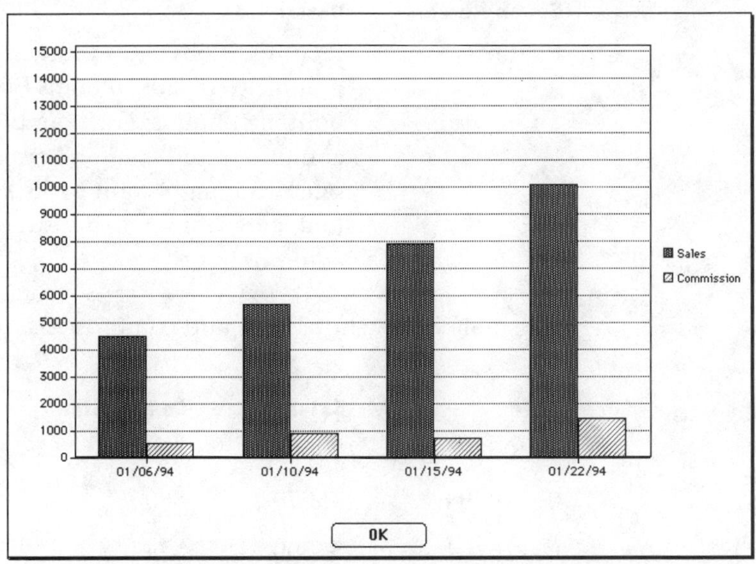

FIGURE 10.3

A stacked column graph

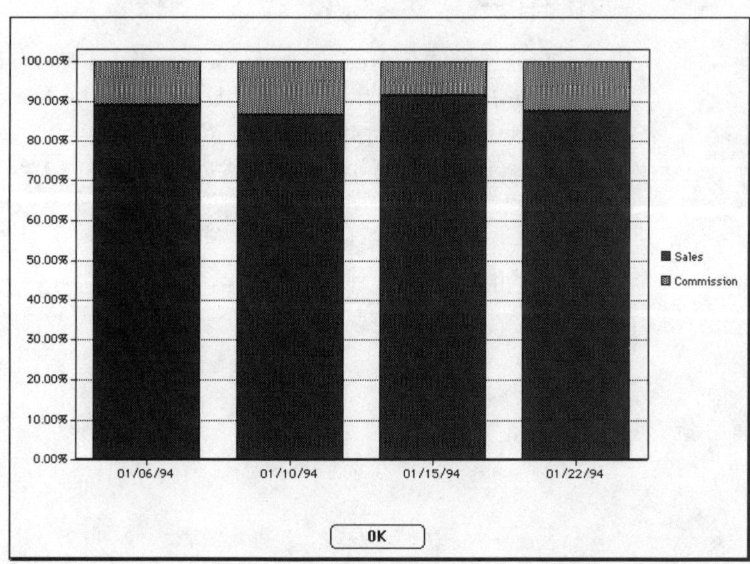

FIGURE 10.4

A proportional column graph

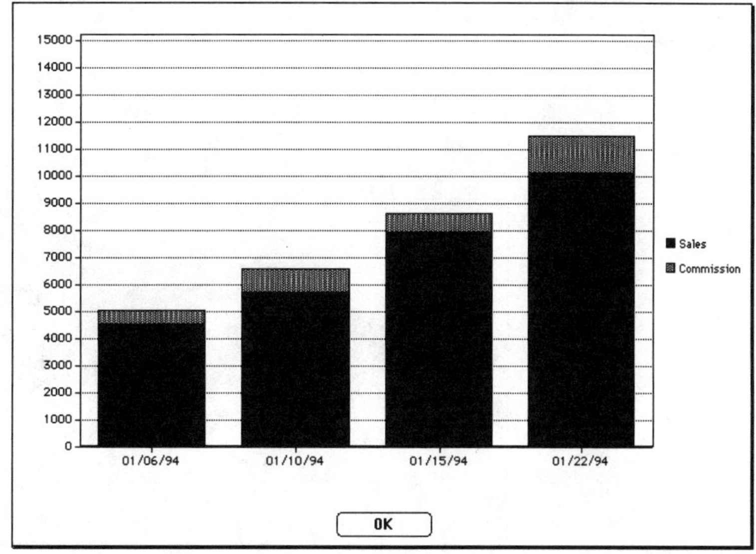

FIGURE 10.5

A line graph

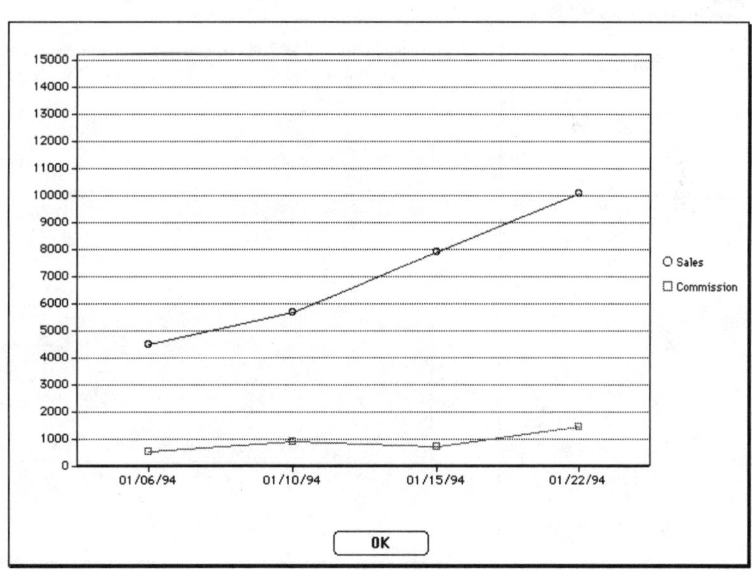

FIGURE 10.6

An area graph

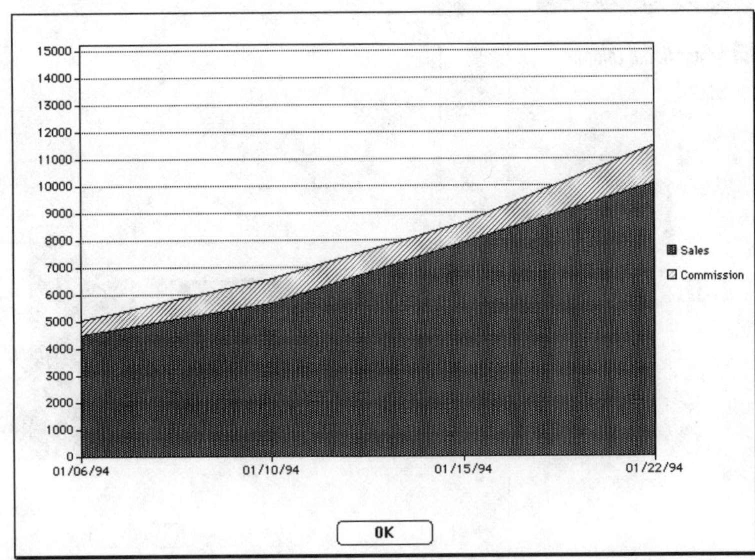

FIGURE 10.7

A scatter graph

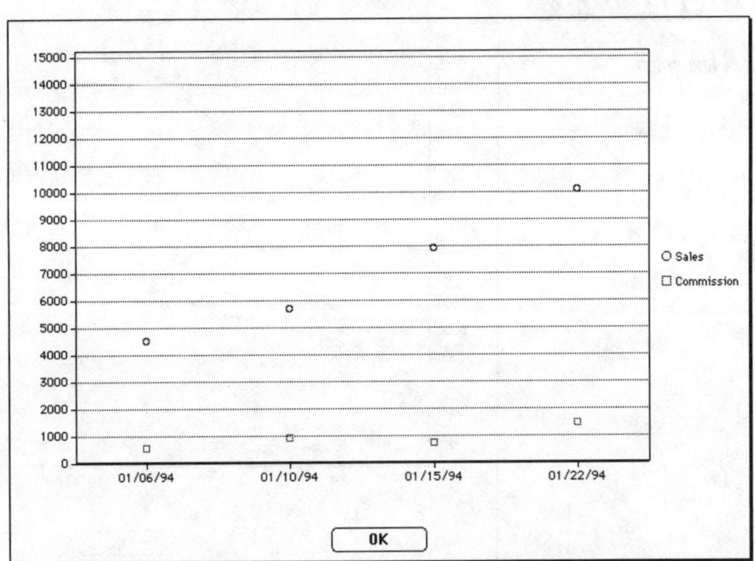

FIGURE 10.8

A pie graph

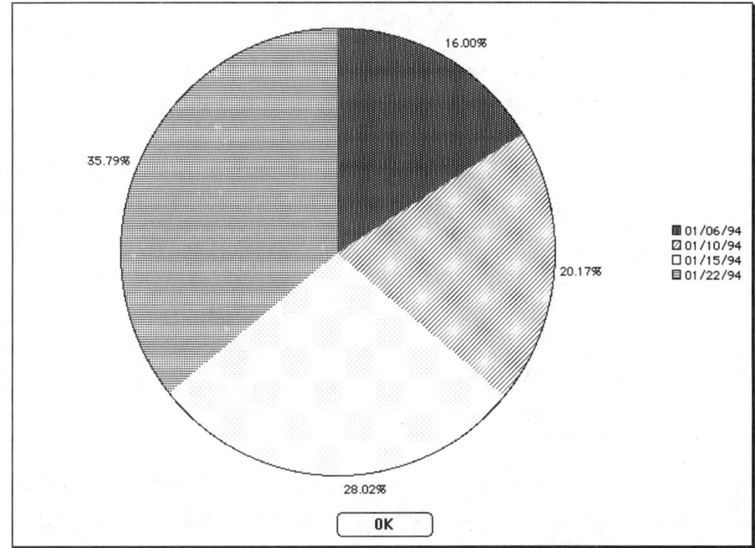

FIGURE 10.9

A picture graph

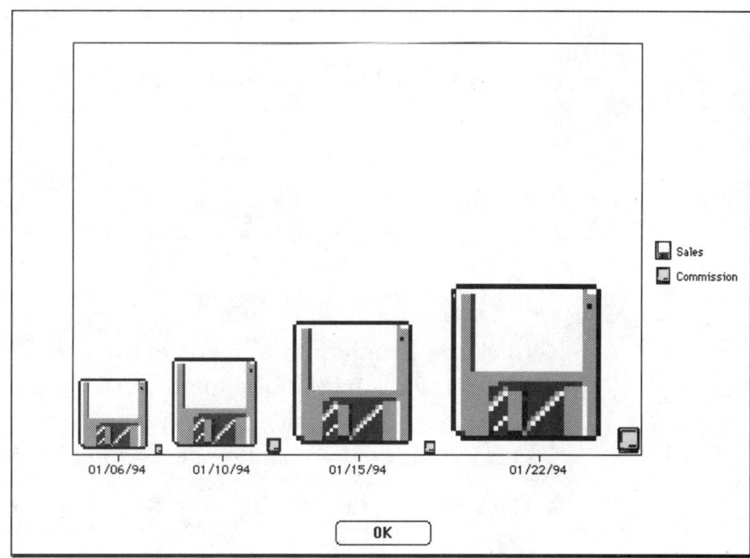

UNDERSTANDING X AND Y AXES

Graphs display information on two axes. The horizontal axis is called the *X axis.* The X axis typically displays the categories of the information that are being graphed. For example, if you were graphing your customers' purchases, you might have the customers' names displayed on the X axis.

The vertical axis is called the *Y axis.* This axis displays the actual data in graph form. For example, the Y axis would display the purchases for each customer displayed on the X axis. Figure 10.2 shows a graph of customers and purchases. Notice that the customers' names are listed horizontally (on the X axis) and the purchases are graphed vertically (on the Y axis).

The X axis can display only one field of information. You can choose to display any one field from the Customers file. While this may seem like a limitation, it really isn't. The X axis displays one field per record. So it wouldn't make any sense to display more than one field on the X axis.

The Y axis on the other hand can graph several fields. For example, you may want to graph several different fields from each record. The Graph Editor allows you to choose several fields to be graphed on the Y axis.

Let's choose fields from the fields list to be graphed and create the graph:

1. Click on the Last Name field to make it the X-axis field.
2. Click on the Balance field to make it the Y-axis field. You may have to scroll down the fields list to select the Balance field.
3. Click the **Graph** button to create the graph. Area graphs use a pattern to fill in the lower portion of the graph. You can select the pattern and color you want for the graph by clicking on the pattern box next to the field in the legend.
4. Click the box next to the word *Balance* to the right of the graph.

5. Select a pattern from the scrollable area and choose a color from the foreground and background color areas.

6. Click the **OK** button.

You can also change the graph type on the fly. To change the graph type, simply select a graph type from the Graph Type menu. Try selecting some of the other graph types.

CHOOSING GRAPH OPTIONS

Once you have created your graph, there are several options you can choose from, depending on the type of graph you have created. These options are selected from the Graph Options dialog box, shown in Figure 10.10.

FIGURE 10.10

The Graph Options dialog box

Graph options...

☒ Group on X-axis

☐ Proportional X-axis

☒ Automatic X-scale

Min: 0 Max: 0

☒ Automatic Y-scale

Min: 0 Max: 0

☒ Grid on X-axis

☒ Grid on Y-axis

Cancel OK

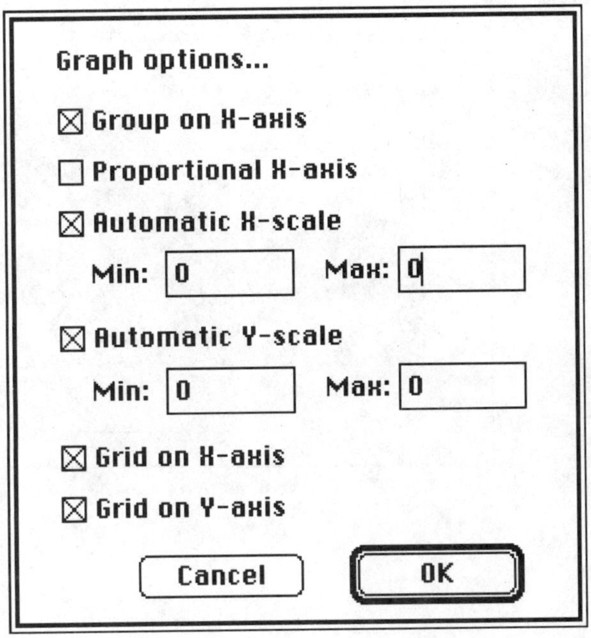

GROUP ON X AXIS

With this option selected, 4D will combine the Y values together for records that have the same value in the field being graphed on the X axis. Look at the data used in Figures 10.2–10.9. Notice that there are two records for the date 01/22/94. With the Group On X Axis option selected, the values in the Sales field are totaled for the two records and graphed as one column. The Commission field is also totaled and graphed as one column. If this option is not selected, each of these two records would be graphed separately. Figure 10.11 shows this data graphed with this option selected, while Figure 10.12 shows the data graphed with this option deselected. The Group On X Axis option is selected by default.

FIGURE 10.11

A Graph with the Group On X Axis option selected

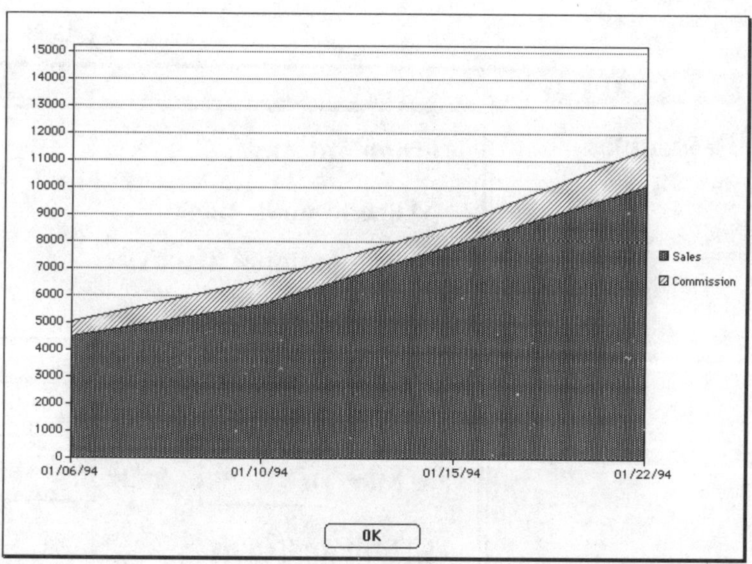

FIGURE 10.12

A Graph with the Group On X Axis option deselected

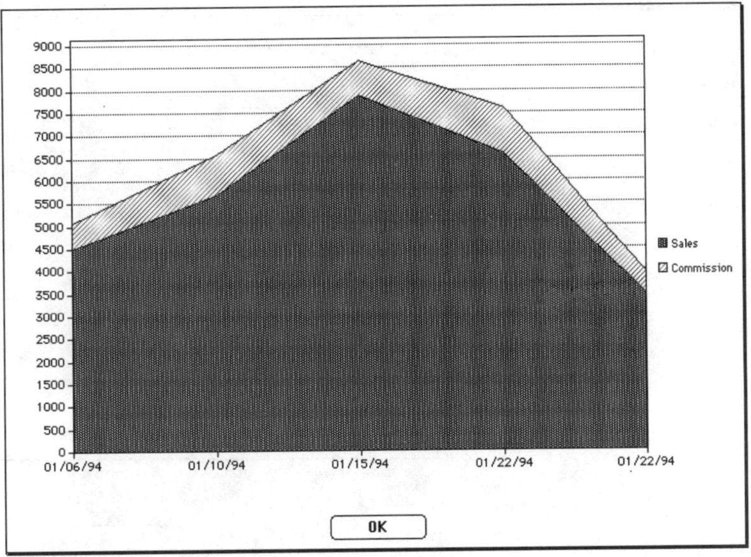

PROPORTIONAL X AXIS

The Y axis is always graphed proportionally to its data. For example, a small value will have a small column and a large value will have a large column. The Proportional X Axis option graphs the data on the X axis proportionally to its value. Consequently, this option will only work if the value being graphed on the X axis is a numeric (Real, Integer, or Long Integer), Date, or Time value. This option only works for scatter and line graphs. Figure 10.13 shows our sales and commission data graphed on a line graph with this option deselected. Figure 10.14 shows the same data graphed with this option selected.

FIGURE 10.13

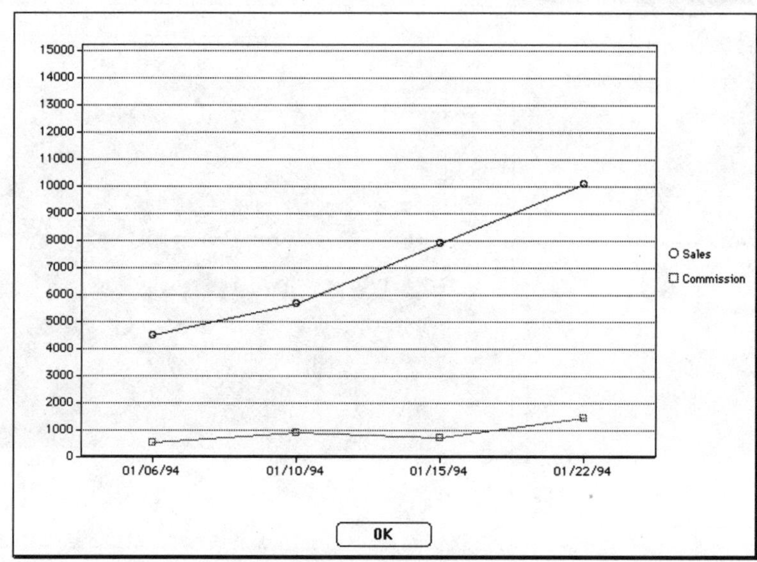

A line graph with Proportional X Axis deselected

FIGURE 10.14

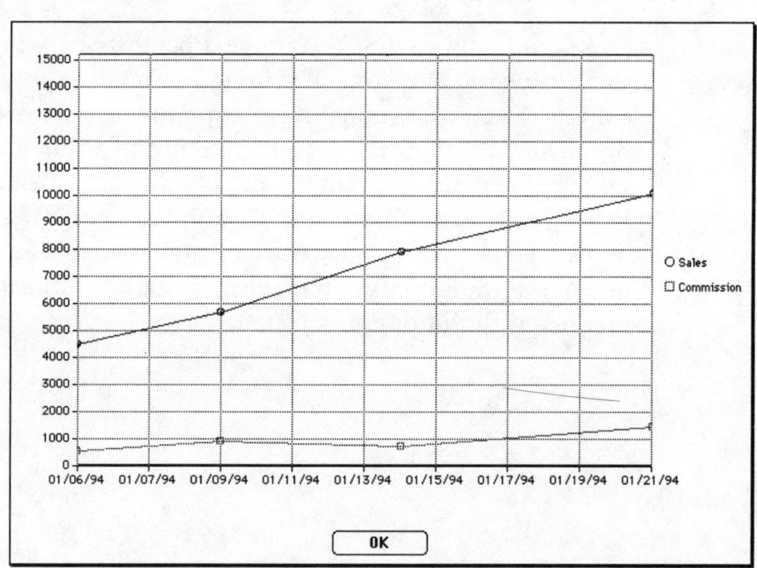

A line graph with Proportional X Axis selected

AUTOMATIC X SCALE

With this option selected, 4D automatically calculates the scale shown on the X axis. While this option is selected by default, you can deselect it if you are creating a scatter or line graph and have the Proportional X Axis option selected. After deselecting the Automatic X Scale option, you can set the minimum and maximum scale settings yourself. Figure 10.15 shows our sales data graphed on a line graph with the Automatic X Scale option selected. Figure 10.16 shows the same data with Automatic X Scale deselected (the minimum is set to 01/01/94 and the maximum to 01/31/94).

FIGURE 10.15

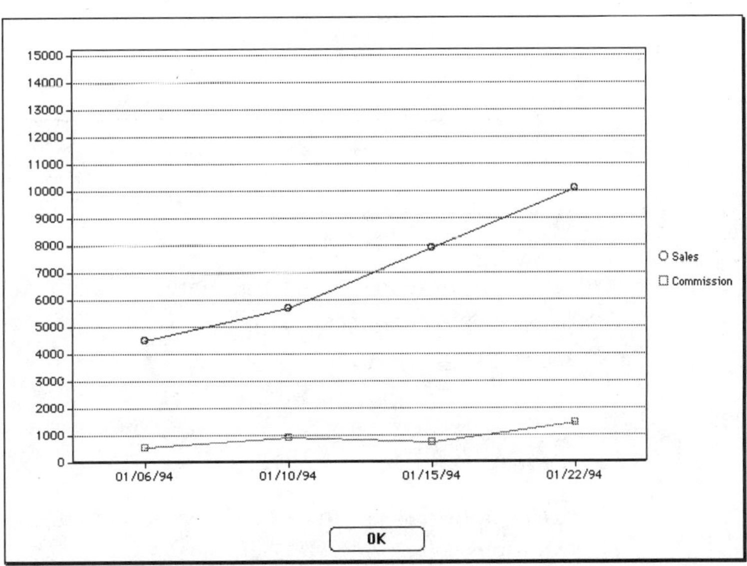

A line graph with the Automatic X Scale option selected

FIGURE 10.16

A line graph with an X scale of 01/01/94 to 01/31/94

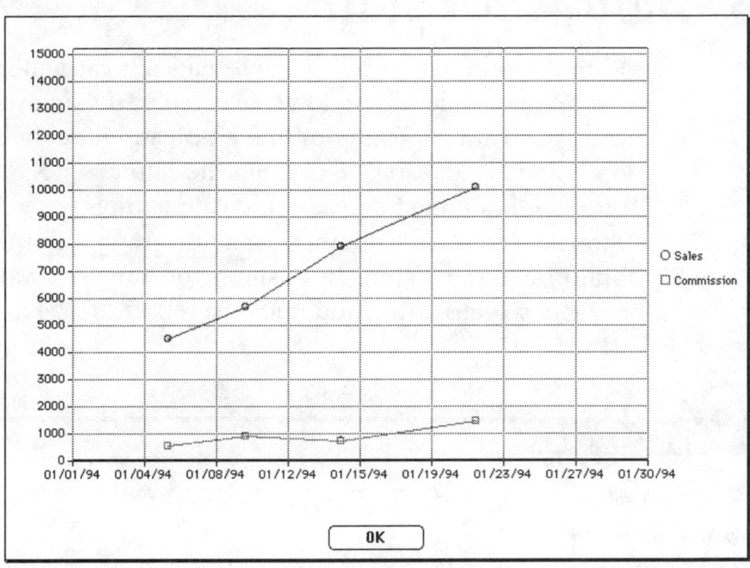

AUTOMATIC Y SCALE

With this option selected, 4D automatically calculates the scale for the Y axis. This option is selected by default and is available for all graphs except pie graphs.

GRID ON X AXIS

When this option is selected, 4D draws vertical lines across the graph. This option is selected by default.

GRID ON Y AXIS

When this option is selected, 4D draws horizontal lines across the graph. This option is selected by default.

CREATING PICTURE GRAPHS

The Graph Editor has the ability to create *picture graphs.* A picture graph is one that uses a picture scaled to the size of a column of data in the graph. Figure 10.17 shows an example of a picture graph.

FIGURE 10.17

An example of a picture graph

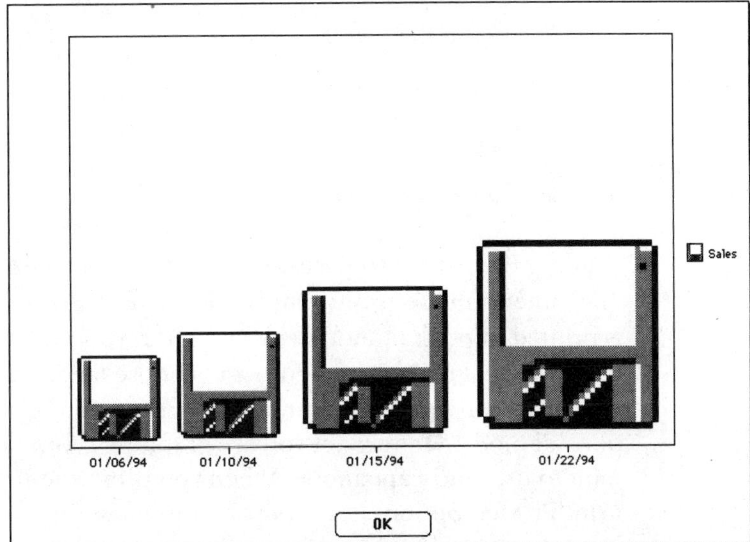

If you don't have any graphics in your scrapbook, find your system software disks and copy the scrapbook file from the disk into your system folder. The scrapbook file that comes with the system software has a few pictures in it.

The Graph Editor's Pictures menu gives you the ability to paste a graphic to one of the fields being graphed on the Y axis. If your graph has multiple fields on the Y axis, you will need to paste a graphic to each field being graphed, If you don't, 4D will use a picture of a Macintosh computer as the default graphic for any fields that don't have one. Let's create a picture graph:

1. Choose Apple ➤ Scrapbook.
2. Find a graphic you want to use in your picture graph.
3. Choose Edit ➤ Copy (⌘-C).
4. Close the Scrapbook.
5. Choose Pictures ➤ Paste To Y1.
6. Choose Graph Type ➤ Picture.

PRINTING GRAPHS

Printing the graphs you create is as simple as printing anything else in 4th Dimension. To print, simply select File ➤ Print. By default, the graph is printed in portrait mode (8½ × 11"). If you want to print in landscape mode, select File ➤ Page Setup and choose landscape mode.

If you are graphing only a few records, you may want to print in portrait mode. However, if you are graphing several records, you will want to use landscape mode. When you print graphs, you can use the Print Preview option. Let's try printing the graph:

1. Choose File ➤ Page Setup.
2. Choose **Landscape**.
3. Click the **OK** button.
4. Choose File ➤ Print (⌘-P).
5. Click the **Print Preview** button.
6. Click **Print**.
7. When you are finished looking at the preview, click **Stop Printing**.

USING GRAPHS WITH OTHER APPLICATIONS

The graphs you create can be used with other applications on your computer. You can copy the graph to the clipboard and, from there, paste it into any program that will accept a picture. For example, you could create a graph, copy it to the clipboard, and then paste it into a document created by a word processor. If you want to keep the graph for a while, you might want to paste it into the scrapbook. Let's copy the graph and paste it into the scrapbook:

1. Choose Edit ➤ Copy (⌘-C).
2. Choose Apple ➤ Scrapbook.
3. Choose Edit ➤ Paste (⌘-V).
4. Close the Scrapbook.

If you are not familiar with the clipboard, you might want to read about it in the system software guide that came with your computer.

WHAT IS GRAPH 2D?

You may have received a file called *Graph 2D* on one of the disks that came with your copy of 4th Dimension. Graph 2D is a set of graphing options that you can install into your 4D database. This set of options is called a *module*. The Graph 2D module gives you all the same features that the Graph Editor gives you plus a few new features. The Graph 2D module is provided free. There are other modules you can buy that add additional functionality and features to 4D. I will discuss Graph 2D and other available modules in *Chapter 20*.

IMPORTING AND EXPORTING RECORDS

11

MAC TRACKS MAC

The Import and Export Editors support three file types **229**

- Text
- DIF
- SYLK

To open the Import Editor **231**

Choose File ➤ Import Data.

Generally, to import a file **231**

You choose a desktop file to import, indicate its file type, and choose the fields that you want the imported data to be filled into.

Featuring

- *The Export Editor*
- *Specifying fields to export*
- *The three export file types*
- *The Import Editor*
- *The three import file types*

WHEN YOU CREATE a new database you will probably enter the records manually and use those records exclusively with that database. However, this may not always be the case. You may already have records in one form or another for some other database or perhaps even for a spreadsheet. Rather than re-enter all of these records by hand, it would make more sense (and certainly save time) if you could somehow transfer those records from the other database or spreadsheet to the new database you have just created. Fortunately, you can transfer data between other applications and 4th Dimension. This transfer process is called *importing.*

The job of using records with a spreadsheet or word processor can be simplified. Rather than bringing your records to these programs, you can bring the programs to your records. 4D Write and 4D Calc are two modules you can buy that can be added to 4D. 4D Write gives you a complete word processor and 4D Calc gives you a complete spreadsheet. With both of these modules you can access the records in your database without exporting them. See ***Chapter 20*** **for more information on these and other modules.**

At some point you may want to use the records you have entered into your database with another program. Perhaps you want to use your customer records with a word processor to print letters to each customer. If you had a database that tracked sales, you might want to use those records with a spreadsheet program to perform some kind of sales analysis. You wouldn't want to have to re-enter all the records in your database into another program (like a spreadsheet) to use the data. Luckily, 4th Dimension provides an option for transferring your records to other programs. This transfer process is called *exporting*.

Importing and exporting (in one form or another) are standard features in most database programs. As a matter of fact, most programs in general give you some method to import and export data. For example, you may have saved a word processing document as a text file so it could be opened by a different word processor or spreadsheet. The difference between programs that have these features is the implementation. Some programs make importing and exporting more difficult than necessary. Fortunately, 4D makes this process easy and painless with the built-in Import Editor and Export Editor.

EXPORTING RECORDS

The word *export* means to move something to another place. When you export data from 4D, you are moving it to another desktop file. You learned in *Chapter 1* that all of your data is stored in the data file. The data file is the file that has the name of your database with *.data* added to the end. Figure 11.1 shows the data file for the Learn 4D database. This file can be used only by 4D, because 4D is storing the data in a fast and efficient format. When you export records from 4D, you are copying one or more of the fields into another desktop file separate from your database's data file. This desktop file has your data stored in one of three common formats that many different programs can read.

FIGURE 11.1

The Learn 4D data file icon

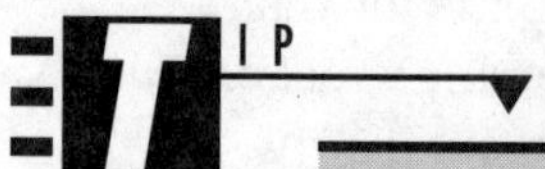

Don't forget that the Quick Report Editor can also be used for exporting records. See *Chapter 8* for details.

4D has a special editor just for exporting records. The Export Editor gives you all kinds of options for exporting your records in many different ways. Figure 11.2 shows the Export Editor.

FIGURE 11.2

The Export Editor

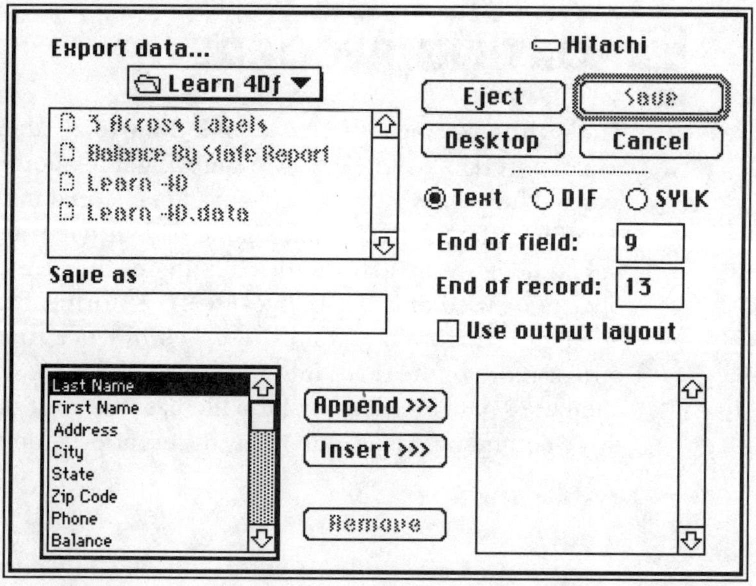

CHOOSING RECORDS TO EXPORT

The first step in exporting records is to select the records you wish to export. You have learned how important 4D's current selection concept is to your 4D database. The current selection is used to determine which records will be exported. Before you access the Export Editor, you might wish to select the records you want to export using the Search Editor or perhaps by selecting the records by hand and using the Show Subset menu item.

Your database doesn't have a large number of records, so we will export all of the records. Let's make sure that all of the records are selected for exporting:

1. Move to the User environment.
2. Choose Select ➤ Show All (⌘-G).

USING THE EXPORT EDITOR

The Export Editor gives you the ability to choose which fields you want exported for each record, what file format you want the export file to be in and where on your disk you want the export file to go.

Let's open the Export Editor.

1. Choose File ➤ Export Data.

The upper-left portion of the Export Editor is used to select where you want 4D to save the export file and to name it. Figure 11.3 shows this portion of the Export Editor. This part of the Export Editor looks similar to many of the Save As dialog boxes you have seen in other programs. By default, 4D will have the folder open that 4D itself resides in. You may want to choose another folder to save the export file in. Let's name the export file and save it on the desktop:

2. Type **Customers Export** as the name of the export file.

FIGURE 11.3

The "Save As" Portion of the Export Editor

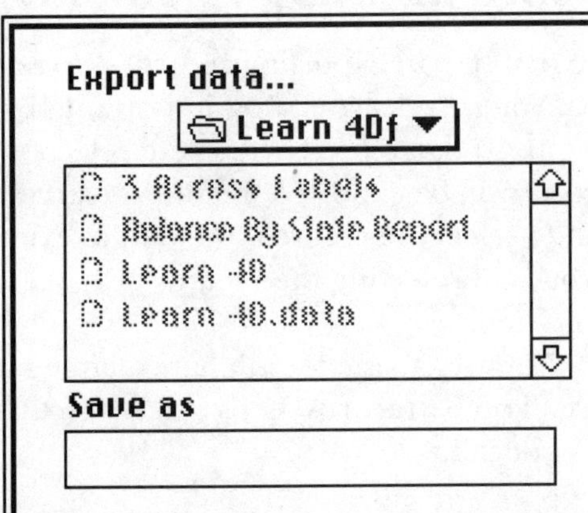

3. Click the **Desktop** button to move to the desktop. If you are running system 6, you won't have a Desktop button. In this case, select the last item in the Folder popup menu (the last item should be your hard disk).

Selecting Fields

Rather than exporting the entire record, 4D lets you choose only the fields you want to export. The scrollable area in the lower-left corner displays the fields from your customers file. This scrollable area is called the *Fields List.* Figure 11.4 shows the portion of the Export Editor.

FIGURE 11.4

The Fields List with a field selected

Not all field types can be exported. Picture and Subfields are not displayed in the Fields List and therefore cannot be exported.

You choose fields from the Fields List and copy them into the scrollable area in the lower-right corner. This second scrollable area is called the *Export List.* Figure 11.5 shows this portion of the Export Editor.

FIGURE 11.5

The Export List with several fields chosen

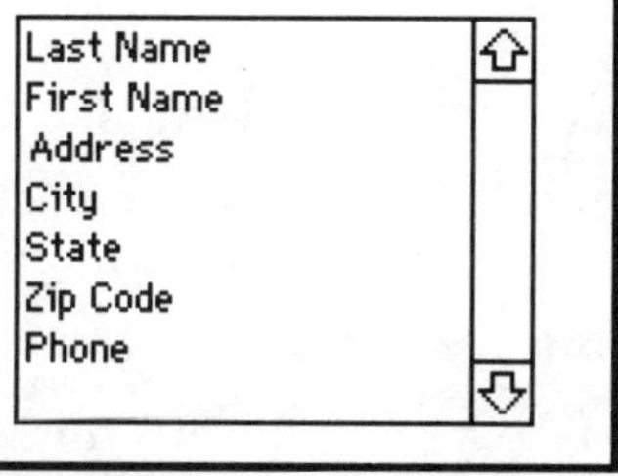

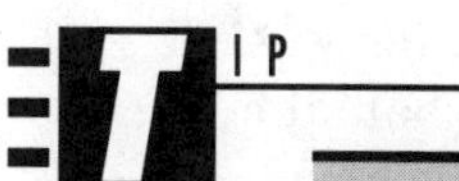

When you export a Boolean field, 4D exports the word *True* or *False*, depending on the value in the field.

The Export List displays the fields from the Fields list that you want to export.

You can use the arrow keys to select fields from both the Fields List and the Export List. The arrow keys work with the selected list. By default, the Fields List is selected (the box around the Fields List tells you that it's selected). To select the Export List, click on it.

When you copy fields from the Fields List into the Export List, it is important to consider the order you copy them in. 4D is going to export the fields in the order they are listed in the Export List. There are three buttons to help you build this list.

Button	Description
Append	Adds the field selected in the Fields List to the end of the Export List. The next field in the Fields List is automatically selected.
Insert	Inserts the selected field from the Fields List into the position selected in the Export List. The field selected in the Export List is moved down one position. The Insert button will not be enabled if a field is selected in both the Fields List and the Export List. The next field in the Fields List is automatically selected.
Remove	Removes the selected field in the Export List from the Export List. This is useful if you accidentally add a field that you really don't want to export.

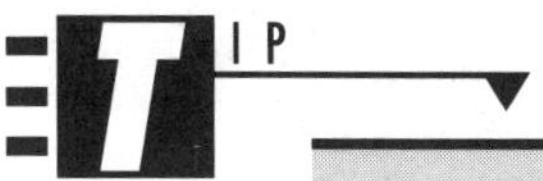

You can double-click on fields in the Fields List to select them and append them to the Export List all in one action.

Let's export the Last Name, First Name, Phone, and Balance fields:

1. Click on the Last Name field in the Fields List to select it.
2. Click the **Append** button to add the Last Name field to the Export List.
3. Click the **Append** button to add the First Name field to the Export List.
4. Add the Phone field to the Export List.
5. Add the Balance field to the Export List.
6. Click the **Save** button to export the records.

To create the export file, you gave your export file a name and specified where it would be created and saved. You also selected four fields from the Customers file to be exported. There are three possible formats for an export file (text, DIF, and SYLK). The default file type is text.

Choosing an Export File Type

The Export Editor can save your records in three different file types: Text, DIF, and SYLK. The file type you choose depends mostly on the program you are going to use the exported data with. For example, if the other program could read only text files, you would select *Text* as the file type.

Text Text (or *ASCII file*) is the default export file type and is the most common format to use. Practically every program that can import data will read a text file. Inside a text file will be all the fields you exported from each record in the current selection. Any program that reads this file will need to know where one field stops and the next field begins. In the text format, 4D adds a special character in between the fields. This character is called a *field delimiter*. By default, the field delimiter will be a tab character. The other program will also need to know where one record stops and the next record begins. 4D adds a character at the end of each record. This character is called a *record delimiter*. By default, the record delimiter is a carriage return (↵).

If you are exporting text fields, you will want to choose another record delimiter instead of using a carriage return. The reason for this is that the user can type carriage returns into text fields. When the program reading the export file finds a carriage return, it assumes that it has found the end of a record. In fact, it may have found a carriage return in the middle of a text field. Consequently, the program wouldn't read the data correctly.

Both the field delimiter and record delimiter can be changed to any character you want. Typically you won't change either of these delimiters because they are standards and just about every program that reads text files expects the field delimiter to be a tab and the record delimiter to be a carriage return (↵). Changing either of these delimiters is simple. In the Export Editor there are End of Field and End of Record boxes. These boxes tell 4D which character to use at the end of the field (the field delimiter) and the end of the record (record delimiter). Notice that the field delimiter is a *9* and the record delimiter is a *13*. The 9 represents a tab and the 13 represents a carriage return (↵). Why are there numbers here instead of the actual characters? Not all characters can appear on the screen or can be printed. This type of character is called a *non-printing character*. Tabs and carriage returns are both this type of character. Also, there are some characters that cannot be typed from the keyboard. So, in order for you to be able to use not-printing characters or characters that cannot be typed from the keyboard as delimiters, you enter numbers that represent the characters instead of the characters themselves. Which numbers represent which characters? To explain this will require a brief history of computers.

A long time ago, in a galaxy far, far away...well, perhaps not too far away. All right, not far away at all, but right here on Earth, a bunch of computer people came across a problem that needed to be solved. You see, computers don't really store or even understand characters you type on the keyboard. They really only understand numbers. So numbers are used to represent characters. Anyway, this bunch of computer people realized that if every computer used a different numbering system, none of the computers would be able to communicate. So, they got together and came up with a set of numbers that represent characters on the keyboard. They called this set the *American Standard Code of Information Interchange* (ASCII for short). Practically all computers use ASCII and can happily communicate with other computers. The number 9 is the number that represents the tab key and the number 13 is the number that represents the carriage return (↵). *Appendix D* shows the entire ASCII set. So, that's where the numbers come from.

While all of this seems complex, it is really quite simple. As a matter of fact, the text file format is the simplest of all formats. Just remember that typically there is a tab between fields and a carriage return between records. Figure 11.6 shows the data you are about to export as it appears in when imported into Microsoft Word. Figure 11.7 shows the data as it appears when imported into Microsoft Excel.

DIF DIF stands for *Data Interchange Format.* The first electronic spreadsheet program (VisiCalc) used this as its file format. All the spreadsheet programs that came later had to be able to read this format. Since spreadsheets are often the place where people begin entering data, 4D can read DIF files.

SYLK SYLK stands for *Symbolic Link.* This format was created by Microsoft and introduced as the format for their first spreadsheet, Multiplan (the predecessor to Excel). Most spreadsheet programs can read the SYLK format.

So, Which Type Do I Use? Again, this really depends on the program that will be reading the export file. If the program can read text files, use the Text file format. This format is very simple and most

FIGURE 11.6

Customers imported into Microsoft Word

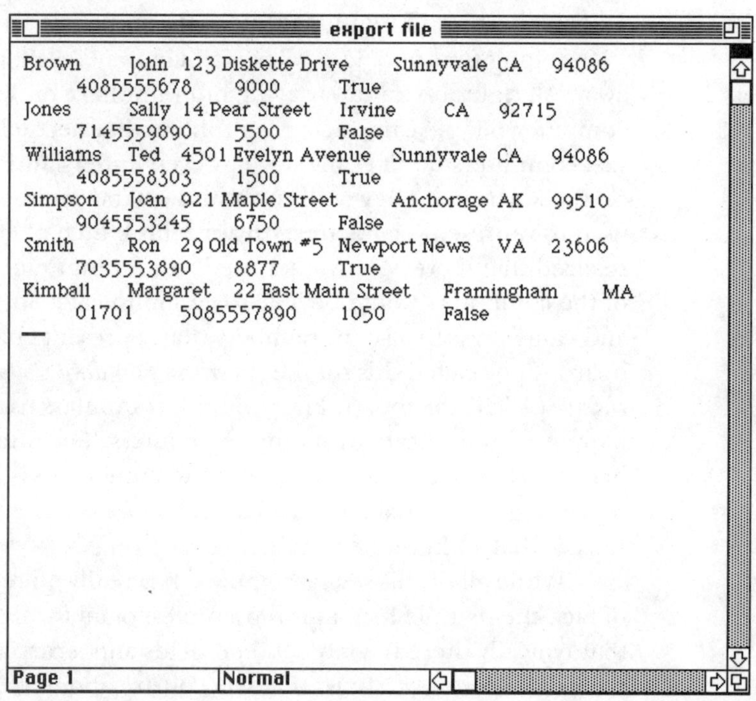

export file
Brown John 123 Diskette Drive Sunnyvale CA 94086
4085555678 9000 True
Jones Sally 14 Pear Street Irvine CA 92715
7145559890 5500 False
Williams Ted 4501 Evelyn Avenue Sunnyvale CA 94086
4085558303 1500 True
Simpson Joan 921 Maple Street Anchorage AK 99510
9045553245 6750 False
Smith Ron 29 Old Town #5 Newport News VA 23606
7035553890 8877 True
Kimball Margaret 22 East Main Street Framingham MA
01701 5085557890 1050 False
Page 1
Normal

FIGURE 11.7

Customers imported into Microsoft Excel

export file

	A	B	C	D	E	F	G
1	Brown	John	123 Diskette D	Sunnyvale	CA	94086	408555567
2	Jones	Sally	14 Pear Street	Irvine	CA	92715	714555989
3	Williams	Ted	4501 Evelyn A	Sunnyvale	CA	94086	408555830
4	Simpson	Joan	921 Maple Str	Anchorage	AK	99510	904555324
5	Smith	Ron	29 Old Town #	Newport News	VA	23606	703555389
6	Kimball	Margaret	22 East Main S	Framingham	MA	1701	508555789
7							
8							
9							
10							
11							
12							
13							
14							
15							
16							
17							
18							
19							
20							
21							
22							
23							
24							
25							

programs have no trouble reading it. Only use DIF or SYLK if you can't use Text for some reason. In the past, the DIF and SYLK formats have changed and not all programs read these formats the same way.

Saving the Export Order on a Layout

If you have a long list of fields you are exporting, you may want to store this list so you can use it again later. 4D can store the fields you want to export and in the order you want to export them by using a layout. When you click the Use Output Layout checkbox, 4D looks at the output layout and exports the fields on the output layout instead of using the Export List. You will learn more about layouts in *Chapter 12*.

IMPORTING RECORDS

The word *import* means to move something from another place to you. When you import data into 4D, you are moving it from a desktop file into your database's data file. When you export records, 4D makes a copy of the data and puts it into a desktop file. When you import data, 4D creates new records in the data file and fills the fields in with the data from the desktop file.

USING THE IMPORT EDITOR

The Import Editor is very similar in operation to the Export Editor. With the Import Editor, you choose a desktop file to import, indicate its file type and choose the fields that you want the imported data to be filled into. The current selection is not relevant to importing because you are creating new records, not working with existing records. Let's open the Import Editor.

- Choose File ➤ Import Data.

The list of files in the upper-left corner is used to select the desktop file you wish to import. If the file you wish to import is in another folder, you will have to use the popup menu to navigate to that folder.

Selecting Fields

When you were using the Export Editor, you chose fields from the Fields List and added them to the Export List. When you are importing data, you choose fields from the Fields List and add them to the Import List. The purpose of the Import List is to tell 4D the order of the data in the desktop file and which fields in the database to import the data into.

In order to import data, you must know the order of the data in the desktop file. Figure 11.8 shows a spreadsheet with some customer data. I will use this as an example for importing.

In the example spreadsheet, there are columns of first names, last names, ages, and states. When saved as a text file, the file will include all of these fields, with tabs separating the columns and carriage returns separating the rows.

FIGURE 11.8

An example spreadsheet

Worksheet1

	A	B	C	D	E	F	G
1	John	Smith	34	IL			
2	Susan	Baker	22	NE			
3	Mary	Peterson	38	OH			
4	Tara	Carson	49	PA			
5	Michelle	Anderson	19	WA			
6	David	Larson	17	MT			
7	Steven	Finkelstein	28	IN			
8	Peter	Piper	69	CO			
9	Scott	Simonton	31	CA			
10	Dorothy	Dodge	74	KS			
11	Maddy	Walker	44	NJ			
12	Cindy	Brady	54	VA			
13	Bobby	Brady	28	SC			
14	Luke	Church	36	ND			
15	Jane	Doe	41	NC			
16	Richard	Lionhart	39	RI			
17	Sally	Raphael	26	NY			
18	Homer	Simpson	35	MA			
19	Marge	Simpson	33	MA			
20	Bart	Simpson	12	MA			
21	Lisa	Simpson	10	MA			
22	Maggie	Simpson	2	MA			
23	Maryann	Johnson	33	WY			
24	Ginger	Westin	56	UT			
25	Phillip	Chadwick	44	CA			
26							

Since we have First Name, Last Name, and State fields in our database, it might seem logical to create an Import List in the following order: First Name, Last Name, State. Figure 11.9 shows what this Import List would look like. We have listed the fields from the database that appear in the text file and in the order that they appear in. The problem is that we have left out one column of information: the age column. If we imported the file using the Import List from Figure 11.9, 4D would put the age into the State field and the state data would not be read in at all.

FIGURE 11.9

An import list

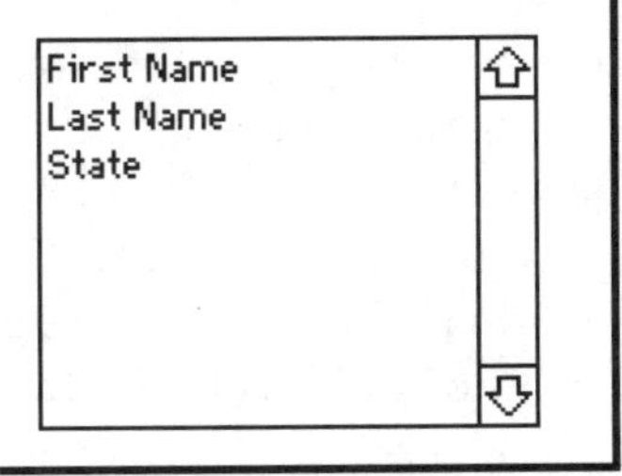

We need to tell 4D to skip the age column and import the state column into the State field. We can do this easily with a slightly different Import List. 4D starts at the beginning of the desktop file and reads to the end. The program *must* read all of the data in the desktop file, though, so it has to put the data from the age column somewhere. To have 4D skip over the data in the age column we will have it put the age data into the State column and then overwrite that data with the state column data. Figure 11.10 shows what our Import List would now look like.

As you can see, the State field is listed twice. The first occurrence of the State field will import the age column. The second occurrence will import the State column. Since the same field is being used twice, the

FIGURE 11.10

A more accurate import list

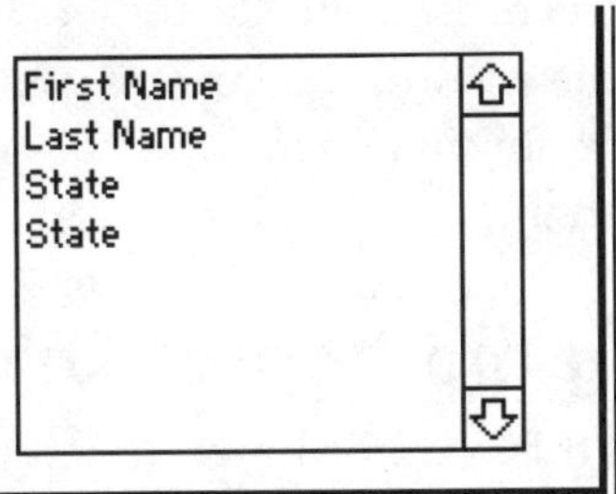

age will go into the State field, then the State column will write over the age data in the State field. So, when you have more information in your desktop file than you want to import, you can use this technique to skip over extraneous data.

Choosing the Import File Type

In order to import a desktop file, you will need know what type of file it is. If it was saved as a SYLK file, you will choose SYLK. If it was saved as a DIF file, you would choose DIF. My recommendation is to use the Text file format as often as possible. The Text file format is the simplest format and the other formats have changed in the past. Most programs that separate data into columns (like spreadsheets) or fields will insert tabs between fields and carriage returns between records. Again, you may have to change delimiters if you are importing data that already has tabs or carriage returns inside the field data.

Getting Some Practice

If you would like to practice importing data, here's what you can do.

1. Make a copy of the Learn 4D*f* folder.
2. Open the copy and export all the fields of all the records in the Customers file.
3. Delete all of the records in the Customers file.
4. Practice importing the file you exported.

Each time you import the file, you will want to make sure you delete all of the records in the Customers file first. Otherwise, you will have lots of duplicate records. Make sure you make a copy of the Learn 4D*f* folder to practice on; that way you will always have your original in case things get messed up.

Saving the Import Order on a Layout

Earlier in this chapter I mentioned that the export order can be saved on a layout. You can also do this with the import order. Using the Layout

Editor, you can place the fields you want to import on a layout in the order you want the data imported. You can then use this layout with the Import Editor to import records. When you click the Use Input Layout checkbox, 4D looks at the input layout and imports the fields on the input layout instead of using the Import List. Figure 11.11 shows a sample layout that would be used for importing the sample spreadsheet into the Customers file. You will learn more about layouts in *Chapter 12*.

FIGURE 11.11

A layout for importing records

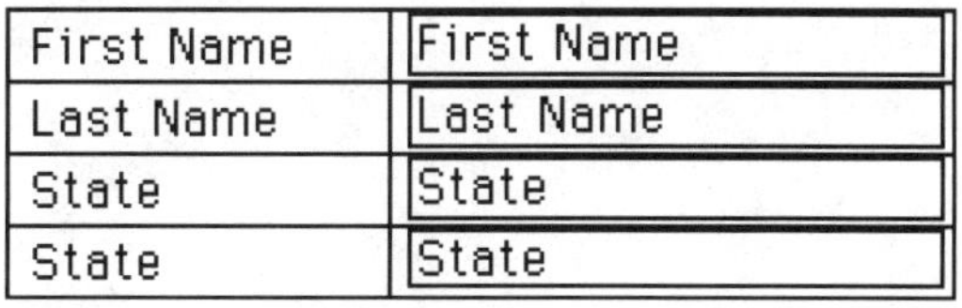

First Name	First Name
Last Name	Last Name
State	State
State	State

CREATING AND CUSTOMIZING LAYOUTS

12

MAC TRACKS MAC

To select a layout as the current input layout 243

1. In the Layout dialog box, click on the layout to select it.
2. Click the **Input** checkbox.

To create a new layout 254

1. Switch to the Design environment.
2. Choose Design ➤ Layout (⌘-L).
3. Click the **New** button.
4. Click on a layout template icon to select it.
5. Select a font size.
6. Type the name of the new layout.
7. Click the **OK** button.

To select multiple objects on a layout to modify them 258

Hold down the Shift key while clicking on each object.

To add a button to a layout — 268

1. Click on the Active Object tool to select it.
2. Draw the button.
3. Type a name for the button.
4. Choose Button from the Type pop-up menu.
5. Choose an automatic action from the Action pop-up menu.

To change the way information in a field is displayed — 277

Use the Format pop-up menu in the Field Definition dialog box.

To control what characters a user can type into a field — 289

1. Double-click on the field in the Layout Editor.
2. Select an Entry Filter from the Entry Filter pop-up menu.

Featuring

- *Creating layouts*
- *Modifying layouts*
- *Formatting fields*
- *Preventing entry errors*
- *Adding balloon help*
- *Building report layouts*

WHEN YOU ENTERED new records or modified existing records, you did this through a screen that 4th Dimension created automatically. This "screen" is called a *layout.* A layout is an arrangement of fields and other objects. You use layouts to interact with the data in your database. These layouts belong to files in your database. Layouts are used to:

- Enter and modify records
- Print labels, reports, and mail-merge documents
- Import and export records
- Create customized dialog boxes

There are only a few steps required to create just about any layout you might need. Once a layout has been created, you can customize it any way you want.

WHAT ARE LAYOUTS?

I have already said that a layout is an arrangement of objects. Layouts are made up of different kinds of objects. A layout will usually have fields to display data from records, text to label the fields being displayed, graphics (such as boxes around the fields), buttons to perform actions like saving the record, and other clickable objects that perform various actions. 4th Dimension has a built-in editor for creating and modifying layouts. The Layout Editor looks and feels a lot like some of the object-oriented drawing programs available for the Macintosh (like MacDraw).

You have probably used MacPaint at least once. MacPaint is a *bitmap-oriented* graphics program. When you draw using MacPaint, the images you create are stored as a series of dots. In an *object-oriented* drawing program (as in the Layout Editor), the images are stored as descriptions. For example, if you draw a rectangle, what is stored (behind the scenes) is a code that represents a rectangle, along with the rectangle's location on the layout, its line width, color, pattern, etc. The format is called PICT (short for picture). The PICT format is a common format on the Macintosh and many graphics programs can import and export PICT images. PICT images usually take up less disk space and are easier to modify than bitmap images.

INPUT LAYOUTS

When you create a new record or double-click on an existing record to modify it, 4th Dimension displays a layout to allow you to make the modifications. How does 4th Dimension know which layout to display? 4D uses the current *input layout* for the file. You select one layout per file to be the current input layout. While you can create as many layouts as you want, only one per file can be selected as the input layout at any moment. For example, you may have several different layouts you use for data entry at different times. When you want to use one of them, you set that layout to be the current input layout. There are three different ways you can select a layout to be the current input layout:

- Using the Layout dialog box in the Design environment
- Using the List Of Files window in the User enviroment
- Using commands in 4th Dimension's procedural language

In the Design environment, you use the Layout dialog box to choose current input and output layouts. Let's try it:

1. Switch to the Design environment.
2. Choose Design ➤ Layout (⌘-L).
3. Click the **Expand** button.
4. Click the Input layout to select it.

You know that 4D automatically creates one input layout and one output layout for each file in your database. It names the these layouts Input and Output respectively. The name of the layout, however, doesn't tell 4D that it should use this layout as an input layout. Notice that there is an *I* next to Input and an *O* next to Output. The *I* indicates that this layout currently is the input layout. The *O* indicates that this layout is currently the output layout. You may occasionally see a layout marked with a *B*. In this case, the layout is selected as *both* the current input layout and the current output layout.

You can create up to 32,000 layouts for your database with 4th Dimension. So don't worry about running out.

To select a layout as the current input layout, you use the Input checkbox. Let's make the Output layout both the current input and current output layout:

1. Click Output to select it.
2. Click the Input checkbox.

Notice that a *B* appears next to the Output layout. This layout is now both the current input layout and the current output layout. If you switched to the User environment at this point and double-clicked on a customer record, the record would open and be displayed using the same layout (Output) that is being used as the output layout.

Notice that Input does not have an *I* next to it anymore. At this point, it is not the current input layout. Let's make it the current input layout:

1. Click Input to select it.
2. Click the Input checkbox.

Notice that the *I* has reappeared next to the Input layout. Once again, Input is the current input layout.

While any layout can be used as an input layout or an output layout, layouts are typically designed for use as one or the other. Input layouts are designed to look like forms and usually display most or all of the fields from the file.

OUTPUT LAYOUTS

Each file has a current output layout. While input layouts are mostly used for data entry, output layouts have many possible uses. The most common use for an output layout is to display the current selection of a file on the screen. You have been using the Customer file's output layout to access records. Another use for output layouts is in printing reports. For example, you might design an output layout in a columnar format (much like a Quick Report) to use for printing a report. Figure 12.1 shows a report printed using an output layout.

FIGURE 12.1

An output layout used to print a report

Customers Report

Last Name	First Name	City
Brown	John	Sunnyvale
Jones	Sally	Irvine
Williams	Ted	Sunnyvale
Simpson	Joan	Anchorage
Smith	Ron	Newport News
Kimball	Margaret	Framingham

Say you have a database that keeps track of invoices. You will have a layout designed to look like an invoice that you will use for printing. Figure 12.2 shows an example of this type of layout. This would appear to be an input layout. However, you are using it for printing so it's an output layout. As we look at the Layout editor and how layouts are used, I will discuss output layouts in more detail.

OTHER USES FOR LAYOUTS

Layouts aren't just for input and output. Although you use input and output layouts to interact with your database, they are not the only means for interaction. Input and output layouts are perfect when the interaction deals with records; however, not all of your interaction will be with records. As you have been reading this book you have seen many of 4D's dialog boxes, which allow you to interact with the built-in functions of the program. There may be times when you want to add some kind of function that is not built-in to 4D. Fortunately, 4D has a powerful programming language that lets you create just about any function you need quickly and easily. Using layouts and 4D's programming language, you can create custom dialog boxes to interact with your database in any way you want. Figure 12.3 shows an example of a custom dialog box that was created using a layout.

FIGURE 12.2

An output layout designed as an invoice

S2 Software

Invoice

19672 Stevens Creek Blvd. Suite 275
Cupertino, CA 95014
408.257.7272

Bill To

Attn: Ms. Betty Wong
Wong International
79 Concord Ave.
Suite 275
Laguna Beach, CA 95014

Ship To

Ms. Betty Wong
President
Wong International
79 Concord Ave.
Suite 275
Laguna Beach, CA 95014

Invoice Number 10321 **Ship Via** Federal Express **Order Date** 10/12/95
P.O. Number 228930 **Client No.** 1864 **Ship Date** 10/12/95

Part No.	Description	Qty	Price	SubTotal
1001	Instant Interface Vol. 1 HD	1	$149.00	$149.00
1010	Instant Code Vol. 1	1	$149.00	$149.00
1017	Inside 4D Disk Offer	1	$30.00	$30.00
1013	Instant TecIndex (Free w/Purchase)	1	$0.00	$0.00

Special Instructions

Subtotal	$328.00
Tax	$27.06
Shipping	$5.00
Order Total	$360.06
Amt. Paid	$0.00
Total Due	**$360.06**

Terms: Net 10 Days

Return this portion with your payment.

Invoice Number 10321
Order Date 10/12/95
Total Due **$360.06**

Billed To:
Attn: Ms. Betty Wong
Wong International
79 Concord Ave.
Suite 275
Laguna Beach, CA 95014

Please make your check payable to S2 Software.
Foreign Orders please remit only International Money Orders payable in US Dollars. Thank You.

REMIT TO:

S2 Software
19672 Stevens Creek Blvd. Suite 275
Cupertino, CA 95014 USA

Thank you for your order!

FIGURE 12.3

A customized search dialog box

Find...

Sandra

Search:

◉ First, Last, Alias & Company

○ Notes

Cancel

OK

WHAT CAN BE PUT ON A LAYOUT?

A layout can contain just about anything you can imagine, including fields from your database, graphics, text, buttons, and many other clickable or enterable (and certainly useful) objects. What you put on a layout depends mostly on what you need. In some cases, your layouts will be simple, with only a few fields and one or two buttons. In other cases, you may be creating layouts that are quite elaborate, with lots of fields, graphics, and buttons that perform all kinds of special functions.

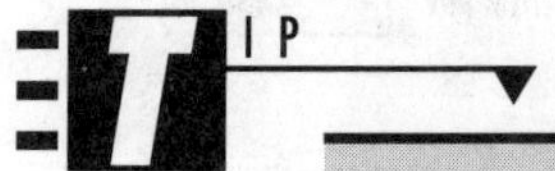

While graphics can make a layout more appealing, they also make the layout take up more room in the structure file and in memory. The more space a layout takes up, the longer it takes to appear on the screen. So, use discretion when creating layouts with lots of graphics.

USING FIELDS ON A LAYOUT

Of course fields from your database can be displayed on a layout. The Learn 4D database has only one file. Later, you will add more files and learn how to add fields from multiple files on the same layout. There are many different ways to display fields. The options you choose will depend largely on what you are doing with the fields. These options will be discussed later in this chapter.

USING TEXT ON A LAYOUT

There are many reasons to have text on a layout. The most common reason is to label the fields from your database. You can also use text on layouts to label groups of fields and provide useful notes that explain how the layout works.

USING BUTTONS AND OTHER CLICKABLES ON A LAYOUT

Buttons are one of the most useful parts of a graphical user interface (like the Macintosh). Buttons perform actions that are used frequently. Also, buttons are not hidden the way menus are. Fortunately, 4D provides you with an easy way to create useful and powerful buttons. You can create round rectangle buttons, radio buttons, checkboxes, icon buttons, and graphical buttons.

4D also provides you with other useful objects that work like buttons. Using the Layout Editor, you can create pop-up menus, scrollable areas, graphs, rulers, thermometers, and more. With all of these different clickable objects you can create an easy-to-use and powerful interface to your database.

USING GRAPHICS ON A LAYOUT

Graphics are an important and useful part of your layout design. With the Layout Editor, you can draw boxes and lines, and set all kinds of attributes about them (like color, line thickness, pattern, etc.). Boxes and lines are useful for grouping fields together or for separating fields that don't belong together. Graphics created with other programs can also be used on your layouts. Any graphic that can be pasted into the Scrapbook can be copied to a 4D layout.

If the database you are creating will be translated into other languages, read the section in the *4th Dimension Design Reference* on Localization. The techniques described will make the translation job go much more quickly and easily.

CREATING LAYOUTS WITH THE LAYOUT TEMPLATES

In order to use a file you have created, you must have at least one layout. You will want to have at least two layouts (one input layout and one output layout). If you haven't created any layouts for a file, 4D will create two layouts (an input layout and an output layout) for you. These layouts are created the first time you leave the Design environment after creating the file. With this feature you can spend less time in the Design environment and get to the job of entering and working with your data. However, you may need to create more layouts to complete the design of your database.

The New Layout dialog box has eight built-in layout templates you can choose from. This dialog box makes creating entire layouts simple and quick. After creating a layout with a layout template, you can make any changes you want using the Layout Editor. There are three templates for creating output layouts and five templates for creating input layouts. Figures 12.4–12.6 show samples of the output layout templates created for the Customers file.

FIGURE 12.4

Output layout template #1

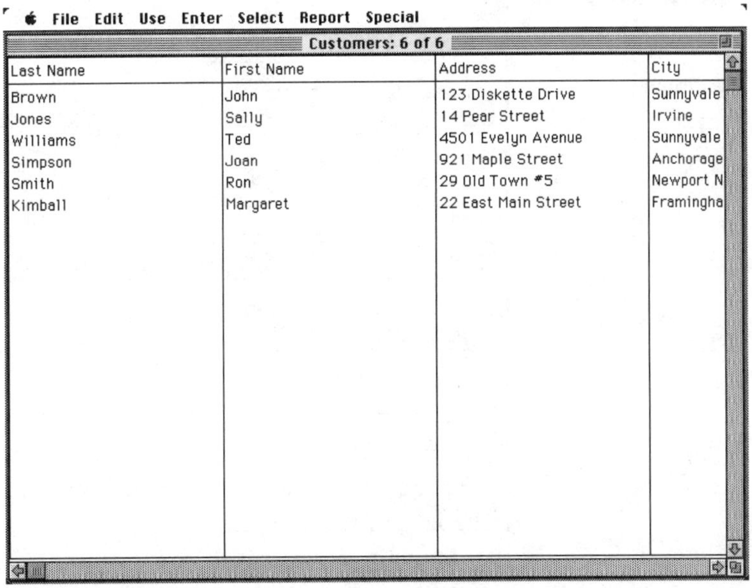
File Edit Use Enter Select Report Special
Customers: 6 of 6
Last Name
First Name
Address
City
Brown
John
123 Diskette Drive
Sunnyvale
Jones
Sally
14 Pear Street
Irvine
Williams
Ted
4501 Evelyn Avenue
Sunnyvale
Simpson
Joan
921 Maple Street
Anchorage
Smith
Ron
29 Old Town #5
Newport N
Kimball
Margaret
22 East Main Street
Framingha

FIGURE 12.5

Output layout template #2

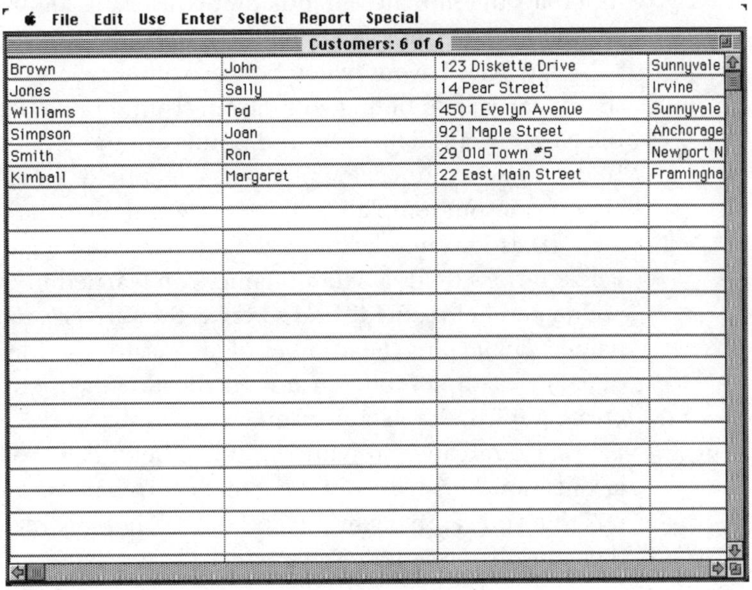
File Edit Use Enter Select Report Special
Customers: 6 of 6
Brown
John
123 Diskette Drive
Sunnyvale
Jones
Sally
14 Pear Street
Irvine
Williams
Ted
4501 Evelyn Avenue
Sunnyvale
Simpson
Joan
921 Maple Street
Anchorage
Smith
Ron
29 Old Town #5
Newport N
Kimball
Margaret
22 East Main Street
Framingha

FIGURE 12.6

Output layout template #3

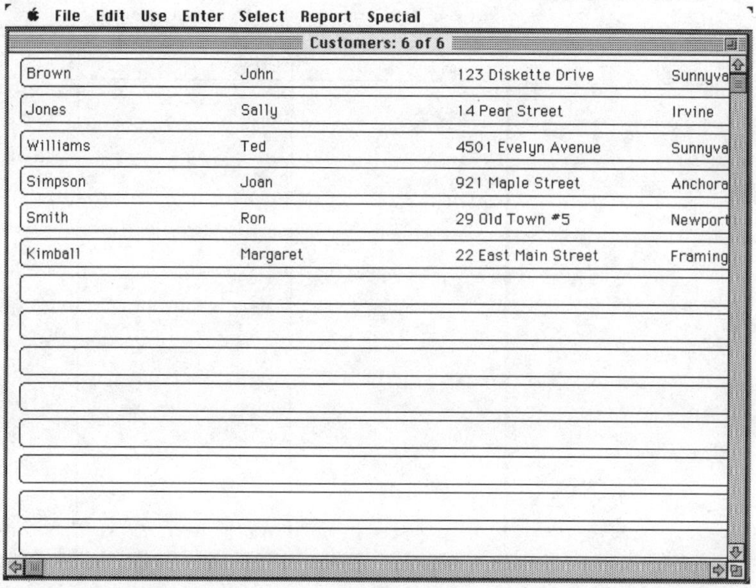

While the three output layout templates look very similar, the five input layout templates all look quite different. Figures 12.7–12.11 show samples of the input layout templates created for the Customers File.

The New Layout dialog box also allows you to create blank layouts so you can start building your layout from scratch. Figure 12.12 shows the New Layout dialog box and points out the eight built-in templates. In the New Layout Dialog box, you select fields from the current file, choose a layout template and font size, and give the new layout a name.

4D assigns new layouts a default name in much the same way that it assigns new fields a default name. You learned in *Chapter 3* that fields are named field1, field2 and so on as they are created. New layouts are named *Layout* plus the number of layouts for the file including the new one. For example, your Customers file already has two layouts. If you create a third, the default name would be Layout3.

Layouts can be renamed just like fields. The rules for naming layouts however, are more flexible. Layout names can include any characters that you can type on the keyboard. The only real limitation is that they must be 15 or fewer characters.

FIGURE 12.7

Input layout template #4

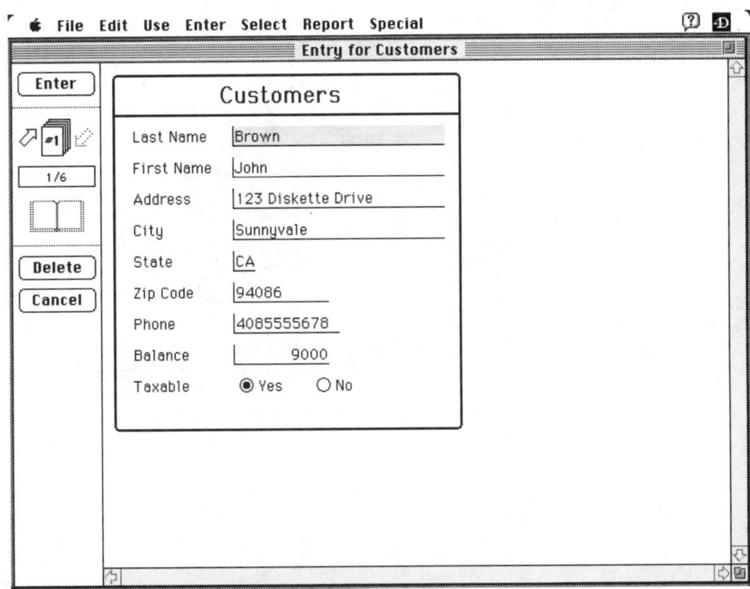

FIGURE 12.8

Input layout template #5

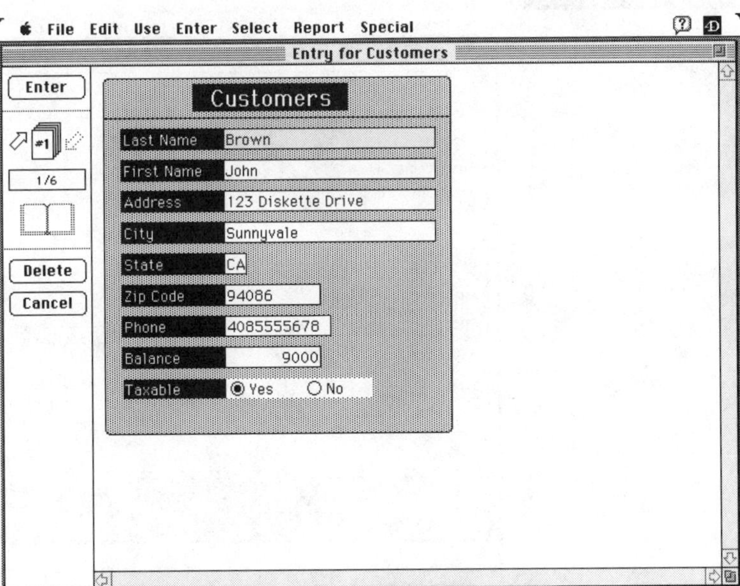

FIGURE 12.9

Input layout template #6

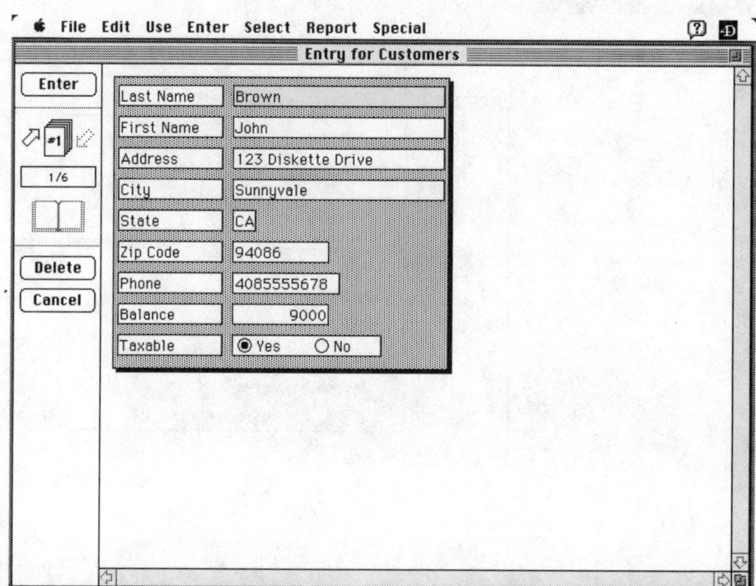

FIGURE 12.10

Input layout template #7

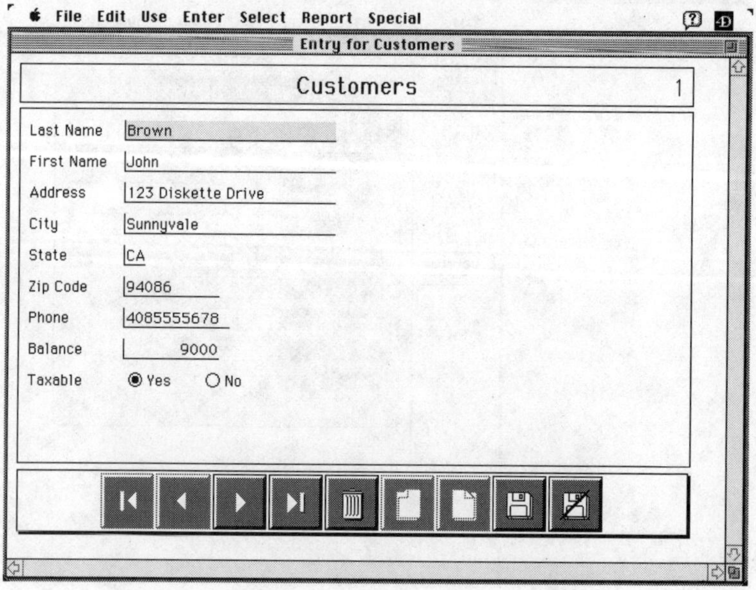

FIGURE 12.11

Input layout template #8

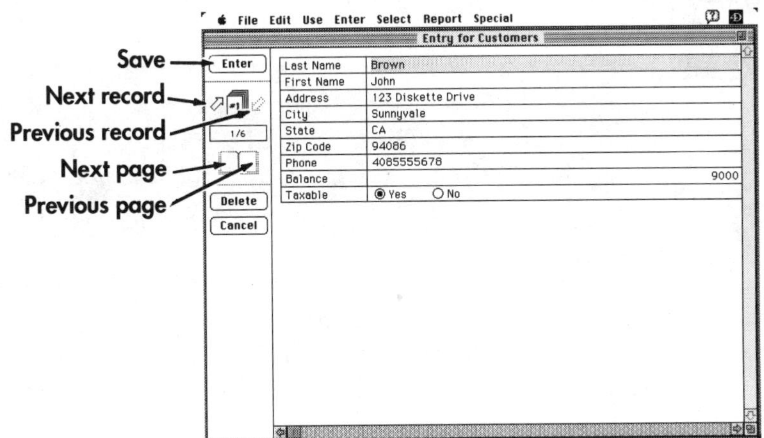

FIGURE 12.12

The New Layout dialog box

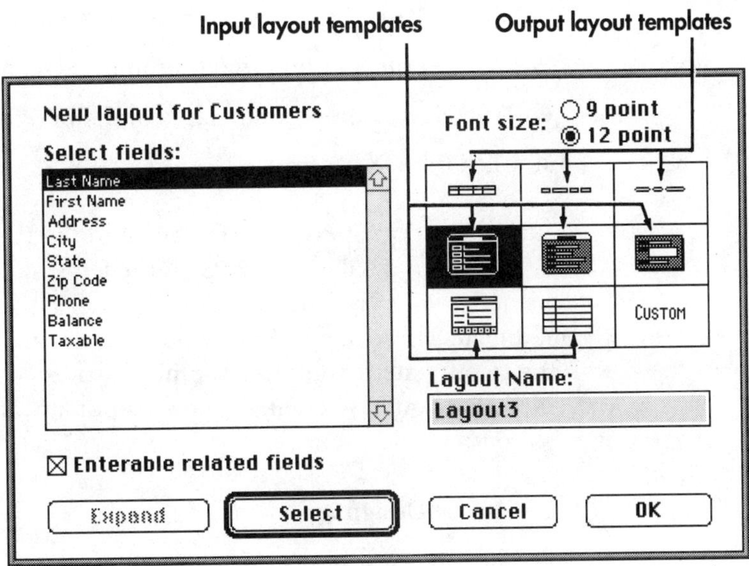

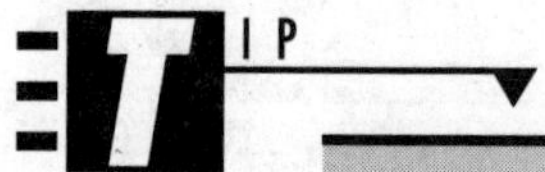

When naming layouts, choose names that reflect what the layout will be used for. For example, an output layout for a balance report might be called *Balance Report*.

You already have input and output layouts for your Customers file. 4D used two of the layout templates (output template #1 and input template #4) to create these default layouts. Let's try building new input and output layouts using two of the other layout templates:

1. Switch to the Design environment.
2. Choose Design ➤ Layout (⌘-L).
3. Click the **New** button.
4. Click on the output layout template #3 icon to select it.
5. Click on the **9 Point** radio button to select it.
6. Type **New Output** as the name of the new layout.
7. Click the **OK** button.

4th Dimension opens the new layout in the Layout Editor. The Layout Editor has a palette of tools on the left side of the window to help you customize your layouts. The Layout Editor also adds four menus to the menu bar. These menus have functions that are also used along with the layout palette tools to customize layouts.

Now that you have created a new output layout, let's create a new input layout:

1. Choose Design ➤ Layout (⌘-L).
2. Click the **New** button.
3. Click on the input layout template #5 icon to select it.
4. Type **New Input** as the name of the new layout.
5. Click the **OK** button.

You have just created a new input layout. Each time you create a new layout or open an existing layout to modify it, 4D opens the layout in a separate window. This makes it easier to copy objects from one layout to another.

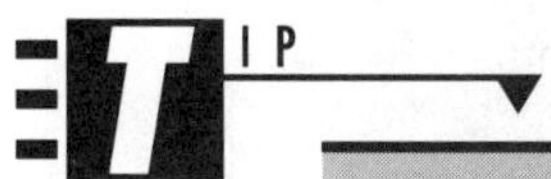

Once you have several windows open it's easy to lose one behind all the others. 4D keeps a list of all of your open layouts at the bottom of the Design menu. If you think you have a layout open in the Layout Editor but can't find the layout on the screen, check the Design menu.

That's all it takes to create a layout using the built-in layout templates. The Input and Output layouts are still selected as the current input and output layouts. The next step is to select New Input and New Output as the current input and output layouts. You can select the current input and output layouts using the Layout dialog box.

1. Choose Design ➤ Layout (⌘-L).
2. Double-click on Customers to expand the list of layouts for the Customers file.
3. Click on New Input layout to select it.
4. Click the Input checkbox.
5. Click on the New Output layout to select it.
6. Click the Output checkbox.
7. Click the **Done** button.

As you can see, the *I* now appears next to the New Input layout and the *O* now appears next to the New Output layout. The User environment's window has already been updated to show the New Output layout. Let's try out these layouts in the User environment.

1. Click on the User environment window or choose Use ➤ User (⌘-U).

2. Double-click on Ted Williams' record to open it.

4D is now using the New Input layout. If the input layout doesn't have any buttons, 4D adds a data entry control panel on the left side of the window. These buttons work just like the buttons in the input layout that 4D created. Figure 12.13 shows the New Input layout with these buttons labeled. Once you add one of your own buttons, this panel will go away. You will learn how to add your own buttons later in this chapter.

3. Click the **Cancel** button to close the record.

FIGURE 12.13

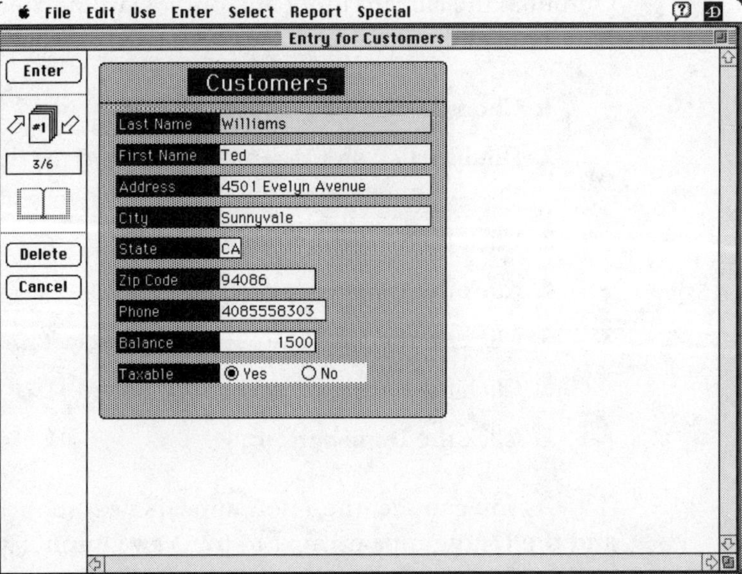

The New Input layout with a data entry control panel

MODIFYING AN EXISTING LAYOUT

You can make changes to your layouts using the layout palette and menus. Figure 12.14 shows the tools in the Layout palette and labels each tool.

You will learn about these tools and the Layout Editor's menus as we explore the Layout Editor. Let's move back to the Layout Editor to begin modifying the New Input layout:

1. Choose Use ➤ Design (⌘-U).
2. Choose Design ➤ Layout: New Input.
3. Click the Zoom box to make the window fill the screen.

FIGURE 12.14

The layout palette

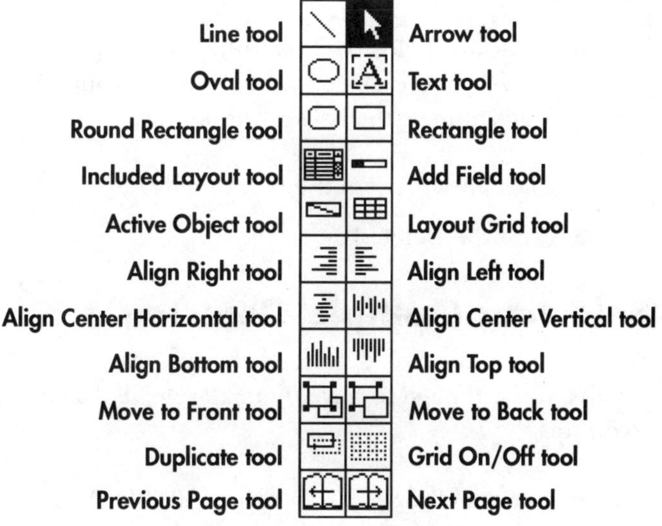

SELECTING OBJECTS ON A LAYOUT

To move, delete, or resize objects, you need to select them. The Layout Editor indicates that an object is selected by surrounding it with small, black squares. These black squares are called *resizing handles.* Figure 12.15 shows a sample layout with a box selected. If you select more than one object, each object will have resizing handles around it indicating that it is selected. To select objects, you use the Arrow tool. When you open a layout in the Layout Editor, the Arrow tool is selected by default. With the Arrow tool selected, you simply click anywhere on an object to select it.

FIGURE 12.15

A box selected in the Layout Editor

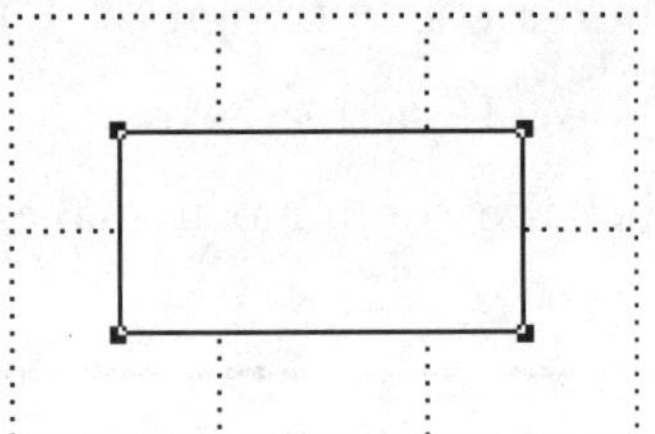

Behind your fields is a box with a grey pattern. When you are first learning how to move objects around on a layout, this box might get in the way. Let's remove the background box:

1. Click anywhere on the box to select it.
2. Press the **Delete** key.

Selecting Multiple Objects

You may want to move, delete, or change several objects at once. To do this, you will need to have them all selected. There are three ways to do this.

- You can choose Edit ➤ Select All (⌘-A) to select all of the objects on the layout.
- You can select multiple objects by holding down the Shift key while you select them. This is commonly called *Shift selecting.*
- You can draw a *marquee* around all of the objects you want to select. A marquee is simply a box that 4D draws on the

screen to allow you to indicate which objects you want to select. Figure 12.16 shows several fields being selected with a marquee. To draw the marquee, move the cursor to any corner of the area you want to select and drag to the diagonally opposite corner.

You can select multiple objects on a layout by holding down the Shift key while clicking on the objects to select them. This is called *Shift-selecting.*

FIGURE 12.16

Objects being selected with a marquee

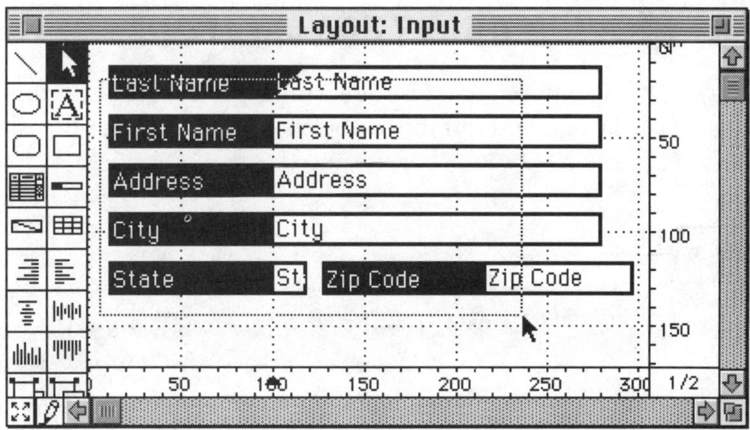

Let's try selecting several objects using the marquee.

1. Click to the left of the text label for the Last Name field.
2. While holding the mouse button, drag to the opposite corner just to the right of the City field.
3. Release the mouse button.

As you can see, the objects that were inside the marquee are selected. Now, let's deselect the selected objects.

4. Click on a part of the layout that has no objects to deselect any selected objects.

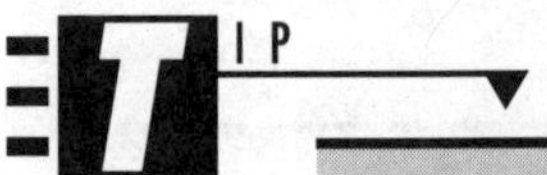

When using the marquee, all objects inside the marquee or partially inside the marquee are selected. If you hold down the Control key while drawing the marquee, only objects completely inside the marquee will be selected.

MOVING OBJECTS ON A LAYOUT

A common need is to rearrange fields, graphics, and other objects on a layout. You can move objects on a layout with the Arrow tool and with the cursor keys.

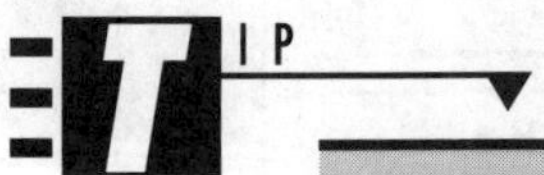

The Layout Editor has a Show Page box in the lower-left corner, just like the Structure Window does. You can click this button to see a reduced view of the layout use the View Frame to easily move to another part of the layout.

You can move any object on a layout with the Arrow tool. Some objects may appear to be one object but are actually several objects together. As in most graphics programs on the Macintosh, you can draw a marquee around several objects to select them all at once.

As you are learning how to use the Layout Editor, you will probably make a few mistakes. If you make a mistake choose Edit ➤ Undo (⌘-Z) to undo the last change you made. If you have made several mistakes, you can change the layout back to the way it was before you opened it by choosing File ➤ Revert To Saved.

Moving Several Objects at Once

The Arrow tool (or cursor keys) can be used to move several objects at once. You can do this by selecting the objects you wish to move and then using the Arrow tool to drag them or the cursor keys to move them one pixel at a time.

The Zip Code field (as with all the fields on this layout) is made up of three objects. The field itself is the black type in the white box. The text label is the white type in the black box. There is also a graphic box surrounding the field and the text label. Let's move these three objects so that the Zip Code field is to the left of the State field. Figure 12.17 shows the Zip Code field in its new position.

1. Draw a marquee around the Zip Code field and text label.
2. Drag the objects to the left of the State field.
3. Use the cursor keys to align the top of the Zip Code field with the top of the State field if necessary.

FIGURE 12.17

The repositioned Zip Code field

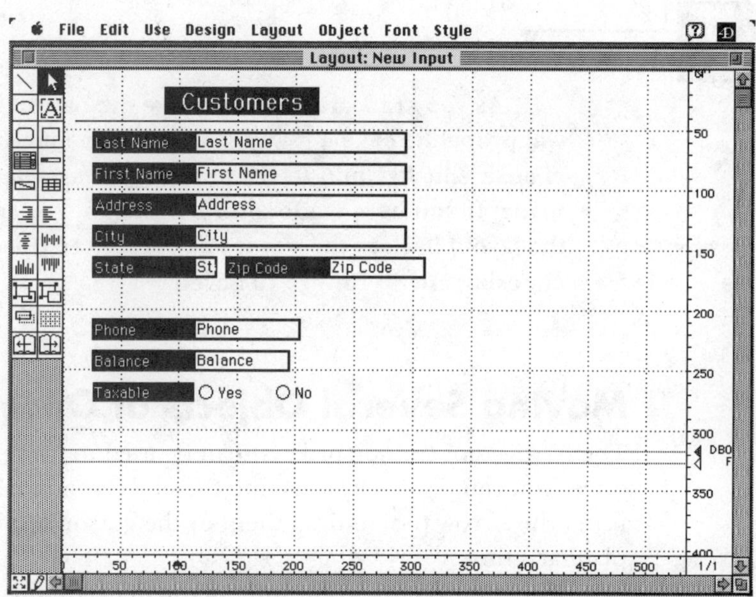

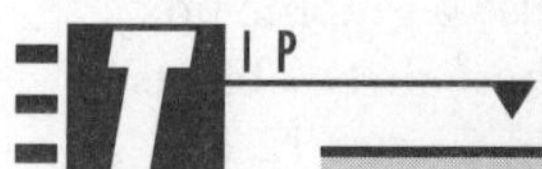

You can store objects you use often in the Scrapbook. When you paste them back on to a layout, they will have the same attributes they had when you copied them into the scrapbook. If you are not familiar with the Scrapbook, consult the documentation that came with your Macintosh.

Now let's rearrange the New Input layout a bit.

1. Select the Customers box and line at the top of the layout.
2. Press the Delete key.
3. Move the Last Name, First Name, Address, City, State and Zip Code fields to the upper-left corner of the layout.
4. Move the Phone, Balance, and Taxable fields to the right of the other fields.

Figure 12.18 shows what your layout should now look like. As you can see, rearranging objects on your layout is easy.

FIGURE 12.18

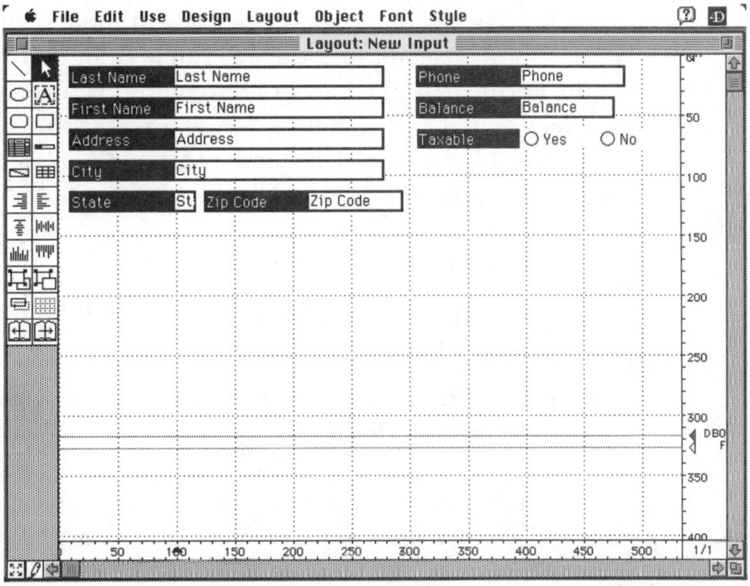

The rearranged New Input layout

TIP

The cursor keys move an object one pixel at a time. If you hold down the Control key while using the cursor keys to move an object, the object will move one grid amount at a time. This grid amount can be set by choosing Layout ➤ Define Grid.

ADDING OBJECTS TO A LAYOUT

There are several tools available for adding objects to your layout. The graphic object tools allow you to draw lines, ovals, and rectangles. The

Add Field tool is used to add fields to the layout. The Active Object tool is used to add buttons, scrollable areas, popup menus, and other kinds of clickable objects to the layout. The Included Layout tool allows you to create an area that will display multiple records from another file.

So far, our layout has only fields and text. If you use the layout now, 4D will add a button bar to the left side of the screen. The button bar, while useful, may not look the way you want or do the things you need it to do. Fortunately, the Layout Editor allows you add your own buttons. As I mentioned earlier, buttons are active objects. Each time you create an active object, you give it a name and select an active object type. Let's add a Save button and a Cancel button to the layout.

1. Click the Active Object tool to select it.
2. In a blank area of the layout, click and hold down the mouse button.
3. Drag to the lower-right to create a rectangle approximately 80 pixels wide and 20 pixels tall.

At this point you have created the active object and told 4D how big it is and where it goes on the screen. Don't worry if the button isn't the right size or in the right place, you can fix it later. As soon as you released the mouse button, 4D presented the Format dialog box. The Format dialog box shown in Figure 12.19 is used to control different attributes of objects on layouts. You will use this dialog box to enter a name for this object, assign the button text, and choose the type of object it will be.

4. Type **bSave** as the name of the button.
5. Choose Button from the Type pop-up menu.
6. Choose Accept from the Action pop-up menu (just below the Type pop-up menu).
7. Press the Tab key to move to the Button Text area.
8. Type **Save** as the button text.
9. Click **OK**.

There are 15 different types of active objects. Figure 12.20 shows all the different types of active objects.

FIGURE 12.19

The Format dialog box

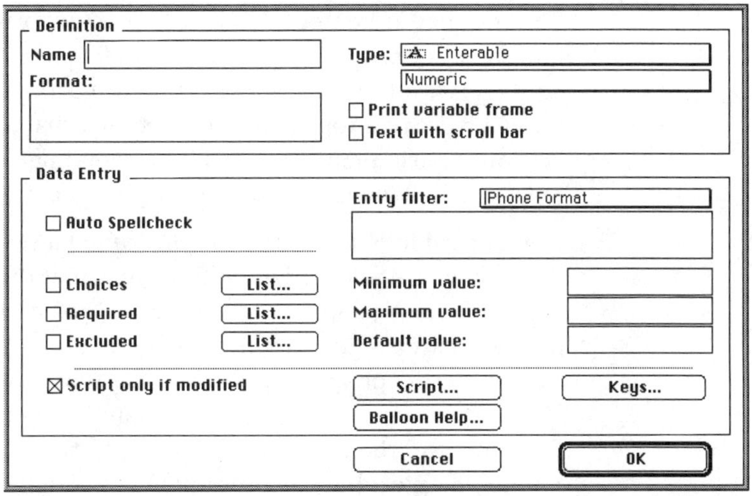

Definition
Name
Type:
Enterable
Numeric
Format:
Print variable frame
Text with scroll bar
Data Entry
Entry filter:
Phone Format
Auto Spellcheck
Choices
List...
Minimum value:
Required
List...
Maximum value:
Excluded
List...
Default value:
Script only if modified
Script...
Keys...
Balloon Help...
Cancel
OK

FIGURE 12.20

The 15 different types of active objects

File Edit Use Design Layout Object Font Style
Layout: Layout5
vName
Save
Grid on
Grid off
Print detail
aNames
aNames

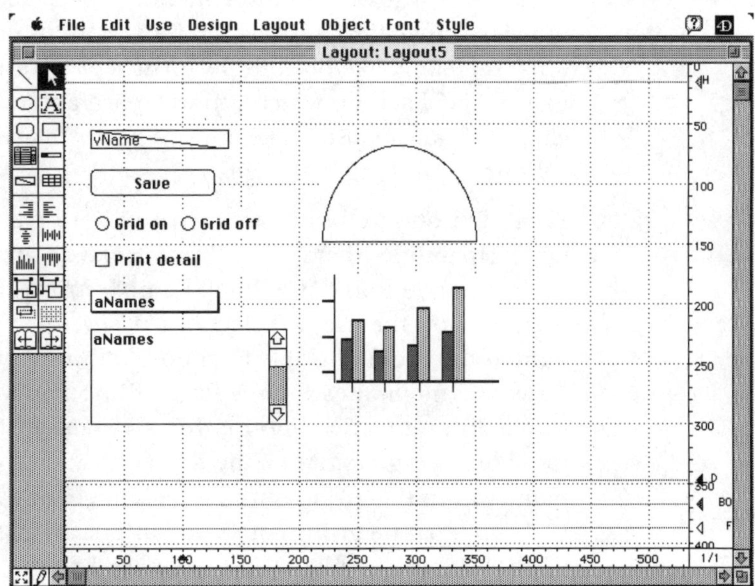

Enterable objects can hold text, numbers, and even pictures. Because they are enterable, the user can enter information into them. Enterable objects look and feel like fields but they don't get saved with the record. Enterable areas are often used to get a piece of information from the user that doesn't need to be stored permanently. For example, you might want to get today's date from the user to use in a search.

Non-enterable objects can hold the same kinds of data the Enterable objects can. The difference is that the user can't enter information into a non-enterable object. What good is having an area of a layout that the user can't enter data into? Non-enterable objects can display data that is put into them by 4D's programming language. For example, you may want to show the user the result of a calculation. You could use an Enterable object but the user might think that it's okay to change the result. By using a Non-enterable object, the user won't be able to change the result of the calculation.

Buttons are one of the most common objects in the Macintosh interface. Specifically, buttons refer to round-rectangle buttons. You can make buttons perform actions using 4D's built-in automatic actions which you will learn about later in this chapter. You can also make buttons perform actions using 4D's programming language.

Radio Buttons are just another type of button and have all the same capabilities that regular buttons have. The difference is in the way you would use them. Radio buttons are typically used to allow the user to select one of several values. If you wanted the user to be able to choose only one of three options, you might create three Radio Button active objects, each with a different label. In order for 4D to understand which radio buttons go together, the first character of each object's name within the group must be the same. For example, if you had two separate groups of radio buttons on a layout, they might have names like aMale, aFemale, bSingle, bMarried, bDivorced.

Checkboxes allow the user to indicate whether they want an option or not. You might use a checkbox instead of two radio buttons. For example, instead of two radio buttons named Male and Female you might have one checkbox named Female.

Pop-up Menus act like pull-down menus. The present a list of choices to the user that they can select an item from.

Scrollable Areas display a list of items that the user can choose one item from. A Scrollable Area has a scroll bar that the user can use to scroll through the list if the entire list doesn't fit in the area displayed on the layout.

Invisible Buttons are buttons that don't have any physical appearance on the layout. Typically, these buttons are used when you want some type of graphic to be a button. You simply paste the graphic on the layout then draw an Invisible Button on top of it. Invisible Buttons don't highlight when clicked.

Highlight Buttons are just like Invisible Buttons. The only difference is that Highlight Buttons invert (highlight) when clicked.

Radio Picture buttons are sort of a combination of Highlight Buttons and Radio Buttons. With Radio Picture buttons you can paste several graphics on a layout and draw a Radio Picture button over each graphic. When the user clicks on a graphic, the graphic will highlight and stay selected. The user can only select one of the graphics in the group. An example of Radio Picture buttons are the page orientation buttons (landscape and portrait) in the Page Setup dialog box.

Graph areas allow you to display graphs as part of the layout. The graph area is controlled using 4D's programming language.

External Objects are controlled by programming code written in languages external to 4th Dimension (like C or Pascal). They are also used by the 4D modules which you will learn about in *Chapter 20.*

Thermometers display a graphical thermometer on the screen. The user can set the thermometer by clicking on it. When you create a thermometer object, you can select the units that the thermometer is divided into.

Rulers display a ruler on the layout. The user can set a point on the ruler by clicking on the ruler with the mouse. Rulers work exactly like Thermometers.

Dials display a dial on the layout. Dials work just like thermometers and rulers.

The Save button you created will allow you to save any changes you make to a record. There is no programming needed because 4D has built-in "automatic actions". These are common functions that you will need for buttons and are assigned by selecting them from the action pop-up menu.

You will also need a button to allow you to cancel any changes you make to a record. Perhaps you make several modifications to a record and decide you don't want to keep any of the changes you have made. Up to now, you have been using the layouts that 4D created for you. The input layouts that 4D creates automatically have a cancel button on them. Let's add a cancel button. The Save button is very similar to what you need for your cancel button. All you have to do is duplicate the Save button and make a few changes to it. Fortunately, 4D has a duplicate tool.

1. Click once on the **Save** button to select it.
2. Click the Duplicate tool.
3. Move the duplicate Save button to the left of the original.
4. Double-click on the duplicate Save button to open the Format dialog box.
5. Change the name from **bSave** to **bCancel**.
6. Press the Tab key and change the button text to **Cancel**.
7. Choose Cancel from the Action pop-up menu.
8. Click **OK**.

ASSIGNING AUTOMATIC ACTIONS TO BUTTONS

4th Dimension has built-in automatic actions that can be assigned to buttons you add to your layouts. These actions make it easy to add buttons that take care of the typical database functions you need from buttons, such as moving from one record to the next. By assigning automatic actions to buttons, you can add functionality to your layouts without having to do any programming. Automatic actions can be assigned to round-rectangle, invisible and highlight buttons. There are 15 different automatic actions that can be assigned to a button.

No Action buttons have no automatic action assigned to them. This is the default setting when you create a button that can have an automatic action. You select No Action when you want to use 4D's programming language to create the action instead of using one of the automatic actions. You can also use 4D's programming language along with an automatic action. You will learn more about how this is done in *Chapter 14.*

Cancel buttons close the record without saving any changes to the record. Clicking a Cancel button also closes the layout. For example, if you double-clicked a record in the output layout to edit it in the input layout, clicking a Cancel button would move you back to the output layout. Cancel buttons can also be used when you create your own customized dialog boxes. You will learn more about creating custom dialog boxes in *Chapter 17.*

Accept buttons save changes made to a record and close the layout. After the record is saved, the Accept automatic action closes the layout. You might think of an Accept button as a Save button.

Next Record buttons save the current record and move to the next record in the current selection.

Previous Record buttons save the current record and move to the previous record in the current selection.

First Record buttons save the current record and move to the first record in the current selection.

Last Record buttons save the current record and move to the last record in the current selection.

Delete Record buttons delete the current record after the user confirms that they want to delete the record.

Next Page buttons move to the next page of the input layout. Layouts can have multiple pages to give you more room to make all necessary fields and buttons fit. A Next Page button gives you the ability to move to the next page of the layout without saving or canceling the record.

Previous Page buttons move to the previous page of the current input layout.

First Page buttons move to the first page of the current input layout.

Last Page buttons move to the last page of the current input layout.

Open Included buttons are used to open a record from an included layout for editing. Included layouts look like small output layouts that display records from other files in the database. You will learn more about included layouts in *Chapter 13.*

Delete Included buttons are used to delete selected (highlighted) records from included layouts.

Add To Included buttons add a new record to a file displayed in an included layout. Again, you will learn more about included layouts in *Chapter 13.*

Now that you have added your own buttons, 4D will not display the data entry control panel for this input layout. If you want to duplicate the other functions of this control panel, you will need to create more automatic action buttons. Fortunately, this can be done quickly and easily as you have just seen when you created your Save and Cancel buttons.

CHANGING AN OBJECT'S APPEARANCE

The appearance of objects on a layout can be altered to look just about any way you want. When you open a layout in the Layout Editor, 4D adds the Layout, Object, Font and Style menus to help you customize the appearance of your objects.

Fields, Text, and Buttons

You are probably used to using Font and Style menus in other Macintosh applications. In a word processor, you select text by highlighting it and then choosing a font from the Font menu or a style from the Style menu. Each object on a layout can have one font, one font size, and any combination of font styles. For example, you can select Helvetica as the font for a field, 12 point as the font size, bold and italic as the font style, and Center as the alignment. You cannot, however, have Helvetica for the first few characters of a field and New York for rest. Typically you won't need multiple fonts when you are entering data. If you do have this need, you might want to consider buying 4D Write. 4D Write is a word processor that you can add to 4D. One of the many things it can do is allow you to have multiple fonts and sizes in one field. For more information on 4D Write see *Chapter 20.*

Let's change the font and style for a field. We are going to use the New York font. If you don't have New York font installed on your computer, just choose some other font you like. Remember, the field is the white box with black text. The white text on the black background is the field label (a text object).

1. Click the Last Name field to select it.
2. Choose Font ➤ New York.
3. Choose Style ➤ Bold.

Let's change the font and style of the First Name field:

4. Click the First Name field to select it.
5. Choose Font ➤ New York.
6. Choose Style ➤ Bold.

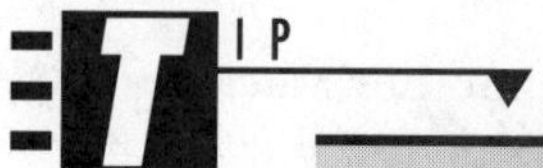

If you find yourself using a particular font, size, or style quite a bit, you might want to set it as the default. By setting a font, size, or style as the default, 4D initially uses these settings when you add objects to the layout. This will save you the extra step of selecting the objects and choosing items from menus. To set the defaults for the Font and Style menus, make sure that no objects are selected then choose a font from the Font menu and a style from the Style menu.

You can also make changes to several objects at the same time. To do this, you simply need to have all the objects you want to change selected before choosing a font, size, or style. You already know how to select an object by clicking on it. To select multiple objects you hold down the Shift key while you click each object to select it. The Shift key is your way to tell 4D not to deselect any objects that are already selected. Let's change the font and style of the First Name and Last Name field back to the Geneva font and Plain style.

1. While holding the Shift key, click on the Last Name and First Name fields to select them.
2. Choose Font ➤ Geneva.
3. Choose Style ➤ Plain.

Text objects and buttons can be changed in the same way. While you might use different fonts for text objects I wouldn't recommend using different fonts for buttons. Round rectangle buttons should be displayed using the Chicago font at 12 point size with a Plain style. If you look at the applications you use on your computer, just about all have buttons that use this font, size and style. Checkboxes and radio buttons also should use this font, size and style. Occassionally, you might need a smaller font size for a button. If this is the case, don't use Chicago. The Chicago font looks fine at 12 point size but at smaller sizes it becomes hard to read and doesn't look nice on the screen. Instead, use Geneva 10 or 9 point size. The Geneva font looks nice at these sizes.

If you are creating a database for someone else to use, you may not know which fonts they have on their computer. If you use fonts they don't have, the objects that are set to those fonts won't appear correctly on the screen. If you want to make absolutely sure that the layouts will appear the same on their screen as on yours, use Geneva and Chicago fonts. These two fonts are system fonts which means they must be installed and cannot be removed. If you want to use a special font and you don't know if the other person will have it, you can use the Font/DA Mover application to install a font into the Structure file. That way the font will be available to your database. If you are running Apple's system 7, you will need Font/DA Mover version 4.1 or greater.

An object's alignment is part of its style. You probably noticed that the Style menu has Default, Left, Center, and Right menu items. These menu items are for setting an object's alignment. For example, if you select a field and Choose Style ➤ Right, the data entered into the field would be aligned with the right side of the field. If you Choose Style ➤ Default, the alignment of the object will be set to the default alignment depending on the data type of the object. For example, numeric fields like Real, Integer and Long Integer will be aligned right by default while Alpha and Text fields will be aligned left by default.

Don't change the alignment of objects unless you have a real need to. Objects will be set to their proper alignment when you create them.

Setting an Object's Color

4th Dimension supports color. This means that if you have a color or grey scale monitor, you can choose different colors for the objects on your layouts. Each object actually has two colors associated with it, the *foreground* color and the *background* color. You set an object's color by selecting the object and choosing Color from the Object menu. The Color menu item displays a submenu (called a hierarchical menu) of all of the foreground and background colors available. If you don't have a color or grey scale monitor (or if your monitor is set to black and white mode) all of the colors on this menu will appear black.

Your computer doesn't run as fast in color as it does in black and white. The reason for this is that color requires more information to keep track of the colors that each pixel on the screen is set to. If you want things to run a little faster, set your monitor to black and white. If you are not sure how to change your monitor from color to black and white, consult the system software manuals that came with your computer.

The foreground color is the color of the text that appears inside the object. For buttons, the foreground color is the color of the button text; for fields, the data you enter will appear in the foreground color.

The background color is the color that the object will be filled with. For example, if you set the foreground color for a field to blue and the background color to red, the data in the field will appear in blue on a red background.

Use color sparingly. Color should be used to accent or draw attention to things. If you use too much color, it can make the layout unattractive and difficult to look at for long periods of time (it probably won't win you any awards either).

Graphics

You can change the appearance of graphics you create with the graphic tools. The Object menu has four items to help you do this:

Menu Item	A Description of the Item
Line Width	Controls the width of the line that makes up the border of the object. There are five preset widths or you can set a custom width.
Fill	Displays a list of patterns. The inside of the object will be filled with the pattern selected.
Border	Displays a list of patterns. The border of the object will be filled with the pattern selected.
Color	Allows you to set the foreground and background colors for a graphic object.

These menu items will work only with graphic objects you create using the graphics tools in 4D or for graphics created in other object-oriented graphics programs like MacDraw.

GETTING OBJECTS TO LINE UP WITH EACH OTHER

Part of making a layout look attractive is aligning objects. If the objects on the layout are all out of alignment, the layout looks messy. The Layout Editor has six tools for aligning objects. To align objects together, select the objects you wish to align and click one of the alignment tools in the tools palette. The alignment tools are (from left to right, top to bottom): Align Left, Align Right, Align Center X Axis, Align Center Y Axis, Align Bottom, and Align Top.

When you align several objects together, 4D chooses one of the objects to align the others to. How does 4D choose one of the objects? Well, 4D doesn't play favorites, but to understand how it chooses you will first need to understand the concept of Object Layers.

Object Layers

Each and every object on a layout has it own layer. This gives you the ability to put objects on top of each other. You can think of a layer as a thin, clear piece of plastic with one object on it. When you click on an alignment tool, 4D aligns the selected objects to the selected object that is behind all the other selected objects. Let's try an experiment with the alignment tools:

1. Create a square using the rectangle tool.
2. Create a circle using the circle tool and place it below and to the right of the rectangle.
3. Select square and the circle.
4. Click the Align Left tool.

Notice that the circle aligned itself to the square. This is because each new object you create is in the top-most layer. Since you created the circle first and the square last, the circle is behind the the square.

If you hold down the Shift key while drawing a rectangle, 4D will constrain the rectangle to a square. If you hold down the Shift key while drawing an oval, 4D will constrain the oval to a circle. This makes drawing squares and circles much easier.

The object that is farthest back may not be the object you want the other objects aligned to. Also, as you create your layout you will probably want to put objects on top of each other or behind each other. Fortunately, the Layout Editor provides you with two tools to move objects to different layers.

To move an object to the frontmost layer, select an object and Choose Object ➤ Move to Front (⌘-F). You can also click the Move to Front tool in the Tools palette instead of using the menu item.

To move an object to the backmost layer, select an object and Choose Object ➤ Move to Back (⌘-B). You can also click the Move to Back tool in the Tools palette instead of using the menu item.

Now, delete the circle and square:

1. Select the circle and square.
2. Press the Delete key or choose Edit ➤ Cut (⌘-X).

FORMATTING FIELDS

Information entered into your database may need to be displayed many different ways for different purposes. At the moment you enter data into your database, you might not know exactly how you will want that data displayed on the screen or on a report. For example, when entering sales figures, you might enter dollars and cents then later decide that you don't want the cents to appear on a report. When you *format* a field, you are telling 4D how you want the data in that field displayed. You might want a sales figure displayed as *$5 567.98* or *5,567*. Perhaps you will use the first format on the screen and the second on a report. Because 4D stores records and formats separately, you can create as many formats for your data as you want and use different formats for different purposes.

Fields (as well as Enterable and Non-enterable objects) are formatted from the Layout Editor. This means that you are not really formatting the field. What you are really formatting is the display of this field on this particular layout. The Field Definition dialog box is used to format fields. You access this dialog box by double-clicking a field in the

Layout Editor or by selecting a field and choosing Object ➤ Format (⌘-K). Figure 12.21 shows this dialog box. The Field Definition dialog box has a Format Display Area that displays the format (if any) for the object. Just below the Format Display Area is the Format pop-up menu. This pop-up menu displays built-in formats that can be applied to the object. Figure 12.21 points out these two items.

FIGURE 12.21

The Format Display Area and Format pop-up menu in the Field Definition dialog box

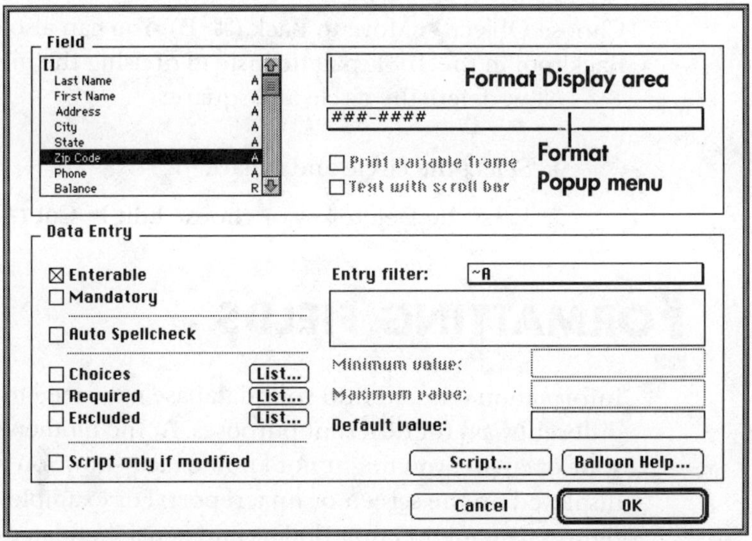

Each data type in 4D has its own formatting. The formatting you apply to an Alpha field won't work with a Date field. For each format there are a few built-in formats to choose from. For Alpha, Real, Integer, Long Integer, and Boolean fields, you can also create your own formats. If you have ever formatted cells in a spreadsheet program, the formatting in 4D will seem very familiar.

FORMATTING ALPHA AND NUMERIC FIELDS

Alpha fields are typically used to store characters and numbers that won't be used in calculations. Say you are storing phone numbers. You aren't going to add two phone numbers together (or do any other kind of math with them) so phone numbers are prime candidates for Alpha fields. You could let the user decide how a phone number should be displayed by simply displaying the phone number exactly the way they entered it. The problem is that not everyone will enter phone numbers the same way. For example, some users might enter 408-555-4444 in the following ways:

4085554444

(408) 555-4444

408/555-4444

408.555.4444

408-555-4444

You end up with phone numbers displayed several different ways, depending on how the user decided to enter them. Instead, you can control how the phone numbers are displayed using formats.

With Numeric fields you might have the same problem. For example, if you are storing sales figures and some have been entered with dollar signs while others have not, the display of the data will be inconsistent. With formatting, you can choose whether you want dollar signs, decimal points, etc. to appear. Let's apply one of the built-in numeric formats to the Balance field:

1. Double-click the Balance field to display the Field Definition dialog box.
2. Select $###,##0.00;($###,##0.00) from the Format pop-up menu.
3. Click the **OK** button.

Now, let's see the effect this format has on the Balance field when we display the input layout:

4. Choose Use ➤ User (⌘-U).
5. Double-click on any record to display it in the input layout.

Using this format, it is now more obvious that the content of the Balance field is a dollar amount.

6. Click the **Save** button.
7. Choose Use ➤ Design (⌘-Y).
8. Choose Design ➤ Layout: New Input.

The format used is the format displayed in the Format Display Area, *not* the format currently selected from the Format pop-up menu.

Place Holders in Formats

With Alpha and Numeric fields you can either choose one of the built-in formats or create your own. An Alpha or Numeric format is made up of placeholders and other formatting characters. When 4D displays the data in a field that has a format, it takes the data from the field and fills it into the placeholder characters in the format. There are four different placeholders you can use in a format. The four placeholders are # (the number sign), 0 (zero), ^ (caret), and * (asterisk).

You choose a placeholder based on the effect you want it to have on leading or trailing zeros. Leading zeros appear to the left of the decimal while trailing zeros appear to the right of the decimal. If a zero appears in a numeric value, the type of placeholder you choose will determine what is displayed in place of the zero.

The pound sign displays nothing in place of a zero. Say you entered the value 5903.9 into a field with the format $###,###.##. The value would appear in the field as $5,903.9. 4D does not recognize the dollar sign or comma as placeholders so it ignores them. The first two pound signs in the format are not displayed because nothing was entered to fill their places. 4D doesn't display the last zero because a # appears as its placeholder.

The zero character displays a zero in the place of a zero or an absent value. So the same value (5903.9) entered into the format $000,000.00 would display as $005,903.90. In most cases you wouldn't want this value to appear in this format. Instead you would use a combination of pound signs and zeros to achieve the format you want. The value 5903.9 when displayed using the format $###,##0.00 would appear as $5,903.90.

The ^ (caret) sign displays a hard space. This means that if a zero or no value at all is entered, a space is inserted. The value 5903.9 when displayed using the format $^^^,^^0.00 would display as $ 5,903.90.

The * (asterisk) sign displays an asterisk. The value 5903.9 when displayed using the format $***,***.00 would display as $**5,903.90. This format is useful when you want to make sure that the person reading the data understands exactly how many places there are to the left of the decimal point.

These formats can be used to format columns in Quick Reports. To format a column, simply click in the detail row for the column you wish to format and type in the format for that column. The format you enter will be used to display that column for all the records in the report as well as totals for that column.

Positive, Negative, and Zero Formats

When you enter a format, it applies to positive, negative and zero values. However, there may be times when you want to have different formats, depending on whether the value is positive, negative, or zero. When entering formats in the Format Display Area, you can indicate positive, negative, and zero formats by separating them with semicolons. For example, the first format is the positive format, the second format is the negative format, and the third format is the zero format. Say you entered the format **$###,##0.00;($###,##0.00);None**. Any positive values entered would be displayed using the postive format *$###,##0.00.* Negative numbers would be displayed using the negative format *($###,##0.00).* If zero was entered (or no value since numeric fields default to zero), the word *None* would appear.

If no zero format is entered, the positive format will be applied to zero values.

FORMATTING DATE FIELDS

Dates are entered in MM/DD/YY format. However, you can display dates in any one of the six built-in date formats. The table below shows these formats and gives an example of each.

Date Format	Example
Short	01/06/94
Abbreviated	Thurs, Jan 6, 1994
Long	Thursday, January 6, 1994
Short2	01/06/1994
Month Date, Year	January 6, 1994
Abbr: Month Date, Year	Jan 6, 1994

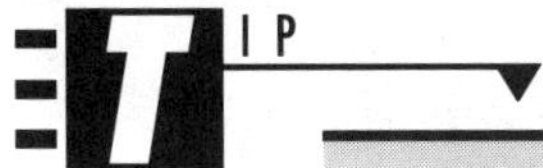

These date formats can be used in Quick Reports. To format a date field in a Quick Report, enter the number of the format in the detail row of the date column on the report. For example, if you had an Invoice Date field on a Quick Report and you wanted it formatted using the Short2 format, you would enter 4 into the detail row of the Invoice Date column.

FORMATTING TIME FIELDS

Time values are entered in 00:00:00 format. However, you can display time values in any one of the five built-in time formats. The table below shows these formats and gives an example of each.

Time Format	Example
HH:MM:SS	03:25:33
HH:MM	3:25
Hour Min Sec	3 hours 25 minutes 33 seconds
HH:MM AM/PM	3:25 AM

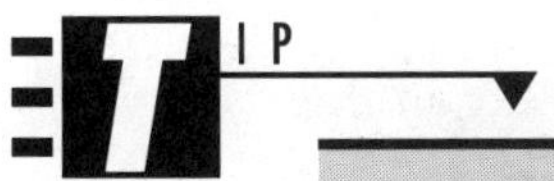

The built-in time formats can be used in Quick Reports in the same way as the date formats. Just enter the number of the format into the detail row of the column displaying time values.

FORMATTING BOOLEAN FIELDS

Boolean fields store only one of two values, true or false. By default, boolean fields appear as two radio buttons labeled Yes and No. You can change the labels that appear next to these radio buttons by entering your own format in the Display Format Area. The format is simple. You enter the true label, a semicolon and the false label. Let's change the Taxable Boolean field so that Tax and No Tax appear instead of Yes and No:

1. Double-click the Taxable field.
2. Type **Tax;No Tax** into the Display Format Area.
3. Click **OK**.

Notice that Tax and No Tax now appear instead of the Yes and No labels. You can also have a Boolean field appear as a single checkbox instead of two radio buttons. To do this, you simply enter the label for the checkbox into the Display Format Area. Let's try it:

1. Double-click the Taxable field.
2. Type **Taxable** in the Display format area.
3. Click **OK**.

Now, a Taxable checkbox appears instead of the two radio buttons. You don't really need the Taxable label on the black background anymore so let's delete it:

1. Select both the Taxable text label (the white text on the black background) and the black box behind it.
2. Press the **Delete** key.

FORMATTING PICTURE FIELDS

The four built-in picture formats control the way pictures are displayed. Pictures are entered by pasting them into the Picture field from the Clipboard.

Truncated (Centered) format means that the center of the picture will be positioned in the center of the field. Any portion of the picture that doesn't fit is truncated. Figure 12.22 shows a picture displayed using the Truncated (Centered) format.

FIGURE 12.22

An example of the Truncated (Centered) picture format

Scaled To Fit format means that the picture will be scaled to fit the size of the picture field on the layout. If the picture is smaller than the size of the field, the picture will be enlarged. If the picture is larger than the size of the picture field, the picture will be reduced in size.

On Background format means that the picture is transparent and any objects behind the picture field will be visible through the picture. Figure 12.23 shows an example of a picture using this format with other fields displayed through the picture field.

Truncated (non centered) format means that the upper-left corner of the picture is placed in the upper-left corner of the field. Any portion of the picture that doesn't fit within the bounds of the field will be truncated.

Scaled To Fit (proportional) is the same as Scaled To Fit with one important difference. With this format, the picture is scaled proportionally.

FIGURE 12.23

A picture field using On Background format

Remember, formats control only how the data is displayed. They do not affect the data itself. In the case of picture fields, this means that if a picture is scaled or truncated, it is only the display of the picture that is changed, not the picture itself.

PREVENTING ERRORS IN DATA ENTRY

People are not perfect (nor are computers for that matter). They make mistakes. Sometimes you won't notice that mistakes in data entry have been made until they appear in 57 different places on an extremely important report that you are about to hand to the president of your company. The best way to prevent mistakes in data entry is to make sure that the data being entered is the kind of data you are expecting. There are plenty of common mistakes that happen during data entry. For example, a user is entering a salary of $50,000 and they accidentally add an extra zero. The formats I spoke of earlier in the chapter are only going to work if the user hasn't entered any formatting characters themselves. Say you have formatted the Phone field with the format (###) ###-####. If your user enters parentheses and dashes into the field, the format will not display properly. You can prevent this kind of data entry error by setting up the field so the user can enter only numbers into the Phone field. The Layout Editor provides you with several tools to check the user's data as it's being entered.

ALLOWING VALUES WITHIN A RANGE

In some cases, you will want to prevent the user from entering data outside of a certain range. With Real, Integer, Long Integer, Date, and Time fields, you can easily define a range of values that are acceptable. In the Field and Object Definition dialog boxes there are areas to enter minimum and maximum values for that field or object. The mimimum and maximum values can be used separately or together. For example, with a mimimum value of 5, the user could enter any value greater than or equal to 5. With a mimimum of 5 and a maximum of 10, the user could enter any value greater than or equal to 5 and less than or equal to 10. If the user enters a value outside of the range, 4D displays a message indicating that the value is outside the range and prevents the user from moving to another field or saving the record.

AUTOMATIC ENTRIES FOR NEW RECORDS (DEFAULT VALUES)

You may have fields where the user is entering the same value in the field for almost every new record they create. You can save the user time and lessen the chances for a data entry error by assigning a default value to a field or enterable object. Say most of your customers are in California. It would save the user time if the State field had the value CA in it when the record was created. If they are entering a customer that is not in California, they can type over the default value. Let's set the default value for the State field to CA:

1. Double-click the State field.
2. Click or Tab into the Default Value box.

3. Type **CA** in the Default Value box.

4. Click **OK**.

This works fine if the value is constant and doesn't change. However, there may be times when your default values change. For example, if you were entering invoices you might have an Invoice Date field. Typically, the date on an invoice is today's date. But if you type **Today's date** into the Default Value box, 4D won't know what to do with it. Instead, there are three built-in stamps you can use. They are #D (current date), #H (current time), and #N (sequence number). To use these stamps, you enter the two character code into the Default Value box.

#D (current date) enters the date from the clock inside the Macintosh. This date is the same date that appears when you open the General Controls control panel.

#H (current time) enters the time from the clock inside the Macintosh. This time is the same time that appears when you open the General Controls control panel.

#N (sequence number) enters a unique long integer value into the field. The first time you enter a record into a file, the sequence number is 1. Each time you save a new record the sequence number for that file is incremented by one. This value continues to increase and numbers are not reused even if records are deleted.

There may be times when your default value needs to change in some way that 4D does not provide automatic entry for. When this occurs, you can use 4D's programming language to enter the default value. You will learn how to do this in *Chapter 17*.

ENTRY FILTERS

One way to prevent errors in data entry is to stop the wrong data from being entered in the first place. Formatting helps because the user sees how the data is displayed once it's entered. But formatting alone won't do the whole job. For example, you could format the Phone field so it displays the phone numbers in a phone number format like (408) 555-1234. In order for this format to work properly, the user must be sure to only enter the numbers and not the formatting characters like the parentheses or dash. Remember, 4D doesn't know that this is a phone number. If the user enters the formatting characters, 4D will format them along with the number and the phone number won't look right at all. Also, when you created the Phone field, you set the maximum length to 10 characters. The phone number with formatting is 14 characters so the user wouldn't be able to enter the entire phone number anyway. As long as the user enters only the 10 digit phone number without any formatting characters, you can assign a format to display the phone number anyway you want. But how do you prevent the user from entering the formatting chararacters? You use an entry filter.

WHAT ARE ENTRY FILTERS?

Entry filters allow you to filter out characters during data entry. Entry filters are assigned to fields or enterable areas on layouts just like Formats. An entry filter tells 4D what characters the user is allowed to enter into a particular field or enterable area on a layout. If the user types a character that is not allowed by the entry filter, 4D will filter out the character and it will never appear in the field. It would be as if the user never typed the character at all. Entry filters also have a format just like Formats. When the user tabs into a field that has an entry filter, the filter's format is displayed. The display format helps the user know what kind of data to enter. In the Field and Object Definition dialog boxes, there is an Entry Filter pop-up menu and an Entry Filter Display Area. Figure 12.24 points out these two items. Like display formats, 4D has several built-in entry filters that are commonly used. Let's choose a display format for the Phone field and an entry filter that only allows the user to enter numbers:

1. Double-click the Phone field to open the Field Definition dialog box.
2. Select (###) ###-#### from the Display Format pop-up menu.

FIGURE 12.24

The Entry Filter pop-up menu and Display Area

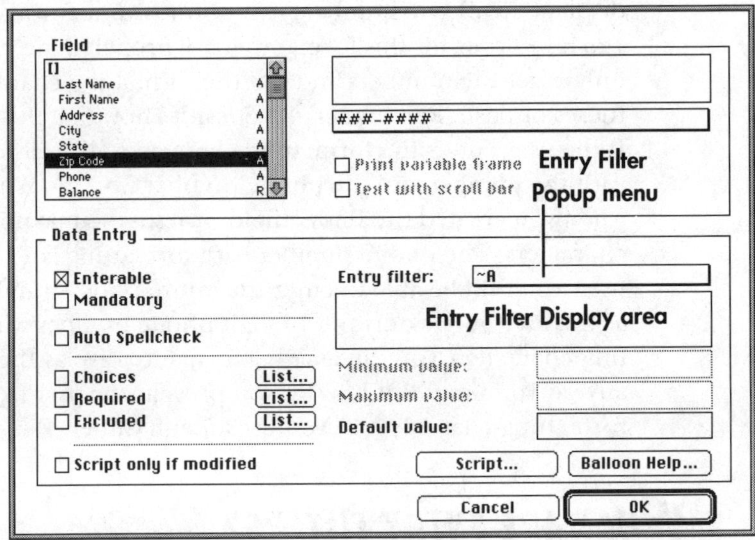

3. Select &9 from the Entry Filter pop-up menu.
4. Click **OK**.

Remember, the entry filter currently displayed in the Entry Filter pop-up menu is not the filter in use. The entry filter in use is displayed in the Entry Filter Display Area.

The entry filter you chose only allows numbers (no letters or formatting characters). This entry filter doesn't have any format along with it. Let's try it out:

1. Switch to the User environment.
2. Choose Enter ➤ New Record (⌘-N).

3. Tab to the Phone field.
4. Try to type your name into the Phone field.

You weren't able to enter your name, were you? That's because the entry filter you chose allows only numbers and your name is made up of letters. You also can't enter commas or dashes or any other characters that are not numbers. Now, let's enter a real phone number:

5. Type **4085551234**.
6. Press the Tab key to leave the Phone field.

You were able to enter this phone number because it is made up of numbers only. Notice that as soon as you tabbed out of the field, parentheses and a dash were added. That's the display format at work. Remember, the display format is for display only. 4D only adds the parentheses and dash on the screen. They are not actually saved in the field.

At this point the user cannot accidentally enter the parentheses or dash. But this is not enough. You want the user to enter the area code along with the rest of the phone number but there is nothing that tells them what to enter. You need something to appear in the field that will let the user know exactly what you expect them to enter.

As I mentioned eariler, entry filters can have formats just like display formats. The purpose of an entry filter format is to give the user an idea of what to enter when they tab into the field. For example, for a phone number, it would be nice to have a format like (###) ### - #### appear in the field to let the user know that they need to enter the area code. One of the built-in entry filters will allow only numbers to be entered and has a format exactly like the one we need. Let's change the entry filter for the Phone field:

7. Click **Cancel**.
8. Choose Use ➤ Design (⌘-Y).
9. Choose Design ➤ New Input.
10. Double-click the Phone field.

11. Choose !_&9(###) !0###-#### from the Entry Filter pop-up menu.
12. Click **OK**.
13. Switch to the User environment.
14. Choose Enter ➤ New Record (⌘-N).
15. Tab to the Phone field.
16. Type **4085551234**.
17. Press the Tab key.
18. Click **Cancel**.

When you tabbed into the field, the entry filter's format appeared. With this format, the user would see the parentheses and know that they need to enter the area code. You probably also noticed that the Phone field on the layout is not wide enough to display the formats. Let's make the Phone field a bit wider so the formats will appear.

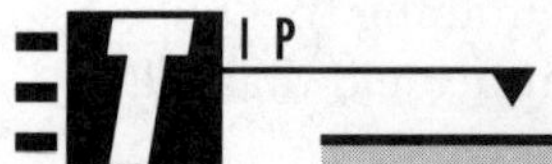

An easy way to resize an object is to click on the object you want to resize to select it. Next, hold down the ⌘ key and press any of the arrow keys to resize the object one pixel at a time in the direction of the arrow key you pressed. If you hold down Control key and the ⌘ key while using the arrow keys, the object is resized based on the grid settings. The grid settings can be changed by Choose Layout ➤ Define Grid.

1. Switch back to the Design environment and open the New Input layout.
2. Click the Phone field to select it.
3. Choose Object ➤ Move To Back (⌘-B) or click the Move To Back tool in the layout palette.
4. Click on the box where the field was to select it.

5. While holding down the Control and ⌘ keys, press the right arrow key twice to resize the box.
6. Choose Object ➤ Move To Back (⌘-B) or click the Move To Back tool in the layout palette.
7. Click on the Phone field to select it.
8. While holding down the Control and ⌘ keys, press the right arrow key twice to resize the field.

Now the field is wide enough to show the formats. I have found that using this method to resize objects can be faster than using the mouse.

The Three Parts of an Entry Filter

The entry filters you have used certainly are effective. At first glance, entry filters look like some kind of secret code. When you look at an entry filter, it's hard to understand how these strange characters tell 4D what to allow into a field. Well, it will all make a little more sense in a moment. An entry filter has three parts: the *initiator*, the *argument*, and the *placeholders*.

The initiator tells 4D that the characters that follow make up an entry filter. There are two characters that can be used as initiators. The first is the ampersand (&). The other character that can be used as an initiator is the tilde (~). When the tilde is used, all characters entered will be automatically converted to uppercase.

The argument tells 4D exactly which characters are allowed to be entered into the field or enterable area. Any other characters will be filtered out. An argument is usually one of four characters.

Character	Description
9	Only allows numbers 0–9
a	Allows upper or lowercase A–Z

Character	**Description**
A	Allows only uppercase A–Z
@	Allows upper or lowercase A–Z and 0–9

The first entry filter you used was &9. With this entry filter, the user can only enter 0–9. If you wanted to allow only *a* through *z* but you wanted everything in uppercase, you could use the entry filter ~a. An argument can also be a range of characters. When you use a range of characters as an argument, the range goes in quotes. For example, if you wanted to allow only the characters *a* through *m*, the filter might look like this **&"a-m"**. You can also use multiple ranges. Say you were keeping track of school grades. School grades are A, B, C, D or F. An entry filter for this type of data would look like this: **&"A-D;F"**. You can use a semicolon (;) to separate ranges inside an entry filter argument.

The placeholders tell 4D how many characters can be entered into the field. The pound sign (#) is used as a placeholder. For example, if you wanted an entry filter that would allow only three numbers, you would write it like this: **&9###**.

One entry filter can contain multiple initiators, arguments and placeholders. For example, the filter **&9###&"A-M"####** allows three numbers and then four letters that are between A and M.

Now that we have made the Phone field wider, let's try out the entry filter we have assigned.

1. Switch to the User environment.
2. Choose Enter ➤ New Record (⌘-N).
3. Tab to the Phone field.

Notice that as you tab into the field, the entry filter's format appears. In each place where you put a placeholder (#), an underscore appears. These underscores are called *display characters.* As you enter a value, the underscores are replaced by the characters you type. If you would rather have a different character appear instead of the underscore, you can replace it in your entry filter. To replace the underscore, add to your entry filter an exclamation point (!) followed by the character that will replace the underscore. As with all other parts of the entry filter, you can have multiple display characters. For example, the entry filter you chose for the Phone field uses an underscore for the first three characters (the area code) and zeros for the rest of the characters.

If the user doesn't type over all of the display characters, the remaining display characters will be saved with the field. This means that if the user only entered the area code, the value saved would be *4080000000*.

4. Type **4085551234**.
5. Try to select any of the formatting characters.
6. Click **Cancel**.

You can't select any of the formatting characters. Formatting characters in entry filters are called *dead characters* and can't be selected. They are there to help the user enter the value and are not saved in the field.

You might use display formats on input or output layouts. Entry filters however, make sense only on input layouts since you typically don't enter data using the output layout.

STORING COMMON FORMATS AND FILTERS

You can see that display formats and entry filters can be very useful in allowing you to control how data is displayed and entered. So far, the database you have created is fairly simple. There is only one file, a few fields, and two layouts. However, databases can become quite large. You might add many more files with each having several fields and layouts. You might find yourself using the same display formats and entry filters for several different fields on many different layouts. A potential problem exists. Suppose you have used the same phone number display format and entry filter in 20 different places on layouts throughout your database. Now you decide to change something about the way you display the phone number or the way the entry filter works. In order to make this change, you will have to remember each location where you used the display format or entry filter and change each manually. This might take a while. I don't know about you, but I don't find typing to be that much fun (and I type pretty fast). Fortunately, you can solve this problem using *Styles.*

Styles are simply display formats and entry filters that are stored in one central location in the database. Each style is given a name and the style names appear automatically in the Display Format pop-up and Entry Filter pop-up menus. When you select a style by name, 4D puts the style name in the Display Format Area or Entry Filter Display Area. The style name is a reference that tells 4D which style to use. This way you can enter display formats and entry filters in one place only. Any time you need to make a change, you change only the style. Any fields or enterable areas that reference this style are automatically updated. Styles are entered through the Styles dialog box shown in Figure 12.25. You access the Styles dialog box from the Preferences dialog box in the Design environment. Let's create a display format and entry filter styles for the Phone field:

1. Switch to the Design environment.
2. Choose File ➤ Preferences.
3. Click the Edit Styles button.

FIGURE 12.25

The Styles dialog box

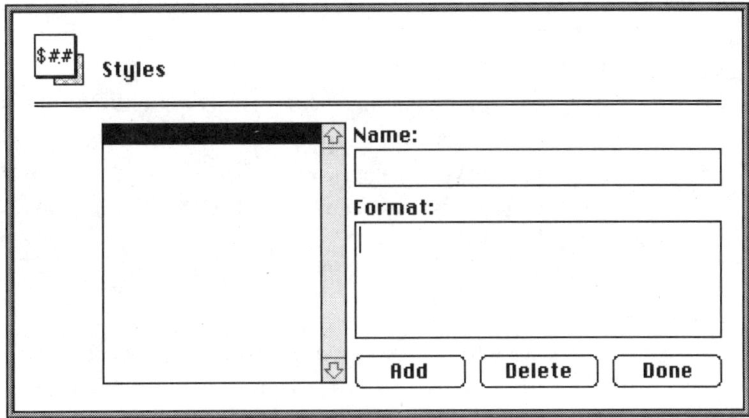

In the Styles dialog box, you have a place to enter the name of the style and the format. The format is the actual display format or entry filter. The scrollable area on the left side of the dialog box is where the list of style names appears. When you want to edit a style, you simply click on its name in the list. Let's enter the display format first:

4. Type (###) ### - ####.
5. Press the Tab key.
6. Type **Phone Format** as the name of the style.

That's all there is to creating a style. Now let's create a style for the phone entry filter:

7. Click the **Add** button.
8. Press the Tab key.
8. Type **&9(###) ### - ####.**
9. Press the Tab key.
10. Type **Phone Filter** as the name of the style.
11. Click the **Done** button.

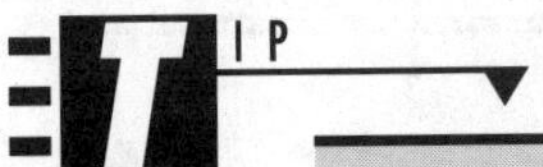

Since styles can be both Display Formats and Entry Filters, it is a good idea to use a naming convention to distinguish between them. Use the word Format for a style that is a Display Format, and Filter for a style that is a Entry Filter.

Now, when we want to apply a display format or entry filter to the Phone field, we won't enter it in directly. Instead, we will just choose the Phone Format or Phone Filter styles. Let's change the display format and entry filter for the Phone field so it uses the styles we created:

1. Switch to the New Input layout.
2. Double-click the **Phone** field.
3. Choose |Phone Format from the Display Format pop-up menu.
4. Choose |Phone Filter from the Entry Filter pop-up menu.
5. Click **OK**.

You can use these styles with any fields you add that would store phone numbers. Any changes you make to the styles are immediately used by all the objects that reference the styles.

In the Display Format and Entry Filter pop-up menus a vertical bar (|) appears. This is just 4D's way of knowing that these are styles and not formats or filters.

USING CHOICE LISTS

One way to prevent errors in data entry is to give a choice or a list of values rather than allowing any value at all. 4D has a built-in List Editor. Using the List Editor, you can create lists of values and attach them to fields or enterable areas. There are three different ways you can use lists:

- To provide the user with a list of choices to select from. This is called a *choices* list.
- To insure that the value entered matches one of the values on a list. This is called a *required* list.
- To insure that the value entered does *not* match one of the values on a list. This is called an *excluded* list.

The List Editor, shown in Figure 12.26, is accessed from the Design environment. Let's open the List Editor and take a look at it:

1. Switch to the Design environment.
2. Choose Design ➤ Lists.

The List Editor has two scrollable areas. The lists scrollable area on the left displays the names of the lists you have created. The items scrollable area on the right displays items from lists and allows you to edit those items.

The List Editor adds two menus to the menu bar. The Lists menu is used to work with lists. The Lists menu has three items:

New is used to create new lists. When you select this menu item, a blank entry is added to the bottom of the lists scrollable area.

Delete is used to delete an entire list. To use this menu item, you must first select a list from the lists scrollable area.

User modifiable is used to indicate whether or not you want users to be able to modify this list. With this menu item checked, the user can edit the selected list when the list is being used as a choices list.

FIGURE 12.26

The List Editor displaying a list

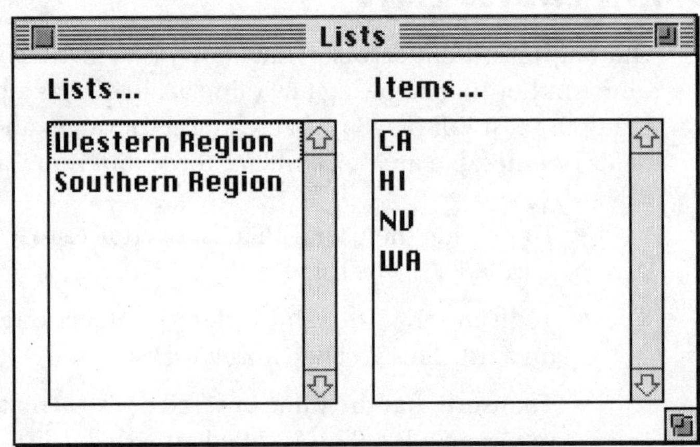

The Items menu has functions that deal with the items on a list:

New is used to add new items to a list. The new item is added to the bottom of the selected list.

Insert is used to insert a new item at a specific position within a list. To insert an item, select an existing item in the item's scrollable area then choose Items ➤ Insert (⌘-I). The item selected (and all other items below it) are moved down one position and a new item is created at the selected position in the list.

Delete is used to delete items from a list. To delete an item, select it in the items scrollable area and choose Items ➤ Delete (⌘-D).

Sort is used to sort items in a list in acsending (A–Z) order. To sort a list, select a list from the list's scrollable area and choose Items ➤ Sort.

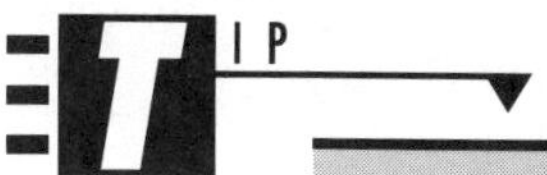

If you hold down the Shift key while choosing Items ➤ Sort, the items will be sorted in descending (Z–A) order.

The database you have created has a State field. Let's create a list of the states in the western sales region:

1. Choose Lists ➤ New.
2. Type **Western Region**.
3. Press the Tab key.
4. Type **CA** and press the Return key.
5. Type **NV** and press the Return key.
6. Type **WA**.

Now, let's create a list of states in the southern region:

1. Choose Lists ➤ New.
2. Type **Southern Region**.
3. Press the Tab key.
4. Create items for the following states:

    CO
    NM
    KS
    OK
    TX
    AR
    LA
    MS
    AL

5. Choose Items ➤ Sort.
6. Click the close box to close the List Editor.

Now that you have created a few lists, you can use these lists to add choices, required or excluded lists to your fields, or enterable objects.

Choices Lists

Choices lists give the user a list to choose from when they tab or click into a field or enterable object. You can add a choices list to a field at the field level or layout level. To add a choices list to a field at the field level, click the Choices checkbox in the Field dialog box, then select a list using the List button. When the user tabs into or clicks in this field in any input layout, the list you select will appear in a window. At this point, the user can click on one of the items in the list and it will be entered automatically into the field. If you always want a particular choices list to appear when the user is entering data into a field, assign it at the field level. In most cases, you will assign choices lists at the field level.

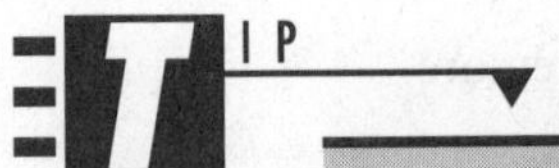

Choices lists assigned at the field level will also appear in the Search Editor when the field is used for searching.

You can also assign a choices list at the layout level. When you assign a choices list through the Layout Editor, the selected list will only display when the user uses the field in this particular layout. You might want to assign a list at the layout level if you don't want the list to appear anytime the field is used in any input layout or when it's used in the Search Editor.

Let's assign the Western Region list as the choices list for the State field on the New Input layout:

1. Double-click the State field.
2. Click the Choices checkbox.
3. Click the List button to the right of the Choices checkbox.
4. The Western Region list is already selected so just click the **Select** button.
5. Click **OK**.

Now that you have assigned to the list to the field, the Western Region list will appear when the user clicks or tabs into the State field in the New Input layout. Let's try out the choices list:

1. Switch to the User environment.
2. Double-click on any record to open it in the input layout.
3. Tab to or click in the State field.
4. Click on NV in the Choices for Western Region window.

Typing the first letter of an item will select it in the list. You can also use the arrow keys to select items through the items in the choices list.

The choices list appears in a window with the name of the list as its title. The choices list window has a Modify button. If you indicated that this list is *User Modifiable* in the List Editor, the user can click the Modify button to access the Special List Editor shown in Figure 12.27. This editor allows the user to add new items to the list, change items on the list, or delete items from the list. Let's add an item to this list from the choices list window.

1. Click or tab into the State field.
2. Click the **Modify** button in the Choices List window.
3. Click the **Append** button.
4. Type **HI**.
5. Click the **Sort** button.
6. Click **OK**.
7. Click **Cancel** to cancel any changes to the record.

FIGURE 12.27

The Special List Editor displaying a list

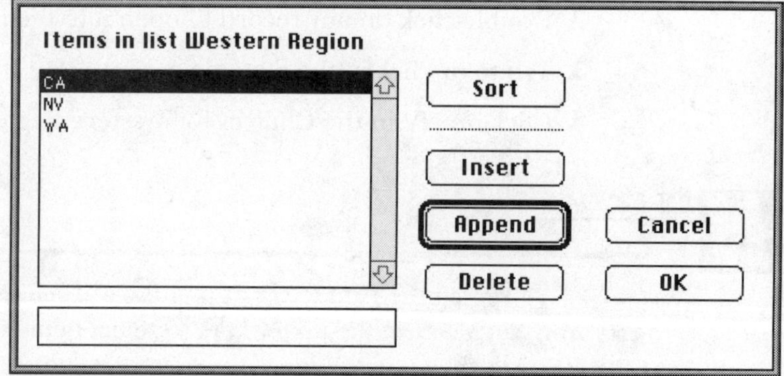

Required Lists

There may be times when you want to require that the value the user enters be one from a list of values. It would seem that using a choices list would accomplish this. However, there is nothing stopping the user from clicking the Cancel button when the choices list appears and then typing in any value they want. Fortunately, 4D has a feature that allows you to indicate that the value entered is required to be on a selected list. Let's choose the Western Region list as the required list for the State field.

1. Switch to the Design environment.
2. Open the New Input layout.
3. Double-click the State field.
4. Click the Required checkbox.
5. Click the **List** button to the right of the Required checkbox.
6. Since the Western Region list is already selected, click the **Select** button.
7. Deselect the Choices checkbox.
8. Click **OK**.

Now, let's try out the required list.

1. Switch to the User environment.
2. Double-click on any record.
3. Click in the State field.
4. Type **NY** and press the Tab key.

The value *NY* is not on the required list. Therefore, 4D will not allow it as a value in the field.

5. Click **OK**.
6. Click the **Cancel** button.

As I mentioned earlier, when you use a choices list, there is nothing stopping users from clicking the Cancel button in the Choices List window and typing in their own value. One way to insure that the user enters a value from the choices list is to make the same list required.

If you assign a required list to a field and the list doesn't have any blank items, the user will not be able to leave the field blank. The reason for this is that 4D is comparing the value they are entering (blank) to the list and not finding a match.

Excluded Lists

Excluded Lists work in almost exactly the same way that Required lists do. The only difference is that in an excluded list, you are creating a list of items that are *not* valid entries instead of creating a list of valid entries.

SPELL-CHECKING

4D can check your spelling as you enter data into Alpha of Text fields or enterable objects. You have probably noticed the Auto Spellcheck checkbox in the Field Definition dialog box. With this checkbox selected, 4D will check the spelling of the value entered in the field provided that you have the 4D Spell module installed. If spelling errors occur, the 4D Spell window appears with suggestions for correction. The 4D Spell module is sold separately. It comes with an installer that adds the spell-checking capability. For more information on 4D Spell, see *Chapter 20.*

CHANGING THE ENTRY (TAB) ORDER

Each layout has an entry order. The entry order is the order that 4D will move from one field to the next as you enter data into fields and press the tab key to move to the next field. By default, the entry order begins with the field in the upper-left corner and ends with the field in the lower-right corner. As you start to rearrange the fields and add other objects, the top-to-bottom, left-to-right entry order may not make sense anymore. Fortunately, 4D gives you the ability to change the entry order.

Look at the layout you have been working on. Originally the fields were all in one column but now you have two columns. By default, 4D is going to move from the Last Name field to the Phone field then from the Phone field to the First Name field. This probably isn't the best order because the user is going to want to enter the First Name immediately after entering the Last Name and then go on to enter the Address. Let's see what the entry order actually looks like: Choose Layout ➤ Entry Order.

4D draws a kind of "road map" to show which field it will go to next when the user presses the Tab key. The black dot indicates that the object is in the entry order and the arrow shows which object is next. Notice that the Save and Cancel buttons are not part of the entry order because you don't enter data into them.

The entry order begins in the Last Name field and proceeds from left to right, ending in the Zip Code field. Figure 12.28 shows the original entry order. It would make more sense if the entry order moved down the left column of fields and then down the right column of fields. To change the entry order, simply click in a field and drag to another

FIGURE 12.28

The default entry order for the layout

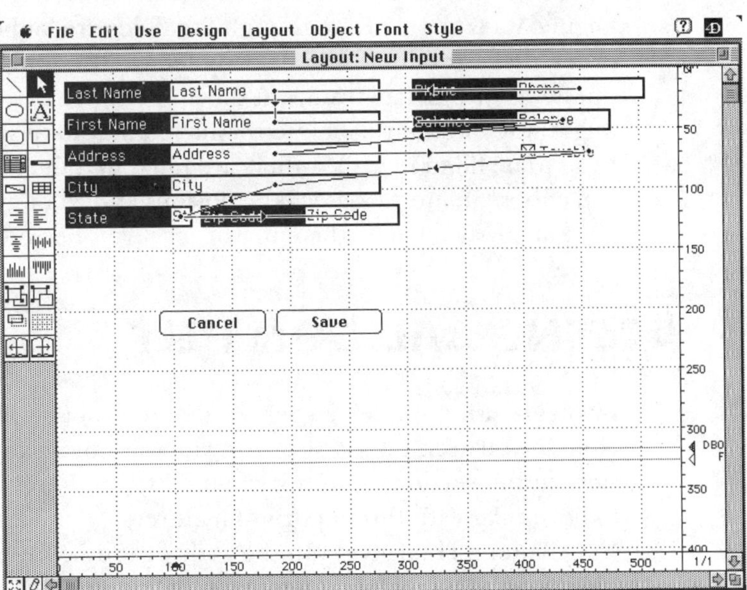

field. Let's change the entry order so that it moves down the columns instead of across:

1. Switch back to Design and open the New Input layout.
2. Click in the Last Name field and drag to the First Name field.
3. Click in the First Name field and drag to the Address field.
4. Click in the Address field and drag to the City field.
5. Click in the City field and drag to the State field.
6. Click in the State field and drag to the Zip Code field.
7. Click the Pointer tool to hide the entry order.
8. Click in the Zip Code field and drag to the Phone field.
9. Click in the Phone field and drag to the Balance field.
10. Click in the Balance field and drag to the Taxable field.

There are some considerations when deciding on the entry order. For example, which field does it make the most sense for the user to begin data entry in? Even though the fields are laid out in a certain order, the entry order may be completely different. You might want to put fields with default values at the end of the entry order since the user might not enter any data into them. You may have some fields that rarely need to be filled in while others are filled in quite often. The entry order you choose in most cases will be obvious and when it's not, experiment. You can always change the entry order if you need to.

ADDING BALLOON HELP

If you are using Apple's system 7, you are probably familar with Balloon Help. If you aren't using system 7, you will not be able to complete the steps in this section; however, you might want to read through it anyway to be familar with this important feature.

Balloon Help gives you the ability to add context-sensitive help to objects on a layout. After users turn Balloon Help on by choosing Show

Balloons from the Balloon Help menu, they can move the pointer across any object and the help balloon for that object will appear. Figure 12.29 shows a help balloon being displayed for a button. This kind of help can be useful in giving the user enough information to answer a question they might have without forcing them to look in a manual.

FIGURE 12.29

A help balloon

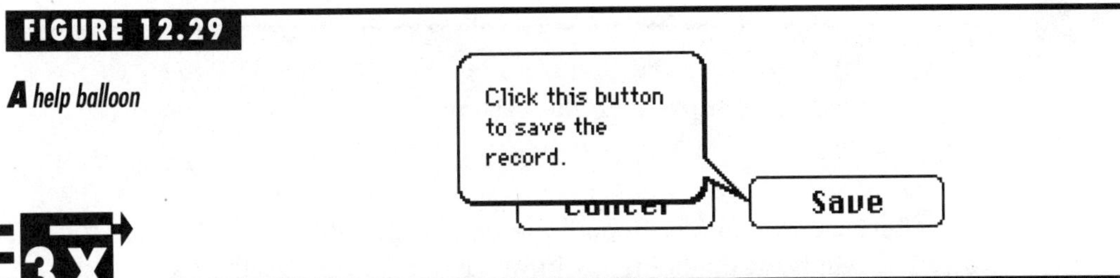

3.X

Support for Balloon Help in the Layout Editor is a new feature added with version 3.0 of 4th Dimension.

Balloon Help for Fields

You can add balloon help to a field at the field level by clicking the Balloon Help button in the Field dialog box. Balloon help text added at this level will appear any time the user has balloon help turned on and moves the pointer across the field in an input layout. Let's add a help balloon to the Balance field at the field level:

1. Choose Design ➤ Structure.
2. Double-click the Balance field.
3. Click the Balloon Help button.
4. Type **The balance is the total amount due from the customer for outstanding invoices.**
5. Click **OK**.
6. Switch to the User environment.
7. Double-click on any record to open it.

8. Choose Show Balloons from the Balloon Help menu.
9. Move the pointer over the Balance field.
10. Choose Hide Balloons from the Balloon Help menu.

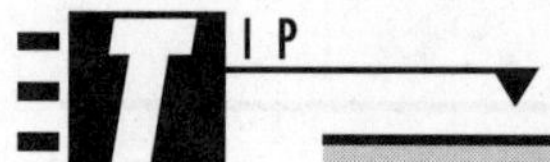

You can turn Balloon Help on and off by holding the Control key and pressing the Escape key.

Because you added the balloon help at the field level, the help for this field will be available in any input layouts where this field appears. Help balloons are also available when the layout is being used for searching with Search by Layout.

Balloon Help messages can be no longer than 255 characters.

Balloon Help for Objects on a Layout

Help balloons can be added to any object on a layout. You add balloon help using the Help Messages dialog box shown in Figure 12.30. This dialog box is used to enter balloon help messages and give them names. You then select the help message you wish to use for a particular object on the layout.

Let's add help balloons to the Save and Cancel buttons:

1. Switch to the Design environment.
2. Open the New Input layout in the Layout Editor.
3. Double-click the **Cancel** button.

FIGURE 12.30

The Help Messages dialog box

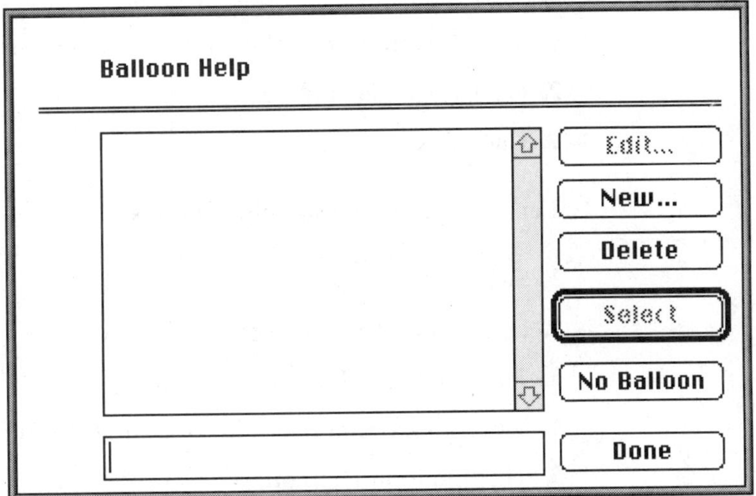

4. Click the **Balloon Help** button.
5. Click the **New** button.
6. Type **Click this button to cancel any changes you have made to the record.**
7. Click **OK**.
8. Type **Cancel Button** as the name of the help message.
9. Click the **Select** button.
10. Click **OK**.

That is all it takes to add a help message and assign it to an object on a layout. Now let's add one to the Save button:

1. Double-click the **Save** button.
2. Click the **Balloon Help** button.
3. Click the **New** button.
4. Type **Click this button to save the record.**

5. Click **OK**.
6. Type **Save Button** as the name of the help message.
7. Click the **Select** button.
8. Click **OK**.

Let's try out these two help balloons.

1. Switch to the User environment.
2. Double-click on any record.
3. Turn Balloon Help on.
4. Move the pointer over the **Save** and **Cancel** buttons.
5. Turn Balloon Help off.
6. Click the **Cancel** button.

The biggest advantage to adding help balloons at the layout level is that they can be shared with other objects on the same layout or on other layouts. For example, when you add more files to your database, you will probably have more input layouts. Your other input layouts will probably have Save and Cancel buttons. You could use the help messages you just created for all the Save and Cancel buttons you create on all of your input layouts for this database.

Some Tips on Writing Balloons

It may seem at first that writing help messages is a fairly easy and straightforward task. However, there are several important guidelines to follow when writing balloons:

- Describe what the user will accomplish by using the item.
- Use the fewest words possible. The shorter the message, the more likely it will be read.

- Write extra balloons for hidden conditions. If checking a checkbox is going to create a condition that is not obvious, let the user know about it.
- Some objects on the screen don't have names. Don't assign them names in your help messages unless the name helps the user.
- If an object on the screen has a name, don't refer to it by name in the help message.
- If there is more than one way to do something, describe the simplest method.
- Only describe the item the user is pointing to. If you start describing other items, your messages can get too complex and difficult to read.

The book *Apple Computer's Macintosh Interface Guildlines* published by Addison-Wesley has a section on writing help balloons. I highly recommend it.

I Think Balloon Help Is Dumb

Some people have criticized Balloon Help as being "too cute to be useful". I must admit that I myself was a critic of Balloon Help until one day when I found a file in my system folder that I didn't recognize. I wasn't interested enough in finding out what this mystery file was to look through a bunch of manuals. Then I remembered about Balloon Help. The Balloon Help message for the file told me that this file was for the Macintosh Quadra 700 and 900 only. I, unfortunately, don't have a Macintosh Quadra 700 or 900 so I deleted the file.

"Too cute" is a criticism that Apple had to overcome in the early days of the Macintosh. I suppose it's mostly cultural. In many Western cultures there is an assumption that anything that is attractive couldn't possibly have any brains behind it. Apple has successfully overcome this criticism and the graphic user interface is now accepted by most as the most intuitive, productive, and easy-to-use interface that a computer can have.

Balloon Help provides the user with an easy to use, context-sensitive help system based on a simple metaphor that anyone who has read a comic strip can understand. If you are developing a database for others to use, remember, they don't know how to use the database (or maybe even the computer) as well as you do. Users are notorious for not reading manuals. Balloon Help is built-in, takes almost no time to add to your database, and is consistent with other applications that take advantage of this easy to use help system.

MULTIPLE PAGE INPUT LAYOUTS

All of the fields from the Customers file fit easily on the New Input layout you have created. However, there may be times when you will need to display more objects than will fit on the screen. Squeezing all of your objects into one screen is not a good solution. You need room to arrange fields and objects into logic groups and place them properly on the layout. Also, if a layout becomes too cluttered, it is more difficult to use. When this situation occurs you have two options:

- Create a layout that is longer or wider than the screen.
- Create a layout with multiple pages; each page being the size of the screen.

If you create a layout that is longer or wider than the screen, the user is going to have to scroll to view some part of the layout. The user may not remember that they need to do this. Also, as the user tabs through the fields, the layout will jump around to show the portion that contains the field the user has tabbed into.

Creating a multiple page input layout is a better solution. Flipping through pages is a metaphor that everyone understands. You can put the most important information on the first page of the layout and less important information on subsequent pages. While there is no actual limit to the number of pages a layout can have, a practical limit is around five pages. The more objects a layout has, the longer the layout will take to open. Also, with more than five pages to navigate through, you might lose the user somewhere along the way.

At the bottom of the layout palette in the Layout Editor there are two icons for moving to the next page or previous page of a layout. When you are on the last page of a layout and you click the Next page icon, 4D asks if you want to add another page to this layout. In the lower-right corner of the Layout Editor is a box that displays the layout page number and the total number of pages that the layout has. Figure 12.31 points out the icons and page numbers.

Although there is no need for a second page to be added to the New Input layout, let's add one anyway to help you understand how to add pages to layouts you might create in the future:

1. Switch to the Design environment.
2. Open the New Input layout in the Layout Editor.
3. Click the Next page icon in the Layout palette.
4. Click **OK**.

You have just added a second page to the New Input layout. Notice that the page indicator in the lower-right corner now reads *2/2*. This means that you are on page 2 of 2 total pages. You use the Next page and Previous page icons to navigate and create pages in the Layout Editor. In order for the user to be able to navigate through the pages of your layout, you will need to add buttons. Fortunately, 4D has automatic actions

FIGURE 12.31

The Layout Editor

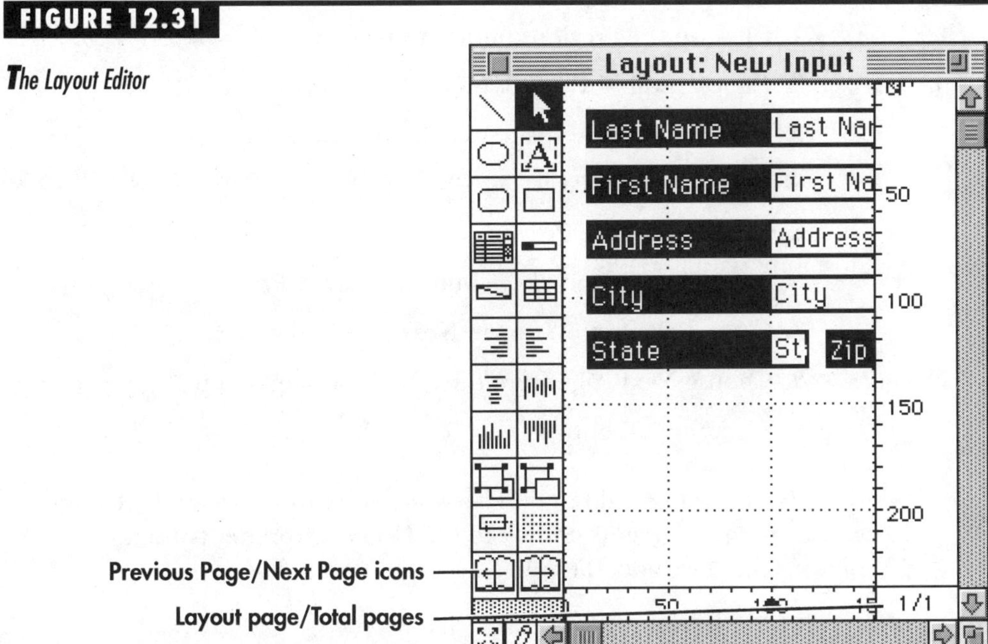

for moving between pages of a layout. Let's add a Previous Page button:

1. Click the Active Object icon in the layout palette.
2. Draw a button about 100 pixels wide by 20 pixels tall in the lower-left corner of your layout.
3. Type **bPrevPage** as the name of the button.
4. Press the Tab key.
5. Type **Previous** as the button text.
6. Choose Button from the Type pop-up menu.
7. Choose Previous Page from the Action pop-up menu.
8. Click **OK**.

Now, when the user moves to this page they will have a button that will take them back to the page they came from. The next step is to add a button to the first page that will take you to this page. You have already created a Previous page button. You can use this button to save you some time when creating a Next page button.

1. Click on the Previous button to select it.
2. Choose Edit ➤ Copy (⌘-C).
3. Click the Previous page icon in the layout palette.
4. Choose Edit ➤ Paste (⌘-V).
5. Double-click the **Previous** button.
6. Change the name of the button to **bNextPage**.
7. Change the button text to **Next**.
8. Choose Next Page from the Action pop-up menu.
9. Click the **OK** button.

By now you should understand how to move between the Design and User environments. Switch to the User environment and try out the buttons you have added to the New Input layout.

CREATING LAYOUTS FOR USE AS REPORTS

So far you have been using layouts to help you find records, edit records, and add new records. Layouts can also be used to create reports and forms. An input layout looks similiar to a form and an output layout looks similiar to a report. You can create layouts that are designed specifically to print forms (like invoices, purchase orders, checks) or reports (like customer lists, daily invoice summaries).

Any layout can be printed. However, the layouts you design for use as input layouts are going to have buttons on them and other objects that you probably wouldn't want showing up on a form. Also, the layouts you design for use as output layouts typically are not going to look exactly the way you want your columnar reports to look. Some layouts you create will be used as input layouts for the screen, some layouts will be used as output layouts for the screen, while others will be used for printing only.

The term "output layout" typically refers to layouts that are used to display several records simultaneously on the screen. However, any time you print, it is the current output layout that is used for printing. You may design a layout for use only in printing a report. Although the layout is never used on the screen, during printing, it is the current output layout. In this case, the output is going to the printer instead of the screen.

OUTPUT CONTROL LINES

You probably noticed that your layouts all have four horizontal lines running across them each with a small triangle in the right ruler. These lines are called output control lines. Each line defines an area of the layout. Figure 12.32 shows the four output control lines. These lines can be moved up or down to increase or decrease the area that they represent. To move a line, you click on the triangle to the right of the line and drag it up or down.

Output control lines are used by output layouts. Consequentially, the output control lines have no effect on input layouts.

FIGURE 12.32

The output control lines

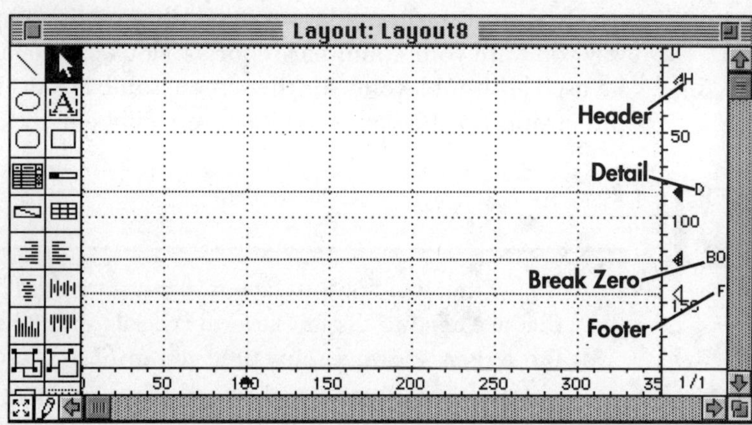

The Header Line

The line marked with an *H*, for example, is the header line. The area from this line to the top of the layout is the header. If you are using a layout as an output layout for the screen, the header area would be at the top of the screen. Figure 12.33 shows an example output layout and points out the header area. If you are using a layout for printing a columnar report, the header area would print at the top of each page. Figure 12.34 shows an example report and points out the header area.

When you are creating output layouts, the most common items that appear in the header area are the column labels. When you are creating layouts for printing columnar reports, you might put the report title, the current date, or the page number in the header area.

FIGURE 12.33

The header area in an output layout

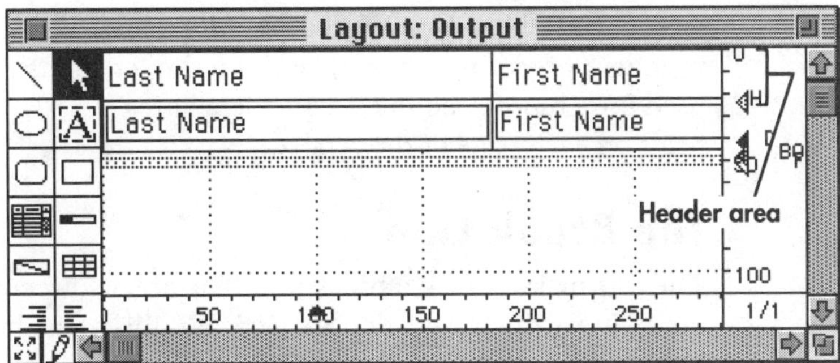

The Detail Line

The line marked with a *D* is the detail line. The area between the D line and the H line is the detail area of the layout. Whether you are using a layout as an output layout or to print a report, the detail area prints once for each record in the current selection. Figure 12.35 shows an example layout and points out the detail area. Typically, the detail area will have

FIGURE 12.34

The header area in a columnar report

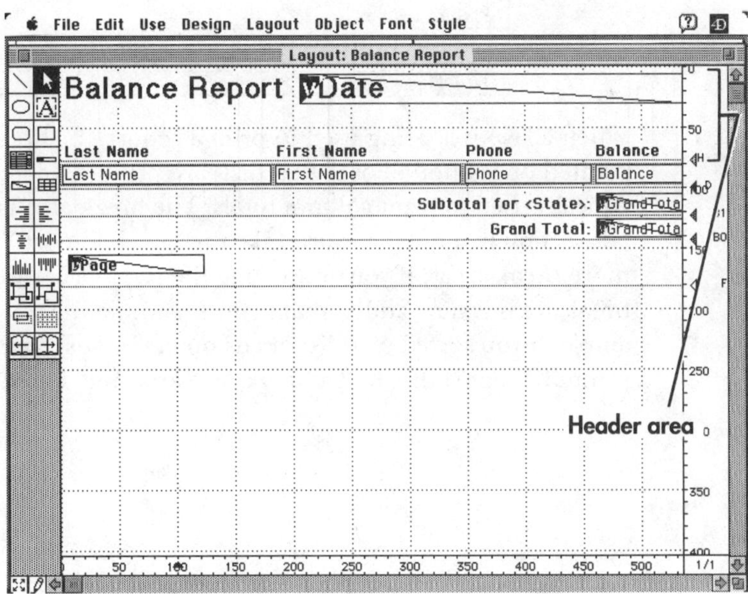

the fields from your file in it. If the layout is used for output to the screen, you will want the detail area to be small to allow the maximum number of records to be displayed on the screen. If the layout is being used for a report, the smaller the detail area is, the more records will print on each page of the report.

The Break Line

The line marked *B0* is a break line. The area between the BO line and the *D* line is the break area. Specicfically, this break line is the break zero line. In an output layout, after the detail area is displayed for every record that will fit on the screen, the break zero area is displayed once.

FIGURE 12.35

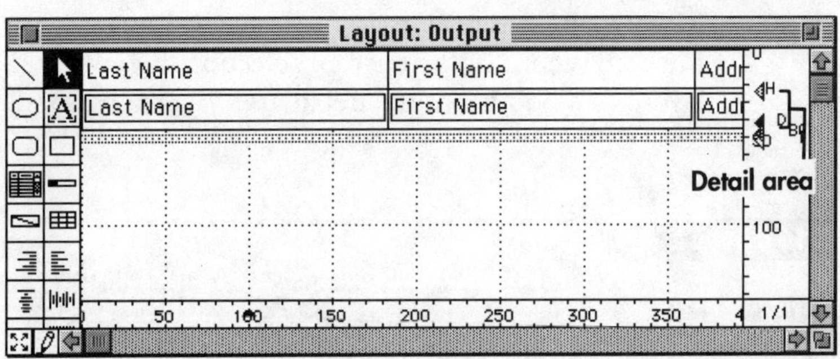

The detail area of an output layout

When a layout is being used to print a report, the break zero area is printed once after all of the records are printed. In a report, this area is typically used to print column totals. The break area is similar to the Totals section in a quick report. Like the Quick Report Editor, you can add more break areas. If you are sorting the records before printing them, break areas can be added that print each time the sort changes. For example, if you sorted your list of customers by Last Name and then printed a report that had a break zero area and a break one area, the break one area would print each time the Last Name changed. If you were sorting two fields, you could add another break area (break area two) that would print each time the second field you sorted on changed. Figure 12.36 shows an example report that is sorted by State and then by Company Name and points out the break one and break two areas.

FIGURE 12.36

An example report showing break areas

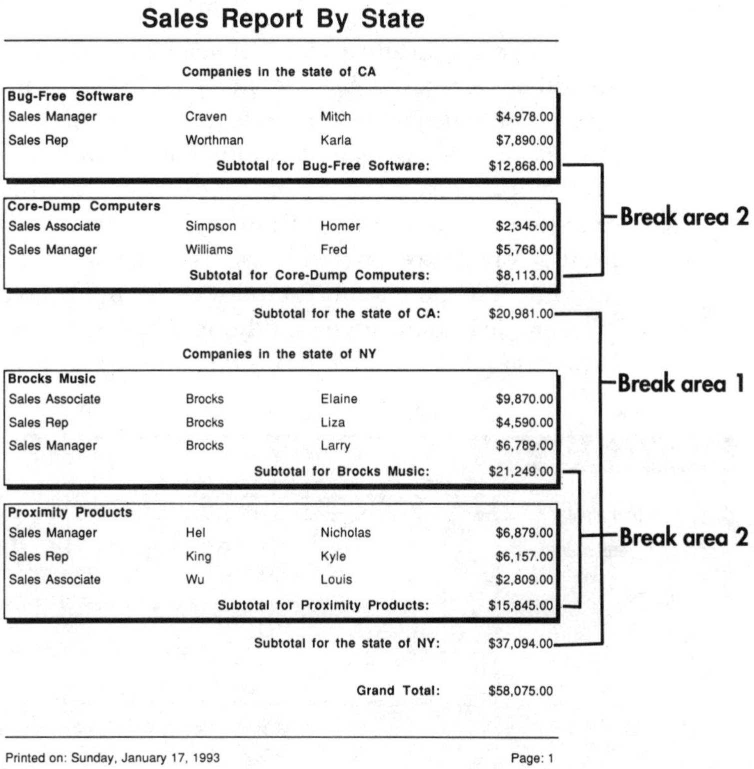

Sales Report By State

Companies in the state of CA

Bug-Free Software			
Sales Manager	Craven	Mitch	$4,978.00
Sales Rep	Worthman	Karla	$7,890.00
	Subtotal for Bug-Free Software:		$12,868.00
Core-Dump Computers			
Sales Associate	Simpson	Homer	$2,345.00
Sales Manager	Williams	Fred	$5,768.00
	Subtotal for Core-Dump Computers:		$8,113.00
	Subtotal for the state of CA:		$20,981.00

Companies in the state of NY

Brocks Music			
Sales Associate	Brocks	Elaine	$9,870.00
Sales Rep	Brocks	Liza	$4,590.00
Sales Manager	Brocks	Larry	$6,789.00
	Subtotal for Brocks Music:		$21,249.00
Proximity Products			
Sales Manager	Hel	Nicholas	$6,879.00
Sales Rep	King	Kyle	$6,157.00
Sales Associate	Wu	Louis	$2,809.00
	Subtotal for Proximity Products:		$15,845.00
	Subtotal for the state of NY:		$37,094.00
	Grand Total:		$58,075.00

Printed on: Sunday, January 17, 1993 Page: 1

Break area 2

Break area 1

Break area 2

To create a break area, hold down the option key and click on a break line. To delete a break area, hold down the ⌘ key and click on the break line you want to delete.

You can also add additional header lines. The header lines you create will be numbered just like the break lines. If you added one header line, it would be labeled H1. The next would be labeled H2 and so on. Each header line is associated with a break line. The H1 area is going to print before the first group of records created by the first field you sorted on. Say you sorted on Last Name and then First Name. The H1 area will print before the records with a specific last name. Next, the records with the same last name will print followed by the B1 area. Figure 12.37 shows an example layout with two additional header areas and two additional break areas. Figure 12.38 shows the same layout printed as a report.

FIGURE 12.37

A layout with multiple header and break areas

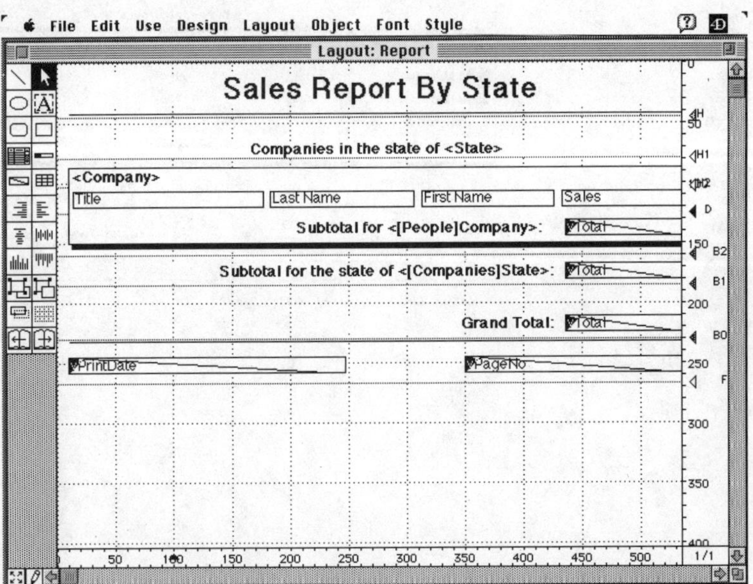

FIGURE 12.38

The same layout printed as a report

Sales Report By State

Companies in the state of CA

Bug-Free Software			
Sales Manager	Craven	Mitch	$4,978.00
Sales Rep	Worthman	Karla	$7,890.00
	Subtotal for Bug-Free Software:		$12,868.00

Core-Dump Computers			
Sales Associate	Simpson	Homer	$2,345.00
Sales Manager	Williams	Fred	$5,768.00
	Subtotal for Core-Dump Computers:		$8,113.00

Subtotal for the state of CA: $20,981.00

Companies in the state of NY

Brocks Music			
Sales Associate	Brocks	Elaine	$9,870.00
Sales Rep	Brocks	Liza	$4,590.00
Sales Manager	Brocks	Larry	$6,789.00
	Subtotal for Brocks Music:		$21,249.00

Proximity Products			
Sales Manager	Hel	Nicholas	$6,879.00
Sales Rep	King	Kyle	$6,157.00
Sales Associate	Wu	Louis	$2,809.00
	Subtotal for Proximity Products:		$15,845.00

Subtotal for the state of NY: $37,094.00

Grand Total: $58,075.00

Printed on: Friday, January 6, 1995 Page: 1

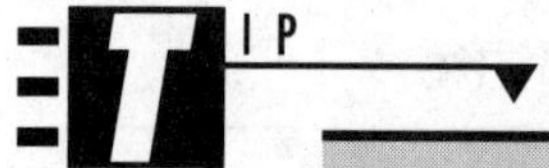

You add and delete additional header areas the same way you add and delete additional break areas.

The Footer Line

The line marked with a *F* is the footer line. The area between the F line and the B0 line is the footer area. The footer area is not displayed on the screen in the User environment. However, it is displayed when the layout is used in the Runtime environment. You will learn how to do this in *Chapter 15*. The footer is the only area that can have buttons in an output layout. Buttons will not function in any other area. You might add buttons to print a specific report, sort the records, search for all of your invoices are past due and display them, etc. Figure 12.39 shows an output layout in the Runtime environment that has buttons in the footer area.

FIGURE 12.39

The footer area of an output layout in the Runtime environment

File Edit

Custom

Last Name	First Name	Address	City
Brown	John	123 Diskette Drive	Sunnyvale
Jones	Sally	14 Pear Street	Irvine
Williams	Ted	4501 Evelyn Avenue	Sunnyvale
Simpson	Joan	921 Maple Street	Anchorage
Smith	Ron	29 Old Town #5	Newport N
Kimball	Margaret	22 East Main Street	Framingha

Print Search Sort Done

When you are printing a layout as a report, the footer area is printed at the bottom of each page. You might place the page number, current date, current time or other useful information in this area when printing a report as shown in Figure 12.40.

FIGURE 12.40

The footer area on a printed report

Sales Report By State

Companies in the state of CA

Bug-Free Software			
Sales Manager	Craven	Mitch	$4,978.00
Sales Rep	Worthman	Karla	$7,890.00
	Subtotal for Bug-Free Software:		$12,868.00

Core-Dump Computers			
Sales Associate	Simpson	Homer	$2,345.00
Sales Manager	Williams	Fred	$5,768.00
	Subtotal for Core-Dump Computers:		$8,113.00

Subtotal for the state of CA: $20,981.00

Companies in the state of NY

Brocks Music			
Sales Associate	Brocks	Elaine	$9,870.00
Sales Rep	Brocks	Liza	$4,590.00
Sales Manager	Brocks	Larry	$6,789.00
	Subtotal for Brocks Music:		$21,249.00

Proximity Products			
Sales Manager	Hel	Nicholas	$6,879.00
Sales Rep	King	Kyle	$6,157.00
Sales Associate	Wu	Louis	$2,809.00
	Subtotal for Proximity Products:		$15,845.00

Subtotal for the state of NY: $37,094.00

Grand Total: $58,075.00

Printed on: Friday, January 6, 1995 Page: 1

You can move an output control line and all the lines below it at the same time by holding down the Shift key while you drag a line.

PRINTING FORMS

Layouts can be used to print full page forms. For example, you might want to print a form that shows account information about a customer. Perhaps you database is tracking invoices. You will probably need a layout that prints an invoice that you can send to the customer. Figure 12.41 shows an example of a layout printed as a form. In these cases, you are printing one record per page instead of multiple records per page. To set up a layout to print this way is simple. All you need to do is make the detail area as large as the page by moving it to the bottom of the layout page.

The layout area you have to work with is about 1245 square feet. When a layout is printed, only so much of the layout will fit on the printed page. The height and width of a layout is based on the Page Setup dialog box. When you have a layout open in the Layout Editor, choosing File ➤ Page Setup will display the Page Setup dialog box and indicate what size page the layout is expecting to print on. If you have your page size set to US Letter, then the height of the layout is 11" and the width is 8½". The height and width of a page is indicated on the layout by grey lines. Figure 12.42 points out these lines that mark the bottom and right side of the layout.

FIGURE 12.41

An expense report form

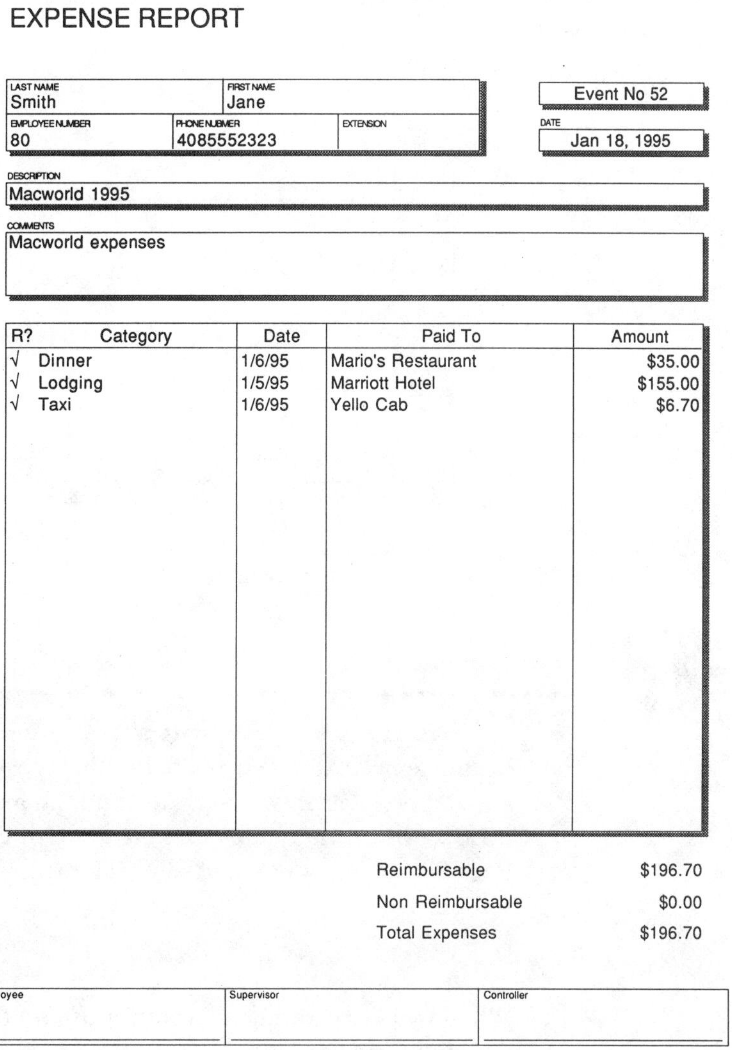

EXPENSE REPORT

LAST NAME	FIRST NAME	
Smith	Jane	
EMPLOYEE NUMBER	PHONE NUMBER	EXTENSION
80	4085552323	

Event No 52

DATE
Jan 18, 1995

DESCRIPTION
Macworld 1995

COMMENTS
Macworld expenses

R?	Category	Date	Paid To	Amount
√	Dinner	1/6/95	Mario's Restaurant	$35.00
√	Lodging	1/5/95	Marriott Hotel	$155.00
√	Taxi	1/6/95	Yello Cab	$6.70

Reimbursable	$196.70
Non Reimbursable	$0.00
Total Expenses	$196.70

Employee	Supervisor	Controller

FIGURE 12.42

The layout width and height lines

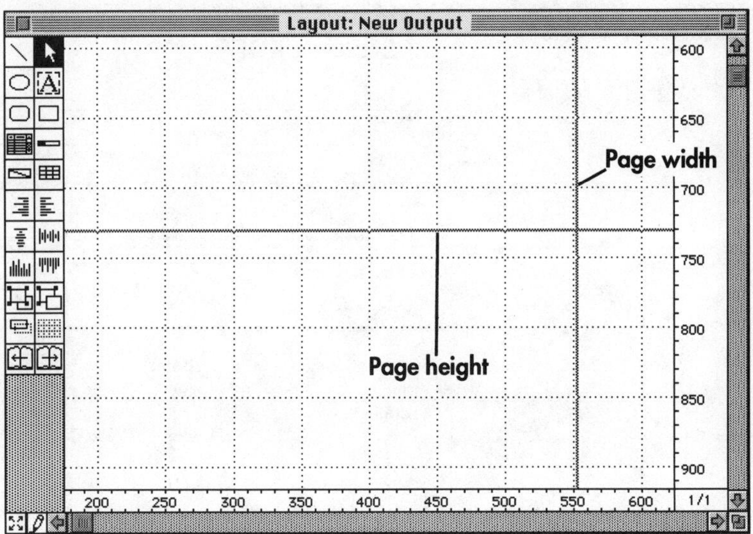

When you are printing to a laser printer, the actual printable area of a page is smaller than page itself. There is about a one half inch margin around the page. You reduce this size of the margin by clicking the Options button in the Page Setup dialog box and selecting the Larger Print Area option.

When you are creating a layout for use on the screen, you can use as much of the layout as you want. However, when you are creating a layout for printing, the layout can be only as wide as one page. If the layout is longer than one page, the additional layout pages will print as additional printed pages.

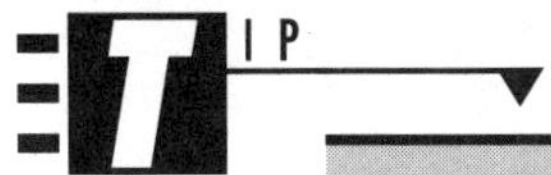

If you are getting extra blank pages when printing, you might have an object below the bottom of the page on the layout.

When you create full page layouts to be printed as forms, make sure that the output control lines are all above the bottom of the printable first page of the layout. Otherwise, 4D will think that the area you want to print is larger than one printable page and an extra blank page will printed.

MAIL MERGE

Another use for full page layouts is for doing a *mail merge*. In most cases, the term "mail merge" means to print a letter with fields from a database inserted inside the text of the letter. If you haven't heard the term "mail merge" before, you have probably heard another term that means basically the same thing: form letter. We have all received form letters at one time or another.

Say you wanted to print letters to your customers letting them know what their current account balances are. You could do this by creating a text object the size of one page, then typing the text of the letter inside the text object. Fields from your database can be inserted inside the text allowing you to use the data from your records in sentences.

Creating a Form Letter

Let's create a form letter:

1. Switch to the Design environment. You can close the New Input and New Output layouts if you wish.
2. Choose Design ➤ Layout (⌘-L).
3. Click the **New** button.

4. Click on the Custom layout template.
5. Type **Form Letter** as the name of the new layout.
6. Click the **OK** button to create the new layout.

Adding Today's Date to the Form Letter

You have just created a blank layout. The next step is to move the detail, break zero, and footer output control lines to the bottom of the page. After that, you might want today's date to appear at the top of the letter. In order to have today's date appear automatically, we need to use a *variable.*

A variable is like a field but the data is not saved. You can think of a variable as a sort of temporary field that is only saved in memory and not on disk. This variable will hold today's date. Next, we will need to give the variable instructions that automatically assign today's date to the variable. We will do this using a *script.* A script is a set of instructions given to an object. You will learn more about scripts in *Chapter 14.*

1. Drag the Header line to the top of the layout.
2. While holding down the Shift key, drag the Detail line to the bottom of the layout page. Make sure that the Footer line doesn't got below the bottom of the page.
3. Scroll back up to the top of the layout.
4. Click on the Active Object tool to select it.
5. In the upper-left corner of the layout, draw an active object about 20 pixels high by 200 pixels wide.
6. Type **vDate** as the name of the object.
7. Choose Non-enterable from the Type pop-up menu.
8. The Format pop-up menu is hierarchical, so choose Date. When you choose Date, another pop-up will appear. Choose Long from that pop-up menu.
9. Deselect the Script Only If Modified checkbox.
10. Click the Script button.
11. Click the **OK** button.

12. Type **vDate:=Current date** into the Script: vDate window.
13. Close the Script: vDate window.

You just created a variable called vDate. The script **vDate:=Current date** tells 4D to assign today's date to the variable vDate. Each time the Form Letter layout is printed, today's date will be printed automatically at the spot where the vDate object is on the layout. Next, you need to create a text object that will contain the text of the letter.

1. Click on the Text tool in the layout palette to select it.
2. Click and hold the mouse button down in the upper-left corner of the layout just below the vDate object.
3. Drag to the lower-right corner of the layout page. Make sure that you don't drag below the Detail line or to the right of the right margin line.
4. Release the mouse button.
5. Scroll back to the upper-left corner of the layout.

Inserting Fields into a Text Object

The text object appears as a large, blank area on the layout with an insertion point flashing in the upper-left corner. Now that you have created the text object, the next step is to insert the text of the letter. You will also want to include some fields from the database in the letter. Let's add the customer's name and address to the top of the letter.

1. While holding down the Option key, click and hold down the mouse button inside the text object.
2. Choose First Name from the Fields pop-up menu.

When you hold down the Option key and click inside a text object on a layout, 4D presents a pop-up menu of the fields from the file that the layout belongs to. When you select a field name from this list, the field is inserted into the text object. When the layout is printed, the contents of the field for the record being printed will be inserted into the letter where the field name appears.

3. Press the spacebar once to enter a space character.
4. Insert the Last Name field into the letter.
5. Press the Return key to move to the next line.
6. Insert the Address field into the letter.
7. Press the Return key to move to the next line.
8. Insert the City field into the letter.
9. Type a comma and a space into the letter.
10. Insert the State field into the letter.
11. Type a space.
12. Insert the Zip Code field into the letter.

Now that you have insert the customer's name and address, let's type the text of the letter.

1. Press Return twice to add a few lines in between the address and the body of the letter.
2. Type **Dear** and a space.
3. Insert the First Name field.
4. Type a colon and press Return twice.
5. Type the following letter:

    You are one of our most valued customers. Your purchases total <Balance;$###,##0.00> this year alone! We are just sending you this letter to let you know that you now qualify for a 10 percent discount on all of your future orders.
    Thank you for patronage.

    Sincerely,
    Nicholas Hel
    Proximity Products, Inc.

When 4D sees the less than (<) and greater than (>) signs, it assumes that whatever is between them is the name of a field or variable. If you add a semicolon you can type a format to format text or numeric values.

The text is in 9 point type which is a bit small. Let's change the font size to 12 point.

1. Select the Arrow tool from the layout palette.
2. Shift-click on the vDate object and the text object to select them both.
3. Choose Style ➤ 12 point.

Printing the Form Letter

Now that you have created the letter, let's print it. We will use the Print Preview function to print the letter to the screen.

1. Switch to the User evironment.
2. Choose File ➤ Print (⌘-P).
3. Click on Form Letter to select it.
4. Click **OK**.
5. Click **OK** in the Page Setup dialog box.
6. Click **Preview on screen** in the Print dialog box.
7. Click **Print** to print the first form letter to the screen.
8. Click the **Zoom** button to view the letter at regular size.
9. Click the mouse anywhere to zoom out.
10. Click the **Next Page** button to view other customer letters.
11. Click **Stop Printing** when you are finished viewing the form letters.

You can see that creating form letters is quite simple. You can make a different layout for each letter and store different letters for different purposes. You can have only one font, font size, and font combination of font styles in a text area. This can be a bit limiting for letters. However, you can get around this limitation by using multiple text areas instead of just one. Another way to create form letters with multiple fonts, sizes, and styles is using 4D Write. 4D Write is a module for 4th Dimension that adds a complete word processor. You can set margins, tabs, fonts, sizes and styles as well as use many other common word processing functions. 4D Write is sold separately. For more information on 4D Write, see *Chapter 20.*

Feel free at this point to switch back to the Design environment and close the Form Letter layout.

MAILING LABELS

The Label Editor is very easy to use and powerful tool for quickly creating and printing labels. However, it has a few of the same limitations in terms of fonts that text objects do. You can use only one font, size, and combination of styles. You also can't add graphics to your labels. There is a solution to this problem.

You may remember the Use Layout checkbox in the Label Editor. Figure 12.43 shows the Label Editor. When you select the Use Layout option, the Label Editor uses the current output layout for printing the

FIGURE 12.43

The Label Editor

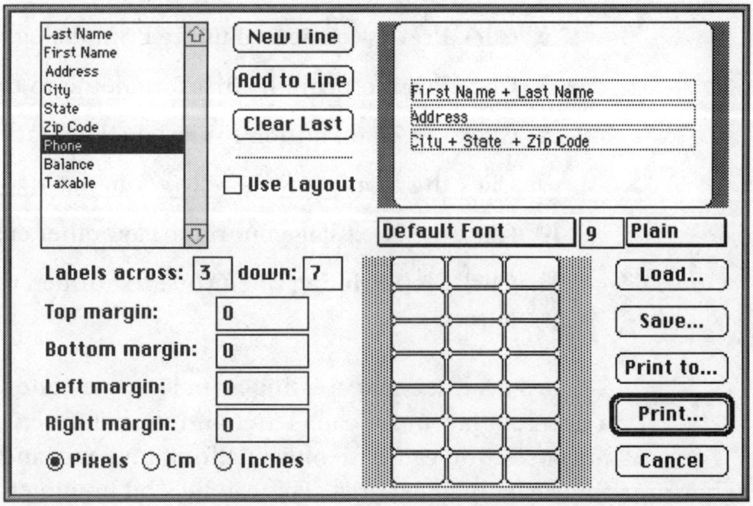

label instead of the fields you have selected in the Label Editor. This means that you can create a layout with graphics, fields, and variables, and use all of the fonts and styles you want. Let's create a layout to use with the Label Editor.

1. Switch to the Design environment.
2. Choose Design ➤ Layout (⌘-L).
3. Click **New**.
4. Click on the Custom layout template.
5. Type **Mailing Label** as the name of the layout.
6. Click **OK**.

The detail output control line defines the height of the labels. If your labels are one inch in height, you would set the detail line at one inch. The width of the label is controlled by the *label width marker*. The label width marker is a small triangle in the horizontal ruler at the bottom of the window in the Layout Editor. Figure 12.44 points out this

FIGURE 12.44

The label width marker

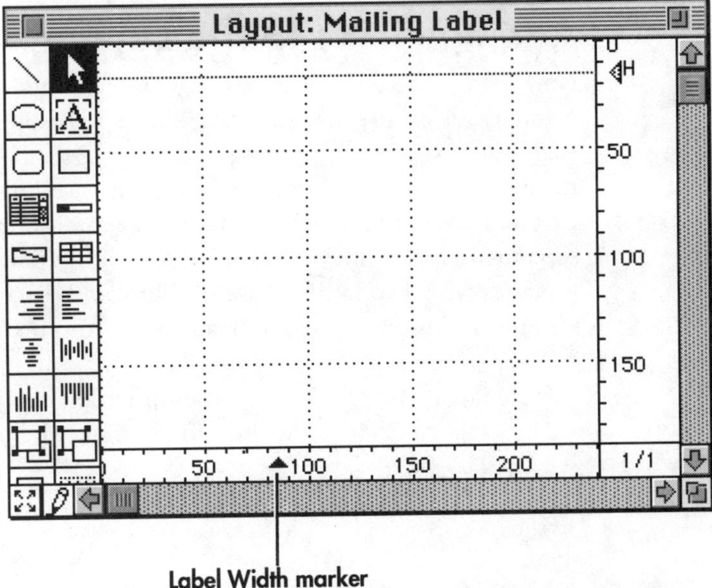

marker. How wide you make the label determines how many labels can be printed across the page. If you have one-up labels, you will want to move the label width marker to the right side of the page.

Setting the Size of the Label

Let's set up the height and width of the label. To make setting the size of the label easier, we can change the type of unit that is used to define the ruler. There are three choices: points, centimeters, and inches. Let's set the rulers to inches. Our labels are going to be one-up and one inch high:

1. Choose Layout ➤ Define Ruler Units.
2. Select Inches.
3. Click **OK**.
4. Move the header line to the top of the layout.
5. Move the detail line to 1 inch.
6. Move the label width marker to the right side of the page (at about 7½ inches).

Adding Fields to the Layout

Now we need to add the fields. If you place the First Name and Last Name fields on the layout, you will have to decide how wide you want each field. Not all names are the same length, so you would have to make the fields long enough for the longest name. This means that most of the first and last names are going to be separated because they are in separate fields. What you want is to have the first name and last name together with a space in between. This can be accomplished using the same technique you used to insert fields into text objects.

1. Create a text object in the upper-left corner of the layout. Figure 12.45 shows how big to make the text object.
2. Insert the First Name field into the text object.

FIGURE 12.45

The first text object on the mailing label.

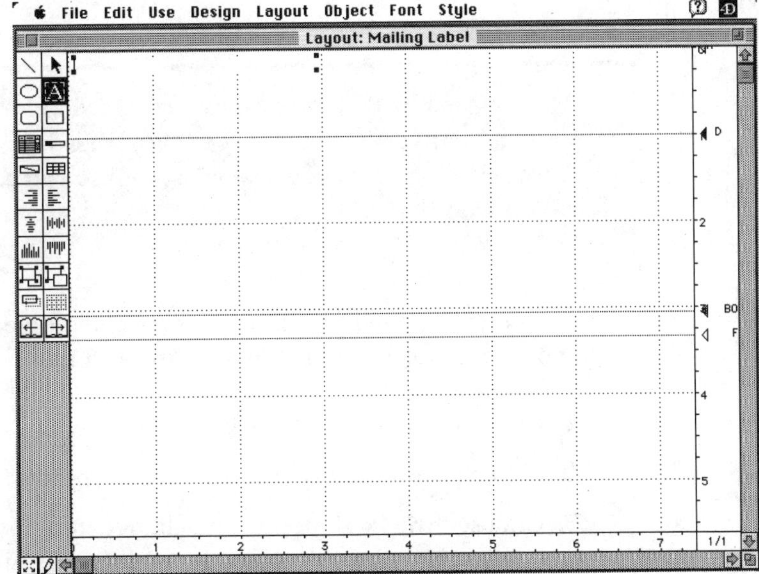

3. Type a space.
4. Insert the Last Name field into the text object.

We will want the customer's name to be in bold and the address in plain text. So we will make a separate text object for the address.

5. Press and hold the ⌘ key and draw another text object below the one containing the First Name and Last Name. Make this the same width but tall enough to hold at least two lines of text.
6. Insert the Address field and press the Return key.
7. Insert the City field and add a comma and a space.
8. Insert the State field and a space.
9. Insert the Zip Code field.

Normally, 4D reselects the Arrow tool after you create an object. If you hold down the ⌘ key when dragging in the Layout Editor, 4D reselects the last tool so you can create an object with that tool.

Let's increase the font size of these two text objects to 12 point and set the object that contains the First Name and Last Name fields to bold.

1. Click on the Arrow tool to select it.
2. Shift-click on each object to select them both.
3. Choose Style ➤ 12 point. The change in point size might collapse the Address object. If this happens, simply click on it and resize it until you can see the City, State, and Zip Code fields.
4. Shift-click the Address text object to deselect it.
5. Choose Style ➤ Bold.

If you Shift-click on an object that is already selected, that object will be deselected and the other selected objects will stay selected.

The last step is to add some graphics to the label to make it look a bit more interesting. Let's draw a box around the text objects:

1. Click on the Rectangle tool and draw a rectangle about three inches wide around the two text objects.

2. Click the Move To Back tool (⌘-B) to move the Rectangle behind the text objects.

Figure 12.46 shows what the finished layout should look like.

FIGURE 12.46

The finished label layout

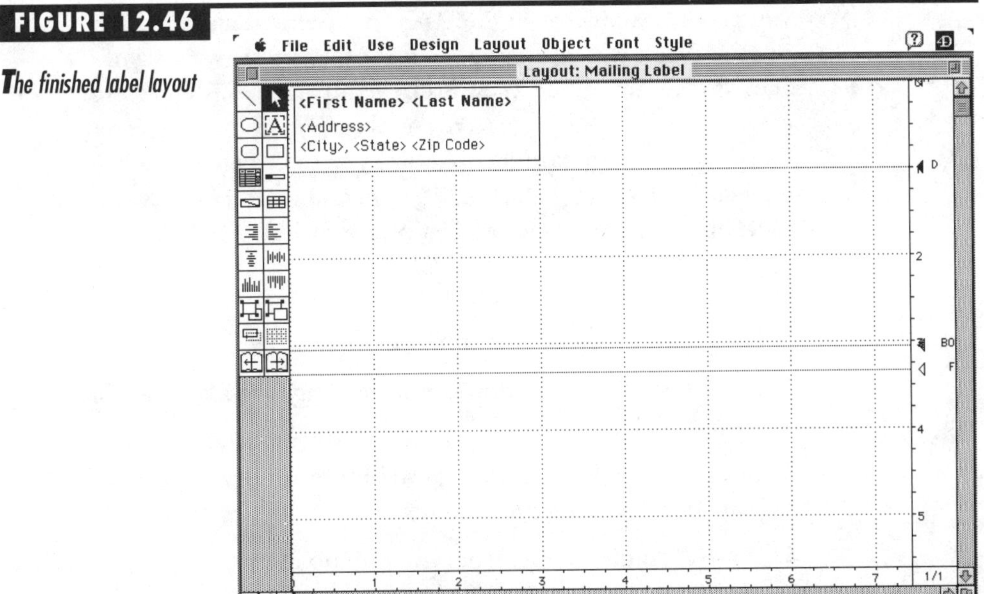

Printing the Labels

Now let's print some labels using this layout. Remember, the Use Layout option in the Label Editor uses the current output layout. So, the first thing we need to do is set the current output layout to the Mailing Label layout.

You have probably seen the List of Files window as you have worked through this book. The List of Files window shows the file names of all the files in your database. You can also switch layouts using the List of Files window. To bring the List of Files window to the front or send it to the back you press ⌘-spacebar. The I and O icons next to the Customers file in the List of Files window are pop-up menus that you use to set the input and output layouts.

Control panels and system extensions have been known to cause conflicts with the ⌘-spacebar key combination. If you press ⌘-spacebar in the User environment and the List of Files window doesn't appear, it means that there is a conflict. For example, the SCSI Probe control panel is known to cause a conflict. Some control panels and system extensions that use key combinations will allow you to change the keys they use. If you can't change the key combination, use ⌘-Shift-Spacebar to toggle the List of Files window.

1. Switch to the User environment.
2. If the List of Files window is not showing, press **⌘-spacebar** to make it appear.
3. Click and hold down the mouse button on the O icon to display the pop-up menu.
4. Choose Mailing Label from the pop-up menu.
5. Choose Report ➤ Labels (⌘-J).
6. Click **OK** in the Page Setup dialog box.
7. Click Use Layout.
8. Click **Print.**
9. Click **Print Preview** in the Print dialog box.
10. Click **Print**.
11. Click **Stop Printing**.
12. Use the List of Files window to set the current output layout to New Output.

You can also switch files and layouts by choosing File ➤ Choose File/Layout (⌘-F).

Feel free at this point to switch back to the Design environment and close the Mailing Label layout.

CREATING COLUMNAR REPORTS

In *Chapter 8* you used the Quick Report Editor to create columnar reports. The Quick Report Editor is by far the fastest way to create these kinds of reports but it has a few limitations. For example, in the Quick Report Editor, you cannot place graphics anywhere on the report. While you do have three different areas that can hold text for the headers and footers, the entire header or footer has to be the same font, font size and style. Also, you can't add graphics to the detail row. So, although the Quick Report Editor is definitely the fastest and easiest way to create columnar reports, there may be times when you need more control over the appearance of the report itself. When you need this level of control, you can use layouts to create columnar reports.

Let's create a columnar report that prints out our customer's last name, first name, phone number (formatted), and balance (formatted). The report will be sorted by State and have balance subtotals for each state that our customers are in. At the bottom of the report we will have a grand total for all of our customers' balances. Figure 12.47 shows what the finished report will look like when it is printed.

FIGURE 12.47

The finished balance report

Balance Report Friday, January 6, 1995

Last Name	First Name	Phone	Balance
Simpson	Joan	(904) 555-3245	$6,750.00
		Subtotal for AK:	$6,750.00
Brown	John	(408) 555-5678	$9,000.00
Jones	Sally	(714) 555-9890	$5,500.00
Williams	Ted	(408) 555-8303	$1,500.00
		Subtotal for CA:	$16,000.00
Kimball	Margaret	(508) 555-7890	$1,050.00
		Subtotal for MA:	$1,050.00
Smith	Ron	(703) 555-3890	$8,877.00
		Subtotal for VA:	$8,877.00
		Grand Total:	$32,677.00

Creating the Report Layout

The first thing we need to do is create a layout. We will need to have the Last Name, First Name, Phone, and Balance fields on the layout. To make creating the layout easier, we will use one of the layout templates.

1. Switch to the Design environment.
2. Choose Design ➤ Layout (⌘-L).
3. Click **New**.
4. Double-click on the Last Name field to select it.

When you double-clicked on the Last Name field, a 1 appeared next to it. You have just selected this field as the first field to appear on the layout when it is created. Let's select the other fields.

5. Double-click the First Name field to select it.
6. Double-click the Phone field to select it.

7. Double-click the Balance field to select it.
8. Click on layout template #2 to select it (column 2 row 1).
9. Type **Balance Report** as the name of the layout.

Figure 12.48 shows what the completed New Layout dialog box should look like.

10. Click **OK**.
11. Click the **Zoom box** to expand the window.

Now you have a layout that has the fields you want already on it. This layout template however, doesn't create a header or break area (for subtotals) or much of a footer. We will need to modify it to complete the report. First, let's format the Phone and Balance fields. You have already created a style for formatting the Phone field, so we can use that style with this layout.

FIGURE 12.48

The completed New Layout dialog box

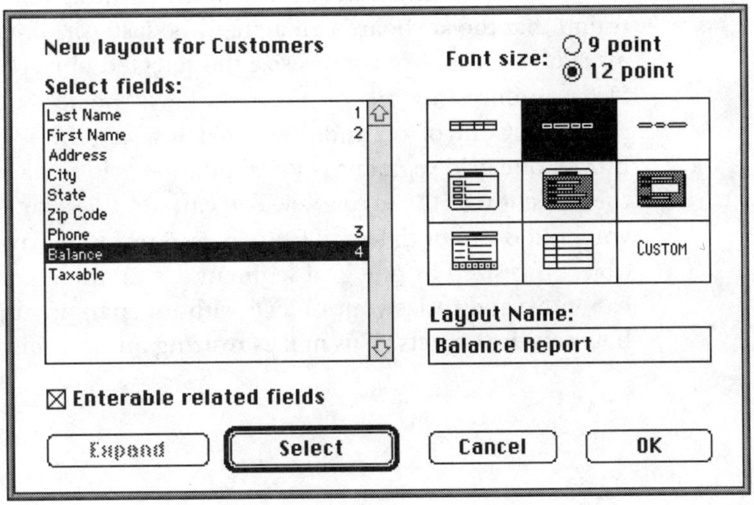

1. Double-click on the Phone field.
2. Choose |Phone Format from the Format pop-up menu.
3. Click **OK**.
4. Double-click on the Balance field.
5. Choose $###,##0.00;($###,#0.00) from the Format pop-up menu.
6. Click **OK**.

If you print the report at this point, you will see that the phone numbers in the formatted form don't quite fit inside the Phone field. The First Name field on the other hand is actually wider than necessary. When you create a layout using the layout templates, 4D estimates how large the field needs to be on the layout based on the type of field it is. For Alpha fields, 4D looks at the maximum number of characters you set in the Field dialog box. In Figure 12.49 you can see that we have set the Phone field to a maximum of 10 characters.

We can make the Phone field wider by making the First Name field narrower. You can use the mouse to make these modifications but I have found that the keyboard can actually be faster in situations like this. You already know that you can resize the selected object by holding down the ⌘ key and pressing one of the arrow keys. You also know that if you hold down the Control key and press an arrow key, the selected object is moved one grid segment (by default, one grid segment is 10 pixels) in the direction of the arrow key. You can use these keys in combination. If you hold down both ⌘ and Control and press an arrow key, the selected object is resized by one grid segment. Using these key combinations, you can move and resize your objects without changing the relative distance between the objects. This makes resizing and moving objects a lot faster,

FIGURE 12.49

The Field dialog box displaying the Phone field

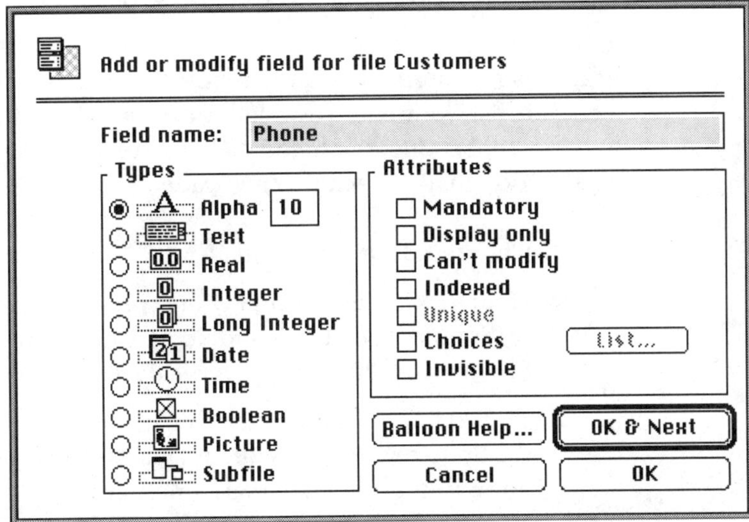

because you don't spending time trying to line objects up with each other using the mouse. Let's try it:

1. Click on the First Name field to select it.
2. While holding down the ⌘ and **Control** keys, press the **Left Arrow** key twice.
3. Click on the dotted line between the First Name and Phone fields.
4. Hold down the **Control key** and press the **Left Arrow** key twice to move the line to the left next to the First Name field.
5. Click on the Phone field to select it.
6. Hold down the **Control** key and press the **Left Arrow** key twice to move the Phone field.
7. Hold down both the ⌘ and **Control** keys and press the **Right Arrow** key twice to make the Phone field wider.

Creating the Header Area

The header prints at the top of every page. You might want to make the header big enough to hold the report title, the field labels, and perhaps a graphic like your company logo. In the header for this report, we will have the report title, the field labels and today's date. The first thing we need to do is make room for the header.

1. Choose Edit ➤ Select All (⌘-A).
2. Hold down the **Control** key and press the **Down Arrow** key eight times. The fields should now be positioned between 80 and 100 pixels on the vertical ruler.
3. The B0 line is on top of the Detail line. While holding down the Shift key, drag the B0 line marker (the triangle) down to the 150 pixel mark on the ruler.
4. Drag the Detail line marker down to the 100 pixel mark on the ruler.
5. Drag the Header line marker down so that it is a few pixels above the fields.

You now have room for the header. The next step is to add the name of the report to the header area.

6. Click on the Text tool to select it.
7. Create a text object about 200 pixels wide in the header area near the left edge of the layout.
8. Type **Balance Report** in the text area.
9. Use the Font and Style menus to set the font, style, and size of the report title to something that looks nice to you (I like report titles to be in large, bold letters).

Now we need labels for the fields. On this report, the reader would know right away what the data was in the columns just by looking at it. However, this is not always the case and it makes the report easier to read if the columns have titles. Let's add column titles for all the fields.

1. Click the Text tool to select it.
2. Create a text object above the Last Name field. Make the object as wide as the field and make sure that the object is above the header line.
3. Type **Last Name** as the name for the column title.
4. Use the Font and Style menus to make the object Geneva, Bold, 12 point.
5. Create column titles for the First Name, Phone, and Balance fields.

It is always helpful to have the date the report was printed on the report itself. This way, if someone reads the report, they will know that the data on the report is accurate to a certain date. If the report is fairly old, they won't confuse the data on the report with current data.

You have already created an object that prints the current date on a layout. This object is called vDate and it is on the Form letter layout. You can copy this object from the Form Letter Layout to the Balance Report layout. This will save you the time of recreating the object again. While this object is simple, and could be recreated quickly, you may create other objects or groups of objects that would take more time to create again.

1. Choose Design ➤ Layout (⌘-L).
2. Click **Expand** to display the list of layouts for the Customers file.
3. Click on Form Letter to select it.
4. Click **Open**.
5. Click on the vDate object to select it.
6. Choose Edit ➤ Copy (⌘-C).
7. Close the Form Letter layout.
8. Choose Edit ➤ Paste (⌘-V).
9. Move the vDate object to the right of the report title.

10. Set the vDate object to the same font, style, and size as the report title. If you have choosen a large font size, you might want to make the vDate object wider to allow the entire date in long format to print.

Adding a Grand Total

Column totals are quite common in reports. Adding column totals to reports is easy. You have already used a variable to display today's date. You will use another variable to store the grand total for the Balance field. To get today's date into the vDate object, you wrote a simple script. Another script is required to put the total for the Balance field into the object you will create to hold it.

1. Click the Active Object tool to select it.
2. Draw an active object about the same size as the Balance field and place it under the Balance field in the B0 area.
3. Type **vGrandTotal** as the name of the object.
4. Choose $###,##0.00;($###,##0.00) from the Format pop-up menu.
5. De-select the Script only if modified checkbox.
6. Click the **Script** button.
7. Click **OK**.
8. Type **vGrandTotal:=Subtotal(balance)** into the Script: vGrandTotal window.
9. Close the Script: vGrandTotal window.
10. Click on the vGrandTotal object to select it.
11. Choose Style ➤ 12 point.
12. Create a text object to the left of the vGrandTotal object.
13. Type **Grand Total:** into the text object.
14. Choose Style ➤ Right.

15. Resize the text object so that it is at least 150 pixels wide.

16. Choose Style ➤ 12 point.

The script of the vGrandTotal variable tells 4D to put the subtotal of Balance field into the vGrandTotal variable. The subtotal function is used to get the subtotal of a field at any break level. Since this variable is in break level zero, 4D knows that you want a subtotal for all the records in the report.

Adding Subtotals by State

While having a grand total is certainly useful, you may also have a need to have totals for all the records in a category. Say you wanted a total for each state where you have customers. One way to accomplish this would be to search the database for all the customers in a state and then print the balance report. You could do this for each state to get the information you needed. While this would work, it would be time-consuming, inefficient and unnecessary. You can get totals by state easily using *subtotals*.

In order to get a subtotal, you need to bring together the records that belong to the same group or category. For example, if you want subtotals by State, you need to have all the records for each state grouped together. You do this by sorting. In 4D you can sort your records on up to 16 fields. Sorting brings all the records with the same values together based on the field you have sorted on. Each time the data in a sorted field changes, a *break* is generated. The term break is used because you are breaking one group of like information out from the next group. A break is simply the point between two records that have different values for the field you sorted on. For example, if you sort by Last Name and then by First Name, a break would be generated each time the Last Name changed and each time the First Name changed. The break generated by the First Name field is called *break one* or *break level one* because it was generated by the first field you sorted on. When the data in the First Name field changes from one record to the next, a break level two will be generated because First Name is the second field you sorted on. While you can sort on up to 16 fields, you can only have 10 break levels (nine plus break level zero). Your balance report has an area called break level zero (B0). Break level zero is generated at the very end of the report. You can create additional break areas. When the break is generated, the corresponding break area is printed.

You have already used the Subtotal function to get the grand total for all the records in the current selection. Because you used the Subtotal function in a script of an object (vTotal) that is in the break zero area, 4D generated a subtotal for that break level. In this case, the total would be for all the records in the current selection. To get a total for each state, we will need to sort the records by State and create a break area to be printed each time the value in the State field changes. Since the State field is the first field we are sorting on, the break area will be break area one (B1). Let's create the break one (B1) area on the balance report layout.

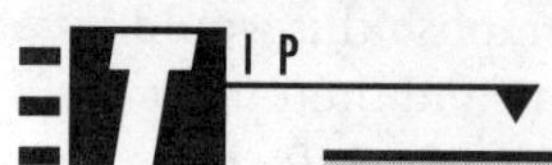

If you hold down the Option key and click on a break line marker, 4D creates another break area. If you hold down the ⌘ key and click on a break line marker, 4D deletes the break line.

1. While holding down the option key, click on the B0 line marker and drag down to the midpoint between the B0 line marker and the F line marker.
2. Drag the B1 line so that it is just below the vGrandTotal object.

The area between the B1 line and the D line is the break level one area. This area will be printed each time the data in the State field changes because the State field is the first field we are sorting on. Although your text says Grand Total, at this point you would get a subtotal for each state since the vTotal object is in the break one area. The next step is to simply duplicate the two items in the B1 area and put the copy in the B0 area. This way, you will have both a subtotal by state and a grand total.

1. Shift-select the Grand Total text object and the vTotal active object.

2. Choose **Object ➤ Duplicate** (⌘-D) or click on the Duplicate tool.
3. Drag the duplicated objects into the B0 area.
4. Click on the Text tool to select it.
5. Change *Grand Total* in the B1 area to **Subtotal for <State>:**.

Now you will have subtotals for each state (break level one) and a grand total at the end of the report (break level zero). By typing <State> into the text, we are embedding the contents of the State field into the text. Each time the break one area is printed, the State will be printed in the break area to let us know which state the total is for.

You might be thinking that 4D is going to confuse the subtotals with the grand total because they use the same variable. In fact, 4D keeps track of subtotals for each break level separately in memory and uses the variable on the layout only to display the results.

The last step is to print the report and see that the subtotals are working. In this case, the Subtotal function is actually helping to generate the breaks. However, it does only half the job. In order to have the break levels generated, you must sort the records. To generate break levels you must sort on one more field than the number of break levels you want. For the balance report, we want one break level so we must sort on two fields. Let's sort by State and then by Last Name. Then we will print the report.

1. Choose Use ➤ User (⌘-U).
2. Choose Select ➤ Sort Selection (⌘-T).
3. Click State.
4. Click Last Name.

5. Click **Sort**.
6. Choose File ➤ Print (⌘-P).
7. Click **Balance Report**.
8. Click **OK**.
9. Click **OK** in the Page Setup dialog box.
10. Select Preview on screen.
11. Click **Print**.
12. Click **Stop Printing** when you are finished viewing the report.

As you can see, the records on the balance report are sorted by State and then by Last Name with subtotals for each state. You could easily sort on more fields and add more break levels.

While the Subtotal function will create break levels, this method will not work if you compile the database with the 4D Compiler. To cause break processing in a compiled database, you must use the BREAK LEVEL and ACCUMULATE commands. For more information on these commands, see your language reference. For more information on the 4D Compiler, see *Chapter 19*.

Creating the Footer

The footer is the area from the F line to the break zero (B0) line. This area prints at the bottom of each page and appears at the bottom of the screen when you are viewing records through the output layout. In the header you put today's date. In the footer, you might want to put the page number. You used the Current date function to assign today's date to the variable vDate. You can use the Printing page function and another variable to hold the page number. Let's add the page number to the footer:

1. Switch to the Design environment.
2. Choose Design ➤ Layout: Balance Report.
4. Drag the footer line down to 180 pixels.
5. Click the Active Object tool to select it.
6. Draw an object in the footer area on the left side of the layout. Make the object about 50 pixels wide and about 20 pixels tall.
7. Type **vPage** as the name of the object.
8. Deselect the Script only if modified checkbox.
9. Click **Script**.
10. Click **OK**.
11. Type **vPage:=Printing page**.
12. Close the Script: vPage window.
13. Choose Chicago 12 point as the font and size of the vPage object.
14. Choose Style ➤ Left.
15. Switch to the User environment and print the Balance Report to the screen.

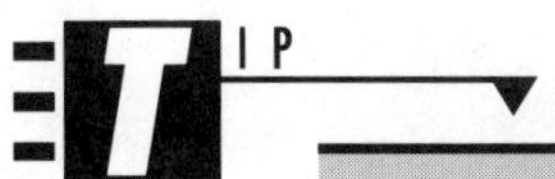

When you click on a layout in the Layout dialog box, 4D displays a preview of the layout in a box on the right side of the Layout dialog box. If a layout is complex, it might take several seconds for 4D to draw this preview. You can prevent 4D from displaying the preview by holding down the option key when you click on a layout to select it.

MANAGING RELATED FILES

13

MAC TRACKS MAC

To redisplay the Relations dialog box — 377

Redraw the arrow between the fields in the related files.

To view records in the many file from the one file — 388

Create an included layout.

To search using fields in a related file — 408

1. Display the file you want a selection of record for.
2. Choose Select ➤ Search Editor (⌘-S).
3. Enter a search criteria using fields from the related file.
4. Click **OK** to begin the search.

Featuring

- *Types of relations*
- *Creating related files*
- *Accessing related files*
- *Searching on related files*
- *Reporting using related files*
- *Deleting related records*

UP TO THIS point all the work you have done has been with one file. Some of the databases you create may only require one file. However, it is likely that most of your databases will require several files to keep track of all kinds of data. In this chapter, you will learn how to work with multiple files.

DATABASE DESIGN

When you first begin thinking about the database you need to build, it might appear that you need only one file. For example, you might need a database to track invoices. You will need to enter the customers name and address on the invoice and enter the products they want to order. If you are using a paper system, you fill this information out on a form (an invoice) which appears to be one record. The invoice itself is one record, however, there are many different kinds of information that make up this record. The invoice contains information about the customer, the fact that the customer made a purchase, the specific products the customer purchased and the quantities. You could enter all of this data into one record in one file. Figure 13.1 shows an example of this kind of database design. This would not be very efficient for several reasons:

- If you sell to the same customer several times, you will have to retype her name and address each time.

FIGURE 13.1

A poorly designed invoicing system

Invoices: 7 of 7

Invoice No	Invoice Date	Customer	Products Sold	Total
1	2/14/95	James T. Kirk	Phaser	$39.95
2	2/18/95	Mr. Spock	Q-Tips	$2.25
3	2/28/95	Scotty	Slim Fast	$3.95
4	3/1/95	Mr. Sulu	Vicks' Vapor Rub	$4.95
5	3/2/95	Mr. Checkov	A Career	$3,295.98
6	3/15/95	Yeoman Rand	A Date with Capt. Kirk	$456.89
7	3/20/95	Lt. Uhura	A Tourist's Guide to Klingon	$12.95

- Storing the same names and addresses over and over is going to waste a lot of disk space.
- If the customer's address changes, you will need to go back and find all of her old records and update them.

Instead of creating an invoices file, you could create a customers file. In the customers file you would store each customer's name and address only *once* and then have *fields* to keep track of each sale you made to them. This design would eliminate the problem of storing the same names over and over. You could store the invoice totals in fields named Total1, Total2, and Total3. For each total field there could be a date field to keep track of the date of the sales. This means that along with the total fields you would also have Date1, Date2, and Date3 fields. Figure 13.2 shows this type of database design. This type of database design is just as inefficient as the first for a number of reasons:

- There is a limit to the number of fields a file can have. That means that there would be a limit to the number of purchases a customer could make. You certainly wouldn't want that!

FIGURE 13.2

Another poorly designed invoicing system

Invoices: 7 of 7

Invoice No	Invoice Date	Customer	Date1	Total1	Date2	Total2	Date3	To
1	2/14/95	James T. Kirk	4/1/95	$45.79	5/12/95	$99.47	6/6/95	
2	2/18/95	Mr. Spock	4/5/95	$45.70	5/5/95	$12.09	6/12/95	
3	2/28/95	Scotty	4/2/95	$34.55	5/23/95	$43.67	6/6/95	
4	3/1/95	Mr. Sulu	4/7/95	$38.04	5/5/95	$176.90	6/9/95	
5	3/2/95	Mr. Checkov	4/8/95	$27.53	5/16/95	$19.73	6/28/95	
6	3/15/95	Yeoman Rand	4/22/95	$34.84	5/28/95	$72.12	6/12/95	
7	3/20/95	Lt. Uhura	4/1/95	$34.09	5/22/95	$28.54	6/14/95	

- If you wanted to search for all the purchases that were made on a certain date, you would have to make sure you always searched all three of the date fields. This might not only be hard to remember to do but is also more work than searching only one field.
- Reporting on this data would be difficult because you can't really separate the purchases (they are all stored in one record). You wouldn't be able to sort your records by purchase date because there are three different purchase dates.

A better solution is to store repeated data in its own file. For example, a customer's name and address are repeated on several invoices, so this information should have its own file. A product's description and price are repeated on many different invoices, so products should have their own files as well. By creating separate files for each type of data, you are storing the data more efficiently because you don't need to repeat the same data over and over. You wouldn't type the same invoice into your invoices file over and over again. The same rule holds true for the other information on the invoice. In the customers file, you need only one record for each customer. In the products file, you need only one record for each product. In the invoices file, you need only one record for each time the user placed an order. Assuming the customer can order as many products as they can afford, you will also need a file to keep track of each product they ordered and are being billed for, as well as the quantity ordered and the price quoted. You might be thinking "our customers never order more than 10 products at a time". That may be a general rule, but it probably isn't true every time. You need to design your database to be flexible. If there is one customer that orders more than 10 products, then the database needs to be able to easily accommodate that order.

Let's continue to assume for the moment that you have a business that sells products. What goes on in your business? Put in its simplest terms: **customers buy products**. This statement tells you immediately that you will need at least three files. You will need one file to keep track of all of your customers. You will need a second file to keep track of their *buys* (invoices) and a third file to keep track of the products you sell. As I mentioned earlier, if the customer might buy several products at once, you will need a file to keep track of this information. On an invoice, these pieces of information are typically called Line Items.

When all of this information is in one file, it is kept together by the simple fact that it all exists in one record. Now, you are breaking this single, flat file into four separate files. If these records are in four separate files, how will the invoice know which customer it's for? How will the line items know which invoice they belong to? How will the products know which invoices they were sold on? This is where the relational part of a relational database comes in.

WHAT DOES "RELATIONAL" MEAN?

The first time you heard the term *relational database* it probably sounded like open-heart surgery; very messy, too complex and years of experience required. It's a very simple and basic concept. For example, there is a relationship between customers and invoices. Invoices are related to customers. The word *relational* simply means that records in one file can be related to records in another. Your customers are related to invoices. Invoices are related to line items and line items are related to products.

In order for the records in one file to know which records in another file they are related to, the two files need to share one piece of common data. For example, when you open a bank account, the bank issues you an account number that uniquely identifies your bank account. Why doesn't the bank simply use your name to identify you? Unfortunately most people's names are not unique. The telephone book proves this. The bank has an accounts file and a transactions file. By issuing you a unique account number, the bank can keep track of which transactions are related to your account and thus keep your information separate from everyone else's.

In your invoicing database, each customer would have a unique customer number to identify that customer. When an invoice is entered, the customer number would be entered on to the invoice to identify the customer that the invoice belongs to. Each invoice would have a unique invoice number and each product would have a unique part number. With these unique values in place, invoices can identify the customer they belong to. Line items can identify the invoice they belong to by the invoice number. The line items will also use the product's part number to identify which product they are related to. Figure 13.3 shows an example of an invoicing system where related files have common fields that relate records in one file to those in another.

FIGURE 13.3

The best way to store invoices and related information

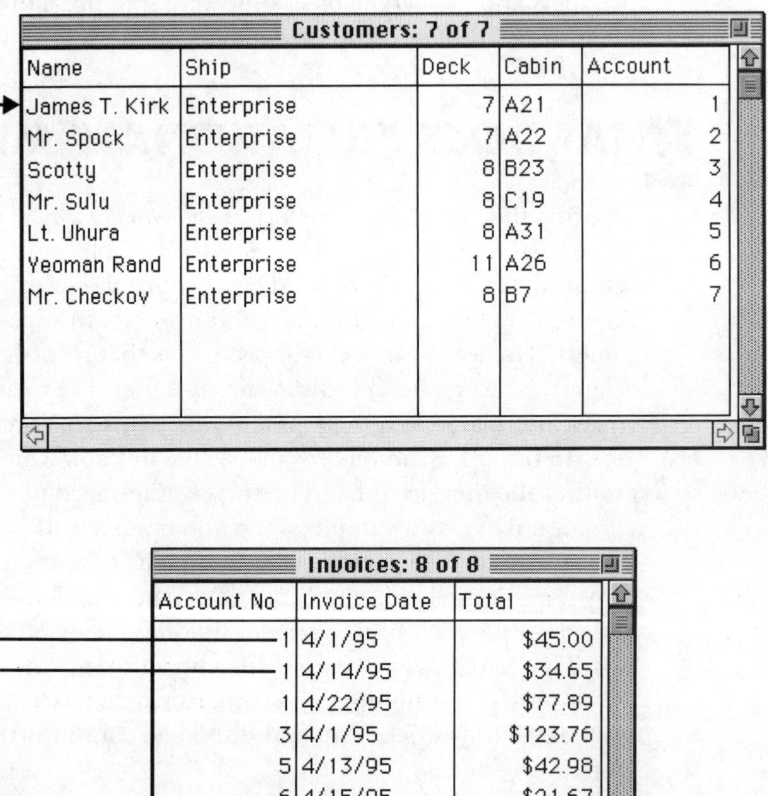

WHY IS A RELATIONAL DATABASE BETTER THAN A FLAT-FILE DATABASE?

A relational database saves you time and money. How is this possible? After all, most relational databases cost more to purchase than flat-file databases. Also, it will usually take longer to build a relational database than it does to build a flat-file database. How can a relational database possibly save time and money? The answer is planning. By planning your database ahead of time you can create a system that more closely matches the real world. In a flat-file system, the same customer will be entered over and over on different invoices. However, there is only one of that customer in the real world. In a relational database, the customer is stored only once. Say you decide to mail out an advertisement to your customers. If you try to print labels from a flat-file database, you will have many labels for the same customer because the customer exists many times on many different invoices. This means you will waste money printing extra brochures and paying for extra postage. You could sort the invoices by the customers name and then look through them to find only the unique names before printing your labels; however, this is going to waste a lot of time. By spending the time up front to design the database correctly, you will save time and money down the road.

Many people think that a relational database is more difficult to use than a flat-file database. This simply isn't true. In fact, when you look at the big picture, a relational database is easier to use. It may take more time and understanding initially to build a relational database. However, once the database is in place, getting accurate information out of the database will be easy. The flat-file database may be easy to create, but you will pay for it in the long run by having to plow through lots of repeated data and by trying to print reports that the data is simply not organized to print. Relational databases allow you to organize your data in ways that match the real world.

You can create flat-file databases with a relational database. The advantage to using a relational database is that, when you are ready, you can create relationships between your files and continue to increase the capabilities of your database as your needs increase. With a flat-file database, your needs may quickly out-grow the capabilities of the database.

TYPES OF RELATIONS BETWEEN FILES

You know now that a relational database is a database that allows you to have multiple files and to relate some of those files to allow them to share information. There are several different kinds of relationships between files. The kind of relationship you choose depends on how the data is used and affects what you can do with the data.

ONE TO MANY

In an invoicing database, *one* customer may have *many* invoices. However, one invoice doesn't belong to many customers. Since one customer can have many invoices and one invoice cannot have many customers, this is called a *one-to-many* relationship. The customer's file is referred to as the *one* file and the invoices file is referred to as the *many* file. A one-to-many relationship between two files is the most common type of relationship in relational databases. If you look back at Figure 13.3, you can see that the relationship between customers and invoices is one-to-many. Here are some examples of common one-to-many relationships:

- One supervisor may have many employees
- One invoice may have many line items

- One home may have many rooms
- One car may have many passengers

If you think about things in life that are related (like cars and passengers), many of them fit into the model of a one-to-many relationship. You will need to spend some time thinking about the relationships that exist between the data you need to keep track of. The most important consideration is whether or not the relationship you believe exists between the data holds true in all cases. For example, your customers will often have one address for billing and another address for shipping. Initially it might appear that the billing address and shipping address fields should be in one file. However, what if one of your customers has two different addresses that they want their orders shipped to at different times? You could create two customer records, one with their first shipping address and another with their second shipping address. This defeats the purpose of having a relational database, though, because you are now storing the billing information twice. If you have even one customer that has more than one shipping address, it is better to create a shipping file. Each record in the shipping file would contain a shipping address for a customer. You can now establish a one-to-many relationship between the shipping file and the customer's file. One customer can now have many shipping addresses. If you have even one customer that has more than one shipping address, it would be better to create a structure that allows for multiple shipping addresses per customer. If you create a database where the customer can have only one shipping address and try to deal with the exceptional customer that has more than one shipping address, you are going to cause yourself problems down the road. It is always better to start off with the right structure (even if it takes longer to create) than the wrong one. The relationship you create between your files has to work in *all* cases. Also, think about the future. Even if you don't have customers right now that have multiple shipping addresses, you might have them some day. It will take you far less time to create the right structure in the beginning than to correct the wrong structure later on.

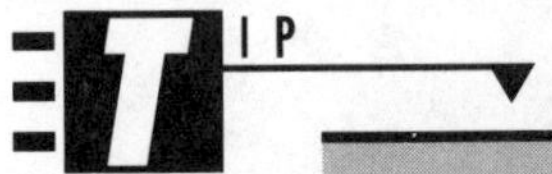

There is a saying that goes something like this: "If you don't have the time to do it right, when are you going to find the time to do it over?"

MANY TO MANY

There may be times when the relationship appears to be one-to-many but isn't. Say you were creating a database to keep track of students and the courses each student is enrolled in. It appears at first glance that this is a one-to-many relationship. One student attends many courses. You could create a students file and a courses file. If you keep track of information about the course they are attending (like the room number, instructor's name, the number of units) you will have a lot of repeated data. For example, if several students are attending the same course, they would all have the same room number, the same instructor, and the same number of units. The relationship between students and courses really isn't a one-to-many. Why isn't it? Well, one student may attend many courses; this is true. However, one course may have many students. This doesn't fit the one-to-many model does it? When you looked at customers and invoices, one customer had many invoices but one invoice did not belong to many customers. With students and courses it goes both ways. *One* student may attend *many* courses and *one* course may be attended by *many* students. This is called a *many-to-many* relationship. There are plenty of examples of many-to-many relationships. Here are a few of them:

- One author may have many books, one book may have many authors
- One compact disc may have many songs, one song may appear on many compact discs
- One company may sell many types of products, one product may be sold by many different companies

A many-to-many relationship is simply two *one* files that share the same *many* file. Let's look at students and courses. The students file would contain information about the student: her name, address, major, and so on. The courses file would contain information about the course: the room number, the instructor's name, and the number of units received for completing the course. The many file that the students and courses file share would contain information about a student attending a course. Let's call this many file *registration.* You might include fields like attendance, fees paid, and registration date. In order for a record in the registration file to be related to both the student and the course, the students file would need to have a field that uniquely identifies each student (say a student ID) and the courses file would need to have a field that uniquely identifies each course (say a course number). The registration file would then contain a student ID field and a course number field. By having both of these fields in one record, you will know for each registration record which student it is related to and which course it is related to. Figure 13.4 shows an example of this many-to-many relationship.

If you think about it, the relationship between invoices and products is a many-to-many relationship. One invoice many have many products on it and one product may be one of many invoices. The many file that they share is the line items file. A line item is a record of the purchase of a particular product.

FIGURE 13.4

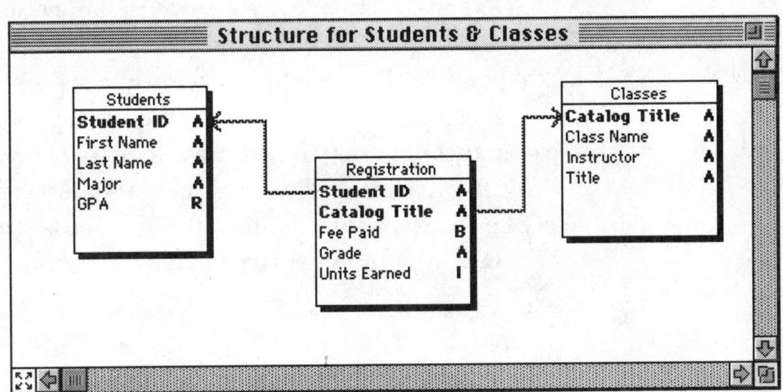

Students and courses is a classic many-to-many relationship.

ONE TO ONE

Another type of relationship is a *one-to-one* relationship. In a one-to-one relationship, each record in the first file has only one related record in the second file and each record in second file has only one related record in the first file. When you think about it, what has really happened here is that one file has been split into two. If there is a one-to-one correspondence between records in two files, the two files really should simply be one file. The fields in the second file should be included in the one file rather than having two separate files.

There is a practical reason for creating a one-to-one relationship and that is record size. The more data you store in a record, the larger the record becomes. The larger the record becomes, the longer it takes to access that record. If you accessed some of the fields most of the time, you could put the most commonly used fields in one file and all of the rest in a related file. This way, when you access the first file, the records would be smaller and, consequently, the speed of access to those records would be faster. Occasionally, when you needed to access the rest of the fields, you could go to the second file. One-to-one relationships are not very common and are mostly used to break up very large files.

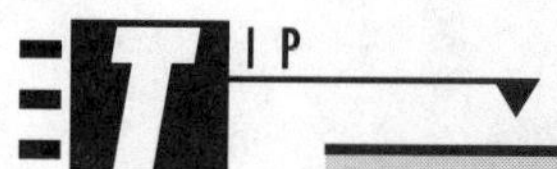

Text and Picture fields can store large amounts of data. If you are storing large amounts of text and pictures, you might consider keeping these fields in a separate file. If you aren't sure whether you need to create a separate file or not, create a test database to test the performance you will get by having all of the fields in one file. If the performance is acceptable, don't split the file. It will be easier to deal with this data as one file instead of two.

A one-to-one relationship looks just like a one-to-many relationship. The only difference is that there is never more than one record that corresponds with a record in a related file.

HIERARCHICAL RELATIONSHIPS

Some types of data don't fit directly into the one-to-many or many-to-many model. For example, say you have a database that keeps track of parts. One part may include many other parts. This seems on the surface to be a one-to-many relationship. One part has many sub-parts. However, those sub-parts are parts themselves and may even contain their own sub-parts. You could create a parts file and a sub-parts file. The parts file would be the *one* file and the sub-parts file would be the *many* file. One part has many sub-parts. In the parts file you might have fields like name, size, weight, and price. You would also have these fields in the sub-parts file. Now you are storing repeated data since the sub-parts will no doubt also have a record in the parts file because they themselves are also parts. Now lets imagine that the price of a part has changed. You would have to go to the parts file and change the price, then go to the sub-parts file and locate every instance of that part in the sub-parts file to change the price. If you needed to create a report showing a part and all of its sub-parts you could do it. However, if you need to create a report that showed each part, all of its sub-parts and all of each sub-part's sub-parts down to the last sub-part of the last sub-part, you couldn't do it because the parts/sub-parts structure you created goes only one level deep. What you need is a way to keep track of a part and all of it's sub-parts no matter how many levels deep it goes. This is called a *hierarchical* relationship. This type of relationship exists when records in the same file are related to each other.

Creating this kind of structure actually does require a one-to-many relationship. The one file would be the parts file and the many file would be the sub-parts file. However, the only fields in the sub-parts file would be the part number (which keeps track of the part that the sub-part is related to) and the sub-part number itself. It takes a little bit of programming to create an interface where the user can see the part and all of its sub-parts but this is how it's done.

At the back of this book, there is an order form to purchase a companion disk for this book. The companion disk contains several databases that were used in this book. One of them is a sample of a hierarchical parts database. If you are going to be creating any type of hierarchical database, you might consider purchasing the disk to have an example to look at.

CREATING RELATED FILES

Now that you have an idea of how to share information between files, it is time to learn how to add more files and to create relationships between those files. In this exercise, you will create an invoices file, a line items file, and a products file.

The first file you will create is the invoices file. Before you create the invoices file, you need to make sure that the Customers file has a field that uniquely identifies each customer. There is the Last Name field and each of our customers does have a unique last name. However, you already know that the Last Name field is not going to be reliable as a unique identifier since you may one day add another customer that has the same last name as an existing customer. So, the first step is to assign something unique to each customer. Let's give each customer a unique account number. You can then use this number to relate our invoices to the customers they belong to.

1. Switch to the Design environment.
2. If the Structure window is not in front, click on it to bring it to the front.
3. Click on the Customers file to select it.
4. Choose Structure ➤ New Field (⌘-F).

5. Type **Account Number** as the name of the field.
6. Select Alpha as the field type.
7. Select the Display Only attribute.
8. Click **OK**.

You have now an Account Number field to store a number that will uniquely identify each customer. It seems like this field should be a numeric field. After all, an account number is a number. However, there is a feature that 4D has to help you find related records that only works with Alpha fields. Since you are not going to be performing calculations on the Account Number field, you can make it an Alpha field to enable you to use this easy lookup feature. I will get to this feature a bit later. You selected the Display Only attribute for this field so that a user doesn't accidentally change an account number. How are you going to get the account numbers into the field? You could remove the Display Only attribute and enter all of the account numbers by hand. Since your database only has a few records, this wouldn't take long. However, what if you had a database with thousands of records. Typing account numbers might take a while. Instead of doing it by hand, you can let 4D do it for you automatically. You know that each file has a current selection. Each record in the current selection has a selected record number. This number is simply the record's position in the current selection. You can assign this selected record number to the Account Number field to give each customer a unique account number:

1. Choose Use ➤ User (⌘-U).
2. Choose Select ➤ Show All (⌘-G).
3. Choose Enter ➤ Apply Formula.
4. Scroll the Fields list (the middle scrollable area) until you see the Account Number field.
5. Click on the Account Number field.
6. Click on := in the Keywords list.
7. Click on Routines to switch the Routines list from pop-up menus to a list of routines.

8. Scroll down through the Routines list until you find String and click on it.
9. Type (to add an opening parentheses to the formula.
10. Scroll down through the Routines list until you find Selected record number and click on it.
11. Type **([Customers])** to add the customers file name to the formula.
12. Type) to add a closing parentheses to the formula.
13. The finished formula should look like this:

    Account Number:=String(Selected record number([Customers]))

14. Click **OK.**

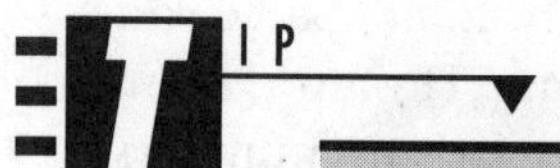

In the Apply Formula dialog box (as well as the Procedure Editor), if you hold down the ⌘ and Shift keys and press a letter, the Routines list will automatically scroll to the first routine that begins with that letter.

Now each customer has a unique account number. String and Selected record number are functions in 4D's language. 4D executes formulas just as you do when you figure out a math problem. 4D starts with what is inside the parentheses and works its way outward. The Selected record number function returned a number to the String function. The String function converted the number from a number into a string (alpha) so that it could be assigned to an Alpha field.

You can't see the account number because the field is new and you haven't added it to any of the layouts yet. Also, you don't want to have to apply this formula every time you want to assign account numbers. What would be better is to have 4D assign an account number each time you create a new customer. Let's add the Account Number field to the New

Input layout and set it up so that 4D automatically assigns an account number:

1. Switch back to the Design environment.
2. Open the New Input layout.
3. Drag a marquee around the entire Balance field and field label to select them.
4. Choose Object ➤ Duplicate (⌘-D) or click the Duplicate tool in the tools palette.
5. Drag the duplicated Balance field below the Taxable check-box and to the right of the City field.
6. Double-click the Balance field to open the Field Definition dialog box.
7. Click on the Account Number field.
8. Type **00000** as the format for this field.
9. Type **#N** as the Default value.
10. Click **OK**.
11. Click on the Text tool to select it.
12. Change the field label next to the Account Number field from Balance to *Account #*.

As you probably remember from *Chapter 12*, the format 00000 will place leading zeros in the places where there is no number. This means that the account number 1 will be displayed as 00001. Also, by adding the default value #N, you are telling 4D to enter the sequence number for the Customers file into the account number field when a new record is created. As I mentioned in *Chapter 12*, the sequence number for each file is incremented when you save a new record. Let's try it:

1. Switch to the User environment.
2. Choose Enter ➤ New Record (⌘-N).

Notice that the Account Number field has a number in it. This number will not necessarily be seven. If you created records and then deleted them, the sequence number was incremented. Don't worry about these numbers being in sequence. What's important is that there are no duplicates.

3. Click the **Cancel** button.

Now that you have unique account numbers for each file and you have set up the Account Number field to generate account numbers for new records, it's time to add the Invoices file.

The Invoices file will contain only the fields that keep track of information about the invoice itself. There will not be any information about the customer (other than the account number) because that will come from the Customers file. Let's add the Invoices file:

1. Switch to the Design environment.
2. Close the New Input layout if it is still open.
3. Make sure that the Structure window is in front.
4. Choose Structure ➤ New File (⌘-N).
5. Click the mouse in the Structure window where you want 4D to create the new file.
6. Choose Structure ➤ Edit File (⌘-R).
7. Type **Invoices** as the filename.
8. Click **OK**.

Now that you have added the file, you can add fields to the Invoices file. Add the following fields:

FieldName	Data Type	Attributes
Invoice Number	Long Integer	Display Only
Account Number	Alpha	

FieldName	Data Type	Attributes
Invoice Date	Date	Display Only
Invoice Total	Real	

Now you have an invoices file with an Account Number field, just like the Account Number field in the Customers file. The two files cannot share information yet, though. The next step is to let 4th Dimension know exactly how they are related. When you create a new invoice, you will enter the customer's account number into the Account Number field on the invoice. 4D needs to know which field it should search in the Customers file to find the matching account number that you just entered. Figure 13.3 has arrows from the invoice account numbers to the customer account number that the invoices match. To let 4D know that the Invoices and Customers files are related, you draw an arrow between them just like the arrows in Figure 13.3. Figure 13.5 shows the Invoices and Customers files with the arrow connecting them.

Let's relate the Invoices and Customers file:

1. Click and drag from the Account Number field in the Invoices file to the Account Number field in the Customers file, then release the mouse button.

FIGURE 13.5

The related Invoices and Customers files

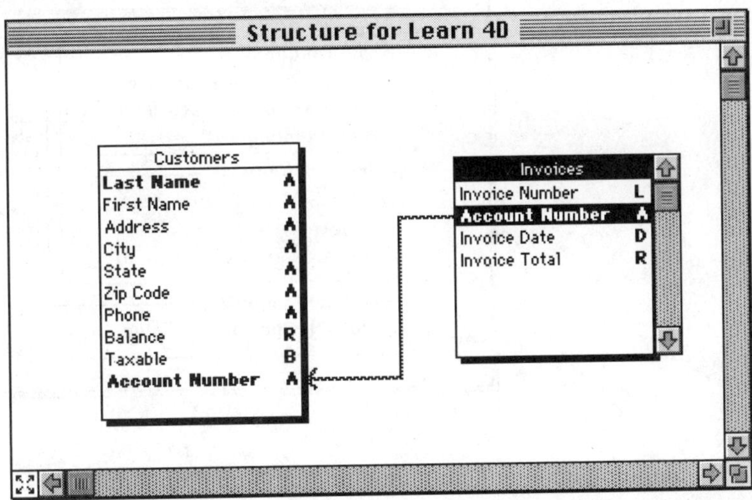

You know that the Customers file is the one file and the Invoices file is the many file. The arrow is always drawn from the many file to the one file. The arrow is pointing to the field that will be searched when a value is entered into the field where the arrow begins.

The arrow that relates files always starts at the many file and points to the one file.

Notice that as you dragged, a line appeared. You are drawing the arrow from the Account Number field in the Invoices file to the Account Number field in the Customers file just as it is drawn in Figure 13.3. When you release the mouse button, the Relations Type dialog box appears. This dialog box allows you to set up options about how you want the relationship between the two files to work. Figure 13.6 shows the Relations dialog box. These options are set just the way you want them.

FIGURE 13.6

The Relations dialog box

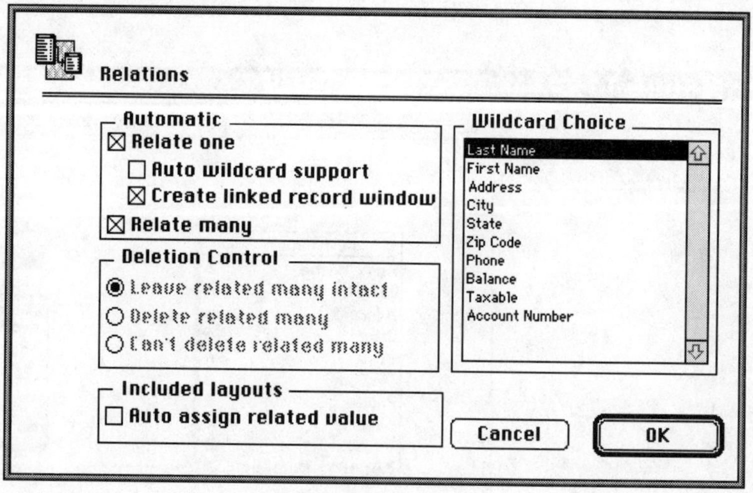

Only fields that can be indexed can be used to relate files. These field types are Alpha, Real, Integer, Long Integer, Date, Time, and Boolean.

2. Click **OK**.

To display the Relations dialog box again so you can change the options, simply redraw the relation arrow between the two fields.

ACCESSING RELATED RECORDS

Relating two files by drawing the relation arrow is all that is required to relate the files. However, you will need some way of accessing the related records. There are two different methods for accessing related files. The method you use depends on whether you are looking at a record from the one file or the many file.

FROM THE MANY FILE

When viewing a record from a many file (like the invoices file) it would be helpful to see fields from the one file (the customer's file) so you can know easily which customer this invoice is for. When you type an account number into the Account Number field on the invoice, 4D searches to Customers file to find the customer record that is related to the account number you entered. 4D also performs this search when you open an existing record. Since there is only one matching customer record, you can put fields from the Customers file one the Invoices Input layout enabling the user to see the contents of those fields when 4D locates the related customer.

At this point you could try entering an invoice. As soon as you switch to the User environment, 4D will automatically create input and output layouts for the Invoices file. If you typed an account number into the Account Number field on the invoice, 4D would find a customer with that account number in the Customers file. However, there are no fields on the Invoices Input layout to show you which customer you selected. Instead of letting 4D create Input and Output layouts automatically, let's create our own. As you create these layouts, you can include fields from the Customers file so that when you use them you will know you have the right customer. The New Layout dialog box allows you to select fields from related files when you create a layout using one of the built-in layout templates. First we will build an output layout:

1. Make sure you are in the Design environment.
2. Choose Design ➤ Layout (⌘-L).
3. Click on Invoices to select it.
4. Click the **New** button.
5. Click Invoice Number and click **Select**.
6. Click on Account Number [Customers] to select it.
7. Click the **Expand** button.

The [Customers] filename appears next to the Account Number field to indicate which file this field is linked to. When you clicked the Select button, 4D placed a 1 next to the selected field. This is to indicate the position that this field will be placed in on the layout when it is created. The New Layout dialog box displays fields from the current file as well as fields from related files. It does this in using an outline style display. When you clicked Expand, 4D displays the fields from the related file. At this point, you can select the fields from the related file that you want displayed on the layout.

8. Click on the First Name field and click the **Select** button to select it.

9. Click on the Last Name field and click the **Select** button to select it.
10. Click on the Account Number [Customers] field.
11. Click the **Collapse** button.
12. Click on Invoice Date and click **Select**.
13. Click on Invoice Total and click **Select**.
14. Click the first template (in the upper-left corner of the templates).
15. Click 9 Point.
16. Type **Output** as the name of the layout.
17. Click the **OK** button.

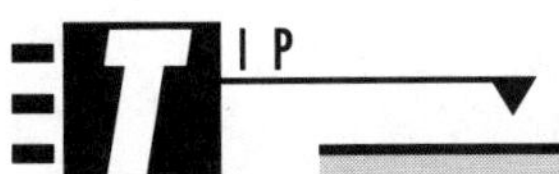

A shortcut to selecting fields in the New Layout dialog box is to double-click on them. The only fields you can't double-click to select are those that have a filename after them. Double-clicking on these fields expands the fields list to show fields from the related file.

Notice that the First Name and Last Name fields are in bold. When 4D creates the layout using a layout template, it puts related fields in bold to let you know that they are from another file.

Now as you view the invoices in the output layout, you will see the customer's first name and last name. As 4th Dimension draws each record to the screen it quickly searches the related file looking for the matching customer. Since the First Name and Last Name fields are on the layout, the contents of these fields from the related customer record are displayed.

The next step is to create an input layout. Let's do it:

1. Choose Design ➤ Layout (⌘-L).
2. Click on Invoices to select it.

3. Click the **New** button.
4. Click on Account Number [Customers] and click **Select**.
5. Click the **Expand** button.
6. Double-click on First Name to select it.
7. Double-click on Last Name to select it.
8. Double-click on Phone to select it.
9. Click on the layout template in the second row, third column.
10. Type **Input** as the name of the layout.

Figure 13.7 shows what the New Layout dialog should look like.

11. Click **OK**.

FIGURE 13.7

The New Layout dialog box

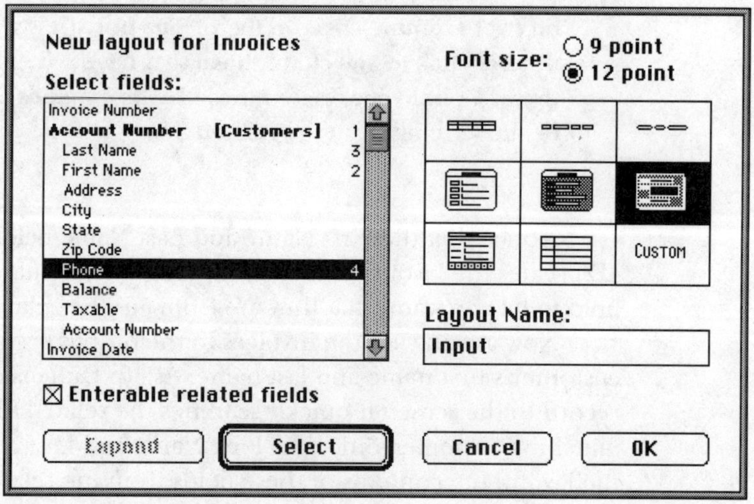

New layout for Invoices
Font size: 9 point / 12 point
Select fields:
Invoice Number
Account Number [Customers] 1
Last Name 3
First Name 2
Address
City
State
Zip Code
Phone 4
Balance
Taxable
Account Number
Invoice Date
CUSTOM
Layout Name:
Input
Enterable related fields
Expand
Select
Cancel
OK

The Enterable Related Fields checkbox in the New Layout dialog box lets you choose if you want the user to be able to make changes to fields from the related one file. This can be useful since the user can update the related *one* record without leaving the *many* record they are entering.

You have created the first part of the input layout. You are going to use a combination of layout templates to create the invoices input layout. Figure 13.8 shows what the input layout should look like so far.

FIGURE 13.8

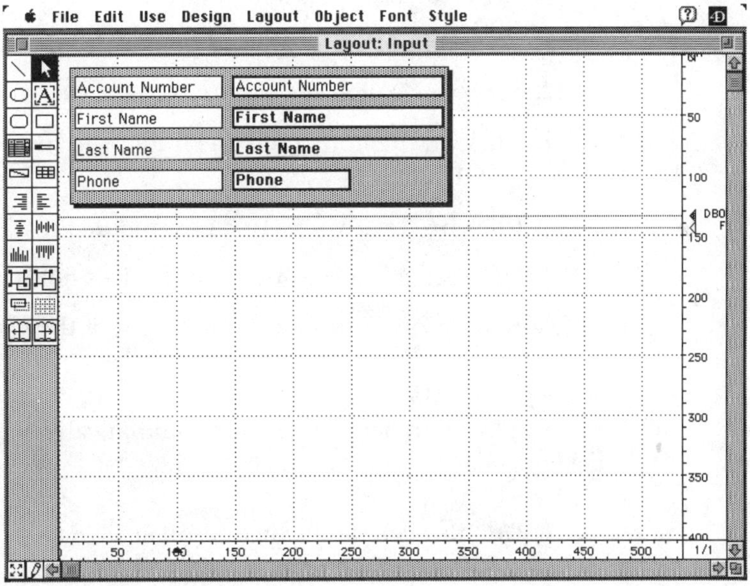

The current state of the invoices input layout

Now you will add the fields from the Invoices file to the Input layout using the Add To Layout menu item. Add To Layout allows you to add fields to the layout using the layout templates.

1. Choose Layout ➤ Add to Layout.
2. Click on the layout just below the box that holds the customer fields.
3. Double-click on Invoice Number to select it.
4. Double-click on Invoice Date to select it.
5. Double-click on Invoice Total to select it.
6. Click on the middle input layout template to select it.
7. Click **OK**.

Now that the Invoice fields are on the layout, you can delete the extra graphics and reposition these fields.

8. Click somewhere on the layout where there are no graphics to deselect any selected graphics.
9. Click on the frame around the invoice fields to select it.
10. Press the **Delete** key.
11. Click on the horizontal line under the Invoices title box and delete it.
12. Click on the Invoices title box and delete it.
13. Draw a marquee around the Invoices fields to select them.
14. Reposition these fields to the right of the Customer fields.

Figure 13.9 shows what the Invoices Input layout should now look like.

You can number the invoices automatically in the same way you assign customer account numbers.

1. Double-click the Invoice Number field.
2. Type **#N** into the Default box.
3. Type **00000** as the format for the field.
4. Click **OK**.

FIGURE 13.9

The Invoices input layout

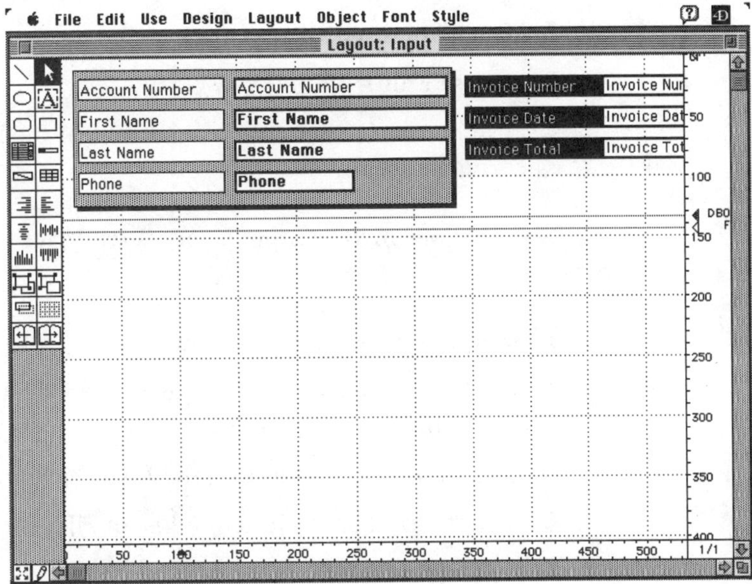

You can also have today's date entered automatically into the Invoice Date field.

1. Double-click on the Invoice Date field.
2. Type **#D** into the Default box.
3. Click **OK**.

You also should have a Cancel button and a Save button on the layout. You already created these buttons for the Customers New Input layout so you can copy them from there.

1. Choose Design ➤ Layout (⌘-L).
2. Double-click on Customers to expand its list of layouts.
3. Double-click on New Input to open it.
4. Draw a marquee around the Cancel and Save buttons to select them.
5. Choose Edit ➤ Copy (⌘-C).

6. Close the New Input layout.
7. Make sure the Invoices Input Layout is in front.
8. Choose Edit ➤ Paste (⌘-V).
9. Position the Cancel and Save buttons in the lower-right corner of the layout.

Now that our invoice input layout is ready, let's try entering a new invoice.

1. Switch to the User environment.
2. If the Invoices file is not displayed press ⌘-spacebar to display the List of Files window.
3. Click on Invoices to display the Invoices file.
4. Press ⌘-spacebar to hide the List of Files window.
5. Choose Enter ➤ New Record (⌘-N).
6. Type **2** into the Account Number field and press the Tab key.

Notice that as soon as you typed 2 and pressed tab, the First Name, Last Name, and Phone fields were filled in with Sally Jones' name and phone number. When you tabbed out of the Account Number field, 4D searched the Account Number field in the Customers file looking for a Customer whose account number is 2. When it found one, that record became the current record for the Customers file. Your invoice has fields from the Customers file on it and those fields display the data for the current record.

Now let's say that you don't know the account number. This could be a problem. You could switch over the Customers file and search for the customer by last name, look at the account number then switch back to the Invoices file. There is an easier way. In the previous chapters, you used the @ (wildcard character) in different database operations like searching. If you type an @ in an Alpha field that is related to another file, 4D displays a selection window that allows you to use the mouse to choose a record. Figure 13.10 shows the Invoices Input layout with the selection window displayed. Let's try it:

1. Click into the Account Number field and replace the 2 with an @.
2. Press the Tab key.

FIGURE 13.10

The selection window

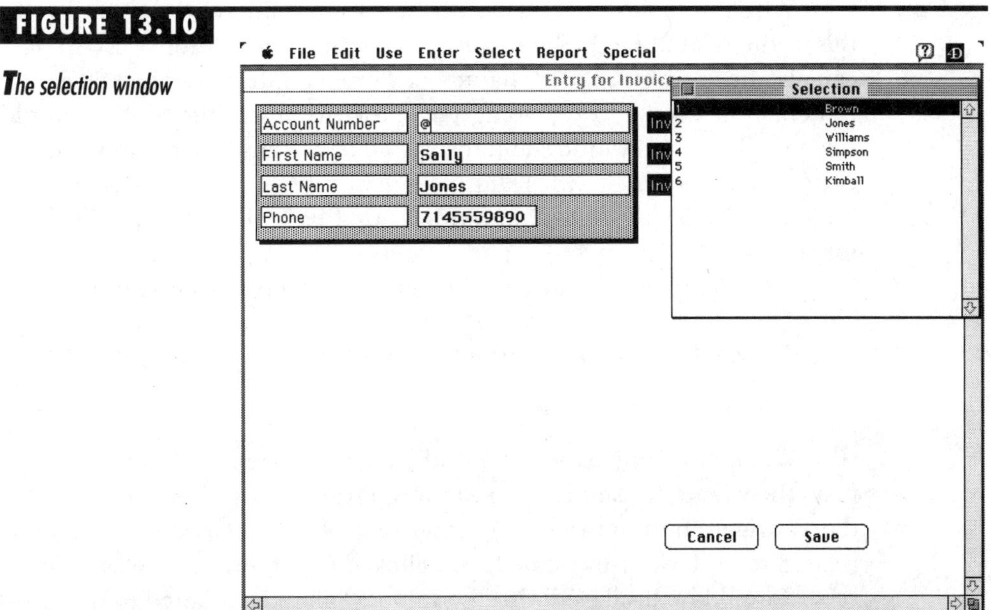

Because you typed @, the selection window shows all of the records in the Customers file. The first column is the Account Number field (the related field) and the second column is the wildcard choice field that was selected in the Relations dialog box.

1. Click on Simpson to select it.

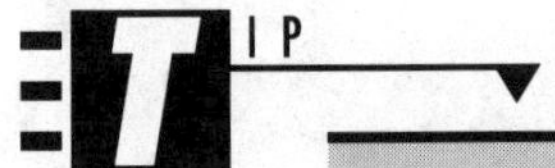

You can use the up and down arrow keys in the Selection window instead of the mouse.

When you click on a record, 4D makes that the related record and fills in the related field (the Invoices Account Number) for you. The @ can also be used with other characters. For example, if you had 20 customers numbered 1 to 20, typing 1@ in the Account Number field would open the Selection window and display all of the customers whose account numbers began with 1. If only one match is found, 4D doesn't bother to display the Selection window and fills in the related field for you.

What happens if it doesn't find a match at all? Let's find out:

2. Type **10** into the Account Number field and press the Tab key.

When 4th Dimension can't find a match in the related file, it displays the Create Linked Record window. From this window you can press the Try Again button to enter another value or press Create It to create a related record with this value. If you clicked Create It, a new Customer record would be displayed with the value 10 already assigned to the Account Number field. This would not be good because you may eventually assign that value to a customer and you would then have two customers with the same account number. You can control whether this window is displayed or not through the Relations dialog box. Let's change this option and the wildcard choice field as well. To display the Relations dialog box, you have to redraw the relation arrow between the Invoices file and the Customers file.

1. Click the **Try Again** button.
2. Click the **Cancel** button.
3. Switch to the Design environment.

4. Choose Design ➤ Structure.
5. Click on the Invoices Account Number field and drag to the Customers Account Number field.

Now that you have the Relations dialog box displayed you can change any of the options. If you don't want the Create Linked Record window to be displayed when the user enters a related value that doesn't exist, deselect the Create Linked Record window checkbox. To have a different field appear in the second column of the Selection window, click on a field in the wildcard choice list.

6. Deselect Create Linked Record Window.
7. Click on First Name in the Wildcard Choice list.
8. Click **OK**.

The Auto Wildcard Support option when selected will automatically enter the @ for the user when they type a value into the related field. The wildcard character does not appear in the field but 4D acts as if the user typed it. This gives the user the advantage of only having to enter a few characters into the field without having to remember to type the @.

With the Created Linked Record window option deselected, the window will not appear if the user types in an account number that doesn't exist in the Customers file. Instead, the First Name, Last Name, and Phone fields will remain blank. In most cases, this would be enough of an indication to the user that they entered an invalid value. If this is obvious for your users, you can use a few commands from 4th Dimension's programming language to present a window with your own message.

FROM THE ONE FILE

If you are looking at a record in a *one* file, you might also need to be able to see the related records in the *many* file at the same time. For example, you will add a Line Items file to the database to allow you to keep track of the products you sell on each invoice. The user will need to be able to see the line items that belong to each invoice. You can view records from a related many file through an *included layout.*

An included layout is a layout from the related many file that is placed (included) on the one file's layout. When you access a record in the one file, 4D automatically locates all of the related records in the many file. These records become the current selection for the many file and can be displayed through an included layout from that file. An included layout looks a lot like an output layout displayed on an input layout.

Let's add a Products file and a Line Items file. Then you can create an included layout to display the line items for each invoice. The Products file will contain information about the products you sell and the Line Items file will contain information about the sale of a product on a particular invoice.

1. Display the Structure window.
2. Choose Structure ➤ New File (⌘-N).
3. Click the mouse below and to the right of the Invoices file to create the new file.
4. Choose Structure ➤ Edit File (⌘-R).
5. Type **Line Items** as the name for the new file.
6. Click **OK**.
7. Add the following fields to the Line Items file:

FieldName	Field Type
Invoice Number	Long Integer
Part Number	Alpha 5
Qty	Long Integer

FieldName	Field Type
Price	Real
Line Total	Real

8. Now drag from the Line Items Invoice Number field to the Invoices Invoice Number field to relate the files.
9. Select Auto assign related value.
10. Click **OK**.

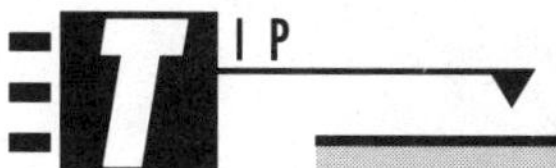

4D draws the relation arrows different ways based on the distance between the related files and the angle between the related fields. If you don't like the way the arrows are drawn, try dragging one of the files to a different location.

The Auto assign related value option keeps the Line Items records related to the invoice they were created from. With this option selected, 4D will copy the Invoice Number from the invoice into the Invoice Number field in the Line Items file when you enter a new line item through an included layout. The next step is to create the Products file.

1. Choose Structure ➤ New File (⌘-N).
2. Click the mouse below the Invoices file to create the new file.
3. Choose Structure ➤ Edit File (⌘-R).
4. Type **Products** as the name of the new file.
5. Add the following fields:

FieldName	Field Type
Part Number	Alpha 10
Description	Alpha 20
Price	Real

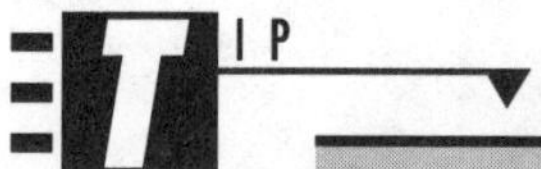

If a file in the Structure window is too long or too short you can click and drag on the bottom of the file to resize it.

6. Drag from the Line Items Part Number field to the Products Part Number field to relate the files.
7. Select Auto wildcard support.
8. Deselect Create linked record window.
9. Select Description as the Wildcard Choice field.
10. Click **OK**.

Notice that the Description field is in the Products file and not in the Line Items file. The description of the product is static; it will not change. The price however is variable, and will change from time to time. You will need to store the price you sold the product for in the Line Items file. Even though you are duplicating the data by storing it in two places, you have to do this so that you can always look back at a particular invoice and see what price was charged for a particular product. When you think about it, you are not really duplicating the Price field. The Price field in the Products file holds the current price of the product. The Price field in the Line Items file contains the price that the product was sold for on that invoice.

When you created the input layout for the Invoices file, you included fields from the Customers file. The Products file is a one file to the Line Items file. When you create the Line Items layout to be included on the Invoices Input layout, you can include fields from the Products file. You will want to include the Description field so that the user can see the description when they enter the part number. Let's create the included layout:

1. Double-click on the Line Items filename in the Structure window to display the Layout dialog box.

2. Click **New**.
3. Click on Part Number [Products] to select it.
4. Click **Select** to include it as a field on the layout.
5. Click **Expand** or double-click on Part Number [Products] to list the fields in the related Products file.
6. Double-click on Description to select it.
7. Click on Part Number [Products].
8. Click **Collapse**.
9. Double-click on Qty to select it.
10. Double-click on Price to select it.
11. Double-click on Line Total to select it.
12. Click on the upper-left layout template.
13. Type **InvoiceIncluded** as the name of the layout.
14. Deselect Enterable related fields.
15. Click **OK**.

Notice that the Description field on the InvoiceIncluded layout is in bold to remind you that this field is from a related file. Before you include this layout on the Invoices Input layout, let's set the format for the Price and Line Total fields.

1. Double-click on the Price field.
2. Choose $###,##0.00;($###,##0.00) from the Format pop-up menu.
3. Click **OK**.
4. Double-click on the Line Total field.
5. Choose $###,##0.00;($###,##0.00) from the Format pop-up menu.
6. Click **OK**.

Now let's include the InvoiceIncluded layout on the Invoices Input layout:

1. Choose Design ➤ Layout (⌘-L).
2. Double-click on Invoices to expand the list of layouts.
3. Double-click on the Input layout to open it.
4. Click on the Included Layout tool to select it. In case you don't remember which tool is it, it's the one that looks like a tiny scrollable area.
5. Position the cursor so that it is lined up with the left side of the box that contains the Customer fields and about one-half inch below it.
6. Click and drag to create a rectangle so that the bottom is at 250 pixels and the right side is at 500 pixels.

When you create an area for an included layout to be displayed, 4D opens the Included Layout dialog box. This dialog box allows you to select the layout that will be included and to select options about how the included layout will behave.

7. Click on [Line Items] to select it.
8. Click **Select**.
9. Click **Expand**.
10. Click InvoiceIncluded to select it.
11. Select Multi-line.
12. Deselect Double-clickable.

An included layout works a lot like an output layout. However, with an included layout you can choose whether or not you want the user to be able to double-click on a record to view it in the input layout. You can indicate which layout should be used for input by selecting the layout and choosing the Full Page option. In this case, no input layout is needed so the Double-clickable option was deselected. This will prevent the user from going to an input layout if she double-clicks on a record in the included layout.

The way an included layout behaves when printed depends on the Print Frame option you select.

The **Variable** option will stretch the included layout as long as possible to insure that all of the related records are printed. If the included layout prints to the bottom of the page, 4D will start at the top of the next page and continue printing the included layout. Figure 13.11 shows the results of printing an invoice with two pages of line items.

The **Fixed (truncation)** option will not change the size of the included layout when printing. Instead, 4D will print only the records that can be printed based on the height of the included area. Figure 13.12 shows the results of printing the same invoice.

The **Fixed (multiple records)** option will not change the size of the included layout when printing. Instead, 4D will reprint the entire layout, printing as many pages as necessary until all of the related records have been printed. Figure 13.13 shows the results of printing the same invoice.

The Auto button sizes the included area on the layout so the area is wide enough to display the entire included layout.

13. Click **Auto**.

The rectangle labeled [Line Items] is the area where the included layout will be displayed. If you need to change the included layout options, you can double-click in this area to open the Included Layout dialog box.

Let's try entering an invoice. We will need to enter a few products first:

1. Switch to the User environment.
2. Press ⌘-spacebar to display the List of Files window.

FIGURE 13.11

The printed result of the Variable Print Frame option

EXPENSE REPORT

LAST NAME	FIRST NAME	
Jones	Jane	
EMPLOYEE NUMBER	PHONE NUMBER	EXTENSION
75	4085551234	555

Event No 52

DATE
Jan 5, 1995

DESCRIPTION
Macworld Expo

COMMENTS

R?	Category	Date	Paid To	Amount
	Air fare	1/4/95	American Airlines	$650.00
√	Taxi-Limo	1/4/95	Yellow Cab	$25.00
√	Lunch	1/4/95	McDonalds	$5.25
√	Dinner	1/4/95	Sensational Seafood	$26.50
√	Taxi-Limo	1/4/95	Yellow Cab	$5.00
√	Fees	1/5/95	Macworld Expo	$20.00
√	Software	1/5/95	BMUG	$100.00
√	Breakfast	1/5/95	Big Breakfasts	$10.25
√	Lunch	1/5/95	McDonalds	$6.25
√	Dinner	1/5/95	Sams' Wharf	$28.00
√	Phone-FAX	1/5/95	AT&T	$5.95
√	Breakfast	1/6/95	Tiffany's	$12.50
√	Fees	1/6/95	Expo Seminar	$20.00
√	Lunch	1/6/95	Arbys	$6.00
√	Taxi-Limo	1/6/95	Cable Car	$3.00
√	Postage	1/6/95	Pac Mail Center	$12.50
√	Dinner	1/6/95	Hard Rock Cafe	$19.00
√	Breakfast	1/7/95	Sandra's Diner	$9.50
√	Taxi-Limo	1/7/95	Yellow Cab	$6.50
√	Software	1/7/95	Cool Software	$79.00
√	Software	1/7/95	Disks R Us	$59.00
√	Lunch	1/7/95	Wendy's	$6.25
√	Taxi-Limo	1/7/95	Yellow Cab	$5.00
√	Dinner	1/7/95	TED's Steaks	$55.00
√	Breakfast	1/8/95	Tiffany's	$12.00
√	Taxi-Limo	1/8/95	Yellow Cab	$4.50
	Lodging	1/8/95	Parc 44 Hotel	$550.12

Reimbursable	$541.95
Non Reimbursable	$1,200.12
Total Expenses	$1,742.07

FIGURE 13.11

The printed result of the Variable Print Frame option (continued)

Employee	Supervisor	Controller

FIGURE 13.12

The printed result of the Fixed (truncation) Print Frame option

EXPENSE REPORT

LAST NAME	FIRST NAME	
Jones	Jane	
EMPLOYEE NUMBER	PHONE NUMBER	EXTENSION
75	4085551234	555

Event No 52

DATE
Jan 5, 1995

DESCRIPTION
Macworld Expo

COMMENTS

R?	Category	Date	Paid To	Amount
	Air fare	1/4/95	American Airlines	$650.00
√	Taxi-Limo	1/4/95	Yellow Cab	$25.00
√	Lunch	1/4/95	McDonalds	$5.25
√	Dinner	1/4/95	Sensational Seafood	$26.50
√	Taxi-Limo	1/4/95	Yellow Cab	$5.00
√	Fees	1/5/95	Macworld Expo	$20.00
√	Software	1/5/95	BMUG	$100.00
√	Breakfast	1/5/95	Big Breakfasts	$10.25
√	Lunch	1/5/95	McDonalds	$6.25
√	Dinner	1/5/95	Sams' Wharf	$28.00
√	Phone-FAX	1/5/95	AT&T	$5.95
√	Breakfast	1/6/95	Tiffany's	$12.50
√	Fees	1/6/95	Expo Seminar	$20.00
√	Lunch	1/6/95	Arbys	$6.00
√	Taxi-Limo	1/6/95	Cable Car	$3.00
√	Postage	1/6/95	Pac Mail Center	$12.50
√	Dinner	1/6/95	Hard Rock Cafe	$19.00
√	Breakfast	1/7/95	Sandra's Diner	$9.50
√	Taxi-Limo	1/7/95	Yellow Cab	$6.50
√	Software	1/7/95	Cool Software	$79.00
√	Software	1/7/95	Disks R Us	$59.00

Reimbursable	$541.95
Non Reimbursable	$1,200.12
Total Expenses	$1,742.07

Employee	Supervisor	Controller

FIGURE 13.13

The printed result of the Fixed (multiple records) Print Frame option

EXPENSE REPORT

LAST NAME: Jones
FIRST NAME: Jane
EMPLOYEE NUMBER: 75
PHONE NUMBER: 4085551234
EXTENSION: 555

Event No 52

DATE: Jan 5, 1995

DESCRIPTION: Macworld Expo

COMMENTS:

R?	Category	Date	Paid To	Amount
	Air fare	1/4/95	American Airlines	$650.00
√	Taxi-Limo	1/4/95	Yellow Cab	$25.00
√	Lunch	1/4/95	McDonalds	$5.25
√	Dinner	1/4/95	Sensational Seafood	$26.50
√	Taxi-Limo	1/4/95	Yellow Cab	$5.00
√	Fees	1/5/95	Macworld Expo	$20.00
√	Software	1/5/95	BMUG	$100.00
√	Breakfast	1/5/95	Big Breakfasts	$10.25
√	Lunch	1/5/95	McDonalds	$6.25
√	Dinner	1/5/95	Sams' Wharf	$28.00
√	Phone-FAX	1/5/95	AT&T	$5.95
√	Breakfast	1/6/95	Tiffany's	$12.50
√	Fees	1/6/95	Expo Seminar	$20.00
√	Lunch	1/6/95	Arbys	$6.00
√	Taxi-Limo	1/6/95	Cable Car	$3.00
√	Postage	1/6/95	Pac Mail Center	$12.50
√	Dinner	1/6/95	Hard Rock Cafe	$19.00
√	Breakfast	1/7/95	Sandra's Diner	$9.50
√	Taxi-Limo	1/7/95	Yellow Cab	$6.50
√	Software	1/7/95	Cool Software	$79.00
√	Software	1/7/95	Disks R Us	$59.00

Reimbursable	$541.95
Non Reimbursable	$1,200.12
Total Expenses	$1,742.07

Employee	Supervisor	Controller

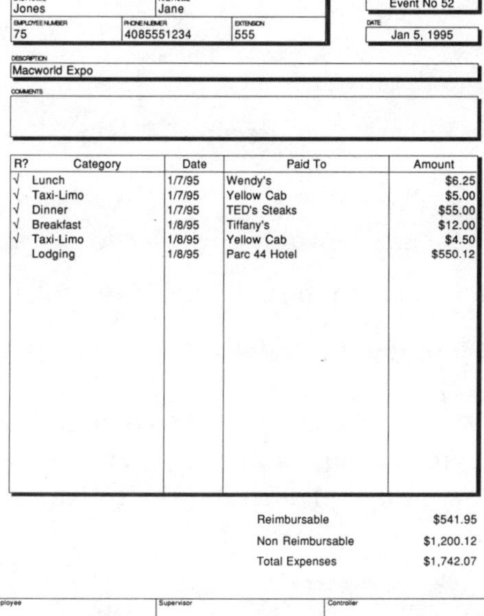

EXPENSE REPORT

LAST NAME: Jones
FIRST NAME: Jane
EMPLOYEE NUMBER: 75
PHONE NUMBER: 4085551234
EXTENSION: 555

Event No 52

DATE: Jan 5, 1995

DESCRIPTION: Macworld Expo

COMMENTS:

R?	Category	Date	Paid To	Amount
√	Lunch	1/7/95	Wendy's	$6.25
√	Taxi-Limo	1/7/95	Yellow Cab	$5.00
√	Dinner	1/7/95	TED's Steaks	$55.00
√	Breakfast	1/8/95	Tiffany's	$12.00
√	Taxi-Limo	1/8/95	Yellow Cab	$4.50
	Lodging	1/8/95	Parc 44 Hotel	$550.12

Reimbursable	$541.95
Non Reimbursable	$1,200.12
Total Expenses	$1,742.07

Employee	Supervisor	Controller

3. Click on **Products**.
4. Press ⌘-spacebar again to hide the List of Files window.
5. Choose Enter ➤ New Record (⌘-N).

The Part Number field has not been set up to automatically assign numbers to new Products, so you will have to enter one manually.

6. Type **1** in the Part Number field.
7. Type **Cat Detector** in the Description field.
8. Type **39.95** in the Price field.
9. Click the **Save** button or press the Enter key.
10. Type **2** in the Part Number field.
11. Type **Fish License** in the Description field.
12. Type **25.00** in the Price field.
13. Click the **Save** button or press the Enter key.
14. Click the **Cancel** button or press ⌘-period.

Now that there are some Products to sell, you can enter an invoice. Let's enter one:

1. Switch to the Invoices file.
2. Choose Enter ➤ New Record (⌘-N).
3. Type **@** in the Account Number field and press the Tab key.
4. Choose a customer from the Selection window.
5. Click anywhere in the included layout to select it.
6. Hold down the ⌘ key and press the Tab key.

Pressing ⌘-Tab creates a new record in the selected included layout. The record is automatically related to the invoice because you selected the Auto assign related value option when you drew the relation arrow. With this option selected, the Invoice Number is copied from the

Invoices file to the Invoice Number field in the Line Items file automatically each time you create a new Line Item. If the Invoice Number field was displayed in the included layout, you would see the number 1 in that field because the Invoices Invoice Number field has the value 1.

Notice that the included layout looks similar to an output layout. When you click on an included layout, 4D displays a flashing triangle in the upper-left corner of the included area to let you know that this included layout is selected. It does this because you may have more than one included layout on the current input layout and 4D needs to know which included layout you wish to work with.

The Part Number field is related to the Part Number field in the Products file. You can enter a part number to relate this new line item to a particular part number and display the description.

1. Type **1** in the Part Number field and press the Tab key.
2. Type **2** in the Qty field and press the Tab key.
3. Type **39.95** in the Price field and press the Tab key.
4. Type **79.90** in the Line Total field.

You have to enter the price and calculate the line total manually. However, in the next chapter you will learn how to instruct 4D to fill in the price and calculate the line total automatically by writing a script.

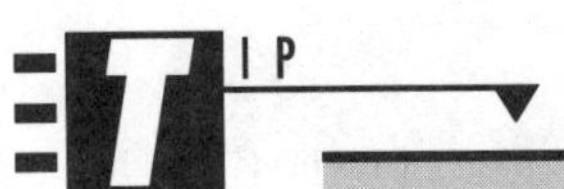

Notice that the scroll bar of the included layouts extends about two pixels below the included layout. You can remove this space by opening the included layout in the Layout Editor and moving the B0 (Break Zero) line up so that it is one pixel below the D (Detail) line.

When you added a line item, you created a record in the Line Items file. This file is completely separate from the Invoices file. This means that canceling the invoice has no effect on the Line Items. The line items you enter will still exist in the Line Items file even if you cancel the invoice. Let's check it out:

1. Click the **Cancel** button.
2. Use the List of Files window to switch to the Line Items file.

The line item you entered is still in the Line Items file even after you canceled the invoice! This is because the Accept and Cancel buttons don't affect records entered through included layouts. This seems to present a problem. If you create a new invoice at this point, it will be invoice number 1. This Line Items has 1 in the Invoice Number field, consequently, this line item would appear on the invoice. There must be some way to tell 4D to only save changes to the Line Items file if you save the invoice. Fortunately, there is a way.

1. Click on the Cat Detector record to select it.
2. Choose Edit ➤ Clear.
3. Click **Yes** to delete the record.
4. Switch back to the Design environment.
5. Choose File ➤ Preferences.
6. Select Automatic Transactions during Data Entry.
7. Click **OK**.

The Automatic Transactions during Data Entry option tells 4D to only save changes to records in an included layout if the parent record is saved. A transaction is something 4D can create to temporarily keep changes to records (including new records and deletion of records) until you tell 4D to save everything or cancel everything. With this option selected, 4D begins a transaction when you create a new record or modify an existing record using a layout that has an included layout from another file. If the parent record is accepted, all changes are saved. If the parent record is canceled, all changes are lost. You can also control transactions using 4D's programming language. For more information on transactions, see your 4th Dimension Programming Reference.

Records in the *one* file are sometimes referred to as *parent records.* Their related records in the *many* file are then referred to as *children.*

Let's enter another invoice, this time, you will cancel the invoice and see if 4D cancels any line items you enter:

1. Switch to the User environment.
2. Switch to the Invoices file.
3. Choose Enter ➤ New Record (⌘-N).
4. Select any customer for this invoice.
5. Enter two line items.
6. Click the **Cancel** button.
7. Switch to the Line Items file.

Notice that the Line Items file is empty. The Automatic Transactions during Data Entry option insures that the line items you entered on the invoice are saved only if you save the invoice itself.

The ⌘-Tab key combination is a convenient keyboard shortcut for adding records through an included layout. However, you might not remember this key combination and there is no key combination for deleting records from an included layout. In *Chapter 12,* I talked about automatic action buttons. Three of the automatic actions that can be assigned to buttons work specifically with included layouts. They are:

Open Included buttons are used to open a record from an included layout for editing.

Delete Included buttons are used to delete selected (highlighted) records from included layouts.

Add To Included buttons add a new record to a file displayed in an included layout.

To make entering line items easier, let's create two buttons for adding and deleting line items.

1. Switch to the Design environment.
2. Open the Invoices Input layout.
3. Click on the Active Object tool to select it.
4. Draw an active object about 90 pixels long and 30 pixels high and just below and to the left of the included layout.
5. Name the object **bAdd**.
6. Choose Button from the Type pop-up menu.
7. Choose Add To Included from the Action pop-up menu.
8. Type **Add Item** as the button text.
9. Click **OK**.
10. Click on the **bAdd** button to select it.
11. Choose **Object ➤ Duplicate** (⌘-D) or click on the Duplicate tool to make a duplicate of the bAdd button.
12. Move the **duplicate** button just to the right of the original bAdd button.
13. Double-click on the **duplicate** button to open the Object Definition dialog box.
14. Change the name of the button to **bDelete**.
15. Type **Delete Item** as the button text.
16. Choose Delete Included from the Action pop-up menu.
17. Click **OK**.

Now you will have these buttons for adding line items and deleting line items. This will make it easier than trying to remember the ⌘-Tab key combination.

In *Chapter 12* you learned how to add balloon help to buttons. You might want to add a help balloon to the Add Item button that reminds the user that the keyboard shortcut for adding line items is ⌘-Tab.

On most invoices, the invoice total appears below the line items. Since you already have this layout open in the Layout Editor, go ahead and move the Invoice Total field so that it is just below the included layout and aligned with the included layouts right side. Figure 13.14 shows how the Invoices Input layout should now look.

FIGURE 13.14

The Input layout with add and delete buttons

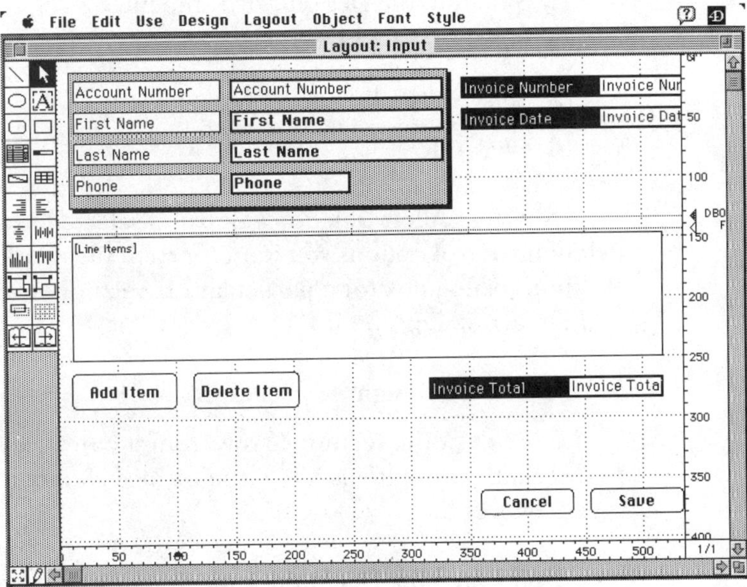

CONTROLLING DELETION OF RELATED RECORDS

When you have related files, another question needs to be answered. What should happen if the user attempts to delete the parent (the one file) record. For example, if the user decides to delete an invoice, what do you want to do with the related line items? You probably don't want to leave records in the Line Items file that have no Invoice record. Do you want to delete the line items? Perhaps you want to prevent the user from deleting the invoice if the invoice has line items. You can have 4D control the deletion of records automatically, using *deletion control.*

Deletion control options are selected when you draw a relation arrow between two files. Before you can select any of the deletion control options however, you have to turn deletion control on. You do this in the Preferences dialog box.

1. Switch to the Design Environment.
2. Choose File ➤ Preferences.
3. Select Allow Deletion Control.
4. Click **OK**.

Now that Allow Deletion Control is selected, you can choose the deletion control options you want for each file relation. To redisplay the Relations dialog box for a particular file relation, you must redraw the relation arrow. Let's try it:

1. Choose Design ➤ Structure.
2. Re-draw the relation arrow from the Invoice Number field in the Line Items file to the Invoice Number field in the Invoices file.

Notice that the Deletion Control options are now enabled. You have three options to choose from:

Leave related many intact means that when the user deletes the related record in the one file, don't delete the related records in the many file. With this option, the many file is left untouched.

Delete related many means that when the user deletes the related record in the one file, the related records in the many file will also be deleted. This is the most likely choice for the relation between the Line Items and Invoices files.

Can't delete related many means that the user cannot delete the related record in the one file if related records exist in the many file. This is the most likely choice for the option for the relation between the Customers file and the Invoices file. You wouldn't want to delete any customers that have invoices because you need to keep their records in order to display their customer information on the invoice.

When a record in a many file has no parent record in the one file, that many record is called an *orphan* (a child without a parent).

1. Select Delete related many.
2. Click **OK**.

You can tell which Deletion Control option is selected without redrawing the relation arrow. In the structure window, relation arrows with Leave related many intact selected display in blue. Relation arrows with Delete related many selected display in green. Relation arrows with Can't delete related many selected display in red.

LINKING MULTIPLE FILES

As you can see, relating two files is quite easy. Relating more files is just as easy. These file relations can go for as many levels as you want. For example, your Learn 4D database now has a three-level relation. The Line Items file is related to the Invoices file, which is then related to the Customers file.

When creating a database structure the best thing you can do is plan before you break ground. In other words, get out a piece of paper and map out what you think the structure will look like. Ask yourself questions like:

- What action or actions will be tracked by the database? (Example: customers buy products.)
- Do I have repeated data that could be stored in a related file?
- Does the structure I have designed account for all possibilities, or are there exceptions which won't fit?

Once you have defined the files you need, determine which files have data that need to be shared. Ask yourself the one-to-many questions. For example, if you were creating a database to keep track of songs and recordings, you might ask yourself these questions:

- Can one song have many recordings? Yes.
- Can one recording have many songs? Yes.

Since the answer was yes both times, the relationship between the two files is a many-to-many relationship. Let's look at another example. Say you were creating a database to keep track of football teams and their players:

- Can one team have many players? Yes.
- Can one player belong to many teams? No.

If you answered yes to one question and no to the other, then it's a one-to-many relationship. The question you answered yes to tells you which file is the one file and which file is the many file. **One team** can have **many players**.

Remember, the relation arrow always starts at the many file and points to the one file.

AUTOMATICALLY UPDATING RELATED FILES

As you enter invoices, it would be nice if 4D could automatically subtract the quantities entered for products from that products inventory. You would of course have to add a few fields to the Products file. For example, you would need a field to keep track of the number of items you have in inventory for each product. You might also want to add a reorder level field. With this field you could print a report and see which items need to be reordered. All of this can be done with 4D's programming language. In the next chapter, you will begin to work with this language. As you understand it more, you will be able to add programming to perform tasks such as these automatically. If you have never used a programming language before, the thought of programming a computer might seem a bit overwhelming. Have no fear. It doesn't take a rocket scientist to program a computer. Anyone can learn programming if she has the desire to learn it.

AUTOMATIC RELATIONS VS. MANUAL RELATIONS

There are two types of relations: automatic and manual. With automatic relations, related records are located automatically when you access a record using a layout. With manual relations, related records are not automatically located unless you use commands in the programming language to tell 4D to locate them. Automatic relations require less setup and no programming. Manual relations require programming but give you more control over your database. You might not ever need to use manual relations. As a matter of fact, by the time you feel comfortable enough with the language to use them, you will probably also understand when to use them. You choose between automatic and manual relations in the Relations dialog box that appears when you draw a relation arrow between two files. When the Relate One and Relate Many checkboxes in the Relations dialog box are selected, those relations are automatic, if you deselect one of these options, the relation becomes manual.

Again, you may never need to change these options. I include this information so that you have an understanding about all of the options in the Relations dialog box.

In the structure window, if a relation between two files is completely manual (the Relate one and Relate many options are both deselected in the Relations dialog box), the arrow will appear as solid black.

SEARCHING ON VALUES IN RELATED FILES

Once you have established relationships between files you can search a file based on fields in a related file. For example, you might want to find all of the invoices for customers that are in California. You are searching for invoices, but the State field is in the Customers file. Since the two files are related, you can search the Customers file.

The confusing part about doing this kind of search is knowing which file to display. For example, if you are searching for all of the invoices that belong to customers in California, which file should you be viewing in the User environment? Well, you are looking for invoices, therefore you should have the Invoices file displayed before you perform the search. That way, 4D will know that you want to create a selection of records for the Invoices file instead of the Customers file. Figure 13.15 shows the Search Editor performing this type of search. Notice that the Invoices file is displayed behind the Search Editor.

FIGURE 13.15

A search using a related file

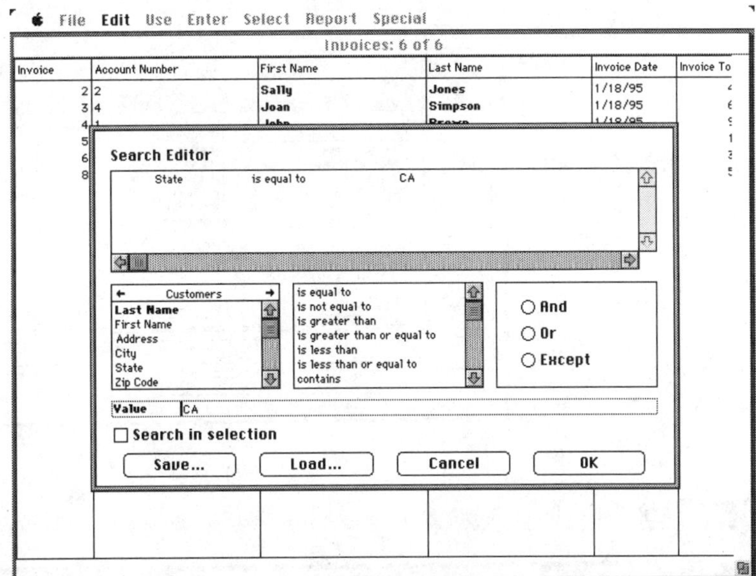

You can even search across multiple related files. For example, you might want to find all of the sales of products to customers in Texas. In this scenario, you would be searching the Line Items file using the State field from the Customers file. The Line Items file is related to the Invoices file and the Invoices file is related to the Customers file. As long as the files are related, you can perform this type of search.

The search criteria I spoke of searches the many file (Invoices) based on a field in the one file (Customers). You can also perform searches on the one file based on a field in the many file. For example, you might want to find all of the customers that have invoices that are dated today so you can print labels to send out their orders. Figure 13.16 shows an example of this type of search.

FIGURE 13.16

Searching the Customers file using a field from the Invoices file

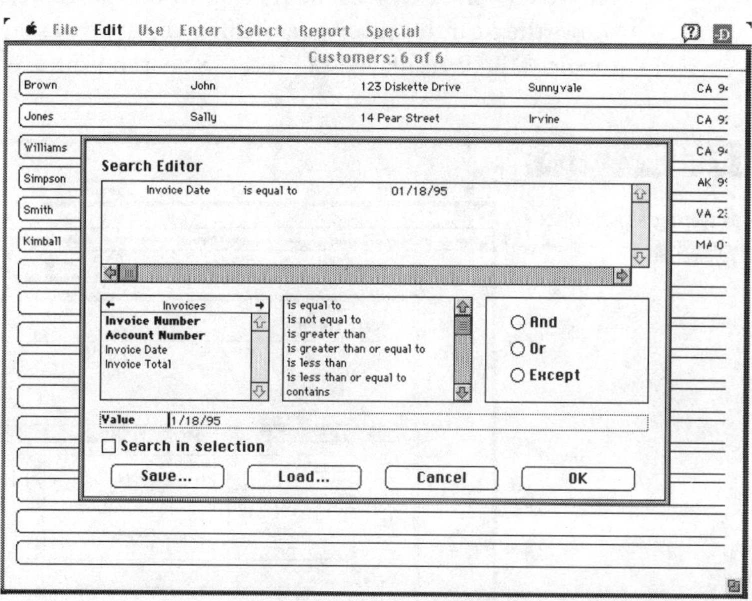

Searches that use related fields don't use indexes. This means that this type of searching will not be as fast as a search that only uses fields from the file being searched. You can improve the speed of searches that use related files using a few commands from the programming language. For more information, see the SEARCH, JOIN, and PROJECT SELECTION commands in the 4th Dimension Language Reference.

SORTING ON VALUES IN RELATED FILES

Fields from related files can be used for sorting as well as searching. For example, you might want to sort your invoices by the state that the customer lives in. In this case, you would display the invoices file then Choose Select ➤ Sort Selection (⌘-T) and choose the State field from the Customers file. Figure 13.17 shows the Sort Editor about to sort the Invoices file by the State field from the Customers file.

FIGURE 13.17

Sorting using a related field

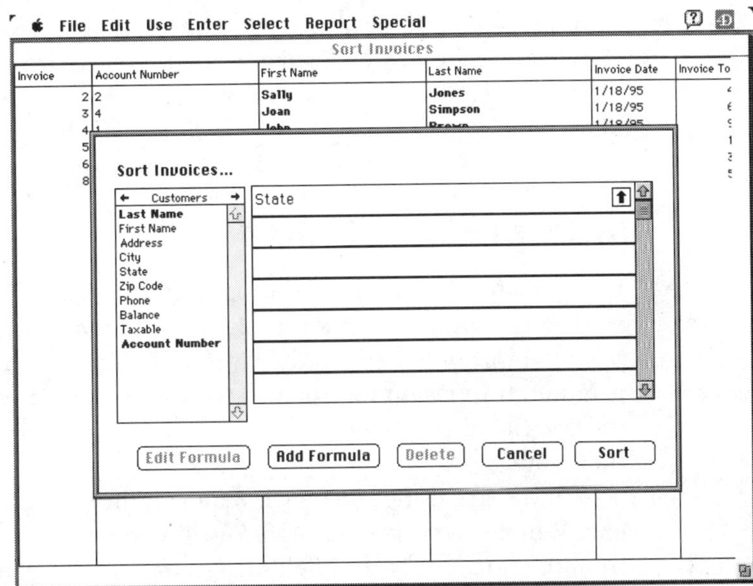

4D cannot use indexes when you sort using related fields. This means that this kind of sorting will not be as fast as sorting the file using one of its own fields.

Reporting on Values in Related Files

You can include fields from related files on your reports. For example, you might want to print a report from the Invoices file that shows a customer's name and address. You might want to print a report from the Customers file that displays a list of invoices for each customer. When you first learned how to display related records, you learned that you use different techniques to display fields from the one file than you use to display fields from the many file. This is also true for printing.

Printing from the Many File

Using related fields when printing from the many file is easy. When you created the Input layout for the Invoices file, you simply added the fields from the Customers file to the layout. The same technique is used when printing. If you want to print a record from the many file with fields from the one file displayed, you just have to add the fields from the one file to the layout.

If you are using the Quick Report Editor to print reports, it is just as easy. When you create the report for the many file, you can add fields from the one file. To add fields from the one file, you click on the left or right arrows in the fields area of the Quick Report Editor to access other files. When you find the related file, drag the fields you want on to the report.

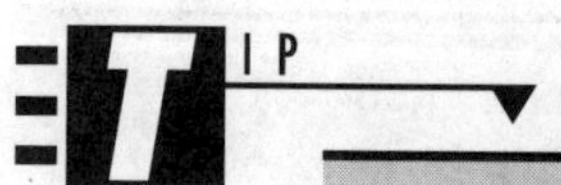

Instead of using the arrow buttons in the Quick Report Editor, you can choose a file by clicking in-between the arrows and display a pop-up menu of the files in the database.

PRINTING FROM THE ONE FILE

To access the related Line Items on the Invoices Input layout, you created an included layout and displayed it on the Input layout. The same technique is used for printing. When you are using a layout for printing and you want the related records from the many file printed along with each record from the one file, you use an included layout. When printing an included layout, remember to choose the Print Frame option (discussed earlier in this chapter) that makes the most sense for the report you are printing. The Print Frame options can be accessed by opening the one file input layout and double-clicking on the included area.

The Quick Report Editor will not print fields from related many files.

WHAT ARE SUBFILES?

So far you have created several files and related them. There is one type of file that you haven't work with yet called a *Subfile.* You probably noticed the Subfile field type in the Field dialog box. In fact, Subfiles are not fields at all. Subfiles can have their own fields (called Subfields) and have their own input and output layouts. Figure 13.18 shows a subfile in the structure window. However, Subfiles cannot be accessed in the way that regular files can. The records in Subfiles can only be accessed through included layouts. Subfile records (called *subrecords*) do not require file relations because they are part of the parent record they were created from. For example, you could add a subfile to the Customers file to keep track of different phone numbers and contacts each customer has. You would create an included layout for the Customers Input layout in the same way you created the included layout for the Invoices Input layout. Figure 13.19 shows a subfile displayed through an included layout.

FIGURE 13.18

A subfile in the structure window

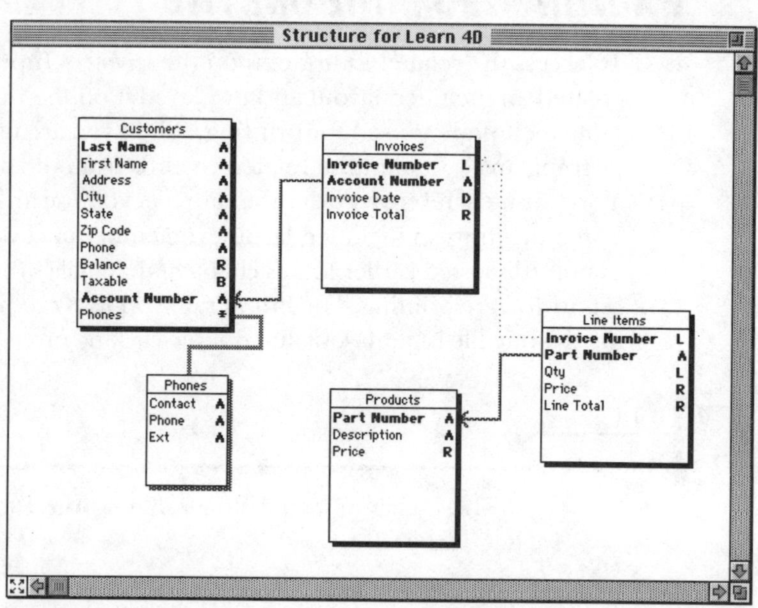

FIGURE 13.19

A subfile in an included layout

Entry for Customers

Last Name Jones
First Name Sally
Address 14 Pear Street
City Irvine
State CA Zip Code 92715
Phone (714) 555-9890
Balance $5,500.00
Taxable
Account # 00002

Contact	Phone	Ext
Bobby	(714) 555-9890	34
Sandra	(714) 555-9899	12

Next Cancel Save

There are some advantages and disadvantages to Subfiles.

- Subrecords are loaded into the computer's RAM memory when you open the parent record they belong to. Consequently, access to subrecords is very fast.
- Because they are loaded into memory, they can use a lot of memory if the parent record has many subrecords.
- It is difficult to report on the data in subrecords because they cannot be accessed independently of their parent record.

Subfiles are useful for keeping track of data that you will never want to print on a report. Phone numbers are perfect for subfiles because they would never be printed on a report. If you did want to print subrecords, they must be printed along with the parent record they belong to.

14

ADDING AUTOMATIC CALCULATIONS USING SCRIPTS

MAC TRACKS MAC

To create an automatic calculation **429**

1. Double-click on an active object in the Layout Editor.
2. Click the **Script: Only If Modified** checkbox.
3. Click the **Script** button.
4. Enter the calculation.

To quickly view a script **439**

In the Layout Editor, hold down the Option key and click on the active object whose script you want to view.

To calculate a date that is x number of days away **443**

Add or subtract the number of days from a date.

To calculate the number of days between two dates 445

Subtract the earlier date from the later date.

To capitalize a last name 447

1. Use the Lowercase function to make the field lowercase.
2. Use the Uppercase and character reference symbols to make the first character of the last name uppercase.

Featuring

- *Creating a script*
- *Arithmetic Operators*
- *Calculations on dates*
- *Calculations on time*
- *Concatenating fields*
- *Common data entry scripts*

IN PREVIOUS CHAPTERS, you have worked with many of 4th Dimension's built-in tools. You have created files and related them to other files as well as created and modified layouts. You now understand 4D's searching, sorting, importing and exporting, reporting, labeling, and graphing capabilities! What else is there? For many of you, what you have learned so far will be enough. You will be able to get most of your work done with what you have learned. However, some of you will need to automate your database tasks further. In this chapter, you will learn about creating automatic calculations to get you started on your way to making your databases even more powerful.

AUTOMATIC CALCULATIONS

There may be times when you need to store data that is not entered manually. Instead, this data is the result of a calculation. For example, the invoice system you have created stores information about the products sold to customers. This information is stored in the Line Items file. When you enter a line item, you enter the part number, quantity and price. At this point you have to manually calculate how much the Line Total will be. The Line Total is the result of a Qty field multiplied by the Price field. Once you have performed this calculation manually, you can enter the amount into the Line Total field. You can save yourself time (and money) by having 4D perform this calculation automatically. By having 4D perform calculations and other tasks automatically, you save yourself the time you would have to take to calculate results and enter them into fields. Another consideration is that there is one thing that a machine is better at doing than we humans. That one thing is performing calculations extremely fast and with consistent accuracy.

While you may not need to build an invoicing system for yourself, invoicing is something everyone generally understands. By automating the invoicing system you are creating, you will acquire skills that you can use in developing whatever database you need.

You can create an automatic calculation so that each time a part is entered, or the quantity or price changes, the Line Total will be calculated. And what about the Invoice Total? The Invoice Total is the sum of all of the Line Totals for each line item on the invoice. Each time the Line Total changes for a line item, that affects the Invoice Total. This calculation can also be made automatic. You automate your calculations using *scripts.*

WHAT ARE SCRIPTS?

A script is a set of instructions that you give to an object on a layout. The objects you place on your layouts can then use the instructions you give them to perform calculations or other tasks automatically. For example, you might want to write a script to calculate the Line Total field for a particular line item. You might want to write a script that automatically changes the customer's last name to the proper case. This way, you could enter her last name anyway you wanted and 4D could automatically make the first letter uppercase and the rest lowercase. The possibilities are endless. The only limitation is your imagination. By adding scripts to your layout objects, you can let the computer do more of the work which means you do less of it. Now that's what I call working smarter, not harder!

HOW DO I WRITE A SCRIPT AND WHERE DOES IT GO?

Scripts are written using 4D's built-in commands and functions. 4D contains hundreds of commands, each of which performs a specific task. Don't worry about learning all of them. You can learn them as you need them. There are probably some that you will never use in your particular database applications and others you will use constantly.

Scripts are sets of instructions that you give to 4D. A script can perform a calculation, perform a task (like printing an invoice), or even make decisions based on the logic that you provide it with. There are three steps to writing a script:

Step one is to understand how solve the problem or perform the task without the computer. For example, if you want to calculate the Line Total field automatically, what is the calculation? Under what conditions should the calculation be performed?

Step two is to know what commands and functions exist to help you solve the problem. 4th Dimension has all of the commands and functions you will need. At first, you won't be sure which commands or functions to use. As you gain experience with 4D, you will get to know 4D's language and be able to use it more and more quickly and efficiently.

Step three is to decide when the computer will know to perform the calculation or task. Most scripts are initiated by the user. Will the user select a pull-down menu? Will the user change a value in a field? Will she click a button? Knowing when the script should execute your calculations is as important as knowing the calculations themselves.

USING NUMERIC FIELDS

4th Dimension has three different data types for numbers: Real, Integer, and Long Integer. You can use any of these data types in your calculations. The only difference between them is the way 4D handles them behind the scenes. Which data type you choose will be based on the kind of result you need.

THE REAL DATA TYPE

Real numbers are basically any number you can think of. A real number can have up to nine decimal places and is the only numeric type that can have a decimal value. This means that if your calculation could result in a number that has a decimal value, you will want to use a Real field or variable to hold the result of your calculation. Reals are often used in business applications because dollar amounts will typically involve cents. A Real number requires 10 bytes of disk space to be stored.

Variables can hold values like fields but do not get stored permanently in records. You will learn more about variables in *Chapter 15*.

THE INTEGER DATA TYPE

Integers can be any number between –32,767 and +32,767. They also must be whole numbers. Use Integers any time you know that the value will fall within this range and will not contain a decimal value. Sales quantities like 22 or 100 usually don't have decimals. Integers require only two bytes of disk space to be stored so they are five times more efficient than Reals.

THE LONG INTEGER DATA TYPE

Long Integers can be any number between –2,147,483,648 and +2,147,483,647. Because they are integers they must be whole numbers. Use Long Integers any time you don't need a decimal value but need a number less than –32,767 or more than +32,767. Long Integers require four bytes of disk space to be stored.

Alphanumeric fields can also hold numbers. Generally, you use Alphanumeric fields for numbers that are not used in calculations (zip codes, phone numbers, ID numbers, etc.).

ARITHMETIC OPERATORS

4th Dimension offers the arithmetic operators shown in the table below for performing calculations.

Operator	Performs	Example
+	Addition	1+1=2
–	Subtraction	1–1=0
*	Multiplication	2*10=20
/	Division	20/2=10
\	Integer Division	4.5\3=1
%	Modulo	3%2=1
^	Exponentiation	2^3=8
()	Grouping	(1+3)*4=16
		1+(3*4)=13

You can also use the following operators to compare numbers:

Operator	**Tests**
>	Greater than
<	Less than
>=	Greater than or equal to
<=	Less than or equal to
=	Is equal to
#	Is not equal to

ORDER OF PRECEDENCE

4th Dimension follows the standard mathematical order or precedence when performing calculations. This means that exponentiation takes place first, then multiplication and division, and finally addition and subtraction. For example, formulas like 2+3*4 and 3*4+2 both produce the same result (14) because the multiplication takes place first.

4D Compiler is another program sold by ACI that makes your computer perform calculations more quickly. If you compile your database with the 4D Compiler, you *must* balance your parentheses. The 4D Compiler will generate an error and will not compile your database. You will learn more about the 4D Compiler in *Chapter 19*.

If you can't remember the order of precedence, use parentheses. When you put parentheses around part of a calculation it forces 4D to perform that part of the calculation first. For example, (3+2)*5 results in 25 because the addition was done first. In most programs that perform calculations, you must have balanced parentheses. This means that you have to have as many opening parentheses as closing parentheses. 4D however, is a bit more forgiving than other applications. It will not produce an error if you don't balance your parentheses but your calculation may not be correct.

NEGATIVE NUMBERS

To enter negative numbers into a field, just precede the number with a minus sign (hyphen). For example, –25 is negative 25 (or minus 25).

AUTOMATING THE INVOICE CALCULATIONS

It would save time during data entry if the Line Total and Invoice Total were calculated automatically by the database instead of having the user do it. Also, computers tend to make fewer mistakes than humans, so having the calculations done by the computer will mean more accurate invoices. Let's use the three-step method I talked about to write the scripts necessary to automatically calculate the Line Total and Invoice Total fields.

Step one is to figure out what the calculations actually are. The calculation for the Line Total is simple:

Line Total = Quantity * Price

The calculation for the Invoice Total is also simple:

Invoice Total = the sum of the Line Total field

Step two is to know what commands and functions exist to help you solve your problem. These calculations will look almost exactly like this in a script. We need only to make a few minor changes. First, 4D will want to know which files the fields come from. When a field is used in a script, the file name that the field belongs to should precede the field name. The file name is placed between brackets ([]). This makes it easier for 4D to know that it is a file name. Also, 4D uses the equal sign

(=) to test the equality of two things. For example, if you wanted to test if the Last Name field was equal to "Smith" you would write:

```
Last Name = "Smith"
```

Certain conventions are used throughout 4D. The fact that filenames are surrounded by brackets ([])is one of them. You may have trouble remembering some of these conventions at first. But have no fear, 4D will let you know when it doesn't understand what you are telling it. These conventions help 4D to understand you and execute your instructions more quickly.

What you want to do is assign the result of the calculation Quantity * Price to the Line Total field. Assignments are made with the assignment operator. The assignment operator is a colon (:), then an equals sign (=). These two symbols together make up the assignment operator. The first calculation would now look like this:

```
[Line Items]Line Total:=[Line Items]Qty * [Line Items]Price
```

You already know how the Invoice Total field should be displayed and how the assignment should be made:

```
[Invoices]Invoice Total:=
```

But what about the rest of the calculation? How do you sum up the Line Total field for all of the line items on an invoice? This is where you use one of 4D's built-in functions. The function you use is called *Sum.* You can use the Sum function to give you the sum of a field. The result returned by the Sum function will be the sum of the values in the field for all of the records in the current selection. Because the Line Items file is related to the Invoices file, each time you open an Invoice, the current selection for the Line Items file becomes the related Line Items automatically. The Sum function requires you to tell it which field to sum. When a function or command needs information to do its job, you give it this information inside of parentheses. Our finished calculation looks like this:

```
[Invoices]Invoice Total:=Sum([Line Items]Line Total)
```

Any time you perform the first calculation the Line Total field will be recalculated. Since the Line Total field has changed and the Invoice Total field is calculated based on the Line Total field, the Invoice Total field must also be recalculated. Consequently, you will want to put these two calculations together:

```
[Line Items]Line Total:=[Line Items]Qty * [Line Items]Price
[Invoices]Invoice Total:=Sum([Line Items]Line Total)
```

Step three is to decide when the computer will know to perform the calculation or task. When you add a script to an object on a layout, you can tell 4D to execute (run) the script only when the user modifies the object. A button or other clickable object is modified when the user clicks it. Fields are modified when the user makes an entry and then exits the field by pressing the Tab key or the Return key or by clicking on a button or in a field.

Since 4D executes a field's script when the field is modified, you need to figure out which fields, when modified, should recalculate the Line Total and Invoice Total. Figuring this out exactly is quite easy. The fields that require this script are the fields that the user can change that are also used in the calculations. If you look at the calculation, the only fields the user can modify are the Qty and Price fields. However, when the user enters a part number 4D will lookup the matching Part Number in the Products file. At this point, you can copy the Price from the Products file into the Price field in the Line Items file. This will save the user the step of having to enter the price herself. The calculation to assign the Products Price field to the Line Items Price field is simple:

```
[Line Items]Price:=[Products]Price
```

Storing the Price in both the Line Items file and the Products file is redundant. However, this is an occasion where redundant information is necessary. You need to store the price with the Line Item for "historical" purposes. Otherwise, you would not be able to go back to an invoice to see what you charged for a product, because the price may have changed in the Products file.

Let's create a script that automatically fills in the Price field:

1. Switch to the Design environment.
2. Open the Line Items InvoiceIncluded layout.
3. Double-click on the Part Number field to open the Field Definition dialog box.
4. Select Script only if modified.
5. Click the **Script** button.

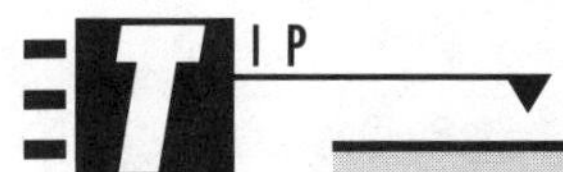

You can write scripts and procedures in 4D using the Listing Editor or the Flowchart Editor. The Listing Editor allows you to write code in lines and the Flowchart Editor allows you to write code using a flowchart. You will be using the Listing Editor. You can tell 4D that you always want to use the Listing Editor so that it won't ask you which editor you want to use. To have 4D default to the Listing Editor, select Listing under Procedure Default in the Preferences dialog box.

6. Click **OK**.

At this point you have two choices. You can type the code in manually or you can use the mouse to click on the parts you need to create the calculations. The best approach is probably a little bit of both.

In the Procedure Editor, the middle scrollable area lists the fields from the current file. All the layouts for the current file are listed below the fields in italics. If you click on a field from the fields list, the field will be inserted into the Procedure Editor. However, the Procedure Editor is not showing the name of the file that these fields come from. If the filename was displayed, it would appear between the left and right arrows. Consequently, the filename won't be inserted along with the field name. Your code would still work without filenames but it wouldn't be as readable. You can display the filename along with the fields by clicking the left or right arrows in the fields list until the Line Items filename appears. There is also a pop-up menu that can be used to select a file. Figure 14.1 shows the Procedure Editor with this pop-up menu displayed.

FIGURE 14.1

The files pop-up menu in the Procedure Editor

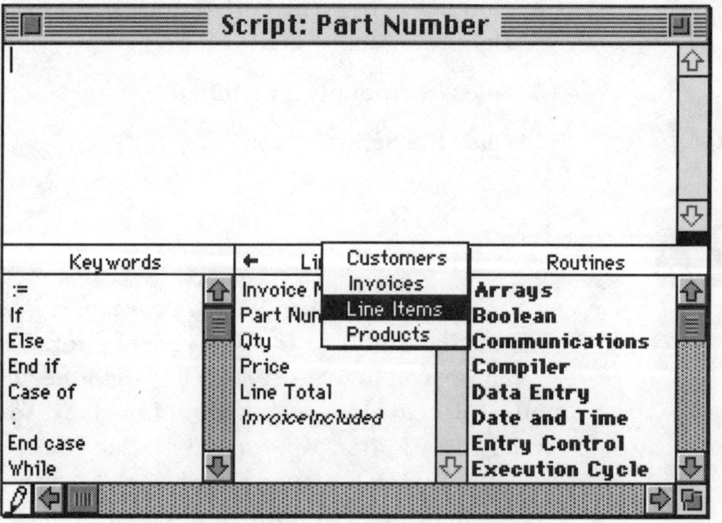

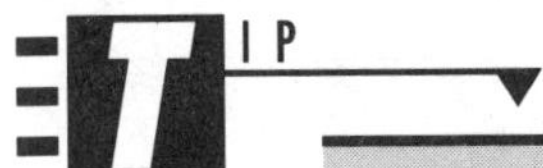

If you click and hold down the mouse button between the left and right arrows in the Fields List, a pop-up menu will appear displaying all of the files in the database. You can select from this pop-up menu to display the fields for a file instead of using the arrow buttons.

7. Locate the Line Items file by click the arrow buttons or using the pop-up menu.
8. Click on the Price field in the Fields List to insert it into the script.
9. Click on := in the Keywords List.
10. Locate the Products file in the Fields List.
11. Click on the Price field in the Fields List.
12. Press the Enter key.

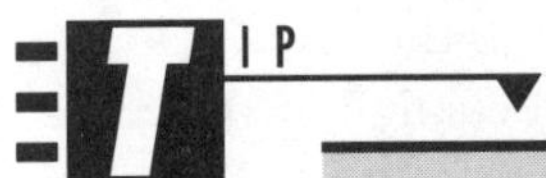

Remember, if you make a mistake you can choose Edit ➤ Undo (⌘-Z) or use the Backspace key to remove your mistake.

When you press the Return key or the Enter key, 4D looks at the line you just entered to see if it recognizes everything you have entered. If it doesn't recognize a field name or filename, 4D will put bullets (•) around it. Figure 14.2 shows the script with bullets around a field.

13. Click the close box to close the Script: Part Number window.

FIGURE 14.2

A misspelled field name will have bullets around it.

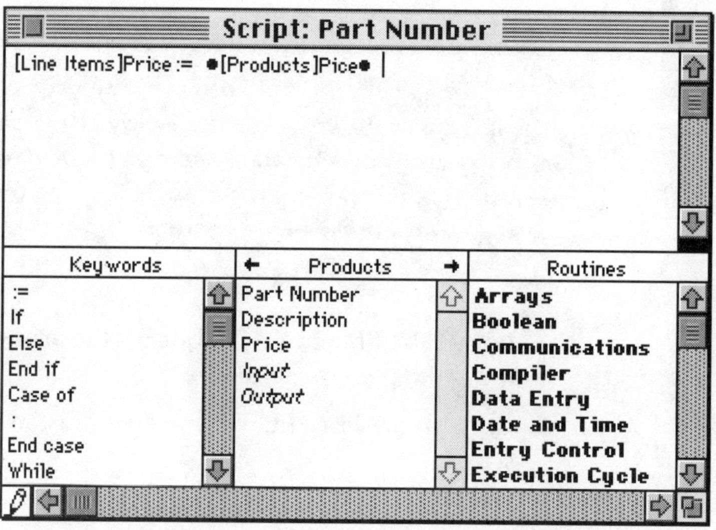

Notice that the Part Number field now has a black triangle in its upper-left corner. This black triangle tells you that this object has a script. Figure 14.3 shows the Part Number field with the black triangle.

Since the Price field will now be filled in automatically, you probably don't want the user to be able to enter anything into the Price field. If the user can still type into the Price field, they might change the price

FIGURE 14.3

The black triangle appears when a field has a script.

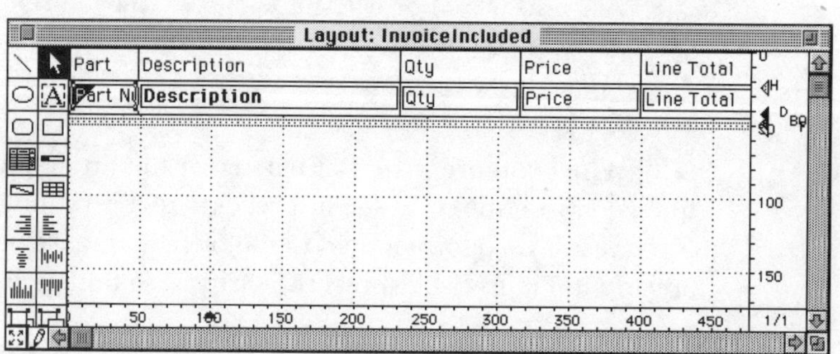

accidentally. To avoid this, let's make the [Line Items]Price field display only. Figure 14.4 shows the Field dialog box for the [Line Items]Price field with the Display only attribute selected.

FIGURE 14.4

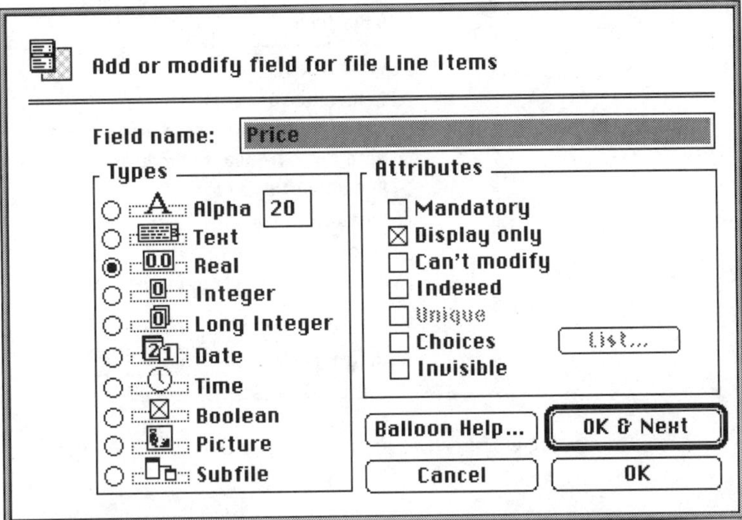

Selecting Display only for the [Line Items]Price field

1. Choose Design ➤ Structure.
2. Double-click on the Price field in the Line Items file to open it.
3. Select Display only.
4. Click **OK**.

Since you will be using scripts and procedures, you will be creating a Listing type procedure. Let's set the Procedure Editor default to Listing. Figure 14.5 shows the Preferences dialog with Listing selected as the Procedure Default.

1. Choose File ➤ Preferences.
2. Select Listing as the Procedure Default.
3. Click **OK**.

FIGURE 14.5

The Preferences dialog box

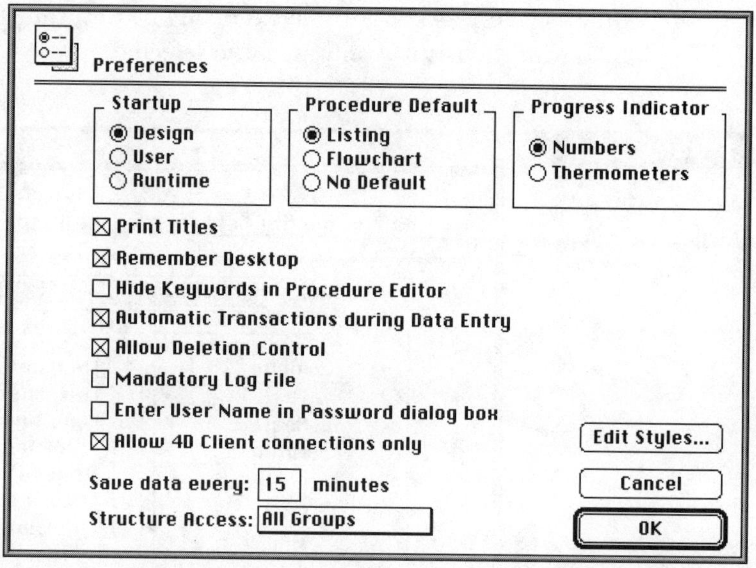

Now that you have entered your first script, let's try it out and see if it works:

1. Switch to the User environment and display the Invoices file.
2. Create a new invoice.
3. Type **1** in the Account Number field.
4. Click on the Line Items area to select it.
5. Click the **Add Item** button.
6. Type **1** in the Part Number field and press the Tab key.

The Price is filled in automatically. Also notice that you can't change the Price field. Let's change the Part Number and see if the Price changes.

1. Click in the Part Number field.
2. Change the Part Number to **2** and press the Tab key.
3. Click the **Cancel** button.

Notice that the Price changes each time you type in a Part Number. When you enter a Part Number, you are modifying that field. Since you selected the Script only if modified option for this object on the layout, modifying the field causes the script to run, which copies the [Products]Price field into the [Line Items]Price field.

When the user changes the Qty field, you will want to recalculate the Line Total since the Qty field is used in the Line Total calculation. The Line Total field is used in the Invoice Total calculation so you will also want to recalculate the Invoice Total. This means that the script for the Qty field should have both Line Total and Invoice Total calculations in it. Let's do it.

Remember, a shortcut to displaying the layouts for a particular file is to double-click on the filename in the Structure window.

1. Switch to the Design environment.
2. Open the Line Items InvoiceIncluded layout.
3. Double-click on the Qty field to open the Field Definition dialog box.
4. Select Script only if modified.
5. Click the **Script** button.
6. Locate the Line Items file in the Fields List.
7. Click on the Line Total field to insert it into the script.
8. Click on := in the Keywords List.
9. Click on the Qty field.
10. Type * into the calculation.
11. Click on the Price field.

12. Press the Return key to go to the next line.
13. Locate the Invoices file in the Fields List.
14. Click on the Invoice Total field.
15. Click on := in the Keywords List.
16. Click on Routines to show the alphabetical list of routines.
17. Scroll down until you find the Sum function.
18. Click on the Sum function to insert it into the script.
19. Scroll to the bottom of the Keywords List and click on the opening parenthesis or just type it.
20. Locate the Line Items file in the Fields List.
21. Click on the Line Total field.
22. Scroll to the bottom of the Keywords List and click on the closing parenthesis or just type it.
23. Press the **Enter** key.

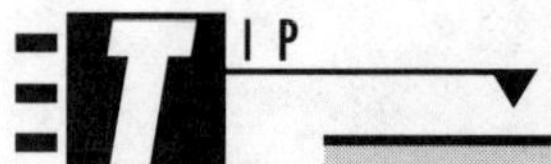

If you hold down the ⌘ key and the Shift key then press a letter, the Routines list will automatically scroll to the first routine that begins with the letter you typed.

You already know that 4D puts bullets around fields if it doesn't recognize them. If 4D recognizes one of its own commands or functions, it will display that command or function in bold. If a command or function you enter doesn't not appear in bold, then 4D did not recognize it. Figure 14.6 shows the script with the Sum function recognized.

Now that you have entered the Qty field script, the Line Total and Invoice Total fields will be calculated automatically. You don't want the user to be able to change the contents of these fields since your script is calculating the values. Let's make these two fields Display only.

FIGURE 14.6

A recognized 4D command displays in bold

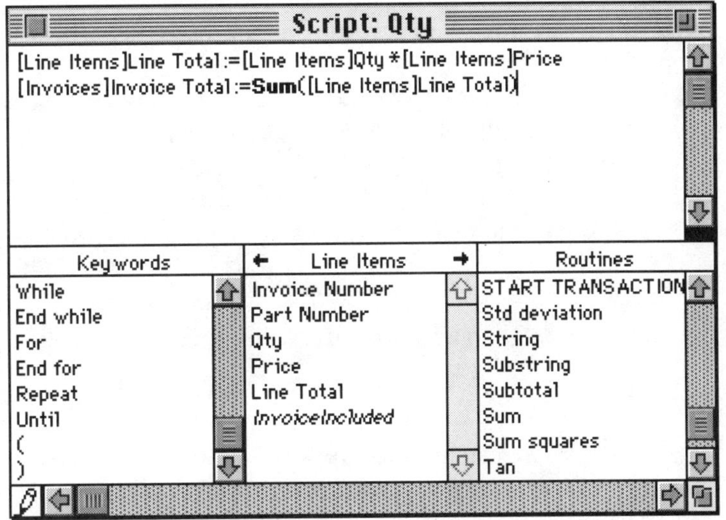

1. Choose Design ➤ Structure
2. Double-click on the Line Total field in the Line Items file to open it.
3. Select Display only.
4. Click **OK**.
5. Double-click on the Invoice Total field in the Invoices file.
6. Select Display only.
7. Click **OK**.

Now that you have entered the Qty field script, let's try it out:

1. Switch to the User environment.
2. Create a new invoice.
3. Type **1** in the Account Number field.
4. Click in the Line Items included layout area.
5. Click the **Add Item** button.

6. Type **1** in the Part Number field and press the Tab key.
7. Type **5** in the Qty field and press the Tab key.

The Line Total and Invoice Total are calculated automatically. Let's enter another Line Item to see that the calculations still work with more than one Line Item.

1. Click in the Line Items included layout area.
2. Click the **Add Item** button.
3. Type **2** in the Part Number field and press the Tab key.
4. Type **3** in the Qty field and press the Tab key.

The calculations work no matter how many line items you enter. However, there is a situation that we haven't considered. What would happen if you changed the Part Number of one of the Line Items you have already entered? Let's try it:

1. Click in the Part Number field for the first Line Item.
2. Change the Part Number to **2** and press the Tab key.

Notice that the Price changed but the Line Total and the Invoice Total were not recalculated. This is because 4D was never told to recalculate these fields should the Part Number change. Fortunately, this is easily corrected. All you need to do is copy the script of the Qty field into the script of the Part Number field. Let's do it.

Windows that were open in the Design environment stay open until you close them. Any windows open in the Design environment are listed at the bottom of the Design menu. You can bring any of these open windows to the front by selecting the item you want from this menu.

1. Click **Cancel**.
2. Switch to the Design environment.
3. Open the Line Items InvoiceIncluded layout.
4. Hold down the Option key and click on the Qty field.
5. Choose Edit ➤ Select All (⌘-A).
6. Choose Edit ➤ Copy (⌘-C).
7. Close the Script: Qty window.
8. Option-click the Part Number field.
9. Click below the first line of the script so that the cursor is on the second line.
10. Choose Edit ➤ Paste (⌘-V).
11. Close the Script: Part Number window.

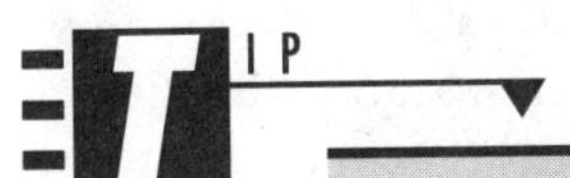

You can open the script of an object on a layout without going through the Definition dialog box by holding down the Option key and clicking on the object.

Now, if the user changes the Part Number after entering a Quantity, the Line Total and Invoice Total will be recalculated.

There is still one last situation that we have not considered, though: What if the user deletes a Line Item by clicking the **Delete Item** button? Since there will be one less Line Item, the Invoice Total will need to be recalculated. How do you solve this problem? Buttons are objects just as fields are objects. Therefore, it would seem logical that you could simply enter the Invoice Total calculation into the script of the Delete Item button. That way, when the user clicked the Delete Item button, the Line Item would be deleted and the script would recalculate the Invoice Total field. There is one catch. Scripts for automatic action buttons execute before the automatic action occurs. This means that the Invoice Total would be recalculated before the Line Item was deleted. Consequently, the Invoice Total would still include the Line Item that was deleted because the calculation occurred before the Line Item was deleted. Fortunately, you can solve this problem with a few 4D commands.

You won't be able to use an automatic action with the Delete Item button. Instead, you will use the *DELETE RECORD* command. The DELETE RECORD command deletes the current record for the file you specify. For example, DELETE RECORD([Line Items]) would delete the current record for the Line Items file. When you click on a record in the Line Items included layout area, that record becomes the current record. After the DELETE RECORD command deletes the record, the current selection for the file will be empty. This means that any other Line Items on the invoice would not be displayed. You need to use another command to tell 4D to redisplay the Line Items that are related to the invoice. You do this with the *RELATE MANY* command.

The RELATE MANY command locates related records in related many files. The Line Items file is the many file to the Invoices file because the relation arrow is drawn from the Line Items file to the Invoices file. Remember, the arrow always starts at the many file and points to the one file. You might have several files that are many files to a one file. Because of this, you will want to tell 4D which of the many files you want to get the related records for. You can do this by passing the field in the one file that has the arrow pointing to it from the many file that contains the related records you need.

Since you now know that filenames appear in brackets, from now on, fields will appear preceded by their filename. For example, the Invoice Number field for the Invoices file will appear as [Invoices]Invoice Number.

In your structure, the [Line Items]Invoice Number field points to the [Invoices]Invoice Number field. You would pass this field to the RELATE MANY command to get the related Line Items for the Invoice after deleting a Line Item. For example, your line would look like this RELATE MANY([Invoices]Invoice Number).

After you have deleted the selected Line Item with the DELETE RECORD command and then redisplayed the related Line Items with the RELATE MANY command, you can recalculate the [Invoices]Invoice Total field. Let's change the Delete Item button:

1. Open the Invoices Input layout in the Layout Editor.
2. Double-click on the **Delete Item** button.
3. Choose No Action from the Action pop-up menu.
4. Click the **Script** button.
5. Enter the following script:

```
DELETE RECORD([Line Items])
RELATE MANY([Invoices]Invoice Number)
[Invoices]Invoice Total:=Sum([Line Items]Line Total)
```

6. Close the Script: bDelete window.
7. While you are here, you might want to format the Invoice Total field for dollars and cents.

Now that you have completed the script for the Delete Item button, let's try it out:

1. Switch to the User environment.
2. Create a new invoice.
3. Type **1** into the Account Number field.
4. Enter two Line Items.
5. Click in the Qty field of the second Line Item to select it.
6. Click the **Delete Item** button.
7. Click **Cancel**.

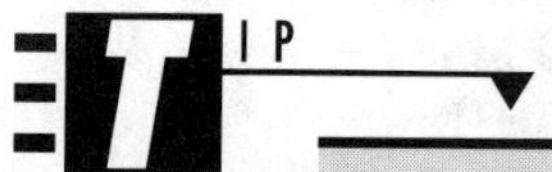

Notice that the Delete Item button is no longer disabled automatically when the Line Items included layout area is not selected. To get the Delete Item button to disable automatically, create another button with the name bDelete and assign it the Delete Included automatic action. You can then place this button on a part of the layout that the user will not see (off to the right or several inches below the Cancel and Save buttons). When 4D disables or enables the bDelete automatic action button, it will disable or enable your Delete Item button because its name is also bDelete and 4D thinks that they are the same button.

The selected Line Item is deleted and the Invoice Total is recalculated. Figure 14.7 shows the Invoice Input layout and the Line Items InvoiceIncluded layout with the scripts you have written. You have

FIGURE 14.7

The layouts and their scripts

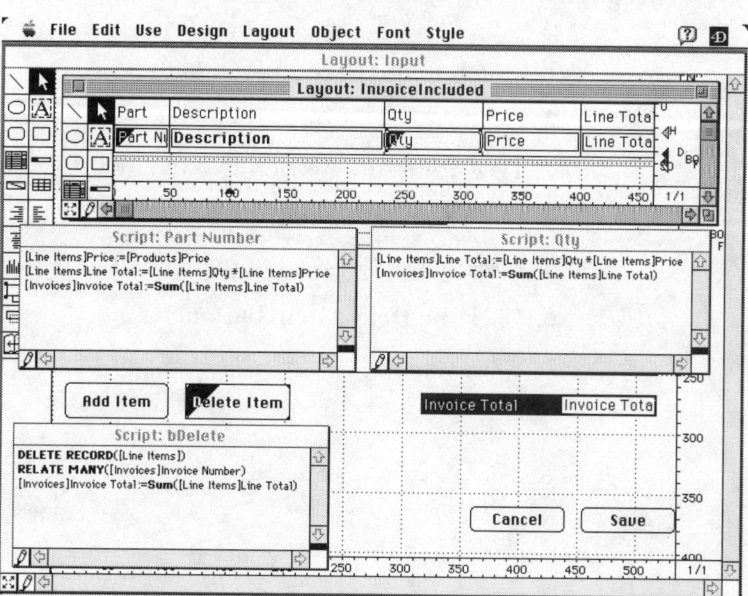

completely automated the calculations necessary for a typical invoice with a few simple scripts.

CALCULATIONS WITH NON-NUMERIC DATA TYPES

You are probably used to thinking of calculations as involving only numbers. If you are using a calculator, numbers are all you have. In 4D, you have types of data other than just numbers. Date, Time, Alphanumeric, Text, even Picture data can be used in calculations.

ADDING DAYS TO A DATE

You can add days to a date. The result of this calculation is a date that is in the future as many days as you added. For example, 12/05/94 + 5 would result in 12/10/94. Let's add a Due Date (Date) field and a Paid (Boolean) field. We can then have 4D automatically calculate the Due Date as being 30 days after the Invoice Date. When an invoice is paid, you could then open the invoice, and click on Paid. Each day, you could search for all of the Invoices that are not paid and have a Due Date that is less than or equal to today's date.

1. Switch to the Design environment.
2. Add the following fields to the Invoices file:

Field Name	Field Type	Attributes
Due Date	Date	Display only
Paid	Boolean	

   Next we need to add these fields to the Invoices Input layout.

3. Open the Invoices Input layout.
4. Draw a marquee around the entire Invoice Date field label and field.

5. Choose Object ➤ Duplicate (⌘-D) or click the Duplicate tool.
6. Position the duplicate field just below the original. Align it with the Last Name field.
7. Use the Text tool to change the field label to Due Date.
8. Double-click on the duplicate Invoice Date field to open the Definition dialog box.
9. Click on Due Date in the Fields List.
10. Remove the #D from the Default value area.
11. Click **OK**.
12. Click the Add Field Tool to select it.
13. Draw a rectangle about 50 pixels wide below the Due Date field.
14. Click on the Paid field in the Fields List.
15. Type **Paid** in the format area to display the Boolean field as a checkbox.
16. Click **OK**.
17. Set the font of the Paid field to Chicago 12 point.

Figure 14.8 shows what the Invoices Input layout should now look like.

Now that you have the fields on the layout, you will need to add a script to calculate the Due Date. Let's assume that you give your customers 30 days to pay their outstanding invoices. When should the Due Date be calculated? You could calculate the Due Date when the Invoice is saved. To do this you would create a script for the Save button that might look like this:

```
[Invoices]Due Date:=[Invoices]Invoice Date+30
```

FIGURE 14.8

The Invoices Input layout

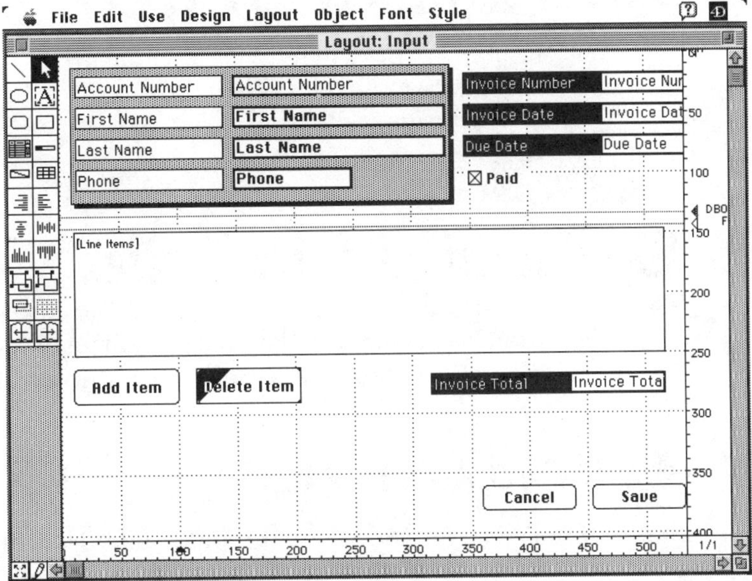

Let's do it:

1. Option-click on the **Save** button.
2. Enter the script listed above.
3. Switch to the User environment.
4. Enter a new invoice and save it.
5. Double-click on the invoice you created.

Notice that the Due Date is 30 days beyond the Invoice Date. Remember, the day of the month will not necessarily be the same since most months do not have 30 days.

SUBTRACTING DAYS FROM A DATE

You can subtract days from a date in the same way you add days. The result of this calculation is a date that is in the past as many days as you subtracted. For example, 12/05/94 – 5 would result in 11/30/94.

Days In-Between Two Dates

You can subtract one date from another date. The result of this calculation is the number of days between the two dates. For example, the result of 12/5/94 – 11/30/94 is 5. The result of the reverse calculation, 11/30/94 – 12/5/94 is –5.

Calculations with Time

Calculations with time work just like dates. The only difference is that when you add or subtract, you are dealing with seconds instead of days.

Adding to a Time Value

You can add a numeric value to a time value. The result of this calculation is a time value that is in the future by the number of seconds you added. For example, the calculation 12:05:10 + 30 would result in 12:05:40.

Subtracting from a Time Value

You can subtract a numeric value from a time value. The result of this calculation is a numeric value that represents the time that is in the past by the number of seconds you subtracted. The result is represented in seconds. For example, the calculation 12:05:10 – 30 would result in 43480. This number can be converted back to a time value with the *Time string* function.

You can subtract one time from another time. The result of this calculation is a time of day prior to the first time by the number of hours, minutes, and seconds of the time subtracted. For example, the result of 12:05:10 – 1:00 is 11:05:10.

CONCATENATION WITH ALPHA AND TEXT FIELDS

You can add Alphanumeric or Text data together. This is called concatenation. For example the result of "Geoff"+" "+"Perlman" would be "Geoff Perlman". You cannot subtract from Alphanumeric or Text fields. However, you can use multiplication! For example, the result of "X"*10 would be "XXXXXXXXXX".

CAPITALIZE THE LAST NAME

To insure that last names always look right, you can write a script to format the Last Name field so that the first character is in uppercase and the rest of the characters are in lowercase. While this won't work for all names, it will work for about 90 percent of all last names. In *Chapter 7*, you wrote a global procedure called Titlecase that you saved and then applied to all of the Customers using the Apply Formula menu item in the User environment. While this worked very well, it won't format any names you enter unless you remember to apply the Titlecase procedure every once in a while. What would be better would be to have the Titlecase procedure run each time a Last Name was entered or changed and only for the Customer that was being edited. Since you have already written the Titlecase procedure, we can simply call (execute) this procedure from the script of the Last Name field. Let's do it:

1. Make sure you are in the Design environment.
2. Open the Customers New Input layout.
3. Double-click on the Last Name field.
4. Select Script only if modified.
5. Click the **Script** button.
6. Type **Titlecase** and press the Enter key.

Notice that Titlecase was converted to italics. 4D converts procedures to italics to let you know that it recognizes the procedure name as being a valid procedure. If you entered a procedure name that you had not created yet, the style of the text would be plain. You will learn more about global procedures in *Chapter 15.*

7. Close the Script: Last Name window.
8. Switch to the User environment.
9. Go to the Customers file.
10. Choose Enter ➤ New Record (⌘-N).
11. Type **PERLMAN** in the Last Name field and press the Tab key.
12. Click **Cancel**.

WHAT DID I JUST DO?

If you have never done any programming before, congratulations are in order. The scripts you have been writing in this chapter are each bits of programming code. It is not all that mysterious. Programming is simply giving the computer instructions on what you want it to do and when you want it to do it. Up until now, you may not have understood the computer's language. You are starting to understand it by writing scripts. You will learn even more about 4D's programming language in the next three chapters. As you learn, you will be able to add more power and functionality to your database. I hope this chapter has taken some of the mystery out of programming and provided you with a bit of understanding on how computers really work.

ADDING CUSTOM MENUS

15

MAC TRACKS MAC

Use the MODIFY SELECTION command.

Use the SET WINDOW TITLE command.

1. Open each layout in the Layout Editor.
2. Choose Layout ➤ Menu Bar.
3. Type **-32000**.
4. Click **OK**.

Featuring

- *Using the Menu Editor*
- *Creating global procedures*
- *Adding standard menus*
- *Activating menus*
- *Accessing the Runtime environment*
- *Adding a custom splash screen*

UP TO THIS point, everything you have done has been in the Design or User environments. There is one environment you have yet to explore: the Runtime environment. The Design environment has its own set of menus. The User environment also has its own set of menus. The Runtime environment removes the User environment menus and displays the menus you create. You create your own custom menus with the Menu Editor.

The menus of the Design and User environments have functions pre-assigned to them. By creating your own custom menus, you can control what menus the user has access to and decide what functionality each menu item will have.

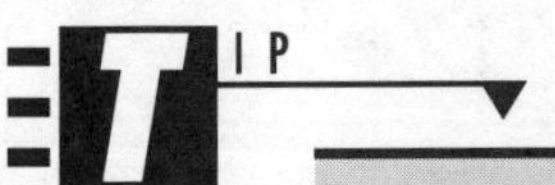

You may have noticed that the Runtime menu item on the User menu is disabled. Once you create menus, the Runtime menu item will be enabled because the Runtime environment then has menus it can display.

To help you learn about menus, you will create menus that are similar to the User environment. Your database will have the following menus:

Menu Name	**Function**
File	For displaying records from the files in your database and allowing users to quit the database when they need to.
Enter	For creating new records.
Select	For searching, sorting, and deleting records.
Report	For printing Quick Reports, labels, and graphs.

At first, these menus will work only with the Customers file. In *Chapter 16* you will learn a technique that allows your menus to work with all of your database files.

USING THE MENU EDITOR

The Menu Editor is used to create custom menus. You use the Menu Editor to create a menu bar. A menu bar is a collection of menus. The computer can only display one menu bar at a time. With the Menu Editor you can create menus, assign keyboard equivalents, enable or disable individual menu items, and assign styles. Figure 15.1 shows menus in the Menu Editor.

The Menu Editor allows you to assign styles to your menu items. However, according to *Apple's Human Interface Guidelines*, styles should be used only for the style menu items in a style menu (like in the Style menu in the Layout Editor. If you would like to know more about creating a proper interface, read *Apple's Human Interface Guidelines* published by Addison-Wesley.

FIGURE 15.1

The Menu Editor

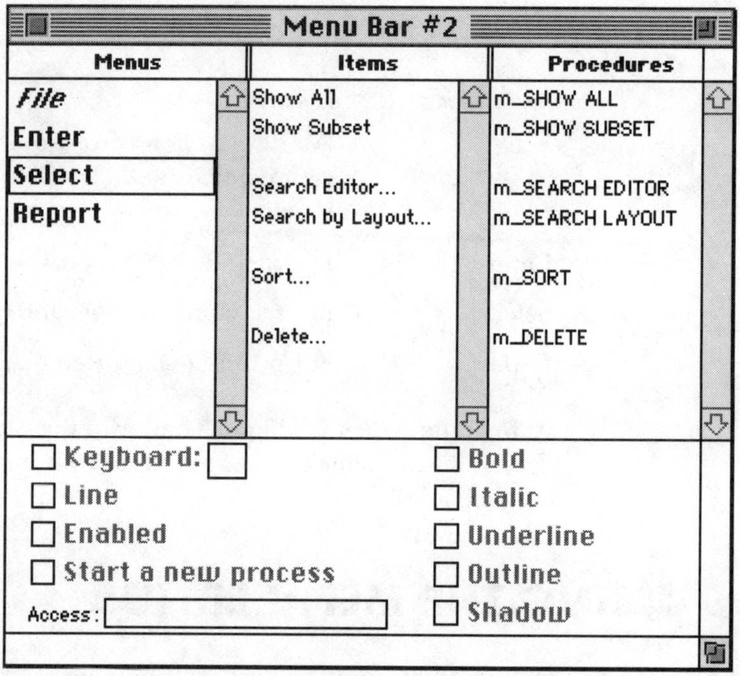

Let's create a menu bar and your first menu:

1. Switch to the Design environment.
2. Choose Design ➤ Menu (⌘-M).
3. Click **New**.

The Menu Editor creates numbered menu bars. The first menu bar you create is menu bar #1, the second is menu bar #2 and so on. The Menu Editor has three scrollable areas. The Menus List displays the menu names. The Items List displays a menu's items when you click on a menu. The Procedures List displays the procedures attached to each menu item. Once you select a menu item, the options in the lower portion of the window will be available.

When you create a menu bar, 4th Dimension adds a File menu with a Quit menu item automatically. You can delete this menu if you don't need it. However, most applications have File as their first menu. There are only two menus that you cannot edit in the Menu Editor: the Apple menu and the Edit menu.

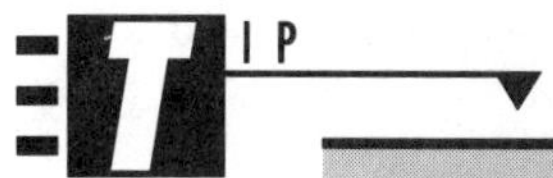

Although you cannot change the Edit menu, you can add your own "About" menu item to the Apple menu. This is done with the SET ABOUT command. See your 4th Dimension Language Reference for more information.

When you type the name of a menu, it will appear in plain style. Notice that the File menu in the Menu Editor is in italics. The word *File* is not typed into the Menu Editor. It is being displayed from a *String List.* Strings of characters can be stored in an STR# resource inside of the structure file. Macintosh applications use resources to store menus, dialog boxes, icons, sounds, and other interface elements of an application. A String List (STR#) is one type of resource. The purpose of using an STR# resource to store the names of your menus and menu items is to make it easier to translate your application into other languages. You can do this by creating one STR# resource for each language your application needs to be in. All of the text that the user sees in your application can be stored in an STR# resource. This includes menus, menu items, text objects on layouts, and button text. Each string of characters in the STR# resource is given an ID number. You can enter this ID number instead of the text itself in your menus, text, and buttons. When you want to create a version of your application in another language, you simply translate your STR# resource into the other language and all of your text appears in that language. The advantage to this is that when you make updates to your application, you can install the STR# resource into the new version in a minute and you have a translated application. The word *File* is in 4D's own STR# resource. If you click on the word *File*, it will change to *:79,1.* The colon (:) lets 4D know that you want to read the text from an STR# resource. The number following the colon is the STR# resource ID and the number following the comma is the ID of the individual string itself. If you are planning on translating your application into other languages, you will want to read the section of the

4th Dimension Language Reference on *Localization.* If you are not planning to translate your application, you do no need to worry about resources and can simply type the names of your menus and menu items into the Menu Editor. I have explained localization so that you will understand why the File menu is appearing in italics.

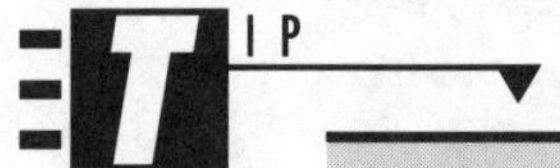

Translating an application into another language is part of *localizing* the application. If you need to do this, make sure you read about 4D Insider in *Appendix A.* 4D Insider makes localizing a 4D database much easier.

4. Click on the word **File** in the Menu Editor to select it.
5. Click on the Quit menu item to select it.

Now that you have a menu item selected, you can choose to assign it a keyboard equivalent, make it a separator line, enable or disable it, set its style, assign it a password access level, and have it start a new process. I will talk about passwords in *Chapter 18.* The Start a new process option will be covered in *Chapter 17.*

The Menu Editor has its own menu. This menu allows you to create new menus, delete existing menus, create new menu items, delete existing menu items and preview the way your menu bar will look when it is used in the Runtime environment. In most applications, the Quit menu item has ⌘-Q as its keyboard equivalent. Let's assign ⌘-Q to the Quit menu item:

6. Select Keyboard.
7. Click in the box to the right of the Keyboard checkbox.
8. Type **Q** into the box.

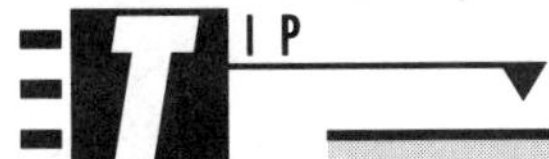

Keyboard equivalents for menu items should always be in uppercase.

Notice that the File menu exists in the menu bar just to the right of the Menu menu. 4D displays the selected menu in the menu bar to allow you to preview the menu you are working on.

Now let's add a Customers menu item to the File menu.

1. Choose Menu ➤ Insert Item (⌘-G).
2. Type **Customers** as the text for this menu item.
3. Click on the Quit menu item to select it.
4. Choose Menu ➤ Insert Item (⌘-G).
5. Select the Line option.

The line is inserted to separate menu items on the same menu that have distinctly different functionality. Now that you have a menu item, you can access the Runtime environment. However, so far, none of your menu items actually do anything. To make your menu items work, you must assign each one a global procedure.

ACTIVATING MENUS WITH GLOBAL PROCEDURES

Menus by themselves don't do anything. A menu is simply an interface tool that allows the user to tell the computer to perform a task. In order for menu items to perform a task, they must have instructions. In 4D, these instructions come in the form of programming code. This programming code goes into a *Global Procedure.* To make a menu item functional, you assign it a global procedure. When the user selects the menu item, the global procedure you assigned to that menu item will be executed. Unlike scripts, global procedures are not attached to anything and can be used by other objects in your database. You have already created one global procedure called Titlecase. While this procedure does a simple task, it is a global procedure none the less.

Global procedures allow you to have even more control over your database. 4D's programming language has hundreds of commands that can be used to create an infinite number of tasks. In this chapter you will write global procedures that are required to create a set of typical menus that you might find in any database application. These global procedures will be slightly more complex than the scripts you wrote in *Chapter 14*. By the end of this chapter, you should have an even better understanding of 4D's programming language. In *Chapters 16* and *17*, we will explore 4D's programming language even further.

ADDING STANDARD MENUS AND FUNCTIONS

There are some common functions that every database needs. You need to be able to access files, search for records, sort the records you find, export records, delete records, print reports, etc. Your next step is to add menus that provide this functionality to your database. You will be surprised at how much you can accomplish with 4D without a whole lot of effort.

The File Menu

You have already began to create the File menu by adding the Customers menu item. So far, this menu item doesn't do anything. The next step is to write a procedure to go with this menu item. What should the Customers menu item do when selected? You are used to working with your files in the User environment. In the User environment, the user works with an output layout that allows her to double-click a record and go to the input layout. Why not duplicate this kind of functionality in the Runtime environment?

The procedure that will go with the Customers menu item should display the output layout for the Customers file and set the window title to display the name of the file (Customers) as well as how many records are in the current selection and how many records are in the file. Let's do it:

1. Choose Design ➤ Procedure (⌘-P).
2. Click **New**.
3. Type **m_CUSTOMERS** as the name of the procedure.
4. Click **OK**.

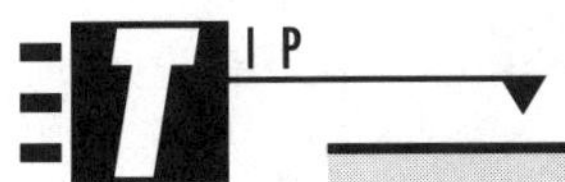

Starting your menu procedures with m_ is a naming convention. By using this convention, your global procedures will be easier to manage because, when sorted, the menu procedures will all sort together. Also, with 4D Insider, you can search for all of the global procedures that begin with m_ and know that these are your menu procedures. For more information on 4D Insider, see *Appendix A*.

The first thing you should do in any procedure is to type a comment with the name of the procedure. Comments are text in a procedure that allow you to write notes to yourself or others about what your programming code does. By typing the name of the procedure in a comment, you will be able to locate which procedure is executing when you trace through your code. Tracing allows you to watch your code execute one line at a time so you can get a better idea about how it works and fix any problems that arise.

1. Type **'m_CUSTOMERS global procedure**.
2. Press the Return key.

If you name your global procedures as closely as possible to the name of the menu item they are assigned to, you will find it easier to locate them.

The most important command in this procedure will be *MODIFY SELECTION.* This command displays the current selection using the current output layout. The user can double-click on a record to go to the input layout and modify it. Before you use this command, you will want to establish the following:

- What selection of records you wish to display initially
- Which layouts should be used for input and output
- What the title of the window should be

For the selection, let's display all of the records in the Customers file. For input and output layouts, you will specify the New Input and New Output layouts that you created. It's a good idea to specify which layouts should be used. If you don't, the MODIFY SELECTION command will use whatever layouts happen to be selected for input and output at the moment. The selected layouts may not be the ones you would want to use. Lastly, you might want the window title to display the name of the file, the number of records in the current selection and the number of records in the file just as it does in the User environment.

Remember, you can use the Keywords, Fields, and Routines Lists when entering global procedures. Whether you choose to type in your code or click on items in the lists, make sure that your procedures match the ones in the instructions.

1. Type **ALL RECORDS**().
2. Press the left arrow key once to position the cursor in-between the parentheses.
3. Click on the Customers filename to insert it into the procedure.
4. Press the Enter key.
5. Press the Return key.

There is no need to type the commands, functions, or filenames in their proper case. 4D will put them in the proper case for you when you press the Enter or Return keys.

Figure 15.2 shows how your procedure should look now. The ALL RECORDS command makes the current selection all the records in the file specified. Many commands and functions require information to do their job. This information (called parameters) is given (passed) to the

FIGURE 15.2

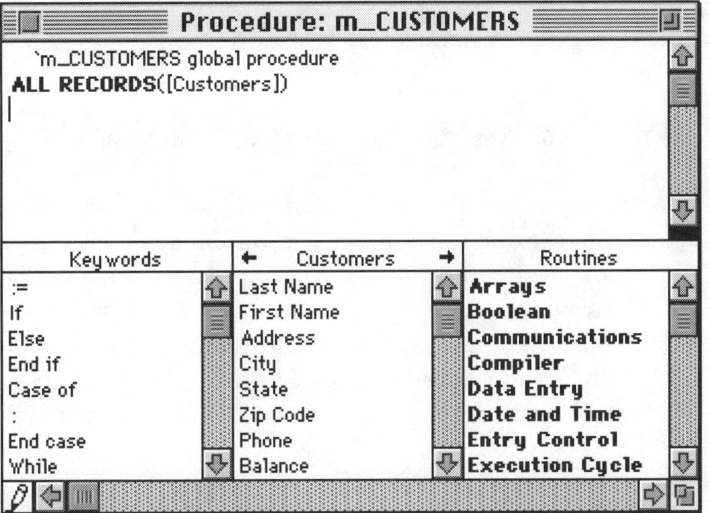

The first few lines of the m_CUSTOMERS procedure

command or function between parentheses. You may end up using another function as a parameter for a command or function. Since you could have several sets of parentheses on one line, it is a good idea to type the parentheses as soon as you finish typing a command or function that requires them. This way, you will always have the right number of parentheses for your code.

When you press the Enter key, 4D determines what you have entered and tries to recognize commands, functions, files, fields, and other things. If you have correctly typed a command or function name, 4D will make that name bold type. If 4D doesn't recognize a filename or field name, it will places bullets (•) around it. Remember that the Enter key and the Return keys are not the same key.

The next step is to set the input layout and output layout:

1. Type **output layout()**.
2. Press the left arrow key once.
3. Scroll the Fields List until you see the layouts for the Customers file listed in italics.
4. Click on New Output to insert it into the procedure.
5. Press the Enter key.
6. Press the Return key.
7. Type **input layout()**.
8. Press the left arrow key once.
9. Click on New Input to insert it into the procedure.
10. Press the Enter key then the Return key.

Figure 15.3 shows what the procedure should look like now. When you click on the name of a layout in the Fields List, 4D assumes that you are passing the name of a layout to a command. All commands that use layouts require two parameters. The first is the name of the file where the layout exists and the second is the name of the layout itself.

Now you will want to set the window title. Remember, the window title in the User environment displays the name of the file, the number

FIGURE 15.3

Setting layouts in the m_CUSTOMERS procedure

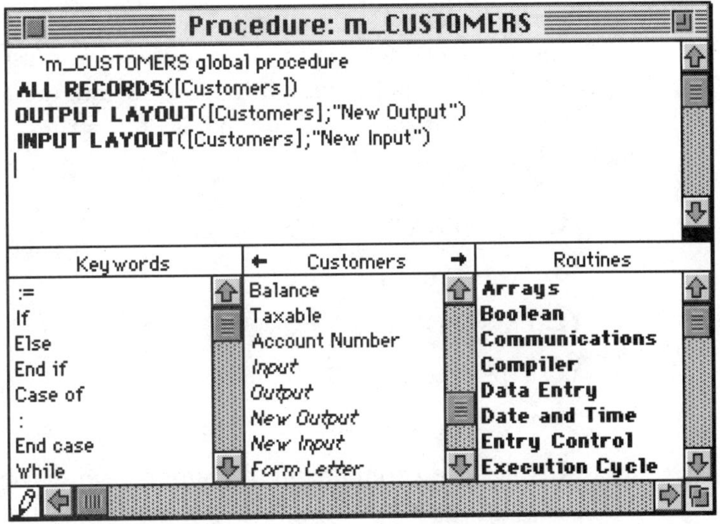

of records in the current selection and the number of records in the file. This line is a bit tricky because it involves one command, three functions, one filename and a lot of parentheses.

1. Type **set window title()**.
2. Press the left arrow key once.
3. Type **"Customers: "+string()**.
4. Press the left arrow key once.
5. Type **records in selection()**.
6. Press the left arrow key once.
7. Click on the Customers filename at the top of the Fields List.
8. Press the Enter key.

Window titles are strings. Strings are characters. When you type a string, you place quotes around it so that 4D knows it's a string. The function *Records in selection* returns the number of records in the current selection for the file specified. You know from *Chapter 14* that you can concatenate strings but you can't concatenate a number with a string. This means that to add the number returned by the Records in selection function, you need to convert the number to a string. This is why the Records in selection function is being passed to the *String* function. The String function takes something that is not a string and returns a copy of it as a string.

9. Press the left arrow key once.
10. Type **+" of "+string()**.
11. Press the left arrow key once.
12. Type **records in file()**.
13. Press the left arrow key once.
14. Click the Zoom box in the right corner of the title bar to expand the window to fill the screen. This will make it easier for you to read long lines of code.
15. Click on the Customers filename in the Fields List.
16. Press the Enter key and then the Return key.

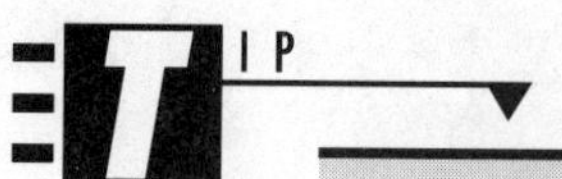

Typing both parentheses first and then using the Left Arrow key to move the cursor between them is a good habit to get into. If you do this, you will be sure to always have a closing parenthesis for each opening parenthesis.

Whew! That is some line of code isn't it? While it looks complex, it really isn't. If you read it from left to right you can see what it is doing. Figure 15.4 shows what the procedure should look like now.

The window title will start with the word *Customers:*. Next, the string of the number returned by the Records in selection function is added. At this point the window title would be *Customers: 6*. Next, the string *of* is added with a space on either side to give you *Customers: 6 of[space]*. Finally, the string of the number returned by Records in file is added to

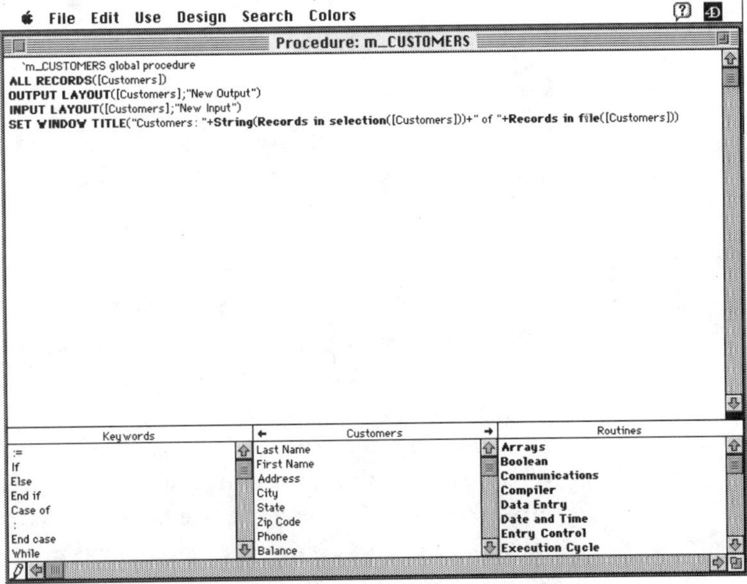

FIGURE 15.4

The m_CUSTOMERS procedure with code to set the window title

complete the window title. Assuming you have all six records in the current selection, once you execute this code, the window title should read as follows: *Customers: 6 of 6.*

Now we need to add the command that does most of the work in this procedure, the MODIFY SELECTION command.

1. Type **modify selection()**.
2. Press the left arrow key once.
3. Click the Customers filename to insert it.
4. Press the Enter key.
5. Click the Zoom box again to shrink the window down to a more manageable size.

There is one last step to do before you can try out your global procedure. You need to assign the m_CUSTOMERS global procedure to the Customers menu item.

1. Choose Design ➤ Menu bar #1.
2. Click on the Customers menu item to select it.
3. Press the Tab key.
4. Type **m_CUSTOMERS** as the name of the procedure assigned to the Customers menu item.

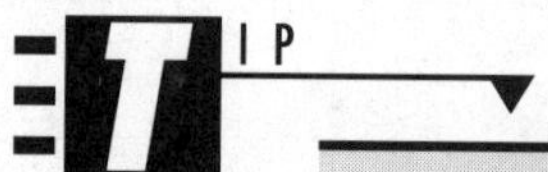

4D has its own naming convention for commands and functions. Commands are in all uppercase (ALL RECORDS, for example). Functions are in titlecase (Records in selection, for example). By naming your procedures and functions using the same convention, it will be easier to remember which procedures are commands (that don't return a value) and which are functions (that do return a value).

You can now try out the menu item you created and the global procedure assigned to it:

1. Switch to the User environment.
2. Choose Use ➤ Runtime (⌘-I).

The User environment menus have been replaced by the menu bar you created. The window that is used by the User environment is also used by the Runtime environment. Since 4D does not know what you want to do next, it displays its own logo in the window until you tell 4D to display something else. Figure 15.5 shows what the Runtime environment should look like at this point.

FIGURE 15.5

The Runtime environment

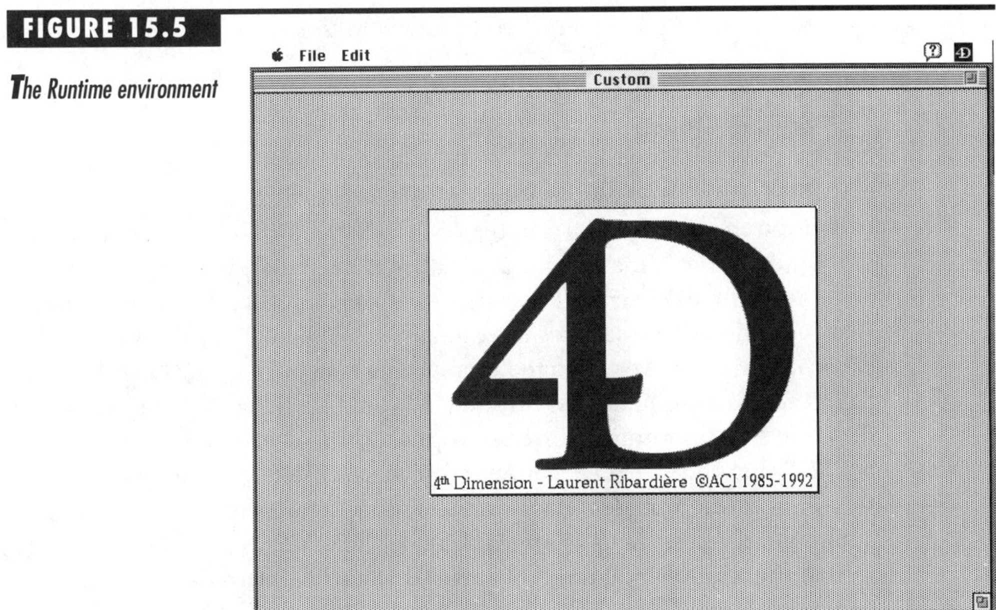

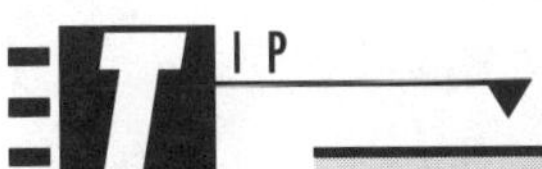

This screen is called the "splash screen" because the 4D logo is "splashed" across it.

3. Choose File ➤ Customers.

The m_CUSTOMERS procedure displays all of the records in the file using the New Output layout and sets the window title. Because your layout doesn't have any buttons on it, 4D adds the **Done** button for you. You need a button to close the layout when you are through with it. You can add your own **Accept** or **Cancel** automatic action buttons if you want. Once you add a button, 4D will no longer add the Done button.

4. Double-click on a record to view it in the input layout.

5. Click **Cancel**.

6. Click **Done**.

4D returns to the splash screen. When you click an Accept or Cancel button in an output layout, the MODIFY SELECTION command ends and the next line of your procedure it executed. In this case, there is no next line to execute. Instead, 4D displays the splash screen. Notice that the window title still has the filename and record numbers in it. This is because it was never changed to anything else once the MODIFY SELECTION command was finished. It would be a good idea if the window title said something more appropriate. You already know that there is a SET WINDOW TITLE command. You can use this command to set the window title for the default window after the MODIFY SELECTION command finishes. Let's change the m_CUSTOMERS global procedure so that the window title reads "Learn 4D Database" when a file is not being displayed.

1. Choose File ➤ Quit (⌘-Q) to switch back to the User environment.

2. Switch to the Design environment.

3. Open the m_CUSTOMERS global procedure.

4. Click below the last line to position the cursor there.

5. Type **SET WINDOW TITLE("Learn 4D Database")** and press the Enter key.

Now when the user returns to the splash screen, the window title will have the name of the database. However, when the user initially opens the database, the window title will still read "Custom". You would probably want the user to see the name of the database in the window title instead of the word Custom. Fortunately, you can set this up easily.

If you create a global procedure and name it STARTUP, that procedure will run when the database is opened. So, if you create a STARTUP procedure and call the SET WINDOW TITLE command in it to set the window title to "Learn 4D Database", the user will see this name instead of Custom. Let's create a STARTUP procedure:

1. Highlight SET WINDOW TITLE("Learn 4D Database").
2. Choose Edit ➤ Copy (⌘-C).
3. Choose Design ➤ Procedure (⌘-P).
4. Click **New**.
5. Type **STARTUP** as the name of the new global procedure.
6. Type **'STARTUP global procedure** as the first line of the procedure and press the Return key.
7. Choose Edit ➤ Paste (⌘-V).
8. Close the STARTUP procedure.

Since the STARTUP procedure will run first, it will set the window title to Learn 4D Database.

If you are using the French version of 4D, you will need to name the procedure DEBUT instead of STARTUP. If you are writing a database which may be used with the French version of 4D as well as versions in other languages, create both a DEBUT procedure and a STARTUP procedure and call the STARTUP procedure from the DEBUT procedure.

The Enter Menu

The Enter menu in the User environment allows the user enter records, make global changes to existing records and use the output layout for modifying records. In the Learn 4D database, you will create an Enter menu that allows the user to create new records. The first step is to create an Enter menu and add a *New record* menu item to it. There is one problem. When the user is at the splash screen, the New record menu item should be disabled because the user is not viewing a file. When the user is viewing a file, the New record menu item should be enabled so the user can select it to create a new record. Let's create the Enter menu and take a look at the way it works in the Runtime environment.

1. Choose Design ➤ Menu (⌘-M).
2. Double-click on Menu Bar #1 to open it.
3. Choose Menu ➤ Append Menu (⌘-R).
4. Type **Enter** as the name of the new menu.
5. Choose Menu ➤ Append Item (⌘-F).
6. Type **New record** as the name of the new menu item.
7. Assign the keyboard equivalent ⌘-N.
8. Deselect Enabled to disable the New record menu item.
9. Switch to the Runtime environment.
10. Pull down the Enter menu.

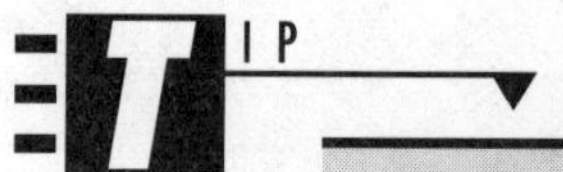

Another way to append a menu item is to double-click below the last menu item in the Items scrollable area.

Figure 15.6 shows what the menu bar should look like now. The New record menu item is disabled. This is appropriate since there is no way to know which file the new record would be for. If your database only had one file, you would know which file the record was for. So far, you have allowed the user access only to the Customers file. In the next chapter, you will learn how to add access to other files.

1. Choose File ➤ Customers.
2. Pull down the Enter menu.

FIGURE 15.6

The Enter menu

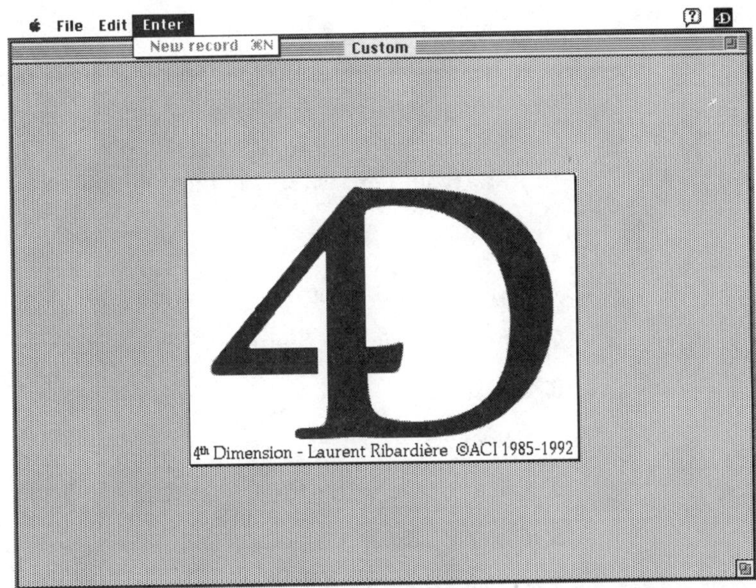

The New Record menu item is still disabled. This is a problem because you will want to be able to enter new records at this point. You need to have this menu item enabled when you are viewing an output layout (during MODIFY SELECTION) and disabled when you are viewing the splash screen (before and after MODIFY SELECTION).

There will be many other menu items that you will want enabled and disabled at different times. I have found that the easiest way to handle enabling or disabling several menu items at once is to have a second menu bar. The second menu bar will look exactly like the first menu bar. The difference will be that the New record menu item will be enabled on the second menu bar and disabled (as it is now) on the first menu bar. The Enter menu already exists on Menu bar #1 so we can copy the Enter menu from there and paste it into Menu bar #2. Let's create a second menu bar.

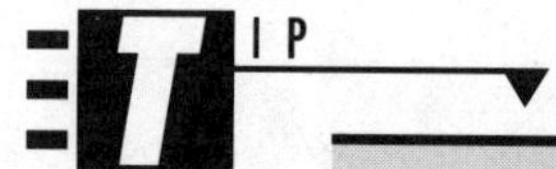

Remember, open windows in the Design environment are listed at the bottom of the Design menu. Selecting a window from here will bring that window to the front.

1. Switch to the Design environment.
2. Choose Design ➤ Menu (⌘-M).
3. Click **New**.
4. Select Menu bar #1.
5. Click on the Enter menu in the Menu Editor.
6. Choose Edit ➤ Copy (⌘-C).
7. Select Menu bar #2.
8. Choose Edit ➤ Paste (⌘-V).
9. Click on the New Record menu item to select it.
10. Select Enabled.

Now you have a second menu bar that has an Enter menu with a New record menu item that is enabled. The next step is to tell 4D to switch to Menu bar #2 before it displays the output layout of Customers, then switch back to Menu bar #1 when the user is finished looking at the Customers and clicks the **Done** button. You can switch menu bars in the Runtime environment with the command MENU BAR. The MENU BAR command is passed a menu bar number and switches the menu bar to the menus on the menu bar you pass it. The output layout is displayed by the command MODIFY SELECTION. When the user clicks the Done button to accept the output layout, the MODIFY SELECTION command is finished. Therefore, the logical place to switch to Menu bar #2 is just before the MODIFY SELECTION command. The logical place to switch back to Menu bar #1 is after the MODIFY SELECTION command. Let's change the m_CUSTOMERS procedure to make the menu bar switch:

1. Open the m_CUSTOMERS global procedure.
2. Place the cursor just to the left of the MODIFY SELECTION command.
3. Press the Return key.
4. Place the cursor on the empty line you created.
5. Type **menu bar(2)** and press the Enter key.
6. Place the cursor at the end of the MODIFY SELECTION([Customers]) line.
7. Press the Return key.
8. Type **menu bar(1)** and press the Enter key.

Figure 15.7 shows how the m_CUSTOMERS procedure should look.

FIGURE 15.7

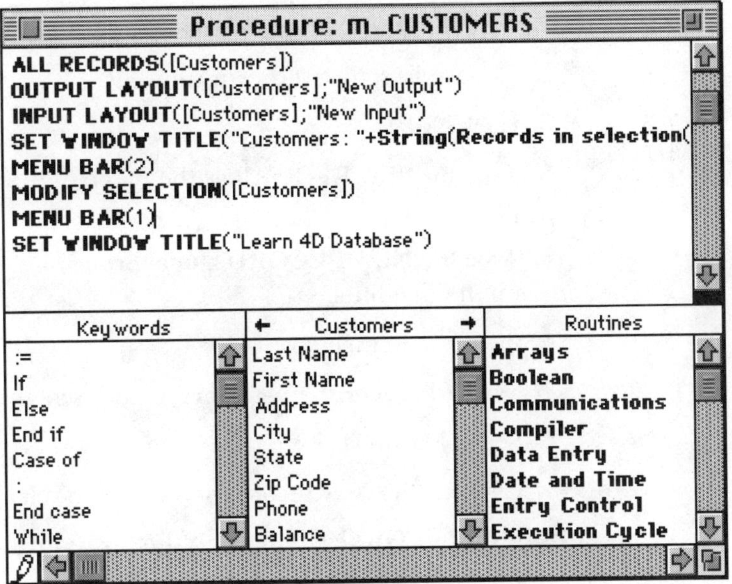

The m_CUSTOMERS procedure using the MENU BAR command

Now when the user chooses File ➤ Customers, the menu bar will switch to Menu bar #2 where the New record menu item is enabled. When the user clicks the Done button, the menu bar will switch back to Menu bar #1. Let's test out this new code:

1. Switch to the Runtime environment.
2. Choose File ➤ Customers.
3. Pull down the Enter menu.
4. Click **Done**.
5. Pull down the Enter menu.

The Enter menu now properly enables and disables. The next step is to write a global procedure that allows the user to create new records. You will call this procedure m_NEW RECORD. MODIFY SELECTION was the important command in the m_CUSTOMERS procedure. The important command in our new procedure will be ADD RECORD. The ADD RECORD command creates a new record and displays it in the current input layout. Let's create the m_NEW RECORD procedure:

1. Switch to the Design environment.
2. Choose Design ➤ Procedure (⌘-P).
3. Click **New**.
4. Type **m_NEW RECORD** as the name of the new global procedure.
5. Type **'m_NEW RECORD global procedure** as a comment on the first line.
6. Press the Return key.
7. Type **add record([Customers])** and press the Enter key.
8. Select Menu bar #2.
9. Click on the New record menu item to select it.
10. Press the Tab key to move to the Procedure scrollable area.

11. Type **m_NEW RECORD** as the name of the global procedure for this menu item.

Figure 15.8 shows the m_NEW RECORD procedure.

FIGURE 15.8

The m_NEW RECORD global procedure

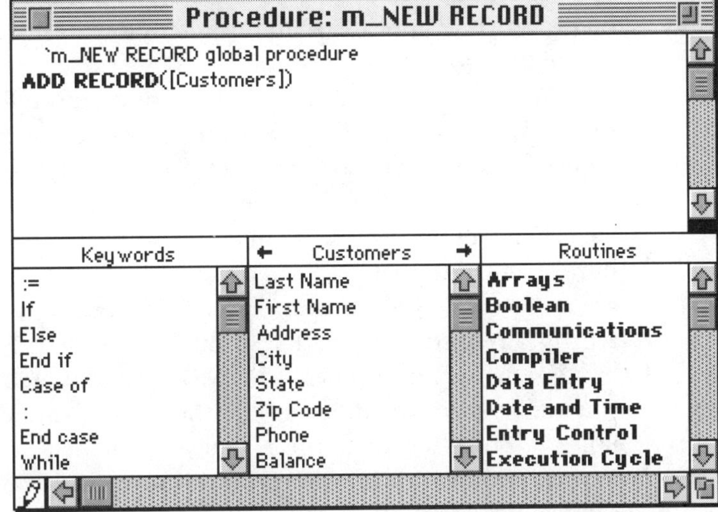

Now that you have created the second menu bar, created the m_NEW RECORD global procedure and assigned it to the New record menu item, let's try out the menu item and see if it creates a new record:

1. Switch to the Runtime environment.
2. Choose File ➤ Customers.
3. Choose Enter ➤ New record (⌘-N).
4. Click **Done**.

The New record menu item is not functioning. Why not? You have created the menu and menu item, created a global procedure, and assigned it. So, why is the menu item not working? When you are not viewing a layout, 4D will execute the global procedure assigned to a menu item when it is selected. However, when you are viewing a layout, you need to expressly tell 4D that you want global procedures assigned to menu items to execute when selected.

The easiest way to handle menus is using *associated menus.* Associated menus allow you to create a menu bar with menus that should appear only when a particular layout is used. In the Layout Editor, you may have noticed that the Layout menu has a menu item called Menu Bar. This menu item is used to associate a menu bar with the layout. The dialog box that appears when this menu item is selected is shown in Figure 15.9.

When you associate a menu bar, you simply tell 4D which menu bar to add to the existing menu bar when this layout is displayed. When you enter the associated menu bar number, you enter the negative of the menu bar number. For example, instead of entering 2, you would enter –2. When a user selects an item on an associated menu, the global procedure assigned to that item will execute. In the Learn 4D database, you are not going to associate any special menus with layouts. Instead of typing a negative menu bar number, you will type a negative, nonexistent menu bar number. When 4D then looks to see which menu bar you have associated and finds that the menu bar doesn't exist, it simply ignores it. The effect of all this is that your menus work. 4D allows you to have 32,000 menu bars. Since you will never have 32,000 menu bars, you can use this number to insure that it is always a menu bar that doesn't exist. Let's associate –32000 as the menu bar for all of the layouts to make the menus work.

FIGURE 15.9

The associated menu bar dialog box

If you want to associate a special set of menus with a particular layout, create a menu bar with those menus on it and then associate the negative of that menu bar number to the layout.

1. Switch to the Design environment.
2. In the Structure window, double-click on the Customers filename to display the layouts for the Customers file.
3. Double-click on the New Output layout to open it.
4. Choose Layout ➤ Menu Bar.
5. Type **-32000** as the associated menu bar number and click **OK**.
6. Close the New Output layout.
7. Open the New Input layout for the Customers file.
8. Enter **–32000** as the associated menu bar number.
9. Close the New Input layout.
10. Associate –32000 with the following layouts:

File	**Layouts**
Invoices	Input, Output Layout
Products	Input, Output

Now that you have associated –32000 with all of your layouts, your menus will work any time you use a layout. Let's try the New record menu item again and see if it works:

1. Switch to the Runtime environment.
2. Choose File ➤ Customers.
3. Choose Enter ➤ New record (⌘-N).

4. Click **Cancel**.

5. Click **Done**.

Your New record menu item works. Any new menus you create will work as well.

The Select Menu

The Select menu in the User environment allows the user to show all the records, view a subset of records, search for records, and sort records. You will create a Select menu that does all of this for the Learn 4D database. The first step is to create the Select menu for Menu bar #2 where all items will be enabled. After that you can copy the menu and paste it into Menu bar #1 and disable all of the menu items. Once you have created the Select menu, you will create global procedures for each menu item. Let's do it:

1. Switch to the Design environment.
2. Select Menu bar #2.
3. Choose Menu ➤ Append Menu (⌘-R).
4. Type **Select** as the name of the new menu.
5. Choose Menu ➤ Append Item (⌘-F).
6. Type **Show All** as the name of the menu item.
7. Assign Show All **⌘-G** as its keyboard equivalent.
8. Choose Menu ➤ Append Item (⌘-F).
9. Type **Show Subset** as the name of the new menu item.
10. Assign Show Subset **⌘-H** as its keyboard equivalent.
11. Choose Menu ➤ Append Item (⌘-F).
12. Select Line and deselect Enabled.
13. Choose Menu ➤ Append Item (⌘-F).
14. Type **Search Editor**... and assign it **⌘-S**.
15. Choose Menu ➤ Append Item (⌘-F).

16. Type **Search by Layout**... and assign it **⌘-L**.
17. Choose Menu ➤ Append Item (⌘-F).
18. Select Line and deselect Enabled.
19. Choose Menu ➤ Append Item (⌘-F).
20. Type **Sort**... and assign it **⌘-T**.
21. Choose Menu ➤ Append Item (⌘-F).
22. Select Line and deselect Enabled.
23. Choose Menu ➤ Append Item (⌘-F).
24. Type **Delete**... as the name of the menu item.

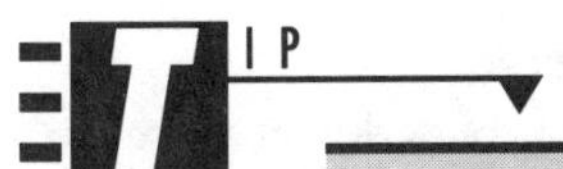

When a menu item is going to ask the user for more information (like the Search Editor menu item) before it can perform its function, the menu item should have an ellipsis (Option-;) at the end.

Figure 15.10 shows what the Select menu should look like. Now that you have the Select menu created, let's copy it and paste it into Menu bar #1 and disable all of the menu items. You will want all of the menu items disabled because Menu bar #1 is used at the splash screen when no file is displayed.

1. Click on Select in the Menus scrollable area to select it.
2. Choose Edit ➤ Copy (⌘-C).
3. Select Menu bar #1.
4. Choose Edit ➤ Paste (⌘-V).
5. Disable all of the items on the Select menu in Menu bar #1.

FIGURE 15.10

The Select menu

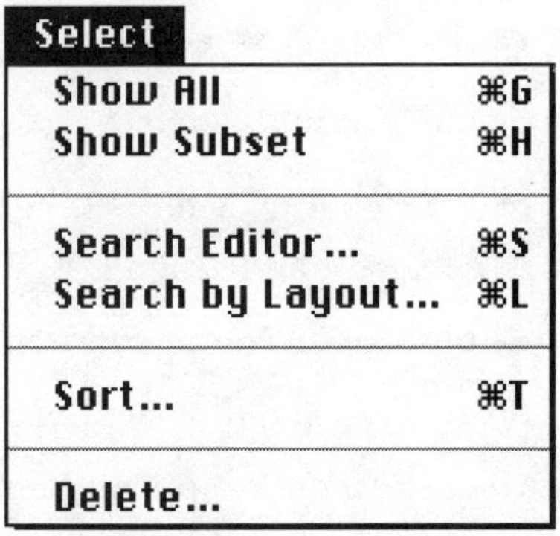

Select
Show All ⌘G
Show Subset ⌘H
Search Editor... ⌘S
Search by Layout... ⌘L
Sort... ⌘T
Delete...

Figure 15.11 shows what the Select menu in Menu bar #1 should look like.

Now that you have the Select menu on both menu bars, let's test it to make sure that all items are disabled at the splash screen and all items are enabled when you are viewing the Customers output layout.

1. Switch to the **Runtime** environment.
2. Pull down the Select menu to see that all items are disabled.
3. Choose File ➤ Customers.
4. Pull down the Select menu to see that all items are enabled.

FIGURE 15.11

The Select menu in Menu bar #1

Select
Show All ⌘G
Show Subset ⌘H
Search Editor... ⌘S
Search by Layout... ⌘L
Sort... ⌘T
Delete...

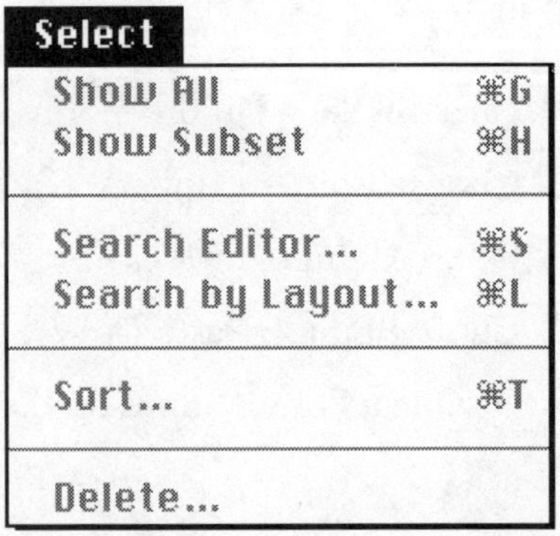

5. Click **Done**.
6. Pull down the Select menu to see that all items are disabled again.

As you can see, the Select menu is now enabled or disabled at the appropriate time. The next step is to write global procedures for each menu item.

The first menu item is *Show All.* You will create a global procedure called m_SHOW ALL that will be assigned to the Show All menu item. m_SHOW ALL should display all the records in the file and update the window title so that it reflects the fact that the current selection is all of the records. You already know that the ALL RECORDS command sets the current selection to all of the records. Any time the current selection changes, the MODIFY SELECTION command will update the screen to show the current selection accurately. You also already have code that sets the window title. You can re-use this code in the m_SHOW ALL procedure. Let's create the m_SHOW ALL global procedure:

1. Switch to the Design environment.
2. Create a global procedure called m_SHOW ALL.
3. Enter the following lines:

```
' m_SHOW ALL global procedure
ALL RECORDS([Customers])
```

Now you need to copy the line of code from m_CUSTOMERS that sets the window title.

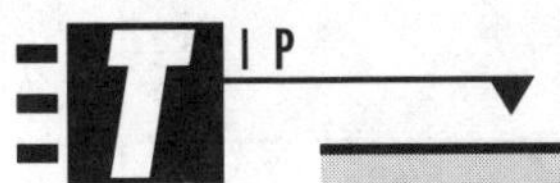

You can highlight an entire line in the Procedure Editor by clicking at the beginning of the line and dragging straight down. This will be faster than dragging horizontally until you reach the end of the line.

4. Open the m_CUSTOMERS procedure.
5. Highlight the line that uses the SET WINDOW TITLE command.
6. Choose Edit ➤ Copy (⌘-C).
7. Close the m_CUSTOMERS procedure.
8. Select the m_SHOW ALL procedure.
9. Press Return to add another line to the procedure.
10. Choose Edit ➤ Paste (⌘-V).

Figure 15.12 shows what the m_SHOW ALL procedure should look like. The last step is to assign the m_SHOW ALL procedure to the Show All menu item on the Select menu in Menu bar #2. Let's do it:

1. Close the m_SHOW ALL procedure.
2. Select Menu bar #2.
3. Click on Select in the Menus scrollable area to select it.
4. Click on the Show All menu item to select it.

FIGURE 15.12

The m_SHOW ALL global procedure

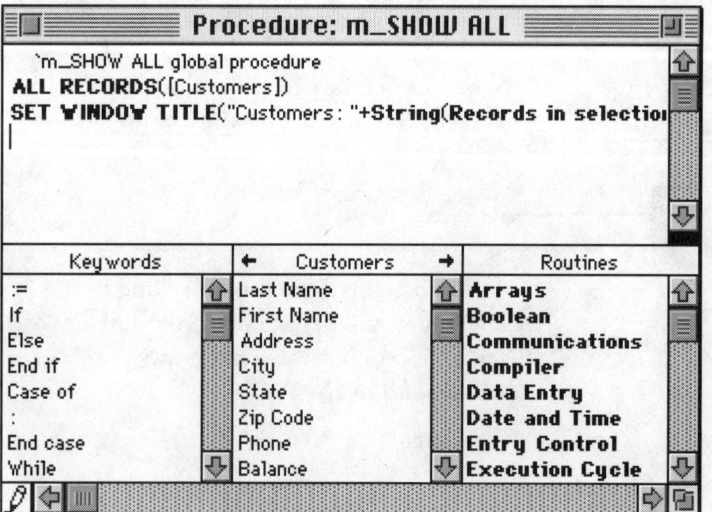

5. Click in the Procedures scrollable area next to the Show All menu item.
6. Type **m_SHOW ALL** to assign it to this menu item.

Now let's try out the Show All menu item and see if it works:

1. Switch to the Runtime environment.
2. Choose File ➤ Customers.
3. Choose Select ➤ Show All (⌘-G).

All the records are redisplayed and the window title is correctly set. Once you have created the search procedures, you will be able to perform searches. After you look at the records found by a search, you may want to look at all of the records in the file again. You will be able to use the Show All menu item to do this.

4. Click **Done**.
5. Choose File ➤ Quit (⌘-Q).

The next menu item is *Show Subset.* This menu item reduces the current selection so that it contains only the highlighted records. Then it sets the window title to show the user how many records are in the current selection. If the user doesn't have any records highlighted, a window should appear that lets the user know that they need to highlight records before selecting Show Subset.

You are going to create a procedure called m_SHOW SUBSET. At the heart of this procedure is the USE SET command. The USE SET command changes the current selection for a file to the records in a set whose name you pass to the USE SET command. A set is simply a list of records. Records can be put into sets in many different ways. There is one set that 4D itself creates for you. This set is called the *UserSet.* When the user highlights records in an output layout, the records are placed in the UserSet automatically. If your procedure calls USE SET("UserSet"), 4D changes the current selection to the records in the UserSet (just the highlighted records). Before you use the UserSet, you will want to check to see if it has any records in it. You can find out how many records are in a set with the function *Records in set.* If the number of records in the User Set is zero, you will want to alert the user that they need to highlight records first. You will use the *ALERT* command to do this. Let's create the m_SHOW SUBSET procedure:

1. Switch to the Design environment.
2. Create a global procedure called m_SHOW SUBSET.
3. Type the following code into the procedure:

```
' m_SHOW SUBSET global procedure
If(Records in set("UserSet")>0)
    USE SET("UserSet")
Else
    BEEP
    ALERT("Please highlight some records first.")
End If
```

You have used an IF statement before. In this case, you are checking to see if the number of records in the UserSet is greater than zero. If it is, then the USE SET command will be executed. If the number of records in the UserSet is not greater than zero, then the computer will beep and display a message that tells the user to highlight some records first.

There is one thing left to do before this procedure is finished. When you use the UserSet, the current selection changes. Therefore, you will want to reset the window title. You will need to copy the SET WINDOW TITLE line of code from your m_CUSTOMERS procedure and paste it into the m_SHOW SUBSET procedure.

1. Open the m_CUSTOMERS procedure.
2. Highlight the line that uses SET WINDOW TITLE.
3. Choose Edit ➤ Copy (⌘-C).
4. Close the m_CUSTOMERS procedure.
5. Select the m_SHOW SUBSET procedure.
6. Click at the end of the USE SET("UserSet") line.
7. Press the Return key.
8. Choose Edit ➤ Paste (⌘-V).

Figure 15.13 shows what the finished m_SHOW SUBSET procedure should look like.

Now you need to assign this procedure to the Show Subset menu item in Menu bar #2.

1. Select Menu bar #2.
2. Assign the m_SHOW SUBSET procedure to the Show Subset menu item.

Now you can try out the Show Subset menu item. Remember, you can hold down the Shift key to highlight several records that are next to each other and hold down the ⌘ key to highlight records that are not next to each other.

1. Switch to the Runtime environment.
2. Choose File ➤ Customers.
3. Select (highlight) a few records.

FIGURE 15.13

The finished m_SHOW SUBSET procedure

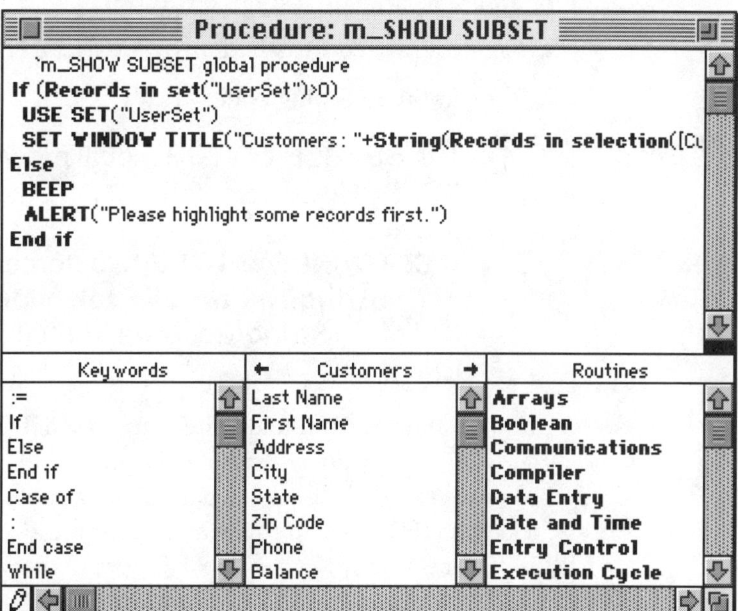

4. Choose Select ➤ Show Subset (⌘-H).

5. Choose Select ➤ Show All (⌘-G).

6. Choose Select ➤ Show Subset (⌘-H).

7. Click **OK**.

When the user has records selected, the Show Subset menu item displays the selected records. Notice also that the window title correctly displays the number of records in the current selection. When the user doesn't have any records selected, the Show Subset menu item tells the user to highlight some records first.

The next menu item is *Search Editor.* For this menu item you will create a procedure called m_SEARCH EDITOR. This procedure should display the Search Editor. If the user performs a search, the window title should be updated. At the heart of this procedure is the SEARCH command. The SEARCH command allows you to tell 4D what to search for. If you don't provide the SEARCH command with any criteria the Search Editor is displayed to allow the user to enter the criteria. Let's create the m_SEARCH EDITOR procedure:

1. Switch back to the Design environment.

2. Create a procedure called m_SEARCH EDITOR.

3. Type in the following code:

```
'm_SEARCH EDITOR global procedure
SEARCH([Customers])
If(OK=1)
   SET WINDOW TITLE("Customers:
    "+String(Records in selection([Customers]))+
    " of  "+String(Records in file([Customers])))
End if
```

In the IF statement, you are checking to see if OK equals 1. OK is not a field. OK is a variable. A variable is like a field but is in memory only and is not saved to disk. This particular variable is set to 1 when the user clicks the **OK** button in the Search Editor and set to 0 if the user clicks the **Cancel** button. You will learn more about variables in *Chapter 16.*

4. Assign the *m_SEARCH EDITOR* procedure to the Search Editor menu item on Menu bar #2.

Now let's test out the Search Editor menu item.

1. Switch to the Runtime environment.
2. Choose File ➤ Customers.
3. Choose Select ➤ Search Editor (⌘-S).
4. Enter the criteria **State is equal to CA**.
5. Click **OK**.

The next menu item is *Search by Layout*. In the User environment, selecting this menu item presents the current input layout and allows the user to use this layout to enter a search criteria. You will create a procedure called m_SEARCH LAYOUT. The heart of this procedure will be the SEARCH BY LAYOUT command. This command does exactly what the menu item by the same name does in the User environment. The m_SEARCH LAYOUT procedure will look exactly like the m_SEARCH EDITOR procedure you just created. The only difference will be the search command used. The fastest way to create this procedure is to copy the m_SEARCH EDITOR procedure and just change what you need to change. Let's do it:

1. Switch to the Design environment.
2. Open the m_SEARCH EDITOR procedure.
3. Choose Edit ➤ Select All (⌘-A).
4. Choose Edit ➤ Copy (⌘-C).
5. Close the m_SEARCH EDITOR procedure.
6. Create a new procedure called m_SEARCH LAYOUT.
7. Choose Edit ➤ Paste (⌘-V).
8. Change the comment line to read **'m_SEARCH LAYOUT global procedure**.

9. Change the SEARCH command to **SEARCH BY LAYOUT**.
10. Assign the m_SEARCH LAYOUT procedure to the Search by Layout menu item in Menu bar #2.
11. Switch to the Runtime environment and test out this menu item.

You have now given the user another way to search for records and learned a little bit more about programming.

The next menu item is *Sort.* In the User environment, this menu item is called Sort Selection and it displays the Sort Editor to allow the user to sort her records. You will create a procedure called m_SORT. The important command in this procedure will be the SORT SELECTION command. This command works in a very similar way to the SEARCH command. You can give this command fields to sort on or not. If you don't tell the SORT SELECTION command how to sort the records, it displays the Sort Editor for you to allow the user to choose how to sort the records. Sorting the records does not change the number of records in the current selection so there is no need to reset the window title. Let's create the m_SORT procedure:

1. Switch to the Design environment.
2. Create a procedure called m_SORT.
3. Type the following code into the procedure:

```
' m_SORT global procedure
SORT SELECTION([Customers])
```

4. Assign this procedure to the Sort menu item in Menu bar #2.
5. Switch to the Runtime environment and test out this menu item.

The last item on the Select menu is *Delete.* You will create a procedure called m_DELETE. In the User environment, the user highlights records and chooses Edit ➤ Clear to delete them. 4D then confirms that the user really wants to delete the records and if the user clicks **Yes**, the records are deleted and the window title is updated. Any records that were not selected remain in the current selection. You will want to your m_DELETE procedure to do the same thing.

The first step is to check to see if the user has highlighted any records. You already know how to do this because you did it in the m_SHOW SUBSET procedure. Highlighted records are automatically put into the UserSet. You can then check to see if there are records highlighted by using the Records in set function to see if there are any records in the UserSet. If there are, you will want to confirm with the user that they really want to delete the records. You can do this with the CONFIRM command.

The CONFIRM command is similar to the ALERT command. The dialog box that it presents is slightly different and you have a **Cancel** button in addition to the **OK** button. If the user clicks OK, the OK variable (the same one you learned about when you wrote the m_SEARCH EDITOR procedure) is set to 1. If the user clicks the Cancel button, OK is set to 0. If OK equals 1, you can use the UserSet to reduce the current selection to only those records that the user selected. The actual deleting of records is done by the DELETE SELECTION command. This command deletes the current selection. Finally, you will want to reset the window title to reflect the fact that the current selection has changed. Let's create the m_DELETE procedure:

1. Switch to the Design environment.
2. Create a new procedure called m_DELETE.
3. Type in the following code:

```
' m_DELETE global procedure
If(Records in set(" UserSet " ) >0)
    CONFIRM( " Delete the selected records? " )
    If(OK=1)
        USE SET( " UserSet " )
        DELETE SELECTION([Customers])
        SET WINDOW TITLE( " Customers:
       " +String(Records in selection
        ([Customers]))+ " of " +String
        (Records in file([Customers])))
    End if
Else
```

```
        BEEP
        ALERT("Please highlight some records first.")
    End if
```

4. Assign this procedure to the Delete menu item in Menu bar #2.

Now let's test out this menu item.

1. Switch to the Runtime environment.
2. Choose File ➤ Customers.
3. Choose Enter ➤ New record (⌘-N).
4. Type in your name, address, and phone number.
5. Click **Save**.
6. Click on your record to select it.
7. Choose Select ➤ Delete.
8. Click **OK**.

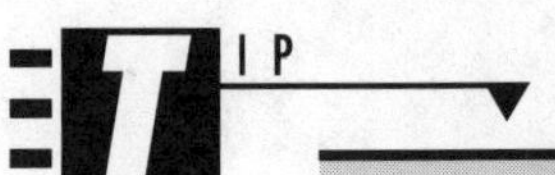

Always confirm an irreversible action like deleting records. This gives the user a chance to change her mind. If the action is not irreversible (like quitting the database), there is no need to confirm it.

The Report Menu

Now the user can enter new records, search for records that meet a criteria, sort records, and delete records. What they cannot do, so far, is print. In the User environment, the Report menu has items that give you access to the Quick Report Editor, the Label Editor and the Graph Editor. You can give the user access to these menu items as well.

The first step is to create a Report menu with Quick, Label, and Graph items. You will add this menu to Menu bar #2, then copy it to

Menu bar #1 as you have done with the Enter and Select menus. Let's do it:

1. Switch to the Design environment.
2. Select Menu bar #2.
3. Choose Menu ➤ Append Menu (⌘-R).
4. Type **Report** as the name of the new menu.
5. Add the following menu items:

Menu Item	Keyboard Equivalent
Quick...	R
Labels...	J
Graph...	K

6. Copy the Report menu and paste it into Menu bar #1.
7. Disable all items on the Report menu in Menu bar #1.

Next, you need to write a global procedure for each one. Fortunately, the procedures to give the user access to the Report, Label, and Graph Editors are quite simple. The Report Editor is displayed by the command REPORT. The REPORT command requires two parameters. The first is the database file you want to report on and the second is the name of a Quick Report file you have stored on disk. If you pass a report name that is on disk, the REPORT command will print the report using the records in the current selection. If you pass the REPORT command nothing (""), an open file dialog box is presented to allow the user to select a Quick Report. However, if you pass the REPORT command a report name that doesn't exist, the Report Editor is displayed to allow the user to create a report. So, to make the Quick Report Editor appear, you need to pass the REPORT command a non-existent filename. There are certain characters that are not allowed in filenames. One of them is Return. By passing Return as the filename, you can be assured that the Report Editor will appear since Return cannot be entered as part of a filename. You already know from earlier chapters that **Char**(13) is equal to a Return. You can pass this as your filename. None of these menu items will change the current selection so there is no need to reset the window title. Let's create the procedures:

1. Create a procedure called m_QUICK.
2. Type the following code into the m_QUICK procedure:

```
' m_QUICK global procedure
REPORT([Customers];Char(13))
```

3. Close the m_QUICK procedure.
4. Assign the m_QUICK procedure the Quick menu item in Menu bar #2.

Now you will create a procedure to give the user access to the Label Editor. You can do this with the command PRINT LABEL. This command works identically to the REPORT command. Let's do it:

1. Create a procedure called m_LABELS.
2. Type the following code into the m_LABELS procedure:

```
' m_LABELS global procedure
PRINT LABEL([Customers];Char(13))
```

3. Close the m_LABELS procedure.
4. Assign the m_LABELS procedure the Labels menu item in Menu bar #2.

Finally, there is the Graph Editor. You can access the Graph Editor with the command GRAPH FILE. This command requires only one parameter which is the database filename you want to graph from. Let's create a m_GRAPH procedure:

1. Create a procedure called m_GRAPH.
2. Type the following code into the m_GRAPH procedure:

```
' m_GRAPH global procedure
GRAPH FILE([Customers])
```

3. Close the **m_GRAPH** procedure.
4. Assign the **m_GRAPH** procedure the Graph menu item in Menu bar #2.

Now you can test the Report menu.

1. Switch to the Runtime environment.
2. Choose File ➤ Customers.
3. Choose Report ➤ Quick (⌘-R).
4. Click **OK**.
5. Choose Report ➤ Labels (⌘-J).
6. Click **OK** in the Page Setup dialog box.
7. Click **Cancel**.
8. Choose Report ➤ Graph (⌘-K).
9. Click **Cancel**.

You have a complete set of menus to work with your database. What menus you need and how to arrange them is really dependent on the database you are creating. If you are not sure what to name your menus or exactly what kind of interface they should present to the user when selected, look at other applications you have on your computer. You can get lots of ideas by looking at the way existing applications handle problems. Also remember that the menus and menu items you create should make sense to you and to the user. They should be intuitive enough that the user will know what a menu item does based on the text. Another important point is that most users prefer buttons to menus because buttons appear in windows whereas menus are sort of hidden. Actions that the user takes each day might be better as buttons instead of menus.

You have created these menus for the Learn 4D database to give you a feel for what is involved in creating menus. As you can see, you don't need to know that many commands to create menus that are quite powerful. You will learn even more about 4D's programming language in the next two chapters.

Changing the Splash Screen Artwork

You can replace the 4D logo with your own artwork. To do this, copy a picture to the clipboard, then go to the Menu Editor and choose Menu ➤ Show Custom menus. When the menus appear choose Edit ➤ Paste (⌘-V). This will replace the 4D logo with your artwork. If your picture was not created with a paint program like MacPaint, SuperPaint, or Studio 8, copy the picture into a paint program first then copy it from the paint program to the clipboard. If the picture was created in a drawing program like MacDraw, any text is still regarded as text. If the font you used for the text in the picture isn't installed on the user's machine, the missing font will be replaced by another font. Copying the picture into a paint program then copying it from the paint program back to the clipboard will convert the picture to a bitmap image (paint format) and insure that picture doesn't change.

In the Menu Editor, you can quickly open the global procedure associated with a menu item by clicking on it and pressing ⌘-P.

ADDING POWER WITH 4D COMMANDS

16

MAC TRACKS MAC

Variables are similar to fields 498

But are held only in memory. They are not saved to disk.

To display a variable on a layout 504

1. Click on the Active Object tool to select it.
2. Draw the active object.
3. Name the active object with the name of the variable you want displayed.
4. Choose Enterable or Non-enterable from the Type pop-up menu.

To get help about a command in the Procedure Editor 505

1. Click on Routines to display all of the commands.
2. Choose Balloon Help ➤ Show Balloons.
3. Move the Arrow over the command you need help with.

To pass parameters to a global procedure 510

Separate the parameters with semi-colons (;).

To display the Debugger 527

Hold down the Option key and click the mouse while your code is executing.

Featuring

- *Using variables*
- *Types of variables*
- *Passing parameters to procedures*
- *Writing functions*
- *Using pointers*
- *Using the Debugger*

UP TO THIS point you have had some experience with 4D Design, User and Runtime environments. In *Chapter 14* you learned about writing scripts to make buttons and fields more powerful. In *Chapter 15*, you learned about writing global procedures to make menus work. In this chapter (as well as the next), you will be exploring 4th Dimension's programming language even further to help you understand more and give you the skills to create very powerful and flexible database applications.

Not all of your databases will require a lot of programming. As a matter of fact, many of the databases you create may not require any programming whatsoever. 4th Dimension certainly makes it easy for you to create powerful database applications without programming. However, the programming language is an important part of 4th Dimension and the better you understand it, the more you can do with 4D.

USING VARIABLES

Up to this point you have stored all of your data in fields that belong to records and are saved on disk. When you are using a programming language, there will often be times when you need to store some information temporarily instead of saving to disk. In business you often have forms that you use for long term storage of information (like the records in your database). You also have a pad of paper you keep on your desk when you need to jot down something like a phone number, a price, a name, etc. You can use the computer's RAM memory like a pad of paper where you can store bits of information. When you want to store information temporarily, you put the information in a *variable.*

RAM stands for *Random Access Memory*. This kind of memory allows you to read values from memory and write values to memory. ROM stands for *Read Only Memory*. This kind of memory allows you only to read values and not write them back.

Variables are like fields in many ways. They have many things in common with fields. They each:

- Have a name
- Have a data type
- Can store a value
- Can appear on layouts
- Can be used in scripts and procedures

You can assign a value to a variable in the same way that you assign values to fields. For example, if you enter a line of code like:

```
Age:=29
```

a variable called Age will be created in memory and the value 29 will be assigned to it. You can perform calculations using variables and store the results in other variables. For example, the following calculation

```
DaysOld:=Age*365
```

will create a variable in memory called DaysOld and store the result of the calculation Age*365 in that variable. After this calculation, the Days-Old variable would contain the value 10585.

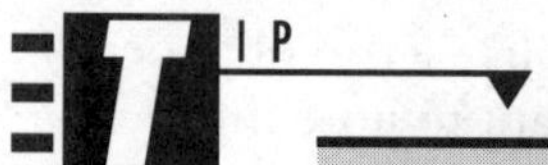

You can use spaces in variable names. However, if you double-click on a variable name that has a space in it (like Today's Date), 4D will select only the word you double-clicked and not the entire variable name. Since variable names themselves are never seen by the user, it is better to not use spaces. This way, when you double-click on a variable name, the entire name is highlighted.

While field names can be up to 15 characters in length, variable names can be only 11 characters in length. If you enter a variable name that is longer than 11 characters, 4D will place bullets around the variable name to let you know that it is too long. Variable names must begin with a letter and cannot contain commas, periods, or other special characters. 4D uses font styles in the Procedure Editor to differentiate between object types. For example, 4D commands and functions are in bold. Fields and variables are both in plain. However, if you get in the habit of including the filename when you use fields in your code, you will easily be able to tell the difference between a field and a variable. The following shows a field and a variable being assigned values.

```
[Invoices]Due Date:=Current date+30
DaysOld:=Current date-!01/06/64!
```

The Colors menu in the Procedure Editor allows you to assign colors to different types of objects in your code. By assigning fields and variables different colors, you will be able to easily tell which are fields and which are variables.

VARIABLE DATA TYPES

Just like fields, each variable has a data type. All of the field types are available as data types. You also have two data types that are available only to variables. How does 4D know which data type a variable is? There are a number of ways. 4D can determine the data type for a variable based on the way you use it. For example, in the following line of code

```
DaysOld:=29*365
```

4D can determine that DaysOld is a number because the result of the calculation is a number. 4D can't be absolutely sure what type of number DaysOld should be (Real, Long Integer, or Integer). Consequently, 4D makes the variable a Real because a Real can hold any number. In the following example

```
Song:="Walk Like An Egyptian"
```

4D determines that the data type of the Song variable is Text. Text variables can hold data from Alphanumeric fields as well as Text fields. In the next example

```
TodaysDate:=Current date
```

4D determines that the data type of the TodaysDate variable is Date because the Current date function returns a date. Typing variables based on the way they are used is called *implicit* variable typing. You can explicitly type variables using the *4D Compiler Directives.*

The 4D Compiler Directives are commands that allow you to indicate the data type of a variable. The 4D Compiler is a product that makes your code execute faster (see *Chapter 19* for more information on the 4D Compiler). If you use the Compiler Directives to indicate the data types of variables, the 4D Compiler can do its job faster because it doesn't have to go through and try to figure out the data types based on their usage. The 4D Compiler Directive commands are:

C_BOOLEAN

C_DATE

C_INTEGER

C_GRAPH

C_LONGINT

C_PICTURE

C_POINTER

C_REAL

C_STRING

C_TEXT

C_TIME

These commands allow you to pass one or more variables to declare them as a particular data type. For example,

```
C_LONGINT(DaysOld,Months,Years)
```

would create the DaysOld, Months, and Years variables and make them the data type Long Integer. 4D will allow you to change the data type. For example, in the following code

```
DaysOld:=10585
DaysOld:="Ten thousand five hundred eight-five"
```

the type of DaysOld is changed from Real to Text. However, after a Compiler Directive, the data type cannot be changed. For example, in the following code

```
C_LONGINT(DaysOld)
DaysOld:=10585
DaysOld:="Ten thousand five hundred eight-five"
```

the Compiler Directive is setting the data type of the DaysOld variable to Long Integer. The next line assigns DaysOld the value 10585 which is a long integer. However, the next line attempts to assign text to the DaysOld variable. Because the C_LONGINT directive was used, this last assignment would not be made. 4D will not generate an error but neither will it make the assignment.

As I mentioned earlier, the 4D Compiler (which you will hear more about in *Chapter 19*) makes your code run faster. If you might use the 4D Compiler one day, you don't want to be changing the data types of your variables, because the 4D Compiler will not allow it.

You may have noticed that there are three directives for data types you haven't used before. These three new data types are:

C_GRAPH

C_POINTER

C_STRING

When you create a graph with the GRAPH command and present the graph on a layout, the graph appears in a variable. The C_GRAPH directive allows you to declare these variables to be of the graph data type.

A *Pointer* is a reference to an object. You can use the C_POINTER directive to declare a variable to be of type Pointer. You will learn more about Pointers later in this chapter.

A String variable is just like a text variable with a few important differences. A String variable can have a maximum length of 255 characters whereas a Text variable can be up to 32,000 characters in length. However, String variables can be accessed more quickly in memory by 4D than Text variables.

TYPES OF VARIABLES

There are three different types of variables. The type of variable you use determines that variable's jurisdiction or domain. The three types are local, process, and interprocess.

Local variables are created when a procedure or script executes and is cleared from memory when it finishes. If you need to store a value temporarily and only for one execution of a procedure or script, use a local variable. In order for a variable to be local, its name must begin with a dollar sign ($). In the following example

```
$DaysOld:=10585
TodaysDate:=Current date
```

$DaysOld is a local variable and TodaysDate is not. Because local variables are created and cleared each time a procedure or script executes, local variables with the same name in different procedures can have different data types. For example, $DaysOld in one procedure might be a Long Integer and $DaysOld in another procedure might be a Text variable.

Process variables can be accessed in any procedure or script. Unlike local variables, process variables are not cleared when a script or procedure is finished. A Process is one distinct database operation. For example, the Design environment is a process and the User and Runtime environments are another process. Since they are separate processes, they execute simultaneously. You can also create your own processes. A Process variable is local to the process that it is being accessed in. When a process is created, all of its process variables are created. When a process finishes, all of its process variables are cleared. You will learn more about processes in *Chapter 17*. Process variables do not have any special character that they begin with. The variables in the following code are Process variables.

```
DaysOld:=10585
TodaysDate:=Current date
```

Interprocess variables hold values that can be shared among all processes. In order for a variable to be an interprocess variable, it must begin with a diamond (♦). You can create the diamond character by pressing Option-Shift-V. You will learn more about interprocess variables in *Chapter 17*. The variables in the following code are interprocess variables:

```
♦DaysOld:=10585
♦TodaysDate:=Current date
```

DISPLAYING VARIABLES

Process and interprocess variables can appear on layouts. They can appear in many different forms. For example, all of the buttons you created were process variables. When the layout is opened, the process variable that is appearing on the layout as a button is set to zero. When you click on the button, the process variable is set to 1. Variables can also appear as enterable and non-enterable active objects. For example, you might want the user to enter a value that you are going to use in a calculation but that won't get stored in a field. In this case, you would use an enterable active object. Basically, all active objects are variables. This means that variables can appear on layouts as any of the active object types.

THE LIFE OF A VARIABLE

The life of a variable is short and sweet. While you may have variables that you use often, they exist in memory only. Local variables die rather suddenly when their procedure or script ends. Process variables meet their demise when the process they live in ends. And interprocess variables shuffle off this mortal coil when you quit 4th Dimension.

Although the life of a variable is short, you will find that variables are a powerful and valuable tool for creating database applications.

GETTING HELP WITH COMMANDS

So far, you have learned about several of 4th Dimension's commands and functions. Some of these commands and functions require you to pass them parameters in order for them to do their job. Which parameters you pass, and in the order in which you pass them, is called *syntax.* In order for a command or function to work properly, you must give it the proper syntax. You can find out the syntax for a command or function by looking it up in the *4th Dimension Language Reference* or by using the Balloon Help that is built-in to the Procedure Editor. Figure 16.1 shows the help balloon for the INPUT LAYOUT command.

The top line of the help balloon shows the syntax. The syntax shows you what 4D expects you to pass this command. In this case, you pass a filename and a layout name. The filename has curly braces ({}) around it. This means that this parameter is optional. Layout however does not

FIGURE 16.1

Balloon Help in the Procedure Editor

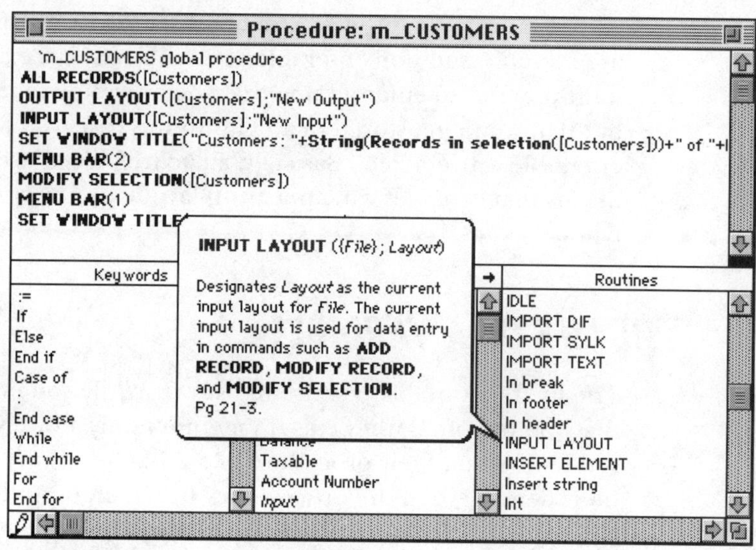

have curly braces around it, so the layout name is required. Figure 16.2 shows the balloon for the Current date function. Notice that there is a dash and a greater than sign followed by the word *date*. The dash and greater sign (->) represent an arrow. The arrow is pointing to *date* to indicate that this function returns a date.

The text for the balloons is stored in the 4D Help file in the System Folder. If this file is missing or has been moved, your balloons will not appear.

FIGURE 16.2

The syntax for a function

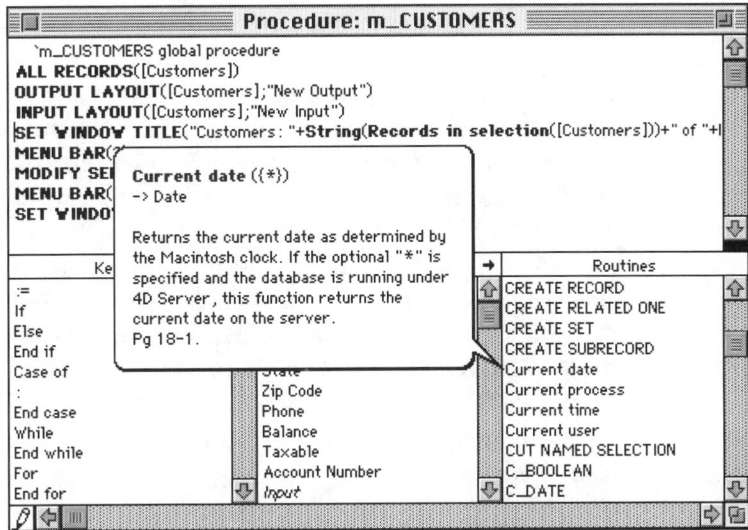

PROCEDURES AND PARAMETERS

In the last chapter, you wrote global procedures that you then assigned to menu items. These menu items execute their assigned global procedure when the user selects the menu item. Global procedures can also be executed from scripts or other global procedures. To execute a global procedure from a script or other global procedure, you simply type the name of the procedure you want to execute at the point in your code where you want it to execute.

The reason for executing one procedure from another is to save time by allowing you to re-use code in several places. Say, for example, you had five lines of code that you had used in two different procedures. If you decide to make a change or fix a problem with any of these five lines of code, you need to change them in both procedures. Instead, you could put these lines of code in another global procedure and call them from the two original procedures.

You have a line of code in the m_CUSTOMERS global procedure that sets the window title for the output layout. When you created other global procedures that needed to set the window title, you copied this code and pasted it into the procedure. However, at some time in the future you might want to change the text of the window title. Since you used this code in many different procedures, you would have to open each procedure and change the line of code that sets the window title. Instead, you can create a separate global procedure called WINDOW TITLE that would have the code in it to set the window title when output layouts are displayed. In your procedures that need to set the window title (m_CUSTOMERS, m_SHOW ALL, m_SHOW SUBSET, m_SEARCH, m_SEARCH LAYOUT, m_DELETE) you can type WINDOW TITLE instead of the line that uses the SET WINDOW TITLE command. When 4D reaches the WINDOW TITLE procedure, it will execute the code in the WINDOW TITLE procedure then continue with the next line after the WINDOW TITLE. When you type the name of another global procedure you are *calling a procedure.* You may have also heard this called *using a subroutine.*

Global procedure names may not be longer than 15 characters. This means that you will sometimes have to abbreviate words to make the name no greater than 15 characters.

Let's modify the procedures that set the window title so that they call a global procedure. The first step is to copy the code from one of the existing global procedures into a new global procedure:

1. Switch to the Design environment.
2. Open the m_CUSTOMERS global procedure.
3. Highlight the line of code that uses SET WINDOW TITLE.
4. Choose Edit ➤ Copy (⌘-C).
5. Create a procedure called WINDOW TITLE.

6. Choose Edit ➤ Paste (⌘-V).
7. Close the WINDOW TITLE procedure.
8. Open the m_CUSTOMERS procedure.
9. Highlight the line that uses the SET WINDOW TITLE command.
10. Type **WINDOW TITLE** in its place and press the Return key.

Figure 16.3 shows what the m_CUSTOMERS procedure should now look like.

4D displays the WINDOW TITLE procedure in italics to let you know that it recognizes that WINDOW TITLE is a global procedure. When 4D reaches the WINDOW TITLE procedure, 4D will open it,

FIGURE 16.3

The m_CUSTOMERS global procedure

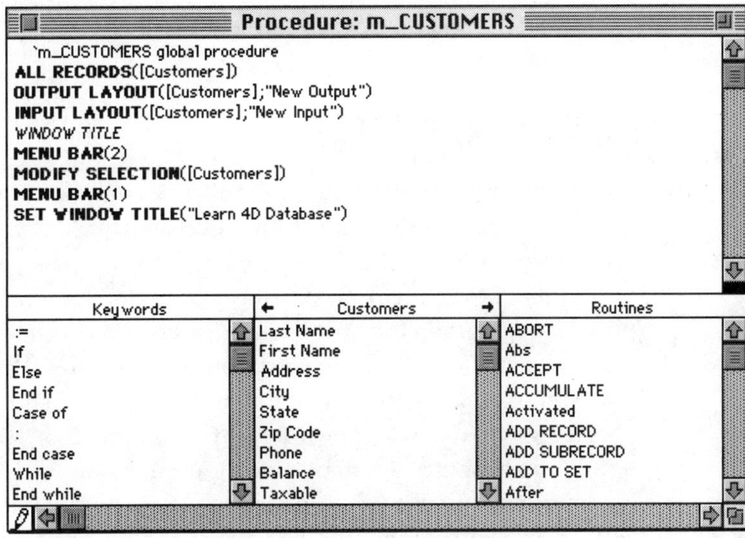

execute any code and then return to the procedure that called WINDOW TITLE. Let's continue:

12. Close the m_CUSTOMERS procedure.
13. Replace the same line that uses SET WINDOW TITLE with the WINDOW TITLE procedure in all of the following procedures:

    m_SHOW ALL
    m_SHOW SUBSET
    m_SEARCH EDITOR
    m_SEARCH LAYOUT
    m_DELETE

Now, anytime you decide to change the way the window title is handled, you can change it in one procedure instead of six different procedures.

PASSING PARAMETERS

You have used several of 4th Dimension's commands and functions. Many of these commands and functions required parameters. You have also written several global procedures. You can pass parameters to your own global procedures. By passing parameters to global procedures, the procedures can perform different tasks based on the parameters or perform some function on the parameters themselves. Parameter passing allows you to create procedures that are more powerful and flexible.

You already know how to pass parameters to a 4D command or function. You pass parameters by placing them inside parentheses after the command or function and separating them with semicolons (;). When you want to pass parameters to your own global procedures, you do exactly the same thing. The parameters you pass are copied into special local variables in the procedure that the parameters are being passed to. These special local variables are numbered. For example, if you passed a procedure three parameters, the first parameter would be copied into local variable $1 in the procedure it's being passed to. The second parameter would be copied into $2 and the third into $3. Say you called the following procedure with the following parameters:

```
MY PROCEDURE(123;"Geoff";DaysOld)
```

The procedure called MY PROCEDURE executes and the local variable $1 has the value 123, $2 has the value Geoff and $3 has whatever value is in the DaysOld variable.

In *Chapter 7* you wrote a procedure called Titlecase. Listed below is the code for the Titlecase procedure.

```
[Customers]Last Name:=Lowercase([Customers]Last
Name)
[Customers]Last Names≤1≥:= Uppercase([Cus-
tomers]Last Names≤1≥)
```

This procedure is useful because the user doesn't have to remember to type the Last Name in the correct case. However, its usefulness is somewhat limited because it works only on the Last Name field. This procedure would be much more useful if it could perform its function on any field or variable. You can alter this procedure to allow it to work with any field or variable. In order to do this, you will need to pass the Titlecase procedure to the text you want capitalized. This text will be copied into the variable $1 in the Titlecase procedure. That means that instead of the [Customers]Last Name, you should have $1. The Procedure Editor has a Replace menu item that makes changes like this easy. Let's change the procedure:

1. Switch to the Design environment.
2. Open the Titlecase procedure.
3. Choose Search ➤ Replace (⌘-R).
4. Type **[Customers]Last Name** into the Find box and press the Tab key.
5. Type **$1** into the Replace by box.
6. Click **Replace**.
7. Choose Search ➤ Replace Next (⌘-T).

8. Choose Search ➤ Replace Next (⌘-T).
9. Choose Search ➤ Replace Next (⌘-T).

At this point, whatever is passed to the Titlecase procedure will be capitalized. Now the code can work on anything instead of just the Last Name field. When you pass parameters, you are passing a copy of the information, not the original. For example, if you now go to the script of the Last Name field and enter the following code

```
Titlecase([Customers]Last Name)
```

as the script for the field, the Last Name field will not be capitalized. This is because when the user types in a last name then Tabs out of the Last Name field, a copy of the contents of the Last Name field will be passed to the Titlecase procedure. The Titlecase procedure will then capitalize the copy but not the original. If you want a copy of the capitalized Last Name to be passed back to the Last Name field, you will need to make the Titlecase procedure a function.

WRITING FUNCTIONS

Some of 4D's commands and functions perform a task (the MODIFY SELECTION command for example), while others return a value (like Records in selection). If a procedure returns a value it's called a *function.* In 4th Dimension, procedures that don't return a value are called *commands* and are in all uppercase (example: MODIFY SELECTION). Procedures that return a value are called functions, and are in (appropriately enough) title case. Getting a procedure to return a value is easy. Simply assign to $0 (dollar sign zero) the value you want returned. When the procedure finishes, the value of $0 will be returned. Let's turn Titlecase into a function:

1. Click below the last line of the Titlecase procedure.
2. Type **$0:=$1**.

Since $1 contains the capitalized copy, you simply assign that value to $0 and you are done. The last step is to change the script of the Last Name field so that it calls the Titlecase function properly.

1. Close the Titlecase procedure.
2. Open the Customers New Input layout.
3. Option-click on the Last Name field to open the script.
4. Change the script so that reads as follows:

```
[Customers]Last Name:=Titlecase([Customers]Last Name)
```

You can now use the Titlecase function to capitalize any field or variable. Passing parameters back and forth between procedures makes them more efficient and more powerful.

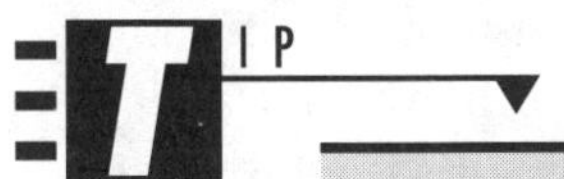

A function by definition can return only one value. If you need to write a global procedure that returns more than one value, you can do this using Pointers. You will learn about Pointers next.

WRITING RE-USABLE CODE WITH POINTERS

You have written several global procedures to give the user access to your database in the Runtime environment. Now you can create a completely customized interface and control what the menus say and do. So far, the procedures you have written will allow the user to access only the Customers file. All throughout your procedures you used the Customers file ([Customers]) to tell the 4D commands and functions which file you wanted to work on. If you wanted to allow the user to have access to other files, you will have to add some code to your procedures. You will want to give the user the same functionality with your other files as you did with the Customers file (searching, deleting, reporting, etc.). Let's take a look at the m_CUSTOMERS procedure:

```
' m_CUSTOMERS global procedure
ALL RECORDS([Customers])
OUTPUT LAYOUT([Customers];"New Output")
INPUT LAYOUT([Customers];"New Input")
WINDOW TITLE
MENU BAR(2)
MODIFY SELECTION([Customers])
MENU BAR(1)
SET WINDOW TITLE("Learn 4D Database")
```

If you wanted to have an *Invoices* menu item under the File menu that would display a list of invoices, how would you do it? You could create a new procedure called m_INVOICES then copy the code above and paste into the new procedure and change the [Customers] filename to [Invoices]. If you wanted to give the user access to other files, you could continue to create duplicate procedures and change the filename each time. This method will work just fine but it is not the most efficient way of getting the job done.

You already know how to pass parameters to procedures. If you could pass something to this procedure to tell it what file to work with, you could use this code for all of your files. Say you put the above code into a global procedure called LIST RECORDS. Then passed it the name of the file you wanted the procedure to list the records for. Your m_CUSTOMERS procedure would then look something like this:

```
' m_CUSTOMERS global procedure
LIST RECORDS([Customers])
```

It seems like this should work but it doesn't. You cannot pass a filename to a procedure. However, you can pass a *reference* to the file. This reference is called a *pointer*.

A pointer is like an address. For example, your address is not you. Your address is where you live or work. As long as you give people your address, they can always find you. As a matter for fact, mail will get to you even if it doesn't have your name on it. It just needs the correct address.

You have probably received several pieces of mail labeled Occupant or Resident. If someone has your address, they can always find you. To a computer, a pointer is the home address of the object that the pointer points to. A pointer is called a pointer because it is *pointing* to the object. Say you created the LIST RECORDS procedure. Your m_CUSTOMERS procedure could call the LIST RECORDS procedure and pass it a pointer to the Customers file. You could then create an m_INVOICES procedure that would also call the LIST RECORDS procedure and pass it a pointer to the Invoices file. Now your LIST RECORDS procedure works for both the Customers file and the Invoices file.

A pointer to a file looks much like the filename itself. You know what a filename looks like in your code ([Customers]). A pointer to a file looks almost identical. The difference is that it starts off with the pointer symbol (»). So a pointer to the Customers file looks like this »[Customers]. Let's change the procedures so they work with pointers:

1. Switch to the Design environment.
2. Open the m_CUSTOMERS procedure.
3. Choose Edit ➤Select All (⌘-A).
4. Choose Edit ➤ Copy (⌘-C).
5. Create a new procedure called LIST RECORDS.
6. Choose Edit ➤ Paste (⌘-V).
7. Change the first line so it reads **LIST RECORDS global procedure**.

At this point the two procedures are identical. You can now remove the code from the m_CUSTOMERS procedure. Then you can call the LIST RECORDS procedure and pass to it a pointer to the Customers file.

1. Select the m_CUSTOMERS procedure.
2. Click to the left of the ALL RECORDS command on the second line and drag down to highlight the remaining lines.
3. Choose Edit ➤ Cut (⌘-X).
4. Type **list records()**.
5. Press the Left Arrow key once.

6. Type the pointer symbol (») by pressing Option-Shift-\.
7. Click on the Customers filename in the Fields list to insert it.
8. Press the Enter key.

LIST RECORDS is displayed in italics to let you know that 4D recognizes LIST RECORDS as one of your global procedures. The pointer symbol goes on the left of the filename to indicate that you are passing a pointer to the file. You know that the first parameter you pass is copied into the local variable $1 in the procedure being called. So, the pointer to the Customers file (»[Customers]) will be copied into the $1 variable in the LIST RECORDS procedure when the LIST RECORDS procedure executes.

Your next step is to change the LIST RECORDS procedure so that it uses the pointer in $1. You will need to replace each reference to the Customers file ([Customers]) with $1». The pointer symbol goes on the right because $1 is a pointer and you want to access what it points to. Because you are setting the input layout and output layout in this procedure, you will want to name all of your input layouts with the same input and all of your output layouts with the same name. Let's change the LIST RECORDS procedure:

1. Select the LIST RECORDS procedure.
2. Choose Search ➤ Replace (⌘-R).
3. Type **[Customers]** in the Find box.
4. Type **$1»** in the Replace box.
5. Click **Replace**.
6. Choose Search ➤ Replace Next (⌘-T) three times to replace all the Customers file references with $1».
7. Change New Input to **Input**.
8. Change New Output to **Output**.

Figure 16.4 shows what the LIST RECORDS procedure should look like.

FIGURE 16.4

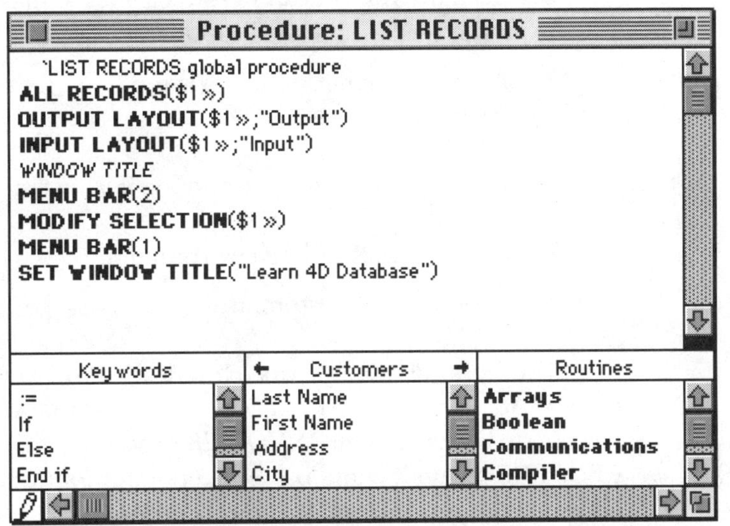
Procedure: LIST RECORDS
`LIST RECORDS global procedure
ALL RECORDS($1»)
OUTPUT LAYOUT($1»;"Output")
INPUT LAYOUT($1»;"Input")
WINDOW TITLE
MENU BAR(2)
MODIFY SELECTION($1»)
MENU BAR(1)
SET WINDOW TITLE("Learn 4D Database")
Keywords
:=
If
Else
End if
Customers
Last Name
First Name
Address
City
Routines
Arrays
Boolean
Communications
Compiler

The LIST RECORDS procedure with pointers

The next step is to make sure that each file has an input layout named Input and an output layout named Output.

1. Choose Design ➤ Layout (⌘-L).
2. Double-click on Customers to display the layouts.
3. Click on the layout called Input to select it.
4. Click the **Delete** button.
5. Click **Yes**.
6. Delete the layout called Output.
7. Click on the New Input layout to select it.
8. In the Name field, type **Input** as the new name for the layout.
9. Click the **Update** button to update the name of the layout.
10. Change the name of the New Output layout to **Output**.

11. Check the Invoices and Products files to make sure that each has a layout called Input and a layout called Output.
12. Change the names of the existing input and output layouts if necessary.

Let's try out your new code and see if it works:

1. Switch to the Runtime environment.
2. Choose File ➤ Customers.

The LIST RECORDS procedure works. You can view your customers. At this point you can easily add access to the Invoices file. All you have to do is create an m_INVOICES procedure that calls the LIST RECORDS command and passes it a pointer to the Invoices file. Let's add a menu item and create the procedure:

1. Switch to the Design environment.
2. Open Menu bar #1.
3. Click on the File menu to select it.
4. Click in-between the Customers and Quit menu items.
5. Choose Menu ➤ Insert Item (⌘-G).
6. Type **Invoices** as the new menu item.

The File menu is a connected menu. This means that the File menu is displayed on both menu bar #1 and #2 but is, in fact, the same menu. So, when you makes changes to the File menu in Menu bar #1 or #2 the change is immediately reflected in the all menu bars that have the File menu connected to them. The File menu is automatically connected to all new menu bars you create. You can connect menus from other menu bars by choosing Menu ➤ Connect Menu. Sharing (connecting) menus with other menu bars means less work for you because a change in one changes the rest.

The next step is to write the m_INVOICES procedure. This is very easy to do since you already have the m_CUSTOMERS procedure, which is very close to what the m_INVOICES procedure will look like. Let's create it:

1. Open the m_CUSTOMERS procedure.
2. Choose Edit ➤ Select All (⌘-A).
3. Choose Edit ➤ Copy (⌘-C).
4. Close the m_CUSTOMERS procedure.
5. Create a new procedure called m_INVOICES.
6. Choose Edit ➤ Paste (⌘-V).
7. Change the first line to read **'m_INVOICES global procedure**.
8. Double-click on the [Customers] file being passed to LIST RECORDS.
9. Replace the [Customers] filename with the **[Invoices]** filename.
10. Select Menu bar #1.
11. Assign m_INVOICES to the Invoices menu item.

Let's try out the new menu item and see if it displays the invoices:

1. Switch to the Runtime environment.
2. Choose File ➤ Invoices.

Because there is only one record in the selection, the MODIFY SELECTION command displays the record in the input layout rather than displaying it in the output layout. Also, notice that the window title says *Customers* instead of *Invoices*. This is because the string "Customers" is being passed to the SET WINDOW TITLE command. The window title is also displaying the number of records in the current selection and the number of records in the file of the Customers file instead of the Invoices file. This is because the WINDOW TITLE procedure is using the [Customers] filename and doesn't know about the file pointer you passed to the LIST RECORDS procedure. How can you make it so that the WINDOW TITLE procedure looks at the file pointer and displays a window title for that file? You can do this with a process variable.

Although the MODIFY SELECTION command displays the input layout when there is only one record in the selection, you can change this behavior. To get the MODIFY SELECTION command to display the output layout first, even when the selection contains only one record, pass an asterisk as a second parameter to MODIFY SELECTION.

Process variables can be accessed by all of your procedures. If you copy the file pointer stored in $1 into a process variable, that variable could then be used by the WINDOW TITLE procedure to know which file it should look at when calling the *Records in selection* and *Records in file* functions. Also, using the *Filename* function and the file pointer, you can find out the filename that the pointer points to and pass this name to *SET WINDOW TITLE* rather than passing the "Customers" string. This way the WINDOW TITLE will always accurately reflect the file you are viewing. Let's change LIST RECORDS procedure and WINDOW TITLE procedures:

1. Switch to the Design environment.
2. Open the LIST RECORDS procedure.
3. Type **FilePtr:=$1** and press the Return key.

Figure 16.5 shows what the LIST RECORDS procedure looks like now.

You created a new process variable called FilePtr. Ptr is short for pointer. You can now use this variable in the WINDOW TITLE procedure to access the file that the pointer points to.

1. Close the LIST RECORDS procedure.
2. Open the WINDOW TITLE procedure.

FIGURE 16.5

The LIST RECORDS procedure

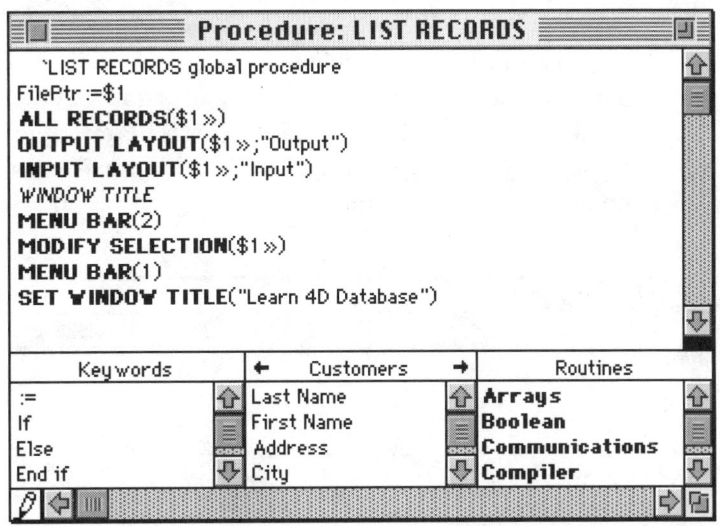
Procedure: LIST RECORDS
`LIST RECORDS global procedure
FilePtr :=$1
ALL RECORDS($1»)
OUTPUT LAYOUT($1»;"Output")
INPUT LAYOUT($1»;"Input")
WINDOW TITLE
MENU BAR(2)
MODIFY SELECTION($1»)
MENU BAR(1)
SET WINDOW TITLE("Learn 4D Database")
Keywords
:=
If
Else
End if
Customers
Last Name
First Name
Address
City
Routines
Arrays
Boolean
Communications
Compiler

3. Click the Zoom box to expand the procedure to fill the window.
4. Double-click on the [Customers] filename passed to the Records in selection function.
5. Type **FilePtr**» to replace the [Customers] filename.
6. Replace the **[Customers]** filename passed to the Record in file function with FilePtr».

The last step is to use the Filename function to get the filename that the FilePtr process variable points to. You want to use the Filename function instead of the string "Customers:" so that the window title will always display the correct filename.

1. Highlight the "Customers:" string including the quotation marks.
2. Type **filename()** and press the Left Arrow key.
3. Type **FilePtr** and press the Right Arrow key.
4. Type **+": "+** to add the colon to the window title.

5. Press the Enter key.

Figure 16.6 shows what the WINDOW TITLE procedure looks like now. Notice that with the Filename function you didn't add the pointer symbol after the FilePtr variable. This is because the Filename function expects a pointer as a parameter and not whatever it is that the pointer points to. Get the point?

FIGURE 16.6

The WINDOW TITLE procedure

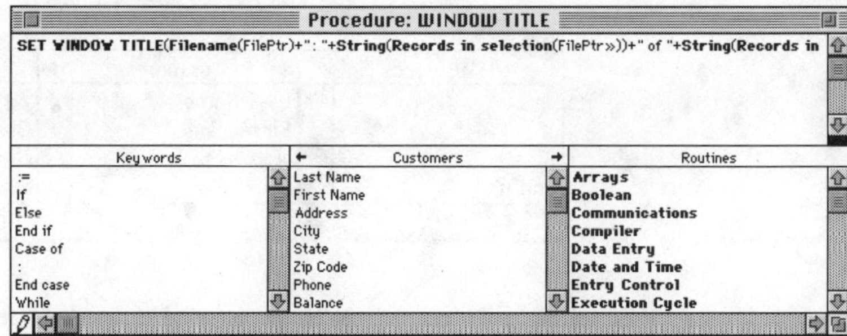

Let's try out this new WINDOW TITLE procedure to see if it works with both files.

1. Switch to the Runtime environment.
2. Choose File ➤ Customers.
3. Press the Enter key.
4. Choose Filc ➤ Invoices.
5. Press the Enter key.

You can now display the records for both files and the window title is displayed properly. What about all of the other menu procedures you wrote? They all use the [Customers] filename. This means that the [Customers] filename in all of the procedures needs to be replaced with FilePtr».

1. Open each of the following procedures and replace any [Customers] filenames with FilePtr».

   m_NEW RECORD
   m_SHOW ALL
   m_SEARCH EDITOR
   m_SEARCH LAYOUT
   m_SORT
   m_DELETE
   m_QUICK
   m_LABELS
   m_GRAPH

2. Switch to the Runtime environment.
3. Choose File ➤ Customers.
4. Try out each menu item to see that it is working on the Customers file.

Using a pointer and a process variable, you have made all of your procedures generic so that they can work with any file. At this point it would be very little work to give the user access to the Products file.

1. Switch to the Design environment.
2. Add a Products menu item to the File menu.
3. Write an m_PRODUCTS procedure (like the m_INVOICES procedure).
4. Assign the m_PRODUCTS procedure to the Products menu item.
5. Test out this new menu item to see that it works.

In this chapter you have been introduced to pointers. You have used a pointer that points to a file. Pointers can actually point to other objects as well (fields, variables, etc.). 4th Dimension is not the only language that uses pointers. C and Pascal are two other programming languages that use pointers. If you learn one of these programming languages someday, you will already be one step ahead because the concept of pointers will not be new to you.

While writing re-usable code requires more preplanning, you can see the benefit. Using pointers, you can write less code and therefore have to maintain less code. Maintenance of programming code comes in the form of adding features and removing bugs. I will talk about bugs next.

GETTING THE BUGS OUT

Computers can only do exactly what they are told to do and do it very fast. Sometimes, we think we are giving the computer enough information to get the job done when, in fact, we have left something out. Other times, we have given the computer all of the instructions it needs but the instructions themselves are not right. When a computer program displays undesirable behavior, it's called a bug.

WHAT ARE "BUGS"?

During World War II Grace Murray Hopper, a mathematician, pioneer programmer, and Naval officer, worked on the Harvard Mark II computer developed at Harvard for the Navy. A mysterious malfunction caused the computer to shut down. The source of the shutdown was an electrical switch that was blocked by a moth that flew into the machine. Grace taped the moth into the Mark II log book and recorded the first actual case of a bug being found in the computer. After that, when an officer asked what they were working on, Grace replied, "we are debugging the computer." This is where the term "bug" came from. It's origin is, quite literally, a bug.

As you use 4D's' programming language you will encounter a few bugs of your own. Look at the following code:

```
X:=1
If(X=2)
    BEEP
End if
```

The program is never going to beep because X is assigned the value 1 and then checked to see if it has the value 2. This is one type of bug. This kind of bug is the result of an error in logic. The computer is doing exactly what it was told to do. The bug is that it is not doing what you want it to do. This is the worst type of bug to fix because you have to look through your code and figure out where your logic went wrong.

Another type of bug involves and error in syntax. In this case, 4D has encountered something in your code that it did not expect. When this occurs, 4D displays the Syntax Error window as shown in Figure 16.7.

In the top portion of the Syntax Error window, 4D displays a message that tells you what the problem is. For example, the error message in Figure 16.7 is informing you that you are trying to perform an operation that can't be used with the data you are using. This would be the case if you tried to add a number and a string together. You can't add a number and a string, so the Syntax Error window is displayed with the message "This operation is not compatible with the two arguments." You can convert the number to a string or convert the string to a number then add them together. In some cases, that would be all you would have to do to fix the bug. The bottom portion of the Syntax Error window displays the line of code where the error occurred.

FIGURE 16.7

The Syntax Error window

This operation is not compatible with the two arguments.

EmpInfo:=Name+" "+StartDate

Abort | Trace | Continue | Edit

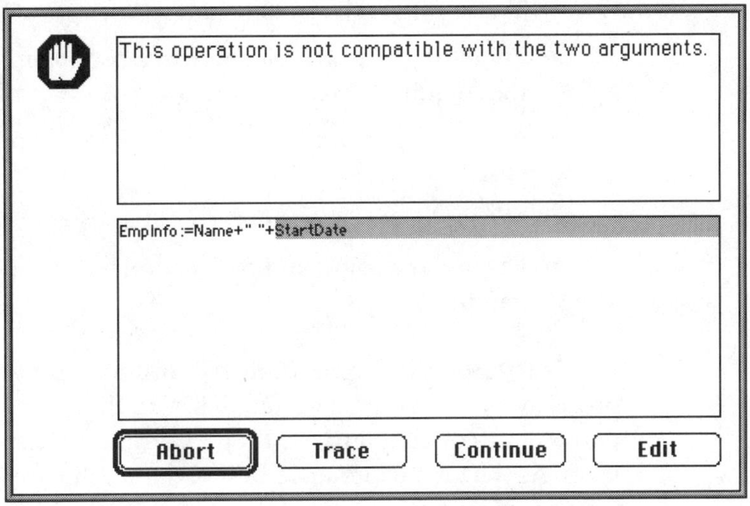

The Syntax Error window has four buttons in it:

Abort stops the code from continuing to execute. You would use this option when you want to stop the procedure from continuing to execute in order to execute another procedure.

Trace opens the Debug window and allows you to watch your code execute one line at a time. I will talk about the Debug window next.

Continue allows 4D to continue executing the rest of the procedure. You should only use this option when the error that displayed the Syntax Error window is not going to have an effect on the rest of the procedure.

Edit switches to the Design environment and opens the procedure in the Procedure Editor.

When the Syntax Error window appears, you will typically look at the error and then switch to the Design environment to fix the bug that caused the error. Some common errors are:

- Misspelling field names, filenames, procedures, and variables.
- Transposing the use of := and =.
- Forgetting to pass a filename to a command or function that requires one.
- Not having the same number of opening and closing parentheses.
- Missing quotation marks around a string.
- Passing to a command or function a data type that it can't handle.

When you first begin using 4D's programming language, you will no doubt become intimately familiar with the Syntax Error window. But don't let this discourage you. Even experienced users of 4D make mistakes. As you gain experience with 4D, you will have fewer errors and you will spend less time staring at this dialog box.

USING THE DEBUGGER

When the Syntax Error window appears, you will often know what caused the error just by looking at the information that the window gives you. This will not always be the case. You may have to look back through your code to find out what is causing the problem. The cause of a bug will not always be obvious when you look at your code. In these situations, the only way to track down the code causing the bug is to watch your code execute one line at a time and monitor values in variables and fields to see where you went wrong. You can do this with the Debugger. Figure 16.8 shows the Debug window. You get to this window in one of four ways:

- Clicking the Trace button in the Syntax Error window.
- Using the TRACE command in a procedure.
- Holding down the Option key and clicking the mouse while a procedure is executing.
- Choosing Process ➤ Trace when displaying the Process List in the Design environment.

FIGURE 16.8

The Debug window

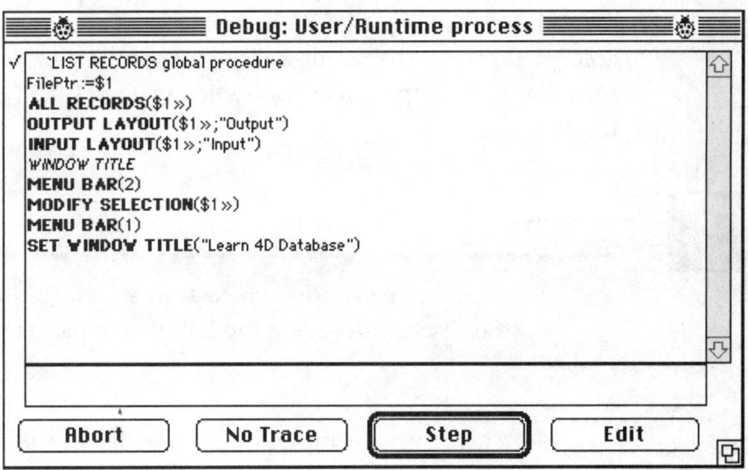
Debug: User/Runtime process
`LIST RECORDS global procedure
FilePtr:=$1
ALL RECORDS($1»)
OUTPUT LAYOUT($1»;"Output")
INPUT LAYOUT($1»;"Input")
WINDOW TITLE
MENU BAR(2)
MODIFY SELECTION($1»)
MENU BAR(1)
SET WINDOW TITLE("Learn 4D Database")
Abort
No Trace
Step
Edit

The Debug window has four buttons in it:

Abort stops the execution of the procedure displayed. This works just like the Abort button in the Syntax Error window.

No Trace closes the Debug window and stops tracing allowing 4D to execute code at its normal pace.

Step executes the next line of code then stops and waits for you decide what you want to do next.

Edit switches to the Design environment and opens the displayed procedure in the Procedure Editor.

The window title of the Debug window tells you which process is being debugged. All code executes inside a process. All of the code in the Learn 4D database is executing in the User/Runtime process. You will learn more about processes in *Chapter 17.* The top portion of the Debug window displays code from the procedure that is currently executing. A checkmark is placed to the left of the line of code that will be executed next. The bottom portion of the Debug window is for evaluating expressions. This means that you can watch the values in fields and variables and test out code. At the end of each expression, 4D places a colon (:) and then the result of the expression. If an expression is a field, variable, or formula, the result will be the contents of that field, variable, or formula. If the expression is a boolean test like X>1, 4D will display true or false.

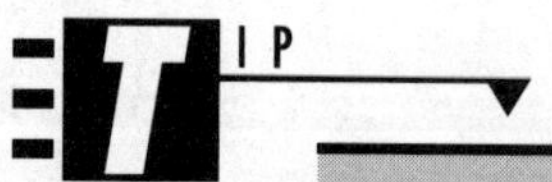

You can resize the expression area by holding down the Option key can dragging the line that separates the two areas.

Here are some examples of expressions in the expression area and what the results would be:

```
[Customers]Last Name   :Williams
[Customers]First Name  :Ted
OK  :1
```

10*25 :250
Records in selection([Customers]) :6
Records in file([Customers])>3 :True
1=1 :True

Each time you click the Step button, 4D executes the line of code that has the checkmark next to it, then it stops and waits for you. This allows you to see the effect that your code has before the next line is executed. All of the expressions in the expression area are re-evaluated when you click the **Step** button. If the line about to be executed is a global procedure, 4D will step into and begin tracing the global procedure.

If a global procedure is about to be executed, hold down the Shift key and click on the Step **button to have 4D execute the procedure without stepping into it. This will save you the time of having to trace through procedures that you know are not the cause of the bug.**

There will be times when you will be tracing a procedure and realize that the code you really need to watch is several lines down in the procedure. Instead of stepping through these lines, you can insert a *breakpoint.*

A breakpoint simply tells 4D to open the Debug window when it reaches a particular line of code. This allows you to click the No Trace button and allow 4D to continue executing code until the line with the breakpoint is reached. To insert a breakpoint, simply click the mouse in the margin where the checkmark is, next to the line of code that where you want 4D to being tracing again. Breakpoints appear in the margin as bullets (•). To remove a breakpoint, just click on it.

By stepping through your code and watching the values of fields and variables, you can usually find out where you went wrong. At first, you will spend quite a bit of time looking up commands to see what they do or what their particular syntax is. Again, don't be frustrated by this. As you gain more experience with 4D and debugging, you will begin to realize what is causing a problem the moment the problem occurs.

If you hold down the Option key and click in the expression area, 4D will display a pop-up menu of your files and fields. When you select an item from the pop-up, it will be inserted into the expression area. If you hold down the ⌘ key and click in the expression area, 4D will display a pop-up menu of 4D's commands and functions.

WHY USE OTHER LANGUAGES?

You may have heard of other languages like C, C++, Pascal, Basic, Fortran, Cobol, SQL, Assembler, etc. With all that 4D can do, you might wonder why anyone would ever use anything else. While 4D is a powerful language, is not suited for every possible programming task. The reason that so many programming languages exist is that they each are specialized for different kinds of programming tasks. For example, if you wanted to write a game program that required lots of animation, you would get the best results using Assembler. And while you could write a database application in Assembler, it would take you at least 1000 times longer than it would if you wrote it using 4th Dimension. There is a saying that a jack of all trades is a master of none. 4D is the master of database applications.

PROGRAMMING TECHNIQUES

MAC TRACKS MAC

To display a progress message during a long operation 563

Use the MESSAGE command.

To build a multi-criteria search 574

Enter a SEARCH command for each criteria and include an asterisk as the last parameter in each SEARCH except the last one.

Featuring

- *Adding dialog boxes*
- *Decision making*
- *The execution cycle*
- *Building searches*
- *Printing*
- *Multitasking*

IN THE LAST chapter you were introduced to several 4D commands and functions. You also learned how to pass parameters to procedures and how to write functions. In this chapter, you will learn about specific commands and functions that will give you even more control over your database applications. The commands and functions that you will learn about in this chapter will give you a better understanding of how to get information from the user, how to process that information easily and quickly, and how to output that information in a format that makes sense.

INTERACTING WITH THE USER

Most people who have purchased a Macintosh bought one because of its graphical user interface (GUI). In the early days, Apple Computer took a lot of flack over the Macintosh because the rest of the industry and a good portion of the market felt that the Macintosh was just a toy. Nothing that pretty could be smart. This turned out to be a classic case of "don't judge a book by its cover." Apple Computer is now the single largest manufacturer of personal computers, and with the appearance of Microsoft Windows, a lot of other computers now have a graphical user interface. Apple has proven that a graphical user interface makes a computer easier to use.

The interface you present to your user in your 4D database is critical to the success of that database. You will spend about half of your development time on the interface. This time includes creating input layouts, output layouts, dialog boxes, and all of the other parts of the database that interact with the user. 4D, as you have already learned, has many built-in features to make creating a clean and intuitive interface fast and easy.

You already know how to create input layouts and output layouts. These layouts are useful when you are presenting information from records to the user. However, there will be times when you need to get information from the user that won't be entered into a record or come from a record. In these cases, you will use dialog boxes.

USING THE BUILT-IN DIALOGS

A dialog box (as the name implies) is used to open a dialog with the user; to exchange information. 4D has four built-in commands that present different types of dialog boxes for different purposes.

The ALERT Command

The ALERT command presents a dialog box with a talking face icon. This is also called a note alert box. You can pass the ALERT command a string of up to 255 characters that will be displayed in the window. The string passed can be between quotes or inside a variable. Figure 17.1 shows a procedure that is calling the ALERT command. Figure 17.2 shows the ALERT dialog box displayed by that procedure. ALERT dialog boxes are used to provide the user with non-threatening information.

FIGURE 17.1

A procedure using the ALERT command

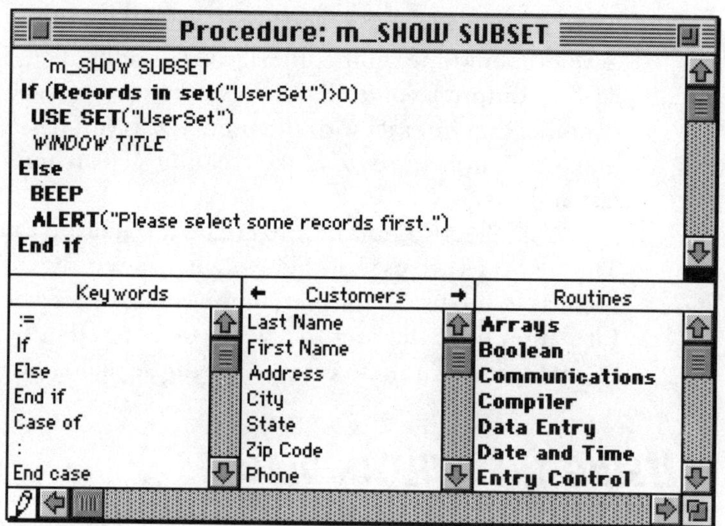

FIGURE 17.2

An example ALERT dialog box

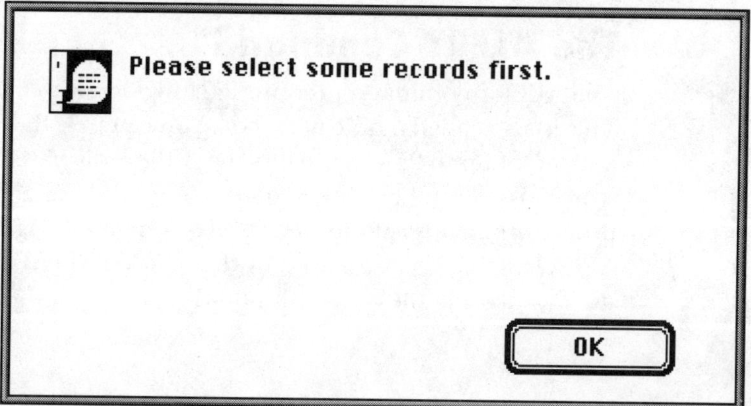

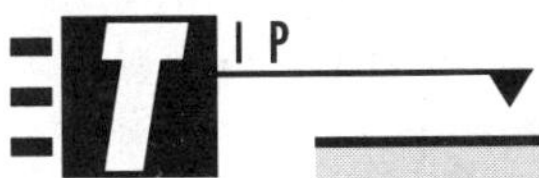

Although the ALERT command will accept a string of 255 characters, you cannot type a string constant (a string of characters between quotes) longer than 80 characters in the Procedure Editor. This means that if you need your ALERT message to be longer than 80 characters, you will need to put some of the string into a variable and concatenate the rest on a second line.

The CONFIRM Command

The CONFIRM command works in a way similar to the ALERT command. You can pass it a string or variable containing a string which is presented in a dialog box. Figure 17.3 shows an example of a CONFIRM dialog box. What makes the CONFIRM command different is the appearance of the dialog and the effect it has on a special variable. The icon in the CONFIRM dialog box is a hand inside a hexagon that represents a stop sign in most locales. The CONFIRM dialog box has two buttons (**Cancel** and **OK**) instead of just one (OK).

FIGURE 17.3

***A** CONFIRM dialog box*

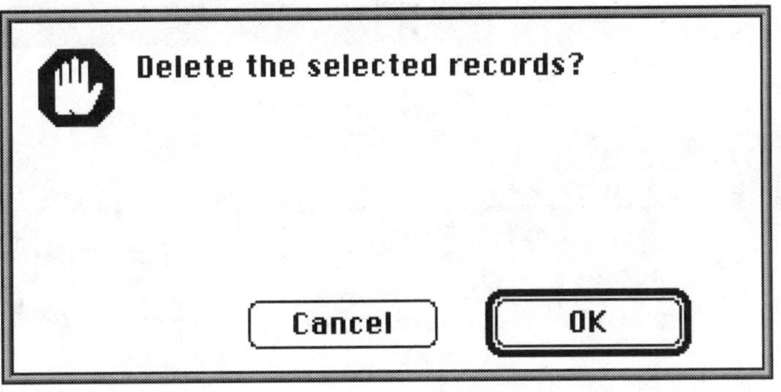

When the user clicks the **Cancel** button, a special variable called OK is set to 0. When the user clicks the **OK** button, the OK variable is set to 1. Therefore, in your procedures you can tell which button was pressed by testing the OK variable. Figure 17.4 shows an example procedure that presented the CONFIRM dialog box from Figure 17.3 and checks to see if the user clicked OK or not.

FIGURE 17.4

A procedure using the CONFIRM command

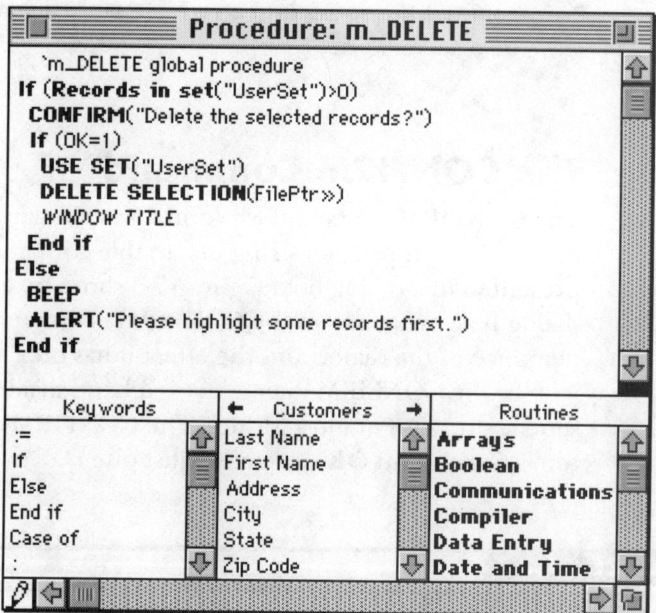

Strings passed to the CONFIRM command cannot be longer than 80 characters.

You should use the CONFIRM dialog box when the user is about to perform an irreversible action that will result in the loss of data. If the action is not going to result in data loss, don't use the CONFIRM command.

Some applications display a confirming dialog box when the user chooses File ➤ Quit (⌘-Q). Quitting an application is not an irreversible action and shouldn't result in data loss. If the user will lose data as a result of quitting, the CONFIRM command should be used to ask the user if they want to save the data before quitting.

The Request Function

The Request function presents a dialog box that allows the user to enter information. You can pass a string to the Request function that will be displayed in the dialog box presented to the user. Figure 17.5 shows an example of a Request dialog box. This dialog box has two buttons (**Cancel** and **OK**) just like the CONFIRM dialog box and like CONFIRM, the OK variable is set based on which button the user clicks.

FIGURE 17.5

An example of a Request dialog box

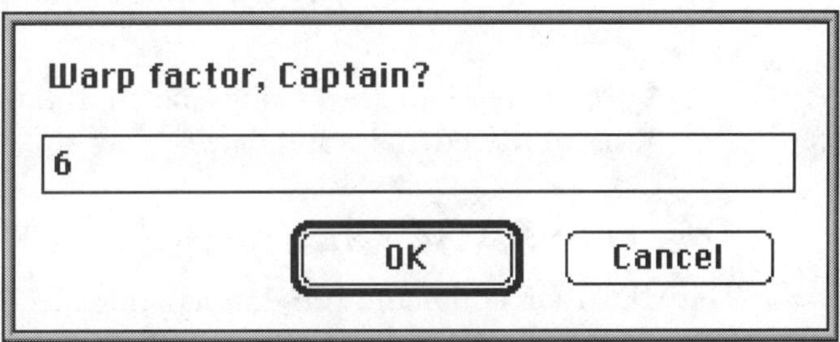

The information entered by the user is a string and is returned by the Request function. This is an important point because you may ask the user for a piece of information that is not a string, like a date. If you need information from the user that is not a string, pass the Request function to a function that will convert the string returned to the type of data you need. Figure 17.6 shows an example of procedure that is asking the user for a date. The Request function is passed to the Date function which converts the string into a date.

FIGURE 17.6

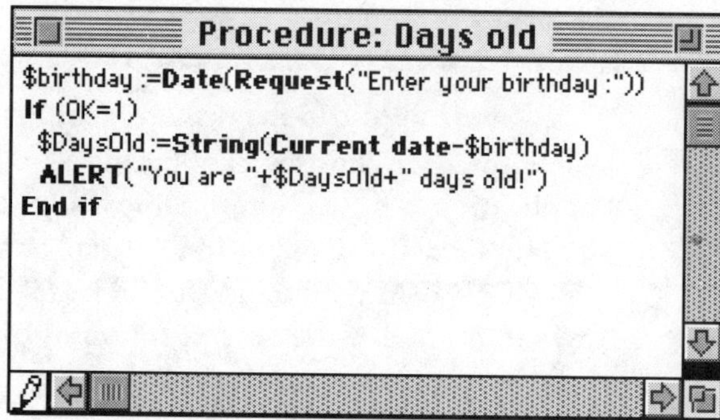

A Request string converted to a Date

Be aware that if you use the Request function to ask the user for a date, the user might enter a date that is not valid, such as *2/31/94.* If you pass this string to the Date function, it will be converted to a date as 3/3/94. You can find out if the user entered a valid date or not using the following steps:

1. Store the date they entered in a variable.
2. Convert a copy of the date to a date.
3. Convert the copy back to a string (with the String function).
4. Test to see if the two strings match. If they don't match, the user entered an invalid date.

The MESSAGE Command

The MESSAGE command presents a dialog box that has no buttons or icons. Figure 17.7 shows an example of a MESSAGE dialog box. The

FIGURE 17.7

Now deleting records...

A MESSAGE dialog box

purpose of the MESSAGE dialog is to present the user with a message while a long operation is in progress. If an operation takes longer than a few seconds, it's a good idea to display some kind of message so the user doesn't think that the machine has stopped (frozen). Figure 17.8 shows a procedure using the MESSAGE command.

FIGURE 17.8

A procedure using the MESSAGE command

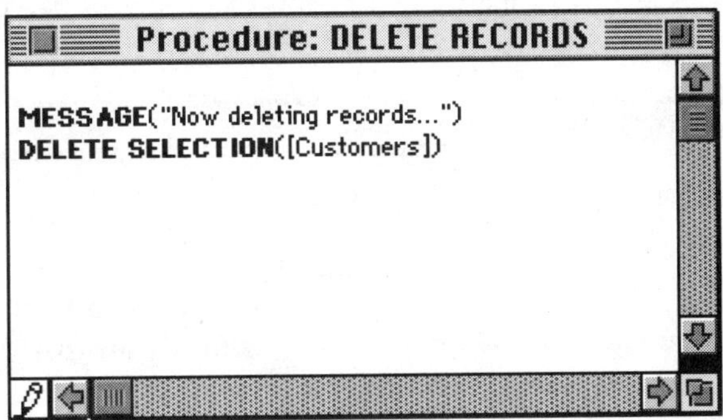

Procedure: DELETE RECORDS
MESSAGE("Now deleting records...")
DELETE SELECTION([Customers])

By default, the MESSAGE command displays the message in Geneva 12 point font. You can change this default font using the Customizer Plus application that came with your copy of 4D. Customizer Plus is discussed in *Appendix A.*

CREATING YOUR OWN DIALOGS

In most cases, one of 4D's built-in dialog boxes will work when you need to ask the user for information or present the user with information. However, there will be times when you need to create custom dialog boxes. Fortunately, you can create custom dialog boxes easily using a layout and the DIALOG command.

Up to this point, the layouts you have created have been used for entering or displaying lists of records. Layouts can also be used to enter or display information that is not necessarily associated with records. This is what dialogs are for. You might require a dialog that looks like an ALERT dialog but allows more than 255 characters or perhaps has different text for the button. You might require a dialog box that allows the user to enter several pieces of information instead of just one. Figures 17.9 and 17.10 show examples of two custom dialog boxes.

FIGURE 17.9

A custom confirming dialog box

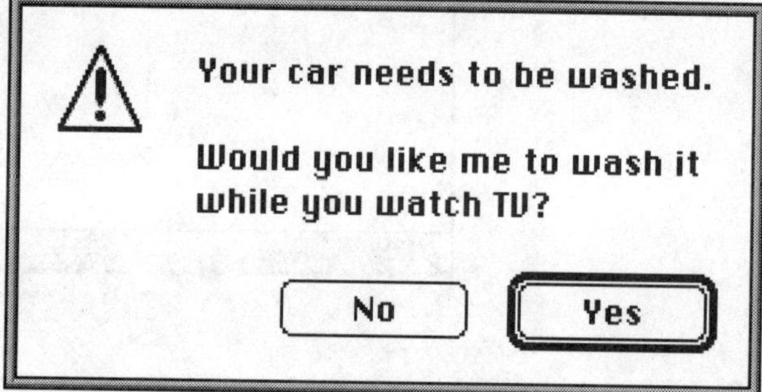

FIGURE 17.10

A custom search dialog box

Creating a custom dialog box requires two steps. The first is to create the layout with the buttons, icons and text you want to display. The second step is to call the DIALOG command to display the dialog box. Figure 17.11 shows the Layout Editor displaying the layout used to create the custom confirming dialog from Figure 17.9.

FIGURE 17.11

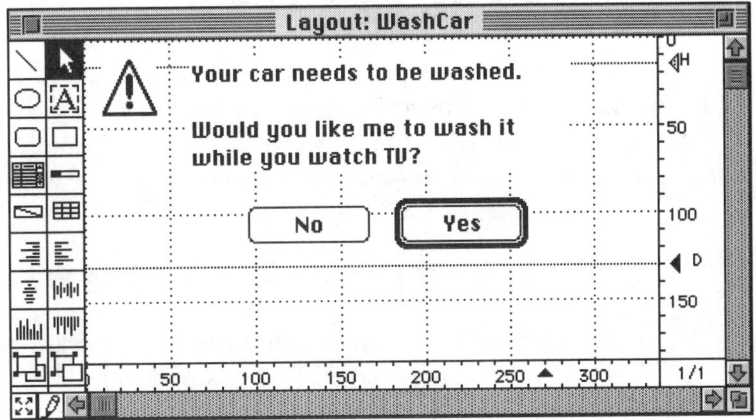

The confirming dialog box in the Layout Editor

Graphics (like the icon) can be pasted in using the Clipboard (accessed from the Edit menu). The text is created using the Text tool in the Tools Palette. The buttons are created with the Active Object tool in the Tools Palette. The right button has been assigned the Accept automatic action and the left button has been assigned the Cancel automatic action. The reason for this is simple. The dialog box will close when either an Accept or Cancel button is pressed. The OK variable is set to 1 when an **Accept** button is pressed and 0 when a **Cancel** button is pressed. If you need two buttons (like in this confirming dialog box) using Accept and Cancel makes sense, because after the dialog box closes, you can test the OK variable to see if the user clicked the Accept button or the Cancel button.

It is common to create a file that will contain all of your layouts that are used for dialog boxes. This file would not contain any records but would give you one place to look when you needed to find one of your dialog layouts.

The DIALOG Command

With the layout created, the next step is to call the DIALOG command. The DIALOG command requires two parameters. The first is the filename where the layout is and the second is the name of the layout itself. Say you created a layout called Search Dialog that was going to be used to create a customized search dialog. The code to present the dialog would look like this:

```
DIALOG([Dialogs];"Search Dialog")
```

When the DIALOG command is executed, the layout will be presented in the currently active window. This means that the dialog layout would replace whatever layout was currently being displayed until the user clicked on an Accept or Cancel button. It might be confusing to the user to see the layout they were working with suddenly disappear. Instead, you can open a new window with the OPEN WINDOW command. This command will open a window of a size and type that you specify. You can also choose the window title you want displayed and add a close box to the window if you desire one. The following code shows the OPEN WINDOW command used to open a new window just before the DIALOG command displays the layout in the window.

```
OPEN WINDOW(100;100;300;300;1)
DIALOG([Dialogs];"Search Dialog")
```

The ability to add a close box to a window is a new feature in version 3.0.

The first four parameters of the OPEN WINDOW command specify the upper-left and lower-right screen coordinates where you want the window opened. One problem is that your database might be used on computers that have different size monitors. Unless you make all of your dialog boxes very small and always open them in the upper-left corner, you are likely to create one someday that will open off screen. To solve this problem, I have written a procedure called CENTER WINDOW that will open a window in the center of the monitor regardless of its size. The following is the code for the CENTER WINDOW procedure:

```
  'CENTER WINDOW(width;height;type;title;close box pro-
cedure)
  '$1 - Window Width
  '$2 - Window Height
  '$3 - Window Type (optional)
  '$4 - Window Title (optional)
  '$5 - Close Box Procedure (optional)
C_INTEGER($1;$2;$3;$sw;$sh;$ww;$wh)
C_STRING(255;$4)
C_STRING(15;$5)
$sw:=Screen width/2
$sh:=Screen height/2+10
$ww:=$1/2
$wh:=$2/2
OPEN WINDOW($sw-$ww;$sh-
$wh;$sw+$ww;$sh+$wh;$3;$4;$5)
```

The CENTER WINDOW procedure uses the Screen height and Screen width functions to figure out the size of the monitor, then does the math to center the window on the screen based on the window's width and height. The comments at the top of the procedure are to remind you what parameters to pass in case you forget.

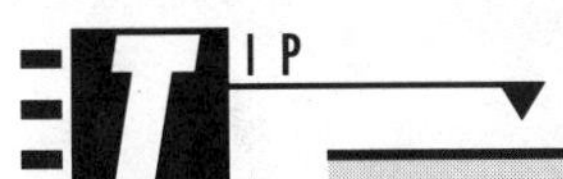

It is quite helpful to put comments at the top of each procedure that remind you what the procedure does and what parameters it expects (if any). While your code will be fresh in your memory when you are writing it, six months from now you will probably forget why you did what you did. Commenting your code takes more time and discipline but pays for itself in the long run.

To use the CENTER WINDOW procedure, you would of course, first create the procedure. Then call the procedure and pass it the width of the window, the height of the window, the window type and window title. The following code shows the CENTER WINDOW procedure being used along with the DIALOG command.

```
CENTER WINDOW(200;200;1;"";"")
DIALOG([Dialogs];"Search Dialog")
```

In this case, the CENTER WINDOW procedure will open a window that is 200 pixels wide and 200 pixels tall. The window will be a *modal* dialog box (type 1). Figure 17.12 shows an example of a modal window. The word *modal* means that the user cannot click outside the window while it is open. In most cases, you will use a modal window for dialog boxes because the dialog layout is in control. If the user clicks on another window, 4D will bring that window to the front but it will not be in control. Since the other window will not function, the user may think that there is something wrong and turn off the computer. If you need a dialog box to stay open on the screen while the user accesses other windows, you can do so using processes. You will learn about processes later in this chapter.

FIGURE 17.12

A modal window

A *modaless* window allows the user to click on other windows. Figure 17.13 shows an example of a modaless window.

FIGURE 17.13

A modaless window

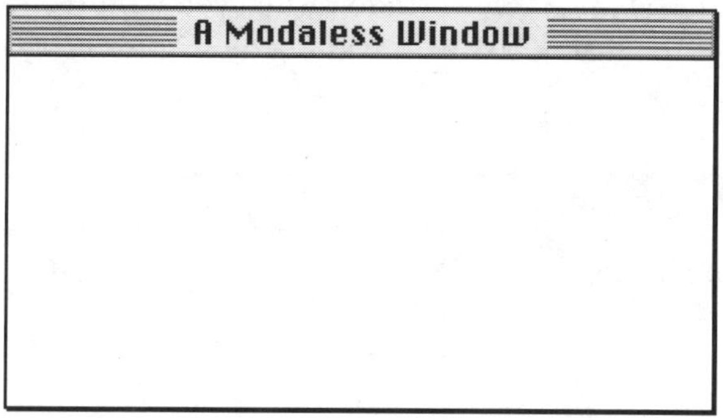

Window Types

There are many different types of windows that can be used within 4D. The type of window you choose is based on what you are going to display in the window. Each type of window has a number that identifies it. 4D provides you access to just about every type of window available on the Macintosh. However, not all of the window types are appropriate for use in your applications.

Figure 17.14 shows a *type 0 modaless* window. This type of window would be used to display input and output layouts. Type 0 windows can also have scroll bars. Commands like MODIFY SELECTION, MODIFY RECORD, and ADD RECORD all ask you to indicate whether or not you

FIGURE 17.14

A type 0, modaless window

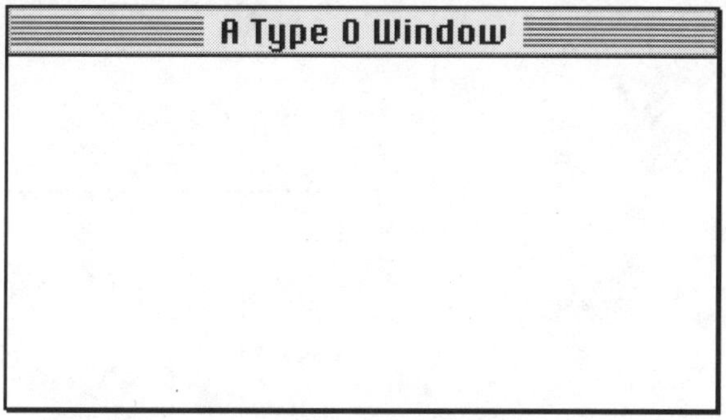

want scroll bars to be displayed. When a type 0 window has scroll bars, it's called a *document* window.

Type 1 windows are modal and should only be used for dialog boxes. The user cannot activate other windows while a type 1 window is open. You use a type 1 window when you want the user to finish with what is in the dialog box before going on. Figure 17.15 shows a type 1 window.

FIGURE 17.15

A type 1 modal window

Type 2 windows are plain rectangles. This window type is rarely used. Type 2 windows are very similar to type 1 windows however they should not be used for dialogs. Figure 17.16 shows a type 2 window.

FIGURE 17.16

A type 2 rectangle window

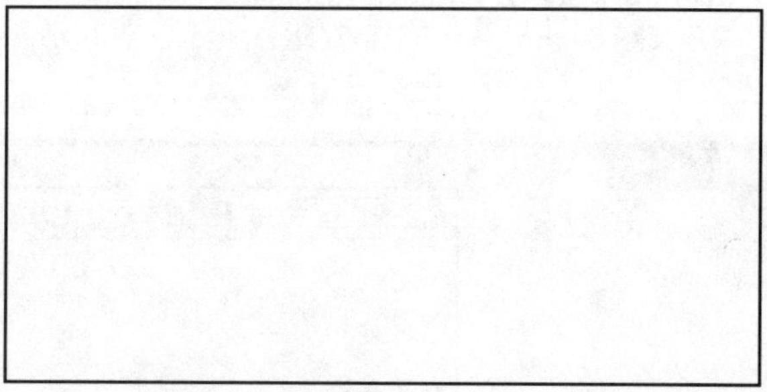

Normally, you can't move windows that don't have a titlebar. However, you can move any window in 4D by holding down ⌘-Control and clicking in the window. This key combination exists to make it easier for you to move windows around when you are creating your database.

Type 3 windows are just like type 2 windows with a drop shadow. Like type 2 windows, type 3 windows are rare and usually are used only for *about* boxes (those boxes that tell the version number and other pertinent information about an application). Figure 17.17 shows a type 3 window.

FIGURE 17.17

A type 3 drop shadow window

Type 4 windows look exactly the same as type 0 windows. The only difference is that type 4 windows are not resizable. You should not use a type 4 window with a command that is going to add scroll bars. If you add scroll bars, a grow box will also be added to the lower-right corner. This will confuse the user because they won't be able to resize the window by clicking on the grow box as they normally would.

Type 5 windows are called *movable, modal* windows. They have a window title so the user can move them. This is the type of window that the System 7's Finder displays when you are copying a file. In most applications, this type of window would be modal to the application meaning that you could click on other windows belonging to other applications but not click on other windows belong to the *same* application. This is not the case in 4D. Figure 17.18 shows a type 5 window.

FIGURE 17.18

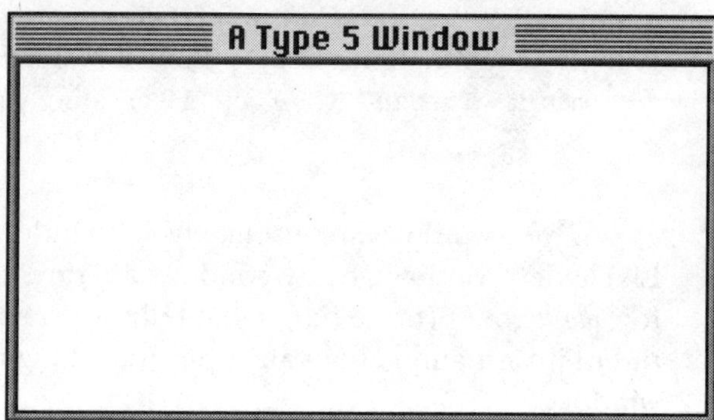

***A** type 5, movable, modal window*

Type 5 windows do not exist in version 6 of Apple's system software. Type 5 windows appear as type 1 windows in system 6. If your database is going to be used on any Macintosh that is running system 6, you might want to use another type of window.

Type 8 windows look exactly the same as type 0 except that they have a zoom box in the upper-right corner. Type 8 windows can have scroll bars. The default window that 4D uses for the User and Runtime environments is a type 8 window.

Type 16 windows have a titlebar but cannot have scroll bars. This type of window is only used in Desk Accessories. It is not recommended that you use this type of window in your applications. Figure 17.19 shows a type 16 window.

FIGURE 17.19

A type 16 window

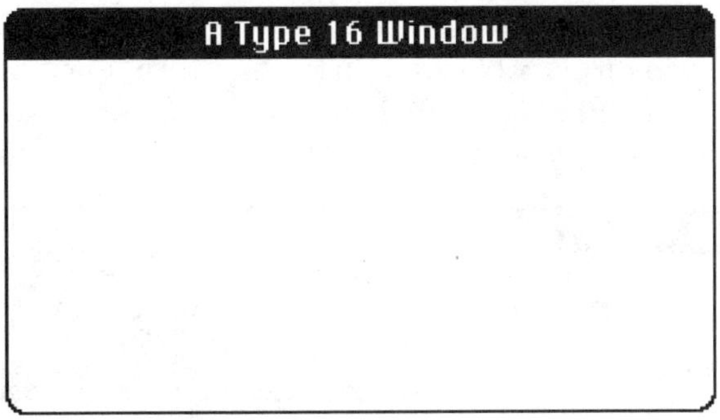

Type 720 windows are called *palettes.* They are a lot like type 0 windows except that they have a different type of titlebar. This type of window is typically only used to create a *floating palette.* Floating palettes are windows that cannot go behind regular, non-floating windows. They always *float* in front of other windows. To make a palette window float, you used the negative value instead of the positive value. For example, a the number to use to create a floating palette is –720. The negative sign tells 4D to make the window float in front of the other windows. Floating windows have their own window layer. This means that floating windows can go behind other floating windows but not behind non-floating windows. Figure 17.20 shows a floating palette window.

FIGURE 17.20

A floating palette window

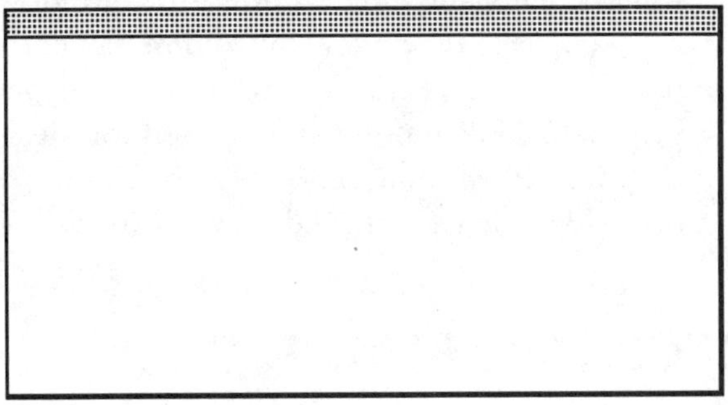

Floating palette windows are often used to hold tools for icons that the user will use constantly. For example, you might want to have a floating palette of icon buttons that have functions the user will access frequently. Figure 17.21 shows an example of such a palette.

FIGURE 17.21

A floating palette of icons

You can add attributes to a floating palette window. The following table shows the attributes and what number to add to –720 in order to have a window that attribute.

–1	When the palette is not the frontmost window, the title bar will be disabled.
–2	Allows the palette to have a window title.
–4	Adds an invisible grow box.
–8	Adds a zoom box.

These negative numbers can be combined to add multiple attributes to a floating palette. For example –720+–2+–8 equals –730. This would create a floating window with a window title and a zoom box.

The type of window you choose depends on what you want the user to be able to do. If you are not sure what type of window would be appropriate, look at other applications for ideas. Also, experiment. One of the nice things about software is that it isn't chiseled into stone. If you don't like one type of window, you can easily change it.

DECISION MAKING

One of the great things about programming is the ability to add your own logic to it. You can have the computer make decisions based on the current situation. For example, after a search that results in no records being found, you might want to have 4D display an alert and notify the user that no records were found. Computers are excellent at making decisions based on the logic you provide them. However, they cannot arrive at this logic on their own. Therefore, the computer's ability to make the right decision is only as good as the logic you provide it. There are two statements that can be used to make decisions. They are the *If* statement and the *Case* statement.

IF...ELSE...END IF

In everyday life you make decisions based on *conditions*. For example, when you get up in the morning, you have breakfast *if* you are hungry. The decision to have breakfast is based on it being true that you are hungry. In 4D, you can make decisions almost exactly the same way using the If statement.

The If statement allows you to test a condition and then have code execute if the condition is true. The condition test is placed in parentheses after the If statement. If the condition is true, all lines of code after the If statement will be executed until 4D reaches the *End if* statement. The following code tests to see if there any records in the UserSet. The UserSet contains records that have been highlighted by the user in an output layout. If there are no records highlighted, the user is presented with an ALERT dialog.

```
If(Records in set("UserSet")=0)
    BEEP
    ALERT("There are no records highlighted.")
End if
```

The value returned by Records in set is being checked to see if it is equal to zero. If it is, then the statement **Records in set("UserSet")=0** is a true statement so the code following it is executed and an ALERT is displayed. If there were records highlighted, the statement would be false and the code would not execute. The condition tested must always result in a *Boolean* value (true or false). Take a look at this next example:

```
If(10/5)
    BEEP
End if
```

This If statement would result in an error. Why? Because 10 divided by 5 (10/5) does not result in a Boolean value. On the other hand, 10/5=2 does result in a Boolean value (true).

The If statement can check multiple conditions. Look at the following example:

```
If((Month of(Current date)=4)&(Day of(Current date)=1))
    ALERT("It's April Fool's Day!")
End if
```

In this example, two conditions are being tested. The Month of function is being passed the Current date to see if the month of the current date is 4 (April). This is the first condition being tested. The & (ampersand) means **AND**, so both the first condition and the second condition must be true. The second condition is using the Day of function to see if today is the first of the month. If both conditions are true, then the ALERT is displayed. You can also test to see if one of many conditions is true. Look at the following example:

```
If((Day of(Current Date)=1)|(Day of(Current date)=15))
    ALERT("Today is payday!")
End if
```

In this If statement, two conditions are being tested. The vertical bar (|) means **OR**. So if either the first condition or the second condition is true, then the ALERT is displayed.

In these examples, a condition is being tested and if the condition is true, code is executed. What if you need to perform some other operation if the condition is false? That is where *Else* comes in. If you add Else to your If statement, you can have code that executes only if the statement is false. Look at the following example:

```
If((Day of(Current date)=1)|(Day of(Current date)=15))
    ALERT("Today is payday!")
Else
    ALERT("Darn! Today is not payday.")
End if
```

If today is the 1st or 15th then the If statement is true so the code between the If line and the Else line will execute. When the If statement is false, then the code between the Else statement and the End if will be executed.

CASE OF...ELSE...END CASE

There may be times when you are testing several conditions, only one of which could be true at the moment. Look at the following example:

```
If(Day number(Current date)=2)
    ALERT("Today is Monday.")
End if
If(Day number(Current date)=4)
    ALERT("Today is Wednesday.")
End if
If(Day number(Current date)=6)
    ALERT("Today is Friday.")
End if
```

This set of If statements is using the Day number function to test to see which day of the week today is. The Day number function returns 1 for Sunday and 7 for Saturday. Each If statement is testing for a different day of the week and then displaying an ALERT that tells the user what day of the week it is. This works fine but it is not the most efficient or fastest way to get the job done. It is not efficient because in this case, only one of the conditions can be true but 4D is going to check each If statement anyway. It not the fastest method for the same reason. A better method would be using a Case statement.

Case statements allow you to check several conditions at once. The code following the first true condition is executed and the rest of the conditions are ignored. A Case statement looks a bit different from a set of If statements. The following Case statement performs the same function as the three If statements above:

```
Case of
    :(Day number(Current date)=2)
        ALERT("Today is Monday.")
    :(Day number(Current date)=4)
        ALERT("Today is Wednesday.")
    :(Day number(Current date)=6)
        ALERT("Today is Friday.")
End case
```

A Case statement begins with *Case of* and ends with *End case*. The conditions go between parentheses just as they do in an If statement. However, in a Case statement, you put a colon (:) in front of the parentheses. This helps 4D to quickly figure out that this condition is part of a Case statement. 4D starts with the first condition and if it is true, executes the code following the condition until it reaches the next condition. Once 4D has finished executing the code, it proceeds to the line after End case. This is more efficient than a series of If statements because as soon as 4D finds a true condition, it executes the code associated with the condition and then continues without taking the time to check other conditions.

Case statements can use Else just like an If statement. If you want something to happen when none of the conditions are true, you could put this after Else in the Case statement. The following example illustrates this:

```
Case of
    :(Day number(Current date)=1)
        ALERT("Today is Sunday.")
    :(Day number(Current date)=7)
        ALERT("Today is Saturday.")
    Else
        ALERT("Today is a weekday.")
End case
```

An important point to remember is that only the first true condition is executed even if multiple conditions are true.

LOOPING

Many times in life you will continue to do a series of actions several times. For example, when you are eating breakfast, you continue to eat until you are no longer hungry. The action of eating continues over and over. Performing the same actions over and over is called a *loop*. It is called a loop because a loop is circular and the idea is that you are performing a set of instructions and then when you get to the last instruction, starting back at the top again.

Augusta Ada Byron (daughter of the poet Lord Byron) is considered to be the first computer programmer and inventor of the operation now known as the loop. The ADA programming language, used mostly by the United States Military, is named after her.

When you are going to perform the same action over and over, there are three possible methods for deciding how many times the action will be performed. There are three different types of loops in 4D; one for each method of determining how many times to perform an action. You might want to execute a set of instructions while a condition is true. You might want to repeat a set of instructions until a condition is true. Or you might want to execute instructions for a certain number of times. There is a different kind of loop in 4D for each of these methods.

REPEAT...UNTIL

A Repeat loop repeats a set of instructions until a condition is true. The instructions will be executed at least once because the condition is tested at the end. The m_NEW RECORD procedure you wrote creates one new record. If you are entering several records, you will have to choose Enter ➤ New Record (⌘-N) once for each record you need to enter. It would be faster if you could tell 4D to continue to create new records until you were finished. The following Repeat loop will do just that:

```
Repeat
   ADD RECORD(vFilePtr»)
Until(OK=0)
```

4D will execute the ADD RECORD command and then check to see if the condition OK=0 is true. OK, as you already know, is a variable that 4D sets to 1 or 0 at different times. When you click an **Accept** button, OK is set to 1. When you click a **Cancel** button, OK is set to 0. This means that the Repeat loop above will add records until you click Cancel. Use a repeat loop when you want the instructions to be executed at least once.

If the code inside the Repeat loop does not somehow cause the condition being tested to be true, the loop will go on forever. This is called an *infinite loop*. If you think your code is executing inside an infinite loop, hold down the Option key and then click the mouse button. This will cause the Syntax Error window to appear and allow you to click the Abort button to stop the loop.

WHILE...END WHILE

A While loop works just like a Repeat loop with one important difference. In a While loop, the condition is tested at the beginning. This means that the code inside the loop may never execute if the condition is never true. Look at this example loop:

```
While(OK=1)
   ADD RECORD(vFilePtr»)
End While
```

It would seem that this loop would work just like the Repeat loop in the last example. If however, OK is not 1 when 4D reaches the loop, the ADD RECORD command will not be executed.

People use Repeat loops and While loops in everyday life. For example, you might use one of the following loops with your children:

```
While(Your Room Is Messy)
   Clean it
End while
Repeat
   Wash the dishes
Until(All Dishes are clean)
```

When I was a kid, these would have been an infinite loops!

For...End For

There are times when you want to execute instructions a specific number of times rather than testing a condition. This is when you would use a For loop. A For loop is the most complex of the three types of loops. The following For loop causes 4D to BEEP ten times.

```
For($i;1;10)
   BEEP
End for
```

A For loop requires three pieces of information. The first is a variable that will hold a number that represents the number of iterations that the loop has run so far. In the above For loop, that variable is $i.

It is common to use i or $i as the variable in a For loop. The i is short for *iteration.*

The next parameter is the starting value of the variable. In the above For loop, the starting value is 1. The third parameter is the ending value of the variable. In the above For loop, the ending value is 10.

When the For loop begins, $i will have the value 1. 4D will execute the instructions in the For loop until it reaches End for. 4D will then check to see if the value of $i matches the ending value. If it does, the loop ends and 4D continues with whatever comes after the loop. If $i is not 10, 4D will increment $i by 1 and go back to the first instruction in the loop.

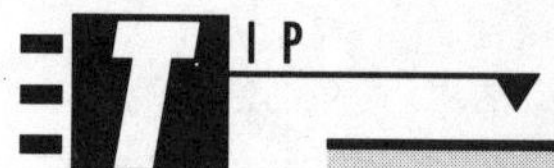

For loops will run faster if the variable used is a local variable. The reason for this is that each time a process variable or interprocess variable changes, 4D needs to check to see if that variable is on a layout so that the new value can be drawn in the layout. Since local variables cannot appear on layouts, 4D doesn't go through this checking process and the loops run faster.

For loops are used when you know how many times you want to perform a set of instructions. In the above example, the loop will execute the instructions 10 times. Functions can also be used to generate more generic loops. Say you wanted to mark all past due invoices. You could add a Boolean field called Past Due and then write a loop like this:

```
For($i;1;Records in file([Invoices]))
  If([Invoices]Invoice Date+30<=Current date)
    [Invoices]Past Due:=True
```

```
            SAVE RECORD([Invoices])
        End if
        NEXT RECORD([Invoices])
    End for
```

In this example, the number of times the loop will execute is determined by the value returned by **Records in file**. The If statement checks to see if the invoice is older than 30 days and if so, sets the Past Due field to true and saves the record with the SAVE RECORD command. The NEXT RECORD command moves to the next record and the whole thing starts over again. All of the instructions between the For statement and the End for statement are repeated as many times as there are records in the file.

The Learn 4D database has a Balance field in the Customers file. You might want to use this field to keep track of the total sales you have had with a customer and subtract the payments she has made so that the field reflects the customer's current balance. Using a For loop you could write a procedure and attach it to a menu that would go through all of your invoices and update the customer's balance. In accounting terms, this is called *posting*. You would need to add a field to the Invoices file that would keep track of the fact that an invoice was posted. Let's call this field **Posted**. The following For loop searches for all unposted invoices, updates the customer's balance, saves the change that has been made to the customer's record, then updates the invoice to show that it has been posted and saves the invoice. This procedure uses the SEARCH command, which you will learn more about later in this chapter. This procedure also uses the RELATE ONE command which looks at the value in the field passed to it and locates the matching (related) record in the file that the field is related to (the Customers file).

```
SEARCH([Invoices];[Invoices]Posted=False)
If(Records in selection([Invoices])>0)
    For($i;1;Records in selection([Invoices]))
        [Invoices]Posted:=True
        SAVE RECORD([Invoices])
        RELATE ONE([Invoices]Account Number)
        [Customers]Balance:=[Customers]Balance+
        [Invoices]Invoice Total
```

```
        SAVE RECORD([Customers])
        NEXT RECORD([Invoices])
    End for
End if
```

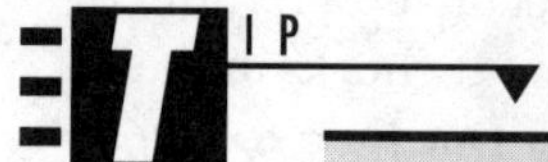

Another reason to use a local variable in a For loop is to avoid problems with nested loops. If you call a procedure inside a For loop and that procedure also has a For loop, the loop is considered to be nested inside the first For loop. If both loops are using the same variable, they won't function correctly because they are both incrementing the same variable. Using local variables solves this problem because the value in a local variable is local to the procedure and cannot be accessed by other procedures.

The variable in the For loop is incremented by 1 each iteration of the loop. There may be times when you want to control the amount that the variable is incremented by. You can do this with a fourth parameter. In the following example, the $i variable will start at 10 and be incremented by 5 each iteration of the loop until it reaches 100.

```
For($i;10;100;5)
End for
```

The loop will have 18 iterations. You can also use this technique to have the variable start at a high number and be decremented until it reaches a lower number. The following example shows a For loop that starts at 100 and is decremented by 20 each iteration.

```
For($i;100;1;-20)
End for
```

THE PROGRESS OF A LONG OPERATION

Most of the example loops in this chapter are short. Their entire execution will take only a few seconds. However, you may create loops that take several seconds, minutes, or even hours to execute, depending on the number of iterations and what the code inside the loop is doing. If a loop (or any operation for that matter) is going to take more than a few seconds to finish, it is a good idea to show the user some indication of the progress of the operation. If the operation is going to take a while, the user can decide to go do something else while the operation runs. When you copy files, the Finder displays a dialog box with a progress thermometer. You can watch how fast the thermometer moves to determine how long the operation will take. If you don't provide the user with some kind of status of the operation's progress, she might assume at some point that the operation is not going to finish and shut off the computer. You can use the MESSAGE command you learned about earlier to show the progress of the For loop in the Past Due example. The following code shows the modified For loop with a MESSAGE command.

```
$records:=String(Records in file([Invoices]))
For($i;1;Num($records))
  If([Invoices]Invoice Date+30<=Current date)
    [Invoices]Past Due:=True
    SAVE RECORD([Invoices])
  End if
  NEXT RECORD([Invoices])
MESSAGE("Processing "+String($i)+" of "+$records+".")
End for
```

Figure 17.22 shows what the MESSAGE dialog box for this loop looks like. In this version of the For loop, a few changes were made to optimize the loop. The value returned by Records in file is converted to a string and then copied into a variable. This is done because Records in file returns a number and this number is going to be concatenated with the rest of the text passed to the MESSAGE command. In order for it to be concatenated, it needs to be converted to a string. The value returned by Records in file is not going to change while this loop is running so it makes sense to copy the value into a variable so that 4D doesn't have to execute the Records in file function over and over each time it goes

FIGURE 17.22

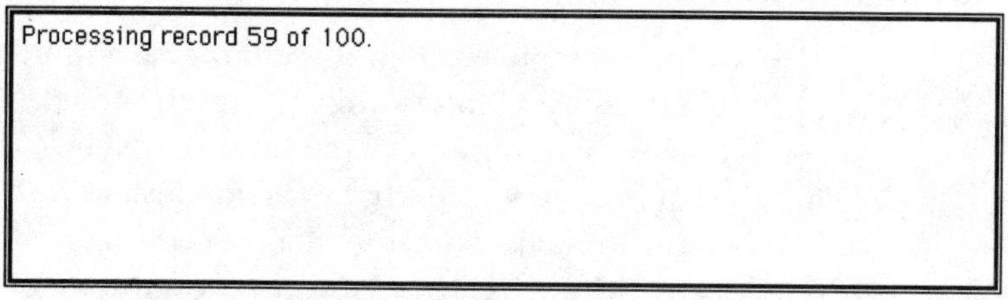

A progress indicator using the MESSAGE command

```
Processing record 59 of 100.
```

through the loop. The $i variable has to be converted to a string with the String function each iteration of the loop because its value does change. In the For statement, the variable containing the value returned by Records in file is converted back to a number with the Num function because the For statement expects it to be a number. This line of code is executed only once for the loop.

THE EXECUTION CYCLE

No, it's not a cheap horror movie. You already know that scripts execute when the object they belong to is modified. Global procedures are executed when they are called inside your code or from a menu. Layouts also have procedures. When are layout procedures executed? They are executed at different times for different reasons. When a layout procedure executes and why it is executing is called the *execution cycle.*

WHAT IS IT FOR?

When a layout is displayed and certain operations occur, 4D runs the layouts procedure to allow you to execute code. For example, when a user double-clicks on a record in the output layout, 4D runs the input layout procedure before the record is displayed. This gives you the opportunity to execute code before the user sees the record. For example, if the user is opening an invoice, you might want to check to see if the invoice is past due and notify the user as soon as the invoice appears. As invoice records are drawn in an output layout, you might want to check for past due invoices and change the font style of the Last Name field to bold as a visual cue.

WHEN DOES IT EXECUTE?

The execution cycle takes place anytime a layout is used for:

- Displaying or modifying data on the screen.
- Importing records.
- Exporting records.
- Printing records.

When a layout is used for any of the above reasons, the layout procedure is executed. In fact it may be executed several times. To take advantage of the execution cycle, you need to be able to test for the reason that the layout procedure is executing so you can have 4D execute your code at the appropriate time. You test the execution cycle with the *execution cycle functions.*

EXECUTION CYCLE FUNCTIONS

These functions are used to test for the reason that the layout procedure is executing. In *Chapter 14* you added a Due Date field to the Invoices file. You also added a script to the Save button so that the Due Date would be filled in automatically (with the Invoice Date plus 30 days) when the user clicked the **Save** button. Unfortunately, this means that the Due Date field is blank when the invoice is created. Using the execution cycle, you could have the Due Date calculated before the record was displayed.

The Before Function

You would want the Due Date filled in *before* the new record is displayed. The layout procedure is executed before the record is displayed. This phase of the execution cycle is called the *before phase.* In the layout procedure you can test for the before phase with the Before function. The Before function returns true when the layout procedure is executing the before phase. For example, the code for the layout procedure to set the

Due Date before the record is displayed, would look like this:

```
If(Before)
   If([Invoices]Due Date=!00/00/00!)
      [Invoices]Due Date=Current date+30
   End if
End if
```

If you did not include the If statement that checks the Before function, the remaining code would execute in all phases of the execution cycle. While this may or may not achieve the results you want (depending on what your code is doing), it would be inefficient because you only want this calculation performed before the record is displayed.

The before phase is executed just before any record is displayed in an input layout. The record is already in memory at this point, so you have access to fields and can make changes to the values in those fields. The before phase is executed for an output layout when it is first displayed and again once for each record as it is drawn in the output layout. When a dialog box is displayed using the DIALOG command, the layout gets a before phase before it is displayed.

The During Function

Each time you change the contents of a field or variable, click on a button, pop-up menu, or scrollable area, or select a menu item, the layout procedure is executed and the *During* function returns true. This is called the *during phase.* In earlier versions of 4th Dimension, scripts did not exist and a lot of the functionality of scripts was handled in the during phase of an input layout procedure. The during phase also occurs in an output layout once for each record as it is drawn in the layout.

When records are drawn in an output layout (to the screen or to a printer), Before and During are true at the same time. This is the only time when two phases of the execution cycle occur simultaneously.

The After Function

When a record has been modified in an input layout and the user clicks an **Accept** button to save the record, the layout procedure is executed and the *After* function returns true. This is called the *after phase.* The layout procedure is executed immediately before the record is saved. Consequently, you can make changes to the record in the after phase and those changes will be saved to disk.

You might want to keep track of the last date that each record was modified on. You could do this in the after phase. Say you had a field called Last Modified in the Customers file. Your input layout procedure could have code that checks to see if the after phase is executing and if so, assign today's date to the Last Modified field. Your code would look like this:

```
If(After)
   [Customers]Last Modified:=Current date
End if
```

The after phase occurs only if the record has been modified. By assigning today's date to the Last Modified field, you will always know when this record was last changed. You could also keep track of what time of day it was changed (using the **Current time** function) and who changed the record (using the **Current user** function).

Other Phases of the Execution Cycle

The phases of the execution cycle described so far are used mainly for input and output layouts. There are other phases of the execution cycle that occur under special circumstances.

Phases for Included Layouts If a layout contains an included layout, the before phase is executed in the included layout's layout procedure for each record displayed in the included layout. After these before phases occur, the before phase for the parent layout is executed. The same is also true of the during and after phases.

Phases for Printing There are execution cycle phases that occur during printing. These phases are:

Before selection returns true before the first record is printed. This phase is useful for setting the initial value of variables before printing actually begins.

In header returns true each time the header area of the layout is printed.

In break returns true each time any break area of a layout is printed. You can use the Level function to determine which break area is printing.

In footer returns true each time the footer area of the layout is printed.

End selection returns true after the last record has been printed.

Phases for Windows Using 4th Dimension's multi-tasking capabilities, you can have multiple windows displayed simultaneously on the screen. To help you manage these windows, there are two special phases that occur. When the user clicks on a window that was behind other windows, the window she clicked on becomes the frontmost window. When a window becomes frontmost, the layout procedure for the layout displayed in that window is executed and the **Activated** function returns true. This is called the *activated phase.*

When the user clicks on a window to make it the frontmost window, the window that was frontmost goes behind other windows. At this point, the layout procedure for that window is executed and **Deactivated** returns true. This is called the *Deactivated phase.*

The Activated and Deactivated functions and phases are new in version 3.0 of 4D.

At this point, it may not be clear when you would use these two phases of the execution cycle. Later in this chapter, you will learn how to add multiple windows to your database allowing you to access files simultaneously. Once you have implemented multiple windows, the need for these phases will be more clear. I mention these phases now so that you will know they exist.

Phases between Processes There is a special phase of the execution cycle called **Outside call**. This phase occurs only when one process calls another process with the CALL PROCESS command. This command simply causes the layout procedure of the process called to be executed and the Outside call function returns true. You will learn more about processes later in this chapter.

The CALL PROCESS, Outside call function, and outside call phase are new features in version 3.0 of 4D.

USING CASE STATEMENTS IN LAYOUT PROCEDURES

If your layout procedure is only testing for one phase of the execution cycle, you can use an If statement. Look at the following layout procedure:

```
If(Before)
   If([Invoices]Due Date<=Current date)
      ALERT("This invoice is past due!")
   End if
End if
```

This layout procedure is only testing for the before phase. In this case an If statement is fine. However, if you are testing for more than one phase of the execution cycle in a layout procedure, a Case statement is more efficient because in most cases, only one phase of the execution cycle will be true at any given moment. Look at the following layout procedure:

```
If(Before)
   If([Invoices]Due Date=!00/00/00!)
      [Invoices]Due Date:=Current date
   End if
End if
If(After)
   [Invoices]Last Modified:=Current date
End if
```

In this layout procedure, the before and after phases are being tested and code is executed. Each time a phase occurs, 4D will have to look at both If statements to see if they are true. Before and After are never true at the same time. In this situation, a Case statement is more efficient. Here is what the same layout procedure looks like using a Case statement:

```
Case of
   :(Before)
   If([Invoices]Due Date=!00/00/00!)
      [Invoices]Due Date:=Current date
   End if
   :(After)
   [Invoices]Last Modified:=Current date
End case
```

This version of the layout procedure will execute faster than the previous version because the Case statement executes faster than multiple If statements.

How Are Scripts Affected by the Execution Cycle?

When the Script Only If Modified checkbox is checked, a script is completely unaffected by the execution cycle. By activating this checkbox you are indicating that you want the script to execute only if the object that the script belongs to is modified and not at any other time. However, when you uncheck this checkbox, the script is affected by the execution cycle.

In input layouts, scripts with Script Only If Modified unchecked will get a before phase and an after phase. This means that if you have code in the script that you want to execute in the before or after phases, you will have to check for those phases in the script. The during phase of a script occurs only when the object is modified.

When you are using MODIFY SELECTION or DISPLAY SELECTION to display an output layout, you can test for the before or during phases if you want the script to execute each time a record is displayed.

When printing, there is no need to have the Script Only If Modified checkbox checked. Scripts are executed just before the object is printed. You don't need to test for any particular phase because the code will be executed only when the object is printed.

BUILDING SEARCHES

Up to this point you have done several searches. For each type of search you have performed, there is an equivalent command in the language. There are two commands that allow you to procedurally build a search with multiple criteria. The two commands are SEARCH and SEARCH SELECTION. With both of these commands you can enter the criteria right into your procedure yourself or create some kind of interface that allows the user to enter criteria.

THE SEARCH COMMAND

The SEARCH command is used to search for records. Using this command is the procedural equivalent of using the Search Editor. As a matter of fact, you have already learned that you use this command to display the Search Editor in the Runtime environment. The SEARCH command requires a minimum of two parameters. They are:

- The filename of the file you want to create a selection of records for
- The fieldname, comparison operator, and value being searched for

Say, for example, you want to search for all of the customers in the Customers file that live in California. You want to find customers so the first parameter would be the Customers file. You are going to search using the State field from the Customers file and you want to find records where the State field is equal to **CA**. You already know how to do this search with the Search Editor. How do you create this search using the SEARCH command? It looks like this:

```
SEARCH([Customers];[Customers]State="CA")
```

The SEARCH command always searches through all of the records in the file. You don't have to worry about what records are in the current selection at this moment. The search above will search the Customers file for all records where the State field is exactly equal to CA. You can also use any of the following comparison operators:

Comparison	Symbol
Equal to	=
Not equal to	#
Less than	<
Greater than	>
Less than or equal to	<=
Greater than or equal to	>=

Performing Wildcard Searches

Say you are searching for a customer by her last name but you can't remember the exact spelling. You already know how to perform a "begins with" search using the wildcard symbol (@). You can use that same symbol here. That search would look like this:

```
SEARCH([Customers];[Customers]Last Name="Perl@")
```

The wildcard symbol works exactly the same way with the SEARCH command as it does with the Search Editor. This means that an "ends with" search looks like this:

SEARCH([Customers];[Customers]Last Name="@man")

and a "contains" search looks like this:

SEARCH([Customers];[Customers]Last Name="@er@")

Searches are not case sensitive. This means that searching for "Sandra" or "SANDRA" will find the same records. If you need to perform a case sensitive search, you can do so using a *formula* search, which you will learn about in this chapter.

Searching with Fields from Related Files

You might be wondering why the filename is necessary as the first parameter when the second parameter clearly indicates which file is being searched. The field used in the search could come from a related file. Say you wanted to search for customers who have an invoice dated today. The file being searched is the Customers file but the field used in the search is the Invoice Date field from the Invoices file. The search would look like this:

SEARCH([Customers];[Invoices]Invoice Date=
Current date)

Because a relationship exists between the two files, you can search one file based on a field from another. This search translates to "find all the customers who have an invoice related to them that has today's date in the Invoice Date field."

In order to search using fields from related files, the relationship between the two files must be automatic. If the relationship is manual, you can temporarily make it automatic with the command AUTOMATIC RELATIONS. See your *4th Dimension Language Reference* for more information.

Using Multiple Criteria

So far, the searches you have seen have used one field. How do you search using multiple fields? Say you want to find all of the customers who live in California and have an invoice dated today. You create multiple searches using multiple SEARCH commands on multiple lines. To create this kind of search, you add a third parameter to the search command. The third parameter is an asterisk (*). The asterisk tells 4D that the search criteria is continued on the next line. The following search finds customers in California that have invoices dated today:

```
SEARCH([Customers];[Customers]State="CA";*)
SEARCH([Customers];&;[Invoices]Invoice Date=
Current date)
```

On the second line, the second parameter is the conjunction. There are three possible conjunctions:

Conjunction	Symbol
And	&
Or	|
Except	#

Notice that the last line of the search doesn't have an asterisk at the end. When 4D doesn't find an asterisk in the third parameter of the SEARCH command, it begins the search. You can also include the asterisk with each line and end with the SEARCH command. The following would perform the same search as the last example:

```
SEARCH([Customers];[Customers]State="CA";*)
SEARCH([Customers];&;[Invoices]Invoice Date=
Current date;*)
SEARCH([Customers])
```

The last SEARCH line has no asterisk so 4D knows that it has the entire criteria and can begin the search.

THE SEARCH SELECTION COMMAND

The SEARCH SELECTION command works identically to the SEARCH command with one exception. The SEARCH SELECTION command searches the current selection instead of the entire file. You can build searches and search using fields from related files just as you can with the SEARCH command. The two commands are functionally the same with the exception of their scope. Like the SEARCH command, if you call SEARCH SELECTION and pass it a filename but no criteria, the Search Editor will be displayed but the Search in selection checkbox will be checked and disabled. This allows you to present the Search Editor to the user and force a search on the current selection instead of the entire file.

SEARCH SELECTION is a new command in version 3. The command that was called SEARCH SELECTION in version 2.0 is now called SEARCH SELECTION BY FORMULA.

WHEN ARE INDEXES USED IN SEARCHING?

The SEARCH and SEARCH SELECTION commands will use indexes to perform searches if any of the fields you are searching on are indexed fields. 4D looks at all of the fields you are searching on and searches the indexed fields first. Using the selection created by this indexed search, it searches on the fields that do not have indexes.

4D may not always use indexes even if they are available. If you are searching on the current selection and the selection is small enough, it is actually faster for 4D to perform the search sequentially rather than take the time to load the indexes to use them in a search.

SEARCHES THAT USE FORMULAS

You need to search on the result of a calculation that involves a field. For example, you might want to find all of the invoices that were created in the month of January of any year. Using the **Month of** function, you can create a search criteria that looks like this:

Month of([Invoices]Invoice Date)=1

Because this search requires a calculation to be performed on a field, you can not use the SEARCH or SEARCH SELECTION commands. Instead, you use **SEARCH BY FORMULA** or **SEARCH SELECTION BY FORMULA**.

These two commands accept two parameters. The first is the file to be searched and the second is the formula. The formula must evaluate to true or false. For example, the formula Month of([Invoices]Invoice Date)=1 is either true for a record or false.

Formula-based searches are always sequential regardless of whether or not any of the fields are indexed.

The SEARCH BY FORMULA command searches the entire file. SEARCH SELECTION BY FORMULA searches only the current selection.

GETTING VALUES FROM THE USER

In all of the example searches, the value being searched for has been typed into the search criteria. However, to make your searches more flexible, you might want the user to enter part or all of the search criteria. You could get the search criteria from the user using the Request dialog or by creating your own dialog box and using the DIALOG command. The following code uses the Request function to get the last name from the user. A wildcard symbol is automatically added to allow the user to enter only a few characters of the last name:

```
$LastName:=Request("Enter a last name to search for:")
If(OK=1)
  SEARCH([Customers];[Customers]Last Name=$Last-
  Name+"@")
End if
```

When a value is typed in to the code rather than entered by the user, the value is said to be "hard-coded".

The following code presents the dialog box shown in Figure 17.23 and allows the user to search on the text entered.

The CENTER WINDOW procedure you learned about earlier is used to open a window. Then the DIALOG command presents the Find Dialog layout as a dialog in the window. If the user clicks the **OK** button, the Case statement looks to see which radio button (r1 or r2) is selected and performs one of two possible searches using the value the user entered in the dialog box into the variable vFind.

```
CENTER WINDOW (330;130)
DIALOG([Dialogs];"Find Dialog")
CLOSE WINDOW
```

FIGURE 17.23

A custom search dialog box


```
If (OK=1)
  Case of
    : (r1=1)
      SEARCH([Contacts];[Contacts]First=vFind+"@";*)
      SEARCH([Contacts]; | ;
      [Contacts]Alias=vFind+"@";*)
      SEARCH([Contacts]; | ;[Contacts]Last=vFind+"@";*)
      SEARCH([Contacts]; | ;[Contacts]
      Company=vFind+"@")

    : (r2=1)
      SEARCH([Contacts];[Contacts]Keywords'
      Word=vFind+"@")
  End case
End if
```

This example dialog is fairly simple. Using the DIALOG command and the available search commands, you can create custom dialog boxes that makes entering complex search criteria fast and easy.

PRINTING

4D offers many different methods for printing out your records. In the User environment, you can choose File ➤ Print (⌘-P) and pick a layout to print the current selection with. The Report menu gives you access to the Quick Report Editor, the Label Editor, and the Graph Editor. There are several commands in the 4D language that allow you to control printing procedurally.

THE REPORT COMMAND

You have already learned quite a bit about the Quick Report Editor. You have also learned how to write a procedure that displays the Quick Report Editor. Using the REPORT command, you can print the current selection using a Quick Report file that you saved to disk. You simply pass to the REPORT command the name of the file that you saved. The following code locates all of today's invoices and prints a sales report.

```
SEARCH([Invoices];[Invoices]Invoice Date=Current date)
If(Records in selection([Invoices])>0)
   REPORT([Invoices];"Sales Report")
Else
   ALERT("There were no invoices today.")
End if
```

Make sure that your Quick Reports are in the same folder as the database. If they are in another folder or even inside a folder that is in the folder with the database, 4D will not be able to find them and will present the user with an open file dialog box.

The Quick Report Editor is a quick and easy way to create columnar reports. It doesn't allow you as much flexibility in the appearance of the report as the Layout Editor does, however, it takes less time. If your reports can be created with the Quick Report Editor, use this first. Later, when everything is working just right, you can take some time to replace your Quick Reports with fancy layouts if you choose.

The PRINT RECORD Command

The PRINT RECORD command prints the current record using the current output layout. PRINT RECORD is useful when you want to give users the ability to print the record they are currently modifying. For example, in an invoicing system, you might want the user to be able to print a new invoice by clicking on a Print button on the input layout. The procedure below is an example of the script you might use. This example script changes the output layout to the printing layout, prints the record, then changes the current output layout back to the layout used to list records on the screen.

```
OUTPUT LAYOUT([Invoices];"Printed Invoice")
PRINT RECORD([Invoices])
OUTPUT LAYOUT([Invoices];"Output")
```

The PRINT RECORD command displays the Page Setup and Print dialog boxes automatically. To prevent these dialog boxes from being displayed, pass an asterisk (*) as the second parameter to the PRINT RECORD command.

```
PRINT RECORD([Invoices];*)
```

THE PRINT SELECTION COMMAND

The PRINT SELECTION command prints the current selection for a file using the current output layout. This means that you need to establish two things before calling this command:

- The current output using the OUTPUT LAYOUT command
- The current selection (using ALL RECORDS, SEARCH, etc.)

The PRINT SELECTION command is basically the equivalent of choosing File ➤ Print (⌘-P) in the User environment (without the choose layout dialog box).

When you use the PRINT SELECTION command, the output control lines on the output layout become very important. Everything between the top of the layout and the H line (the header area) is the header and will print at the top of every page. Everything between the H line and the D line (the detail area) will print once for each record. This is where your fields should be if you want them to be printed. Everything between the D line and the BO line (the break zero area) will print once at the end of the report. Everything between the B0 line and the F line (the footer area) will print at the bottom of every page. Figure 17.24 shows the Balance Report layout you created for the Learn 4D database.

The layout is designed to print subtotals for Customers by state. Let's assume that we want to create a procedure that prints this report showing all of the Customers. The procedure would look like this:

```
ALL RECORDS([Customers])
OUTPUT LAYOUT([Customers];"Balance Report")
SORT SELECTION([Customers];[Customers]State;>;[Cus-
tomers]Last Name;>)
BREAK LEVEL(1)
ACCUMULATE([Customers]Balance)
PRINT SELECTION([Customers])
OUTPUT LAYOUT([Customers];"Output")
```

The ALL RECORDS command establishes the current selection. The OUTPUT LAYOUT command sets the output layout to the Balance Report layout. The SORT SELECTION command is sorting the current selection by State. Why is the State field sorted twice? Break areas are printed when data in a field that is sorted changes. You have to sort on

FIGURE 17.24

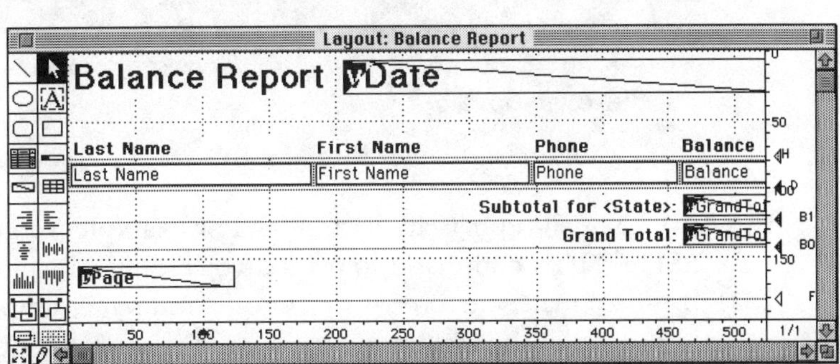

The Balance Report layout

one more field than the number of break levels you want. The layout has break area 1 so you need to sort on two fields. The reason you need to sort on one more field is that 4D doesn't generate breaks for the last field you sort on. If you want to generate a break for the last field you sorted on, sort on the last field twice. The BREAK LEVEL command tells 4D how many break levels there are. Your procedure will run without this command. However, you will need this command to generate break levels if you use the 4D Compiler. The 4D Compiler is a separate product that makes your code run faster. You will learn more about the 4D Compiler in *Chapter 19.* The ACCUMULATE command tells 4D what fields or variables you want to be able to subtotal with the Subtotal function. This command is also required if you are going to use the 4D Compiler. Finally, we come to PRINT SELECTION which prints the current selection using the output layout. The PRINT SELECTION command will present the Page Setup and Print dialog boxes to the user. Once the user clicks **OK** in the Print dialog box, 4D will pass control to the output layout procedure. If any of the objects on the layout have scripts with the Script Only If Modified checkbox unchecked, the scripts will run right before the object is printed. The OUTPUT LAYOUT command is called again at the end to reset the output layout to the layout used to list records on the screen. You need to do this mostly when you are testing your procedures. Without resetting the output layout, the User environment would display the Balance Report as the output layout when you were done printing the report.

You can use the BREAK LEVEL command to generate page breaks. The second parameter of the BREAK LEVEL command is the break level that you want a page break to occur at. See the *4th Dimension Language Reference* for more information.

Not all reports are columnar. For example, you can use the PRINT SELECTION command to print invoices. Each invoice usually takes a full page. To make each record print on a full page, simply move the H line to the top of the layout and move the D line to the bottom of the page.

The bottom of the page is marked by a thick horizontal line. By making the detail area very large, each record takes up more of the page when it prints. In this case, one record would take up the entire page.

Page Numbering

If you want to put the page number on the report (in the header area or footer area) you can do so using the **Printing page** function. This function returns the number of the page that is printing.

THE PRINT LAYOUT COMMAND

The PRINT LAYOUT command prints the area between the header and the detail line. You use this command when the PRINT SELECTION command won't do the type of printing you need. For example, say you have created a dialog box that looks like a calendar and you want a **Print** button in the dialog that prints the calendar. In this case, you aren't printing records, you are simply printing the layout itself.

You can also use the PRINT LAYOUT command to print several layouts on one page. The PRINT LAYOUT command prints the layout into the computer's memory. The next time you call the PRINT LAYOUT command, the layout being printed is added to the bottom of the first one printed until the page fills. Once the page is full, 4D sends the page to the printer to be printed. If the page doesn't fill, the page is not printed. To force the page to be printed, you use the FORM FEED command. Always call the FORM FEED command after the last call to PRINT LAYOUT. This way, if there is anything left in memory that didn't get printed, the FORM FEED command will force the remaining information to be printed. The following example code uses the Mailing Label layout you created for the Customers file to print copies of a mailing label for the current record. You might put this code in a button on the Customers input layout if you need to print multiple shipping labels for the Customer.

```
$labels:=Num(Request("How many labels do you want?"))
For($i;1;$labels)
   PRINT LAYOUT([Customers];"Mailing Label")
End for
FORM FEED
```

This is a good example of where PRINT LAYOUT is used. You really couldn't print a variable number of labels for a Customers with the PRINT SELECTION command because it prints each record once. However, the PRINT LAYOUT command simply prints the area between the header and detail lines. So, you can keep printing this area over and over to print multiple copies. The FORM FEED command at the end makes sure that the last page prints.

Use the PRINT SELECTION command when you can. If it won't do what you need, the PRINT LAYOUT command usually will. The PRINT LAYOUT command gives you a lot more control over the printing process than PRINT SELECTION. However, along with the control comes the responsibility to handle the entire printing process including printing headers and footers at the appropriate time, moving through the records, and even displaying the Page Setup and Print dialog boxes (with the PRINT SETTINGS command).

THE POWER OF MULTITASKING

Everything you have done so far with 4D you have done one step at a time. You created a file, then entered records into it. You searched for records, you sorted records, and then printed a report. Each task was done in sequence, one after the other. In the real world however, you don't really do one task at a time. For example, while you are reading this book, you might also be listening to some music. In this case you are doing two tasks at the same time (reading and listening). If you use your computer to print long reports, you probably find something else to do while the report is printing. In this case you are performing two tasks at the same time. You are printing your report and doing something else like reading your mail or talking on the phone. You are able to perform multiple tasks simultaneously. When a computer can perform multiple tasks simultaneously it is called *multitasking*.

In the early days of the Macintosh, you could use only one program at a time. If you were using your word processor and needed something out of your database program, you had to quit the word processor before you could open the database program to get the information you wanted. This meant a lot of quitting one program to open the next then quitting that program to go back to the first one again.

It would seem that all of this monkeying around, switching from one program to the next would keep the Macintosh pretty busy. In fact, most of the time, the Macintosh is just idling, waiting for you to move the mouse or press a key on the keyboard so it can perform some task. Apple made changes to the Macintosh Operating System and created Multi-finder and then System 7 to allow the Macintosh to distribute this idle time to other programs allowing you to have multiple programs open at the same time. You can write a letter in your word processor and have your database open at the same time. You can even be printing a long report from your database (using the background printing feature in the Macintosh Operating System) and writing your letter at the same time. This is called *multitasking*.

Like the Macintosh, 4D is also idling most of the time when you are using it. You might choose a menu item to display a list of records and then a few seconds later double-click on one of the records to edit it. Those few seconds of idle time are an eternity to a computer. With version 3.0 of 4D, you can tell 4D to give that time to other procedures that are running simultaneously.

Why would you want to run several procedures at the same time? Well, say you are entering new records and you suddenly realize that you need to print a very large report that will take 15 minutes to print. Now you have to stop entering records to print the report. 15 minutes later, you can go back to entering records again. With multitasking, you can instruct 4D to run the code that prints the report as just one of its many tasks. This allows you to continue to enter new records while the report is printing. With this method, it doesn't matter how long it takes for the report to print because you can continue working while it prints.

To 4D each task is called a *Process*. You can instruct 4D to execute a procedure in a new process. This means that 4D will treat this procedure (and all other procedures called by it) as one of 4D's many processes. 4D constantly switches from one process to the next giving each a few ticks (a tick is a 60th of a second) of time to execute some code before going on to the next process. The constant looping through processes causes the illusion that all of the processes are executing at the same time. In fact, since there is only one microprocessor, the computer can only perform one task at a time. However, since 4D is switching very quickly between tasks, you get the equivalent effect of having all of the processes (procedures) executing at the same time.

Multitasking is a new feature in version 3 of 4D.

ADDING MULTIPLE WINDOWS

One of the benefits of having 4D create processes that execute your code is being able to have multiple active windows. In the Learn 4D database, you have been using only one window. You have designed the database so that you can easily switch between files. However, all of the display is in one window so you can't look at a list of products and a list of customers at the same time. If the m_CUSTOMERS procedure was running in one process, and the m_PRODUCTS procedure was running in another process, they would be running at the same time so you could view both lists at the same time.

Up to this point, all of the layouts are displayed in the default window. This window is used by the User environment and the Runtime environment. In fact, the User and Runtime environments are running in one process called the User/Runtime process. If you start a new process, 4D will display a new window as soon as it encounters a command that displays a layout (like MODIFY SELECTION). If you open a window with the OPEN WINDOW command before the command that displays a layout, 4D will use the window you opened. Let's add this multiple window capability to the learn 4D database.

1. Switch to the Design environment.
2. Open Menu Bar #1 in the Menu Editor.
3. Click on the File menu to display it.
4. Click on the Customers menu item.

4D also creates a new process called the Indexing process when you index a field. It does this so that indexing a field of a file that already has many records in it won't tie up 4D. You can continue to work while the index for the field is being built.

You probably noticed the *Start a new process* checkbox before. If you check this checkbox, 4D will create a new process when the user selects this menu item. 4D will then execute the procedure attached to this menu item in the new process.

5. Click the Start a new process checkbox.
6. Click on the Invoices menu item.
7. Click the Start a new process checkbox.
8. Click on the Products menu item.
9. Click the Start a new process checkbox.
10. Switch to the Runtime environment.
11. Choose File ➤ Customers.
12. Choose File ➤ Products.
13. Move the Products window down and to the right.

You now have separate windows for Customers and Invoices. You can switch back and forth between them by simply clicking on a window. No extra code is required. This is all you need to do to add multiple windows to your databases. In fact, you can even look at multiple windows displaying the same file. This allows you to see different selections at the same time.

1. Click on the Customers window.
2. Choose Select ➤ Search Editor (⌘-S).

3. Search for customers in California.
4. Choose File ➤ Customers.

You now have two Customers windows. One shows all of the customers and the other is showing only customers in California. This is another benefit to having multiple windows. If you decided to print a long report with the Quick Report Editor, you could continue using all of the other windows.

As I mentioned before, the User and Runtime environments are in a process called the User/Runtime process. The Design environment is in another process called the Design process. You can access all of these process at the same time. This means that you can be using a layout in one window and editing it in the other. Let's try it:

1. Click on the default window with the 4D logo in it to bring it to the front.
2. Resize the window to make it as small as the other windows.
3. Choose File ➤ Quit (⌘-Q).
4. Switch to the Design environment.
5. Resize the Structure window to make it as small as the other windows.

Notice that all of the windows are displayed. Figure 17.25 gives you an idea of how to arrange the windows so you can see all of them easily.

You can switch between the Design environment (the Design process) and the processes you created to display customers and products, simply by clicking on the respective windows.

6. Click on the Structure window to bring it to the front.
7. Choose Design ➤ Layout (⌘-L).
8. Open the Products Output layout.

As you can see, you can edit a layout and use it at the same time. The reason you can do this is that each is in a separate process. The

FIGURE 17.25

Multiple windows

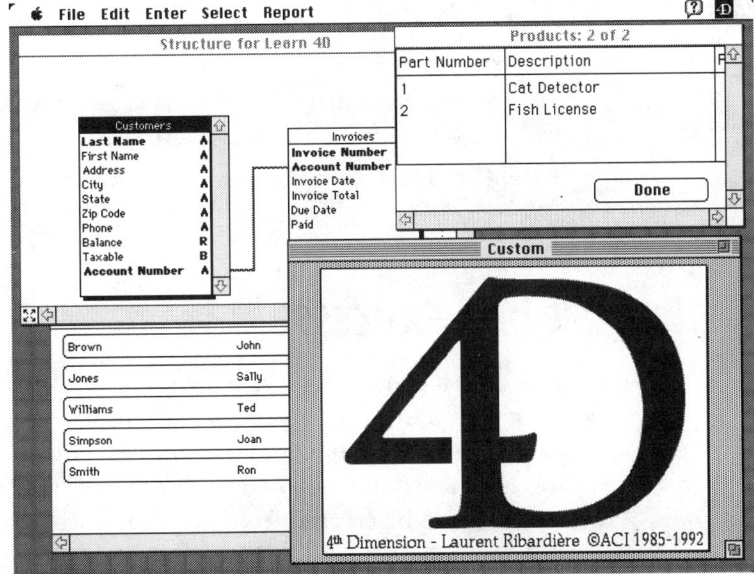

Layout Editor is open in the Design process and the Customers and Products are displayed in other processes.

1. Click on the Description field in the Layout Editor.
2. Choose Style ➤ Bold.

Notice that the Description field in the Products window did not turn to bold. The reason for this is that this field was not bold when the layout was originally displayed in the other process. If you open a new window now, the Description field will be in bold. Let's try it:

3. Click on the Products window to bring it to the front.
4. Choose File ➤ Products.

In this new window, the Description field is in bold because the field was bold when the layout was displayed.

When you switch to another process from the Design process, 4D automatically saves any changes you have made in the Design environment.

THE LIFE OF A PROCESS

How long does a process live? When you create a process, you specify a procedure to run in the new process. When that process finishes executing (reaches its last line of code), the process ends.

You have learned how to create processes using the Menu Editor. Processes can also be created from the User environment by choosing Special ➤ Execute Procedure (⌘-E) and clicking the New process checkbox. Another way to create a new process is with the function *New process.* This function allows you to procedurally create new processes.

HOW MANY PROCESSES CAN I CREATE?

The number of processes that can co-exist is limited only by the amount of memory you have allocated to 4D at the Finder. If you give 4D more memory (presuming of course that you have the memory to give), 4D can create more processes. The more processes you have, the more memory 4D requires. Also remember that 4D is switching between these processes constantly. This means that more processes that are running, the more work there is for 4D to do. The faster your computer is, the faster 4D can switch between these processes and the less you will notice it.

THE NEXT STEP

In the last four chapters you have learned quite a bit about 4D's programming language. What is the next step? I would suggest that you read through the *Language Reference.* Even if you don't understand it all, you will probably get a lot out of it. Also, later on when you need to write a script or procedure, you might remember some small bit of information that will steer you in the right direction. All of the reading in the world however, cannot replace the thing you need the most of: experience. The best thing you can do is get in with both feet and build your database. As you come across functions that require programming, spend the time to figure out how to write the procedures you need. At first, it might be frustrating if you have never done any programming before. You are not alone. Once you get some experience with programming, you will find that it gets easier and easier.

There are other resources to help you learn. The ACI developer program is one of them. As a member of the ACI developer program, you receive technical notes every month. These technical notes give you tips and techniques for solving problems you might face as you develop your applications. For more information on the ACI developer program, contact your local ACI distributor.

If you have access to a modem, there is the ACI US forum on CompuServe. This forum has thousands of users that access it regularly. You can ask questions, read messages of interest, download example and demo databases and get the latest news from ACI. You can even direct questions to technical support through the forum.

There is an independent magazine available called Dimensions. This magazine is published every other month and is full of articles and examples. Dimensions is published by Blackledge Publishing in Winona, Minnesota. Their phone number is 507-452-0023.

Many Apple Users Groups have 4D SIGs (*special interest groups*). If you have the extra time, consider attending your local 4D SIG monthly meeting. Talking with other users of 4D and exchange ideas can dramatically reduce the learning curve. Contact your local ACI distributor for the local 4D SIG near you.

ADDING PASSWORDS

18

MAC TRACKS MAC

You add passwords to your database **596**

To control the kind of access that each user has to the database.

To create users and groups **600**

Choose Design ➤ Passwords in the Design environment.

To enable the built-in password system **601**

Assign a password to the Designer.

To add a user to a group 604

In the Password Access Editor, drag the user over to the group.

To limit access to the Design environment 612

1. Create a Developers group.
2. In the Design environment, choose File ➤ Preferences.
3. Choose the Developers group from the Structure Access pop-up menu.

Featuring

- *Creating users and groups*
- *Adding users to groups*
- *Attributes of the Designer*
- *Attributes of the Administrator*
- *Limiting access to the environments*
- *Changing passwords*

PASSWORDS PROVIDE A means of controlling access to information. If you use an automated teller machine (ATM), you have a password. If you have a calling card from your phone company, you have a personal identification number (PIN) which is another type of password. Practically everyone has used some kind of password. 4D provides an extensive password system to allow you to control access to all the different areas of your database and of 4D itself.

WHY USE A PASSWORD SYSTEM?

You may not need a password system. If you are the only user of your database and the data in the database is not sensitive, you might not need to put a password on the database. A password system is typically used when there is going to be more than one user accessing the database. When several users are going to access the same database, you will probably want to control what portions of the database they have access to. Another possibility is that you want to make sure that only authorized people have access to the database. In both of these cases, implementing a password system will solve the problem.

Passwords systems are designed to provide a level of security. If you don't need the security, it is probably best if you don't put a password on the database. However, if you do need to control the ways that your users access your database, 4D's password system will allow you to do that easily.

WHAT DOES THE PASSWORD SYSTEM PROTECT?

4D's built-in password system lets you protect many different items in your database. Using the password system, you can decide which environments (if any) the user has access to. Within each of 4D's environments, you can control the actions that the user can take. In the Runtime environment, you can control which menu items the user has access to. In the User environment, you can control which files, layouts, and procedures the user can access. You can even control the type of access the user has to each file. For example, you may want the user to be able to view records but not to change them. In the Design environment, you can control the type of editing a user can perform on a file as well as which layouts and procedures they can edit.

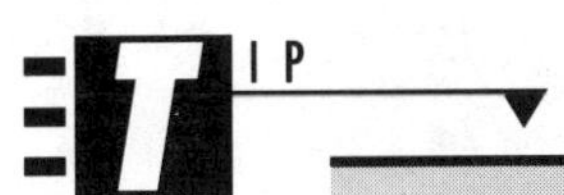

If your only reason for using the password system is to prevent your users from accessing the Design environment, there is another way to do this. You can use the 4D Compiler to compile your database. The 4D Compiler makes your programming code execute much faster. You can then give your users the compiled version of the database to use. The Design environment cannot be accessed in the compiled version of a database. This gives you the ability to prevent access to the Design environment without using the password system. You will learn more about the 4D Compiler in *Chapter 19.*

OPENING A PROTECTED DATABASE

With the password system enabled, users will be asked to enter their passwords when they open the database. As the database designer, you can choose from two different dialog boxes that the user can use to enter her password. Figure 18.1 shows the default dialog box that lists all users and gives the user a place to enter her password.

In this dialog box, the user simply clicks on her name, then types her password and clicks the **OK** button. If the password entered doesn't match the password for the user selected, 4D will beep to let the user know that it doesn't recognize her password. This dialog box is quite easy for the user to use. For most of you, the default log on dialog box will be sufficient.

FIGURE 18.1

The default log on dialog box

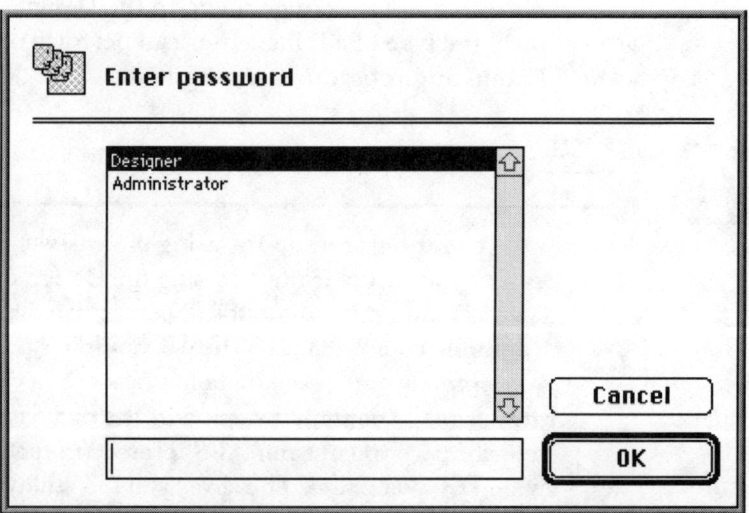

Some of you may require a system that is more secure. The default log on dialog box shows the entire list of users. This means that anyone who sees this list can use this information to find out a user's password. Fortunately, 4D provides another password dialog box that doesn't list the users. Figure 18.2 shows this alternative dialog box.

FIGURE 18.2

The Enter User Name dialog box

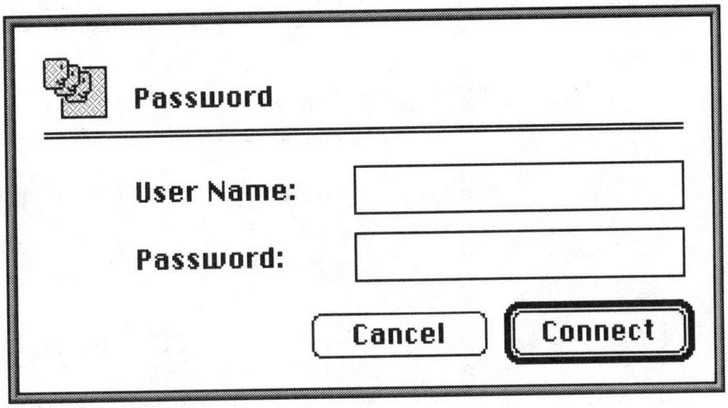

Password

User Name:

Password:

Cancel Connect

If you want to be able to switch users without closing the database, you can display the log-on dialog box by calling the CHANGE ACCESS **command. This command is very useful when you are testing your password system and want to log on quickly as different users.**

In this dialog box, the user must enter both her user name and password. This provides an additional level of security, because the list of users that have access to the database is never displayed. To select this dialog as the default log on dialog box, choose File ➤ Preferences in the Design environment and select the Enter User Name in Password Dialog option.

In both dialog boxes, the password is masked by pictures of locks as the user enters it. Figure 18.3 shows the Enter User Name dialog box with a password entered.

FIGURE 18.3

A masked password

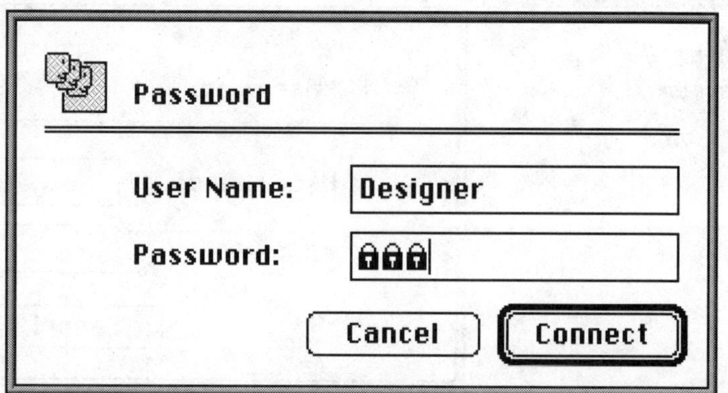

If you have used mainframe systems, you have probably been locked out at least once for entering the wrong password. Many systems allow the user to enter a password three times. If the user doesn't get the right password, the system locks that user out after the third failed attempt. 4D does not do this and will allow a user to try as many times as she has the patience for.

USERS AND GROUPS

The password system is based on *users* and *groups*. Using the password system, you create users and groups. The users are then put into groups you have created. The groups are necessary because all access is based on groups. If you give a group access to an object, all of the users in that group will have access to that object. The password system editor is called the Password Access Editor. Figure 18.4 shows the Password Access Editor. You can access the Password Access Editor from the Design environment.

FIGURE 18.4

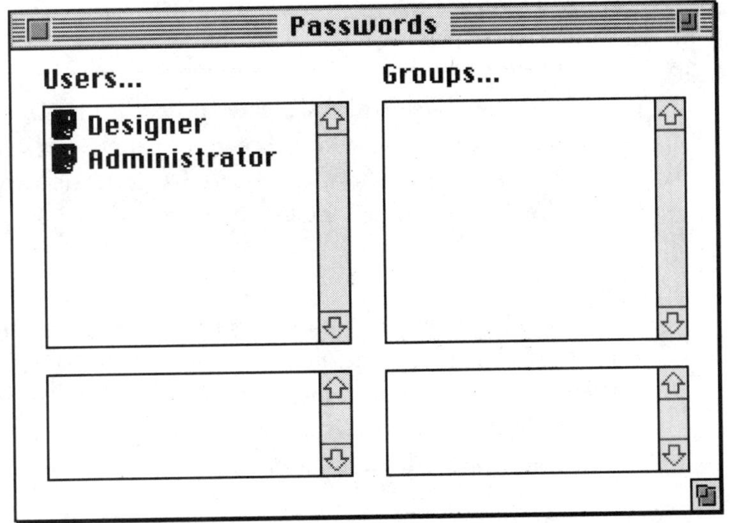

The Password Access Editor

When you create a database, 4D automatically creates two users, the Designer and the Administrator. These two are the only users who can create new users and groups or edit information about users. The icons of the Designer and Administrator are black. This is to distinguish the fact that 4D itself created these users.

THE DESIGNER

The *Designer* is you, the designer of the database. The Designer has access to everything in the database. The only objects that cannot be edited by the Designer are any users and groups created by the administrator. The Designer can move users in and out of groups, but cannot edit information about the users or groups created by the Administrator.

You can change the name of the Designer user if you want, because the Designer is simply the first user in the Password Access Editor. The Designer can only makes changes to users or groups that he or she created. The icons of any users or groups created by the Designer are white.

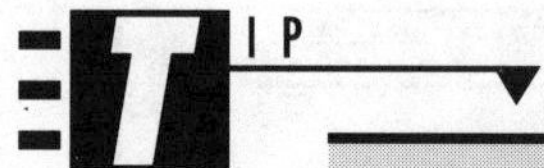

Any users who will have access to the Design environment should be created by the Designer. If these users are created by the Administrator, the Designer will not be able to change the users' passwords.

Once you assign a password to the Designer, the password system is enabled. The next time a user opens the database, they will have to enter their password. If you remove the Designer's password, the password system is disabled and users will no longer have to enter their passwords when they open the database.

THE ADMINISTRATOR

The *Administrator* is typically the person in charge of maintaining users that don't have access to the Design environment. The Administrator is a regular user with three important exceptions. The Administrator can:

- Create users and groups.
- Change user's names, passwords, and other information.
- Can save the users and groups he or she created to a disk file.

Many times, the Designer and Administrator are different people. The Designer builds the database and the Administrator (along with other users) is using the database. When the Designer delivers a new version of the database, any changes to users created by the Administrator will be lost. This can be avoided using the Save Groups menu item in the Password Access Editor. Before installing a new version of the database, the Administrator can access the Password Access Editor and choose

Password ➤ Save Groups. This will save the users and groups created by the Administrator to a disk file. The Administrator can then install the new version of the database and then reload the users and groups by choosing Passwords ➤ Load Groups in the Password Access Editor. Following this procedure will preserve any changes that were made to the users or groups that the Administrator created. Because of this, users that are not accessing the Design environment should be created by the Administrator. The icons of users and groups created by the Administrator are gray.

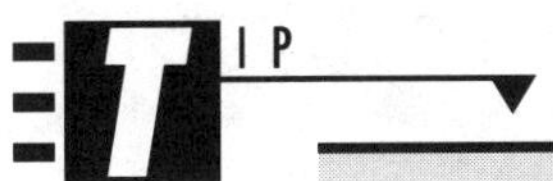

You may not want the Administrator to have access to the Design environment. In this case, you can write a global procedure that calls the EDIT ACCESS command. This command will open the Password Access Editor. By creating this global procedure, you can give the Administrator access to the Password Access Editor without giving her access to the Design environment.

GROUPS OWNERS

Each group has an owner. Only group owners can access the Password Access Editor. If the owner user is not the Designer or Administrator, she can move users in and out of only the groups she owns. She cannot create new users and groups or edit existing users or groups. The Designer and Administrator are the only users who can set the owner of a group by double-clicking on the group in the Password Access Editor. Figure 18.5 shows the Edit Group dialog box that is used to edit the name of the group and select the group's owner.

FIGURE 18.5

The Edit Group dialog box

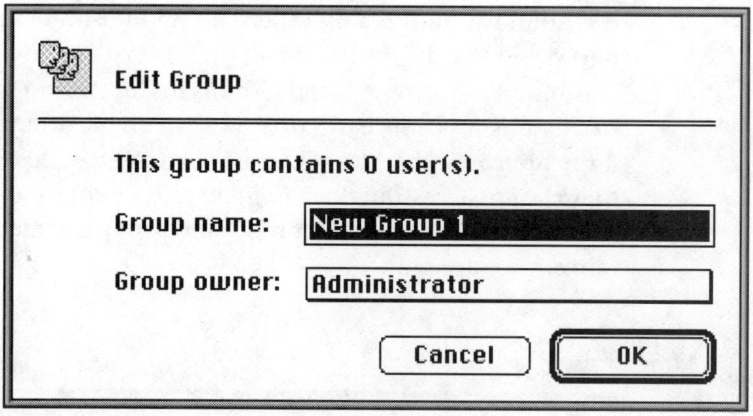

Edit Group

This group contains 0 user(s).

Group name: New Group 1

Group owner: Administrator

Cancel OK

CREATING NEW USERS

Adding new users to the password system is easy. You simply open the password edit and choose Passwords ➤ New User (⌘-N). The Edit User dialog box will appear, allowing you to enter information about the user. This dialog box is shown in Figure 18.6.

FIGURE 18.6

The Edit User dialog box

Edit User

User name: Designer

Password: *****

Startup procedure:

Last use: 4/1/94

Number of uses: 1

Default owner of objects created by this user: All Groups

Cancel OK

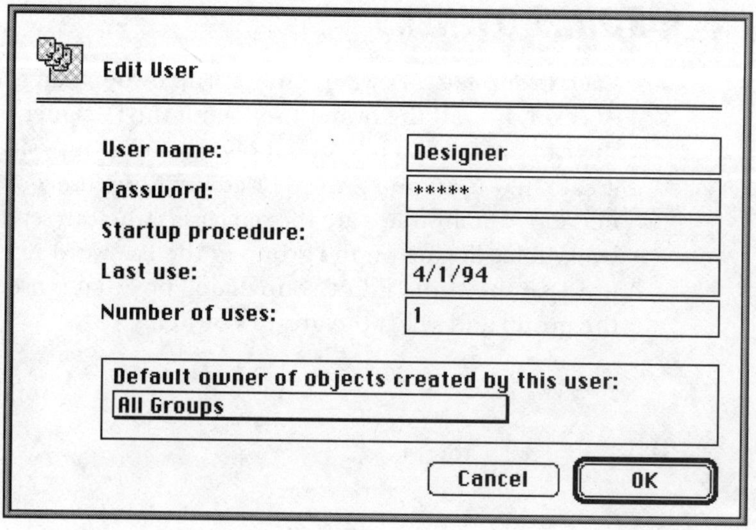

In this dialog box, you enter the following information about the user:

User name is the name of the user. The user name can be up to 30 characters long and does not have to be unique.

Password is the text the user will have to enter when they open the database. Passwords are the only features of 4D that are case-sensitive. This means that 4D sees *Sandra* and *sandra* as two different passwords. The password can be up to 15 characters long. Once you type a password and close the Edit User dialog box, you will not be able to see the password again. The next time you open the Edit User dialog box the password will be masked with asterisks. There is no way to find out what password a user entered once this dialog box is closed.

Startup procedure is the name of a global procedure you want to run when a user opens the database. This can be useful when you have different actions you want to take place for different users when they log on. For example, you might have different menu bars for different users. The startup procedure could be a global procedure that calls the **MENU BAR** command and specifies the menu bar for this user.

Last use is the last date on which the user opened the database. 4D updates this automatically. This is useful for keeping track of the usage of the database.

Number of uses is the number of times the user has opened the database. This is also useful for tracking the usage of the database.

Default owner of objects created by this user allows you to select a group of users that will have the ability to edit the files, layouts, and procedures that this user creates.

Be careful when creating new users and groups, as they cannot be deleted once they are created.

Let's add some users and groups to the Learn 4D database. Make sure you make a backup copy of your Learn 4D database before you add passwords just in case something goes wrong.

1. Switch to the Design environment.
2. Choose Design ➤ Passwords.
3. Double-click on Designer to edit it.
4. Click in the Password field.
5. Type **cat** as the Designer password.
6. Click **OK**.

Now that you have assigned a password to the Designer, the password system is enabled. The next step is to assign a password to the Administrator:

1. Double-click on Administrator.
2. Click in the Password field.
3. Type **fish** as the password for the Administrator.
4. Click **OK**.

At this point, you should re-open the database and log on as the Administrator. This way, all of the users you add will be editable by the Administrator.

5. Choose File ➤ Open Database.
6. Open the Learn 4D database.

7. Click on Administrator.
8. Type **fish** as the password.
9. Click **OK**.
10. Choose Design ➤ Passwords.

Now let's add a new user to the password system:

1. Choose Passwords ➤ New User (⌘-N).
2. Type **Arthur Dent** as the name of the new user.
3. Move to the Password field and type **dent** as the password.
4. Click **OK**.

You wouldn't want to use a person's last name as her password because it would be too easy to guess. Last names are being used here for demonstration purposes only.

That is all there is to it. Go ahead and add the following list of users:

User	Password
Ford Prefect	towel
Zaphod Beeblebrox	gold
Trisha McMillan	moped
Marvin	android
Douglas Adams	42

Now that you have added users, you need to create groups and assign users to the groups. Let's create three groups: one for users that do data entry, one for users who perform accounting functions, and a third for managers. By creating these three groups, we can define three distinct levels of access.

1. Choose Passwords ➤ New Group.
2. Type **Data Entry** as the group name.
3. Click **OK**.

Notice that the Administrator is now listed in the lower-right scrollable area. This area shows all the users who are in the selected group. The Administrator is the owner of the Data Entry group, so he or she is by default a member of the group. If you click on the Administrator in the Users list, the groups the Administrator is a member of will appear in the scrollable area in the lower-left corner. Figure 18.7 shows how the Password Access Editor looks when the Data Entry group and Administrator user are selected.

FIGURE 18.7

Viewing users and groups

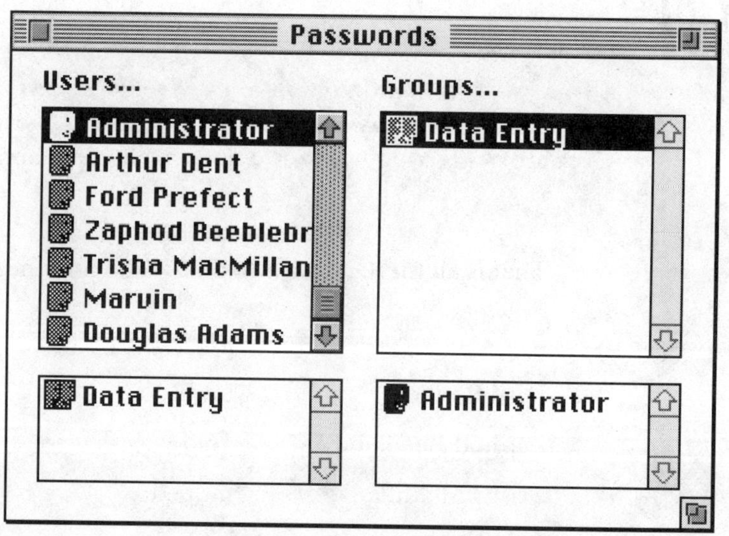

The next step is to put users into the Data Entry group. You do this by dragging a user to a group. Figure 18.8 shows a user being dragged to a group.

Let's assign Arthur Dent and Ford Prefect to the Data Entry group:

1. Click on **Arthur Dent** and drag over to the Data Entry group.

FIGURE 18.8

Assigning a user to a group

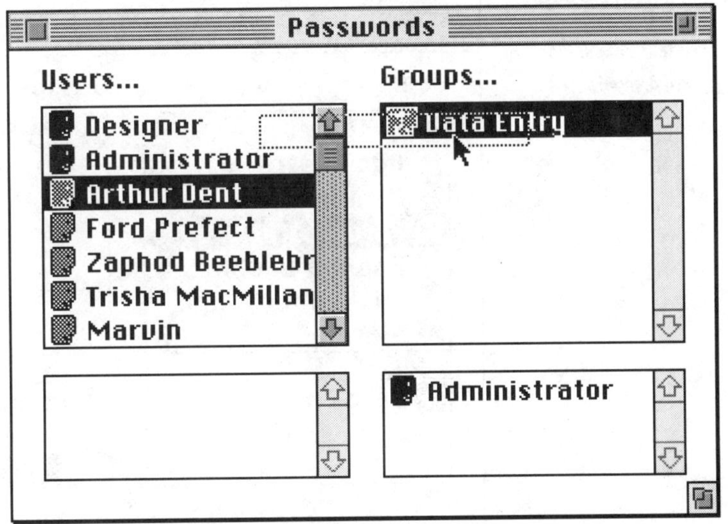

2. Click on **Ford Prefect** and drag over to the Data Entry group.

Notice that Arthur Dent and Ford Prefect are now listed as users in the Data Entry group. Figure 18.9 shows what the Password Access Editor should look like now.

Let's add the other two groups:

1. Create an **Accounting** group.
2. Place **Trisha McMillan** and **Marvin** in the Accounting group.
3. Create a **Managers** group.
4. Place **Zaphod Beeblebrox** and **Douglas Adams** in the Managers group.

Groups have an icon with two faces while users have an icon with one face. This makes it easier to tell them apart.

FIGURE 18.9

The current state of the Password Access Editor

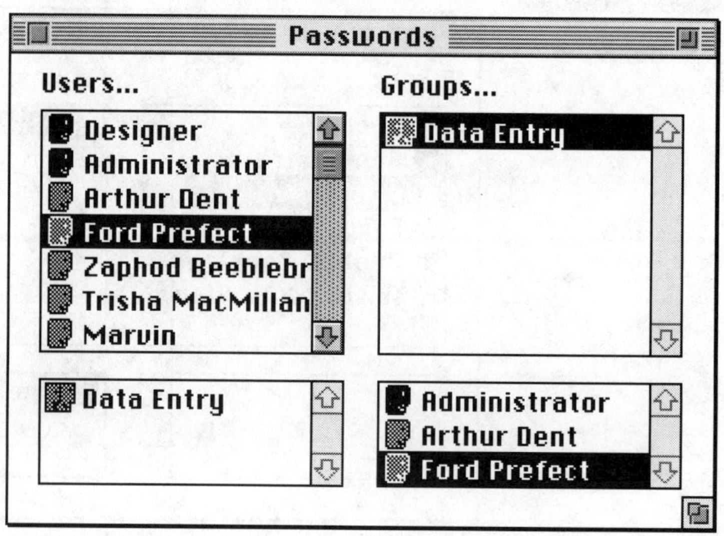

Data Entry users will have the lowest level of access. They should be able to enter new invoices and new customers but nothing more. Accounting users should be able to do everything that the Data Entry users can do. You could put all of the Accounting users in the Data Entry group to make sure that they have the same access that the Data Entry group has. This is unnecessary because groups can be members of other groups. All you need to do is make the Accounting group a member of the Data Entry group. You do this by dragging one group on top of another. Let's do it:

1. Drag the **Accounting** group over the Data Entry group.
2. Scroll to the bottom of the users in the Data Entry group.

Notice that Accounting is now listed as a user. Accounting is in italics to remind you that this is a group and not a user. All members of the Accounting group will now also have the privileges of the Data Entry group.

Managers will have the highest level of access. They will have their own special privileges, but should also have all the privileges that the members of the Accounting group have. Let's make the Managers group a member of the Accounting group:

3. Drag the **Managers** group over the Accounting group.

The Managers group is now a member of the Accounting group. It is also now a member of the Data Entry group because the Accounting group is a member of the Data Entry group. There is one group left to create.

As a database designer, there may be parts of the database you want to restrict access to. For example, you might want to restrict access to a menu item that is not fully functional yet. So that you will have this capability, let's create a Developers group. You will need to log on as the Designer before creating this group.

1. Choose File ➤ Open Database.
2. Open the Learn 4D database.
3. Click on Designer.
4. Type **cat** as the password.
5. Click **OK**.
6. Make sure the Password Access Editor is open.
7. Choose Passwords ➤ New Group.
8. Type **Developers**.
9. Choose Designer as the group owner.
10. Click **OK**.

Now that you have a Developers group, you can use this group to restrict access to the Designer only. At the moment, there is only one Designer—you. However, at some point you may want to have several designers, and each could be put into the Developers group. At this point, you have not assigned access to anything in the database. Assigning access to objects in the database is what you will learn about next.

LIMITING ACCESS

Using the password system, you can *limit* access to practically every part of the database. You can also limit each user's access to the different environments in 4D. For example, you would probably want to limit most users to the Runtime environment only. You might limit the Administrator to the User and Runtime environments and give Designers access to all three environments. The kind of access you give each user really depends on your particular situation.

THE DESIGN ENVIRONMENT

You probably would not want your users poking around in the Design environment. Who knows what kind of trouble they might get into? In this case, you will want to allow only members of the Developers group to have access to the Design environment. You can limit this access through the Preferences dialog box in the Design environment. Figure 18.10 shows the Preferences dialog box.

In this dialog box you can limit access to the Design environment by selecting a group from the Structure Access pop-up menu. Only members of the group you select will have access to the Design environment. Although the name implies that you are only protecting access to the Structure window, in fact you are protecting access to the entire Design environment. Users that do not have access to the Design environment will see the Design menu item in the Use menu disabled. Let's set this access:

1. Choose File ➤ Preferences.
2. Choose Developers from the Structure Access pop-up menu.
3. Click **OK**.

Currently, you have 4D set in the Preferences dialog box to open the Design environment when a user opens the database. If the user doesn't have access to the Design environment, 4D will open the User environment instead.

FIGURE 18.10

The Preferences dialog box in the Design environment

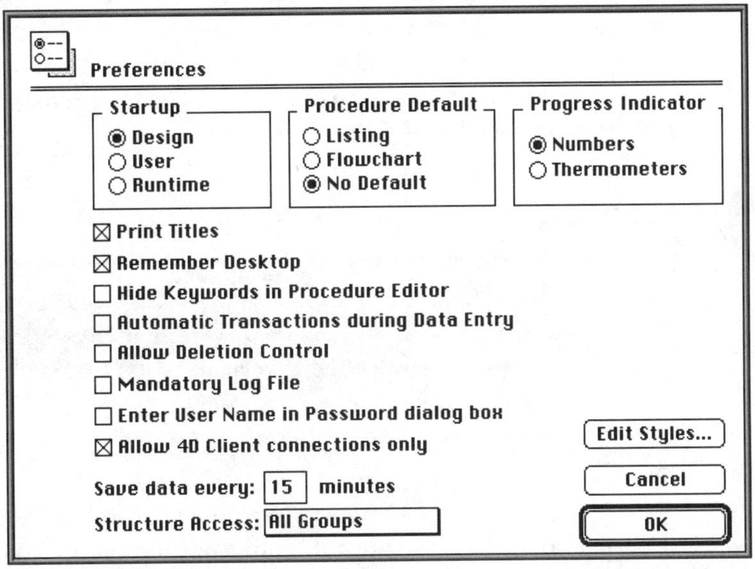

THE USER ENVIRONMENT

Once you have added menus to your database, you might want to prevent the user from accessing the User environment. In the Runtime environment, if the user chooses an enabled menu item that does not have a procedure associated with it, 4D will switch to the User environment if the User environment is available. The user can also switch to the User environment if she presses Option-f. This special key combination is primarily to allow Designers to switch to the User environment in case there isn't a menu item they can choose to do so. Fortunately, there is a simple way to prevent the user from switching to the User environment.

To do this, you must assign a startup procedure to the user in the Edit User dialog box. The global procedure you assign does not have to be an existing procedure. If you type anything at all in the Startup procedure area, 4D will prevent the user from accessing the User environment. Should she choose a menu item in the Runtime environment that doesn't have a procedure, 4D will quit back to the Finder. If the user presses Option-f, 4D will again quit back to the Finder. This prevents the user from accessing User environment. If you are not assigning a startup procedure but would like to prevent the user from accessing the User environment, just type a character (like Z) in the Startup procedure dialog box. You would probably never name a global procedure with only one character. By using one character, you will be reminded that this isn't a global procedure—just a method of security.

The User environment is available only in 4th Dimension and 4D Client (the user software that comes with 4D Server). 4D Runtime is a special version of 4D that limits the user to the Runtime environment only.

In some cases, you will want the user to have access to the User environment, but you want to limit what she can do. In the User environment, you can limit the user's access to layouts and procedures as well as limit what she can do to records in each file.

Files

For each file in the database, you can limit a group's access. What you can limit comes in the form of four separate actions that the user could take. You can choose which group can

- Load (view) records.
- Save (make changes to) records.
- Add new records.
- Delete records.

This access is set in the File Attributes dialog box. You access this dialog box by choosing Structure ➤ Edit File (⌘-R). Figure 18.11 shows this dialog box. To assign access privileges, you simply select a group from the pop-up menu next to the action you want to control. By default, all groups have the ability to load, save, add, and delete records. By choosing a group from one of the pop-up menus, you limit a particular action to the members of that group only.

FIGURE 18.11

The File Attributes dialog box

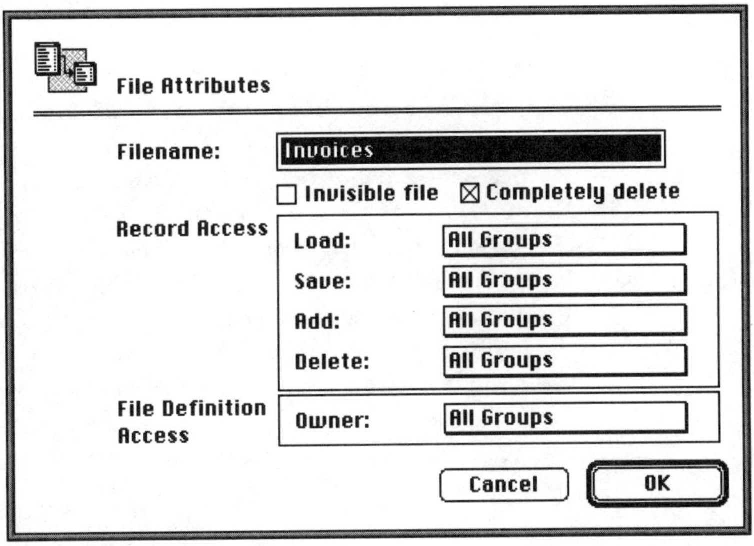

If the user tries to perform an action she doesn't have privileges for, 4D will present an error message. Figure 18.12 shows the error message displayed when a user attempts to delete a record without having the privileges for deleting records.

FIGURE 18.12

The Error dialog box showing a privilege error

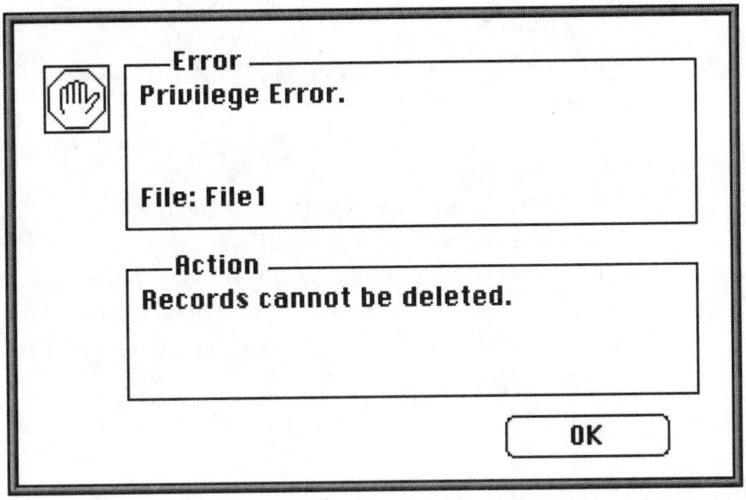

Record access affects the User and Runtime environments. However, it doesn't make sense to use these Record Access pop-up menus to control access for the Runtime environment. It wouldn't make sense to allow the user to select a menu item that will add a new record, only to have 4D present the user with an error message. In the Runtime environment, you can control a user's access to menu items. This prevents the user from using menu items she doesn't have access to. It is better stop the user at the menu before she attempts to perform the action. You will learn more about menu access later in this chapter.

You can also assign access to the File definition through the File Definition Access pop-up menu. The members of the group you select will be the only users that can add new fields or edit existing fields of this file in the Design environment. You might use this feature if you had more than one group of developers and wanted to make sure that each group didn't make changes to another group's files.

Layouts

You may have certain layouts that you don't want the user to have access to (special reports for example). You can limit access to a layout using the Access pop-up menu in the Layout dialog box. Figure 18.13 shows this dialog box.

Only the members of the group you select will have access to the layout in the User environment. To assign access to a layout, you simply select a layout and choose a group from the Access pop-up menu. From this dialog box you can also choose which group of users will have the ability to edit the layout in the Design environment. This access is limited using the Owner pop-up menu.

FIGURE 18.13

Assigning access to a layout

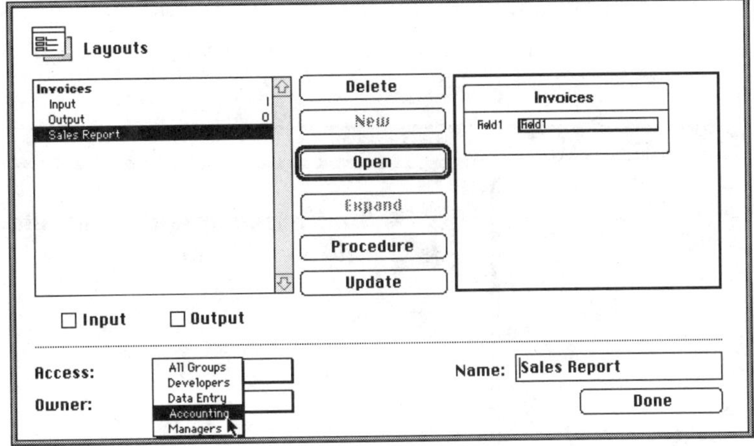

Procedures

There may be many global procedures that you don't want the user to accidentally execute by choosing Special ➤ Execute Procedure (⌘-E). You can assign access to each global procedure using the Access pop-up menu in the Procedure dialog box. You can also use this dialog box to assign the group that can edit this procedure in the Design environment.

If a user has access to the Design environment but does not have access to a global procedure, that user can still trace the global procedure with the Debugger. This will allow him or her to view the procedure but not edit it.

THE RUNTIME ENVIRONMENT

In the Runtime environment, you control access by assigning groups to menu items. This is done using the Access pop-up menu in the Menu Editor. Only members of the group you select will have access to the menu item. If a user selects a menu item and she does not have access privileges for that menu item, 4D will display a “friendly” error message. Figure 18.14 shows the error message the user sees in this situation.

FIGURE 18.14

The privilege error message for menu items

Your password does not allow you to use this menu item.
OK

CHANGING PASSWORDS

Even if a user has access to the Design environment, she cannot change her own password unless she is the Designer or Administrator. However, you can give the user the ability to change her own password using the CHANGE PASSWORD command. This command allows you to pass a string that becomes the current user’s new password.

If you choose to give this option to your users you must be careful. You will want to force the user to enter the new password twice so that you can compare the first password they type in to the second. If the passwords don’t match, force the user to start over again and enter a new password. This is important to do to prevent the user from incorrectly typing her new password and locking herself out of the database. Also, remember that passwords are case-sensitive. When comparing strings, 4D sees *SANDRA* and *sandra* as the same. This means that you must compare the ASCII values of each character in the two passwords to make sure that they are the same case. The procedure listed below takes two passwords, compares them, and then changes the user’s password if they match exactly.

You may not want others to see the password the user is entering. If you create a custom dialog box, you can mask the variable that the user types her new password into using the password font that 4D uses when the user opens the database and enters her password. The password font does not display on the Font menu in the Layout Editor. To set your password variable to the password font, call FONT(vPassword; "%Password") in the before phase of your dialog's layout procedure.

```
$password:=Request("Enter new password:")
If (OK=1)
  $verify:=Request("Enter it again to verify it:")
  If (OK=1)
    If (Length($password)=Length($verify))
      $PasswordErr:=False
      For ($i;1;Length($password))
        If (Ascii($passwords$ir)#Ascii($verifys$ir))
          $PasswordErr:=True
        End if
      End for
      If ($PasswordErr)
        BEEP
        ALERT("The passwords don't match. Please try
        again.")
      Else
        CHANGE PASSWORD($password)
      End if
    Else
      BEEP
      ALERT("The passwords don't match. Please try
      again.")
    End if
  End if
End if
```

Don't forget your Designer password. If you forget your password, you will not be able to get into the Design environment. If you are locked out of the Design environment, you can't make changes to the database. Your only choices at this point would be to try typing whatever you think your password might be (this could take awhile) or to re-create the database from scratch (this could also take awhile). If you do forget your password, there is one thing I can suggest. Don't waste your time trying to remember the password you assigned. Chances are a thousand monkeys sitting at typewriters would type out one of Shakespeare's plays before you remember your password. Instead, think about what you would use as a password if you where going to assign one today. Continue trying these passwords. If you are lucky, the logic that gives you passwords to try will be the same logic that produced your original password. After all of this, if you find yourself unable to remember your password, consider how useful your database has been up to this point. If it hasn't been useful, which considering your current situation seems more likely, you may get some satisfaction from the knowledge that it won't be troubling you any longer.

CONTROLLING ACCESS TO 4D MODULES

If you are using 4D Server to allow multiple users to have access to your database and you have any of the 4D modules installed, you can control access to those modules. You will want to control access to the modules to ensure that the users that need to use the module, have access to it. Say you have purchased 4D Write. When you purchased 4D Write for use with 4D Server, you purchased a certain number of concurrent users for 4D Write. Each time a user opens the database, she will use one of these licenses. This does not create any problems provided that you have purchased a license for as many users of 4D Write as you have users for 4D Server. For example, if you have a ten-user license for 4D Write and a ten-user license for 4D Server, 4D Write will always be available to each user. However, if you have a ten-user license for 4D Write and a twenty-user license for 4D Server, the first ten users will be able to use 4D Write. The eleventh concurrent user who opens the database will not have access to 4D Write because your license is for ten 4D Write users only. You may have purchased a ten-user 4D Write license because only ten of your users need to use 4D Write. The eleventh user may need access to 4D Write but can not access it because the first ten users have used up all the licenses.

You can solve this problem using the External Package Access dialog box in the Password Access Editor. This dialog box displays all of the modules that are installed along with a pop-up menu of password groups. You can click on a module and select a group. This gives only the users in that group access to the selected module. To solve the problem described above, you could create a group called **4D Write Users** and put the ten users that use 4D Write into that group. Any users who open the database and are not in the 4D Write Users group will not have access to 4D Write. Figure 18.15 shows the External Package Access dialog box with 4D Write selected and the 4D Write Users group assigned. You will learn more about the 4D modules in *Chapter 20.*

FIGURE 18.15

The External Package Access dialog box

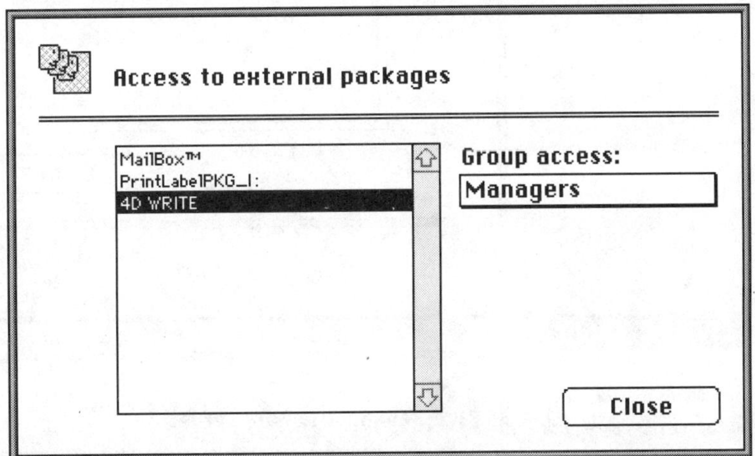

PATH FILES

4D Client is the software a user uses to access a database running with 4D Server. 4D Client is the functional equivalent to 4th Dimension. When the user opens a 4D Server database, the user is presented with a dialog box that allows her to choose which 4D Server database she wants to open. If the network the user is connected to has only one zone, the dialog box shown in Figure 18.16 will be displayed. However, if the network has more than one zone, the dialog box in Figure 18.17 will be displayed.

FIGURE 18.16

The single zone, 4D Server selection dialog box

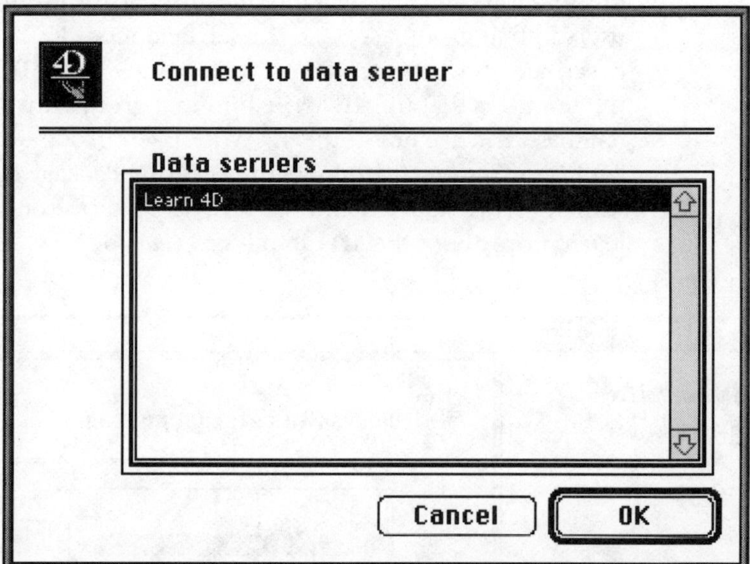

FIGURE 18.17

The multi-zone, 4D Server selection dialog box

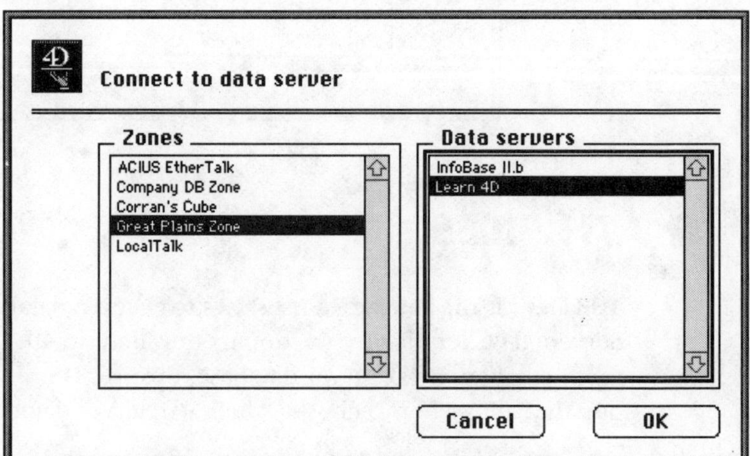

If you are using passwords, the user will have to enter her password after choosing a 4D Server database and click **OK**. If your network has only one zone, this procedure for opening a database might be long and difficult for the user to remember. To solve this problem, the Password Access Editor in 4D Client allows you to create a path file. A Path file is a desktop document that contains the name of the 4D Server database and the zone that the database is in on the network. Figure 18.18 shows the path file icon. To open a database, the user simply double-clicks on this document, never seeing the 4D Server selection dialog box. The first window the user sees is the password dialog box. You can also choose to have the user's password saved in the path file. If you choose this option, the user will not have to enter her name or password when opening the database because 4D Client will enter it automatically.

FIGURE 18.18

A Path file

INCREASING
PERFORMANCE
WITH THE
4D COMPILER
19

MAC TRACKS MAC

To explicitly tell the Compiler the data type of a variable ***633***

Use a compiler directive.

To test your database code for possible design flaws ***636***

Use the 4D Compiler's Range Checking option.

Featuring

- *What computers understand*
- *What is a compiler?*
- *Why code runs faster*
- *Variable typing*
- *Compiler errors*
- *Compiler options*

COMPUTERS CAN DO some pretty amazing things. They can help you write a letter, tell you the time, and keep track of your checkbook. Computers are also used to design cars, enable medical researchers to find cures and treatments, and in general, to make life better (and definitely more interesting).

In earlier chapters you learned about 4th Dimension's procedural language. You learned how to use this language to easily and automatically make changes to the records in your database. When you look at 4D's language, it would almost seem that the language that a computer understands is very similar to your own language. This couldn't be farther from the truth. The language that a computer understands looks nothing at all like your language. To make using your database easier, 4D provides you with a language that is closer to a spoken language than what the computer really understands. As 4D executes the instructions you have given it, it translates its own language into something that the computer can understand. The 4D Compiler makes this translation a lot faster, and consequently, your database runs faster.

What Do Computers Really Understand?

Believe it or not, computers are idiots. They understand very little and cannot make decisions on their own. As a matter of fact, when left to themselves they are quite happy to sit and do nothing. What they are good at is doing what we tell them to do and doing it terribly fast. We tell computers what to do using a programming language which is then translated into the computer's language.

A computer's brain is called a *microprocessor.* It is this microprocessor (or chip) that does most of the work. The microprocessor only understands two things: 1 and 0. That's it. That is all a computer can understand. This language of 1's and 0's is called *machine language.*

In order for the computer to understand any program it must be translated into machine language. Computer languages like C, Pascal, BASIC, FORTRAN, and 4th Dimension's language are called *high-level* languages because they are more readable than the lowest level language (machine language). These high-level languages, which use natural language commands, were developed to make it easier to write computer programs without having to work with only 1's and 0's.

For the computer to understand these high-level languages, they must be translated into machine language. This translation can occur in two methods, known as *interpreted* and *compiled* programs. In interpreted programs, the programming code in the program is translated while the program is running. For example, in 4th Dimension's interpreted mode, each time 4D reaches a line of code in a procedure or script, that line is translated into machine language and then executed. In compiled programs, all of the programming code has been translated into machine language all at once by a program called a *compiler.* Once a program has been compiled, no more interpretation is required because the instructions are now stored in machine language. Consequently, your code executes much faster (3 to 1000 times faster, to be exact).

What Is a Compiler?

A compiler is a special application program that translates a high-level computer language into machine language. There are different compilers for each type of high-level language, such as C, Pascal, etc., and even for different vendor's brands within each of these languages. The compiler for 4th Dimension is called *4D Compiler.*

When you compile your 4D database using the 4D Compiler, it will create a new structure file that contains all of your database procedures translated into machine language. You use the same data file for both an interpreted or uncompiled database and a compiled one, as your data information is independent from your structure file procedures.

WHY SHOULD I COMPILE MY DATABASE?

Compiling your database has several advantages, including increasing the speed of your application, checking your code for errors that may affect how the program works, protecting your database code from deliberate or inadvertent modification, and merging your database with 4D Runtime to create a double-clickable, stand-alone, single user application.

For many users, increasing the speed of the application is the most important reason to compile their application. A compiled 4th Dimension database can run up to 1,000 times faster, depending on the type and number of procedures it uses and how it was written. There are two reasons for this increase in speed. The code has already been translated into machine language and so it can be executed immediately, which is much faster than translating each line individually in interpreted mode. Secondly, when the program is compiled, the variables you use are referred to by the address in memory where they reside instead of by their name. In interpreted mode, 4D looks up the variables you use to find the address in memory where they are stored. In compiled mode, 4D uses the addresses directly instead of having to constantly look them up. Consequently, access to variables is much faster.

Another advantage to compiling your database is using the code checking features of 4D Compiler. When you compile your database, the 4D Compiler runs a systematic check of all your code, analyzing each statement for logical and syntax errors. When an error is detected, the compiler generates an error message or warning, and these are written to a special error file that you can use interactively with your interpreted database to debug and correct your errors. The 4D Compiler won't create a compiled application until you have fixed all the errors it has located.

You can also use the Range Checking option to further test your code for possible design flaws or execution problems that can't be detected during compilation because they can occur only when the compiled database is in use. For example, once your database compiles without errors, and if you have compiled with Range Checking selected, you simply test your database by running it through its paces. If any additional error is detected, an informative message explaining the problem will be displayed. Range Checking slows down compiled databases and is used only as the last development diagnostic check for your database.

The compiler also generates a text file called a Symbol Table. This contains an alphabetized index of all your interprocess, process, and local variables, including their type and usage, arrays with their type and dimensions, and all procedures and functions, including their parameter types. This list is very useful in debugging and diagnosing error messages reported by the compiler and as a guide to the contents of your database.

There are many cases when you will want to prohibit any modifications to your database code. A compiled database is protected from modifications because it prohibits access to the Design environment. In a compiled database, the structure and the procedures cannot be viewed or changed by the user. When you hear someone refer to the "source code for your 4th Dimension database," they mean the uncompiled copy of your structure file. That's because the compiled database structure file can't be changed, updated, or uncompiled. In order to make changes, you must change your uncompiled structure and recompile it. Remember that when you compile a 4D database, the compiler makes a compiled duplicate of your uncompiled structure file, and leaves the uncompiled structure file intact.

You can also use the 4D Compiler to create a single user, double-clickable, stand-alone application. To do this, you simply compile your database and merge it with a copy of *4D Runtime.* This is done during the compilation process, by selecting "Merge with Runtime" and choosing the name of a copy of 4D Runtime located on your hard disk. You must purchase a copy of 4D Runtime for each individual merged application you create to distribute, and it is important to use the same version of 4D Runtime as that of the 4th Dimension application used to create the structure file. 4D Runtime is a copy of the 4th Dimension database engine, and when merged with your structure file, allows users to operate your compiled database without having a full copy of 4th Dimension on their Macintoshes. When 4D Runtime is merged with your application, it will run only that application in single user mode and cannot be used to design or run any other 4th Dimension databases.

HOW DO I COMPILE MY DATABASE?

Unlike many other compilers, 4th Dimension's compiler is very easy to use. You simply select the database to be compiled and choose from a variety of compilation options, and it does all the translation chores for you. You can save your choices as a project, so that you can recompile again after any modifications simply by opening a project with your saved settings.

Before you use the 4D Compiler to compile your database, you should prepare your database for compilation. This process is known as "preparing your code for the compiler," and consists of typing your variables and making sure that each procedure, global procedure, variable and external procedure have a unique name.

For most compilers, you must declare or define all the types of your variables before running the compiler. Just like assigning a type to a field when you created it with the Structure Editor. A variable must be one of the following types: Boolean, Date, Graph, Integer, Long Integer, Picture, Pointer, Real, String (alphanumeric), Text, or Time. Arrays also have specific types, such as Array Boolean, Array Date, etc.

The compiler is going to translate all your variables into machine language and create a master list of all of this information, including each object's name, its place (or memory address) and its type. In order for the compiler to do this efficiently it has to be able to identify each unique object in your database, so your procedures and variables can't have the same name. Because the compiler can't change an address in memory for variables of different sizes (and the type determines the memory size), your variables need to be consistently of the same type throughout the database. For example, if you have a variable in one procedure, vSalary, that contains a real number, like a dollar amount, you can't use it in another procedure and assign it another type, such as a string, like **vSalary:="Total Salary"**.

A single character or number in memory is called a *byte.* Different types of variables take up different amounts of memory. Real numbers take 10 bytes, integers take 2 bytes, long integers take 4 bytes, and dates and times take 6 bytes. Text variables, Picture variables and arrays do not have a fixed size since the size of the data in them can change.

Unlike other compilers, the 4D Compiler helps you with this typing process because it can automatically type most variables for you by determining their type based on your usage of the variable in your procedure or script. For example, if it reads a procedure that contains **vSalary:=Subtotal([Employees]Salary)**, 4D Compiler knows that the Subtotal function returns a number so 4D Compiler types the vSalary variable as a Real.

In the above example, vSalary can contain different real numbers at different times within the database, but it can't ever contain data that is not a real number. Remember, interprocess and process variables must be of the same type within the entire database, and local variables must be of the same type within the procedure or script that they execute in.

However, even 4D Compiler can't always type your variables automatically, especially in cases where it might not be obvious what type they are. So it helps if you pre-declare some of your variables. This is what the Compiler Directive commands are used for. The following is a list of compiler directives:

C_BOOLEAN

C_DATE

C_INTEGER

C_GRAPH

C_LONGINT

C_PICTURE

C_POINTER

C_REAL

C_STRING

C_TEXT

C_TIME

By using compiler directives, you are pre-declaring the type for the variable. This way, the compiler knows ahead of time what the data types are and you can use the Compilation Path option to tell the compiler to skip the typing phases where it goes through your code to figure out what types your variables are. By skipping these phases, your compilation time will be reduced.

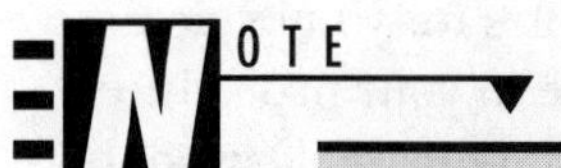

Variables of type integer are automatically converted to long integers by the compiler. The reason for this is that a long integer takes only two more bytes of memory and can hold much larger numbers. Also, if you try to assign a value greater than 32,767 to an integer variable, you will overflow it, which can cause an error. With long integers, you are less likely to have an overflow error because a long integer can hold values of over 2 billion.

You can type or declare your variables within the procedure they execute in (this is the only way to pre-declare a local variable) or within a separate procedure that is never used directly by your application. For example, you can create a procedure called **Compiler**, with all the declared variables in it. The compiler will read that procedure during compilation, and since the Compiler Directives take precedence over any usage of a variables within your scripts, the compiler can correctly type your variables in one pass.

Another advantage to pre-declaring all your variables using the Compiler Directives instead of 4D's automatic typing, is that you can make your database faster and avoid compilation errors. For example, 4D will automatically type a variable as a real number if it is a number. However, in your code you might be using this variable as a long integer. If you are doing math with this variable, you would want to use a compiler directive to type the variable as a long integer. The reason for this is that the microprocessor can perform math functions more quickly on long integers than it can on real numbers. By pre-declaring your variables, you also limit your chances for errors during compilation due to variables being used as more than one type. For more information on preparing your code for the compiler, refer to the 4D Compiler documentation.

Once you have prepared your code, you are ready to compile your database. The very first and most important step is to make a backup copy of your uncompiled structure file. Always perform operations like compiling and database maintenance on a backup copy of your database just for safety purposes.

Using the 4D Compiler is easy. Just double-click on the 4D Compiler application, and choose File ➤ New (⌘-N), to create a new compiler project, or Choose File ➤ Open (⌘-O) to select an existing project. The 4D Compiler settings window will be displayed. Figure 19.1 shows this window.

FIGURE 19.1

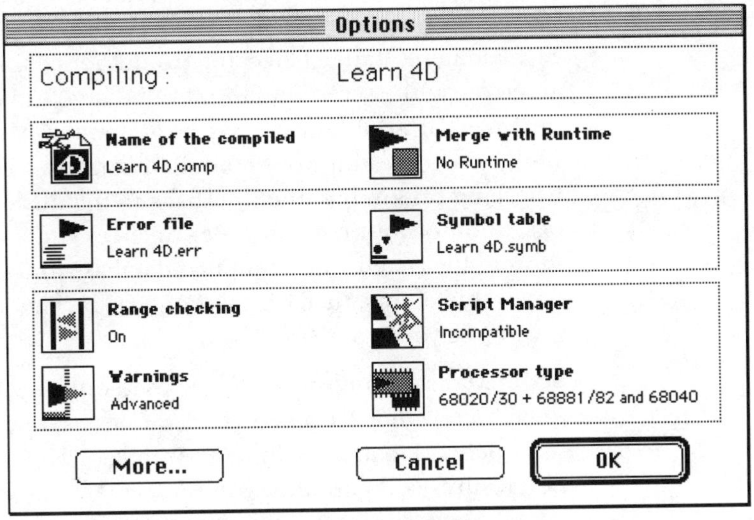

The 4D Compiler settings window with some options selected

Options
Compiling : Learn 4D
Name of the compiled
Learn 4D.comp
Merge with Runtime
No Runtime
Error file
Learn 4D.err
Symbol table
Learn 4D.symb
Range checking
On
Script Manager
Incompatible
Warnings
Advanced
Processor type
68020/30 + 68881/82 and 68040
More...
Cancel
OK

Simply select the options you need for this compilation, and click OK to compile your database. The compiler options are explained briefly below.

Compiled Database Name option allows you to choose the name for the compiled version of your database. If the original and compiled database are to have the same name, they must be located in different folders. The compiler will prevent you from overwriting your uncompiled structure file.

Merge with Runtime is optional. You use this option to choose the copy of 4D Runtime on your hard disk that you want to merge your compiled structure with.

Error File is optional and is used to generate a text file of errors found during compilation. The default name shown in the standard file dialog box must be used if you want to have the ability to open your uncompiled structure and view the errors detected by the compiler.

Symbol Table is optional and generates a text file that lists the data types for all the variables in your database. The symbol table is used for debugging and as a reference.

Range Checking is optional and is used to insure that you don't go beyond the limits of a variable. For example, if you had an array with 10 elements in it and you tried to use the 11th element, Range Checking would notice this and report an error on the screen. Without the Range Checking option, a system error would most likely be generated. Use this option while you are testing your compiled database. The Range Checking option has one drawback in that it slows down the execution of your code in order to check it. Once you have thoroughly tested your compiled database and removed all detectable errors, turn off the Range Checking option and recompile your database.

Script Manager option should be used only if your database is to be used with a 4D version that uses non-Roman character sets, such as Japanese, Chinese, Arabic, or Hebrew. This option insures compatibility with these character sets.

Warnings has three options: Off, Basic, and Advanced. These options govern the display of informative messages in the error file. During your initial compilation and debugging phases, using the Advanced mode is recommended as it gives the most extensive information. Warnings are issued by the compiler when it spots a potential error in your code.

Processor Type allows you to select the type of microprocessor of the Macintosh that the application will run on. You should select the highest processor for all of the computers that your database will run on. By doing this, the compiler will generate code that takes advantage of the advanced capabilities of the microprocessor you select and math coprocessors (if they are available) to make your code as fast as possible. If you aren't sure what processors your database will be running on, then select the lowest setting (68000), so the application can run on all models of Macintosh. Remember that code compiled for a 68020/30 machine won't run on a 68000 machine, and an error will be generated when you try to start the database. You may want to compile several versions of your database if users are running everything from the Mac Plus to the Quadra, so that each machine class can have the fastest compiled application possible.

Clicking the More button takes you to a second page of options which was not available in version 1 of the 4D Compiler. Figure 19.2 shows page two of the compiler options.

Optimization allows you to choose between two kinds of compilation. The Normal option compiles your code. The Optimized option also compiles your code but makes it smaller and run faster than the Normal option. You might be wondering why you would ever choose the Normal option if the Optimized option creates faster compiled code. The reason is simple. The Optimized option takes about 30% longer to compile and generates code that will only run on a 68020 or better processor. The Macintosh Plus, SE, Classic and the original Portable all have the 68000 processor. If you are using any of

FIGURE 19.2

The second page of compiler options

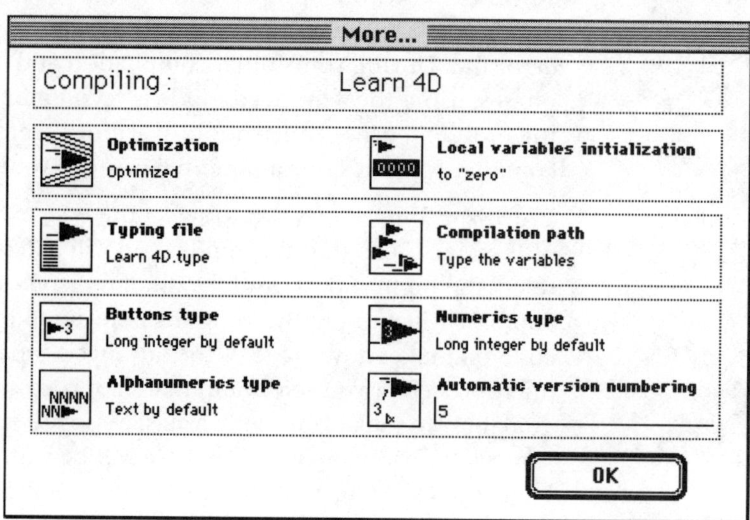

these machines and have not added an accelerator board with a 68020 processor (or better) you cannot run a database compiled with the Optimized option.

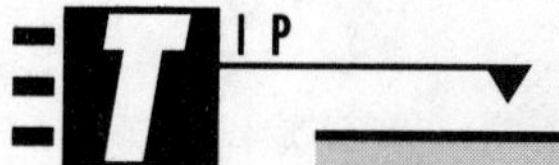

Because the Optimized option takes longer to compile (about 30% longer), at first use the Normal option. Later, when you are ready to deliver the database to the user or use it yourself, compile with the Optimized option.

Local Variables Initialization option allows you to choose how 4D will treat local variables when a procedure is executed. The default setting is Zero. This means that when a procedure is run, 4D will assign a null value to each variable based on its data type. For example, an integer, long integer, or real number variable would be assigned zero. A date variable would be assigned 00/00/00. The second option is Random Value. This option assigns local variables the random value 7267. While this is not really a random value, it does have purpose. By selecting this option you can easily locate any variables that you haven't explicitly assigned an initial value to. If you haven't assigned a value to a variable before using it, it will have the value 7267. When you see this value appear in your calculations or on the screen, you will know that you have not assigned an initial value to that variable before using it. You use this option in preparation for the third option which is No initialization. Once you are sure you have assigned every local variable a value before using it, you can select No initialization. By selecting this option your compiled code will run slightly faster because 4D doesn't have to bother with assigning values to your local variables each time a procedure is executed. You can think of this like programming a phone number into a speed dialer. Once you program the number into your phone, you can just push one button to dial it.

Typing File creates a text file on disk with compiler directives for all of your interprocess, process, and parameter variables. You can copy the text from this file and paste it into a procedure in your database. If you name this procedure COMPILER, the next option can use these directives to type your variables without going through all of your procedures to figure out the data types of your variables. This makes compiling a lot faster.

Compilation path allows you to inform 4D Compiler as to which variables in your database already have compiler directives. The default setting is Type The Variables. This option causes the compiler to go through your code looking for variables and figuring out the data types based on the compiler directives and usage of the variables. The second option is Process And Interprocess Variables Are Typed. This option tells the compiler that you have entered compiler directives for all process and interprocess variables into a procedure called COMPILER. Since these variables are all typed, 4D Compiler can skip the typing phase and go directly to the compilation phase, typing your local variables as it compiles your code. By skipping directly to the compilation phase, the time it takes to compile your code is reduced substantially. The third option is All Variables Are Typed. When selected, the compiler assumes that you have typed every variable including local variables. This enables the compiler to skip to the compilation phase and begin compiling without even bothering to type local variables. This provides you with the fastest possible compilation.

Buttons Type gives you the option to select Long Integer or Real as the data type for button variables. Unless you are using your button variables to store values, you should select Long Integer because long integers take up only 4 bytes (characters) in memory while real numbers take up 10 bytes in memory.

Numerics Type gives you the option to select Long Integer or Real as the data type for numeric variables. If most of your calculations don't involve decimal values, select Long Integer to save memory.

Alphanumerics Type gives you the option of Text or Fixed String. Text variables use less memory but take longer to access than Fixed String variables. Fixed String variables take up more memory typically, but are faster to access than Text variables.

The default typing options like Buttons Type, Numerics Type, and Alphanumerics Type only operate on variables that don't have compiler directives.

Automatic Version Numbering gives you the option to have the compiler add a VERS resource to your structure file which will show the version number of your database in the Get Info window from the Finder. This option increments the non-release number automatically each time you compile. If you want to increment the version number itself, you can open the structure file with Resedit or any other resource editor and manually set the version number.

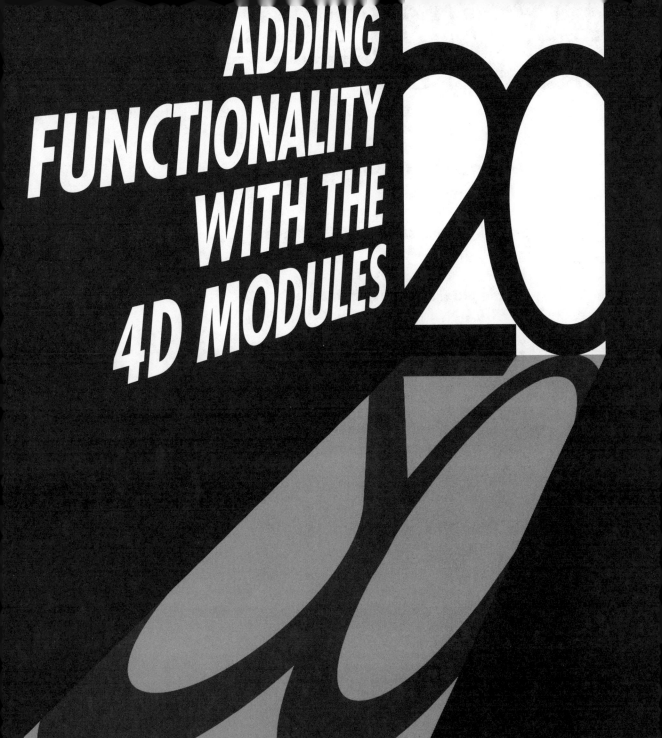

ADDING
FUNCTIONALITY
WITH THE
4D MODULES
20

MAC TRACKS MAC

TRACKS **MAC** TRACKS

To add CAD drawings to your database **659**

Use 4D CAD.

To do a thorough spellcheck of your database **660**

Use 4D Spell.

To make your 4D database a front end **660**

Use 4D SQL Server, 4D D.A.L, or 4D Oracle.

Featuring

- *4D Modules*
- *Text, graphics, charting, and spreadsheet modules*
- *Front-end modules*

DATABASES ARE USED to hold information and give you fast access to that information. Often the data needs to be used in conjunction with other applications like word processors or spreadsheets in order to get the result you want. 4D gives you the ability to export your records to a text file which can then be used with other applications. However, as your database grows, it will take longer and longer to export the records because there are more and more of them. There is another more elegant solution. Instead of taking your data to the other application, you can bring the other application to your data. You can do this using *4D modules.*

WHAT ARE THE 4D MODULES?

The *4D modules* are add-on programs for 4D that allow you to increase the functionality of your database as needed. Using the modules lets you build integrated database applications that can perform a full range of business functions. The modules can be used independently, they can share data between each other, and they can manipulate the information within your 4th Dimension database in many different ways, without your having to import and export data to other Macintosh applications.

Each module adds a specific type of functionality:

Module	**Function**
4D Write	Word processing application
4D Calc	Spreadsheet application
4D Draw	Object-oriented drawing application
4D Chart	2D and 3D charting application
4D CAD	Computer Aided Design application
4D Spell	Spell checker
4D SQL SERVER	SYBASE SQL interface application
4D D.A.L.	Interface application for any RDBMS supported by DAL
4D ORACLE	Interface application for communication with Oracle databases

Your database can use one, several or all of the modules simultaneously, depending on the extra features you need. The modules are easy to install and remove and can be shared by different databases. Each module contains additional language commands and functions that let you procedurally control the module from within your 4th Dimension database.

You can also use the special built-in *hot links* feature to share information between the 4D Write, 4D Calc, 4D Draw, 4D Chart, and 4D CAD modules. One or several modules can be Hot Linked together. When a module document, graph, drawing, or spreadsheet is published as a Hot Link to another module, and when that Hot Linked module's information is changed, it is automatically updated in the other linked module. For example, if a spreadsheet from 4D Calc is included in a 4D Write document, when the spreadsheet is changed, the changes will flow through and update the spreadsheet displayed in the 4D Write document. This is very useful for management of complex documents that contain frequently updated information. For the modules to share information via hot links, they must all be installed in the same database.

HOW ARE THE MODULES INSTALLED?

Each module comes with its own special installer application that lets you decide where to install the module. Each module can be installed either inside the structure file of your database, or in a special external procedure file called a *Proc.Ext* file. One, several, or all modules can be installed in a structure file or within one Proc.Ext file. You must choose either the structure or the Proc.Ext file for the location of modules for a single database, as it is not recommended for some of them to be in the structure and some of them in a Proc.ext file.

Selecting the location is a matter of personal preference. Modules installed in the structure file can be used only by that database, eliminating the need for the separate Proc.Ext file in the database folder. Installing them in the structure also increases the overall size of your database, depending on the size of the modules and the number of them you have installed. Installing modules in a single Proc.Ext file allows you to make copies of that Proc.Ext file and place a copy in each database folder to share the modules among several databases at once. If you install the module(s) in a Proc.Ext file, it must reside in the same folder as your database.

Whichever location you choose, you must avoid duplicate installation of a module—that is installing it in the structure and also placing a Proc.Ext with that module in the database folder. If this happens, the database won't open. To get the database to open again, you must remove the Proc.Ext file from the database folder or deinstall the duplicate module from either the Proc.Ext or the structure file.

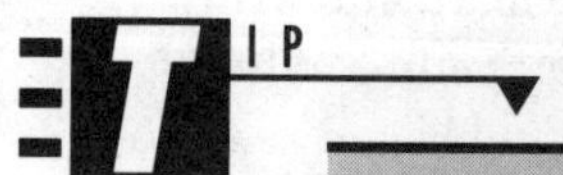

You must use each module's installer program, and not the 4D External Mover to install them. If you are using modules in a Proc.Ext file, remember that only one Proc.ext file can be in use (in the same folder) for each database, although several databases can share copies of one Proc.ext file.

Modules in either location can be updated, removed, or reinstalled at any time, without affecting the data in your database.

To share modules in a multi-user application using 4D Server, you must have a license for the number of users who will be using the module simultaneously. 4D Server automatically tracks the number of users for each module, and will deny access to excess users, releasing the slot for the next available user when a user exits the database. Using the password system, you can setup groups of users that should have access to a particular module. This way, users that don't use a module won't use up a license for it when they log in to the database.

INSTALLING A MODULE

To install a module, follow these steps:

1. Double-click on the module application installer icon.
2. When the installation window appears, if this is the first time you've used the module, personalize the program by typing in your name and company name. The installation message area will read, "No file is selected." Figure 20.1 shows the installer window.
3. To create a new Proc.Ext file, click New. To open an existing Proc.Ext file or a structure file, click Open.
4. If you are creating a New Proc.Ext file, a standard Macintosh file dialog box will be displayed, with Proc.Ext entered as the new file name. Select the folder where you want to save the new Proc.Ext file, and click Save. The installation message area will now show the name of the selected file and say that the module is not installed.

FIGURE 20.1

The 4D Write installer window with no file selected

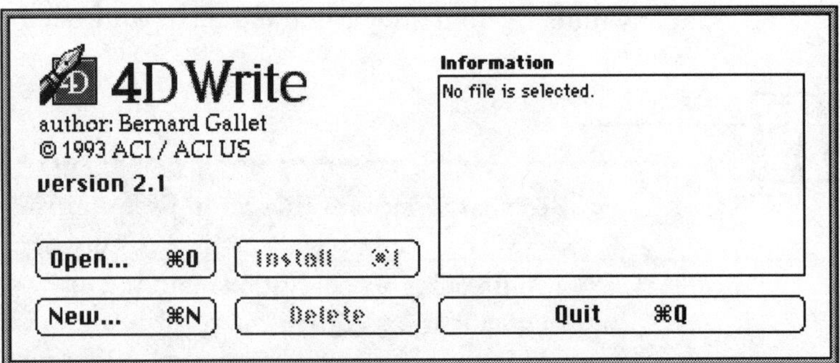

If you are installing the module into an existing Proc.Ext or into your database structure, select the Proc.Ext or the structure file from the standard Macintosh file dialog box displayed and click Open. If you are installing into a structure file, the database must be closed before you run the module installer. The installation message area will show the name of the selected file and say that the module is not installed.

5. Click Install. When the installation is complete, the message area says "Installation has been correctly installed!"; click Quit to exit the installer. Figure 20.2 shows the installer window with a module installed in a Proc.Ext file.
6. Now reopen your database to use your new module. If you are using a Proc.Ext, be sure it is placed in the same folder as your database before you reopen that database.

FIGURE 20.2

The 4D Write installer window with a module installed in Proc.Ext

4D Write
author: Bernard Gallet
© 1993 ACI / ACI US
version 2.1
Information
4D Write has been correctly installed!
Open... ⌘O
Install ⌘I
New... ⌘N
Delete
Quit ⌘Q

REMOVING A MODULE

To remove a module, launch the module application as you did to install it. Select the structure or Proc.Ext file from the open file dialog box that you want to remove the module from. The installation message area will show the name of the file and a message stating that the module is already installed. To remove it, click Delete. When you see the message that the module has been successfully removed, click the Quit button to exit the installer.

WHAT DO THE MODULES DO?

Each module is an application with a specific purpose. All of them can be easily integrated into your database application. Each of the modules is described below to give you an idea about them and what you might use them for.

4D WRITE

The *4D Write* module adds complete word processing capabilities to your database. Using 4D Write, you can create an advanced mail-merge system, document management system, database publishing system, and other types of databases that require the creation and organization of many letters, contracts, articles or other documents.

You can use 4D Write as an external area on your input layout or as a separate independent window in the User environment. You can have several different 4D Write areas of different sizes on one layout. Each 4D Write area is a self-contained application and has its own menu bar, scroll bars, and keyboard equivalents. You can zoom any 4D Write area to full screen size for easier editing and viewing.

A 4D Write document can be saved as a separate Macintosh document, as a template to your hard disk, or within a field to a record in your database. Saving documents to a field in a record means that you can create a file full of records, each with its own separate document. If you include other fields in each record, such as subject, name, and date, you can use the 4D language to search for a document on those fields as well, thus creating an integrated document tracking system.

Documents saved as a template can be used by many documents in many records, and the changes made to a template will be updated for each document using that template in each record. This is an easy way to create form letters and other standardized documents.

4D Write contains all standard word processing features. Each document can be about 32 pages long and can be saved in 4D Write, RTF, or text format, as well as many other formats for popular Macintosh applications. 4D Write uses the Claris XTND translators to allow you to open documents created by other applications as well as to save your 4D Write documents in other applications' formats. You have complete control over changing font, size, style, color, and alignment of text, including setting tabs, adjustable line spacing, headers and footers, page breaks and page numbering, and ruler settings for each paragraph. You can hide, show, copy, and paste rulers; hide and show margins; and hide and show invisible characters and pictures. Editing features include Search/Replace commands, a full undo command, graphic scaling, and the ability to use all the 4D standard date, time, alpha, and numeric formats.

4D Write documents can be printed as part of a layout in a report, as a separate document, like a letter, or as a mail-merge document using references to fields from your database.

One of the most important features of 4D Write is its ability to include references to fields from your database. Field references can be inserted in any 4D Write document by placing the cursor in the document where you want the field information and selecting from the 4D Write popup menu of files and fieldnames, or by typing the field name for the current file or a related file between the <> symbols, like this: <[Customers]Customer name>. When the document is printed with the current selection of record(s), the information from the database replaces the reference. This feature is used to create templates for form letters or other boilerplate documents that you create frequently, and also to build personalized mail-merge letters. Figure 20.3 shows a 4D Write area on an input layout.

Another important feature of 4D Write is the ability to completely control the 4D Write area with its procedural language. 4D Write contains over 40 commands that let you completely customize it within your database application. You can procedurally set margins, tabs, font, size, color, style, the appearance of the 4D Write menu bar, rulers, text editing, and other features.

FIGURE 20.3

4D Write on an input layout displaying a letter

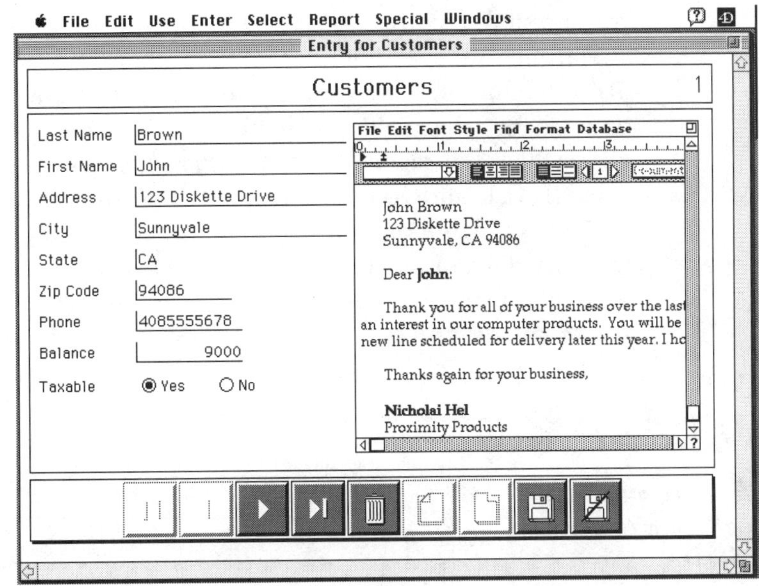

You can use procedures to insert field references or call 4D procedures to perform other data manipulation tasks, such as loading a customer's purchase information or invoice information into a mail-merge letter automatically. You can use the 4D commands within 4D Write to automatically insert calculations or other database information into the document, for example you can create a procedure that totals all the products ordered by a customer and insert both the line item for each product and a totals line for the order.

Some of the most common uses of 4D Write are to add document management capabilities to your database. One typical use is creating a file of correspondence records, which contains 4D Write mail-merge documents for customer orders, invoices, dunning letters, thank-you notes, or sales inquiry responses. Another is a database publishing application, which would use 4D Write documents to store catalog-page product information or newsletter articles. You can create a complete business document manager for such items as monthly sales reports by using 4D Write, 4D Calc, and 4D Chart to gather statistics from your database—such as customer purchase or sales data—and display them in a 4D Write report using included spreadsheets and graphics that are automatically updated when the database information changes. Because you can store pictures and formatted text in 4D Write, you can create a reference archive of news articles or other documents and use the 4D commands to search for and retrieve the documents by subject, date, or any other field information you have created in your database. Figure 20.4 shows a 4D Write window in the User environment with data from 4D Calc and 4D Draw included through the use of hot links.

4D Write is a very powerful organization and presentation tool when used in conjunction with your 4D database application. However, despite its many features, it is very easy to install and configure within your database, and is a very useful addition to your 4D library.

FIGURE 20.4

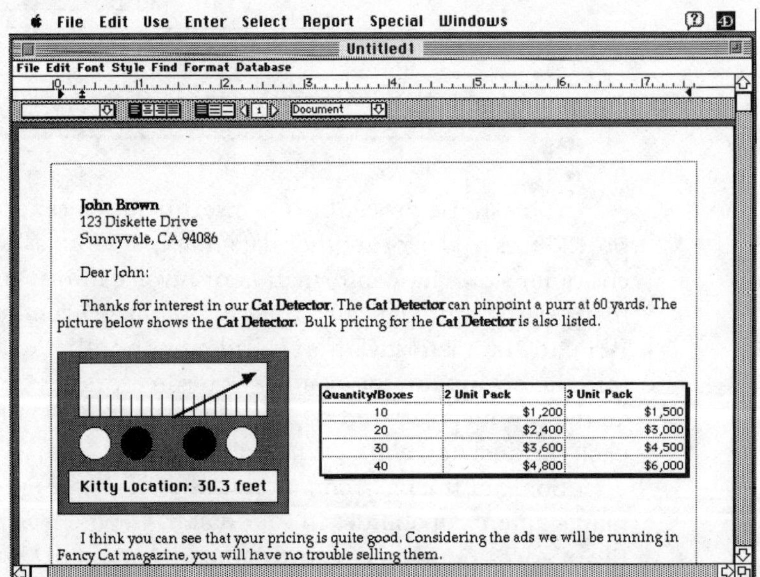

A 4D Write window with hot links from 4D Draw and 4D Calc

4D CALC

4D Calc allows you to add fully integrated spreadsheet capabilities to your database. Some of the most common uses for 4D Calc are to display product, marketing, or sales information in spreadsheet format, presenting enterable expense report forms, creating budgets, financial forecasts, and other analyses, and other spreadsheet tasks that need to use information drawn directly from your database. Using 4D Calc is much easier than importing and exporting data to another spreadsheet application, as changes to your database or your 4D Calc spreadsheet can be updated automatically without having to manually transfer, retype, or even cut and paste any data.

You can use 4D Calc as an external area on your input layout or as a separate independent window in the User environment. Figure 20.5 shows a 4D Calc area on an input layout.

FIGURE 20.5

A 4D Calc area on an input layout

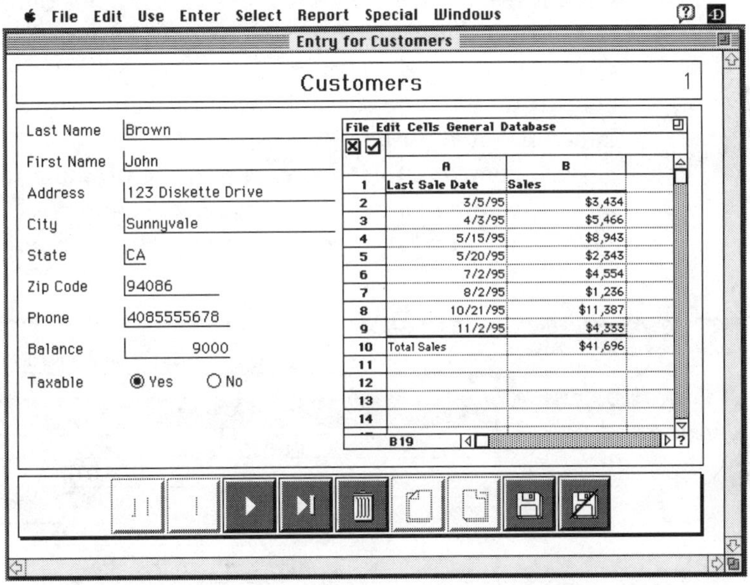

You can have several different 4D Calc areas of different sizes on one layout. In the User environment, you can have multiple 4D Calc spreadsheets open at once. Each 4D Calc area is a self-contained application, and has its own menu bar, scroll bars, and keyboard equivalents. You have an option to zoom any 4D Calc area to full screen size for easier data entry and viewing. You can use 4D Calc in layouts and within the User environment as a separate application, both in the same database.

A 4D Calc spreadsheet can be saved as a separate Macintosh document, as a template to your hard disk, or within a field to a record in your database. Saving documents to a field in a record means that you can create a file full of records, each with its own different spreadsheet. A spreadsheet saved as a template can be used in many records, and the changes made to a template will be updated for each spreadsheet using that template in each record. This is an easy way to create budgets, financial analyses, expense forms, and other standardized spreadsheets. Figure 20.6 shows a 4D Calc window in the User environment.

4D Calc contains all standard spreadsheet features, and is fully interactive with your 4th Dimension database. You can customize a 4D Calc spreadsheet to any size up to 8190 rows by 256 columns. You can perform manual and automatic calculation, have variable row height and column width, and select discontinuous row, column and range selections. You can name cells for easier reference and also search within values, formulas or text.

You have complete control over the presentation of your spreadsheet, including changing font, size, style, and color for each cell, cell alignment and rotation, custom row and column titles, modifiable grid

FIGURE 20.6

A 4D Calc window in the User environment

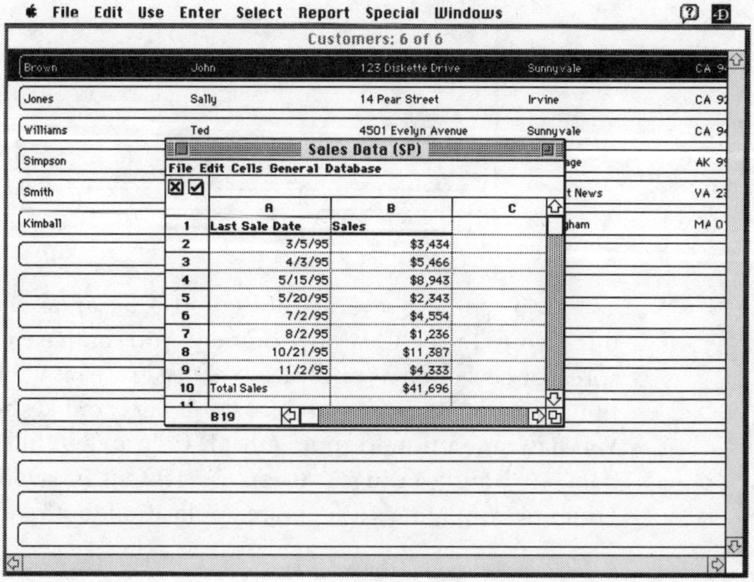

color, borders, multiple lines within a cell, and scaled and transparent graphics. You can hide or show row and column titles, grid by region, scroll bars, and menus. Editing features include row and column insert and delete, fill down and fill right, and the ability to clear formulas, values or formats from any cell. 4D's standard graphing capability is also provided, so you can graph your data on your spreadsheet as well.

4D Calc spreadsheets can be printed as part of a layout in a report or as a separate spreadsheet. When you print your spreadsheet, you can add custom headers and footers that include the date, time, and page number; you can print formulas, have discontinuous print areas, and show or hide any included graphics. Spreadsheets can be saved in 4D Calc or *tab delimited* format. Other saved formats can be added with the use of custom 4D externals.

One of the most important features of 4D Calc is its ability to include any combination of 4D fields, commands, variables, or user-defined functions or external routines to a formula in a cell. You can also completely control the 4D Calc area with the procedural language. 4D Calc contains over 40 built-in functions and 70 commands that let you completely customize it within your database application. Using these powerful integrated features lets you create a spreadsheet that takes information directly from your database and automatically presents it for you. For example, you could create a spreadsheet for a marketing analysis of your customers, and each time a new customer record was added to the database, the spreadsheet would update the demographic information totals automatically.

4D Calc is a very powerful spreadsheet analysis and presentation tool when used in conjunction with your 4D database application.

4D DRAW

The *4D Draw* module adds object-oriented drawing capabilities to your database. Using 4D Draw you can create graphic representations of your data, such as organizational charts, floor plans, wiring diagrams, computer network layouts, product manufacturing flow diagrams, and other types of technical illustration, diagramming, mechanical design, or other graphical representations.

You can use 4D Draw as an external area on your input layout or as a separate independent window in the User environment. You can have several different 4D Draw areas of different sizes on one layout. Each 4D Draw area is a self-contained application, and has its own menu bar, scroll bars, and keyboard equivalents.

A 4D Draw area can be saved as a separate Macintosh document, as a template to your hard disk, or within a field to a record in your database. Saving drawings to a field in a record means that you can create a file full of records each with its own different drawing.

4D Draw contains all of the standard draw program features along with some additional special features. Each drawing can be up to 120" × 120" in size and drawings can be reduced and enlarged from 2.8% to 800%. You can have custom rulers, which you can hide or show, ruler lines, object attributes, page breaks, the menu bar, the scroll bars, and the tool palette. You can create text, line, oval, rectangle, polygon, and arc objects. You have complete control over object presentation, including fill and line colors and patterns, line widths, arrow or cross line endpoints, corner rounding, object rotation, and alignment of text and objects, and have multiple fonts, styles, colors, and sizes in a text block. You can select or lock objects by attribute, group and ungroup, smooth and unsmooth, Send to back or Move to front, draw from the center or edge, add and remove handles from polygons, reshape polygons and arcs, and place, size and scale objects using the mouse or the keyboard. You can search for objects by attribute, such as color, line weight, fill pattern, type, or name.

You can also import or open drawings from other object-oriented drawing programs, paint programs, or documents saved in EPSF (Encapsulated PostScript format).

4D Draw drawings can be printed as part of a layout or as separate drawings. 4D Draw drawings can be saved as 4D Draw, MacPaint, PICT, and EPSF formats. Figure 20.7 shows a 4D Draw area as part of an input layout.

One of the most important features of 4D Draw is its ability to reference fields in the database in your drawings and associate drawn objects to records in your database. You can reference 4D fields, variables, commands and functions within any text block on your drawing. For example, you can create an employee organizational chart drawing and use the employee name and title fields text from your database records and insert it into the drawing. You can also insert pictures from fields in your database into your drawing, for example a picture of an employee or a

FIGURE 20.7

A 4D Draw area on an input layout

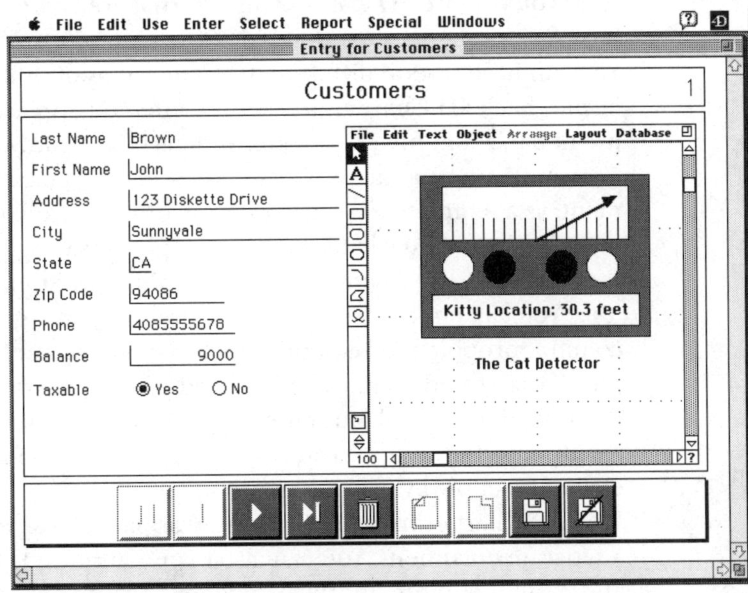

manufacturing part. You can also control the 4D Draw area with its procedural language. 4D Draw contains over 120 commands that let you completely customize it within your database application. 4D Draw knows when a user has performed some action within a drawing, so you can customize your drawing using 4D procedures to react to that action. For example, when a user clicks on a drawn object you could prevent or allow changes or modifications to it. When a user adds or deletes an object, for example a part on a manufacturing diagram, you could update your database information to show that the part has changed.

4D Draw is a very powerful drawing presentation tool when used in conjunction with your 4D database application.

4D CHART

4D Chart adds graphing capabilities beyond those that are built-in to 4D. With 4D Chart you can create 2D and 3D graphs from data in 4D fields, hot links from other modules, and even the clipboard. 4D Chart gives you the ability to completely manipulate all of the graphic elements of your graphs in a object-oriented drawing environment.

You can use 4D Chart as an external area on your input or output layout or as a separate independent window in the User environment. You can have several different 4D Chart areas of different sizes on one layout. Each 4D Chart area is a self-contained application and has its own menu bar, zoom box, close box, and keyboard equivalents.

A 4D Chart area graph can be saved as a separate Macintosh document, as a template to your hard disk, or within a field to a record in your database. You can also export graphs by saving them as PICT documents that can be opened by most graphics programs.

You can choose from many different types of graphs, including column, proportional-column, stacked-column, line, area, scatter, pie charts, scaled-picture, and stacked-picture graphs. You can change the scale of the graph, and use any picture from the Clipboard to customize a picture graph. You can change the pattern and color of graph elements simply by clicking on them.

4D Chart graphs can be printed as part of a layout in a report or as a separate document. You can also copy your graphs to the Clipboard and paste them into another document or into a picture field within your database.

The most important reason to use the 4D Chart module instead of the Graph Editor is to take advantage of the ability to completely control the 4D Chart area with the procedural language. 4D Chart contains over 100 commands that let you completely customize it within your database application. You can use the commands instead of manually using the Graph editor, to place information into a graph, create and save graphs, and change the appearance of a graph, such as its type, scale, color and pattern.

Using the 4D Chart module also lets you use the built-in hot links feature to share data with other modules. You can publish a picture of a graph for display in another module, for example within a 4D Write document. Any changes you make to the data are updated automatically in the other linked modules. Figure 20.8 shows a chart created with 4D Chart.

4D Chart will be available from ACI in 1994.

FIGURE 20.8

A chart created with 4D Chart

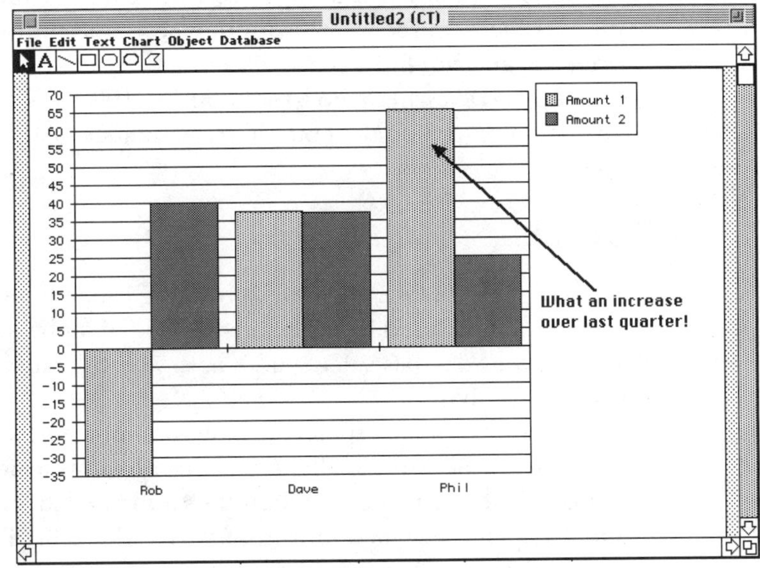

4D CAD

4D CAD adds integrated *computer aided design* (CAD) drawing capabilities to your database. Using 4D CAD you can create complex architectural drawings, technical illustrations, mechanical blueprints, and other complex design documents.

You can use 4D CAD as an external area on your input layout or as a separate independent window in the User environment. You can have several different 4D CAD areas of different sizes on one layout. Each 4D CAD area is a self-contained application and has its own menu bar, scroll bars, and keyboard equivalents.

A 4D CAD area can be saved as a separate Macintosh document, as a template to your hard disk, or within a field to a record in your database. Saving documents to a field in a record means that you can create a file full of records each with its own different document.

4D CAD contains all of the standard computer aided design program features along with some additional special features. It will include import and export capabilities, several different save formats, and like the other modules, the ability to reference fields from your database, associate objects to records in your database, and utilize the 4D procedural language and hot links between modules.

4D CAD is scheduled to ship during 1993. Contact ACI for more information regarding the complete capabilities of 4D CAD.

4D SPELL

The 4D Spell module adds spell-checking capabilities to your database. 4D Spell can be used to check the spelling of alpha and text fields or variables in your database. 4D Spell is a very useful data-entry validation tool for your database.

To set automatic spell checking for alpha and text fields or variables, check the Auto Spellcheck check box in the Field Definition or Object Definition dialog box. When the Auto Spellcheck feature is checked and 4D Spell is installed in your database, those fields or variables will be spell checked during data entry in the User or Runtime environments. If spelling errors occur, the 4D Spell window appears with suggestions for correction.

You can also use 4D Spell to check and correct your spelling in the Design environment, including text areas in your layouts and menu bars.

4D Spell is currently available in French, and the English language version is scheduled to ship during 1993. Contact ACI for more information regarding the availability and features of 4D Spell.

4D SQL SERVER

4D SQL Server lets you use a 4D database to receive and transfer information from a SYBASE SQL Server database on another computer platform. You can create a 4D database that acts as an intelligent client front end and use it with 4D SQL Server to access host data from a SYBASE SQL Server database. Together 4D and 4D SQL Server let you build complete custom client/server applications that allow users to manipulate host SYBASE data using a custom, user-friendly interface in 4D on their Macintosh. You can also use 4D SQL Server as a prototyping tool and a data management tool for SQL Server.

To use 4D and 4D SQL Server as a client front end, you create your 4D database and use 4D SQL Server's almost 100 commands and functions and access to the full range of DB-Library commands, which allows access to both high- and low-level calls. 4D SQL Server automatically handles many of the DB-Library commands and allows you to communicate with a SQL Server at initialization, login, to transmit commands, to execute commands, retrieve results, and logout.

4D SQL Server communicates with the other RDBMS using its own included set of over 50 additional commands which support SQL programming, additional included routines to move data between 4D and the server, and using a programming technique called *contexts* (or a group of binds). A bind is a link between two items or data objects, for example a field in the SQL database and a 4D field of the same type that contains the same information, like product name or product cost. 4D Data objects include fields, variables and arrays. Binding the two objects together allows for retrieval and transfer of data from one object to another. Contexts are simply a combination or set of bindings, grouped together to make it easier to control procedures like updating, inserting and deleting information in the database. 4D SQL Server lets you create contexts graphically, by selecting items from each database displayed in popup menus and scrolling lists, making it much easier to program and design your 4D database front end.

To reduce network traffic and optimize your server efficiency, the data you retrieve from the host can be integrated with your local 4D data, to perform data-entry validation, allow users to make ad hoc queries, and to generate reports using the Quick Report editor or custom report layouts. You can take advantage of 4D's built-in features, including full use of its Macintosh interface tools (this means you can supplement your host data with sound and video animation). When you connect to other servers, 4D SQL Server maintains the security and access privileges of the host system.

4D SQL Server can be used as a prototyping tool for testing database designs, as your data structure created in 4D can be duplicated onto SQL Server using the DB Clone file function.

Using 4D SQL Server as a data management tool you can control host server processes and the configuration of SYBASE SQL Server. You can also create and edit SQL Server stored procedures, rules, and triggers directly from within 4D using its Macintosh text editing tools, so you don't have to use a host-based text editor. SQL Server and DB-Library are Secure trademarks of SYBASE, Inc.

4D D.A.L

4D D.A.L lets you use a 4D database as an intelligent client front end to access information from one or multiple *Relational Database Management System* (RDBMS) servers on different computer platforms and networks. 4D D.A.L can communicate with any mainframe or minicomputer RDBMS that is supported by Apple Computer's Data Access Language (DAL), such as DB2, Informix, Ingres, Oracle, RDB, Sybase, Tandem Non-Stop SQL, and others. Together 4D and 4D D.A.L let you build complete custom client/server applications that maximize use of your Macintoshes, ensure the most efficient use of servers, and reduce network traffic.

You create the client or front end as a 4D database application on the Macintosh. The 4D D.A.L externals are installed in the structure file of the database, and a DAL driver is installed with the system software. The user then needs to use only this 4D application to interact with other host RDBMS servers. Using 4D with 4D D.A.L you can build a custom, user-friendly Macintosh interface for users to manipulate host data from many different databases. You can also use 4D D.A.L as a prototyping tool for RDBMS applications.

4D D.A.L communicates with the other RDBMS using its own included set of over 50 additional commands, which support SQL programming, additional included routines to move data between 4D and the server, and by using a programming technique called *contexts* (or a group of binds). A bind is a link between two items or data objects, for example a field in the RDBMS and a 4D field of the same type that contains the same information, like product name or product cost. 4D Data objects include fields, variables and arrays. Binding the two objects together allows for retrieval and transfer of data from one object to another. Contexts are simply a combination or set of bindings, grouped together to make it easier to control procedures like updating, inserting and deleting information in the database. 4D D.A.L lets you create contexts graphically by selecting items from each database displayed in popup menus and scrolling lists, making it much easier to design and program your 4D client database front end.

When you connect to other servers, 4D D.A.L maintains the security and access privileges of the host system. Host data retrieved through 4D D.A.L can be combined with local 4D data, to perform data-entry validation, allow users to make ad hoc searches or queries, and to generate reports using the Quick Report editor or with custom report layouts created in 4D. You can combine in a single 4D database the host data retrieved from multiple other RDBMS on different servers, and create comprehensive analysis and reports and perform other complex data manipulation. Once the host server data has been retrieved into 4D, it can also be used in any of the other modules, such as 4D Write, 4D Calc, 4D Draw, 4D CAD, and 4D Chart. Because the user interacts only with the 4D Client database, you can take advantage of the full use of its Macintosh interface tools including supplementing the retrieved host data with sound and video animation.

4D ORACLE

4D Oracle gives you complete access to data in an Oracle Server database that exists on any platform. There is no need for any additional software on either the client or server side to make the connection between Oracle Server and 4th Dimension. If you are familiar with Oracle, you will find the commands provided in 4D Oracle to be familiar.

Fields, variables and arrays can be bound to Oracle columns for transparent access to data. 4D Oracle also provides a graphic interface to allow the user to easily create SQL queries. These queries can be automatically turned into code that will allow you to generate the query procedurally. 4D Oracle also has a cloning function that allows you to create Oracle tables that match your 4D database files. The important 4D concept of a "current selection" is extended to 4D Oracle to allow the user to browse Oracle rows without having to load the data into 4D files.

4D Oracle and 4th Dimension make for a fast and easy connection between these two powerful database systems.

ALLOWING MULTIPLE USERS WITH THE 4D SERVER

21

MAC TRACKS MAC

4D Server is 669

The multi-user, client/server version of 4th Dimension.

4D Server is faster than file-sharing databases because 669

Most of the database operations are performed on the server machine instead of on each user's (the client) machine.

To set up your database with 4D Server 670

1. Install 4D Server on your server machine.
2. Copy your database on to the server machine.
3. Double-click on 4D Server to open it.
4. Open your database.
5. Install 4D Client on each user's machine.
6. Double-click on 4D Client and open your database.

TRACKS MAC TRACKS

Featuring

- *Multiple users*
- *Client/server technology*
- *4D Server vs. 4D*
- *Setting up 4D Server*
- *Hardware considerations*
- *Record locking*

WHEN YOU CREATE a database, you may initially intend to have only one user that accesses the database. At some point, it may become necessary to have multiple users accessing the database at the same time. There are two different ways you can handle this.

You could give a copy of the database to each user. The only problem with this is that each time you change the structure, layouts, procedures, menus, or the data itself, you have to give a new copy to each user. The more users you have, the more trouble this is going to be. Also, since each user is accessing a copy of the same database, any changes they make will be made only in their own personal copy and not in everyone else's copy.

A more elegant solution would be to have all of your users accessing the same structure file and the same data file simultaneously. As users made changes to the data, the other users would immediately see these changes because they would all be using the same data file. Also, if you as the designer made changes to the structure, you would have to replace only the one structure file that all of your users are accessing instead of replacing one on each user's machine. This is where 4D Server comes in.

What Is the 4D Server?

4D Server is the multi-user, client/server version of 4th Dimension. Using 4D Server you can have all of your users access your database at the same time. You can create your database with 4th Dimension and when you are ready to have multiple users access the database, you purchase 4D Server.

Many other multi-user databases use file-sharing technology to allow multiple users. This means that the database resides on a machine that all users can access through your network. Anytime a user wants to work with the database, the data she wants to use is transferred from the file server to her local machine. For example, when a user searches an indexed field, the index table is copied from the file server over the network to the user's machine where the search is then performed. Once the user's machine has figured out which records were found, it then might go back to the file server to get those records to display them on the screen. With file-sharing, multi-user databases, the file server is nothing more than a central storage place for the database. The file server machine itself is doing very little. Also, because all of the database manipulation is done from the user's machine, there is a tremendous amount of network traffic created by all of the data being transferred between the file server and the users machine. Most file-sharing databases perform marginally well with a few users. However, as soon as the number of users increases, file sharing databases become sluggish.

4D Server uses *client/server* technology. This means that instead of just having a file server that stores the data, there is an application running on the file server that carries most of the database access burden. For example, when a user performs a search, the search criteria (which is quite small) is sent across the network to the 4D Server application running on the file server machine. 4D Server performs the search and reports back how many records were found to the client (the user's machine). The index table doesn't have to be copied over to the client because the search is performed on the file server not on the client. Also, since the file server machine is doing the search, the speed of the search is at the speed of the file server machine. For example, if the user was using a Macintosh Classic and 4D Server was running on a Quadra 800, the speed of the search would be at the speed of the Quadra not the speed of the Classic.

When the user displays an output layout, the client software sends a list of the fields displayed on the layout as well as fields used in scripts to the 4D Server. The 4D Server then determines how many records can be displayed and sends back only the data that will fit on the screen. In file sharing databases, there is no server application helping out so the entire record has to be transferred back to the client in order to display anything. Also, because there is an application running on the file server controlling the database, commonly accessed layouts, procedures, and records are stored in memory on the file server for faster access. In a client/server database, there are two applications sharing the workload. This means less network traffic, faster access to data, and much better overall performance, because there are two computers doing the work where there was really only one before.

HOW IS THE 4D SERVER DIFFERENT FROM 4D?

4th Dimension and 4D Server both use the same file format and have practically the same features. You have complete compatibility between the two products. The difference is in the way they handle your database. This means that you can create a database with 4th Dimension and then use it with 4D Server when you are ready to have multiple users access the database. 4D Server gives you access to the Design, User, and Runtime environments. This means that you can have multiple designers all working on the structure at the same time. As a matter of fact, your designers can even be working on the structure while other users use the database! Because 4D Server gives you access to the User environment, you can create a database in the Design environment and in no time have it available to your users in the full-featured User environment. With 4D Server, you can have a multi-user, client-server database up and running in less than a day.

HOW DO I SET UP 4D SERVER?

4D Server is actually two applications, 4D Server and 4D Client. 4D Server is the application that runs on the file server machine and handles most of the searching, sorting, and other database activities. The Client application runs on each user's machine and handles displaying layouts, executing code, and communicating searches and sorts to the 4D Server for execution.

To use 4D Server, you need to have a network connecting your computers. LocalTalk (the network that comes built-in to every Macintosh) can be connected between several computers in a few minutes.

Setting up 4D Server is easy. The 4D Server as well as your database are installed on to the file server. The 4D Server software has a main window that displays information about the database is it serving as well as information about each user that is connected to the database. Figure 21.1 shows the 4D Server window.

FIGURE 21.1

4D Server's window

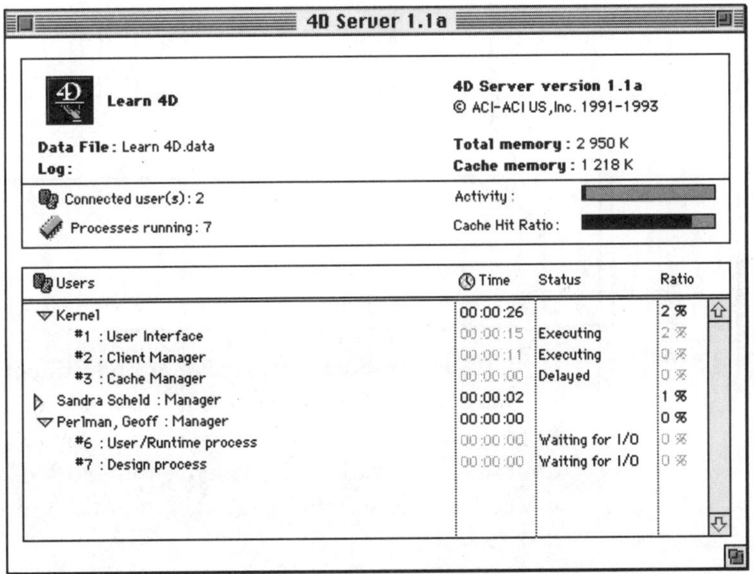

The Client software is installed on each user's machine that will need access to the database. Once this is done, you simply double-click on the 4D Server to launch it and open your database. This makes the database available to all users that have 4D Client installed. Now that the database is up and running with 4D Server, your users simply double-click on 4D Client and select the 4D Server database they wish to access.

Figure 21.2 shows the window that the user uses to select a database to connect to. That is all there is to it! You can set up 4D Server in a matter of minutes. It has to be hands down the easiest client/server database application to install and begin using.

FIGURE 21.2

4D Client connecting to a 4D Server database

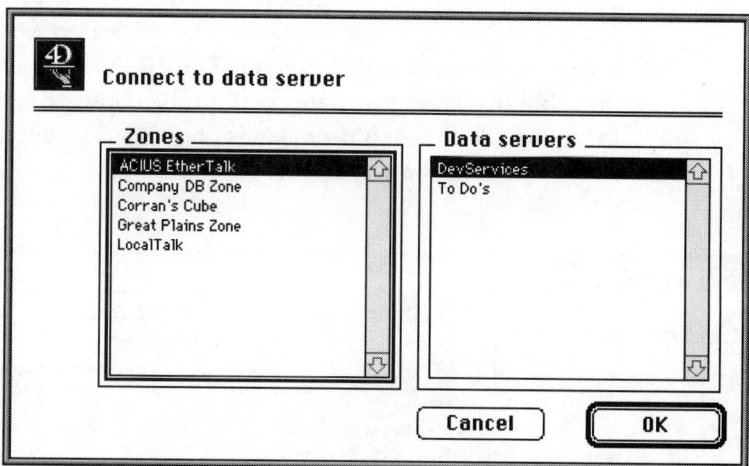

4D Server does not require any additional networking software to run. This means that you don't have to purchase AppleShare or even use the file sharing capabilities that are built-in to System 7. This also gives you added security since the user can access the database but not the file server hard disk itself.

WHAT CONSIDERATIONS SHOULD I MAKE WHEN SWITCHING TO 4D SERVER?

There are two areas to consider when making the switch from single user to multi-user: hardware and database design. Both of these areas are going to impact the performance of your database. The database design however, also impacts the functionality of your database. Each of these areas are important in the overall success of your multi-user database.

HARDWARE CONSIDERATIONS

There are three parts that factor into the performance of the database in terms of hardware. These three parts are the client machine, the network, and the server machine.

The *client machine* is responsible for executing code and redrawing the screen. The faster the client machine is, the faster code will execute and the faster any results coming back from the server can be displayed. The amount of memory allocated to 4D Client on each user's machine also impacts performance. The more memory available to 4D Client, the more layouts, procedures, and other structure-related data can be kept in memory on the client. By keeping layouts and procedures in memory, the 4D Client avoids having to reload frequently used layouts and procedures across the network. What kind of computer will perform well as a client machine? This is not an easy question to answer. Performance is a word that is quite relative. What is fast to one person may be slow to another. The best way to judge is to see 4D Server in action and decide for yourself if the machines being used as clients are performing at an acceptable speed.

The *network* is responsible for transferring data between the 4D Client software and the 4D Server software. Records, layouts, procedures, menus, and other data are transferred between 4D Client and 4D Server as the users access the database. In the past, the type of network in use greatly impacted the performance of the database. This is much less true today. You may find that LocalTalk (the network built-in to every Macintosh) gives you the performance you need. As the amount of data being transferred over the network increases, you may need to switch to a faster network like Ethernet. The data transfer increases as the records in your database get larger (by adding more fields) and as you add more users that use the network to access the database. If you haven't installed a network yet, you might want to start with LocalTalk and see if you can get the performance you want from this built-in and inexpensive solution. If you need more performance, you can install an Ethernet network which is about five times faster than LocalTalk. Keep in mind however, that Ethernet will not make searching and sorting any faster. Most of your searches and sorts are executed by 4D Server on your file server machine. What Ethernet will increase is the speed at which the data is transferred between 4D Client and 4D Server.

Ethernet is about five times faster than LocalTalk. Think of LocalTalk as a road with one lane in each direction. Compared to LocalTalk, Ethernet is like having a multi-lane freeway running in both directions. Most of Apple Computer's mid- to high-range Macintoshes now come with Ethernet built-in. This means that the expense of switching to an Ethernet network is much more reasonable than it was in the past.

The *server machine* that will run 4D Server and your database is the single most important piece of hardware in terms of performance. Because the server machine handles all searching, sorting, saving of records, and database access, the speed of the server machine is critical to the performance of the database. When you are deciding how much money to spend on a server machine or which of your existing machines to use as a server, get the fastest machine you can afford. The amount of memory installed on the server is also a factor. As users access records, layouts, procedures, etc., 4D Server loads this data from the hard disk into memory. It does this because access to memory is significantly faster than access to a hard disk. Once the data is in memory on the server, 4D Server can access the data in memory instead of having to reload it constantly from the hard disk. The more memory you have installed on the server and available to the 4D Server application, the more of your database 4D Server will hold in memory and the hence the faster the access to that data will be. The 4D Server software shows a thermometer that displays the Cache/Hit Ratio. This ratio shows how often 4D Server gets the data it needs from memory versus the hard disk. Once your database has been running for awhile, the Cache/Hit Ratio will tell you if you need more memory or not. If the thermometer shows mostly full, you have plenty of memory. If the thermometer is showing under 50 percent, you might want to consider adding more memory. The amount of memory you have allocated to 4D Server may not be enough to hold everything being accessed in memory and 4D Server may be removing data from memory to make room for recently requested data. The hard disk connected to the server machine also impacts performance. When 4D Server goes to the hard disk to get some data, it has to wait for the disk to deliver the data before it can continue. The faster the hard disk, the faster it can respond to requests from 4D Server and the faster 4D Server can get back to handling the next request made to it. Also remember that typically, the more users you have, the more data you have. This means that you may need a hard disk with much greater capacity than the one you are using now. If you are unsure how much room you will need, purchase the biggest one you can afford. It is always better to have too much room instead of too little.

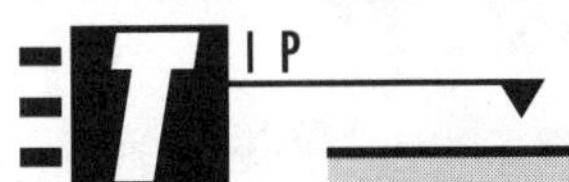

The performance of any particular machine is often misjudged by the processor's clock speed. For example, a Macintosh IIci has a clock speed of 25 MHz. The Macintosh Centris 610 is also 25 MHz but runs at about twice of the speed of a Macintosh IIci. When deciding on a server, find out how fast the machine you are considering is, relative to other machines.

DATABASE DESIGN CONSIDERATIONS

When you use your database in *single-user* mode, only one user is accessing the records at any given time (hence the term). However, when you use 4D Server, several users can access the records in your database simultaneously. When one user is modifying a record, 4D Server locks that record to other users. This prevents other users from attempting to modify the record while someone is editing it. While the record is locked, others cannot edit the record but they can view it. When the user that is modifying the record saves or cancels the record, 4D Server unlocks the record, making it available again for editing by other users. In most cases, when a user accesses a record that is locked, 4D will inform the user that the record is being edited and by whom. Figure 21.3 shows the dialog that is displayed when a users accesses a locked record.

FIGURE 21.3

The locked record dialog box

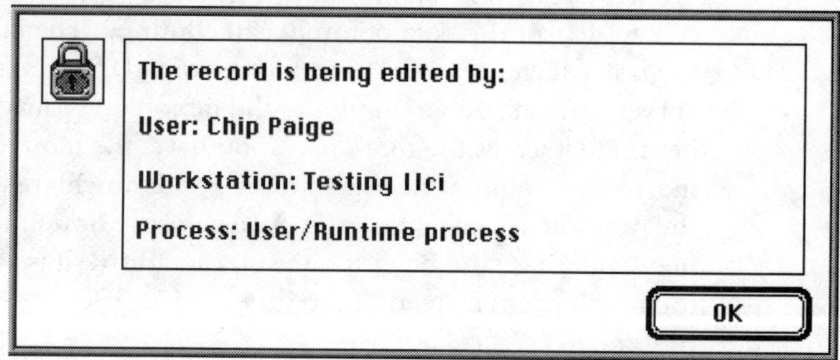

Record locking is a database behavior you may not have had to deal with in the past. For the most part, 4D will handle record locking and informing the user for you. You may run into situations where you need to check to see if a record is locked before you attempt to modify it. This is especially true when you are executing procedures that you have written that modify several records one after another. What's important at this stage is to remember that record locking does occur and you may have to plan for it when writing procedures and deciding how your users will access your records.

The way your database is designed can greatly impact the performance of the database. For example, you already know that searching and sorting on indexed fields is generally much faster than the same operations performed on non-indexed fields. This does not mean however, that you should index every field. The more fields you have indexed, the longer it will take 4D Server to save the record because all of the index tables have to be updated as well as the record itself. The size of your records will also impact performance. While the size of a record does not usually affect the speed of a search or sort, it will affect how quickly records are transferred from the server to the client. Try not to add any fields that aren't really necessary. Also remember that subfiles, picture fields, and text fields can hold a tremendous amount of data and consequently make records quite large. Use these field types sparingly. Because all code is executed by 4D Client, you will want to avoid formula-based operations like Search by Formula, Apply Formula, and using formulas when sorting. The reason for this is that the formulas you create are themselves code. This means that they will execute on the client machine, and consequently, the operation is handled by 4D Client instead of 4D Server. Formula-based operations cause each record they access to be loaded across the network to the client machine to allow the formula to be used on them. This can cause a lot of network traffic and produce slower performance.

Printing to networked printers can cause quite a bit of network traffic. For example, if the user prints a report to a laser printer on the network, the data has to travel from the 4D Server to the 4D Client then back out over the network to the printer. If you have several users printing to different network printers all at the same time, you may see a performance lag. You may want to consider installing a non-networked printer at each station that will need to print often to avoid network traffic.

There are many other factors that can affect network and overall database performance. Access to file servers, network modems, and electronic mail all can create tremendous amounts of network traffic. These types of network activities should be considered when looking for ways to decrease network traffic and thus increase performance.

The best thing you can do is test out your database with your computers and your network. I have given you some tips on what to do and what not to do to get the best performance out of your database. However, every situation is unique and you will need to test out your database with your equipment and network to determine if the performance is acceptable or not. Generally speaking I think you will find the performance of 4D Server to be more than acceptable. In many cases you may find that as you add more users, you will not notice any difference in the performance of the database. Switching from a single-user database to a multi-user just doesn't get any easier than it is with 4D Server.

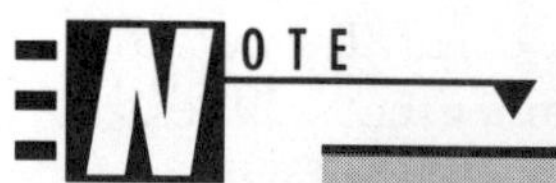

There is a new feature in version 1.1 of 4D Server that increases its performance significantly. As users access file structures, layouts, procedures, and menus these items are transmitted across the network to the user's computer. In version 1.1 (and greater) these items are stored in a file in the Preferences folder which resides in the system folder so that they don't have to be retransmitted over the network the next time the user accesses them. If the item accessed has changed, 4D Server will automatically retransmit the changed version. This reduces network traffic and can significantly improve the display and use of large file structures, complex layouts, and long procedures. The file that stores this structure information in the Preferences folder has the same name as your database, with .rex as its extension. For example, your Learn 4D database would have a file called Learn 4D.rex in each user's Preferences folder. You can create the .rex file manually by placing a copy of the structure file in your Preferences folder and renaming it *database.rex* (Learn 4D.rex, for example).

4D APPLESCRIPT

AppleScript is a language developed by Apple Computer to allow end users to have more control over the information stored on their computers. The language is very simple (similar to Hypercard's Hypertalk language) and provides the user with the ability to generically communicate with any application that supports AppleScript. For example, you might want to create a script that checks to see whether a 4D Server database is running and if so, search for certain records and copy information from those records to the clipboard. In order for an application to respond to an AppleScript request, it must be expecting to receive them. 4D Server 1.1 supports AppleScript through an application called 4D AppleScript.

In order to use AppleScript to access data in a 4D Server database, you must have the AppleScript extension installed in your System Folder, a script editor of some kind (Apple Computer sells one), and the 4D AppleScript application running on your machine. 4D AppleScript acts as a translator between 4D and AppleScript (hence the name). When you send an AppleScript message to 4D AppleScript, it contacts the database you are referring to and translates your requests into something that 4D Server understands directly. The example script below checks to see whether a database called "Learn 4D" is running and informs the user of the answer.

```
tell application "4D AppleScript"
   copy (exists database {location:"Learn 4D",
protocol:ADSP}) to isRunning
   if (isRunning) then
      Display Dialog ("Yes, the database is running.")
   else
      Display Dialog ("No, the database is not running.")
   end if
end tell
```

There are many uses for AppleScript. For example, you could use AppleScript to locate certain records in one 4D Server database and then copy them to another 4D Server database. In an effort to make the scripts you write more re-usable, AppleScript uses a generic set of terms called the AppleScript database suite for databases. For example, Records are referred to as rows, all of the values in a field for a selected group of records are referred to collectively as a column, database files are referred to as tables, and a field value for a single record is referred to as a cell.

4D AppleScript is provided free with 4D Server 1.1. Contact ACI or your local distributor for more information.

4D OPEN

You can of course access a 4D Server database using 4D Client. However, there may be times when you would like to access the records in a 4D Server database from another application. You can do this using 4D Open.

4D Open is a set of procedures (libraries) that allow you to write code in C or Pascal that can connect to a 4D Server database. This means you can write applications that act as a front-end to a 4D Server database or write extensions for existing applications (such as Quark Xpress or Canvas) that can access data in your 4D Server database directly. When you connect to 4D Server using 4D Open, you simply appear as another client. 4D Open allows you to perform almost all of the database operations that you can perform with 4D Client such as creating new records, searching, sorting, modifying, and deleting. The 4D Open libraries for C and Pascal will initially be available for the Macintosh only. However, ACI plans to release 4D Open for 4D (as a set of externals), 4D Open for Windows (C/C++), and 4D Open for Microsoft's Visual Basic (also running under Windows). Once 4D Open for Windows and Visual Basic is available, you will be able to create a windows front-end to your 4D Server databases. Contact ACI for more information.

4D REMOTE ACCESS

AppleTalk Remote Access from Apple Computer allows a user to connect to an AppleTalk network through a modem. Once connected, you can then access 4D Server Remote databases on the network using 4D Client running locally on your computer. Because AppleTalk Remote Access also allows the user to perform other functions (like connect to electronic mail or access AppleShare file servers) it carries with it extra overhead that is not needed to access a 4D Server Remote database.

4D Remote Access installs into 4D Client and allows the user to access a 4D Server database on a remote network through a modem without using AppleTalk Remote Access. Because 4D Remote Access only allows access to 4D Server Remote databases, the overhead is removed and significantly better performance is achieved. 4D Remote Access will be available in 1994. Contact ACI for more information.

DATABASE MAINTENANCE

MAC TRACKS MAC

TRACKS **MAC** TRACKS

Featuring

- *Making backups*
- *Storing backups*
- *4D Backup*
- *Log files*
- *Mirroring*
- *Using 4D Tools*

A DATABASE APPLICATION, LIKE a car, has many different parts to it. And like a car, a database needs a certain amount of maintenance. As a matter of fact, the part of a database that handles searching, sorting, creating records, and other record-related activities is called the "database engine." This engine, unlike a car, is not the part of your database that needs maintenance. The part of your database that needs maintenance is the data itself. The purpose of database maintenance is to keep your data as secure and healthy as possible to minimize data loss and down time if and when it occurs.

WHAT KIND OF MAINTENANCE DO I HAVE TO DO?

Keeping your 4th Dimension database in top shape requires two types of regular maintenance, making copies of your active database structure and data files and compacting your database. The third kind of maintenance task you will rarely perform is repairing a damaged database file.

MAKING BACKUPS OF YOUR DATA OR BACKING UP YOUR DATABASE

In computer terminology, "backing up" is the process of making a duplicate copy of your active work files, to use in case of an emergency, such as data corruption or data loss. The process of returning your database to a prior, undamaged condition is called "restoring" your data. Remember that your backup is only as good as your ability to easily and completely restore that backup, that is, in keeping your database in working condition on your computer.

There are several very good reasons to back up your database on a planned, regular basis. Computers are mechanical devices, and so sometimes, albeit rarely, they can suffer mechanical failures. Power failures and other problems can also corrupt or damage data, and cause you to lose data from your database files. Human error is another cause of damaged or lost data, due to incorrect usage of the computer or database itself. Accidental deletion of important records or even removal of entire files from the hard disk and other such events can leave you in a situation where you need to restore your database to a prior, usable condition. In addition, in case of accident, fire, or theft of your computer hard drive, you will want to have a recent copy of your valuable data stored away safely, so you can begin working again.

Backing up your data is not difficult, and it has been made even easier in recent years with advances in hardware and software technology that automate most of the backup process for you. The first decision to make is how often you need to back up your data. My dentist has a poster on his office wall that reads, "Only floss the ones you want to keep!" This same advice applies to data backups—only back up the data you want to keep! If you only modify the data in your database once a week, then a weekly backup would be sufficient. If your database is in heavy use each day, like adding, changing, and deleting many records, you will want to perform a daily backup. Another rule of thumb is to "backup as much as you can afford to lose." If you can't afford to lose a week's worth of work, then back up every two days or daily. One easy way to perform a daily backup is to create five or seven (depending on your office usage) backup tapes or disk cartridges, labeled for each day of the week. At the close of business on Monday, you use the Monday tape or disks, on Tuesday, use the Tuesday tapes or disks, etc.

Most people don't keep backups until their hard disks crash and they lose everything at least once. This kind of trial by fire is not the best way to learn the importance of a good backup system. Backing up your database, simply put, is disaster insurance.

It is also a good idea to create an extra backup that is stored off-site, or away from your office at an employee's home, or in a bank safety deposit box, or whatever is most convenient. If you are going to store your only backups at the office, be sure to obtain a fireproof safe designed specifically for magnetic media, as regular safes are designed to protect paper, which burns at a much higher temperature than computer media. Storing backups off-site as well as in a magnetic media fireproof safe together are the recommended backup configuration for any important business database. Again, if you keep backups off-site, be sure that the backups are recent ones or they won't be as useful to you if you need them.

After you have decided how often you need to back up, and what additional copies are needed for your off-site and safe storage backups, you need to decide what backup method to use. This is a personal choice, dependent upon how much you want to spend and the speed and ease of both backing up and restoring your data. There are several methods available, which require additional computer hardware. The old method of backing up by copying the data file onto a floppy disk probably won't work, as most data files will be too large to fit onto a floppy disk; besides, swapping floppy disks in and out of your computer disk drive is a very slow backup method! The preferred methods use either magnetic tape, a removable hard drive cartridge, or an optical drive cartridge.

The most convenient way to backup your database is to use the 4D module, 4D Backup. For more information, see *Using 4D Backup* below.

Whichever method you use, the important thing to remember is to backup your data often! It is also important to back up your structure file before performing any operations on it, such as adding or removing 4D modules or externals, using Customizer Plus, ResEdit, or 4D Mover with it, compiling your database, or compacting your database. All of the above operations access the structure file and leave it vulnerable to the vagaries of unforeseen power failures, computer crashes or user error. You'll work easier knowing that you're modifying a copy of your database and if any problems occur, your original is safe and still usable!

USING 4D BACKUP

4D Backup is a module you can buy that is designed not only to make the backup process easier but to also to make the disaster recovery process as complete as possible. 4D Backup consists of two parts. The first part is a module that installs into your database. This module allows you to procedurally perform complete as well as incremental backups. 4D Backup includes over 30 commands that allow you to automate any part of the backup or recovery process. The second part of 4D Backup is a stand-alone application that allows the user to choose from the many different backup and recovery options. Figure 22.1 shows the 4D Backup main window.

FIGURE 22.1

The 4D Backup main window

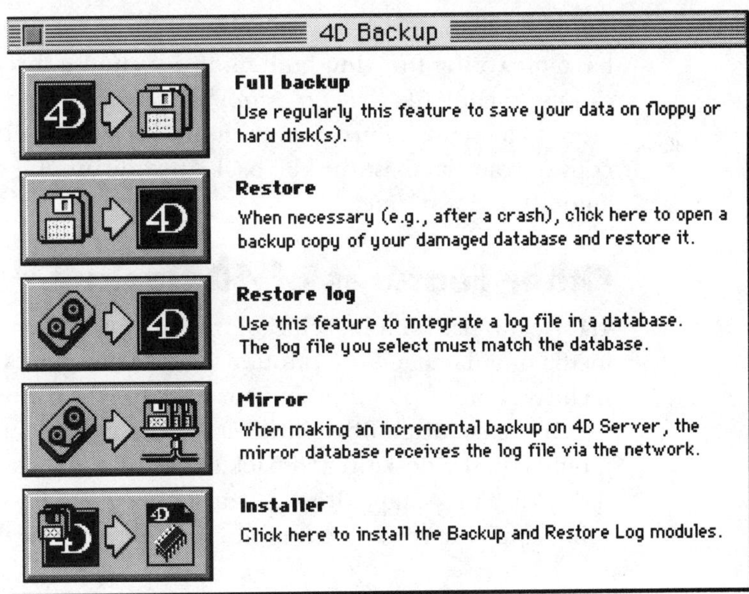

4D Backup
Full backup
Use regularly this feature to save your data on floppy or hard disk(s).
Restore
When necessary (e.g., after a crash), click here to open a backup copy of your damaged database and restore it.
Restore log
Use this feature to integrate a log file in a database. The log file you select must match the database.
Mirror
When making an incremental backup on 4D Server, the mirror database receives the log file via the network.
Installer
Click here to install the Backup and Restore Log modules.

The Log File

One of the options of 4D Backup is to have it create and maintain a log file. The log file keeps track of every addition, edit, or deletion that occurs in the database. Should you experience a mechanical failure or damaged database, you can restore your last complete backup, then have 4D Backup rebuild the datafile by recreating each action stored in the log file. Because the log file contains the date, time, and user information for each action, you can also use the log file to recover from a user error. For example, say a user accidentally deleted a large number of records. You can restore your last complete backup and then use 4D Backup to recreate all edits from the log file up to the point where the user deleted the records.

The log file is not designed to be a replacement for a backup. Rather it is designed to be used with a complete backup. For example, you could make a complete backup every three days and use a log file to keep track of changes to the database in-between your complete backups. You can even create sets of backups automatically that 4D Backup will cycle through when creating full backups.

Mirroring Your Database

The term *mirroring* means to have an exact copy of your data. 4D Backup has a mirroring function built-in. If you choose this option, 4D Backup can use the log file to keep a copy of your datafile up to date. In the event of a media failure, you can quickly switch over to the mirrored copy of your database and be back up and running with a minimum amount of down-time.

Other Features of 4D Backup

4D Backup has built-in, self-repairing features that can be used if bad media or a damaged file is found. This feature gives you an extra layer of security should you find that your backup is also damaged.

For maximum flexibility, 4D Backup can use any volume that mounts on the desktop as a backup destination. This means that floppy disks, hard disks, tape drives, even volumes that have been mounted using AppleShare can be used for backing up your database.

COMPACTING YOUR DATABASE

As you work with your database, it develops holes or spaces where data no longer exists or doesn't fit in the same amount of space that it used to. 4th Dimension will reuse some holes if it can find something that fits in that same space, but it may not be able or have information to fill them all. Holes are created when you design your database and modify or delete layouts and procedures; and they are also created in your data file when you modify and delete records. Compacting is the process of removing the holes in the structure file and the data file.

There are two advantages to compacting your database. Removing the holes causes the database to shrink in size, so it takes up less room on your hard disk. For example, it is important to compact your database after you have deleted many records, as 4D will not reuse the disk space until the database is compacted. It also makes the database more efficient and in some cases, it will work faster. You should compact your database just after you have deleted a large amount of records, and otherwise at least weekly or monthly, depending on the amount of usage. It is also a good idea to compact your database before compiling it.

You compact your database using a special utility called *4D Tools* that came with your copy of 4th Dimension. Here are some steps to take when compacting a database:

1. Make a copy of your database structure and data file before compacting.
2. 4D Tools makes a duplicate of your database structure and data files. Be sure you have enough room on your hard disk for these duplicates.
3. Launch 4D Tools by double-clicking its icon.
4. Select the database to compact from the standard Open File dialog box and click Open. If you are using the password system, only the Designer or Administrator will be able to open the database.

5. Choose Utilities ➤ Compact.
6. Enter a name for the new, compacted database and click Save. 4D Tools will create a new copy and compact your database structure and data file.

When done, 4D Tools will automatically quit back to the Finder. That's all there is to it. You can immediately begin using the compacted copy of your database.

REPAIRING DAMAGED DATABASE FILES

A database can be damaged if there is a mechanical or power failure at a critical moment. For example, when 4th Dimension is saving records to disk or performing other disk intensive activities, a power failure or mechanical failure can cause the wrong data to be written to the wrong place on the disk or even be erased. If the hard disk where the database is stored becomes damaged, this could also affect your database. If your database is damaged, when you attempt to launch it, you will get an error message that says, "Unable to open database. Database has been damaged." If this occurs, you have two choices. If you have an undamaged, usable backup, delete the damaged database and restore the clean backup. This method is almost always preferable. If you don't have a backup, or it is not as recent as you'd like, you can run 4D Tools and attempt to repair the damaged database. Here are some steps to take should your database ever become damaged:

1. Make a copy of your "damaged" database structure and data file before attempting repair your database. Be sure you don't copy over the last undamaged backup when you do this!
2. 4D Tools makes a duplicate of your database data files during the Recover by Tags process. Be sure you have enough room on your hard disk for the duplicate data file.
3. Launch 4D Tools by double-clicking its icon.

4. Select the database to repair from the standard Open File dialog box, and click Open. Remember, if you are using the password system, only the Designer or Administrator can open the database with 4D Tools.
5. Choose Utilities ➤ Check & Recover.
6. Select the first radio button option, "Check Only and Create a Log," and click **OK**. 4D Tools will now analyze the database for damage, and create a text file "Journal" detailing any damage found. Your database won't be changed using this option.
7. Restart 4D Tools and open the damaged database again.
8. Select the second radio button option, "Check and fix damaged record or indexes," and click **OK**. This time 4D Tools will attempt to repair any damaged records or indexes. Another Journal text file will be created. Review the Journal file after 4D Tools has completed this task, to determine what damage was corrected.
9. If the Journal file reports that the database is still damaged or recommends "Recover by Tags," restart 4D Tools again, and reopen the damaged database.
10. Select the third option, "Recover by tags duplicating the data file (takes time)," and click **OK**. 4D Tools will now attempt to fix the data file by looking for records by their tags or markers that are stored with a record when it is created. It will create a new data file called *database.temp*, and this data file may contain records that were previously deleted. The Recover by tags option should be used only as a last resort if the second option fails to recover the data file.
11. If either option 2 or 3 appeared to be successful, restart the database in single user mode and review the data, to confirm the database's usability. If any other problems occur during this testing phase, your best bet is to completely delete the damaged structure and data file and restore your most recent backup copies. A second pass of repair using 4D Tools will not help.

Remember, 4D Tools is meant as a last resort when you find that all redundant backups systems have failed (or don't exist at all).

SORTING FILES IN YOUR DATABASE

You can use 4D Tools to permanently sort all the records in a file. This is similar to the Sort File command that was available in version 2. This kind of permanent sorting is used mainly for files with static data, because new records added to a sorted file are not inserted in the sort order. Here are the steps to take to sort your database:

1. Make a copy of your database structure and data file before sorting any files.
2. Launch 4D Tools by double-clicking its icon.
3. Select the database to sort files in from the standard Open File dialog box and click Open.
4. Choose Utilities ➤ Sort.
5. Select the File to sort and click **OK**.
6. The 4D Sort editor will be displayed. Select the file and fields and sort direction, just as you normally would using the Sort editor. Sorts using formulas are not allowed.
7. Click **Sort**. During this process, 4th Dimension will sort the file, rebuild all the indexes for that file, and save the records in the new sorted order. Remember that for large databases, rebuilding the indexes can be a time consuming job.

When you repair your database using the Recover by Tags method, previously deleted records may reappear. To insure that this does not happen, click in the Completely Delete check box in the File Attributes dialog box. With this option selected, deletion of records will take longer but will also insure that deleted records cannot reappear in repaired databases.

4D DEVELOPMENT UTILITIES

THIS CHAPTER LISTS some of the development utilities available for 4th Dimension. New utilities are being developed all the time, though, so keep in touch with ACI to stay abreast of them.

4D CUSTOMIZER PLUS

4D Customizer Plus can be used to customize the resources within your 4th Dimension applications, databases and related files, and modules. Customizer Plus can be used to customize 4th Dimension, 4D Client, 4D Server, 4D Structure files, 4D data files, Proc.Ext files, 4D Compiler, 4D Insider, and the 4D Write and 4D Draw modules. You can even customize Customizer Plus itself using ResEdit, a resource utility.

CUSTOMIZING 4TH DIMENSION AND 4D CLIENT

You can customize ten different resources in your 4th Dimension application or 4D CLIENT application:

Keys	Change the default keyboard equivalents for saving a record, canceling a record and adding a record to an included layout.
Windows	Change the size and position of the User and Runtime environment main window, such as full screen with title or without title, constant size, etc. This is also used to hide the splash screen in the Runtime environment.
Preferences	Set the preferences for the spinning beach ball, for printing, and for the 4D stack size.
Translation	Select the language for 4D commands and functions and for localization.
Fonts	Change the default fonts for the structure window, procedure editor, messages created using MESSAGE command, and laser printer font for printed procedures.
Scripts	Define Script Manager functions, including procedure editor styles, print method, Zero ASCII code, character following zero, menu font, menu item font, comparison mode, TRIC resources and date calculation method, all used when localizing your database for use with non-Roman languages.
Buttons	Change the default buttons that are used in the Layout Editors sample input layout Template #7.
Procedures	Change the default color settings assigned to the items in the Procedure Listing editor, such as fields, files, process variables, procedures, etc.

Memory	Set several memory usage parameters, such as cache memory, kernel memory, minimum flushed, and number of data cache blocks per cache pointers, as well as memory range parameters for different memory settings.
Stacks	Set the default stack size for standard 4D processes, including on event call, on serial port call, user generated processes, menu generated processes, client tasks on the Server, backup and restore.

CUSTOMIZING 4D SERVER

You can customize four different resources in your copy of 4D Server: Preferences, Script Manager, Memory, and Stacks. Customizing these resources is the same as customizing them as described above in the *Customizing 4th Dimension and 4D Client.*

CUSTOMIZING 4D STRUCTURE FILES

You can customize any 4D structure files, uncompiled or compiled, or those compiled and merged with 4D Runtime. You can customize Keys, Windows, Preferences, the WEDD resource and the Compatibility resource for a structure file. Because the Keys, Window, and Preferences resources have been described above in the section *Customizing 4th Dimension and 4D Client,* we will only explain the other two here:

WEDD Resource	Locks a data file to a particular structure file. Used to prevent the use of incompatible or old structure or data files.

Compatibility Resource	Used to control compatibility of certain routines, such as on event call, on serial port call, mono-transactions, semaphores, automatic flush after transaction, and activated/deactivated call, between databases created in version 2.0 and version 3.0 of 4th Dimension.

CUSTOMIZING DATA FILES

You can customize your data files by including a WEDD resource. (See *Customizing 4D Structure Files* above.) Unless you use Customizer Plus to add a WEDD resource, there is no WEDD resource and no locking present in either the structure or data file of your database.

CUSTOMIZING PROC.EXT FILES

You can customize a Proc.Ext file by adding an Update resource, which controls the updating of modules between 4D Server and 4D Client. When modules are installed or removed using the installer into a Proc.Ext on the server (when it is not running), the "4D4D" resource counter is updated, which reflects the change. When the Client next connects to the server, if the client's and server's counters are different, the module from the server is updated or copied to the Client. If the module resources are changed without using the installer, the counter must be incremented manually using the Update resource to enter the new counter value in the Update signature box.

CUSTOMIZING 4D WRITE

You can customize your master copy of 4D Write Installer, a copy of 4D Write installed in a structure file, or one installed in a Proc.Ext file. You can customize the 4D Write Separators resource and the 4D Write Preferences resource.

Customizing the Separators resource lets you define both line-break and word-break characters. A line-break is *at* which character a line will break and wrap to the next line. A word-break character is a character that will not be selected when you double-click on a word.

You can use the Preferences resource to select the minimum height and width of a 4D Write area, to hide or display the font alert about converting fonts in a document to available fonts, and whether or not to use the predefined keyboard shortcuts with your newly created style sheets. The Preferences resource also allows you to control the default left and right margins as well as the default indentation.

CUSTOMIZING 4D DRAW

You can use Customizer Plus to customize the Preferences resource in 4D Draw. The Preferences resource lets you set the keys used for horizontal and vertical locking constraints of drawn objects; select if PICT graphics are pasted as one or a collection of separate objects; change the behavior of the selection rectangle; remove the automatic snap-to-grid alignment; prevent the Save dialog from appearing; display a partial 4D Draw area without tool palette, menu bar, or scroll bars; and change the suffix attached to 4D Draw documents in external windows.

CUSTOMIZING 4D COMPILER

You can customize the Translation and File Creator resources for the 4D Compiler. You can store these resources in either the 4D Compiler application or within the 4D Compiler Preferences file, located in your System folder. Resources stored in the Preferences file will be kept when you install new versions of the compiler, otherwise you will have to reselect your preferences for these resources.

The Translation resource lets you set the language for the error type, 4D commands and functions that are in the compiler error messages and error file.

The File Creator resource lets you specify which text editor application to use to open the Error file, Symbol table file, and Typing file created by the compiler.

CUSTOMIZING 4D INSIDER

You can customize the Translation resource in 4D Insider. The translation resource lets you select the language in which all the 4D commands appear when using 4D Insider.

CUSTOMIZING CUSTOMIZER PLUS

Customizer Plus can be modified so that resource icons can be hidden from users so they can use Customizer Plus but not change those hidden resources. You can also install your own button control panel as the default button panel for input layout Template #7. You must use ResEdit to customize Customizer Plus in both these cases.

4D EXTERNAL MOVER PLUS

External Mover Plus is a utility that lets you move external procedures from one database structure or Proc.Ext file to another, without having to use a resource mover like ResEdit.

You can copy all types of externals from one file to another; create new Proc.Ext files; delete externals from files; display and change information about external procedures, packages and hooks; add, modify, and delete parameters and set the type of the value returned by a function, for externals and external packages; and generate reports on the contents of external files. External Mover Plus can be used with all the external types that work with 4th Dimension, including procedures, packages, drivers, hooks, tasks, and compressions.

4D INSIDER

4D Insider is a cross-referencing utility for your databases. You can use 4D Insider both to help you design your database and to document your finished database. Using 4D Insider, you can view your procedures, variables, structures, externals, lists, and layouts from your database in their own separate window. The cross-referencing information, which shows where each of these objects is used in your database as well as which objects they use, can be printed showing none, some, or all of the elements for that object item, and can be output to an ASCII text file that you can read with your word processing application. 4D Insider can also export your procedures to a text file. Using 4D Insider, you can globally search for and replace any database object with any other database object. If you need to translate your application into different languages, 4D Insider can reduce the time it takes by creating a STR# resource containing all of the unique strings used in your layouts and menus. 4D Insider can then insert references to these items. You can use 4D Insider simultaneously as you develop your database, using MultiFinder in System 6.x, or under System 7.x. The current version of 4D Insider is 1.1. Version 2.0 (due in 1994) will provide all the ability to copy files, layouts, procedures, and menus from one database to another. As you become an advanced 4D database designer, you will find 4D Insider very useful in developing, managing, and documenting your complex 4D databases.

4D EXTERNAL KIT

4th Dimension was designed with an open architecture to allow developers to add new commands and features, called *External Extensions* (commonly called *externals*). Externals are written in another language, such as C, Pascal, FORTRAN, or assembly. When correctly written and installed, externals enhance the capability of your database and perform seamlessly as part of your database.

The 4D External Kit is a guide for Macintosh programmers to use in creating 4D externals. It contains reference manuals that provide background information on creating externals, and a description and an explanation of the Entry Points and Access Libraries for writing externals. It also contains several example externals written in Pascal, C, and FORTRAN, documentation for the examples, and the Access Libraries for Pascal.

The 4D External Kit is for use by advanced Macintosh programmers only. It does not teach you how to program externals, nor does it provide a development system to write the externals in.

CHANGES IN 4D VERSION 3.1

VERSION 3.0 OF 4th Dimension offers many exciting new features, as well as significant enhancements to existing ones. This appendix covers the important changes from version 2.0 to 3.0, including a list of commands that are no longer used.

TRUE TIME-SLICED MULTITASKING

Multitasking is now available when running your database. In the User/Runtime environments, you can create processes that allow you to perform various database tasks simultaneously.

Since more than one process cannot be executed at the same time, when you open multiple processes, 4D slices the total processing time so that execution is divided between all open processes. Execution alternates between the processes so rapidly that the processes appear to be executing simultaneously.

CLIENT/SERVER ARCHITECTURE FOR MULTI-USER

Multi-user with 4D Runtime has been replaced with a true client/server architecture consisting of a designated server Macintosh networked to many client Macintoshes. The 4D Server software runs on the server and the 4D Client software runs on each client. The 4D Client computer workstations request information from the 4D Server computer.

You can create and use your database in both single and multi-user mode. The single user version is 4D version 3.0 or 4D Runtime version 3.0. The multi-user version is a combination of 4D Server and 4D Client, using a database developed with either 4th Dimension 3.0 or 4D Server itself.

4D Server has several benefits over other the file-sharing, multi-user architecture of many other multi-user products. Since data is stored and analyzed on the server, the number of network passes from the workstations to the server decreases to only two per operation, thereby significantly increasing speed. Also, many users can access the database at the same time. The Design, User, and Runtime modes are now concurrent. This means that you can be designing a layout in the Layout Editor and with the click of your mouse, be entering records into another window that is part of the Runtime environment.

MULTI-USER DEVELOPMENT ENVIRONMENT

Using 4D Server in multi-user, multiple developers can use Design, User, and Runtime mode simultaneously. You can even work on the database design in the Design environment while other users continue to add and modify data in the User or Runtime environments. You can add and modify scripts, procedures, objects, and data in a multi-user mode. This allows for faster application development time since multiple developers can work in the Design environment of the database at the same time.

Processes

Processes are like separate 4D environments that allow you to perform tasks such as designing a layout, writing a procedure, entering a new record, printing a report, etc. The ability to create and execute multiple processes at the same time extends multitasking capabilities to your databases.

Processes allow you to have multiple active windows because each process can have one active window. No additional code is required to create multiple active windows. All you need to do is select a checkbox in the Menu Editor.

Global variables are local to the process they are being used in. Because of this, global variables are now referred to as *process variables.* There is a new kind of variable called an *interprocess variable.* Interprocess variables are available throughout the database and are shared by all processes. They are primarily used to share information between processes.

Floating Windows

You can now create floating windows. These windows are in their own layer above the regular window layer. Floating windows in the floating window layer act just like non-floating windows except that they never go behind your non-floating windows. A floating window will always be active even though there could be another active window at the same time. There can be one floating window per process. Floating windows are meant to be used as palettes and not for data entry, as they can only accept mouse clicks. Keystrokes are sent to the frontmost, non-floating window.

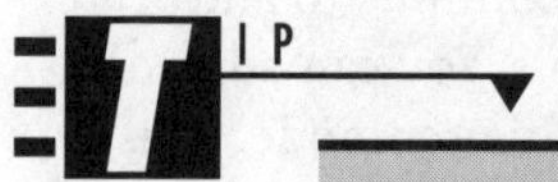

If you display a type 1 (modal) window, it will be displayed in front of all windows, including floating windows.

BALLOON HELP

You can now add help balloons to fields and active objects on layouts. You can create balloon help, either in the field dialog box (to have it appear in all layouts in which the field is used) in the field definition dialog box, or in the object definition dialog box (to have the help appear in that particular layout). Balloon help for a field or object in a layout will override the help associated with the field in the field dialog box.

In order to use balloon help, the user's Macintosh must be running System 7 and have balloon help activated. You can provide users with additional information about using the layouts in your database by creating help messages that explain the functions of fields and active objects.

4D has its own balloon help in the Procedure editor. You can view the syntax for commands and functions by placing the pointer over the command or function in the Routines list.

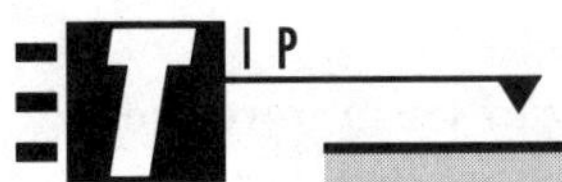

You can toggle balloon help on and off using the Control-Esc **key combination.**

INVISIBLE FILES AND FIELDS

You can now make a file or field invisible to users in the User and Runtime environment editors. Invisible files and fields are not displayed in all Search Editors, the Sort Editor, Graph Editor, Label Editor, Quick Report Editor, Import and Export Editors, and the Apply Formula Editor. You make a file or field invisible by selecting the Invisible check box in the File Attributes or Field dialog box. Invisible files can be used in procedures and scripts and can appear on layouts.

THE DEBUGGER

The debugger can now debug multiple processes simultaneously. Using the debugger, users can step through their code as it executes to locate errors.

THE PROCEDURE EDITOR

A new menu item has been added to the Procedure Editor's Search menu. The Goto Line menu item allows you to find a specific line of code, making it easy to find errors detected by the compiler, which flags syntax errors by the line number in which they occurred.

THE PASSWORD EDITOR

There is now an additional password dialog box you can select to request that 4D present users an Enter Password dialog box where they enter their user name and password without seeing a list of user names.

Because 4D and 4D Server now allow for multiple developers to have access to the Design environment, you now have the ability to give Group level access to the Design environment. This is done from the Structure Access pop-up menu in the Preferences dialog box. From this pop-up menu, you select a group. All the users in the group you select will have access to the Design environment.

The Designer has access to the structure, all files, layouts, procedures, and menus. The Designer cannot be locked out of any part of the Design environment.

When using modules with 4D Server, the licensing of those modules is handled by 4D Server. As users log in to 4D Server, they use up licenses for each module. The Password menu in the Password Editor now gives you the ability to control which groups can use each module that is installed. When a user logs in, they will use up a license only for the modules that you have given them access to.

Because you can now have multiple users accessing the Design environment, you can now indicate which group can edit the objects created by each user. When you set up a user's password, you can select the group that will have design access to the layouts and procedures that the user creates.

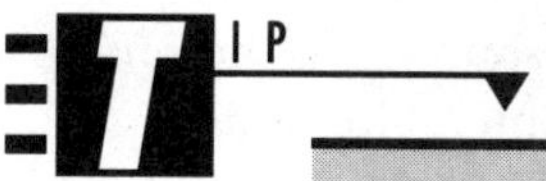

Each developer may wish to decide for herself at what point she want the objects she creates to be accessed by other developers. To allow this, create a group for each developer and assign this group as the group that can edit objects created by this user. That way, no other developer will have access to the objects that any particular developer creates. When a developer is ready to give other developers access to an object, she can simply change the access to that particular object.

CONNECTED MENUS

Connected Menus let you share menus among several different menu bars. You create a single menu definition, such as a Reports menu, and connect it to several menu bars. It is much easier to manage the instances of single menus this way. This means you can make a single menu, and change the menu items, disable or enable menu items, or place or remove checkmarks on items, and those changes flow through to all other *instances* or uses of that same menu in the connected menu bars.

LOCALIZATION

Localization is the process of translating all the text in your database to different languages for use in other countries. To make this translation process easier, you can design your database to access string resources (STR#) for the text that appears in menus and menu items, buttons and static layout text.

The purpose of using the STR# resource is that you can create one for each language. When you have an update of your database, you can simply paste in the STR# resource for a particular language. You can use ResEdit to create new or modify existing string resources. In the version 3.0 Menu editor, when entering menu names or menu items as a string resource, if you single-click on the item you can see the name of the item read from the resource. It is recommended that you place resources in the database's structure file. For more information on localization, see the *4th Dimension Design Reference.*

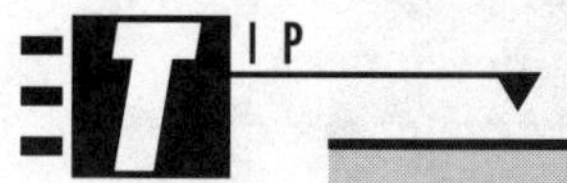

You can use 4D Insider to localize your database. 4D Insider can go through all of your layouts and menus and create a list of all the unique static text objects, button text and menu items. It then creates a STR# resource in your structure file and inserts references to these strings in your buttons, static text, and menu items. Using this feature, you can automate the most time-consuming portion of localizing a database.

MOVING BETWEEN ENVIRONMENTS

The Design environment now runs concurrently with the User and Runtime environments. You can switch between the Design and User and the User and Runtime environments by selecting the environment name from the Use menu. To go into the Runtime environment, you must go through the User environment first; in version 3.0 the Runtime menu item only appears in the Use menu in the User environment. If you have multiple environment windows open, you can just click on the environment's windows to switch to that environment.

NEW COMMANDS AND FUNCTIONS

4th Dimension 3.0 adds 35 new commands and functions to 4D's programming language. These new commands are listed below. For more information on each command see *Appendix C* or your *4th Dimension Language Reference.*

Activated

BRING TO FRONT

CALL PROCESS

CLEAR NAMED SELECTION

COPY NAMED SELECTION

Count tasks

Count user processes

Count users

Current process

CUT NAMED SELECTION

C_GRAPH

Deactivated

DELAY PROCESS

DISTINCT VALUES

FILTER EVENT

Frontmost process

HIDE PROCESS

JOIN

LOCKED ATTRIBUTES

New Process
Outside call
PAUSE PROCESS
PROCESS ATTRIBUTES
Process state
PROJECT SELECTION
REDUCE SELECTION
RESUME PROCESS
SCAN INDEX
SEARCH SELECTION
SEARCH SELECTION BY FORMULA
SET INDEX
SET ITEM
SHOW PROCESS
USE NAMED SELECTION
User in group

REVISED COMMANDS

Many existing 4th Dimension commands and functions were revised for version 3.0 to add new functionality. These revised commands are listed below. For more information on each command see *Appendix C* or your *4th Dimension Language Reference.*

ARRAY TO SELECTION
CHECK ITEM
DISABLE ITEM
ENABLE ITEM
MENU BAR
ON EVENT CALL

ON SERIAL PORT CALL

OPEN WINDOW

SEARCH

SEARCH SELECTION

SEARCH BY FORMULA

SELECTION TO ARRAY

Semaphore

DISCONTINUED COMMANDS

Because using multiple processes is progammatically the same as having multiple users, the following commands are no longer supported in version 3.0. If you are converting a version 2.0 database to version 3.0 to use with 4D Server, you are not using these commands anyway, as they don't work in version 2.0 in multi-user mode.

NEW DATA FILE

OPEN DATA FILE

SORT FILE

CHANGES IN 4D 3.1 AND 4D SERVER 1.1

This portion of this appendix covers changes in 4D version 3.1 and 4D Server version 1.1. When you open your version 3 database with either 4D 3.1 or 4D Server 1.1 for the first time, 4D will automatically convert the database to the new version. You will no longer be able to open the database with any version of 4D prior to 4D 3.1 or 4D Server 1.1, so make sure you make a copy of the database before opening it with either of these new versions.

MAXIMUM NUMBER OF FILES

The maximum number of files in a single database has been increased from 100 to 255.

MAXIMUM SIZE OF THE DATA FILE

The maximum size of the data file has been increased from 1 gigabyte to 128 gigabytes. The data file can be divided into 2 gigabyte segments which can be stored on different volumes (hard disks). Each segment has a maximum size of 2 gigabytes. 4D uses the segments in the order that they were created. If more room is created in one segment by deleting records, this space will be reused before additional space is created in other data file segments. Data file segments can be created by using the Split button in the New Database dialog box (when you initially create the database) or by choosing Data ➤ Add New Data Segments in the Design environment.

If the database was created with a version of 4D earlier than 4D 3.1 or 4D Server 1.1, the maximum size of the first data file segment will be 1 gigabyte. To increase the maximum size of this segment to 2 gigabytes, compact the database with 4D Tools.

INVISIBLE FILES AND FIELDS

Invisible files and fields now appear in italics in the Structure window of the Design environment.

COMPLETELY DELETE OPTION

This new option insures that deleted records cannot be recovered accidentally. When records are deleted using the DELETE SELECTION command, 4D simply keeps a list of these records so that they are no longer accessible. These "holes" in the database are then refilled with new records. If a database becomes damaged and the Recover By Tags option is used to recover the records, deleted records may also be recovered. To insure that deleted records for a particular file will not be recovered, click the Completely Delete check box in the File Attributes dialog box for that file. This will cause record deletion to take longer, but will prevent deleted records from being recovered.

ONLY 4D CLIENT CONNECTIONS OPTION

This new option allows you to control whether or not a 4D Server database will allow applications other than 4D Client to connect (using 4D Open) to the database. By default, this option is selected.

NEW COMMANDS AND FUNCTIONS

4th Dimension 3.1 adds six new commands and functions to 4D's programming language. These new commands are listed below. For more information on each command see Appendix C or your *4th Dimension Language Reference.*

ADD DATA SEGMENT

COMPRESS PICTURE

COMPRESS PICTURE FILE

Picture size

PRINT RECORD

READ COMPRESS PICTURE FROM FILE

SAVE PICTURE TO FILE

4D COMMANDS AND FUNCTIONS

THIS APPENDIX PROVIDES you with a summarized description of all of the commands and functions of 4th Dimension version 3.x. Functions can be used within commands or by themselves. Most commands and functions can be passed parameters (arguments). When passing parameters to a command or function, you must use the correct syntax and data types for the parameters you are passing. Additional information about each command or function can be obtained from the help balloons in the Procedure Editor. For detailed information about each command and function, refer to your *4th Dimension Language Reference.*

You need be concerned with the commands and functions contained within this appendix only if you need to go beyond what 4D can do without the programming language.

ARRAYS

The *array* commands and functions allow you to create, resize, search, sort, and delete arrays. Arrays are basically lists in memory. They are used on layouts to create scrollable areas and pop-up menus. Arrays are also used in programming when it is easier or more convenient to work with a list of values rather than several individual variables.

Command	Function
ARRAY BOOLEAN(array name; size1; {size2})	Creates or resizes a one- or two-dimensional boolean array of elements in memory.
ARRAY DATE(array name; size1; {size2})	Creates or resizes a one- or two-dimensional date array of elements in memory.
ARRAY INTEGER(array name; size1; {size2})	Creates or resizes a one- or two-dimensional integer array of elements in memory.
ARRAY LONGINT(array name; size1; {size2})	Creates or resizes a one- or two-dimensional long integer array of elements in memory.
ARRAY PICTURE(array name; size1; {size2})	Creates or resizes a one- or two-dimensional picture array of elements in memory.
ARRAY POINTER(array name; size1; {size2})	Creates or resizes a one- or two-dimensional pointer array of elements in memory.
ARRAY REAL(array name; size1; {size2})	Creates or resizes a one- or two-dimensional real array of elements in memory.
ARRAY STRING(string length; array name; size1; {size2})	Creates or resizes a one- or two-dimensional boolean array of elements in memory.

Command	**Function**
ARRAY TEXT(array name; size1; {size2})	Creates or resizes a one- or two-dimensional boolean array of elements in memory.
ARRAY TO LIST(array; list; {linked array})	Copies an array to a choices list, creating the list if it doesn't exist.
ARRAY TO SELECTION(array1; field1 {;...; arrayN; fieldN})	Copies one or more arrays into fields for records in the current selection.
COPY ARRAY(source; destination)	Duplicates an array.
DELETE ELEMENT(array; where; {number of elements})	Deletes one or more elements from an array.
DISTINCT VALUES(field; array)	Creates a sorted order text array from the current selection in the current process, containing the distinct value of an indexed field, regardless of the type of field.
Find in array(array; value; {start})	Returns the number of the first element in the array that matches the value given, starting the search at the element number specified by start.
INSERT ELEMENT(array; where; {number of elements})	Inserts one or more array elements into an array. Elements are inserted above the element number "where" and elements beyond "where" are moved down by the optional parameter number of elements.

Command	Function
LIST TO ARRAY(list; array; {linked array})	Creates an array from the list and copies the data from the list into the array.
SELECTION TO ARRAY(field1; array1 {;...; fieldN; arrayN})	Creates one or more arrays and copies data from the field or fields of the current selection into the array or arrays. For 4D Server, the array is created on the server and sent in its entirety to the workstation.
SELECTION TO ARRAY(file; array1 {;...; fieldN; arrayN})	Creates an array of record numbers for the file. For 4D Server, the array is created on the server and sent in its entirety to the workstation.
Size of array(array) -> Number	Returns the number of the elements in the array.
SORT ARRAY(array1 {; ...; arrayN}; {direction})	Sorts one or more arrays in ascending or descending order.

COMPILER DIRECTIVES

The *compiler directives* are used to state explicitly the data type of a variable. When the database is compiled by the 4D Compiler, the 4D Compiler first looks through the database for these directives to determine the data types of variables. If a variable doesn't have a compiler directive, the compiler will attempt to figure out the variable's data type based on the way the variable is being used. By declaring all of your variables with compiler directives, you can greatly reduce the time it takes to compile your database.

Directive	Comments
C_BOOLEAN(variable1 {;...; variableN})	Used to declare and type boolean variables.
C_DATE(variable1 {;...; variableN})	Used to declare and type date variables.
C_INTEGER(variable1 {;...; variableN})	Used to declare and type integer variables.
C_LONGINT(variable1 {;...; variableN})	Used to declare and type long integer variables.
C_PICTURE(variable1 {;...; variableN})	Used to declare and type picture variables.
C_POINTER(variable1 {;...; variableN})	Used to declare and type pointer variables.
C_REAL(variable1 {;...; variableN})	Used to declare and type real number variables.
C_STRING(size; variable1 {;...; variableN})	Used to declare and type string variables.
C_TEXT(variable1 {;...; variableN})	Used to declare and type text variables.
C_TIME(variable1 {;...; variableN})	Used to declare and type time variables.

DATABASE STRUCTURE

The *database structure* commands and functions allow you to get information about the structure of your database. With these commands, you can write generic, re-usable code to determine how many files the database has, how many fields a particular file has, as well as get the attributes of the fields. You can also get pointers to files and fields for generic access to the database.

Command	Function
Count fields(file number) -> Number	Returns the number of fields in the file.
Count fields(file pointer) -> Number	Returns the number of fields in the file.
Count files -> Number	Returns the number of files in the database.
DEFAULT FILE(file)	Sets the default file to simplify and clarify procedures and make code that is not file specific.
Field(field pointer) -> Number	Returns the field number of the field.
Field(file number, field number) -> Pointer	Returns a pointer to the field.
FIELD ATTRIBUTES(field pointer; type; {length}; {index})	Assigns to variables the type, length, and index information of the field specified by the field pointer.
FIELD ATTRIBUTES(file number, field number; type; {length}; {index})	Assigns to variables the type, length, and index information of the field specified by the file number and field number.
Fieldname(field pointer) -> String	Returns the fieldname specified by field pointer.
Fieldname(file number, field number) -> String	Returns the fieldname specified by file number and field number.
File(field pointer) -> Number	Returns the file number of the field.

Command	Function
File(file number) -> Pointer	Returns a pointer to the file.
File(file pointer) -> Number	Returns the file number of the file.
Filename(file number) -> String	Returns the name of the file of the file number.
Filename(file pointer) -> String	Returns the name of the file for the file pointer.
SET INDEX(field; index;{ *})	Creates or removes an index for the field. If the asterisk is included, the index is built asynchronously.

DATA ENTRY AND MANAGING RECORDS

These commands and functions are used to add, delete, or edit records and navigate through them.

Command	Function
ADD RECORD({file}; {*})	Adds a new record to the database for the specified file. The new record is displayed in the current input layout and becomes the current record for that file.
CREATE RECORD({file})	Creates a new empty record but doesn't display it. It exists in memory only until a SAVE RECORD is executed. Use it instead of ADD RECORD to assign data to a record without displaying it.
DELETE RECORD({file})	Deletes the current record from the file.

Command	Function
DISPLAY RECORD({file})	Displays the current record of the file in the current input layout.
DISPLAY SELECTION ({file};{*})	Displays the current selection for the file, but does not allow the user to modify any records.
DUPLICATE RECORD({file})	Duplicates the current record in the file. Use SAVE RECORD to save the duplicate record.
FIRST RECORD({file})	Makes the first record of the file the current record and loads it from the disk.
GOTO RECORD({file}; record)	Selects the record as the only record in the selection and loads the record from the disk.
GOTO SELECTED RECORD({file}; record)	Moves to the record and makes it the current record without changing the current selection of the file.
LAST RECORD({file})	Makes the last record of the file the current record and loads it from the disk.
Modified record({file}) -> Boolean	Returns TRUE if the user has modified the record but not saved it.
MODIFY RECORD({file}; {*})	Allows the user to modify a record in an input layout.
MODIFY SELECTION ({file}; {*})	Displays the current selection of the file in the current output layout and allows the user to modify the record when in the input layout.
NEXT RECORD({file})	Makes the next record of the current selection the current record and loads it from the disk.

Command	**Function**
ONE RECORD SELECT({file})	Makes the current record the only record in the current selection for the file.
POP RECORD({file})	Pops a pushed record and its subrecords, if any, off the file's record stack and makes the record the current record.
PREVIOUS RECORD({file})	Makes the previous record of the current selection the current record and loads it from the disk.
PUSH RECORD({file})	Pushes the current record and its subrecords onto the file's record stack.
Record number({file}) -> Number	Returns the absolute record number for the current record. It returns –1 if there is no current record, and it returns –3 for new records that have not yet been saved.
SAVE RECORD({file})	Saves the current record of file.
Selected record number({file}) -> Number	Returns the position of the current record within the current selection of the file.
Sequence number({file})	Returns the next sequence number for the file.

DATA OBJECTS INFORMATION

The *data objects* functions are used to get information about data objects such as the type of object.

Command	Function
Count parameters -> Number	Returns the number of parameters passed to a procedure.
Get pointer (name) -> Pointer	Returns a pointer to a variable.
Is a variable (parameter) -> Boolean	Returns TRUE if the parameter is a pointer to a variable. Returns FALSE if the parameter is a pointer to a field.
Self -> Pointer	Returns a pointer to the object whose script is executing. Only valid in a script, cannot be called from a global procedure.
Type (parameter) -> Number	Returns the data type of the parameter, a field, or a variable.

DATE FUNCTIONS

The following are *date* functions:

Command	Function
Current date({*}) -> Date	Returns the current date from the Macintosh system clock.
Date(date string) -> Date	Returns a date from a non-alphabetic date string like 01/06/94.
Day number(date) -> Number	Returns a number representing the weekday on which the date falls, with Sunday starting as 1. It also returns 1 for dates of 00/00/00.
Day of(date) -> Number	Returns the day of the month of the date.

Command	**Function**
Month of(date) -> Number	Returns a number for the month of the date.
Year of(date) -> Number	Returns the number of the year of the date.

DOCUMENTS AND THE SERIAL PORT

These commands are used to read and write to files on disk as well as communicate through the *serial port* to a *modem* or any other serial device.

Command	**Function**
Append document (document; {type}) -> Document reference	Opens an existing Macintosh document for writing. Text written to the open document is appended to the end of the document.
CLOSE DOCUMENT (document ref)	Closes the open Macintosh document and saves it to disk.
Create document (document; {type}) -> Document reference	Creates a new Macintosh document and returns a document reference to it.
DELETE DOCUMENT (document)	Deletes any document or application on any disk. Deleting is a permanent operation that cannot be undone.
ON SERIAL PORT CALL(serial procedure; {process})	Installs a procedure as the interrupt procedure that 4D calls automatically for serial port events.

Command	**Function**
Open document (document;{type}) -> Document reference	Opens an existing Macintosh document for reading or writing data from the beginning of the document.
RECEIVE BUFFER (receive var)	Reads the serial port that was previously initialized with SET CHANNEL.
RECEIVE PACKET({document ref}; receive var; number of char)	Reads data from the serial port or from a document and transfers the number of characters specified into receive var.
RECEIVE PACKET({document ref}; receive var; stop char)	Reads data from the serial port or from a document until the stop character is read and transfers all characters except the stop character into receive var.
RECEIVE RECORD({file})	Reads data from the serial port or a document opened by the SET CHANNEL command and receives it into a file. The record must be: sent with SEND RECORD, received into a new record for the file made with CREATE RECORD, and finally saved with SAVE RECORD.
RECEIVE VARIABLE(variable)	Receives variable sent by SEND VARIABLE from the document or serial port previously opened by SET CHANNEL.
SEND PACKET({document ref}; packet)	Sends a packet of data to the serial port or to the Macintosh document specified, or the last serial port or document previously opened with the SET CHANNEL command.

Command	**Function**
SEND RECORD({file})	Sends the current record to the serial port or Macintosh document opened by the SET CHANNEL command.
SEND VARIABLE(variable)	Sends the variable to the serial port or Macintosh document previously opened by SET CHANNEL.
SET CHANNEL	Puts the characters in the buffer into receive var and clears the buffer.
SET CHANNEL(operation; {document})	Creates, opens, and closes one document that can be read from or written to.
SET CHANNEL(port; setup)	Opens a serial port, setting the protocol and other settings information.
SET TIMEOUT(seconds)	Sets the amount of time a serial port command has in which to complete its action.
USE ASCII MAP (*; I/O)	Restores the default ASCII map. If I/O is 1, it is reset for output; if 2, it is reset as the input map.
USE ASCII MAP(mapname; I/O)	Loads the ASCII map from the disk for use during import and export of records or text. If I/0 is 1, it is loaded as the output map; if 2, it is loaded as the input map.

GRAPHING

The *graphing* commands are used to create and manipulate graph areas on layouts.

Command	Function
GRAPH(graph area; graph number; x field; yfield1 {;...; yfield8})	Draws a graph from data in arrays or subfields in a Graph Area on a layout.
GRAPH FILE({file})	Displays the Graph window and lets the user select the fields to be graphed.
GRAPH FILE({file}; graph number; x Field; y Field1 {;...; yField8})	Draws the graph using the specified fields and data from the current selection of the file.
GRAPH SETTING(g;xmin;xmax;ymin;ymax;xprop;xgrid;ygrid;title1 {; ...;title8})	Changes the settings for a graph already displayed using the GRAPH command.

IMPORTING AND EXPORTING

These commands are used to *import* and *export* to and from files on disk. Layouts are used to determine which fields should be used and in what order.

Command	Function
EXPORT DIF({file}; document)	Writes DIF type data from the records of the current selection to a Macintosh text document on the disk.
EXPORT SYLK({file}; document)	Writes SYLK type data from the records of the current selection to a Macintosh text document on the disk.
EXPORT TEXT({file}; document)	Writes TEXT type data from the records of the current selection to a Macintosh text document on the disk.

Command	**Function**
IMPORT DIF({file}; document)	Reads DIF type data from a Macintosh text document into a file.
IMPORT SYLK({file}; document)	Reads SYLK type data from a Macintosh text document into a file.
IMPORT TEXT({file}; document)	Reads TEXT type data from a Macintosh text document into a file.

LAYOUT MANAGEMENT

The *layout* commands are used to close layouts, navigate through a layout, and set the current input and output layouts for files.

Command	**Function**
ACCEPT	Saves a new or modified record (and its subrecords, if any). Layouts displayed with the DIALOG command can also be closed with ACCEPT.
CANCEL	Closes the current input layout, output layout, or dialog box. Any changes made to a record are not saved.
FIRST PAGE	Displays the first input layout page. Changes the current input layout page to the first page.
GOTO PAGE(page number)	Changes the display of the current input layout page.
INPUT LAYOUT({file}; layout)	Sets the current input layout for the file.

Command	**Function**
LAST PAGE	Displays the last input layout page. Changes the displayed input layout page to the last page.
Layout page -> Number	Returns the number of the currently displayed input layout page.
NEXT PAGE	Changes the displayed input layout page to the next page.
OUTPUT LAYOUT({file}; layout)	Sets the current output layout for the file.
PREVIOUS PAGE	Changes the displayed input layout page to the previous page.
REDRAW(included file)	Used to update the included layout when a value, its field, or subfield is changed procedurally.

LAYOUT AREA ATTRIBUTES

These commands and functions are used to work with objects on a *layout*. Using these commands you can work with text from a enterable area, set the choice list to be used by an area, prevent the user from leaving a field that doesn't match particular criteria, as well as many other data entry error checking tasks.

Command	**Function**
GET HIGHLIGHT(text object; first; last)	Puts the first and last characters of the highlighted text into variables.
GOTO AREA(data entry area)	Moves the insertion point to the data entry area on an input layout.

Command	Function
HIGHLIGHT TEXT(text object; first; last)	Highlights a text selection, and moves the cursor to that text object if necessary.
INVERT BACKGROUND(text variable)	Changes the background of a text variable on a layout on the screen or when printing to an ImageWriter printer.
Last area -> Pointer	Returns a pointer to the last or current enterable object area where the cursor was or just left.
Modified(field) -> Boolean	Returns TRUE if the user has modified the field.
Old(field) -> String, Number, Date, or Time	Returns the value of the field before it was modified. For a new record, Old returns an empty value.
REJECT	Rejects the entire data entry area (input layout) and does not accept the record.
REJECT(field)	Rejects only the field and the cursor remains in that area, forcing the user to enter a correct value.
SET CHOICE LIST(text object; list)	Sets the choice list for the text object displayed in the current layout.
SET ENTERABLE(text object; boolean)	Sets the state of the text object displayed in the current layout to either enterable or non-enterable.
SET FILTER(text object; filter)	Sets the character filter for the text object displayed in the current layout.
SET FORMAT(object; format)	Sets the display format for the text object displayed in the current layout.

LAYOUT OBJECT ATTRIBUTES

These commands are used to set the condition and appearance of *objects* on the layout that is currently in use.

Command	Function
BUTTON TEXT(button; button text)	Changes the text of the button.
DISABLE BUTTON(button)	Dims a button and makes it inactive to prevent it from being used.
ENABLE BUTTON(button)	Enables a button and makes it active.
FONT(object; font name)	Changes the object display font into font name.
FONT SIZE(object; size)	Changes the font size for the object.
FONT STYLE(object; style number)	Changes the font style for the object.
SET COLOR(object; color)	Sets the foreground and background colors for object.

LAYOUT EXECUTION CYCLE

The *layout execution cycle* functions are used to determine what action has caused the layout procedure to execute.

Command	**Function**
Activated -> Boolean	Returns TRUE in a layout procedure when a window becomes the front-most window. A window becomes frontmost by the user clicking on it or by calling the BRING TO FRONT command.
After -> Boolean	Returns true in an input layout procedure when a new or modified record is accepted. The After phase is generated only when ADD RECORD, MODIFY RECORD, or MODIFY SELECTION is used or if a record is accepted in the User environment.
Before -> Boolean	Returns TRUE before the layout is displayed or printed, and is usually used to initialize fields and variables.
CALL PROCESS(process)	Calls the Outside call phase of the frontmost layout window of process. Passing –1 instead of a process reference number will redraw all the windows of any process that contains interprocess variables.
Deactivated	Returns TRUE in a layout procedure when the frontmost window of the frontmost process moves to the back. A window is deactivated when a new window is opened, when the user clicks on another window or when the BRING TO FRONT command is called on another process.

Command	Function
During -> Boolean	Returns TRUE when any modification is made to a record or when the record is saved. The During phase is usually used to manage data entry tasks, such as calculations, data validation tasks, and updating fields or variables.
In break -> boolean	Returns TRUE in an output layout procedure when a Break area is about to be printed. Returns TRUE in an output layout procedure just before a Break area is about to be printed.
In footer -> boolean	Returns TRUE in an output layout procedure when a Footer area is going to be printed.
In header -> boolean	Returns TRUE in an output layout procedure when a Header area is about to be printed.
Level -> Number	Returns the level number during the In Break or In Header phase of the execution cycle for an output layout during report printing.
Outside call -> Boolean	Returns TRUE if CALL PROCESS has been called for this process, and for only the frontmost window of the process which was called by the command CALL PROCESS.

LOGICAL FUNCTIONS

Logical functions are typically used to test the value of an boolean object or to test a condition.

Command	Function
TRUE -> Boolean	Returns the Boolean value TRUE.
FALSE -> Boolean	Returns the Boolean value FALSE.
Not(boolean) -> Boolean	Returns the negation of Boolean, changing TRUE to FALSE or FALSE to TRUE.

MATH FUNCTIONS

These functions return the results or calculations on Real, Integer, and Long Integer data types.

Command	Function
Abs(number) -> Number	Returns the absolute [unsigned and positive] value of (number).
Dec(number) -> Number	Returns the decimal or fractional part of a number. Dec is always a positive number or zero.
Exp(number) -> Number	Raises the natural log base (e=2.71828182845904524) by the power of the number. Exp is the inverse function of Log.
Int(number) -> Number	Returns the integer portion of the number without rounding. Negative numbers are truncated toward zero.
Log(number) -> Number	Returns the natural Napierian log of the number. Log is the inverse function of Exp.
Mod(number1; number2) -> Number	Returns an integer remainder of number1 divided by number2. The "%" operator can also be used to calculate the remainder.

Command	Function
Num(boolean) -> Number (0 or 1)	Returns 0 if Boolean is FALSE. Returns 1 of Boolean is TRUE.
Num(string) -> Number	Returns the string as a numeric value.
Random -> Number	Returns a random integer value between 0 and 32,767 inclusive.
Round(number; places) -> Number	Returns the number rounded to the number of decimal places given.
Trunc(number; places) -> Number	Returns a number with its decimal part truncated by the number of decimal places specified.

MANAGING MENUS

The *menu* commands and functions are used to set the menu bar to be used and to change the condition of items in the menus.

Command	Function
CHECK ITEM(menu; menu item; mark; {process})	Places or removes a check mark next to the menu item specified, for the specified process.
DISABLE ITEM(menu; menu item; {process})	Dims a menu item and makes it inactive to prevent it from being selected.
ENABLE ITEM(menu; menu item; {process})	Enables a menu item and makes it active.
MENU BAR(menu bar number; {process})	Replaces the current menu bar.

Command	Function
Menu selected -> Number	Returns the Macintosh menu-selected number or 0 if no menu item was selected. Menu selected works only if an input or output layout is displayed.
SET ITEM(menu; menu item; menu name; {process})	Sets the text for the menu item in the menu. In a connected menu, it will change the menu item text in all menus.

DISPLAYING MESSAGES

The message commands are used to communicate with the user.

Command	Function
ALERT(message)	Displays an alert box with a message and an OK button.
CONFIRM(message)	Displays a Caution dialog box with a message and OK and Cancel buttons.
DIALOG({file}; layout)	Presents a layout, usually in a type 1 modal or type 5 moveable modal window, to get information from the user or present information to the user. Fields are non-enterable in dialogs.
ERASE WINDOW	Clears the contents of a window opened with OPEN WINDOW and moves the cursor to the upper-left corner of that window.
GOTO XY(x; y)	Positions an invisible cursor in a window opened by OPEN WINDOW when a layout is not being displayed.

Command	Function
MESSAGE(message)	Displays a message on the screen in a temporary window that is erased as soon as a layout is displayed or the procedure is done executing.
MESSAGES OFF	Turns off the 4D progress thermometers that are displayed during time-consuming processes.
MESSAGES ON	Turns on the 4D progress thermometers that are displayed during time-consuming processes. The messages are on by default.
Request(message; {default response}) -> String	Displays a dialog box containing a message, a text input area with optional default response value and OK and Cancel buttons.

MISCELLANEOUS COMMANDS

Command	Function
SELECT LOG FILE	Only used when 4D Backup is installed in the database. Same as selecting Log File from the File Menu in the User environment.
SET ABOUT(item text; procedure)	Changes the About 4th Dimension item in the Apple menu to item text. The installed procedure can open a custom dialog box to give version information about your database.
ADD DATA SEGMENT	Displays a dialog box that allows the user to add new data segments to the data file.

MULTI-USER COMMANDS AND FUNCTIONS

These commands are used mostly in databases that are going to be used with 4D Server for *multi-user access* to the database. These commands mostly deal with record locking. Records can be locked in single-user databases when several processes are being used. For more information on processes, see the *4th Dimension Language Reference.*

Command	Function
CLEAR SEMAPHORE (semaphore)	Removes the semaphore flag.
LOAD RECORD({file})	Loads the current record of the file.
Locked({file}) -> Boolean	Returns TRUE if the current record of the file is locked. Returns FALSE if the record is unlocked.
LOCKED ATTRIBUTES({file}; process; user; machine; process name)	Returns the process number, user name, machine name, and process name for which the record has been locked. In single-user mode, it returns process and process name only if a record is locked, and user and machine return empty strings.
READ ONLY({file})	Sets the state of the file to read-only. All records loaded after READ ONLY are locked.
READ WRITE({file})	Sets the state of the file to read-write. A record loaded after READ WRITE will be unlocked if no other user has locked the record yet.

Command	Function
Semaphore(semaphore) -> Boolean	Returns TRUE if semaphore exists. If semaphore does not exist, the semaphore is created and returns FALSE. Used as a simple message between multi-user workstations.
UNLOAD RECORD({file})	Unloads the current record. If the record is unlocked for the local user, it unlocks the record for all other users.

PASSWORDS

These commands affect the use of *passwords*.

Command	Function
CHANGE ACCESS	Lets the user change to a different user name without quitting the database.
CHANGE PASSWORD (password)	Changes the password of the current user.
Current user -> String	Returns the name of the current user. If the user entered as a Guest, it returns an empty string.
EDIT ACCESS	Lets the user access the password system's Password Access editor.
User in group(user; group) -> Boolean	Returns TRUE if user is in the group.

PICTURES

These commands are used to load, compress, and save pictures.

Command	Function
SAVE PICTURE TO FILE(document ref;picture)	Saves the picture passed to the document referenced.
READ COMPRESS PICTURE FROM FILE(document reference;method;quality; picture)	Compresses the Picture (using the method and quality) loaded from the document referenced.
Picture size(picture) -> number	Returns the size (in bytes) of the picture.
COMPRESS PICTURE FILE(document reference;method;quality)	Compresses the picture stored in the document referenced without loading the picture into memory.
COMPRESS PICTURE(picture;method; quality)	Compresses the picture (stored in a variable or field) using method and quality.

PRINTING REPORTS

These commands and functions are used to *print* records using quick reports and layouts to create reports. Layouts can be printed without records as well to create reports that don't derive their data directly from records.

Command	Function
ACCUMULATE (data1{;...; dataN})	Specifies the field(s) or variable(s) to be subtotaled when printing a layout report.
BREAK LEVEL(level; {page break})	Determines the number of break levels in a report and whether to page break while printing.
FORM FEED	Prints out any remaining data that has been sent to the printer and ejects the page. Used with PRINT LAYOUT to force page breaks and print out the last page.
PAGE SETUP({file}; layout)	Sets the page setup for the printer to the layout's page setup
Printing page -> Number	Returns the printing page number when using PRINT SELECTION or Print from the User environment.
PRINT LABEL({file}; {*})	Prints labels using the current selection of records and using the current output layout. Displays the printer dialog boxes before printing unless the asterisk parameter is used.
PRINT LABEL({file}; {label document})	Prints labels with the current selection of records using the Label editor to select the output and the label setup that is defined in the label document.
PRINT LAYOUT({file}; layout)	Prints the layout with the current values of fields and variables, without any break processing, record processing, form feeds, headers, or footers.
PRINT RECORD ([file];{*})	Prints the current record of the file using the current output layout.

Command	Function
PRINT SELECTION ({file}; {*})	Prints the current selection of the file using the current output layout.
PRINT SETTINGS	Displays the printer dialog boxes, the Page Setup dialog box, and the Print Settings dialog box.
REPORT({file}; document; {*})	Prints a report for the file, using the Quick Report editor.
Subtotal(data; {page break}) -> Number	Returns the subtotal for the field or variable for the current or last break level in a sorted selection during printing with PRINT SELECTION or from Print in the User environment.

PROCEDURE EXECUTION CONTROL

The following commands are for controlling *procedure execution.*

Command	Function
ABORT	Terminates procedure execution.
EXECUTE(statement)	Executes one line of code.
FILTER EVENT	Removes events from the event queue. Used in an ON EVENT CALL procedure.
FLUSH BUFFERS	Saves all the data in memory buffers to the disk.
IDLE	Used only in compiled databases in user defined procedures where no 4th Dimension commands are executed and a process must be interrupted.
NO TRACE	Turns off the 4D Debugger.

Command	**Function**
ON ERR CALL(error procedure)	Installs that procedure as the procedure 4D calls when an error occurs.
ON EVENT CALL(event procedure; {process})	Installs that procedure as the procedure 4D calls when an event occurs. Events are only recognized when a procedure is executing.
TRACE	Turns on the 4th Dimension Debugger.
QUIT 4D	Quits 4th Dimension and returns to the Finder.

PROCESSES

4th Dimension is divided into *processes.* These processes all execute simultaneously allowing you to have multiple database tasks running at the same time. Using processes you can allow users to be more productive by allowing them to use the database while time-consuming tasks like printing long reports or batch updating large selections of records are done behind the scenes. The process commands allow you to create, manipulate, and communicate between processes.

Command	**Function**
BRING TO FRONT(process)	Brings the windows of the process to the front.
Count tasks -> Integer	Returns the number of all processes open on a workstation or in a single user 4th Dimension database. Includes the User/Runtime process, Design Process, Cache manager process, and Indexing process.

Command	**Function**
Count users -> Integer	Returns the number of users connected to the server. For a single user 4th Dimension database, it returns 1.
Count user processes -> Integer	Returns the number of open processes except for the Design process, Cache manager process and Indexing process.
Current process -> Process reference number	Returns the process reference number of the process from which this command is called.
DELAY PROCESS(process; duration)	Delays the execution of the process for a number of ticks (1 tick = 1⁄60th of a second). The process remains in memory.
Frontmost process({*}) -> Integer	Returns the number of the process with the frontmost window(s).
HIDE PROCESS(process)	Hides all the interface elements including all windows and the menu bar of the process until the next SHOW PROCESS.
New process(procedure; stack; {process}) -> Process reference number	Launches a new process and returns a reference number to that process.
PAUSE PROCESS(process)	Stops the execution of process until it is continued by the RESUME PROCESS command.
PROCESS ATTRIBUTES(process; name; state; time)	Returns the name, state, and cumulative time taken by process in ticks.

Command	Function
Process state(process) -> Integer	Returns the status number of the process state. In 4D Server, this command returns the process state on the workstation and not on the server.
RESUME PROCESS(process)	Resumes a process that has been paused.
SHOW PROCESS(process)	Displays all the windows belonging to the process, but does not bring the windows to the frontmost level.

PROGRAMMING

The following commands are used in *programming.*

Command	Function
Case of... Else... End case	Used to control procedure flow. Used to separate the execution of code statements in global procedures, layout procedures and object scripts.
For(counter; start value; end value; {increment})... End for	A programming loop structure used to execute code statements a specified number of times.
If (boolean) _ Else _ End if	A programming statement used to control procedure execution based on the results of a TRUE/FALSE test. If Boolean is TRUE, the next code statements are executed until Else or End If is reached.
Repeat _ Until(boolean)	A programming loop that executes one or more code statements until the Boolean is FALSE.

Command	**Function**
While(Boolean)... End while	A programming loop that executes code statements as long as Boolean is TRUE.

SEARCHING RECORDS

Use the following commands in *searches*.

Command	**Function**
SEARCH({file})	Allows user to build a search argument using the Search Editor to perform the search on the entire file and return a selection of records for the file.
SEARCH({file}; search argument; {*})	Performs an intelligent search on the entire file using the search argument and returns a selection of records for the file. Built searches are created by executing multiple search commands using the asterisk parameter.
SEARCH BY FORMULA({file}; {search formula})	Searches every record in the file for those that match the search formula and returns a new selection of records for the file.
SEARCH BY INDEX({search argument1} {;...; search argumentN})	Searches on indexed fields only for all records in the file that match the search argument.
SEARCH BY LAYOUT({file}; {layout})	Searches the entire file for the data that the user enters in the layout.

Command	Function
SEARCH SELECTION BY FORMULA({file}; {search formula})	Searches every record in the selection for those that match the search formula and returns a new selection of records for the file.
SEARCH SELECTION({file})	Presents the Search editor and allows the user to specify search criteria. Searches the current selection of the file in the process and returns a selection of records.
SEARCH SELECTION({file}; {search argument}; {*})	Searches the current selection of the file in the process using the search argument and returns a selection of records for the file. Built searches are created by executing multiple search commands using the asterisk parameter.
SEARCH SUBRECORDS (subfile; search formula)	Searches the subfile for all subrecords that match the search formula and creates a new subselection of subrecords.

SELECTIONS OF RECORDS

Use these commands for *selecting* records.

Command	Function
ALL RECORDS({file})	Selects all the records from the file and makes them the current selection. The first record of the file becomes the current record and that record is loaded from the disk.

Command	**Function**
APPLY TO SELECTION({file}; statement)	Applies one line of code or a global procedure to every record in the current selection of the specified file.
Before selection({file}) -> Boolean	Returns TRUE just before the first record is printed when using the PRINT SELECTION command.
CLEAR NAMED SELECTION(name)	Clears the selection named from memory. Does not affect files, selections, or records.
COPY NAMED SELECTION({file]; name)	Copies the current selection of the file to the named selection. The default file for the process is used if the file is not specified.
CUT NAMED SELECTION({file]; name)	Creates a named selection and places the current selection of the file into it.
DELETE SELECTION({file})	Deletes the current selection of records from the file.
End selection({file}) -> Boolean	Returns TRUE just before the last record footer is printed when using the PRINT SELECTION command.
JOIN(many file; one file)	Generates a selection of records in the one file based on the selection of records in the many file.
PROJECT SELECTION(field)	Generates a selection of records in the many file based on a selection of records in the one file.
Records in file({file}) -> Number	Returns the number of the records in the file.
Records in selection({file}) -> Number	Returns the number of records in the current selection.

Command	**Function**
REDUCE SELECTION (file; number)	Returns the first specified number of records from the current selection and creates a new selection of records for the file in the current process.
SCAN INDEX(field; number; direction)	Returns a selection of the number of records, for the direction < from the end of the index, or > from the beginning of the index.
USE NAMED SELECTION(name)	Makes the records in the named selection the current selection for the file to which it belongs.

SETS

The follow commands are used with *sets.*

Command	**Function**
ADD TO SET({file}; set)	Adds the current record of the file to the set.
CLEAR SET(set)	Removes the set from memory.
CREATE EMPTY SET({file;} set)	Creates a new empty set for the file.
CREATE SET ({file}; set)	Creates a new set for the file and places the current selection in it.
DIFFERENCE(set1; set2; result set)	Compares two sets and returns a set with only records that are in set one and not in set two.
INTERSECTION (set1; set2; result set)	Compares two sets and creates a result set containing only items that are in both sets.

Command	Function
Is in set(set) -> Boolean	Returns TRUE if the current record for the file that set belongs to is in the set and returns FALSE if the record is not in the set.
LOAD SET({file}; set; document)	Loads from a Macintosh document the set from that file that was saved to that document using the SAVE SET command.
Records in set(set) -> Number	Returns the number of records in the set. Returns 0 if the set does not exist or if there are no records in the set.
SAVE SET(set; document)	Saves the set to a Macintosh document on the disk.
UNION(set1; set2; result set)	Creates a result set that contains all the records from two sets.
USE SET(set)	Makes the records in the set the current selection for the file to which the set belongs.

SORTING RECORDS

Use the following commands when *sorting* records.

Command	Function
SORT BY FORMULA(file; expression1; {direction1} {;...; expressionN; {directionN}})	Sorts the current selection of the file by the expression(s).

Command	Function
SORT BY INDEX	Use only for compatibility reasons for databases created with version 1.0 of 4th Dimension.
SORT SELECTION({file})	Displays the Sort dialog box and lets the user specify the sort fields and direction. Sorts the current selection of the file.
SORT SELECTION(file; field1;{direction1} {;...; fieldN; {directionN}})	Sorts the current selection of the file according to the field and direction parameters.
SORT SUBSELECTION (subfile; subfield1; {direction1} {;...; subfieldN; {directionN}})	Sorts the current subselection of the subfile of the current parent record.

PLAYING SOUNDS

These commands control when *warning beeps* sound.

Command	Function
BEEP	Makes the Macintosh beep or emit whatever beep sound is set in the Control Panel for sound.
PLAY(sound name; {channel})	Plays the sound resource named.

STATISTICAL FUNCTIONS

These commands have *statistical* applications.

Command	Function
Average (series) -> Number	Returns the arithmetic mean or average of a series of numbers.
Max(series) -> Number	Returns the maximum value in a series of numbers in a field or subfield.
Min(series) -> Number	Returns the minimum value in a series of numbers in a field or subfield.
Std deviation (series) -> Number	Returns the standard deviation of series of numbers for a field or subfield.
Sum(series) -> Number	Returns the sum total of all values for a series of numbers for a field or subfield.
Sum squares(series) -> Number	Returns the sum of squares for a series of numbers for a field or subfield.
Variance (series) -> Number	Returns the variance for a series of numbers in a field or subfield.

STRING FUNCTIONS

Strings are text or alphanumeric data. For example *Geoff* is a string that is five characters long. The string functions allow you to manipulate data stored in Text and alphanumeric fields as well as data stored in Text variables and Fixed string variables.

Command	**Function**
ASCII(character) -> Number	Returns the ASCII value of the character.
Change string(source; what; where) -> String	Changes a string of characters and returns the new string.
Char(ASCII code) -> String (1 character)	Returns the character of the ASCII code.
Delete string(source; where; number of chars)	Deletes characters from a string and returns the resulting string.
Insert string(source; what; where) -> String	Inserts a string into source before the "where" character and returns the resulting string.
Length(string) -> Number	Returns the number of characters that are in the string.
Lowercase(string) -> String	Returns a string with all the alphabetic characters in lowercase.
Position(find; string) -> Number	Returns the position of the first occurrence of find in the string. Returns 0 if the find string is not found.

Command	Function
Replace string(source; old string; new string; {how many}) -> String	Replaces all occurrences of old string in the source with the new string and returns the resulting string.
String(date;{format}) -> String	Returns a date as a string, using the MM/DD/YY format, unless another format is specified.
String(number; {format}) -> String	Returns a number as a string, optionally formatted.
String(time; {format}) -> String	Returns a time as a string, using the HH:MM:SS format, unless another format is specified.
string ≤ position ≥ string -> String (1 character)	Returns the character at the specified position.
Substring(source; first char; {number of chars}) -> String	Returns the portion of the source string between the first character and the last character defined by the number of characters.
Uppercase(string) -> String	Returns the string with all alphabetic characters in uppercase.

SUBRECORDS

These commands allow you to manage data stored in *subrecords.* Remember that these functions can only manipulate the subrecords for the currently selected parent record.

Command	Function
ADD SUBRECORD(subfile; layout; {*})	Adds a new subrecord to the subfile using the specified subfile layout. There must be a current parent file record. The subrecord is kept in memory and is not saved to disk until the parent record is saved.
ALL SUBRECORDS (subfile)	Selects all the subrecords of the subfile and makes them the current subselection.
APPLY TO SUBSELECTION (subfile; statement)	Applies one line of code or a global procedure to every subrecord in the current subselection of the specified subfile.
Before subselection(subfile) -> Boolean	Returns TRUE when the current subrecord pointer is before the first subrecord.
CREATE SUBRECORD (subfile)	Creates a new subrecord for the subfile and makes it the current record. The new subrecord is not saved until the parent record is saved.
DELETE SUBRECORD (subfile)	Deletes the current subrecord of the subfile.
End subselection(subfile) -> Boolean	Returns TRUE when the current subrecord pointer is after the end of the current subselection.
FIRST SUBRECORD(subfile)	Makes the first subrecord of the current subselection the current subrecord.
LAST SUBRECORD(subfile)	Makes the last subrecord of the current subselection the current subrecord.

Command	**Function**
MODIFY SUBRECORD(subfile ; layout; {*})	Displays the current subrecord in the layout and allows the user to modify it.
NEXT SUBRECORD (subfile)	Makes the next subrecord of the current subselection the current subrecord.
PREVIOUS SUBRECORD (subfile)	Makes the previous subrecord of the current subselection the current subrecord.
Records in subselection(subfile) -> Number	Returns the number of subrecords in the current subselection of the subfile.

TIME FUNCTIONS

These commands are used with *time* functions.

Current time({*}) -> Time	Returns the current time from the Macintosh system clock.
Time(time string) -> Time	Returns the time specified by time string given in HH:MM:SS format and in 24-hour time.
Time string(seconds) -> String	Returns the time as a string in 24-hour format, given time in number of seconds since midnight.

TRANSACTIONS

Transactions allow you to make modifications to several records from different database files and then procedurally decide whether or not to keep the changes or not.

Command	**Function**
CANCEL TRANSACTION	Undoes all changes made to records since the last START TRANSACTION command.
START TRANSACTION{(*)}	Starts a transaction and all changes to the database will be stored temporarily in memory until it is accepted or canceled.
VALIDATE TRANSACTION	Accepts the transaction started by START TRANSACTION and saves the changes to the database that occurred.

TRIGONOMETRIC FUNCTIONS

The following are *trigonometric* functions.

Command	**Function**
Arctan(number) -> Number	Returns in radians of the angle whose tangent is number.
Cos(number) -> Number	Returns the cosine of a number, expressed in radians.
Sin(number) -> Number	Returns the sine of the number expressed in radians.
Tan(number) -> Number	Returns the tangent of the number, given in radians.

VARIABLES

The following command are for use with *variables*.

Command	**Function**
CLEAR VARIABLE(variable)	Removes the contents of a global variable from memory and makes it undefined.
LOAD VARIABLE(document; variable1 {;...; variableN})	Loads the variable(s) from a Macintosh document created by the SAVE VARIABLE command.
Nil(variable) -> Boolean	Returns TRUE if the value of the variable is a nil pointer (»[]). Variable must be of type pointer.
SAVE VARIABLE(document; variable1; (;_; variableN})	Saves the variable to a Macintosh document on the disk.
Undefined(variable) -> Boolean	Returns TRUE if variable is not defined, and FALSE if variable is defined.

WINDOWS

The following commands are for use with *windows.*

Command	**Function**
CLOSE WINDOW({docRef})	Closes the window opened by OPEN WINDOW.
EXTERNAL WINDOW(left; top; right; bottom; type; title; area) -> Longint	Opens a new, modaless window and displays an external area, returning a reference number used to access that external area.

Command	Function
OPEN WINDOW(left; top; right; bottom; {type}; {window title}; {close box})	Opens a new window of the dimensions of the first four parameters of the optional type, an optional window title, and an optional close box.
Screen height -> Number	Returns the height of the screen in pixels.
Screen width -> Number	Returns the width of the screen in pixels.
SET WINDOW TITLE(title)	Changes the title of the current window.

ASCII CHART

CHARACTERS 0–127 ARE the standard ASCII characters; these will not change from font to font. Characters 128–255 will change, however.

Character	ASCII Value	Character	ASCII Value
NUL	0	CR	13
SOH	1	SO	14
STX	2	SI	15
ETX	3	DLE	16
EOT	4	DC1	17
ENQ	5	DC2	18
ACK	6	DC3	19
BEL	7	DC4	20
BS	8	NAK	21
HT	9	SYN	22
LF	10	ETB	23
VT	11	CAN	24
FF	12	EM	25

Character	ASCII Value
SUB	26
ESC	27
FS	28
GS	29
RS	30
US	31
sp	32
!	33
“	34
#	35
$	36
%	37
&	38
‘	39
(	40
)	41
*	42
+	43
,	44
–	45
.	46
/	47
0	48
1	49
2	50
3	51
4	52
5	53
6	54
7	55
8	56
9	57
:	58
;	59
<	60
=	61
>	62
?	63
@	64
A	65
B	66
C	67
D	68
E	69
F	70
G	71
H	72
I	73
J	74
K	75

Character	ASCII Value
L	76
M	77
N	78
O	79
P	80
Q	81
R	82
S	83
T	84
U	85
V	86
W	87
X	88
Y	89
Z	90
[	91
\	92
]	93
^	94
_	95
ù	96
a	97
b	98

Character	ASCII Value
c	99
d	100
e	101
f	102
g	103
h	104
i	105
j	106
k	107
l	108
m	109
n	110
o	111
p	112
q	113
r	114
s	115
t	116
u	117
v	118
w	119
x	120
y	121

<table>
<tr><th>Character</th><th>ASCII Value</th><th>Character</th><th>ASCII Value</th></tr>
<tr><td>z</td><td>122</td><td>}</td><td>125</td></tr>
<tr><td>{</td><td>123</td><td>~</td><td>126</td></tr>
<tr><td>|</td><td>124</td><td>DEL</td><td>127</td></tr>
</table>

4th DIMENSION KEYBOARD SHORTCUTS AND ICONS

4TH DIMENSION KEYBOARD SHORTCUTS

TABLE E.1 *4th Dimension Keyboard Shortcuts*

TO DO THIS...	USE THIS SHORTCUT...
Starting up 4th Dimension	
Open Data file dialog box	Option key-hold while opening any structure file
User and Runtime Environment	
Call Debugger	Option-Click while code is executing
Exit RunTime environment to User environment	Option-f
Add record to included layout	⌘-Tab
Select a radio button boolean field item from a group	Type the first letter during data entry, press spacebar, or press Y and N
Check and uncheck a Check box boolean field during data entry	spacebar or Y and N
Scroll to an item in a choices list	Type character
Stop events from being passed to ON EVENT CALL procedure	⌘-Option-Shift-Control-Backspace

TABLE E.1 *4th Dimension Keyboard Shortcuts (continued)*

TO DO THIS...	USE THIS SHORTCUT...
Display Choice of Mode palette for a picture field	Double-click the picture field
User Environment Only	
Create a new record	Double-click in any blank area on an output layout
Bring List of Files to front in User environment	⌘-spacebar
Bring List of Files window to front when using multiple OS on Mac	⌘-Shift-spacebar
Prevent display of layout preview when selecting a layout in the Choose File/Layout dialog box	Option-click to select layout
Structure Editor	
Create a new field	Select file image; ⌘-F
Compress data in Picture field	Option-click on Picture field radio button
Procedure Dialog	
Expand or Collapse the Procedure List	Either ← or →

TABLE E.1 4th Dimension Keyboard Shortcuts (continued)

TO DO THIS...	USE THIS SHORTCUT...
Select procedure name in list	⌘-Shift-letter(s)
Procedure Editor	
Display procedures by category or individually alphabetized	Click on the "Routines" header
Change files via popup menu in Filename bar	Click on filename between cycle arrows and hold mouse down
Open highlighted procedure	⌘-P
Open highlighted layout name	⌘-L
Enter Commands	Enter the command's first few letters and @
Pointer symbol	Shift-Option-l
Pointer symbol	Option-l
_ Time variable symbol	Option-T
_ Interprocess variable symbol	Option-Shift-V
Check syntax of current line of code	Enter
Check syntax of entire procedure	⌘-Enter

TABLE E.1 *4th Dimension Keyboard Shortcuts (continued)*

TO DO THIS...	USE THIS SHORTCUT...
Layout Dialog	
Open Layout Dialog with only the selected file's layouts listed	Double-click the filename bar in Structure window
Sort Layout names in list	Option-Hold-Open Layout Dialog
Prevent display of layout preview when selecting a layout	Option-click to select layout
Layout Editor	
Open Position dialog for object	Control-Double-click the object
Open Script for object	Option-click the object
Select last layout tool used	⌘-click in the layout area
Select only objects completely enclosed by marquee	Control-drag
Shrink or grow object by one pixel	⌘-← or →
Nudge object by 1 pixel	← or →
Move object 1 grid at a time	Control- ← or →
Number a series of active objects from left to right	Option-select Objects on Grid from Layout menu
Draw 1 pixel border around selected object	⌘-Shift-click

TABLE E.1 ***4th Dimension Keyboard Shortcuts (continued)***

TO DO THIS...	USE THIS SHORTCUT...
Draw 1 to 9 pixel border around selected object	⌘-number 1 through 9
Create break or header control marker	Option-click B or H marker
Delete break or header control marker	⌘-click B or H marker
Move all control lines below a control marker	Shift-Hold-Drag a control marker
⌘ symbol (displays in Chicago font only)	Control-Q
Checkmark symbol (displays in Chicago font only)	Control-R
Insert field reference in a text area, master file popup	Option-click in text area for popup list
Insert field reference in text area, all files and fields popup	Shift-Option-click
Debugger	
Commands Popup menu	⌘-click-hold
Files & Fields Popup menu	Option-click-hold
Resize expression window	Option-click-drag
Step without tracing (stepping into) global procedure	Shift-click on Step button

TABLE E.1 *4th Dimension Keyboard Shortcuts(continued)*

TO DO THIS...	USE THIS SHORTCUT...
Open Debug window for process about to be created with the New process function	Control-click on Step button
	+
Menu Editor	
Append a new menu or menu item	Double-click in space below last menu or item in list
Open highlighted procedure	⌘-P
List Editor	
Sort items in a list in descending order	Hold down the Shift key and choose Items ➤ Sort.
Process List	
Bring a processes window to the front	Double-click on the name of the process in the process list.
Import Data Dialog	
Select fields for import	Double-click on field name
Quick Report Editor	
Change a field that the report is sorted on	Drag a field from the Sort Area to a field on the report

4TH DIMENSION ICONS

ICON	NAME	FUNCTION
	4th Dimension	Double-click on this icon to open an existing database or create a new one.
	4D Client	Double-click on this icon to access a database running on 4D Server.
	4D Server	Double-click on this icon to open a database with 4D Server.
	4D Structure file	The structure file contains all of the files, fields, layouts, scripts, procedures, menus, and lists that make up your database. When you want to give another user a new version of your database and let her keep her data, give her a copy of this file.
	4D Data file	The Data file contains all of the actual data you have entered into your database.
	4D Balloon Help	This file contains all of the balloons for the Design and User environments. This file belongs in the System Folder.
	4D text file	When you export using the Export Editor, the file created is given this icon.

ICON	NAME	FUNCTION
	Apply Formula Editor file	When you save a formula from the Apply Formula Editor dialog box, the file created is given this icon.
	Search Editor file	When you save a search criteria from the Search Editor dialog box, the file created is given this icon.
	Quick Report Editor file	When you save a quick report from the Quick Report Editor dialog box, the file created is given this icon.
	ASCII Map	When you save an ASCII map from the Edit Input ASCII Map or Edit Output ASCII Map menu items in the Special menu, the file created is given this icon.
	Variable file	When you use the SAVE VARIABLE command to save a variable to disk, the file created is given this icon.
	Set file	When you save a set (like the UserSet) to disk with the SAVE SET command, the file created is given this icon.
	Compiled Structure	When you compile your database with the 4D Compiler, the compiler creates a duplicate compiled structure with this icon.

ICON	NAME	FUNCTION
	Label Editor file	When you save a label format in the Label Editor, the file created is given this icon.
	Users and Groups file	When you save Users and Groups in the Password Editor, the file created is given this icon.
	4D Preferences file	This file stores preferences about you copy of 4D and should always be in the System Folder.
	4D Backup log file	When you install 4D Backup, you can have 4D create a transaction log. These log files are given this icon.
	4D Path file	When you are using 4D Client, the Password Editor gives you the ability to create a file that stores the location of the database and optionally, the user's password. The user can then simply double-click on this document to open the database without having to know where the database is located.

ICON	NAME	FUNCTION
	Res file	If you have externals or modules installed in your 4D Server database, they are copied into a *.res* (short for resource) file in the user's Preferences Folder in the System Folder the first time the user accesses the database, or anytime the externals or modules are reinstalled. The .res file is named with the name of the database and *.res* added to the end of the name.
	Hot Links file	When you create hot links between different 4D modules, 4D creates this file to keep track of those links.
	4D AppleScript	This application allows you to communicate with 4D Server via AppleScript.

Index

A note to the reader: This index differentiates between *mentions* of items and *explanations* of items. Explanations are listed as **bold** page numbers, while mentions are listed as regular text. Numbers in *italics* refer to pages with figures or tables.

Symbols & Numbers

A

C

D

E

G

H

M

N

O

Q

R

T

Y

Z

A First Word About the Mac.

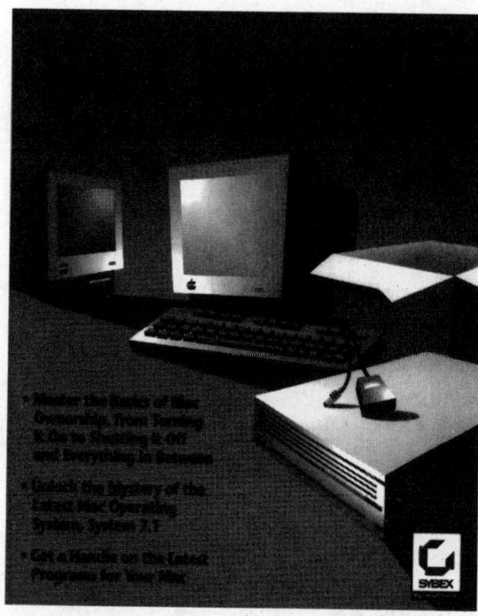

300 pp. ISBN: 1316-8.

Your First Mac is an engaging, friendly handbook for anyone who's just bought a Mac or is thining of purchasing one and wonders what to do next. It's one-stop shopping for the Mac beginner.

This handy guide gives you complete coverage of the basics of Mac ownership, a comprehensive look at System 7.1 and detailed coverage of every major program category. You'll learn how to buy applications that help you get the most from your Mac.

You'll also find troubleshooting tips at the end of each chapter and plenty of timesaving notes, tips and warnings. You'll be remiss if you own a Mac and don't own this book.

SYBEX. Help Yourself.

2021 Challenger Drive
Alameda, CA 94501
1-510-523-8233
1-800-227-2346

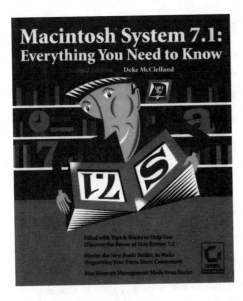

Inside 4th Dimension® by Geoff Perlman

Companion Disk Offer

.earn 4D the easy way...

'he Inside 4th Dimension Companion Disk makes earning 4th Dimension faster and easier. The Com-)anion Disk contains all of the databases, forms and eports used in this book, including a chapter by hapter version of the Learn 4D example database.

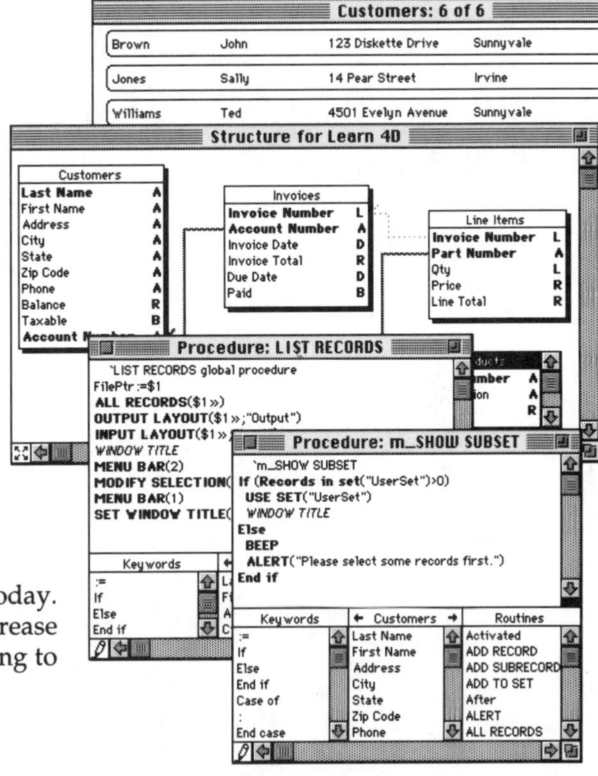

The perfect learning companion...

Exploring the Disk examples will make it easier to ınderstand and apply what you have learned. As /ou read each chapter, compare your Learn 4D latabase with the example Learn 4D databases that come on the Disk. The completed Learn 4D database comes with hundreds of records and sample text locuments to allow you to test out searching, sorting, mporting and reporting.

Order your Inside 4th Dimension Companion Disk today. It's the smart way to save yourself hours of time and increase your return on the investment you've made in learning to program with 4th Dimension.

Order Form

Yes! I want the inside track on learning 4D. Send me the Inside 4D Companion Disk today!

NAME	
COMPANY	
ADDRESS	
CITY	
ST./PROV.	POSTAL CODE
COUNTRY	
WORK NO.	( )
FAX NO.	( )

SYBEX is not affiliated with S2 Software and assumes no responsibility for any defect in the disk or programs.

Inside 4D Companion Disk $30/ea.

- Enclose your check payable to S2 Software.
- Price includes shipping. Allow 2 weeks for delivery.
- Foreign orders add $5 and pay by International Money Order in USD only.
- CA residents add 8.25% sales tax of $2.48.

Mail To:

Inside 4D Disk Offer
S2 Software
19672 Stevens Creek Blvd. Suite 275
Cupertino, CA 95014
Phone Orders (US only): 408-257-7272

FREE BROCHURE!

Complete this form today, and we'll send you a full-color brochure of Sybex bestsellers.

Please supply the name of the Sybex book purchased.

____

How would you rate it?

- ____ Excellent
- ____ Very Good
- ____ Average
- ____ Poor

Why did you select this particular book?

- ____ Recommended to me by a friend
- ____ Recommended to me by store personnel
- ____ Saw an advertisement in ______________________
- ____ Author's reputation
- ____ Saw in Sybex catalog
- ____ Required textbook
- ____ Sybex reputation
- ____ Read book review in ______________________
- ____ In-store display
- ____ Other ______________________

Where did you buy it?

- ____ Bookstore
- ____ Computer Store or Software Store
- ____ Catalog (name: ______________________)
- ____ Direct from Sybex
- ____ Other: ______________________

Did you buy this book with your personal funds?

- ____Yes
- ____No

About how many computer books do you buy each year?

- ____ 1-3
- ____ 3-5
- ____ 5-7
- ____ 7-9
- ____ 10+

About how many Sybex books do you own?

- ____ 1-3
- ____ 3-5
- ____ 5-7
- ____ 7-9
- ____ 10+

Please indicate your level of experience with the software covered in this book:

- ____ Beginner
- ____ Intermediate
- ____ Advanced

Which types of software packages do you use regularly?

____ Accounting	____ Databases	____ Networks
____ Amiga	____ Desktop Publishing	____ Operating Systems
____ Apple/Mac	____ File Utilities	____ Spreadsheets
____ CAD	____ Money Management	____ Word Processing
____ Communications	____ Languages	____ Other ______________ (please specify)

Which of the following best describes your job title?

____ Administrative/Secretarial ____ President/CEO

____ Director ____ Manager/Supervisor

____ Engineer/Technician ____ Other ____________________
(please specify)

Comments on the weaknesses/strengths of this book: ____________________

Name ____________________

Street ____________________

City/State/Zip ____________________

Phone ____________________

PLEASE FOLD, SEAL, AND MAIL TO SYBEX

SYBEX, INC.
Department M
2021 CHALLENGER DR.
ALAMEDA, CALIFORNIA USA
94501

SEAL

THE LAYOUT EDITOR TOOL PALETTE

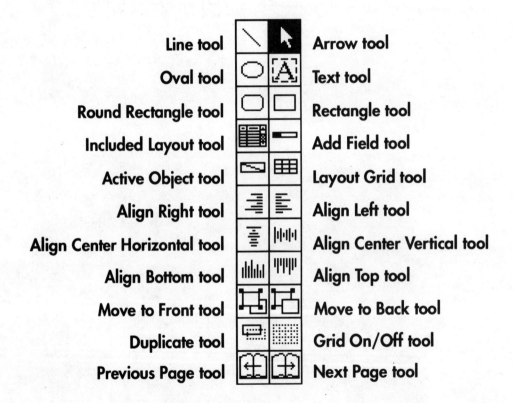

Line tool	Arrow tool
Oval tool	Text tool
Round Rectangle tool	Rectangle tool
Included Layout tool	Add Field tool
Active Object tool	Layout Grid tool
Align Right tool	Align Left tool
Align Center Horizontal tool	Align Center Vertical tool
Align Bottom tool	Align Top tool
Move to Front tool	Move to Back tool
Duplicate tool	Grid On/Off tool
Previous Page tool	Next Page tool